U.S. S
an Ur

A WASHINGTON QUARTERLY READER

U.S. Security in an Uncertain Era

edited by

BRAD ROBERTS

MIT Press
Cambridge, Massachusetts
London, England

Zbigniew Brzezinski, "Order, Disorder, and U.S. Leadership," *TWQ* 15, no. 2 (Spring 1992); Alberto R. Coll, "Power, Principles, and Prospects for a Cooperative International Order," *TWQ* 16, no. 1 (Winter 1993); Patrick J. Garrity and Sharon K. Weiner, "U.S. Defense Strategy After the Cold War," *TWQ* 15, no. 2 (Spring 1992); Caroline F. Ziemke, "Military Planning Beyond the Cold War: Lessons for the 1990s from the 1920s and 1930s," *TWQ* 14, no. 1 (Winter 1991); Gary L. Guertner, "Deterrence and Conventional Military Forces," *TWQ* 16, no. 1 (Winter 1993); Joseph F. Pilat and Paul C. White, "Technology and Strategy in a Changing World," *TWQ* 13, no. 2 (Spring 1990); W. R. Smyser, "Vienna, Versailles, and Now Paris: Third Time Lucky?" *TWQ* 14, no. 3 (Summer 1991); François Heisbourg, "The Future of the Atlantic Alliance: Whither NATO, Whether NATO?" *TWQ* 15, no. 2 (Spring 1992); Hugh De Santis, "The Graying of NATO," *TWQ* 14, no. 4 (Autumn 1991); Adrian A. Basora, "Central and Eastern Europe: Imperative for Active U.S. Engagement," *TWQ* 16, no 1 (Winter 1993); James E. Goodby, "Peacekeeping in the New Europe," *TWQ* 15, no. 2 (Spring 1992); Stephen R. Covington and John Lough, "Russia's Post-Revolution Challenge: Reform of the Soviet Superpower Paradigm," *TWQ* 15, no. 1 (Winter 1992); James C. Clad, "Old World Disorders," *TWQ* 15, no. 4 (Autumn 1992); John Chipman, "Third World Politic and Security in the 1990s: 'The World Forgetting, By the World Forgot'?" *TWQ* 14, no. 1 (Winter 1991); Geoffrey Kemp, "Regional Security, Arms Control, and the End of the Cold War," *TWQ* 13, no. 4 (Autumn 1990); Edward C. Luck and Toby Trister Gati, "Whose Collective Security?" *TWQ* 15, no. 2 (Spring 1992); George Weigel, "Religion and Peace: An Argument Complexified," *TWQ* 14, no. 2 (Spring 1991); Brad Roberts, "Arms Control and the End of the Cold War," *TWQ* 15, no. 4 (Autumn 1992); Lewis A. Dunn, "Four Decades of Nuclear Nonproliferation: Some Lessons from Wins, Losses, and Draws," *TWQ* 13, no. 3 (Summer 1990); George H. Quester and Victor A. Utgoff, "U.S. Arms Reductions and Nuclear Nonproliferation: The Counterproductive Possibilities," *TWQ* 16, no. 1 (Winter 1993); Graham S. Pearson, "Prospects for Chemical and Biological Arms Control: The Web (Deterrence," *TWQ* 16, no. 2 (Spring 1993); Thomas G. Mahnken, "The Arrow and the Shield: U.S. Responses to Ballistic Missile Proliferation," *TWQ* 14, no. 1 (Winter 1991); Janne E. Nolan, "The Global Arms Market After the Gulf War: Prospects for Control," *TWQ* 14, no. 3 (Summer 1991); Michael Moodie, "Transparency in Armaments: A New Item for the New Security Agenda," *TWQ* 15, no. 3 (Summer 1992); K. Subrahmanyam, "Export Controls and the North–South Controversy," *TWQ* 16, no. 2 (Spring 1993); Avner Cohen and Marvin Miller, "How to Think About—and Implement—Nuclear Arms Control in the Middl East," *TWQ* 16, no. 2 (Spring 1993); Gerald Segal, "Managing New Arms Races in the Asia/Pacific," *TWQ* 15, no. 3 (Summer 1992); Charles C. Flowerree, "On Tending Arms Control Agreements," *TWQ* 13, no. 1 (Winter 1990).

Library of Congress Cataloging-in-Publication Data

U.S. security in an uncertain era : a Washington quarterly reader / edited by Brad Roberts.
    p. cm.
    "All articles have been previously published in the Washington quarterly"—CIP galley.
    Includes bibliographical references.
    ISBN 0-262-18155-X. —ISBN 0-262-68080-7 (pbk.)
    1. National security—United States. I. Roberts, Brad.
II. Washington quarterly. III. Title: US security in an uncertain era.
UA23.U26 1993
355'.033073—dc20   93-10056
                                                        CIP

Contents

Introduction

WITH THE END of the Cold War the challenges of formulating U.S. defense and security policies have magnified considerably. For over five decades, the East–West conflict substantially structured the national strategy, defense planning priorities, and military needs of the United States. Its passing has certainly enhanced U.S. security. But it has also brought a new era of instability as well as a changing domestic political context to the formulation of policy.

In these unfamiliar and uncertain times, policy cannot rest on the outdated assumptions of past decades. But the new environment has not taken sufficient shape to evoke a clear national consensus about the content of U.S. security policy for the 1990s and beyond. Effective policies that secure and advance U.S. interests require both the setting aside of old analytical frameworks and a careful assessment of new realities. They also require the integration of defense policy with the other diplomatic, economic, and political instruments of national and international security. These conceptual tasks have begun haltingly in the last few years, sometimes because international crises have compelled fresh thinking and sometimes because thoughtful individuals have set themselves to the work of sorting through new issues.

Journals are uniquely positioned to facilitate this process of creating intellectual capital for a new era. They fill an important niche in the market of ideas between the daily media, where the press of reportage tends to crowd out analysis of trends beyond the headlines, and the book world, where ideas are slower to enter the public debate. Journals capture new arguments as they are developing. The best will draw upon the most creative thinkers to stimulate innovative directions for analysis and policy.

This volume consists of a selection of articles from *The Washington Quarterly*, a journal of international policy issues published by the MIT Press for the Center for Strategic and International Studies of Washington, D.C. The journal is committed to intellectual leadership in this field, to stimulating its readers to think afresh about statecraft, international security, and, more broadly, the international engagement of the United States. It seeks to achieve this goal in a number of ways. Its authors represent a diversity of political viewpoints and areas of expertise. In addition to policymakers and analysts in both main political parties, this group includes experts from overseas whose views are not often heard in the United States and younger scholars whose ideas deserve a broader hearing. Articles are drawn together in clusters in order to lay open the connections among issues and the complexity of policy choices. The journal also emphasizes commissioned essays, rather than unsolicited materials, in order to lead rather than follow the public debate.

The articles included here appeared

in the journal between winter 1990 and winter 1993. Of the nearly 200 essays published during this period, these stand out as having the most impact on the current debate about U.S. security. The journal's interests range considerably wider than this subject, however. A companion to this volume, published in early 1992 and entitled *U.S. Foreign Policy After the Cold War* (Cambridge, Mass.: MIT Press, 1992), gives an idea of its range. That volume draws together outstanding articles from the journal on the redistribution of power in the international system; how U.S. interests are evolving in various regions; ways to update policy instruments; the new policy challenges of the global economy, the environment, and demographics; and traditional questions about the international commitment of the United States.

The chapters in this volume have been selected because of their continuing salience for the large, ongoing project of redefining U.S. national and international security policies. Each probes an issue brought to prominence by the post–cold war security environment. Together they present a coherent agenda for thinking about and acting on the challenges confronting the United States. To be sure, parts of some essays have been overtaken by events. Please note that authors have not been asked to update their essays—in a rapidly changing world, this is a never-ending task. But all make arguments that remain relevant in any review of U.S. security policy in the post–cold war era. Please note further that all biographies are current to January 1, 1993, and that they may have changed from the time of original publication. The views presented here are the authors' alone and should not be attributed to any institutions with

which they are affiliated or to the publishers, CSIS and MIT Press.

Chapter I introduces fundamental questions of U.S. grand strategy in an evolving international system. It points to the themes of order and disorder in the new era, explores the basic choices confronting the United States in its world role, and emphasizes the virtues of integrating those choices into a coherent course of action.

Chapter II focuses on the challenge of formulating defense policy in peacetime. The articles included here examine planning priorities and budgets but look beyond them to the essentials of military strategy (for example, what kind of deterrence best serves U.S. interests?) and of the generation of the technology necessary to support this strategy. Historical perspectives are included where they are useful in establishing precedents for current choices.

Chapter III examines the changing European security agenda. Do we confront a new era of peace, or of war, or both? The articles examine the future of the North Atlantic Treaty Organization (NATO) and the Atlantic Alliance more generally, as well as the peacekeeping and peacemaking tasks in Central and Eastern Europe.

Chapter IV explores new themes of international security. This began as a chapter on regional security, but the material in the journal clearly suggests that the old regional security agenda has been transformed as the political and military problems within the regions have begun to have an impact well beyond their confines. Articles examine the implications of disintegrating Soviet power for the international system, the growing problems confronting the developing countries, and the escalating debate about whether collective security is the best way to manage relations among states.

Chapter V reviews the elements of the emerging North–South dialogue on international security. Articles examine the proliferation of nuclear, chemical, and biological weapons and advanced delivery systems, as well as the general arms market. Questions related to strengthening existing treaty regimes and to creating new regional or global measures are also addressed. Each essay moves from the description and analysis of new global problems to prescriptions for policy.

The editor owes a debt of gratitude to the many authors who have lent their time, energy, and expertise to composing the articles included here. He is also grateful to his colleagues at the journal and especially to Yoma Ullman, Denise Miller, and Lynn Northcutt de Vega, whose own commitment to excellence is reflected in this volume.

Brad Roberts
Washington, D.C.
February 15, 1993

I. U.S. Security in the 1990s

Order, Disorder, and U.S. Leadership

Zbigniew Brzezinski

THE PHRASE "NEW world order" has become a subject of widespread debate and a target of intellectual critique. Two commentators have staked out important parts of the debate. One is Henry Kissinger, who has argued:

> [T]he widespread perception that the Gulf War certified America as the last remaining superpower misses the real significance of that conflict. That war marked a glorious sunset to the Cold War world, not a new dawn for the period of American predominance. America remains militarily the strongest nation, but the spread of technology and reduced military budgets make this a declining asset.[1]

The other is James Schlesinger, who has written:

> Although the world after the Cold War is likely to be a far less dangerous place because of reduced risks of a cataclysmic clash, it is likely to be more unstable rather than less. The Bush administration has coined the phrase "new world order." If the phrase means that the world order has been sharply *altered* from the strict divisions of the Cold War, then

clearly it is correct. If it means that the world order will be *novel*, marked by a new stability, then it is unduly utopian. The world order of the future will revert to that which existed before 1939, and most notably after World War I: It will be marked by power politics, national rivalries, and ethnic tensions.[2]

Both men make valid and important points. It is right to emphasize the reality of the superpower status of the United States in the new post–cold war world but at the same time to point to the limitations of that status. It is also right to emphasize the potential that what follows the Cold War could be even more unstable and dangerous than the Cold War itself.

But in evaluating the quite significant limits to American power, we must appreciate also the fact that the U.S. role in the world is likely to be the most important of any in determining whether international relations become increasingly well ordered or sink instead into increasing disorder. And in assessing the dangers ahead, it is important to recognize that the likelihood of increased conflict depends very much on what the United States does—or does not do—with respect to specific existing political problems. The "new world order" thus depends very much on the United States—on the choices it makes and the leadership it seeks to exercise.

Zbigniew Brzezinski is a counselor at CSIS; Robert Osgood Professor of American Foreign Policy, the Paul Nitze School of Advanced International Studies, The Johns Hopkins University; and former assistant to the president for National Security Affairs.

The future of world order will depend upon the resolution of basic problems within three important regions where order is at issue. In defining the emerging geostrategic agenda, it is useful to think of the world map and then to draw a straight line from Brussels to Tokyo, then from Tokyo to Cairo, and then back to Brussels. At the points of this triangle are the key geostrategic zones within which developments will shape the larger global order. This triangle spans, after all, Europe, the Far East, and the Middle East. Within each region, a critical local agenda remains at issue. Successful efforts to deal with each agenda will bear fruit internationally, whereas failure could be of enormous importance in prompting both crisis and calamity. Within each region, success requires U.S. engagement and leadership.

Brussels and the European Project

Brussels is, of course, symbolic of the future Europe, which stands today at a critical stage in the process of unification. There is little doubt about where the economic dimension of that process is headed. Remaining economic barriers in Europe are being swept away and the process will continue to move forward whatever intermediate obstacles may crop up. But will it also move forward politically and militarily? Would this be desirable from the standpoint of international order? What role should the United States play in this regard? Nothing in history suggests that the unification of Europe can be confined to the economic dimension alone. To be real and meaningful, unification must move to the political and eventually to the military domain. In fact, this process is well under way. The Maastricht

Summit was an important milestone in the progressive emergence of Europe as well as an indicator of the path ahead. Some progress was made on the basis of compromise, some of the seemingly insurmountable obstacles were overcome, and an agreement emerged acceptable to all. It is reasonable to expect that it will continue, although because Europe consists of a complex of sovereign states with different traditions and historical orientations, objections and obstructions along the way are inevitable. Europe will not speak with a single political voice or employ its military force with coherence any time soon. But the secular trend toward expanding economic cooperation, both in depth and scope, matched increasingly by growing political and military cooperation, is clear.

A fully united Europe will not arrive very quickly, but when it does arrive, the cause of international order will be well served. A more united Europe will be an important asset to a more stable world. Unity would help terminate the traditional intra-European power conflicts that have been so destructive historically, especially by anchoring Germany within the international community. European unity can also provide the point of departure for a more effective response to the difficulties that are being confronted today by the post-Communist world, particularly in Central Europe. Only a more united Europe can create a context in which the very difficult sociopolitical transformations now taking place within Central Europe can successfully be pursued.

From a U.S. point of view, therefore, what happens in Europe makes a difference. The United States can be of some importance in influencing to some degree how rapidly Europe moves toward unity. Ill-conceived policies might actually hinder European integration. The United States therefore should not be shy in registering its opinions when difficult choices are being made. At the moment, the United States should be outspoken in its support for the Franco–German approach to a future Europe. This approach makes the best sense in the long run because it is more likely than the alternatives to create structures that overcome historical conflicts. It would also ensure the solid incorporation and integration of Germany. Further, it would lead to a Europe that would become a more forceful and critically constructive element on the world scene. This is a choice that the United States can exercise, and U.S. involvement is important.

Tokyo, the Far East, and Regional Security

The easternmost point of the triangle symbolizes the salience and increasing international importance of the Far East, with Japan in the lead. This has become a truism. Despite the new prominence of East Asia, few analysts have recognized the emerging pattern of international relations within the region. There we see the emergence of a cluster of independent and increasingly powerful states that are not assimilated within a multilateral framework of political or military or even economic cooperation. In many respects, the emerging international scene in the Far East is very reminiscent of traditional international politics, especially in some ways of Europe before World War II or even World War I—that is to say, uneasy coexistence and the potential for conflict between individual and increasingly powerful nation-states.

The new power of the individual states is hard to miss. Japan's economic success is also bringing it some kinds of political power. Even its military power is no longer negligible: Japan is the fourth military power in the world. Its military potential will continue to expand.

But Japan is not the only power in the Far East. China is emerging on the scene, and it is almost a certainty that China will thrust outward within the next decade. Chinese economic growth is remarkable. Its gross national product (GNP) currently grows on average about 6 percent per annum, a figure that may go up to about 9 percent in the near future. China is bound, therefore, to make its weight felt increasingly. One early manifestation of this trend is its sales of weapons to places like the Middle East and North Africa. Both Chinese ambitions and Chinese assertiveness are likely to grow.

The political predilections of China's current leadership are only a partial obstacle to a larger role. China's political freeze is likely to be undermined within the next three to five years as the old regime fades from the scene. Once the gerontocracy disappears, conflict between the increasingly market-oriented economy, particularly of coastal China, and political restraints, especially the ideological type, will come to a head. This will lead to some moderation, but probably not to rapid progress toward democracy. Rather, an authoritarian regime similar in essential political and economic respects to the early days of Taiwan and South Korea is more likely.

Korea may well become united within the next decade. In so doing it might emerge also as a nuclear power. This would be bound to have a powerful impact on Japan; it would certainly complicate the relationship between Japan and China and whatever remains of the Soviet Far East.

Further west is, of course, the regional power of India, with its nuclear potential and its hegemonic aspirations.

For the United States, therefore, the important question is what kind of multilateral security structure is likely to be possible in the Far East. What should be done to make certain that the Far East does not replicate the power conflicts that so dominated Europe in the course of the twentieth century? Here, too, the U.S. role is going to be important, not as a dominant, dictating power, but certainly as a critical participant in—and catalyst of—a process that might contribute to the emergence of some new multilateral dialogue and then a multilateral framework of security in the region. Such a framework is genuinely needed. U.S. strategy must anticipate that need by taking initiatives regarding such questions as, for example, security on the Korean peninsula.

In brief, in the Far East as in Europe challenges related to future order and disorder cannot be ignored. There is a clear need in both regions for a constructive process leading to the creation of new structures. To be sure, the specific characteristics of those structures must vary significantly from one region to another. The Far East is unlikely to experience anything like the degree of economic and political integration evident in Europe—at least not in the near future. It is the security agenda that is critical in the Far East.

Efforts to design and implement a multilateral structure of cooperative security within East Asia will be made easier by the U.S. role there. The paramountcy of U.S. power affords it significant leverage in a part of the world concerned about local sources of instability and potential international crises. There appears to be a widespread appreciation of the risk that the emergence of independent powers in the region could produce conflicts unless efforts are made now to create some sort of structure.

Cairo, the Middle East, and Peace

The third point of the triangle, Cairo, is symbolic, of course, not only of the importance of the Middle East but also of the salience of the problems that this region confronts. Here, too, the U.S. role is likely to be of critical importance.

For the first time in modern history, the Middle East is not the object of big power competition—whether it be Turkey and Russia, Britain and France, the United States and Britain, or in recent decades the United States and the Soviet Union. The Middle East finds itself today subject to the domination of one power alone: the United States. This is the result of the Persian Gulf War. It is also the consequence of the collapse of the Soviet Union, which today plays only a supportive role to U.S. policy in the region. Thus there is an unprecedented opportunity to move forward toward some degree of stability in the region. Again, U.S. influence will be decisive. The U.S. role will be critical with regard to two important issues: proliferation and peace.

The dissemination of weaponry of high destructiveness in the region has emerged as a sharp international policy challenge. It is an issue that bears on U.S. relations with many countries in the region. Looking ahead, it is likely that the nuclear weapons interests of Iran may become as critical to the United States as were Iraq's over the last year. Clearly, initiatives to deal with that problem are needed. These initiatives must be regional—they cannot be imposed from outside. They must address the problem on a comprehensive basis, taking into account also the reality of Israeli nuclear weapons if any regimen of self-restraint in the region is to be adopted.

Even more immediate is the U.S. role in the peace process. One cannot envisage more propitious circumstances for progress toward peace between Arabs and Israelis than those currently prevailing.

The Arabs for the first time since the Suez crisis of the mid-1950s have no one other than the United States to whom to turn—both subjectively and objectively. They have simply no alternative but to accept the reality of American preponderance and, in the absence of movement toward peace, continued Israeli political and military preponderance with American support.

For the Israelis, economic circumstances plus the likelihood of large-scale immigration from the Soviet Union make their country more dependent than ever before upon U.S. political and financial support. The Likud government seems inclined to emulate what the Arabs have done before them: "never to miss an opportunity to miss an opportunity" (to quote Abba Eban). It is thus isolating itself internationally and undercutting itself in U.S. public opinion. Weakened domestic support for Israel translates of course, into enhanced U.S. leverage.

Thus, both parties to the conflict are highly susceptible to U.S. leverage. Not to exercise that leverage would be a very serious mistake. The opportunity for peace would very likely disappear suddenly, leaving the region to revert to intensified and certainly protracted conflict with destructive and dynamic consequences. Without U.S. leadership and pressure, the parties will never reach agreement on their

own. The notion that simple face-to-face negotiations might somehow miraculously solve the problem is a mirage or an evasion, or probably a little bit of both, depending upon who is advocating it.

The Crisis of Post-Communism

Thus, Europe, the Far East, and the Middle East constitute the three points of the global triangle where constructive U.S. intervention can make a difference in terms of what shape the future takes. But there is still the area enclosed by the different sides of the triangle: the post-Communist world.

The remarkable implosion of the Soviet Union must be recognized. No other historic case comes to mind involving a sociopolitical collapse as massive as the one experienced by the Soviet system. It is a complete collapse simultaneously of the economic and of the political systems, and it is a collapse without the slightest hope of any redemption. It thus has no analogy, for example, to the Great Depression into which the United States and the capitalist system were plunged in the late 1920s and early 1930s. This simultaneous collapse of political economic institutions is accompanied by a total collapse of will, perspective, and faith.

No one should lament the Soviet Union's passing. But we must be clear-eyed about the consequences. The collapse has created a vacuum, with potentially very dangerous consequences. It has also created a situation calling for a Western response. The West must act to avert the immediate dangers. But it must also act so that the failure of communism does not subsequently become the failure of democracy as well. The failure of communism is directly and organically linked to the great philosophic and strategic struggle that was waged over the last 40 years, and its defeat in that struggle opens the gates to the eventual success of democracy. But if that success does not occur, the prospects are either chaos or some attempt to establish a different form of order based on nationalism, crypto-fascism, or what you will.

The situation today in the erstwhile Soviet Union is literally on the knife's edge. There is a palpable sense of despair and desperation, uncertainty, fear, resignation, and in some cases, lack of understanding of what is happening. In December 1991, the illusions of the Gorbachev leadership that some form of union might be preserved are fast dissipating. The question is, what comes next. Here one must be very careful not to transgress the boundaries between analysis, prognosis, and simple prophecy. The latter is a foolish but popular undertaking these days. Careful analysis and prognosis can identify possible options. The most likely and obvious option is protracted chaos, continued decay, socioeconomic dissolution of existing fabrics, and—probably for a long time to come—no recovery. That is the optimistic conclusion. The more pessimistic involves varieties of force, a breakdown of order, and a kind of escalating chaotic sociopolitical conflict, or a coup—a coup by the army in order to save the union and "preserve order."

The December 1991 independence of Ukraine must be seen as a very critical stage in the dissolution of the central authority. Its independence left the central government as little more than a shell. It rests on only one of the four former pillars of Soviet power. The Communist party has been abolished. The repressive state apparatus has been decentralized and largely taken over by the republics. The economic central controls have been completely taken over by the republics. This leaves the army, which still exists in a residual sense but is being subjected to a lot of pressures for its dissolution and integration into the republican fold.

To some degree, Mikhail Gorbachev may well be positioning himself for the possibility of a coup—and even legitimating it. Some of his autumn 1991 statements about the threat posed by Boris Yeltsin's economic reform programs to the benefits of socialism, his increasingly desperate note of anxiety regarding the future of the union, and his references to the dangers of civil war may be more than expressions of genuine concern and judgment; they might also be statements to be used later to justify some declaration of state emergency. Gorbachev might justify such a declaration and follow it up with military action as an act of necessity that in no way compromises his commitment to continued perestroika. Only in that way is he likely to save his own position. If this does not happen, then Gorbachev's days are literally numbered and the center will fade from the scene.

Key, of course, to this scenario is the Soviet military. Just who controls these forces is in dispute today. Most Western commentary has focused on the effective command and control of the nuclear system, which is still being maintained by authorities that in the past have been associated with the political center and to some degree still are. The question of nuclear control has been a distraction from the main issue: the progressive breakdown of authority within the conventional army. There have been instances in which units, even large-scale units, have defied orders to relocate. The overall cohesion of the armed forces is in jeopardy. This may be a necessary aspect of the process of devolution of central power to constituent republics, something which in most respects is desirable, but it creates a potentially dangerous transitional stage, during which some senior officers are bound to see a mortal danger to an institution to which they are deeply committed and which to them might well seem to be the only guarantee of civilized power.

Allegedly, the political control of the old guard over the military has been abolished by order of President Yeltsin. But as of late November 1991, only 36 political officers had been dismissed out of several tens of thousands. Such officers constitute a specific political danger because they might very well be mobilized to exercise some degree of last-gasp authority in some form of perhaps abortive but nonetheless dangerous military coup. Such a coup might be directed against Yeltsin and Gorbachev and new governments in other republics, or it could be legitimated by Gorbachev, as argued above. It is doubtful that such a coup would succeed in the long run, but certainly it would exacerbate the situation and it could plunge the country into a burst of very intense violence.

The only possible solution for the crisis of the Soviet Union is some agreement regarding an open economic space, plus a minimal agreement regarding some consultative political institution as a substitute for what was the union government. Nothing less than that will do. Nothing more than that would be accepted by the different union republics. (Postscript: The December 1991 agreement to create a Commonwealth of Independent States should be seen as an important but still tentative step in this direction.) The West must rec-

ognize that such an agreement may not long survive. The West must also prepare itself for the possibility that the collapse in the Soviet Union could become dynamic, meaning that social disintegration within the former union might become uncontrollable, possibly spilling over into other regions.

Particularly vulnerable to such dynamic collapse would be the fragile emerging political and economic institutions of Central Europe. The countries of Central Europe remain very vulnerable and their economic and political progress is undergoing ever greater difficulties, with the West insufficiently attentive or engaged. Hence, the West could well confront in the not too distant future the painful reality that its victory over communism has produced not a genuine success for democratic institutions with a free market mechanism, but is rather plunging an enormous portion of the critical heartland of Eurasia into an intensifying crisis with essentially unforeseeable consequences.

This points to another agenda item for the West and particularly the United States. It is imperative to create somewhere a successful conceptual and practical model of the transition from communism to democracy and the free market system. No precedents, models, or even concepts exist. The only places where this can actually be done now are Hungary, Poland, and Czechoslovakia. Thus, while dealing with the crisis in the Soviet Union, the West must not desist from ensuring that some or all of these three countries successfully manage the transition—and soon. A successful model will be a critical asset. If these three countries fail, whatever the short-term successes in keeping some people afloat in the former Soviet republics, in the long run the international community would not be able to deal with the structural and organic problems that would arise. Therefore, in addition to dealing with the regions and republics, the United States must concentrate much more effectively on creating a successful model of transition somewhere, which will then become an example to others.

The United States has not been doing enough to shape these events toward desired results. The reasons are not difficult to understand. It is in part a problem of misfocused attention: the U.S. government throughout much of 1991 has been mesmerized by the notion of continuing to deal with an increasingly mythical center in the Soviet Union. But there is also a practical complication for the West: over the last couple of years the West has plowed between $8 and $12 billion into the Soviet economy in the form of loans, grants, joint ventures, and philanthropic aid—almost every penny of which has disappeared. No one seems able to account for it. This must be the biggest theft in financial history and is an appalling story. Most Western aid to the Soviet Union not only has been wasted but has literally been requisitioned by a corrupt and fading political elite. The West has helped the wrong people, instead of establishing new relationships with new governmental structures in the former republics.

A more significant and long-term aid commitment by the West and especially the United States to post-Communist entities in Central Europe and the Soviet Union will result only if the costs of *not* acting come clearly into focus. If Soviet transition leads to wholesale collapse and conflict, with massive social and political consequences throughout the former republics that also spread into Central Europe, the costs to the United States in terms of military budgets and global insecurity would likely far outstrip the costs it might incur now if it were to exert itself just a bit more. Certainly the same applies to the European Community. There are, of course, things that might be done that do not necessarily involve the transfer of funds but would simply help the economies of these countries to grow, such as lowering tariffs on exports from them. For example, if the United States is committed to the success of the formerly Communist states in the same way that it has been committed to the success of the developing world, incentives must be found for the creation of trade-motivated growth along the lines of the newly industrializing countries in Asia. This requires adjustments in the trade policies of both the United States and the European Community, something both have been reluctant to consider.

Of course, neither the United States nor Europe has sat by idly as the Soviet empire has crumbled. But nor have they worked with the sense of urgency warranted by the genuinely historical magnitude of not only the opportunity but also the threat. The torpid pace of Western efforts will only be magnified by the dynamics that are accelerating within the erstwhile Soviet Union. Time has grown shorter and the issue has become more urgent. This situation requires a more concerted initiative by the United States in coordination with both its European and Japanese partners and the multinational institutions.

Order or Disorder and U.S. Leadership

A new world order is not upon us. A genuinely new order may take decades to evolve. Looked at in long-term historical perspective, the world appears to be moving toward a more supranational order. But moving from one historical phase to another is not like taking a leap. It is an evolutionary process. The elements of the past coexist with novel elements. The international system of the 1990s is very different from what it was in the late 1930s, in part because of technology and in part because perceptions have changed, and a continued refashioning of the international system must be envisaged. Certainly 40 years from now the international system is likely to be much more supranational and interdependent than it is today, although many elements of state sovereignty will continue to exist in different parts of the world.

World order in the interim requires not just U.S. engagement but also U.S. leadership. Within each of the regions of the globe where issues of order remain unresolved, U.S. influence, patience, power, and relative wealth will be critical factors in the progress toward order or the descent into disorder. In Europe, Asia, and the Middle East, U.S. leadership must

take on new forms. But in recognizing the importance of the three points of the triangle, U.S. leaders must understand also the risks of disorder of genuinely historic character within the triangle. The United States must take the lead in focusing international efforts to address very seriously the developing crisis of massive and historical magnitude that is mushrooming before our very eyes in that part of the world until recently called the Soviet Union. This crisis could well get out of control before too long and disrupt any progress made elsewhere toward a new world order.

This essay is based on remarks delivered to the International Club of Washington on December 3, 1991.

Notes

1. Henry Kissinger, "What Kind of New World Order?" *Washington Post*, op. ed., December 3, 1991, p. A–21.

2. James Schlesinger, "New Instabilities, New Priorities," *Foreign Policy*, no. 85 (Winter 1991–92), p. 4.

Power, Principles, and Prospects for a Cooperative International Order

Alberto R. Coll

In 1943, as the eventual outcome of World War II was becoming clear, but well before the Cold War had begun, the historian Carl Becker wrote an essay with the apt title *How New Will the Better World Be?*[1] In it he took a hard look at the world around him and tried to dampen some of the more utopian enthusiasms of his contemporaries about the new age of peace that the collapse of fascism and the founding of the United Nations (UN) supposedly would mark. Today, Americans have a similar challenge before them, to discern whether the period of international relations ahead will be either new or better.

One thing seems certain. The prospects for a cooperative world order will depend to no small extent on the degree to which the United States has a sober appreciation for the role of both power and principle in international politics. Such an appreciation is not foreign to the American tradition. The American presidents most successful in the conduct of foreign affairs have been well aware of the indissoluble connection between power and prin-

Alberto R. Coll is principal deputy assistant secretary of defense for Special Operations and Low-Intensity Conflict. He has taught previously at the Naval War College and Georgetown University.

ciple, of the necessity for shaping U.S. policies with due regard for both realities of power and the constraints and possibilities posed by moral principles. As president, Washington, Jefferson, Monroe, Lincoln, Wilson, the two Roosevelts, Truman, Eisenhower, Kennedy, and Reagan were all realists determined to safeguard U.S. power. But they also appreciated the importance of grounding and articulating their policies and strategies in terms of moral principles congruent with the character of the American polity.

Americans often think of the relationship of power to principle as one of tension and even conflict. It is important to remember that it can also be one of mutual reinforcement. U.S. principles need U.S. power every bit as much as U.S. power needs U.S. principles. Without power to back them up, those principles wither in the harsh environment of international politics. Yet, without principles to energize and impart a guiding vision to it, U.S. power either lies dormant or drifts purposelessly or misdirected. Moreover, the principles are in themselves a source of power, as Americans discovered repeatedly in both world wars and throughout the Cold War. Besides infusing Americans with vitality, their principles attract others around the world who share them, joining their resources to those of the United States in a common purpose. As Americans seek to construct a co-operative world order in the 1990s and beyond they will have to exercise their power in the world while remaining faithful to their principles. And they will have to develop policies and strategies that reflect a dynamic interaction between the requirements of their power and those of their principles.

Two opposite dangers loom ahead. The first is that Americans will over-estimate the capacity of principles un-aided by power to shape a more decent international order. The second is that, in a fit of cynicism and despair over their mounting domestic problems, Americans will succumb to the temptation of assuming that raw economic or military power is all that matters in today's world. Either outcome reflects a false understanding of the true character of politics and human nature and would bode ill for cooperative security.

The Requirements of Power

Promoting a cooperative international order will require Americans to pay attention simultaneously to the requirements of both their power and their principles. With regard to the requirements of U.S. power, it is possible to sketch two policy objectives that, while promoting U.S. security, will also encourage the development of a more cooperative international system. These are to nurture and strengthen U.S. alliances in Europe and the Pacific Basin and to integrate multilateral institutions and practices more thoroughly into the fabric of U.S. foreign and defense policy.

The first of these objectives has been widely accepted to this day and may seem prosaic enough, but it is in danger of being gradually discarded as a result of economic squabbles among the allies and of weariness among the American people with the responsibilities it implies. The second objective is far from accepted today, yet will be vital to a constructive U.S. role in the future ordering of international politics and economics along lines beneficial to U.S. interests. Both of these objectives must be pursued at a difficult time when U.S. economic resources will be limited as a result of the current U.S. fiscal crisis.

Nurturing and Strengthening U.S. Alliances in Europe and the Pacific Basin. Secretary of Defense Richard B. Cheney has rightly emphasized that the network of alliances of which the United States is a part is its single most important political-military asset, more valuable than any weapon or military unit it possesses. Those critics who urge the United States to withdraw from its existing alliances forget that those alliances are a series of partnerships through which the United States significantly leverages its investments in security, enabling the nation to protect and promote its global interests far more extensively and cheaply than it could standing alone. Over the next few years the alliances will be under great strain as a result of economic tensions and the belief of some that, with the Soviet threat no longer a stimulus, the alliances are neither sustainable nor desirable. The United States must not yield to such pressures.

In truth, the U.S. alliances with Europe and Japan embody long-term U.S. interests that go well beyond the containment of Soviet or Russian power. Although the Soviet threat provided the initial impetus for their formation, the alliances have nurtured over the last half century a community of economic and political interests that now has a life of its own and that provides ample justification for preserving the alliances as its political-military backbone. This community of interests will be as important to Americans in the future as it was during the cold war years, if not more so.

By the second decade of this century, long before the outbreak of the Cold War and the formation of the North Atlantic Treaty Organization (NATO), it had become clear to many thoughtful Europeans and Americans that Great Britain was no longer capable of maintaining the European balance of power and that without an active U.S. political and military role in European affairs Europe would be torn by the traditional rivalries of such great powers as Germany and Russia and might become dominated by one of them, with harmful consequences for U.S. interests. To varying degrees, Theodore Roosevelt, Alfred Thayer Mahan, and Elihu Root shared this view. At the end of World War I the United States's greatest mistake was not its refusal to join the League of Nations; by itself, U.S. membership in the League, absent any willingness to use American power in support of the League's policies, would not have averted the coming of World War II. Its greatest error was, rather, to refuse France's request for an Anglo–American military guarantee in the event of future German aggression. Such a guarantee, if embodied in effective military arrangements among the three countries, would have given France the requisite security with which to pursue a conciliatory policy toward Weimar Germany in the 1920s and later a firmer policy toward Nazi Germany in the 1930s.

The implications of that failure are history, and they weighed heavily in the minds of the American and European architects of NATO. Within the protection afforded by NATO, European states have for several decades been able to lay aside their traditional security anxieties, even as far as accepting German reunification with much less opposition than would have seemed possible. It is also because of NATO that Europe and the United States are free to follow a magnanimous policy of friendship and assistance toward the former Soviet republics today.

Although it is natural to expect that over time the U.S. contribution to NATO will decline from its cold war levels, NATO can and should survive. Its maintenance and strengthening will be immensely useful to American and European interests for several reasons. First, NATO will continue to have a stabilizing effect on European affairs, calming security anxieties and deterring any future forces that may seek to overturn Europe's current status as a peaceful, democratic community of free peoples. Under NATO's roof, European integration will continue, ancient interstate rivalries will be moderated, and separatist tendencies within major European states will not be as difficult to accommodate as they would be in a system without an overarching security framework.

Second, NATO will act as a magnet, drawing toward the European–Atlantic security community states at present outside it. It is not inconceivable that some day most East European states and many of the former Soviet republics will join NATO. NATO then would have an effect on them similar to its eventual effect on Portugal, Spain, and Greece: by drawing them toward Europe it would also draw them more firmly toward democracy and free markets, eroding old authoritarian and statist traditions.

The U.S.–Japanese alliance is also rooted in common interests that go

15

well beyond the containment of Soviet or Russian power. By the end of the nineteenth century U.S. interests as a Pacific power were already being affected by the growing rivalries among Russia, Japan, China, and Korea. In the future, the stability of the Pacific Basin and a strong U.S.–Japanese relationship will be more important to the United States than ever before. The U.S. economy needs the vast markets of the Pacific Rim, and it benefits enormously from Japanese investment capital and technology and the impetus toward greater productivity provided by Japanese competition. By making it unnecessary for Japan to maintain large offensive military capabilities, and by reassuring other regional powers about the U.S. commitment to a peaceful, stable Pacific Basin, the alliance helps to hold in check traditional rivalries among Asian powers that otherwise could unravel into unrestrained military competition, conflict, and aggression.

By anchoring German and Japanese security in a broader multinational security community, the Atlantic and Pacific alliances respectively play a key role in discouraging what has been described as the "renationalization" of both countries' security policies. Such a renationalization is not desired by most Germans and Japanese or by their neighbors. Preventing it is a signal contribution to international order.

Integrating Multilateral Institutions and Practices More Thoroughly into the Fabric of U.S. Foreign and Defense Policy. Fiscal realities will dictate considerable reductions in U.S. military forces and in the economic resources available to the United States for foreign assistance. This means that the nation will have to use its available assets more imaginatively and with greater versatility. The United States will need to

look for ways to enhance its diplomatic and political leverage by joining its resources to those of others in pursuit of common objectives. Multilateral institutions and practices provide such an opportunity.

At the height of the Cold War the usefulness of certain multilateral institutions such as the United Nations was limited by the hostility of the Soviet bloc and of a group of third world states that, emboldened by Soviet support, felt confident in obstructing U.S. policy. On some occasions, such as with the infamous "Zionism is racism" resolution, the UN actually helped to inflame rather than calm the tensions of international politics. For the time being, however, Russia is following a pro-Western course, the People's Republic of China is too eager for Western economic ties to act as an obstructionist power, and many third world states have little incentive to alienate the United States and its allies gratuitously.

While these conditions last, the UN is potentially more useful than ever before for promoting both international cooperation and Western security. This is neither a call for multilateralism for its own sake, nor another incantation of the supposed goodness and efficacy of the United Nations. It is simply an acknowledgment that, as long as the core of the UN leadership is a concert of states with which the United States has considerable common interests, the institution can be useful in promoting policies that benefit both Americans and the larger international community. Such a hardheaded realist as Winston Churchill had a similar outlook toward the League of Nations up until the mid-1930s.

It goes without saying that this argument is true as well of other multilateral institutions that traditionally have been friendlier than the UN to Western interests. With regard to at least three important issues the United States can accomplish far more through multilateral efforts than by acting on its own: (1) encouraging the integration of the former Soviet Union into the community of democratic and capitalist states loosely known as the West; (2) slowing the proliferation of ballistic missiles and nuclear, chemical, and biological weapons; and (3) organizing peacekeeping and peace-enforcement operations to defuse selected conflicts around the world.

As former President Richard M. Nixon has reminded us, helping the former Soviet republics to join the family of liberal democratic nations is not only in accordance with the highest principles of the United States, it is also in its national interest. Although the United States has much to offer the new republics in the way of political-military incentives such as arms reduction arrangements, much of the investment capital and economic assistance will have to be provided through multilateral efforts in which the United States joins its resources to those of others. Such investments in a democratic, capitalist order in the heart of Eurasia will enhance both future U.S. security and future prospects for a more cooperative international order.

Enough can never be said about the horrendous perils posed to contemporary democratic civilization by the rapid worldwide spread of weapons of mass destruction. It is only a matter of a few years before numbers of such weapons will be in the hands of regimes willing to use them. An effective U.S. strategy to slow down and disrupt proliferation will require a multilateral effort on the diplomatic, economic, political, and military fronts. The acquisition of these weapons is a long and complex process with numerous stages, each of which is vulnerable to disruption and obstruction through diplomatic pressures, carefully targeted economic sanctions and regulations, and covert as well as overt military operations. Only with the support of other interested parties and under the legitimacy and moral authority provided, however loosely, by multilateral institutions, can the United States hope to succeed.

The third area in which multilateralism can pay generous dividends for the United States is in peacekeeping and peace-enforcement operations. The United States cannot afford to become involved everywhere with substantial military resources, but there are conflicts in which, for a relatively small investment of political capital and military power, it can encourage constructive settlements that benefit its long-term interests. Two such kinds of conflicts come to mind.

In one, the security of the United States is not threatened directly but its interests are affected considerably, as they would be by a conflict between Russia and Ukraine or between Greece and Turkey that threatened to escalate to major war. In the second kind of conflict, such as Serbia's war against its Balkan neighbors, or a possible future civil war in Peru, U.S. interests may not be affected immediately in substantial ways, but the long-term consequences can be highly corrosive to the fabric of regional stability and eventually undermine important U.S. objectives. In neither of these cases should the United States intervene unilaterally, yet it is not in its interests to remain indifferent.

The ongoing war in the old Yugoslavia is a case in point. For almost a whole year, as the war among Serbia, Croatia, and Bosnia widened, many insisted that it was peripheral to U.S.

17

interests and that, beyond offers of support to the European Community's mediation efforts, U.S. policy should not exercise any forceful leadership to settle or contain the conflict. Eventually, and perhaps too late, it was realized that, as a matter of practical realism, the United States could not afford to remain on the sidelines. First, American indifference to Serbian aggression and Serbian atrocities would send a dangerous signal to potential would-be imitators in Eastern Europe and the former Soviet Union about the will of the United States and the Atlantic Alliance to shape Eastern Europe's political future. The prospects for orderly democratic reform and peaceful interstate relations in this region would suffer a severe setback if Serbia's policies were not sharply reined in. Second, if allowed to burn uncontrollably, the war might spread and draw into it outside parties such as Greece, Bulgaria, Turkey, Germany, and Russia, imperiling European peace and NATO's cohesiveness in highly dangerous ways. Finally, the threatened migration of millions of refugees from the conflict to Austria and Hungary posed an urgent humanitarian and political challenge requiring not merely a regional, but an international solution. In retrospect, with the hindsight rarely available to statesmen, it appears that the United States should have taken a more vigorous lead in defusing the conflict, in a multilateral context, in the fall of 1991 instead of waiting for others to do so. The war's human and economic costs would have been lower, and a settlement acceptable to all parties and to the long-term interests of the United States and the Atlantic Alliance would have been more feasible than it is now.

There will be other conflicts of this kind where it will be desirable for the United States to be engaged, while limiting the extent and risks of its engagement. By joining others in a peacekeeping or peace-enforcement effort, the United States can leverage its political and military power considerably and reduce the risks and costs of its involvement. As we move into an era of ever deadlier military technologies and virulent ethnic and religious struggles, multilateral peacekeeping and peacemaking operations that can defuse conflicts and promote settlements will become increasingly relevant to both U.S. security and international order.

The Requirements of Principle

The requirements of principle also present opportunities for policies that will benefit U.S. security while encouraging a more cooperative international order. Two sets of principles drawn from the American tradition offer such an opportunity. They are an appreciation of the value of international order and the prudent encouragement of liberal, capitalist democracy.

All great American statesmen have recognized that the United States exists in a particular kind of international society or order that, by facilitating the peaceful conduct of relations among states, benefits the United States considerably. The institutions and practices of diplomacy, of international law or what the Founding Fathers called "the Law of Nations," and of international morality, however blurred their boundaries and substance sometimes are, are intrinsic elements of such an order. Formal respect for them has always been part of the American tradition, even at the height of such intense struggles as the Cold War.

One of the greatest U.S. assets in international politics is the credibility of the United States as a power that succeeds more often than not in paying attention to the concerns and interests of its allies and friends and the rules and customs of international society. The value of such credibility is incalculable, especially at a time when, contrary to popular misperceptions, the United States will need its allies and friends more, not less, in the arduous task of shaping the international security environment. As the global conventional forces of the United States shrink and its economic resources become relatively less dominant, its credibility in Europe and Asia as a power that can be trusted to act responsibly will become proportionately more important as an asset. And key to that credibility's strength will be the kind of international order, including the framework of international principles and practices, that the United States supports.

Defining such an international order brings one close to three core prohibitions that U.S. foreign policy has supported over the last eight decades and that serve to strengthen both U.S. security and the prospects for a more cooperative international order. They are the impermissibility of armed aggression as an instrument of foreign policy, of war crimes, and of human rights violations egregious enough to classify as crimes against humanity. An international order grounded in these prohibitions is one in which the United States will be more secure.

These prohibitions, though formally embodied in international law since the Nuremberg trials, have been part of the Western moral tradition for several centuries. They are a set of minimalist norms that prevent pluralism from degenerating into chaos and unrestrained violence. They place restraints on the conduct of states, but they do not seek to uproot established cultural traditions or political systems.

Indeed, they presuppose a pluralistic world of different cultures, religions, and political and economic systems.

As a practical matter, the United States will have to act in concert with other states to enforce the prohibitions when they are violated. Such enforcement will be problematic, and often the norms will be honored more in the breach than in the keeping. What is important is that the United States and other interested parties summon the requisite will and resources to articulate and enforce the prohibitions on enough occasions to maintain them alive as generally authoritative norms whose violation carries significant costs, thereby raising the threshold at which potential violators consider it convenient to disregard them.

Enforcing the prohibitions against aggression and egregious human rights violations may require U.S.–led and coordinated multilateral peace-enforcement operations in which military force is used against the will of some of the warring factions to facilitate or impose a particular kind of diplomatic settlement. Such operations are extremely complex politically and militarily, and the United States should be highly selective in undertaking them. But they should be part of the armory of political instruments through which the United States, in a multilateral context, helps to shape the international political and security environment in ways that are favorable to its long-term interests and values.

The U.S. military is likely to resist involvement in peace-enforcement operations, citing the specter of Vietnam and similar "quagmires." Although such protestations deserve a fair hearing, they should be treated as useful warnings rather than inviolate counsels. The U.S. military will tend to be wary of any use of military power that falls short of the Desert Storm paradigm, which Gen. Colin Powell has approvingly described as "overwhelming force." In the world ahead, however, the requirements of shaping the international security environment will often call for the use of force at levels far short of, and in ways quite different from, "overwhelming force."

Although the prohibitions against aggression, war crimes, and egregious human rights violations embody positive human values to which Americans are strongly attached, they do not capture the whole range of principles to which the United States has been committed since its founding. One would have to add a principle that, though highly desired by many around the world, is still far from universally cherished. It is the principle of freedom, both in its political dimension of democracy and in its economic dimension of capitalism. It is in the interests of the United States to promote freedom and to help it take root in those societies where it can flourish, even while recognizing that not all societies are either capable of it or want it.

In the aftermath of the cold war victory we must not succumb to the temptation of ascribing to freedom a historical inevitability and triumphal universality that, historically, it has never had. Most philosophers and historians, including some within the liberal tradition itself, would warn us that freedom requires a delicate balance between the enjoyment of rights and the exercise of responsibilities, between creativity and restraint, between the desires of the individual and the needs of the community, that few societies are able to achieve for more than a flickering historical moment. The implication of this warning should be to instill in U.S. foreign policy a degree of modesty and circumspection at odds with the natural enthusiasm of Americans. The United States should

support freedom around the world, but always in the context of this modesty and of a prudential appraisal of the kind of world in which Americans live. The history of U.S. foreign policy since 1914 represents an effort to strike such a prudential balance.

Prospects for a Cooperative World Order

It is difficult to predict how successful the United States will be in building a more cooperative international order. The world is being shaped simultaneously by forces of integration and disintegration. Viewed from one angle, modern communications, technology, trade, and the appeal of political and economic freedom have the potential to create a global democratic capitalist society where international cooperation will be more successful than in the past. But from another perspective, the post–cold war world does not look as comforting.

In addition to the current intensification of international economic competition, which sooner or later could have political ramifications destructive of international cooperation, the new world is facing an unexpected development. From California to Czechoslovakia, old ethnic and cultural identities are surfacing with vigor, threatening to overwhelm the integrating processes of democracy and technology with the disintegrating effects of ethnicity and tribalism. In a manner eerily reminiscent of Fyodor Dostoevsky's "underground man," many people are rebelling against the depersonalized, desacralized character of modern society by searching for new sources of identity and meaning, in the process discovering some very ancient ones. Throughout history, ethnic and tribal politics have been peculiarly resistant to either an ethic or statecraft of prudence. Its norm has been instead total annihilation of the enemy—not a reassuring prospect in an age of weapons of mass destruction.

Meanwhile, democratic societies everywhere—not only the new ones in Eurasia and in the Third World but also more established ones such as the United States—are facing a complex array of problems that are diminishing their governability or capacity to provide effective government. First, modern democracies have dangerously shifted the ground of their legitimacy from the principle of freedom to the guarantee of perpetually greater economic prosperity. It is questionable, however, whether a political arrangement based on the promise of ever rising living standards can endure for long. Long recessions and depressions have always been part of the economic cycle, and there is no reason to think it will be otherwise in the future. At some point there could be a major economic global contraction, and modern mass democracies will be vulnerable to authoritarian leaders or ideologies that artfully promise renewed prosperity.

Second, democratic legal systems are gradually evolving into enormously complex and burdensome institutions for facilitating individual fulfillment rather than simply protecting life and liberty. The long-term durability of a legal order whose prevailing maxim is to get for yourself the most that the law allows you to have is also questionable. As Thomas Jefferson pointed out, as soon as everyone tries to push the law to its uttermost limits, the social foundation that makes possible a legal system in the first place begins to crumble.

Third, Charles Krauthammer and others have reminded us that Western democratic society is the first in history to combine individual liberty with mass hedonism.[2] The result has been the creation of a democratic, capitalist mass culture whose dominant values—unrestrained individualism, consumerism, and the rejection of authority—paradoxically undermine the very virtues of self-discipline, hard work, and thrift necessary for the long-term viability of both capitalism and political liberty. As we look at the decline of that society over the last 30 years—a decline that has been masked by economic prosperity and the spectacular collapse of communism—we need to ask ourselves how long a society combining the liberty of democracy with an ethic of mass hedonism can endure.

Regarding all these vulnerabilities of democracy, it is also useful to note that, like its rival political systems, democracy has failed to address thus far the most pressing social and economic problems generated by modern urban society and technology, including the widespread alienation, loneliness, and sense of futility pervading much of our collective life.

Although democracy, in Churchill's words, may be the worst system of government except for all the others, it is possible that over the long run some democratic societies will collapse under the weight of their inadequacies and revert to forms of traditional authoritarianism that offer a degree of social discipline and economic security in exchange for limits on individual freedom. Such authoritarianisms, of which there remain plenty in the 1990s, do not augur well for peaceful international relations. It is thus an open question whether a global democratic society will take root long or deeply enough to advance significantly the prospects for international cooperation.

It is not clear today, any more than it was to Carl Becker in 1943, whether we are entering a world that is either new or better. In the face of these uncertainties, the United States must remain hopeful yet sober. As incurable optimists, Americans must not allow their hopes to outrun their prudence. They will have to balance the requirements of their power with those of their principles, for their strength will lie precisely in the way in which they can relate principles to power for mutual reinforcement. But Americans must also remember that international society remains anarchical, and that the best way to construct a cooperative international order is not to place their hopes in such institutions as collective security or the United Nations as if they had a life of their own apart from the values, direction, and effective strength that nations bring to them. A much sounder way to improve the prospects for international cooperation is to look for ways in which the United States and its allies, who together wield enormous power, can put that power behind policies that further U.S. national and common security while simultaneously strengthening the fabric of that international society to which Americans are inexorably tied and upon whose stability and welfare they so heavily depend.

The views in this article are the author's alone and do not necessarily represent those of the U.S. Department of Defense.

Notes

1. Carl Becker, *How New Will the Better World Be? A Discussion of Post-War Reconstruction* (1944; Freeport, N.Y.: Books for Libraries Press, 1971).

2. Charles Krauthammer, "The Issue-Thin Campaign," *Washington Post*, September 11, 1992, p. A–23.

II. Peacetime Defense Policy

U.S. Defense Strategy After the Cold War

Patrick J. Garrity and
Sharon K. Weiner

IN A SPEECH delivered literally hours before Iraq's invasion of Kuwait on August 2, 1990, President George Bush outlined the key components of a new, post–cold war defense strategy for the United States. The new strategy shifted emphasis from a major global conflict with the Soviet Union toward regional military contingencies and envisioned maintenance of a Base Force structure that would be roughly 25 percent smaller than the 1990 force by the middle of the decade. The administration's relatively cautious view of the post–cold war world seemed to be validated by Iraq's aggression and the shift to the right in Moscow a few months later, and the budget agreement in the fall of 1990 appeared to promise a level of funding that would support the Base Force.

But the world has continued to change, as has thinking about defense strategy—and the willingness of the U.S. public to support defense investments on the scale envisioned. In the aftermath of the Desert Storm victory, strong pressures for further defense spending cuts reemerged, not least of which was a federal budget deficit about to exceed $350 billion. The apparent breakup of the USSR and the

demise of any significant short- or midterm military threat from that state or its successors further undermined the defense strategy consensus. Looking ahead to the 1992 congressional budget cycle, the defense budget is likely to be in free fall.

This essay examines the emerging national debate over the direction of U.S. defense policy. It is not a discrete subject because in fact the defense debate has become a principal vehicle for discussing the much larger issue of the place of the United States in the post–cold war world. Rather than anticipate some of the political debate and jockeying during an election year, this article instead identifies and evaluates the most important issues that will emerge with the accelerated defense build down.

The New Defense Strategy of 1990

The point of departure in the debate about a new U.S. defense strategy must be the Bush speech of August 1990 and its basic concepts and recommendations.[1] The Base Force and strategy outlined then were organized around two basic ideas.

The first was the shift in U.S. defense planning toward regional contingencies and away from the Soviet threat. The rationale was straightforward. The military threat posed by the

Patrick Garrity is a staff member at the Center for National Security Studies, Los Alamos National Laboratory. Sharon Weiner is a doctoral candidate in political science at MIT.

Soviet Union was seen to have waned considerably, although in the first half of 1990 many in the administration considered the reappearance of that threat to be possible in the long and medium terms as well as the short term. The focus shifted to the rise of would-be regional hegemons such as Iraq and to global issues such as shifting demographics, ethnic and religious problems, economic stagnation, and sharp differences in living standards and humanitarian conditions that would be likely to fuel old conflicts or give rise to new ones. Secretary of Defense Richard B. Cheney argued that "the end of the bipolar world could unleash local, destructive forces that were previously kept in check."[2] The purpose of U.S. military power would be to act as a stabilizing factor in key regions by deterring conflicts, dampening local arms races, and protecting U.S. interests and allies should conflicts occur. Regional threats against vital U.S. interests were deemed sufficiently robust to warrant the maintenance by the United States of a military force of superpower quality.

But the administration acknowledged the necessity of maintaining such a force within domestic fiscal realities—meaning a sharply declining military budget. The design of the Base Force structure was driven by projected levels of defense spending that came to be incorporated into the 1990 Budget Enforcement Act (BEA). The BEA limited all discretionary spending, including defense, for fiscal years 1991–1995. These limits translated into an 11.3 percent decline in real defense budget authority in FY 1991 followed by decreases of roughly 3 percent per year for the next four years. If BEA limits remain in force, by FY 1996 defense budget authority will have declined to approximately the amount spent in FY 1980 ($243

billion in constant 1992 dollars). But because of so many factors intervening since the autumn of 1990, including not least the failed Soviet coup and the growing political pressure to focus resources on the domestic agenda, it is very likely that the funding "floor" upon which the Pentagon constructed its Base Force is likely to become a ceiling instead.

The 1990 version of the defense strategy can be summarized as follows. It established four primary goals: deterrence, forward presence, crisis response, and reconstitution. The means to achieve these goals was to be a Base Force subdivided into Atlantic, Pacific, Contingency, and Strategic force packages. These in turn were to be supported by four basic military capabilities in space, transportation, research and development (R&D), and reconstitution.[3]

Deterrence remains the primary purpose of the U.S. military. In the nuclear arena, the Bush administration has focused on deterring the deliberate use of nuclear weapons by whatever state or entity should inherit the nuclear legacy of the USSR, although in fall 1991 there has been growing concern about accidental or unauthorized use of nuclear weapons, particularly during the breakup of the USSR.[4] Dangers associated with the proliferation of weapons of mass destruction and sophisticated delivery systems in the developing world have also been brought into sharp focus by revelations about the extent of the nuclear programs of Iraq and North Korea, but given the uncertainties of deterrence of such states, emphasis had been placed on strategic defenses, theater defenses, and diplomacy.

In the nonnuclear, conventional area, thinking about deterrence has undergone a radical shift. No longer do senior military leaders focus on preventing a major global war with the USSR beginning in Europe. Instead, the administration emphasizes the emergence of a strategic environment requiring forces capable of deterring a broad range of contingencies from regional wars to insurgencies, interruptions in the flow of trade and commerce, terrorism, and other forms of low-intensity conflict.

Forward presence is prized as a way to demonstrate U.S. engagement as the preeminent military power but it will be at a lower level than embodied in the forward deployments of the cold war era. It is defended as a way to maintain alliance relations, deter aggression, deflect regional arms races, and prevent the power vacuums that invite conflict. In regions where the United States has compelling interests, such as Europe and East Asia, it will continue permanently to deploy forces as long as they are needed and welcomed. But the size of these forward deployments will decline, and in some cases may be replaced with less permanent and visible forms of presence such as military exercises and visits, infrastructure and logistics arrangements, military assistance, disaster relief, other forms of humanitarian assistance, and peacekeeping efforts.

Crisis response capabilities are required as a way to compensate for the diminution of forward-deployed forces. The administration assumes that regional crises will tend to remain localized but will vary in character and in the amount of time for advance warning and response. Thus the strategy emphasizes flexible military options, power projection, transportation, and a high state of readiness.

Reconstitution has been seen as a basic insurance policy against a resurgence of a future "Soviet" threat and more generally against future uncertainties in the international environ-

ment. Reconstitution entails the ability to deploy wholly new military capabilities above those in the Base Force. By demonstrating a U.S. ability to deploy a credible defense faster than a would-be global adversary could generate an overwhelming offense, the Department of Defense (DOD) hopes to prevent a remilitarization of great power relations, to deter war if remilitarization cannot be prevented, and to wage it successfully if war cannot be deterred. The ability to reconstitute is a function of the maintenance of a quality defense industrial base, U.S. technological superiority in key areas, and military leadership and warfighting skills.

The force posture to accomplish the military goals of the new defense strategy is contained in the Base Force with its collection of four force packages—Atlantic, Pacific, Strategic, and Contingency.[5] These force levels have been defended as the minimum necessary to sustain the strategy, and Secretary Cheney has warned that "cutting below these levels would not leave us with needed capabilities, even under quite positive future trends."[6] The Base Force would emerge after a build down over five years, ending in FY 1995. Military active duty strengths would be reduced from FY 1990 levels of 2.07 million to 1.65 million, and reserve end strengths from 1.13 million to 906,000, for total personnel reductions of approximately 20 percent from FY 1990 levels. Overall, reserve forces are to decline by approximately the same percentage as active forces.[7] The Base Force concept envisions 12 active army divisions, 6 reserve divisions, and two cadre divisions (versus 18 active and 10 reserve divisions in the FY 1990 force structure); 12 naval carrier battle groups and 448 ships (versus 15 and 536); and 15 active and 11 reserve tactical fighter wings (versus 22 and 12).[8]

The four force packages of the Base Force are organized in terms of geographic and functional areas. The Atlantic Force, to include the areas of Europe, the Mediterranean, the Middle East, and Southwest Asia, would consist of greatly reduced forward basing and deployment in Europe with heavy reinforcements from the continental United States. The Pacific Force is primarily maritime in character with little change from previous strategy, except for plans for reduced deployments in Japan and South Korea. The forces for crisis response would be found in a Contingency Force composed of rapidly deployable light units, special operations forces, and command, control, communications, and intelligence (C³I) systems. These forces would operate under regional commanders and would be based predominantly in the United States. Lastly, land, sea, and bomber-based nuclear forces fall under the Strategic Force.

The goals of the new defense strategy and the Base Force are to be supported by four underlying capabilities. Space and space-based systems would provide early warning, intelligence, surveillance, navigation, command, control, and communications, space control (antisatellite or ASAT), and force application (space-based defenses). Transportation, consisting of prepositioned equipment and mobility assets such as the C–17 aircraft and improved sealift, would be essential to support the new strategy's emphasis on rapid response. To assure continued U.S. technological superiority, the United States would retain a strong research and development program. Finally, to hedge against future unanticipated threats, the new strategy calls for an ability to reconstitute

forces and military industrial capacity as necessary.

This defense strategy rests on a set of assumptions about the international environment and the politics of budget making in the United States that have changed substantially since the strategy was articulated and "endorsed" by the Congress in the FY 1992 defense budget process. As Representative Les Aspin (D–Wis.), chairman of the House Committee on Armed Services, has observed:

The first revolution irreversibly ended the Warsaw Pact threat to Western Europe and the right response was judged to be a 25 percent reduction in our forces. If this second revolution results in the end of the Soviet military threat to the United States, can't we go further? Some say no, that we must hold at the 25 percent reduction. I don't think that position can be held if the Soviet threat is really gone.[9]

Indeed, there is a widely held expectation today that the defense budget will be reduced over the mid term by 40 or 50 percent rather than the projected 25 percent. Defense spending could decline to a level between $150 to $200 billion (in constant FY 1992 dollars) by the late 1990s, well under the Bush administration's planned $243 billion. Such a budget would clearly not be adequate to support the Base Force.

Senior Pentagon officials have publicly declared their intention to fight to maintain the projected funding levels. In General Colin L. Powell's terms: "We can't redo our strategy and structure every Monday morning based on events in Red Square."[10] But in late 1991, there were press reports that the administration was quietly preparing more cuts, down to 10 active army divisions, 9 carrier battle groups, and 20 active and reserve tactical fighter wings.[11] Further reductions of this magnitude will obviously call into question many of the premises and goals of the new defense strategy.

Rather than simply discard the Base Force and the new defense strategy, however, the Bush administration and Congress should use them as the starting point in the lengthy process of adjusting defense policy to account for a fundamentally altered national security environment. To do so during a presidential election year will be extremely difficult and unlikely to produce consensus. It will also obscure many of the fundamental issues with which the process of adjustment must deal. These are the focus of the following discussion.

U.S. Interests and Military Power

The basic definition of U.S. interests has not been seriously at issue since the late 1940s. Those interests were the reconstruction of postwar Europe and Asia, the expansion of a liberal trading system, and containment of communism, all under the aegis of forceful U.S. leadership. Over time, this definition has led to a certain level of defense spending (of 5 to 10 percent of GNP), a certain type of military force structure and strategy (varied, globally deployed conventional and nuclear forces operating under a policy of flexible response), and a strategic goal (to deter war, and if deterrence failed, to terminate war at the lowest possible level of violence on terms acceptable to the United States and its allies). These are all very much in doubt today. Redefinition by the U.S. body politic of its concept of the national interest and of the means to pursue that interest will inevitably lead to new strategic goals, force structures, and levels of defense spending.

Despite its rhetorical concessions to growing economic and transnational concerns, the Bush administration's view of the world is fundamentally strategic and military in character. It believes that U.S. military power imbues Washington with the unique ability to provide for the stability and defense of key regions and thus gives it the political leverage necessary to move toward a new international order. This order is to be based on U.S. principles and led by the United States in partnership with its key allies in the industrial world.

There are other views of the world and of U.S. interests therein, however, that would point toward much smaller U.S. military forces based on a different kind of defense policy. These alternatives have not yet emerged full-blown on the U.S. political scene. Nor is it likely that political consensus on national interests in the post–cold war era will emerge quickly or through a single, decisive debate. A durable approach will emerge only gradually through a series of specific decisions about particular issues. The outcome of the 1992 election will be critical in this respect, as will international developments whose emergence and outcome cannot be foreseen. This said, some of the most likely lines of argument have already emerged. They are not mutually exclusive: it is possible to embrace several of them with different degrees of emphasis.

One line of argument concerns a broadening of the definition of "defense" to one of "national security" or even "international security." This view is implicit in some of the legislative actions of Senator Sam Nunn (D–Ga.) and Representative Aspin, such as the unsuccessful effort to shift $1 billion from the defense budget to provide for food aid to the former Soviet Union. The argument here is that money that was once spent to provide military security should in part be diverted to meet other emerging challenges to U.S. interests in the new strategic environment, such as the prevention of chaos in the strategic space once occupied by the USSR. This view does not reject the importance of maintaining a global military capability, but it holds that there are other tools for maintaining and enhancing regional and global stability besides armed forces and that the size of the defense budget and the character of the U.S. military structure should reflect this fact.

A second position has a very specific definition of "national security" in the context of the new strategic environment: economic security. It holds that the traditional military competition among the great powers has been replaced by a geoeconomic struggle.[12] The Europeans (particularly the Germans) and the Japanese have emerged as a new kind of industrial-technological superpower, in large part because, secure under the U.S. military umbrella, they have invested resources that would otherwise have gone to defense into building up their economic strength. The United States must now follow suit if it is not to become a second-rate power in the areas that truly matter, or so goes the argument.

This position tends to see military spending and economic-technological strength as being in direct opposition: the defense budget should be cut and the resources diverted to help gear up the U.S. economy to meet the Japanese and European economic challenge. Above all, the United States should cease providing Japan and Europe with a free ride in the security arena. This implies that the United States should cease to provide ex-

tended nuclear deterrence to its allies, withdraw forward-deployed forces in Europe and the Pacific, and develop regional-contingency forces only to meet threats to U.S., and not allied, interests.

For some, the emphasis on geo-economics takes on a strongly nationalist, neo-isolationist hue. Thus adherents of this viewpoint assert that Germany and Japan are not simply more competitive or clever than the United States but are actually overtly hostile to U.S. interests and economic well-being. The United States is seen to be in an economic conflict with its putative strategic allies, for which U.S. opponents are organizing themselves into regional trading blocs. Many adherents of this point of view are therefore strong supporters of a Western Hemisphere free trade zone. Among conservatives who hold this nationalistic view, regional military balances and conflicts outside the hemisphere should not be of concern to the United States; U.S. defense policy should focus instead on defending the sea and aerospace lines of communication to and from the United States.

A third perspective, held by many congressional Democrats but also by a growing number of Republicans, is likewise concerned about U.S. well-being, but it defines U.S. interests primarily in domestic terms rather than in the context of international relations. It would be unfair and inaccurate to characterize this perspective as isolationist, but it does assume that, with the collapse of the Soviet Union, the attention and resources of the country should be refocused primarily on the well-being of U.S. citizens at home. The threat to this well-being, generally stated, is a declining standard of living and quality of life. It includes such issues as the loss of U.S. economic competitiveness, the rising rate of crime, lack of affordable health care, the drug problem, a deteriorating service infrastructure, and so on.

From this perspective, there is no foreign policy problem of such magnitude today that it should command funds and attention ahead of these domestic challenges. The defense budget is seen primarily as a pool of resources that should be diverted as rapidly and as extensively as necessary to meet domestic concerns. The allocation of remaining funds in the Pentagon's accounts will also be influenced by domestic concerns: which weapon systems to fund, which bases to close, the size of the reserve forces and so on, will be judged largely on their impact on the U.S. people (or, less politely, on their impact in specific congressional districts), and not on abstract strategic calculations.

A fourth perspective on U.S. interests is internationalist in character. With the end of the Cold War, the United States has the opportunity to work toward a basic restructuring of international politics and toward a new military relationship among the great and lesser powers. From this perspective, the United States should focus its attention on integrating its national military posture with that of appropriate multinational coalitions and international bodies (for example, the United Nations). It should also work with other states to create military postures that are inherently and mutually defensive in character—for instance, by eliminating capabilities that might support ground invasions or long-range bombardment. Such a restructuring would not only save money directly for the United States, it would also foster international cooperation and trust that, over time, might remove many

of the sources of national tension and conflict that led to the creation of large military establishments in the first place.[13]

There are, of course, many possible variants on these lines of argument. New alternatives may emerge in the course of the next few years as Congress and the administration debate the particulars of national security and military policy. But as can be seen from the above trends, the prospect for a major shift in the direction of U.S. defense strategy is very real.

However U.S. interests come to be defined over the next few years, the role of U.S. military power in the nation's security policy must be in accordance with those interests. Most important, the case for the defense establishment must begin with a recognition that the world has fundamentally changed and that U.S. military power will in all likelihood be a subordinate element in the new equation of national purpose.

The Bush administration has made the case that military power underpins the U.S. claim to superpower status and global leadership. This is undoubtedly true, but it will not be sufficient to persuade those who define superpower status in other terms. DOD will increasingly be judged by its impact on the long-term health of the U.S. economy. This has led to a desire to redirect Pentagon research to support economic competitiveness, although this probably should be resisted in part because there are more direct and efficient ways to foster the development of commercial technologies and industries than through defense spending. But at the very least, the department should take care to do no harm. It should seek to tap much more directly into commercial research, development, and production.

It should endeavor to not monopolize scarce resources and talent and act instead as a smart and supportive customer.

More broadly, the United States must cease thinking about and justifying its military capability primarily in terms of deterring a specific, ill-intentioned adversary. The central strategic challenge for the foreseeable future will not be deterrence, but rather fostering political conditions in which relations among the great industrial powers remain friendly, and preventing what competition does emerge from spilling over into the military domain. In many policy areas, such as supporting peaceful and democratic change in Eastern Europe and the former Soviet Union, this will not involve U.S. military power. But the continued existence of substantial U.S. military capabilities may be essential to reassure other great powers that they need not (re)enter the military arena in a major way. This will not be an easy case to make to Congress and the American people, but it is likely to be more persuasive than the search for nonexistent threats.

In shaping future force structure and military doctrine, the Pentagon will also be well advised to take into account its "customer"—the U.S. people and their elected representatives in Congress. In some cases, such as the active-reserve mix, this will require that the military accept some compromises. Rather than throw up its hands, it should seek creative solutions within the boundaries created by the political process.

The Pentagon is also likely to find the greatest political support for those technologies and weapons that can meet the Desert Storm criteria: they must offer the potential for rapid and decisive operations with low U.S. military casualties (from hostile and friendly fire) and with low civilian exposure. To be sure, war can never be guaranteed to be neat and clean and quick, and there are very real dangers in basing the political case for the U.S. military force structure on "user friendly" grounds. But in an era of effective U.S. military superiority, the Desert Storm criteria are not unreasonable standards for the U.S. public to set for the professional military.

Military Requirements Absent the Threat

For the past four decades, the Soviet Union has provided U.S. military planners with an obvious benchmark against which to determine the appropriate quantity and quality of U.S. forces. To be sure, even during the Cold War, the process of determining U.S. military requirements was hardly devoid of politics or of controversy, and the Pentagon was never able to come close to generating the "minimum risk force" against the USSR that conservative planning criteria would have indicated. But there was a consensus in the United States and the West that no strategically significant gaps should emerge in the military capabilities of the two sides.

Until the failed coup of August 1991 and the subsequent collapse of the Union, the Soviet military remained a familiar threat. This is no longer the case. And although a revived Iraq or a desperate North Korea remain important planning contingencies, there is no longer any substantial political support for military planning based on specific threats. As General Powell himself remarked: "I'm running out of villains. I'm down to Fidel Castro and Kim Il Sung. . . . I would be very surprised if another Iraq occurred."[14] The challenge is now said to be "planning against uncertainty and instability." But there is no obvious way to set spending levels or design a force structure without reference to a specific threat.

The Bush administration has yet to come to grips with this problem. With its focus on regional conflicts, the administration has implicitly generated a set of military requirements based on the need to fight two such conflicts although it has not made this explicit in the Base Force concept.[15] Those seeking deeper budget cuts believe that a contingency force enabling simultaneous or sequential operations in two regions is excessive. Given current fiscal realities, political factors are likely to compel planners to size military forces for only a single major regional contingency.[16]

But such an approach to overall size offers little in the way of guidance about the proper character of U.S. military capabilities and plans. In the absence of a new and politically persuasive planning rationale, the level and direction of military spending will be driven almost exclusively by domestic considerations. Some such considerations are both necessary and legitimate: who could quarrel with the need to cut the federal deficit or address pressing domestic concerns? But some considerations are less defensible. Special interests could skew the force structure and severely limit U.S. options. The desire of many members of Congress to keep the level of reserve forces relatively high and to fund some weapon programs beyond their useful life is but one example.

There are a number of methods that might be employed to guide the planning process and assist the administration and Congress to reach some consensus about defense policy. One technique involves the formulation and evaluation of generic threats, for instance, a "Green Threat" posed to the Persian Gulf by one or more hostile regional military powers in the Middle East in the mid-1990s, a "Red Threat" posed to Europe by a large, medium-to-high-technology continental power in the early twenty-first century, and an "Orange Threat" posed to U.S. maritime interests in the Pacific by a high-technology power toward the year 2010.[17] (The political sensitivities created by devising such generic threats are, of course, obvious.) Other generic threats need not be region-specific; they could include Grenada and Panama-style rescue and intervention missions, low-intensity conflicts, counternarcotic operations, and the like.

The planner uses these generic models to consider alternative force structures and operational plans and, given a reasonable estimate of the available funding, calculations can also be made of the extent to which the forces/capabilities should be active or in the reserves, or whether they must be reconstituted. This planning process should be aimed at deriving a set of force structure requirements that will meet a range of the most plausible and important of these generic threats, even if the force structure is not optimized for any particular case. To be sure, these generic threats should not be treated as being equal: the Green Threat is probably both more likely and more imminent than the Orange Threat, and therefore should have greater weight.

Another approach drops any reference to specific threats and focuses instead on identifying specific benchmarks in critical military-technical areas. This is analogous to the former British naval standard to match and best the combined capabilities of the next two most substantial navies. In the nuclear arena, for example, the United States could decide to maintain a stockpile at least equal to those of all combined non-Soviet (or non-Russian) nuclear forces. If a benchmarking approach is adopted, however, qualitative standards are likely to prove more useful than quantitative ones. For instance, the United States could decide to ensure that its deployed aerospace capability in strategic bombers, fighter aircraft, and space launch systems is qualitatively equal to or better than that of any other nation, friendly or hostile.

A third approach to generating military requirements could focus instead on modernization and force improvement. The United States could seek to improve its absolute capability to achieve certain military objectives on a steady basis, regardless of the actions of potential enemies. Some of these objectives, such as moving a military force a certain distance in a specific amount of time, might be relatively straightforward. Others might be much more strategically ambitious: for instance, to master the technologies and operational concepts associated with the so-called revolution in military affairs.[18] If this goal were adopted, the United States would seek to perfect its ability to conduct a Desert Shield/Desert Storm type of conflict and especially to determine the course and outcome of future large-scale military operations through a strategic air campaign against even the most sophisticated possible opponent. Baseline objectives could also be set for the less intense military operations that are likely to be prevalent in the post–cold war environment.

Careful thought will undoubtedly suggest other approaches to the generation of military requirements in the absence of specific and well-defined threats. Because each method has its advantages and drawbacks, the best course for defense planning may be a combination of methodologies under the rubric of a national net assessment process. Some such means must be found to provide this administration (and its successors) with an intellectual framework for fighting the inevitable political battles within the Pentagon and in Congress about the future size and character of U.S. military forces.

The Character and Purpose of U.S. Nuclear Forces

For most of the first three years of its tenure, the Bush administration remained a staunch defender of the centrality of nuclear deterrence in U.S. defense policy. According to the latest National Security Strategy: "Even in a new era, deterring nuclear attack remains the number one defense priority of the United States."[19] The administration was occasionally willing to accede to political reality, for example, in canceling the Follow-on-to-Lance (FOTL) tactical nuclear system in the face of obvious German opposition, but for the most part it retained relatively conservative views on nuclear matters.

President Bush's September 1991 speech appears to indicate a sea change in the U.S. government's perspective on nuclear weapons. The speech was in part a tactical effort to preempt some of the political pressures that were mounting against controversial programs such as the B–2 bomber and the Strategic Defense Initiative (SDI). But the administration has also clearly shifted its strategic emphasis away from deterring a deliberate Soviet nuclear attack and toward ensuring the control and safety of nuclear weapons in whatever entity succeeds the Soviet Union.[20] (Similar concerns might likewise arise if the Chinese central government should be weakened as the current generation of political leaders passes from the scene.) And of course, the prospect of proliferation in the Third World and in such hitherto unlikely places as East–Central Europe further points toward the end of the familiar, and relatively stable, nuclear terrain of the past several decades.[21]

The shift in the administration's attitude toward nuclear weapons has accelerated existing political pressures to delegitimate them. With the disappearance of the Manichean character of the East–West conflict, the destructive capacity of nuclear weapons appears increasingly in tension with the political and moral requirements of the new era. Also, the clear U.S. conventional superiority as manifested in the Persian Gulf War would seem to render moot the principal long-standing military justification for nuclear weapons—that they were needed to compensate for presumed Western conventional *inferiority.*

Under these changed circumstances, the prospect of nuclear civil war in the former Soviet Union, and of Iraqi (or North Korean or Iranian) nuclear bombs, seems therefore to point toward trading "excess" U.S. nuclear capability in a series of political deals aimed at eliminating the most dangerous manifestations of nuclear multipolarity. (It has also breathed new life into the U.S. ballistic missile defense program, which has now been reoriented toward defending against accidental, unauthorized, and third country launches.) One example of this approach is to be found in Korea, where U.S. withdrawal of tactical nuclear weapons from South Korea is being used to try to get a handle on North Korea's nuclear program by compelling Pyongyang to open its nuclear facilities to international inspection.

If taken to its logical conclusion, this approach will rapidly lead the United States to cease to regard nuclear weapons as the cornerstone of its national security and to "segregate" any remaining nuclear forces from its force structure and strategy. Already some U.S. military officials are speculating about the emergence of an overtly countercity targeting strategy that would reverse a decades-long priority on holding at risk enemy military (especially nuclear) capability. If policy continues in this direction, the United States will likely drift toward a policy of "existential deterrence," with much smaller nuclear stockpiles (on the order of 1,000 to 2,000 weapons), much less diverse forces, and no deployment of ground-based or air-launched nuclear forces outside U.S. territory. In the event that an existential nuclear deterrent posture were adopted, the United States would also likely reduce or terminate its nuclear testing and modernization programs. Although the savings from these steps would be relatively modest, they might allow Washington to delay or truncate reductions in conventional forces.[22]

The United States may choose not to move quite this far, however. A good case can be made that nuclear weapons played a major and perhaps decisive role in deterring East–West war throughout the Cold War. If the drawdown on nuclear weapons proceeds too far, the case can also be made that a dangerous political and even military vacuum would be created, especially if great power relations at some time again deteriorate. In addition, for political reasons, the United States would be likely to have difficulty regenerating a nuclear force of the size and quality existing today if deep cuts proceed.

In any case, the United States must reassess the concepts that have dominated its thinking about nuclear weapons over the last few decades. In particular, the concept of deterrence is likely to become a much less attractive means of justifying military programs and policies of any kind. Deterrence will be viewed as unnecessary and provocative in relations with the other major powers (including the former Soviet Union, or whatever entities may emerge from its breakup), and probably ineffective in the case of rogue regional powers like Iraq.

The current shift in the focus of U.S. nuclear policy away from the traditional Soviet threat and toward the more likely threats of accidental or unauthorized launch, terrorist activities, or the use of a few weapons by third world leaders, seems sensible. But this shift requires more than a few simple changes in declaratory policy or a retargeting of forces. Nuclear weapons policy must reflect careful thinking about the persons they are designed to deter, the relationship between deterrence and defense against nuclear attack, how far any such deterrence can (and should) be extended to allies, and whether the ability to destroy an adversary that possesses only a few crudely built nuclear weapons is of any value at all.

The Character of the U.S. Conventional Force Structure

In the new strategic environment, the nuclear force posture is likely to attract less attention than the maintenance of effective conventional forces. This will involve debates over military roles and missions, the importance of readiness, the need to modernize the remaining force structure, and the like.

One of the most interesting such issues concerns the trade-offs between a "balanced" force and a more specialized one. During the Cold War, the United States created a balanced military force structure through which to deter and, if necessary, wage global war. This included a variety of capabilities that came at considerable expense: large and militarily effective ground forces, tactical aviation, naval surface and attack submarine fleets, strategic nuclear forces, and their associated supporting infrastructure (e.g., transportation and space). At a time when the threat of global war has all but vanished and defense resources are declining markedly, it is natural to examine this structure in order to eliminate unnecessary components and to optimize the remainder for the most likely future conflicts. Certain elements of the existing structure will be high on the budget-cutters' hit list: ground forces, strategic nuclear forces, and attack submarines.[23]

Because of the very uncertain strategic environment, DOD is reluctant to move too rapidly away from a balanced force structure. Moreover, strong institutional interests will also cause the Pentagon to resist excessive cuts in any one service. This does not mean that priorities cannot be set; rather, it implies that the United States should not move irrevocably out of any major arena of combat, for example, armored warfare, naval aviation, or amphibious assault. From DOD's perspective, even if such moves could be justified in a narrow military sense—a debatable point—they might cause potentially hostile states to conclude that the United States had opted out of a critical military arena and to move into that arena accordingly. One genuinely unique aspect of U.S. military capability is its broad character. No other power can hope to match the United States across the full range of military activities.

This is one of the greatest barriers to a remilitarization of great power relations.

The problem with this approach is that, by continuing to try to do everything well despite much lower budgets, DOD may end up doing nothing well. The services insist that they will not allow their forces to go "hollow" (i.e., become poorly trained, undermanned, or badly maintained) as they did during the 1970s, and that they will accordingly cut force structure rather than sacrifice readiness. But if the budget falls to anywhere near $150 billion, a balanced force structure may well become impractical because, at least by traditional standards, the services emphasize that they need a certain minimum force structure for coherence (as a rotation base, and for training and career development).

There is likely to be substantial criticism of this business-as-usual approach, coupled with calls to emphasize U.S. technological strengths and/or new types of military contingencies that do not require a balanced force. One possibility would be to sharply reduce ground forces in favor of a maritime/aerospace focus. This approach might be seen to move with the tide of the revolution in military affairs, that is, toward stealthy, standoff, precise, tailored, and eventually autonomous weapon systems that operate in the context of a highly advanced information gathering and processing system. The strategic air campaign that was waged against Iraq is the prototype of this revolutionary type of warfare. It would also be possible to emphasize forces that are optimized for the so-called lesser regional contingencies, or lower-intensity conflicts.

One way to grapple with this problem is to increase the emphasis on core competencies. These are distinct combinations of technologies, organizations, and ways of doing business at which a state is inherently or especially good. Core competencies allow the United States to excel over a broad range of military activities, to provide considerable and sustained advantages over potential competitors, and to adapt quickly and favorably to changing circumstances.[24] Such competencies include information management and aerospace systems in the area of technology. With respect to warfighting, the United States has comparative and absolute advantages in such areas as C^3I; long-range, autonomous, precision-strike capabilities; the ability to gain and maintain air superiority; joint and combined operations; and long-range power projection and intervention capabilities. In the intelligence arena, the United States has core competencies in remote, multispectral technical collection and processing systems.

The development, maintenance, and enhancement of core competencies should be thought of as a dynamic and innovative and not as a static process. Obviously, the United States cannot rest on its laurels in any of these areas. But it must also be prepared to recognize that some core competencies may no longer be as essential or appropriate to the changing strategic environment and to disinvest accordingly. Finally, the United States must be alert to the need to identify, promote, and develop appropriate new core competencies, for example, flexible manufacturing (technological/industrial); ballistic missile defenses (warfighting); and economic/technological forecasting (intelligence).

As the defense budget decreases, the services should also incorporate "jointness" much earlier in the planning and budgeting process in an attempt to provide a coordinated fighting force more efficiently. If individual service inputs are the point of departure for these processes, the end product will have a certain amount of redundancy and duplication. Useful as such duplication often is in combat (by adding an element of flexibility), the military may soon find it an unaffordable luxury. To avoid duplication, the military may find itself budgeting and planning on the basis of functional rather than service distinctions. Such functional areas include power projection, rapid deployment forces, close air support, special operations and low-intensity conflict, the use of space, and transportation.

Sustaining an Adequate Military-Technology-Industry Base

In the aftermath of World War II, the United States created, for the first time in its peacetime history, a substantial, dedicated military-technology-industry (MTI) complex. It was not only the primary tool used in waging the Cold War—indeed, some believe it is the reason that the Cold War was won—but it also had a substantial impact on the performance and trajectory of the overall U.S. economy.

Whether this MTI base should continue in its present form—if at all—is a major question for the 1990s. To be sure, even if the current defense budget were to be cut in half, substantial funds will still be spent on research, development, testing, and evaluation (RDT&E) and on procurement. Thus there is no reason to believe that the MTI base will collapse. But current trends point toward a significant reduction in the size and, more important, the quality of that base.

Perhaps the most essential issue with respect to the composition and character of the MTI base concerns

the role of technology in future U.S. national security policy. The Bush administration's new defense strategy continues the post–World War II emphasis on developing and deploying cutting-edge military technologies. This emphasis was widely seen to have borne its full fruit in the stunning performance of U.S. military hardware during the Persian Gulf War. But the broad-scale development of technology and its incorporation into deployed weapon systems is very expensive. The argument for slowing the development and deployment of military technology is made by some on the grounds that without a Soviet competitor the United States would simply be engaging in an arms race with itself, although over time, other powers might seek to compete with the U.S. in armaments development in order to avoid being left too far behind. U.S. technological restraint, in this view, is a necessary precondition to more peaceful relations among the great powers, to the containment of regional arms races, and to the prevention of further proliferation of advanced military systems to rogue states.

Even those who would prefer that the United States continue its technological emphasis would admit that reduced defense spending must also translate into less money for RDT&E and for the procurement of a new generation of advanced weaponry. There are a variety of ways to cope with the implications of such cuts for the quality of what remains. For instance, the United States could essentially skip the next generation of weaponry (especially weapon platforms) and focus on upgrades to current systems and on advanced R&D for follow-on generations. Alternatively, DOD could decide to move on to the next generation and to pay for this procurement by accepting a much smaller deployed force. The most likely course will be a compromise between these two extremes—one of selective and focused modernization. The danger is that this selective modernization will be guided not by careful strategic calculations but by politically driven outcomes in the Pentagon and in Congress.

Whichever course the United States chooses, it must have an MTI base capable of supporting present and future military requirements. The Bush administration has by and large adhered to the policy that the future character of the MTI base is best determined by direct defense needs and by market forces. It has strenuously resisted efforts by Congress (and by certain parts of the executive branch) to pursue a de facto industrial policy in the name of preserving the MTI base or to use military spending to promote dual-use technologies. Opponents of the Bush administration's approach argue that a laissez-faire attitude toward the U.S. military and technological infrastructure will lead to a "hollowing out" of the MTI base: U.S. firms will choose or be forced to leave the defense sector, those that remain will lack competition and will be second rate compared with equivalent civilian sectors, and much of the technological and industrial competence necessary for a healthy MTI base will flow offshore. Critics of the administration's approach are particularly concerned about the viability of second- and third-tier suppliers, about which the Pentagon evidences little concern.[25]

Finally, efforts to preserve the viability of the MTI base must deal with the issue of foreign dependency. Most U.S. high-technology weapon systems already contain foreign-owned or built components, but there is little information about the extent, and little agreement about the importance, of this dependency. The Bush administration tends to be relatively unconcerned with this issue, on the grounds that the globalization of the civil and military technology and industrial bases is inevitable and beneficial. Any large-scale effort to establish a "Fortress America" MTI base would be not just counterproductive but also protectionist and industrial policy by another name. In effect, the Bush administration argues that the United States cannot logically seek to rely more heavily on its allies for joint defense activities while at the same time proclaiming their unreliability as suppliers of technology.

The majority of congressional opinion and a substantial body of outside experts are far more concerned about the dangers of foreign dependency, which could well increase in the wake of defense reductions and the continued decline of the U.S. MTI base. They foresee circumstances in which the United States might be engaged in a regional conflict from which key allies have chosen to stand aside. In war the United States would seek to surge the production of critical weapons, but its ability to do so might be held hostage to foreign governments unwilling to allow their national firms to supply the necessary subcomponents (just as the United States sought to do to European governments in the Siberian gas pipeline affair). Congressional pressure for action is likely in this area over the next several years as part of a more general effort to address the perceived loss of U.S. technological leadership.

Whether DOD ultimately adopts a traditional or an activist approach to the MTI base, it must consider the best way to do business with much less money. Two particular sets of reforms should be pursued vigorously.

First, the Pentagon should explore

new ways to conduct R&D and to maintain production capability without necessarily procuring large numbers of finished products or distorting the civilian economy. One approach is to prototype a small number of weapon systems, enough to sustain competitive design teams, maintain and modernize manufacturing capacity, and allow the military to exercise and develop operational concepts.[26] These production prototypes would be produced in large quantities only if they demonstrated a real military advantage or if an emergent threat warranted a generational modernization. If neither situation occurred, useful improvements derived from the prototype would be incorporated into the Base Force and another round of prototyping would begin.

A second reform would focus on breaking down the barriers between the civil and military technology and industrial bases. For several decades, military technology was more productive than its civilian counterparts in many critical areas. Today, this is no longer generally true: the civilian electronics industry, for example, is more advanced and innovative than the military. The problem is compounded by a set of governmental rules and regulations that tend to segregate the MTI base from the civil sectors. Many companies simply refuse to do business with DOD (or with any government agency); others carefully separate themselves into civilian and military divisions, even though they may do substantially the same work.

This "ghetto-ization" of the MTI base has several potentially serious consequences for DOD that could well be greatly exacerbated as defense spending declines. For instance, military hardware will not be as technically advanced as it could be—a fact that could become a major problem if other states that possess advanced civilian technologies are able to "militarize" those technologies. Even if this does not occur, the segregation of the MTI base means that U.S. military technology will be more expensive than it need be, with the attendant opportunity costs.

A number of reforms have been proposed to remedy the situation. These include a thorough overhaul of the Pentagon's acquisition system, including the onerous process of establishing and verifying military specifications ("milspecs"), and changes in many laws and procedures that are intended to ensure competition and prevent fraud, waste, and abuse, but that actually have the effect of driving up costs and discouraging firms from entering or staying in the defense business.[27] Such reforms have been stifled in the past, in part because the Pentagon acquisition bureaucracy and congressional committees gain much of their power through their ability to monitor and enforce these requirements. These interests will not easily give way now, especially as the size of the MTI base decreases and the relative stakes of reform increase. But the dramatic decline in defense spending may also create a unique political opportunity to fix—or better yet, to completely supplant—a procurement system that had largely broken down even in a time of relative plenty.

Other Issues

The issues discussed above by no means exhaust the defense agenda that will confront the administration, Congress, and American people. Some other basic questions must be answered before a coherent, sustainable defense strategy can be implemented:

- To what extent should U.S. military planning rely on (or demand) the contribution of allies, given the fact that the familiar cold war alliance patterns are likely to change substantially, if not disappear entirely, over the coming decade?
- With the complete demise of the traditional Soviet threat, and the absence of any other global threat on the horizon for at least this decade, what is the proper purpose and orientation for a policy of reconstitution?
- Can innovative forms of arms control be used to limit the potential threats to U.S. national security—for example, regional military capabilities, especially advanced conventional weapons, and weapons of mass destruction—so as to justify lower levels of U.S. defense spending?
- Given changing U.S. interests, where might U.S. military forces be required to fight in the future? Will the Third World (other than the Persian Gulf) matter? Are there realistic contingencies for the use of large-scale military power in Europe?
- To what extent can (or should) military capabilities be diverted to nontraditional functions, for example, drug interdiction, environmental monitoring and cleanup, and humanitarian assistance?

Conclusion

Defense spending in the mid-1990s and beyond is likely to be driven to levels far below those anticipated as recently as autumn 1990. Such reductions, coupled with the collapse of the Soviet threat, will compel another restructuring of U.S. military capabili-

ties and quite possibly a further reorientation of U.S. defense strategy.

Perhaps the most important restructuring that must take place concerns not budgets, force structures, or military requirements, but the U.S. perspective on the world. Over the past 40 years, the United States has based its national security policy on waging a near war against a serious, global adversary. Now that this near war has ended, there is a real risk that the United States will fall victim to its traditional postwar impulse to dismantle its military capability beyond prudent levels. This concern has been well stated by Secretary Cheney:

Unfortunately, if you look at the historic record, we have never, ever gone through one of these periods and gotten it right. We've always screwed it up. Every single time when it's happened previously we've been so quick to cash in the peace dividend, to demobilize that force, that within a very short period of time we find that our weakness in and of itself becomes provocative and tempts others to do things they shouldn't attempt; that we always end up having, once again, to commit the force some place—we get in trouble some place in the world and have to send in the troops; that we find ourselves with troops that are not well trained or well equipped, not prepared to go to war.[28]

But this legitimate concern should not obscure the fact that the United States is no longer in a wartime situation. The manner in which DOD did business during the Cold War is not appropriate to the new strategic environment. Those in the U.S. government who have the responsibility for the future of the U.S. military must first and foremost develop the appropriate peacetime mentality. They must adjust to the fact that the United States will no longer be engaged in a highly dynamic competition in military hardware and doctrine—an arms race—with a sophisticated and ambitious global rival. This does not mean that history has ended and that military power is irrelevant; far from it. Rather, it means that those who wish to avoid Secretary Cheney's nightmare should seek ways to sustain the appropriate level and character of U.S. military capabilities through mechanisms that make sense in a much more complex and multifaceted world.

Notes

1. Key official statements about the new defense strategy and the Base Force include the remarks by President Bush to the Aspen Institute Symposium, Aspen, Colo., August 2, 1990; statement of General Colin L. Powell, chairman of the Joint Chiefs of Staff, before the House Committee on Armed Services, February 7, 1991; statement of Secretary of Defense Richard B. Cheney before the Senate Committee on Armed Services in connection with the FY 1992–93 budget for the Department of Defense, February 21, 1991; Joint Chiefs of Staff, *1991 Joint Military Net Assessment* (Washington, D.C.: Department of Defense, March 1991); statement of the Undersecretary of Defense Paul Wolfowitz before the Senate Committee on Armed Services, April 11, 1991; statement of Admiral David E. Jeremiah, vice chairman of the Joint Chiefs of Staff, before the Senate Committee on Armed Services, April 11, 1991; *National Security Strategy of the United States* (Washington, D.C.: The White House, August 1991); and statement of General Colin L. Powell before the House Appropriations Committee, Subcommittee on Defense, September 25, 1991. Unless otherwise noted, the description and analysis of the new defense strategy and the Base Force are taken from these documents.

2. Statement of Secretary of Defense Richard B. Cheney before the House Committee on Armed Services in connection with the FY 1992–93 budget for the Department of Defense, February 7, 1991.

3. A more elaborate summary of the new defense strategy and the Base Force concept can be found in Sharon Weiner, *National Security in the Post–Cold War Era: A Description of the New U.S. Defense Strategy and the Base Force Concept*, CNSS Briefing (Los Alamos, N. Mex.: Center for National Security Studies, July 1991).

4. "While we have traditionally focused on deterring a unitary, rational actor applying a relatively knowable calculus of potential costs and gains, our thinking must now encompass potential instabilities within states as well as the potential threat from states or leaders who might perceive they have little to lose in employing weapons of mass destruction." *National Security Strategy of the United States*, p. 26.

5. These four force packages will not correspond with the regional and functional commanders in chief (CINCs), as had originally been rumored. At least under the 1991 concept of the Base Force, there is likely to be very little reorganization or consolidation of the existing command structure.

6. Statement of Secretary of Defense Richard B. Cheney before the House Committee on Armed Services in connection with the FY 1992–93 budget for the Department of Defense, February 7, 1991.

7. In the Defense Authorization Bill for the first year of the build down, Congress proved unwilling to accept the cuts in reserve forces requested by DOD. Instead of the requested cut of 105,076 in FY 1992 and 79,800 in FY 1993, Congress approved cuts in reserve forces of 37,580 in FY 1992 and 28,641 in FY 1993.

8. It should be noted that, outside of DOD, there was widespread agreement among defense analysts that the defense spending limits projected by the Bush administration would not be adequate to support the Base Force at its official size. See, for example, the testimony of Dr. Gordon Adams, director, Defense Budget Project, before the Senate Budget Committee on defense planning for FY 1994–FY 1995, July 16, 1991.

9. "The Coming Defense Debate: A Floor Statement" by Representative Les Aspin (D–Wis.), U.S. House of Representatives,

October 3, 1991. The first revolution referred to by Aspin took place from December 1988 to November 1989. It included such events as the fall of the Berlin Wall and the withdrawal of Soviet forces from Eastern Europe. The second revolution refers to the events that occurred in the former Soviet Union after the failed August 1991 coup.

10. *The Base Force: A Total Force,* summary talking points. Presentation by General Colin L. Powell to the Senate Appropriations Committee, Subcommittee on Defense, n.d. [1991].

11. Eric Schmitt, "Pentagon Making a List of Choices for Spending Cuts," *New York Times,* November 24, 1991, pp. 1, 32.

12. Edward Luttwak, "Do We Need a New Grand Strategy?" *National Interest,* no. 15 (Spring 1989), pp. 3–14.

13. William W. Kaufmann and John D. Steinbruner, *Decisions for Defense: Prospects for a New Order* (Washington, D.C.: Brookings Institution, 1991), pp. 67–76.

14. "Powell Outlines Plan for Small, Versatile Force of the Future," *Army Times* (April 15, 1991), p. 4.

15. The requirement for sequential, instead of simultaneous, operations in two major regional contingencies seems to be driven basically by limitations in lift capacity and not by limitations in force structure. This said, it is conceivable that the United States could conduct defensive operations (which in principle require fewer forces than offensive operations) in two theaters simultaneously, or defend in one theater while assuming the offensive in another.

16. It might also be possible to justify force structure size based on the need simultaneously (or sequentially) to fight one major regional contingency and one lesser regional contingency, or to fight two lesser regional contingencies.

17. These generic threats should not be based on worst case projections but should represent a reasonable projection of what a "Red Threat" in the year 2001 would look like, based on a full intelligence analysis and the net assessment process.

18. The DOD view of the so-called revolution in military affairs is discussed in Cheney, statement before the Senate Committee on Armed Services, February 21, 1991.

19. *National Security Strategy of the United States,* p. 25.

20. The administration has to date pursued a policy of actively discouraging the dispersion of nuclear weapons among the breakaway republics in favor of supporting the continued control of these weapons by a central authority.

21. As State Department Counsellor Robert B. Zoellick has remarked: "The dangers that we, and the Soviets, will face in the future are more likely to come from rogue third parties than from one another. So it makes sense that our arms control thinking shift increasingly to the risks of proliferation and regional conflicts." Statement before the Subcommittee on the Middle East of the House Foreign Affairs Committee on relations of the United States with the Soviet Union and the republics, October 2, 1991, p. 18.

22. Congressional Budget Office, *Implications of Additional Reductions in Defense Spending,* CBO Staff Memorandum (Washington, D.C.: Congressional Budget Office, October 1991), pp. 31–33.

23. Even when the United States maintained a "balanced" force structure during the Cold War, certain areas, for example, mine/countermine activities, received relatively little attention and funding. These areas of neglect may well increase during the build down.

24. For a discussion of the notion of core competencies in business, see C. K. Prahalad and Gary Hamel, "The Core Competence of the Corporation," *Harvard Business Review,* no. 3 (May–June 1990), pp. 79–91. We are indebted to David Andre for calling this subject to our attention.

25. The problem of the subtiers is discussed in *Deterrence in Decay: The Future of the U.S. Defense Industrial Base,* Final Report of the CSIS Defense Industrial Base Project (Washington, D.C.: Center for Strategic and International Studies, May 1989).

26. See, for example, U.S. Congress, Office of Technology Assessment, *Redesigning Defense: Planning the Future of the U.S. Defense Industrial Base,* OTA-ISC-500 (Washington, D.C.: U.S. Government Printing Office, July 1991); and Paul H. Richanbach et al., *The Future of Military R&D: Towards a Flexible Acquisition Strategy,* IDA Paper P-2444 (Arlington, Va.: Institute for Defense

Analyses, July 1990). One criticism of this concept is that the production of a limited number of production prototypes will not be sufficient to identify and work out all the manufacturing problems that inevitably emerge under full-scale production. This is a fair point, but because full-scale production runs are likely to be quite limited for the next decade or more, prototyping and limited rates of production will be the only means to maintain any direct manufacturing activity for many weapon systems.

27. See, for example, Jeff Bingaman, Jacques Gansler, and Robert Kupperman, *Integrating Commercial and Military Technologies for National Strength* (Washington, D.C.: Center for Strategic and International Studies, 1991); and *Redesigning Defense*.

28. Transcript of Secretary of Defense Richard B. Cheney's meeting with the editorial board of the *San Diego Union*, November 12, 1991, p. 2.

Military Planning Beyond the Cold War: Lessons for the 1990s from the 1920s and 1930s

Caroline F. Ziemke

THE UNITED STATES military establishment of the 1990s faces a period of retrenchment as the ongoing disintegration of the Warsaw Pact, along with internal economic and political turmoil in the Soviet Union, portend effective removal of the principal threat upon which U.S. military planning has rested since 1945. As the likelihood of major war in Europe recedes, and political pressure to reduce the burden of defense on the U.S. economy escalates, a significant, long-term abridgment of military budgets seems certain. Budgetary austerity and a mutable political environment are nothing new: since 1945, the armed forces have coped with cyclical congressional and presidential miserliness that has included the Truman administration's postwar demobilization, Eisenhower's "New Look," and the lean years of the post-Vietnam era. What is new is budgetary austerity combined with the apparent decline of the most persuasive, immediate military threat. Although it is unlikely

Caroline F. Ziemke is a research staff member at the Institute for Defense Analyses in Alexandria, Virginia. She holds a Ph.D. in military history and strategic studies from the Ohio State University.

that the post-1990 United States will return to the stubborn isolationism and military unreadiness of the pre–World War II years, the U.S. armed services have already entered what promises to be an extended period of fundamental and traumatic realignment.

Changes are coming too fast for the military, the political leaders, and the defense analytic community to formulate rational responses. The temptation is strong, therefore, to look to history for quick answers. Analogies are, however, hard to find. Post–World War II demobilization involved major force reduction and restructuring but unfolded in the absence of a long-term sense of strategic security: the Cold War was already under way when the hot war of 1939–1945 ended. Demobilization and defense reform following the Korean and Vietnam wars took place in the context of relatively constant superpower competition.

The absence of recent analogies, then, leads back to the pre–World War II decades: the last extended period of U.S. force planning without the Soviet threat. Following World War I, Americans—war-weary and disillusioned with European politics—were eager to return to the business of economic growth and were relatively secure in their continued strategic insularity. Germany—defeated, demoralized, and in a political and economic shambles—seemed an unlikely, or at most remote, long-term threat. Japan, a formidable U.S. competitor in the Pacific, nonetheless seemed only a distant threat. Congress and the White House—suspicious of army and navy motives in calling for the establishment of a large postwar military structure and permanent mobilization base—shared the desire to scale down the armed forces as far and as quickly as possible. Over time, what began as postwar demobilization became prolonged military dwarfism and minimal readiness.

The purpose of this paper is to present a brief, comparative analysis of the interwar force planning experience to determine how the armed services coped with austere budgets and the absence of a persuasive external threat and to test the oft-cited similarities between "then" and "now." The conclusions represent an effort to match the lessons of the interwar experience with the challenges force planners face today. The results are less conclusions than implications and suggest approaches rather than solutions.

The Military Planning Context

In turning to history for lessons, it is important to keep in mind the different threat environments in which interwar and current military planners ply their trade. Interwar U.S. armed services planned against quite specific threats: a naval war with Japan, and a major, coalition war on the European continent in which Germany would be the principal opponent. The army and navy both based their interwar planning on the assumption that the next war would be big, protracted, and operationally similar to World War I.

They faced no lack of threats, only the difficulty of convincing a war-weary, later isolationist, and even later economically traumatized political establishment that it should devote major financial resources to building military capabilities to meet them. While the post–cold war world is hardly devoid of threats to U.S. security and interests, it seems likely that the conventional, global superpower war will recede as the principal basis for military force planning.

Germany in 1918 and the Soviet Union in 1990 both represent diminishing threats, but the long-term consequences of their respective declines are fundamentally different. The Versailles Treaty used reparations, a "war guilt" clause, and strict limits on future German military forces to complete and prolong the effects of military defeat. Germany became a pariah nation, ripe for revanchism and possessing the necessary elements for economic and military revival: a literate, relatively homogeneous labor force; a solid technological and industrial base; a well-developed, if foundering, economy; and a solid tradition of military professionalism. Britain, France, and the United States all recognized the likelihood of a renewed German threat; that they chose not to rearm against it was a conscious decision based on overwhelming domestic political opposition to preparing for another major ground war on the Continent.

The Soviet Union's "defeat" in the Cold War, while it has not brought the humiliation of military surrender, has nonetheless triggered political and economic setbacks more complex, and probably more enduring, than Germany's military defeat in World War I. Any significant reversal of the ongoing decline of the Soviet military threat seems increasingly improbable and would, at any rate, be a long time in coming. The Soviet Union, nonetheless, retains enormous military capabilities and should not be dismissed as a potential future threat as Germany was between 1920 and 1938.

It is also important to remember that there were actually two interwar periods. Isolationism, economic optimism, and a general sense of strategic invulnerability drove budget and force structure cuts in the 1920s. The military establishment of the 1930s—after over a decade of atrophy—faced two rapidly rising, widely separated military threats: Germany and Japan. U.S. strategic security was dwindling, but economic collapse made a rapid military buildup politically and fiscally impossible.

The transformation of U.S. national status and self-perception since 1945 has fundamentally changed the context of military planning. In 1920, the United States was a rising economic star, but its geographic insularity allowed it the luxury of military isolationism. In 1990, the United States is a military superpower leading a global system of mutual security—just the sort of "entangling alliance" that U.S. diplomatic tradition from George Washington to Franklin Roosevelt openly eschewed. Americans can no longer afford the luxury of the strategic complacency of the 1920s and dare not risk the military unreadiness of the 1930s.

The United States Navy

Despite demobilization fever, the navy in 1920 seemed relatively immune to drastic cuts for three reasons. First, the navy was the U.S. traditional first line of defense, a symbol of national strength and, as such, it enjoyed fairly consistent political support. Second, the "big navy" party, the Repub-

licans, controlled the White House during the 1920s, and a former assistant secretary of the navy took it over in 1933. Third, War Plan ORANGE, which posited naval war against Japan, was considered the most feasible U.S. military scenario for the foreseeable future and gave the navy a clear, independent mission and a politically defensible, if chronologically remote, basis for its postwar planning.

A series of naval arms limitation treaties offset some of the navy's political and strategic advantages by the mid-1920s, frustrating its efforts to modernize the fleet. Products of diplomatic as well as military negotiation, the treaties compromised some of the operational and strategic concepts that underlay naval planning. In particular, a nonfortification pledge—according to which the United States agreed not to build badly needed naval bases west of Hawaii in exchange for a Japanese pledge not to fortify the formerly German-mandated islands—complicated interwar operational planning and undermined the navy's ability even to defend existing U.S. interests in the Pacific. Most damaging to the ultimate success of naval arms control was the lack of attention to verification and enforcement, which left the treaties with no teeth and made compliance largely voluntary.[1] The navy tried to modernize as much as possible within treaty limits, but successive budget cuts, particularly after the severe post-1929 economic collapse, kept the fleet well below treaty strength.

The navy's fundamental concepts changed little from the World War I model through the interwar years. Treaty limits on construction of new large surface combatants did force the navy to adjust some of its priorities. In an effort to counter Japan's strategic advantages in the Pacific, the navy emphasized the capabilities least subject to treaty limits, focusing on support capabilities and "treaty-free" carrier aviation, submarines, and "fleet trains" to increase force projection and fleet defense.

The most impressive technological innovations came out of the navy's two new arms: naval aviation and submarines. Similarly imaginative doctrines and strategies were slower in coming, and as a result new capabilities tended to be grafted on to traditional concepts of fleet operations.[2] Defensive-minded submarine doctrine neglected more promising capabilities like commerce raiding (the United States had, after all, declared war on Germany in 1917 in reaction to U-boat attacks on "neutral" U.S. shipping) and offensive mine-laying.[3] Technological progress likewise outstripped doctrinal innovation for carrier air, although naval aviators were, as a group, more effective in pressing their interests than were their subsurface colleagues. Despite the Navy Department's prescient identification of Japan as the next U.S. wartime enemy, the use of submarines to "bleed Japan white" and the aircraft carrier's position as the cornerstone of the Pacific naval battles of World War II emerged out of wartime necessity, not prewar planning.[4]

While personnel problems were common throughout the interwar military, the navy was relatively better off than the other services in that regard. Promotion was slow, but duty was active and varied, and the navy still enjoyed its traditional image as a vehicle for vocational training, social mobility, and personal adventure. Naval Academy graduates dominated the upper ranks of the interwar navy. Younger officers and graduates of civilian universities on the cutting edge of technological know-how concentrated in the more innovative but less presti-

gious arms—aviation and submarines. As a result, tactical and technological innovation often ran head-on into traditionalist doctrines and strategies.[5]

Navy fortunes improved during the 1930s; in no small measure thanks to the efforts of two of its most powerful and enthusiastic supporters: President (and former Assistant Secretary of the Navy) Franklin D. Roosevelt, and House Military Affairs Committee Chairman Carl Vinson. Japan's 1936 renunciation of the Washington Naval Treaties triggered a series of Naval Acts that removed legal and budgetary barriers to fleet modernization (although the Depression limited available resources). By 1939, naval readiness was still low, but significant numbers of new ships in all classes were under construction with New Deal work relief programs underwriting the labor costs.

Because the navy accurately anticipated the coming threat, it was relatively well prepared for the war it fought from 1941 to 1945. The navy's institutional conservatism, however, left some operational weaknesses on the eve of war: excessive reliance on battleships, defensive submarine doctrine, underdeveloped amphibious capabilities, and a general tendency to force new capabilities into old concepts.[6] As a result of its Pacific-centered strategy, the navy was ill-prepared for the Battle of the Atlantic (notwithstanding its antisubmarine experience in that ocean during 1917 and 1918), and the resulting deficiency of its convoy and antisubmarine warfare (ASW) capabilities proved the major and most costly failure of the early U.S. war effort. One of the yardsticks of effective military planning, however, is flexibility, and although interwar naval planning did not anticipate every wartime contingency (nor could it be expected to have done so), it did succeed in building forces and doctrines capable of adapting over time to wartime challenges.

The United States Army

While its readiness suffered relatively more from fiscal austerity than that of the navy, the interwar army's greatest handicap was the lack of a politically salable threat upon which to base its operational planning. The army knew it probably faced another coalition land war in Europe, but political realities—not the least of which was the lack of a direct, visible, major "European" threat—prevented it from openly adopting that scenario as the basis for force modernization. These factors, together with its World War I experience and Congress's determination to "arm solely for defense," forced the army to focus instead on maximizing its latent potential.

In the prevailing political and economic atmosphere, the army had few real options. Postwar legislation reduced army manpower from 280,000 in 1920 to 125,000 in 1924; in 1939, manpower levels would still be 90,000 short of 1920 authorizations. After 1924, manpower levels stabilized, but army equipment continued to deteriorate well into the 1930s.[7] Congressional appropriations for army weapons modernization did not increase until 1936 and then only because World War I equipment was finally used up or worn out and had to be replaced. While operational readiness in the 1920s and 1930s sank to the lowest levels in its history, the army turned its attention to plans to harness its vast, untapped, industrial, material, and manpower potential in the event of another major war.[8]

Despite the effort and expertise in-

volved, manpower policies developed in the absence of clear scenarios fell short of the challenge of the 1940–1941 mobilization. Mobilization planners, in concentrating on cadre divisions and rapid force expansion, failed to consider some important practical concerns: providing basic equipment for large numbers of new recruits; the effects of stringent enlistment requirements; the need to stockpile strategic materials not readily available on the continent; and the strains of mobilization on an archaic staff system that concentrated all decision-making authority in the person of the chief of staff.[9] Still, the army's efforts bore valuable fruit: its experience cooperating with civilian agencies and industry in developing mobilization plans, which the navy avoided, served the army (and the other services) well when war finally came.

World War I left the army's infantry-minded operational concepts essentially unchanged, and the General Staff assumed the next war would look much like the last. As a result of congressional intransigence, limits on modernization resources, the army's emphasis on manpower mobilization, and a cautious research and development philosophy, army weapons modernization throughout the period proceeded at a snail's pace.[10] The army was, until the late 1930s, reluctant to standardize and produce new weapons until they were nearly perfect: the M1 rifle was in development for 19 years. Although the speed of technological advancement raised legitimate concerns over standardizing and producing obsolete weapons, too often the effect was to leave the army with no weapons at all.[11] Chief of Staff General Malin Craig (1935–1939), alarmed that the army was at least two years away from even minimal combat readiness, froze research and development in 1936 and endeavored to rearm as quickly as possible with whatever equipment was available, foreign or domestic.[12]

The most frequently cited wartime effect of slow interwar offensive modernization was the deficiency of U.S. armor relative to German and Soviet capabilities. In 1930, the army had 1,115 tanks, all of World War I vintage, and the first new standard tank model appeared only in 1938. Armor doctrine, based on World War I operations, robbed tanks of their greatest assets—speed and shock—by tying their employment to the support of slow-moving infantry. Not until the first independent armored force appeared in 1940, in response to the success of German blitzkrieg tactics in Poland and France, did the army undertake any systematic development of armor's independent capabilities.[13]

Force readiness proved an even more pervasive weakness than equipment. The army's 10-division structure (9 infantry plus 1 cavalry), which manpower authorizations limited to around 50 percent strength (at best), combined with manpower and budgetary restrictions to make realistic operational training impossible until 1941. Field commands existed only on paper, and the bureaucratic nature of most duty created a generation of "desk officers" with minimal operational command experience and insufficient familiarity with army doctrine and practices. The stultifying nature of the resulting duty undermined morale and, along with low pay, slow promotion, and the low status of army service, made recruiting and retaining talented officers and enlisted men difficult.[14]

Even after the outbreak of war in Europe in 1939, army readiness improved slowly, and the gap between army requirements and capabilities widened. Congressional allocation for defense did not exceed domestic spending (miniscule by today's standards) until well after Pearl Harbor; throughout the war the army's share of combat responsibility continued to outstrip its share of resources relative to the other three services.[15] Until 1941, Congress refused to appropriate sufficient funds to enable the War Department to begin industrial mobilization and strategic stockpiling. That, in turn, led to heavy wartime dependence on synthetics and replacements and placed a premium on the energy and management skills of individual leaders like Army Chief of Staff General George Marshall.[16]

The interwar army suffered more than any other service from poor civil–military relations and the general political mood, two factors that combined to rule out effective army operational planning for the most likely scenario. Army leadership did, however, understand and deal with the nature of the challenge ahead—mobilization, perhaps in the distant future, for a major, overseas ground war—although it vastly underestimated the scope of the task. The army's greatest miscalculation, however, was in its emphasis: it developed mobilization plans at the expense of operational doctrine and readiness, for which the World War II army paid a high price in early combat operations.[17]

The United States Marine Corps

Because the Marine Corps shared the navy's threat—Japan—its prewar planning proved similarly prescient and brought significant operational success in World War II. The institutional context of marine planning was, however, fundamentally different. Since its inception in 1775, the United States Marine Corps had fought an almost continuous battle to retain its autonomy. Under the leadership of Commandant John A. Lejeune (1920–1929), the interwar marines capitalized on an earlier, peripheral interest in amphibious operations to create a new mission, tying their doctrine to U.S. strategy and navy operations and guaranteeing the corps' continued independence.[18] The Marine Corps developed the kind of balanced, all-arms capabilities that a Pacific war would require (and the army and navy were unlikely to establish), making the corps' mission all the more unique.[19]

Marine advocates of amphibious doctrine challenged both the traditionalist view of the corps as a ground expeditionary force and conventional wisdom that the Gallipoli landings of 1915 had proved amphibious assaults against defended shorelines infeasible, even suicidal. Close study of the Gallipoli campaign and successful German landings on the Gulf of Riga (1917) led the marines to draft their first concept for amphibious assault of defended islands in 1921. Despite a strong start, amphibious capabilities languished during the late 1920s in the face of scarce resources and conflicting missions.[20]

The Marine Corps' first complete amphibious doctrine manual (1934) provided the basis for all U.S. (and most Allied) amphibious doctrine during World War II.[21] Fiscal shortages limited testing and training, and operational capabilities advanced slowly until the late 1930s. Some important lessons nonetheless emerged from the few large-scale amphibious exercises of the 1930s: the unsuitability of existing navy landing craft, the need for specialized amphibious equipment, and the importance of logistical planning to ensure that the necessary equipment would be available when and where it was required.[22]

The marines also made impressive advances in air-ground support practices as a result of deployment against Sandino guerrillas in Nicaragua during the late 1920s. Marine aviation was from the beginning defined in terms of ground operations leading to a marine close support doctrine that was integral to overall amphibious doctrine. Marine aviators incorporated operational experience, tactical training at the U.S. Army Air Corps Tactical School, and operational training with marine ground and amphibious units in developing unparalleled air-ground doctrine. Two factors undermined marine close support capabilities: a responsibility for both air superiority and fleet defense that diverted scarce marine aviation; and the navy's development of higher performance aircraft that, in practice, proved incompatible with existing air-ground communication capabilities.[23]

The interwar corps benefited from successive commandants who understood the importance of politics. During challenges to marine independence from the War Department and the White House, the corps' survival depended on congressional support (as it would again in the late 1940s). During the 1920s, Lejeune built a public relations network (which later became the envy of the other services) to promote within Congress the image of the Marine Corps as a "reliable, austere, essential, and effective combat force."[24] Even the most skillful lobbying, however, could not overcome the budgetary impact of the Depression, and marine readiness declined during the early 1930s. Overseas deployments in the late 1920s slowed amphibious development until the creation of the Fleet Marine Force in 1933 set aside a designated portion of the corps specifically for amphibious training and indoctrination. From that point on, amphibious assault was the corps' primary wartime mission and specialized training for such operations its principal peacetime activity.[25]

On the eve of World War II, two major deficiencies limited Marine Corps readiness: equipment and manpower capabilities well below the requirements of its doctrine; and a continuing lack of realistic training to iron out problems with doctrine, equipment, or techniques. The marines modified two civilian boat designs—the Higgins "Eureka Boat" and the Roebling "Alligator"—into the amphibious shipping for personnel (LCVP) and equipment (LCVM), and amphibian tanks (LCVT) that would serve throughout World War II, but they were not available in sufficient numbers until after the war started.[26] Navy neglect of logistics and combat engineering, furthermore, left it unprepared to exploit amphibious gains; and coordination of navy gunfire support with amphibious assaults was dismal and would remain so until the navy agreed to allow a marine officer to supervise offshore fire support, beginning in late 1941.[27]

That amphibious operation proved indispensable to Japan's defeat and that their conduct progressed so far between the wars is testimony to the performance of Marine Corps leadership in the face of a variety of obstacles. The marines stand out as the only U.S. service in the interwar period to recognize fully the importance of combined arms operations and to develop doctrine and capabilities to implement them. The fact that the other services ignored joint, amphibious, and close air support operations made marine progress in those areas all the more decisive in Europe as well as the Pacific. If the Marine Corps

played no role in the Normandy invasion, aspects of its doctrine certainly did.[28]

The United States Army Air Corps

The interwar development of the Army Air Corps centered on its ambitions for organizational autonomy.[29] Unlike the marines, Air Corps leaders were military revolutionaries: where the marines identified closely with the navy and its mission, airmen harbored a view of war fundamentally different from that of their parent service, the army. World War I offered little operational experience with offensive aviation, and postwar army leadership tended to view the airplane as just another weapon to support ground missions and certainly not one with the revolutionary potential that its more enthusiastic proponents claimed for it. Believing that air power's full potential depended on its liberation from surface force concepts, Air Corps leaders fought an uphill battle throughout the interwar period for operational and organizational autonomy.

The Air Corps' position seemed hopelessly weak during the 1920s. Not only was it a small, fully subordinate service, but as a new branch its officer corps was younger, and the hopelessly stagnant promotion lists offered little prospect of any significant increase in the percentage of air officers reaching the highest levels of army leadership. The Air Corps, furthermore, had few institutional allies: the War and Navy Departments staunchly opposed Air Corps autonomy, successive presidential administrations were hostile to air power, and Congress remained indifferent.[30] By 1921, the air arm was virtually extinct, its World War I equipment worn out and dangerous.

Frustration over the army General

Staff's conservatism led airmen during the late 1920s and 1930s to circumvent the military establishment to advance their cause. General Billy Mitchell, both before and after his court-martial in 1926 (for insubordination after he accused the army—and, indirectly, President Calvin Coolidge—of criminally neglecting the safety of military aviators), led a public and often rhetorically intemperate campaign to build popular support for air power. The campaign was a popular success but an institutional disaster that solidified resistance to air autonomy within the military establishment and made the U.S. Navy a perennial enemy.[31] A succession of presidential boards considered modernization and reorganization of U.S. air power but saw no clear and present foreign air threat to justify major changes. The Air Corps made modest gains in its status but on the eve of World War II remained organizationally subordinate to the army.

A quieter, and ultimately more successful, revolution unfolded at the Air Corps Tactical School (ACTS), where airmen built their own theory of air warfare—a theory that was wholly inconsistent with prevailing national and army policy and void of empirical foundation. Strategic bombing as an operational concept independent of specific circumstances and universally applicable gave the interwar Air Corps two things it badly needed: an independent and potentially decisive combat mission and an operational basis for its interwar force planning. In 1931, the Air Corps moved ACTS to Maxwell Field, and in the geographic and intellectual isolation of south-central Alabama set about developing its strategic bombing capabilities. Airmen did not let the prevailing political antipathy and resulting lack of adequate material capability deter progress on the theoretical aspects of strategic bombing, nor did they waiver in their conviction that the next war would validate their theories if the military establishment provided the means and opportunity to implement them.[32]

The tactical air mission did not fare so well. Captains George C. Kenney and Claire Chennault made some advances at ACTS during the 1920s, and although their efforts were abandoned during the 1930s, their concepts resurfaced to the army's good fortune during the Central Pacific campaign. The army, engrossed in mobilization planning, made few operational demands on the Air Corps until the eve of war. As a result, tactical aviation doctrine and capabilities (for close air support and troop carrier operations) languished through the 1930s, as became painfully obvious during the army's first major operational exercises in the fall of 1941. Tactical aviators had no idea how to cooperate with the ground forces they were supposed to support, and, as Army Air Force Chief of Staff General Henry ("Hap") Arnold noted, air-ground capabilities were "just awful."[33]

Modernization of U.S. military aircraft between the wars was a mixed success. The financial constraints on the Air Corps were significant but less a function of subordinate status (representing less than 10 percent of the War Department organization, the Air Corps received roughly 20 percent of its budget) than of chronically low army funding overall.[34] The national policy of "arming solely for defense" hurt the Air Corps relatively more than the surface army because many combat aircraft types—fighter escorts, attack aircraft, and bombers larger than the B–17—were impossible to sell to Congress on defensive grounds.[35] Under the guise of coast defense, the Air Corps developed a long-range, heavy payload, bombardment aircraft (the B–

17) but army–navy agreements limited the offshore range of land-based aircraft and prevented testing larger, truly strategic bombers. In cooperation with the civilian aviation industry, however, the Air Corps had by 1939 developed prototypes or requirements for all its wartime bomber aircraft, including the B–29. Most wartime cargo aircraft, including the stalwart and long-lived C–47 (DC–3), were direct adaptations of civilian models.

Strategic bombing and coast defense represented only two-thirds of the Air Corps' stated mission. Tactical aviation did not keep pace with bombardment aircraft. The Air Corps had no written doctrine for tactical operations, no operational experience supporting ground forces, and no doctrinal requirement for the bomber escorts (like the P–51) it eventually used to support ground force operations. As a result, in 1939, the United States had no fighter or attack aircraft on a technological par with either its own heavy bombers or British and German fighter types. The tactical workhorses of World War II, the P–38 (1941), P–40 (1941), P–47 (1942), and P–51 (1943) all became operational well after the outbreak of war in Europe.[36]

The Air Corps on the eve of Pearl Harbor suffered a significant doctrines–capabilities gap, and as General Arnold noted, "we had plans, but not planes." Air Corps doctrine—at least for offensive bombardment—was sound and ready for war, but the aircraft necessary to carry it out would not be available for two years.[37] In cooperation with the Royal Air Force and ground commanders in North Africa, Tactical Air Force commanders worked out an ad hoc doctrine by late 1943, but theater air commanders continued, for the most part, to view air-ground cooperation as a diversion of limited resources from their primary mission: long-range strategic bombing. Overall, however, the interwar Air Corps fulfilled its two principal goals: it built a flexible and potentially decisive military instrument, and it laid the operational and doctrinal foundations for the independent, post–World War II air force.

The Military Establishment

While declining defense budgets and vague threats complicated interwar military planning, the poor state of civil–military relations proved most debilitating over the long run. At no time during the twentieth century has politics more diligently circumscribed military capabilities, or more completely excluded the services from the decisions that governed their fates, than during the two decades following World War I. In its approach to Asia (where U.S. involvement was active) and Europe (where it was not), U.S. foreign policy consistently drew lines that it—either directly or by implication—dared revisionist powers like Japan and Germany to cross. During an era in which U.S. diplomacy still dealt heavily in ultimatums, political leaders nonetheless allowed—indeed, encouraged—military preparedness to drop to perilously low levels. Through it all, the army and navy remained steadfastly united on one issue: the danger of the spreading gap between declared foreign policy goals and existing U.S. military capabilities.

That gap widened even after the outbreak of war in Europe. Congress in particular did not take seriously warnings of the rising specter of war until after the fall of France in June 1940 and the ensuing Battle of Britain. Even then, political support for the military mobilized slowly until the Japanese forced the United States into the war on December 7, 1941. The consequences of lingering unpreparedness might have been disastrous had not a series of extraordinary presidential initiatives—cash-and-carry (1939), the destroyers–bases deal (1940), and the Lend–Lease Act (1941)—kept the Allies in the fight and effectively bought the United States two years in which to rebuild its military capabilities.

Disconnections between declared national strategies and actual military capabilities are not uncommon in peacetime and have, in fact, been a constant (and ultimately successful) element of U.S. cold war strategy. For such calculated risks to pay off, however, they must involve a delicate balance of political, economic, and military concerns. The irresponsibility of the interwar political establishment's risk-taking lay in its exclusion of the military from the national strategy process. As a result of outdated and unfounded suspicions, Congress dismissed as self-serving alarmism all military warnings that national strategy and expanding threats were spreading military capabilities too thinly.

The traditional role of the U.S. military professional as a passive player in the policy-making process did little to remedy the sad state of civil–military relations. Too often, military attempts to join in the process were heavy-handed or politically naive. Such was the case in 1920, when the army submitted a postwar force plan that called for a peacetime army of 500,000, universal military training, and the establishment of a General Staff. Congress—already impatient with defense talk, eager to cut federal spending, and generally suspicious of "Germanic militarism"—rejected the plan resoundingly and did not quickly forget the army's political faux pas.[38] Army leadership never succeeded in finding a political niche, and its influence on

political decisions that affected its fate remained minimal. The navy and Marine Corps were somewhat more successful in overcoming civilian suspicions, in part through the lobbying efforts of the Navy League and skillful use of public relations to improve their image among voters and, consequently, Congress. Overall, however, none of the services really succeeded in breaking the political barriers that excluded them from policy-making for defense.

Beyond the realm of civil–military relations, interwar operational readiness suffered from the organizational effects of force reductions. Over the course of two decades, the sluggish promotions system, low social status of military service, meager pay, and often tedious duty took their toll, driving talented officers and enlisted personnel out of the military and seriously undermining the morale of those who remained in uniform. Operational stagnation is not necessarily an inevitable by-product of force reductions if mechanisms are in place to keep peacetime service active and career progression steady. All of the services suffered under stagnant promotion systems and low salaries, but the navy and Air Corps, both of which offered the prospect of technical training and adventure, and the Marine Corps with its virile, elite image, all fared better than the largely bureaucratic interwar army.

Because billets were limited, the majority of the interwar officer corps were service academy graduates. Although military education fostered esprit and leadership qualities, the lack of diversity among senior military officers contributed to the operational conservatism of the interwar services and prevented the services—particularly the more conservative navy and army—from taking full advantage of

55

the talent and technological expertise of officer candidates from civilian universities. Many of the bright and ambitious young minds of the interwar military (whether from the academy or not) congregated in the new arms—aviation and submarines—where the duty was more rewarding but organizational influence was limited.[39] As a result, the service branches with the least institutional clout often fostered the most innovation.

As is often the case in periods of traumatic political and budgetary change, the interwar services had little success in cooperating to solve their mutual problems. Interservice rivalry is a constant of U.S. military policy, but during the interwar period rigid organizational separation and the dearth of cooperation at the strategic, operational, or doctrinal levels aggravated the debilitating effects of low budgets and poor civil–military relations—with some chilling consequences for World War II.[40] The strict operational division between land-based and sea-based air defense and the lack of coordination between army and navy commanders within Hawaii contributed to the most traumatic military defeat of the war: the Japanese attack on Pearl Harbor.[41] The relative inexperience of U.S. forces with joint operations also contributed to some initial problems in combined operations with Allied forces.[42]

Both the War and Navy Departments developed a certain strategic "tunnel vision" as the threat solidified. Navy/marine preoccupation with the Pacific strategy, army preoccupation with manpower mobilization, and the Air Corps preoccupation with its independent capabilities all led to important planning omissions. Logistical planning was a surprisingly low priority for a military establishment facing what it knew would probably be a protracted, global conflict conducted far beyond the home supply base and requiring a logistical tail unparalleled in military history. Transport was in short supply in all the services: landing craft (marines, and later, army), sealift (navy), troop carrier and cargo aircraft (air force), and trucks, especially tanker types (army). Wartime production offset some of the shortfalls, but others—especially amphibious shipping and cargo aircraft—had to compete for resources as combat attrition brought on soaring replacement demands. Communication capability, especially air-ground communication, was also quantitatively and qualitatively inadequate. In short, although each of the services anticipated the basic nature of the threats ahead, they vastly underestimated the scope of the operational challenges those threats presented.

Given the political and economic limits within which it operated, the military establishment (including each of its component services) developed sound and relatively effective capabilities for the threat it eventually faced. Despite the historical image of the interwar years as the Dark Ages of military preparedness, each of the services proved able to mobilize for, and ultimately win, a major, global war within a not unreasonable period of time, although their success derived in part from the advantages of two years of wartime warning (September 1939–December 1941) and two great power allies (Great Britain and the Soviet Union). Although it is possible to argue that a higher level of U.S. military preparedness might have deterred German and Japanese adventurism during the late 1930s, U.S. political leadership, more than the military establishment, bears the burden of responsibility for any lack of resolve in that area. Given the constitutional and statutory mandate within which it operated (far more restrictive than today's), the interwar military establishment performed, in most cases, as well as—and in some, better than—might reasonably have been expected.

Implications for the Future

If the history of the interwar period is any guide (the working assumption of this paper being that it is), then it suggests a number of important implications for future military planning.

It is not safe to assume that because civil–military relations are reasonably good now, they will continue to be so forever. In fact, there are already warning signs that the Defense Department will have to work much harder in the future to avoid being overridden on questions of national strategy, or worse, cut out of the process altogether. For example, the center of gravity in the current debate over defense restructuring seems to have shifted toward Capitol Hill. As Senator William S. Cohen (R–Me.), among others, has suggested, in that venue the chances are virtually nil that long-term strategic and national defense interests will outweigh short-term budget pressures in determining the future of the U.S. defense establishment.[43] In the long run, active Defense Department participation in the "demobilization" process can forestall the kinds of arbitrary budget and force structure cuts that plagued all of the services after World War I. The armed services, for their part, need to be aware of changing political priorities, avoid public statements or actions that appear unduly self-serving or alarmist, and perhaps be prepared to sacrifice some readiness in the interest of maintaining their voice in defense policy over the longer term.

Interservice rivalry tends to escalate during periods of rapid political change and strategic uncertainty, but in contrast to the interwar period, the current defense establishment can benefit from the existence of civilian and military agents specifically tasked with maintaining interservice cooperation. Two independent and potentially competitive civilian agencies—the Department of War and the Department of the Navy—oversaw the interwar military services: the few (generally voluntary) joint army and navy planning efforts during the 1930s tended to be viewed with suspicion by Congress and the civilian bureaucracy. In today's system, the Office of the Secretary of Defense, as the civilian arbiter of military affairs, can take the initiative in ensuring that the natural tendency of the services to diverge under institutional stress does not result in more permanent damage to interservice relations. The Joint Chiefs of Staff should likewise keep service unity a high priority to avoid any undermining of important joint capabilities.

Readiness and general high force quality are more difficult to maintain in peacetime, but the lack of an immediate threat does not make these factors less important. Smaller forces need not become stale provided force reduction plans keep mechanisms in place that allow for steady career advancement and the continued operational orientation that keeps military service interesting and challenging. Peacetime forces organized to maximize readiness (perhaps even beyond immediate requirements) and allow active, realistic training and exercises also help keep doctrines current. Beyond the obvious military advantages, such steps will fend off the low morale, high attrition, low social status, and general sense of ennui that plagued the interwar services.

Declining defense budgets present

obvious problems for keeping doctrine and capabilities up-to-date, but as both the successes and failures of interwar force modernization show, there are ways to minimize deterioration. Extended research and development, prototyping of radically new systems to evaluate their potential, and more limited production of interim systems can all contribute to keeping doctrines, capabilities, and warfighting concepts dynamic. Involvement in such activity, by providing challenging duty, will also help keep military service competitive with civilian careers in peacetime.

Arms-control agreements, both nuclear and conventional, are likely to have a significant impact as well on future force structures and capabilities. As the naval arms-control treaties of the 1920s demonstrate, arms control can either undermine or facilitate force modernization—sometimes both. The overall effectiveness—or ineffectiveness—of the interwar agreements was determined, in large part, by their dearth of verification and enforcement mechanisms. As the interwar period provides the last extended experiment in conventional arms control, a more comprehensive review of where it succeeded and where it failed could provide some timely insights.

In the event that the present Soviet withdrawals continue, it seems likely that the U.S. military posture will take on an increasingly defensive character. The implications of that shift for long-term military readiness will depend on where Congress, the White House, and the defense establishment draw the parameters of defense. The often naive and overly simplistic definitions of defensive weapons—as reflected in the interwar congressional policy of "arming solely for defense"—contributed, directly or indirectly, to most of the shortfalls of U.S. military capabil-

ities during World War II. In the nuclear era, the lines between offense and defense—never explicit to begin with—have become more indistinct and their implications for national defense policy more vital.

The military establishment of the 1990s indeed faces a degree of reassessment and restructuring, unparalleled since the post–World War II demobilization, that will fundamentally change the structure of U.S. military capabilities. The present retrenchment of the Soviet empire, however, also offers an unprecedented opportunity to realign strategy, force structures, and commitments to make U.S. military capabilities more responsive across a range of contingencies below the level of a global conflict between the North Atlantic Treaty Organization (NATO) and the Warsaw Pact. What the interwar experience teaches us, ultimately, is that a relative balance of strategy, commitments, and capabilities cannot be achieved if force restructuring is treated as a purely fiscal exercise.

Abbreviated defense budgets are an inevitable product of post–cold war demobilization, but if today's civilian and military leadership—unlike their interwar predecessors—take care to join forces in responding to the changing threat, force restructuring poses few problems for the political standing or long-term readiness of the U.S. armed forces. Through such an approach to the post–cold war environment, moreover, civil–military relations in the 1990s can avoid the mutual suspicion and strategic naïveté that decimated military preparedness in the 1920s.

The conclusions drawn in this paper are the author's and are not necessarily endorsed by the Institute for Defense Analyses or by the Department of Defense.

The author wishes to acknowledge the extensive advice and support she received from General William Y. Smith, Dr. Victor Utgoff, and Ms. Mary M. Evans in the preparation of this article. Responsibility for any inaccuracies, omissions, or other lapses of judgment is, of course, the author's alone.

Notes

1. Ronald Spector, "Military Effectiveness of the US Armed Forces, 1919–1939," in *Military Effectiveness*, vol. 2, *The Interwar Period*, Allan R. Millett and Williamson Murray, eds. (New York: Allen & Unwin, 1988), pp. 72–73.

2. Allan R. Millett and Peter Maslowski, *For the Common Defense* (New York: Free Press, 1985), p. 374.

3. Ronald Spector, *Eagle Against the Sun* (New York: Free Press, 1985), pp. 19–21.

4. Spector, "Military Effectiveness," p. 89.

5. *Ibid.*, p. 77.

6. Russell F. Weigley, *The American Way of War* (New York: Macmillan, 1973), pp. 264–265.

7. Mark S. Watson, *The United States Army in World War II*, vol. 4, pt. 1, *Chief of Staff: Prewar Plans and Preparations* (Washington, D.C.: GPO, 1950), pp. 17, 150–151.

8. Russell F. Weigley, *History of the United States Army* (New York: Macmillan, 1967), pp. 402–403.

9. Watson, *Chief of Staff*, pp. 82–84.

10. Weigley, *History of the United States Army*, p. 409.

11. Spector, "Military Effectiveness," pp. 74–75.

12. Watson, *Chief of Staff*, pp. 42–44.

13. Martin Blumenson, "Kasserine Pass, 30 January–22 February, 1943," in *America's First Battles: 1776–1965*, Charles E. Heller and William A. Stofft, eds. (Lawrence, Kan.: University Press of Kansas, 1986), p. 228.

14. Spector, *Eagle Against the Sun*, pp. 11–13.

15. Allan R. Millett, "US Armed Forces in the Second World War," pp. 48–49; and Earl F. Ziemke, "Military Effectiveness in World War II," p. 282, in *Military Effectiveness*, vol. 3, *The Second World War*, Allan R. Millett and Williamson Murray, eds. (New York: Allen & Unwin, 1988).

16. Blumenson, "Kasserine Pass," p. 240.

17. See Blumenson, "Kasserine Pass," and Jay Luvass, "Buna," in Heller and Stofft, *America's First Battles*.

18. Victor H. Krulak, *First To Fight: An Inside View of the US Marine Corps* (Annapolis, Md.: Naval Institute Press, 1984), p. 15.

19. Jeter A. Isely and Philip A. Crowl, *The Marines and Amphibious War* (Princeton, N.J.: Princeton University Press, 1951), pp. 22, 27.

20. Allan R. Millett, *Semper Fidelis: The History of the United States Marine Corps* (New York: Macmillan, 1980), pp. 321–322, 328–329.

21. The navy adopted the marine doctrine, *A Tentative Manual for Landing Operations*, in 1938, and the army copied it virtually verbatim for its own 1941 doctrine. Isely and Crowl, *The Marines*, p. 52; Weigley, *American Way of War*, p. 262.

22. Isely and Crowl, *The Marines*, pp. 30–32.

23. Millett, *Semper Fidelis*, p. 335.

24. Krulak, *First to Fight*, p. 13.

25. Isely and Crowl, *The Marines*, p. 34.

26. *Ibid.*, p. 69.

27. *Ibid.*, pp. 69–70; Weigley, *American Way of War*, p. 262.

28. Weigley, *History of the United States Army*, pp. 262–265.

29. The United States Army Air Corps remained, throughout the interwar period, a subordinate branch of the army. Because of its fundamentally different mission, and to facilitate parallel comparison with the present military structure, however, this paper treats it separately. The air arm also underwent a series of name changes. The Air Service became a coequal combat arm in 1920. Congressional legislation created the subordinate, but semiautonomous U.S. Army Air Corps in 1926. In 1934, the War Department created the GHQ Air Force to oversee operational units in peacetime. In World War II, the GHQ Air Force became the U.S. Army Air Forces, which were administratively subordinate but operationally coequal to army ground commands. To avoid confusion, this essay will use the name that predominated for most of the period: U.S. Army Air Corps.

30. Wesley F. Craven and James L. Cate, *The*

Army Air Forces in World War II, vol. 1, *Plans and Early Operations, January 1939– August 1942* (Chicago: University of Chicago Press, 1948), p. 20.

31. *Ibid.*, pp. 22–24.

32. See Thomas Greer, *The Development of Air Doctrine in the Army Air Arm, 1917–1941* (Washington, D.C.: GPO, 1985).

33. Watson, *Chief of Staff*, p. 240.

34. Millett and Maslowski, *For the Common Defense*, p. 383.

35. *Ibid.*, p. 35.

36. Craven and Cate, *Army Air Forces*, pp. 109–110.

37. *Ibid.*, p. 150.

38. Millett and Maslowski, *For the Common Defense*, p. 366.

39. Spector, "Military Effectiveness," p. 77.

40. Weigley, *History of the United States Army*, p. 408.

41. Elliot A. Cohen and John Gooch, *Military Misfortunes: The Anatomy of Failure in War* (New York: Free Press, 1990), p. 51.

42. Millett, "The US Armed Forces in the Second World War," pp. 64–72.

43. William S. Cohen, "Whither NATO or Will NATO Wither?" Remarks before the Washington Strategy Seminar/National Strategy Information Center, June 22, 1990.

Deterrence and Conventional Military Forces

Gary L. Guertner

THE SEARCH FOR a U.S. national security strategy periodically opens major policy debates that push policymakers in new, sometimes revolutionary directions. The collapse of the Soviet Union and the end of the Cold War have given rise to a national debate unmatched since the end of World War II. Dramatic changes in the international system have forced Americans to reevaluate old strategies and look for new focal points amidst the still unsettled debris of the bipolar world. At issue is the role of the United States in a new world order and its capabilities to defend and promote its national interests in a new environment where threats are both diffuse and uncertain and where conflict is inherent yet unpredictable.

The degree of uncertainty requires flexibility in U.S. military strategy and significant departures from cold war concepts of deterrence. This paper examines new options for deterrence. Its primary thesis is that new conditions in both the international and domestic environments require a dramatic shift from a nuclear dominant deterrent to one that is based on conventional forces. The paper identifies the theories and strategies of nuclear deter-

Gary L. Guertner is director of research at the Strategic Studies Institute, U.S. Army War College. His latest book is *Deterrence and Defense in a Post-Nuclear World* (New York: St. Martin's Press, 1990).

rence that can also be applied to modern conventional forces in a multipolar world.

One obstacle to analysis of that transfer is semantic. The simultaneous rise of the Cold War and the nuclear era produced a body of literature and a way of thinking in which deterrence became virtually synonymous with nuclear weapons. In fact, deterrence has always been pursued through a mix of nuclear and conventional forces. The force mix changed throughout the Cold War in response to new technology, anticipated threats, and fiscal constraints. There have been, for example, well-known cycles in both U.S. and Soviet strategies when their respective strategic concepts evolved from nuclear-dominant deterrence (the "massive retaliation" of Dwight D. Eisenhower and its short-lived counterpart under Nikita Khrushchev), to the more balanced deterrent (John F. Kennedy to Ronald Reagan) of flexible response, which linked conventional forces to a wide array of nuclear capabilities in a "seamless web" of deterrence that was "extended" to U.S. allies in the North Atlantic Treaty Organization (NATO).

Early proponents of nuclear weapons tended to view nuclear deterrence as a self-contained strategy, capable of deterring threats across a wide spectrum of threat. By contrast, the proponents of conventional forces have always argued that there are thresholds below which conventional forces pose a more credible deterrent. Moreover, there will always be nondeterrable threats to U.S. interests that will require a response, and that response, if military, must be commensurate with the levels of provocation. A threat to use nuclear weapons against a third world country, for instance, would put political objectives at risk because of worldwide reactions and the threat of escalation beyond the theater of operations.

The end of the Cold War has dramatically altered the "seamless web" of deterrence and has decoupled nuclear and conventional forces. Nuclear weapons have a declining political-military utility below the threshold of deterring a direct nuclear attack against the territory of the United States. As a result, the post–cold war period is one in which stability and the deterrence of war are likely to be measured by the capabilities of conventional forces. Ironically, the downsizing of U.S. and allied forces is occurring simultaneously with shifts in the calculus of deterrence that call for conventional domination of the force mix.

Downsizing is being driven by legitimate domestic and economic issues, but it also needs strategic guidance and rationale. The political dynamics of defense cuts, whether motivated by the desire to disengage from foreign policy commitments or by the economic instinct to save the programs in the defense budget richest in jobs, threaten the development of a coherent post–cold war military strategy. This paper identifies strategic options for a credible deterrence against new threats to U.S. interests. Most can be executed by conventional forces, and present conditions make a coherent strategy of general, extended conventional deterrence feasible.

Critics of conventional deterrence argue that history has demonstrated its impotence. By contrast, nuclear deterrence of the Soviet threat arguably bought 45 years of peace in Europe. The response to this standard critique is threefold. First, conditions now exist (and were demonstrated in the Persian Gulf War) in which the technological advantages of U.S. conventional weapons and doctrine are so superior to the capabilities of all conceivable adversaries that their deterrence value against direct threats to U.S. interests is higher than at any period in American history.

Second, technological superiority and operational doctrine allow many capabilities previously monopolized by nuclear strategy to be readily transferred to conventional forces. For example, conventional forces now have a combination of range, accuracy, survivability, and lethality that allows them to execute strategic attacks, simultaneously or sequentially, across a wide spectrum of targets that include counterforce, command and control (including leadership), and economic elements.

Third, critics of conventional deterrence have traditionally set impossible standards for success. Over time, any form of deterrence may fail. The United States will always confront some form of nondeterrable threat. Moreover, deterrence is a perishable commodity. It wears out and must periodically be revived. Failures of deterrence provide the opportunity to demonstrate the price of aggression, rejuvenate the credibility of deterrence (collective or unilateral), and establish a new period of stability. In other words, conventional deterrence can produce long cycles of stability instead of the perennial or overlapping intervals of conflict that would be far more likely in the absence of a carefully constructed U.S. (and allied) conventional force capability.

How the United States responds to deterrence failures will determine both its credibility and the scope of international stability. Figure 1 summarizes reasonable standards for judging conventional deterrence.

Long periods of stability may or may not be attributable to the success of deterrence. In any case, no deterrence system or force mix can guarantee an "end to history." Paradoxically, stability is dynamic in the sense that forces are constantly at work to undermine the status quo. Those forces, also summarized in figure 1, mean that deterrence failures are, over time, inevitable. Readers may have difficulty associating the events in column 1 of the figure with periods of "stability." Regrettably, such is the nature of international politics.

The United States should, therefore, base its military strategy on weapons that can be used without fear of self-deterrence or of breaking up

coalition forces that provide political legitimacy and military capability. If the United States is serious about deterring regional threats on a global scale, this strategic logic will push it into a post–cold war deterrence regime dominated by conventional forces.

A Deterrent Based on Conventional Forces

Conventional deterrence has a future, but one very different from its past, in which it was subordinated to nuclear threats and strategic nuclear theory. The United States now faces a multipolar international political system that may be destabilized by a proliferation of armed conflict and advanced weaponry. To secure stability, security, and influence in this new world order, the United States can use the military prowess it demonstrated in the Persian Gulf War to good advantage. Using that force effectively, however, or threatening to use it, requires the formulation of a coherent

Figure 1
Conventional Deterrence and International Stability

Period of Stability →	Deterrence Failure →	Stability Restored	OR Instability Spreads
• Military technology advances	• Crisis or war	• Aggression is countered	• Aggression succeeds
• Weapons proliferate	– Collective security	• Conventional forces and doctrine demonstrate capabilities	• Deterrence fails
• Political and economic conflicts flare	– Collective defense	• Conventional deterrence revitalized	• Utility of aggression demonstrated
• Incentives for war increase	– Unilateral action	• New period of stability begins	• Period of instability extended in scope and duration
• Risk of miscalculation increases		• U.S. interests protected	• U.S. interests at risk
• Deterrence fails			

strategy of "general extended conventional deterrence" and the prudent planning of general purpose forces that are credible and capable of underwriting a new military strategy.

Neither proponents nor critics should judge this analysis in isolation. Conventional deterrence cannot succeed unless it is reinforced by supporting policies and concepts. The strategic concepts in the current National Military Strategy document that appear to have the greatest synergistic value in support of conventional deterrence are:

- technological superiority;
- collective security;
- forward presence;
- strategic agility; and
- theater defenses.[1]

Technological Superiority. Expected reductions in the overall force structure will make the force-multiplying effects of technological superiority more important than ever. Space-based sensors, defense-suppression systems, "brilliant weapons," and stealth technologies give true meaning to the concept of force multipliers. This broad mix of technologies can make conventional forces decisive provided they are planned and integrated into an effective doctrine and concept of operations.

The conflicts most likely to involve the United States will be confrontations with less capable states that have trouble employing their forces and their technology in effective combined arms operations. As Anthony Cordesman has concluded in his assessment of the Persian Gulf War,

the U.S. can cut its force structure and still maintain a decisive military edge over most threats in the Third World. It can exploit the heritage of four decades of arming to fight a far more sophisticated and combat ready enemy so that it can fight under conditions where it is outnumbered or suffers from significant operational disadvantages.[2]

Exploiting technology to get economies of force will require investments where the payoff in battlefield lethality is greatest. Given the threats that U.S. forces are most likely to confront in regional contingencies, these technologies will include:

- battle management resources for real-time integration of sensors-command-control and weapon systems that make enemy forces transparent and easily targeted;
- mobility of conventional forces to fully exploit technological superiority and battlefield transparency;
- smart conventional weapons with range and lethality; and
- component upgrades for existing delivery platforms to avoid costly generational replacements. This means limited procurement of new tactical fighters, tanks, bombers, submarines, or other platforms that were originally conceived to counter a modernized Soviet threat.

Technology that leads to unaffordable procurement threatens the U.S. military with force multipliers of less than 1.0. Net decreases in combat-capable forces can best be avoided through combinations of selective upgrading and selective low-rate procurement.

Technological superiority will also depend on concurrent political strategies. Technology is a double-edged sword; it can act as a force multiplier, but the laws of science apply equally to potential U.S. adversaries. Multilateral support for the nonproliferation of both nuclear and critical conventional military technologies can be an equally effective means for preempting threats to U.S. interests and for underwriting conventional deterrence.

Collective Security. Collective security has become explicitly incorporated in the National Military Strategy. It is broadly defined to include both collective security (activities sanctioned by the United Nations [UN]) and collective defense arrangements (formal alliances such as NATO). These are linked informally in what could, if promoted by the United States, form transregional security linkages—a "seamless web" of collective action.[3]

The potential value of collective security to conventional deterrence is difficult to quantify because it requires the United States to link its security to the capabilities and political will of others. Its potential must always be balanced against the risk that collective action may require significant limitations on unilateral action. Nevertheless, there are three compelling reasons for the United States to embrace collective security.

- Allies or coalition partners are essential for basing or staging the range of capabilities required to fully exploit technologically superior forces against a regional hegemon.
- The American public shows little enthusiasm for an active role as the single, global superpower. Collective deterrence is politically essential for sharing not only the military burden, but also the increasingly salient political and fiscal responsibilities.
- Patterns of collective action, as demonstrated in the Persian Gulf War, give conventional deterrence

credibility and capabilities that the United States can no longer afford or achieve on its own. Even though collective action and shared capabilities may limit U.S. freedom of action, these limits are reassuring to others and may contribute more to stability than attempts by the world's only superpower to unilaterally impose deterrence—nuclear or conventional.

Forward Presence. The post–cold war shift in U.S. military strategy from large-scale forward deployments of military forces to limited or intermittent forward presence is linked to the credibility of both conventional deterrence and collective security.[4]

U.S. forces abroad will continue to be viewed as the most visible symbols of U.S. resolve and commitment to regional stability. They are vital components of both short- and long-range stability because they

- demonstrate U.S. leadership, commitment, and capabilities for collective security, collective defense, and peacekeeping operations;
- contribute to the preservation of regional power balances and provide disincentives for the nationalization of regional defense policies and of arms competitions; and
- contribute to the containment of security obstacles that, absent a U.S. presence, could disrupt regional economic integration and political union, both vital components of long-term regional stability.

The forward presence of U.S. military forces as part of collective security or collective defense regimes has a deterrent value in excess of its immediate military capabilities, provided that these symbols of U.S. commitment are backed by the strategic agility to bring credible military force to bear at decisive points and at decisive times in a crisis.

Strategic Agility. Strategic agility is a generic concept that reflects the dramatic changes in cold war forward deployment patterns that fixed U.S. forces on the most threatened frontiers in Germany and Korea. Old planning assumptions have given way to new requirements to meet diffuse regional contingencies. Simply stated, U.S. forces will be assembled by their rapid movement from wherever they are to wherever they are needed. Strategic agility requires mobile forces and adaptive planning for a diverse range of options. Many of these options signal U.S. commitment and demonstrate military capabilities short of war. Joint exercises, UN peacekeeping missions, and even humanitarian/disaster relief operations provide opportunities to display power projection capabilities and global reach despite reduced forward deployment of forces.

Theater Ballistic Missile Defenses. Nuclear and chemical weapons proliferation make theater air and antitactical ballistic missile defenses important components of conventional deterrence. The next states that are likely to acquire nuclear arms are under radical regimes that are openly hostile to U.S. interests (North Korea, Libya, Iran, and Iraq, if UN intervention fails).[5] The success of such regional powers in creating even a small nuclear umbrella under which they could commit aggression would represent a serious challenge to U.S. global strategy.

Theater defenses in support of conventional deterrence need not be a part of the grander objectives of the Strategic Defense Initiative or its most recent variant, Global Protection Against Limited Strikes (GPALS). The layered, space-based weapons architecture of these costly systems seems, at best, technologically remote and, at worst, a vestige of the Cold War.[6] What is needed in the near term is a global, space-based early warning, command and control network that is linked to modernized, mobile, land-based theater defense systems (Patriot follow-on or Theater High-Altitude Area Defense [THAAD] interceptors designed for greater defense of countervalue targets such as cities).

Theater Strategic Targeting with Conventional Forces

Uncertainties about nondeterrable nuclear threats make it all the more imperative that the United States also have credible warfighting options. Nuclear preemption prior to an attack is not plausible, and there are uncertainties as to whether any president or his coalition partners would authorize a response in kind, even if the enemy used nuclear weapons first. More plausible are the range of conventional options afforded by modern, high-tech weapons that have a theater strategic capability for both denial and punishment missions. The broad outline of a conventional deterrence strategy would include:

- conventional preemption of the nuclear/chemical infrastructure and key command and control nodes to deny or disrupt an attack (deterrence by denial);
- threats of conventional escalation to countervalue targets (economic) if nuclear weapons are used (deterrence by punishment);
- threats to seize enemy territory (deterrence by punishment);

- countervalue retaliation by conventional forces if deterrence and preemption fail (deterrence by punishment); and
- theater antitactical missile and air defenses (deterrence by denial).

The air war against Iraq demonstrated the limitations of counterforce targeting against missiles and nuclear/chemical infrastructures. Nevertheless, the impact of the coalition's technological superiority was felt throughout Iraq, particularly at the nerve center and heart of the Iraqi government and its war-making capability. The success of the stealth systems and precision bombing capabilities projected some of the same physical and psychological aspects as weapons of mass destruction without the liabilities of this type of weapon. Operations that could target Saddam Hussein and his war-making potential without causing widespread, indiscriminate destruction of the Iraqi people provided a counter to Saddam's attempts at influencing world opinion. Such precision prevented Saddam from successfully painting the coalition's actions as war on the Iraqi people.[7]

The imperfect capability of deterrence by denial (even with nuclear weapons) and the unknowable responses to threats of retaliation and punishment leave theater antitactical ballistic missile defenses as the last line of defense for U.S. and coalition forces. On balance, conventional deterrence that combines attempts to dissuade, capabilities to neutralize or capture, credible threats to retaliate, and the ability to defend is more credible against regional powers than nuclear threats. Together, these capabilities dramatically reduce the coercive potential of third world nuclear programs. This does not mean, however, that nuclear forces have no role to play in the future of deterrence.

The Role of Nuclear Weapons in a Deterrent Dominated by Conventional Forces

The National Military Strategy 1992 states that the purpose of nuclear forces is "to deter the use of weapons of mass destruction and to serve as a hedge against the emergence of an overwhelming conventional threat."[8]

The dilemma confronting the United States is still the same classic problem that confronted strategists throughout the Cold War. Nuclear weapons fulfill their declared deterrence function only if they are never used. Yet, if everyone knows that they will never be used, they lack the credibility to deter. The most credible means to resolve this dilemma is through a combination of declaratory policies and military capability that emphasizes the warfighting capabilities of conventional forces with strategic reach.[9]

There is, however, a potential paradox of success if aggressive third world leaders believe that only weapons of mass destruction can offset U.S. advantages in conventional military power. Under such circumstances, theater nuclear weapons can have important signaling functions that communicate new risks and introduce greater costs for nuclear aggression that inflicts high casualties on U.S. forces or on allied countervalue targets.

Nuclear signaling can take the form of declarations by the president or the Department of Defense (DOD) that U.S. ships deploying to a hostile theater of operations have been refitted with nuclear weapons carried by dual-capable aircraft (DCA) and Tomahawk

Land Attack Missiles (TLAM).[10] Deployment options alone can play a critical role in the strategic calculus of aggressors who possess uncommitted nuclear capabilities.

The role of strategic nuclear forces is also directly related to the problems of reorienting the National Military Strategy from a global to a regional focus. The first problem is determining the force structure after the combined reductions of the Strategic Arms Reduction Treaty (START), unilateral initiatives, and the Bush–Yeltsin summit. The combined results will be dramatic cuts in U.S. strategic forces from some 12,000 warheads to 3,500 or less.[11] These cuts are prudent responses to the collapse of the Soviet Union and give the United States and its allies a long-sought opportunity to pull back from the nuclear brink where they so often found themselves during the Cold War. Moreover, these reductions are consistent with obligations under the Nuclear Non-Proliferation Treaty (NPT). They should be accompanied by strong U.S. endorsements of the treaty and support for the strengthening of the nonproliferation regime as a critical NPT review conference approaches in 1995.

The credibility of U.S. support for nonproliferation will also be affected by the declaratory policies and targeting strategy for a smaller strategic nuclear force structure. The most comprehensive review of the problem to date suggests that the United States could be moving in the right direction provided that the strategic role of conventional forces dominates future planning. A report by the Joint Strategic Target Planning Staff Advisory Group, chaired by former Secretary of the Air Force Thomas C. Reed, recommends major changes in the Single Integrated Operational Plan (SIOP).

The cold war SIOP contained carefully calibrated strike options against the former Soviet Union. In its place, the panel recommends an Integrated Strike Employment Plan (ISEP) with a "near real time" flexibility to cover a wider range of targets with a smaller force structure. The proposal identifies five categories of plans:

- *Plan Alpha* is a conventional force option against selected strategic targets of "every reasonable adversary."
- *Plan Echo* is a nuclear option for theater contingencies or "Nuclear Expeditionary Forces."
- *Plan Lima* is a set of limited SIOP-like nuclear options against Russian force projection assets.
- *Plan Mike* is a more robust version of *Plan Lima* with graduated attack options in the 10s, 100s, and 1,000s.
- *Plan Romeo* is a strategic nuclear reserve force (SRF) to deter escalation, support war termination, and preclude other nuclear powers not directly involved in an ongoing crisis from coercing the United States.[12]

In their current form, these recommendations are excessive and favor a nuclear force structure that is not well suited for credible deterrence in the new world order. If they were misinterpreted as official policy, the United States could be accused of a double standard in proclaiming the value of nuclear weapons at the same time that it was asking others to forswear them.

In the case of the former Soviet Union, U.S. targeting policy should be muted. Prudence dictates that advantage be taken of every opportunity for mutual reductions of force levels and confidence-building measures such as lower alert rates, improved command and control structures, and cooperative steps to improve the safety of nuclear storage, transportation, and destruction procedures.[13]

Russia will remain a nuclear power with a potential to threaten the United States and its allies. On the other hand, it is no longer the center of a hostile global movement or the leader of a powerful military alliance threatening Europe with overwhelming force deep in its own territory. Russian behavior is shaped more by its need for Western aid and technology than by U.S. military capabilities. It is difficult to conceive credible scenarios in which even the most reactionary Great Russian nationalist could find in nuclear weapons the tools that could be used against the West in preplanned ways to coerce concessions or that might tempt revisionist leaders to adopt reckless and inflexible positions. The United States will and should, along with its British and French allies, retain nuclear options, but it is premature in the extreme to plan robust nuclear attacks against the "force projection assets" of a state that is struggling for democracy and economic reforms.[14]

Even though the United States may be a benevolent superpower, the political impact of global nuclear targeting is more likely to stimulate rather than deter nuclear proliferation. An alternative set of declaratory policies that are consistent with nonproliferation includes commitments to deep cuts in nuclear forces coupled with a *defensive* strategy of direct retaliation against nuclear attacks on U.S. territory. Direct retaliation is one of the few credible missions for strategic nuclear forces in the post–cold war world. Extending deterrence should be a function of conventional forces (the option embodied in Plan Alpha above).

Global retargeting of nuclear forces is an unfortunate concept that is more likely to put U.S. interests at risk in the long run. Marshal Yevgenii I. Shaposhnikov, commander in chief of the Russian Armed Forces, struck a more positive image in his correct observation that retargeting frightens people. It is better, he said, to discuss "nontargeting," which lowers the level of alert to "zero flight assignments of missiles."[15]

The marshal's formulations are too vague to serve as the basis of national policy. Nevertheless, his point should not be dismissed. The objectives of national military strategy are more likely to be achieved through the *implicit* flexibility to respond to nuclear aggression from any source rather than *explicit* declarations of global nuclear targeting. Many regional crises may be precipitated by the proliferation of nuclear weapons and ballistic missiles. U.S. strategy will, therefore, require a delicate balance lest it give incentives to that very threat. A reassuring posture, in the eyes of regional actors and global partners, will require reexamination and "denuclearization" of deterrence in a new multipolar world.

Finally, and above all, this paper's primary purpose has been to recommend the option of using modern conventional forces for strategic purposes. A reliance on offensive nuclear weapons carries enormous risks that have already brought the United States and its allies to the brink of war during several cold war crises. The American public has every right to expect that the Cold War's principal legacy of danger not be deliberately extended into the new world order.

A conventional dominant deterrent will require full emancipation from cold war thinking. As Fred Iklé has wisely noted, strategic thought "remains locked into place . . . by dated nuclear arsenals," and these forces remain tied to imaginative scenarios that "persist, like a genetic defect."[16]

Freeing U.S. military strategy from its nuclear past will require deeper cuts in the existing strategic nuclear force structure and in strategic defense spending. The Bush–Yeltsin summit was a dramatic step, but one that when fully implemented will leave the United States with nearly as many strategic nuclear warheads as it deployed in 1970, the period when serious efforts were just beginning for negotiated limits on Soviet and U.S. nuclear forces.[17]

Deeper cuts will be required to win congressional support for a conventional force structure that is capable of meeting the regional contingencies in the new national military strategy. Failure to clearly address how and why the U.S. force structure must change will result in an impotent mix of nuclear and conventional forces that will neither deter nor be capable of meeting threats to U.S. interests.

The views expressed in this article are those of the author and do not necessarily reflect the official policy or position of the Department of the Army, the Department of Defense, or the U.S. government.

Notes

1. These strategic concepts are drawn from *The National Military Strategy 1992*, released by the chairman of the Joint Chiefs of Staff in January 1992. Some have been narrowed in scope for ease of analysis. For example, the NMS lists strategic deterrence and defense as one of the four foundations on which U.S. strategy is built. This paper narrows this strategic concept to conventional deterrence and theater defense.

2. Anthony H. Cordesman, "Compensating For Smaller Forces: Adjusting Ways and Means Through Technology" (Paper presented at the Third Annual Strategy Conference, U.S. Army War College, Strategic Studies Institute, Carlisle Barracks, Pa., February 14, 1992), p. 2.

3. For a detailed assessment of collective security and U.S. strategy, see Inis Claude, Jr., Sheldon Simon, and Douglas Stuart, *Collective Security in Asia and Europe* (Carlisle Barracks, Pa.: U.S. Army War College, Strategic Studies Institute, March 2, 1992). Ironically, the administration's pledge to support growing UN peacekeeping activities is under attack by members of Congress because of a long-standing agreement that makes the United States responsible for 30 percent of the cost of every operation. Japan and the West Europeans could conceivably relieve part of the perceived inequity, but Congress should also examine these costs in the larger context of collective security and global stability. See Don Oberdorfer, "Lawmakers Balk at Peacekeeping's Cost," *Washington Post*, March 4, 1992, p. A–17.

4. *The National Military Strategy* describes forward presence operations to include forward stationed troops, forces afloat, periodic rotational deployments, access and storage agreements, military exercises, security and humanitarian assistance, port visits, and military-to-military contacts.

5. Leonard S. Spector, "Deterring Regional Threats from Nuclear Proliferation" (Paper presented at the Third Annual Strategy Conference, U.S. Army War College, Strategic Studies Institute, Carlisle Barracks, Pa., February 14, 1992), p. 31 and appendix A.

6. In his testimony before the House Armed Services Committee on December 10, 1991, CIA director Robert Gates stated that only missiles from Russia and the People's Republic of China (PRC) could threaten the territory of the United States. He did not expect direct risks from other countries for at least another decade. See *Statement of the Director of Central Intelligence*, pp. 16–17.

7. Colonel Douglas Craft, *An Operational Analysis of the Persian Gulf War* (Carlisle Barracks, Pa.: U.S. Army War College, Strategic Studies Institute, August 1992).

8. *The National Military Strategy 1992*, p. 13.

9. A major thesis of this paper is that conventional deterrence must occasionally give way to conflicts that demonstrate capabil-

ities, thereby strengthening deterrence for a new phase of stability. The bombing of Hiroshima and Nagasaki had much the same effect on nuclear deterrence.

10. President George Bush's unilateral initiatives in September 1991 eliminated ground-launched tactical nuclear weapons and withdrew them from surface ships and submarines. Some sea-based weapons are scheduled for destruction. Others are in storage whence they can be redeployed for the "signaling" purposes advocated here.

11. President Bush's January 1992 initiative pledged cuts in strategic nuclear warheads up to 50 percent below START-permitted ceilings of approximately 8,000 warheads. At the Bush–Yeltsin summit on June 17, 1992, dramatic breakthroughs were announced that included the agreement to reduce strategic nuclear warheads to a range of 3,000 to 3,500 by 2003, the lowest levels since 1969. The flexible ceiling reflects agreement to deploy asymmetrical force levels. More important, the Russians agreed to destroy all their land-based intercontinental ballistic missiles (ICBMs) with multiple independently targeted reentry capacity (MIRV), the core of their strategic force structure, and the most long-standing goal in U.S. arms negotiating strategy. The United States also agreed to reduce its deployed submarine-launched ballistic missiles (SLBM) forces by 50 percent. See R. Jeffrey Smith, "Arms Talks Devoid of Usual Anxieties," *Washington Post*, June 18, 1992, p. A–38, and Thomas L. Friedman, "Reducing the Russian Arms Threat," *New York Times*, June 17, 1992, p. A–11.

12. Thomas C. Reed and Michael O. Wheeler, "The Role of Nuclear Weapons in the New World Order," JSTPS/SAG Deterrence Study Group, Department of Defense, Washington, D.C., October 19, 1991, pp. 33–34. See also R. Jeffrey Smith, "U.S. Urged to Cut 50% of A-Arms," *Washington Post*, January 6, 1992, p. A–1.

13. These latter steps are well under way. Congress allocated $400 million to assist Russian efforts to transport, store, and destroy nuclear weapons, and on March 26, 1992, the State Department announced the appointment of Retired Maj. Gen. William F. Burns, former director of the U.S. Arms Control and Disarmament Agency, to head the U.S. delegation on Safety, Security, and Dismantlement of Nuclear Weapons (SSD Talks). Moscow has agreed to U.S. assistance in the production of containers for fissile material from dismantled nuclear weapons, conversion of rail cars for secure transport, construction of storage facilities, training in nuclear accident response, accounting procedures, and ultimate disposition of enriched uranium and plutonium. See Department of State Press Release, March 26, 1992.

14. Open discussions of nuclear targeting in the press were followed by equally controversial reporting of threat scenarios that were developed in the Office of the Chairman of the Joint Chiefs of Staff. These scenarios included a hypothetical NATO counterattack if Russia invaded Lithuania. There is virtually no support in NATO or in the U.S. Congress for such a course of action. The scenario does, however, raise the question of what the United States should do in the event of a Russian-initiated civil war to reunite the former Soviet Union. Russian nationalists could indeed threaten nuclear retaliation against Western intervention. History suggests, however, that Western response would be political and economic, but not military, thus making nuclear threats irrelevant. "Threat" scenarios are discussed by Barton Gellman, "Pentagon War Scenario Spotlights Russia," *Washington Post*, February 20, 1992, p. A–1.

15. Marshal Yevgenii I. Shaposhnikov, interview in *Red Star*, February 22, 1992, pp. 1–3. Quoted in Foreign Broadcast Information Service, *Central Eurasia*, February 24, 1992 (FBIS-SOV-92-036), p. 8.

16. Quoted in Michael J. Mazarr, "Nuclear Weapons After the Cold War," *The Washington Quarterly* 15 (Summer 1992), p. 198.

17. As noted in note 11, the Bush–Yeltsin summit agreement would reduce U.S. strategic nuclear warheads to 3,000–3,500 by 2003. In 1970, a period when the Soviets achieved strategic nuclear parity with the United States, U.S. strategic nuclear warheads numbered 3,780. Data compiled from *The Military Balance*, 1969–1972 editions (London: International Institute for Strategic Studies). Ironically, the Strategic Arms Limitation Talks (SALT I) initiated by President Richard M. Nixon in 1969 resulted, over time, in a fourfold increase in U.S. strategic nuclear warheads.

Technology and Strategy in a Changing World

Joseph F. Pilat and Paul C. White

THE CERTAINTIES THAT have governed U.S. strategy and diplomacy in the decades since World War II are dissolving in dramatic fashion. Proclamations of the end of the Cold War, and even the end of history, are heard as communism collapses. Events in the Communist world have captured the headlines, sometimes overshadowing the seemingly global resurgence of democracy and market forces. Equally important as signs of the changing world are the accelerating diffusion of political, military, and economic power; the global proliferation of advanced weaponry; the rise of terrorism and the drug trade; and ongoing regional conflict in certain strategic areas. Not since the late 1940s has the international security environment been so fluid, uncertain, and, despite the euphoria signaled by those who believe that history has come to an end, so fraught with instability.

Despite the remarkable progress of the current East–West arms control agenda, threats to U.S. and Western interests persist. Although the Soviet military threat probably is receding, due to political and economic devel-

opments in the Soviet Union and Eastern Europe, Soviet military capabilities remain formidable and, even if significant Soviet force reductions are achieved in the future, it is by no means clear that overall Soviet military capabilities will decline if remaining forces are modernized and reorganized. Furthermore, in the years ahead, new challenges to the West will be posed by the emergence of regional powers in the Third World and the prospect of the militarization of the Pacific Rim countries. In addition, the United States will face a special challenge in the economic power of an integrated Europe and an ever-more prosperous Japan. Although these challenges are real, the shape of things to come is not at present fully understood. Despite the potential dangers of the 1990s and beyond, defense spending is certain to decline, perhaps dramatically.

Will it be possible to ensure Western security in the decades ahead? If so, how? The West was confronted by a similar situation in the late 1940s and early 1950s, as new and imperfectly understood threats to its interests emerged. There was uncertainty about how to meet those threats while building the peace. There were many who looked to technology at a time when wartime forces were being demobilized rapidly. In a seminal 1945 report on defense technologies, *Toward New Horizons,* one observer

Joseph F. Pilat is a staff member with the Los Alamos National Laboratory's Center for National Security Studies (CNSS) and director of the Center's Conventional Forces Assessment Project. Paul C. White is division leader of the Applied Physics Division of Los Alamos and served previously as deputy director and acting director of CNSS.

predicted the rising importance of revolutionary new technologies, including nuclear weapons, intercontinental ballistic missiles (ICBMs), supersonic and unmanned aircraft, and global navigation and communications.[1] In the decades since, U.S. technological superiority, along with an infrastructure jointly involving the government, military, and industry and capable of exploiting that superiority, has provided for Western security. However, in contrast to the decade after World War II, the United States today faces a more diffuse and uncertain international security environment with a defense technology infrastructure that is unraveling and becoming less adaptable and responsive. If history offers lessons about meeting such challenges, will we be able to learn from them?

Future Military Requirements and Force Structures

To some extent, military forces by necessity are designed without a perfect definition of national security objectives and strategy. Forecasts of the military threat always are imprecise, yet they are the foundation of force structure as well as strategy, national security objectives, and research and development (R&D) requirements. They are especially uncertain in a time of dramatic change. Yet, as one reflects on the positive and negative dimensions of the emerging international security environment, not all that one surveys is the shifting sand of a strategic desert. The Soviet military threat has never been the sole reason for U.S. international engagement, and with the perceived waning of that threat it is important to ask whether the United States should in general decrease its presence and influence in the world. Strategic retreat would be

irrational; isolationism may be appealing to many Americans but is not feasible. The alliances established by the United States in the postwar period remain essential to U.S. security for the foreseeable future and, as President George Bush made clear at a news conference after his meeting with the heads of state and government of the North Atlantic Treaty Organization (NATO) following the Malta "summit," the United States will remain engaged in Europe. As Bush stated,

Although this is a time of great hope—and it is—we must not blur the distinction between promising expectations and present realities. We must remain constant with NATO's traditional security mission. I pledged today that the United States will maintain significant military forces in Europe as long as our allies desire our presence as part of a common defense effort. The U.S. will remain a European power, and that means that the United States will stay engaged in the future of Europe and in our common defense.[2]

If the United States is to remain engaged in Europe and elsewhere in the coming years, current force levels and structures will require changes if they are to be responsive to the changing international security environment and to emerging political, economic, diplomatic, and military challenges. The focus on forces able to fight a high-intensity conflict in Europe against the Warsaw Pact, with the assumption that these forces would be adequate for lesser conflicts, may be sufficient no longer. The contingencies outside of Europe undoubtedly will be more demanding in the future. Given the emerging threat environment, and the prospect of reduced forward basing, the need for multi-purpose forces with global reach appears increasingly critical. This implies an emphasis on more flexible and mobile forces and greater strategic lift capabilities. It will be extremely difficult to achieve the flexibility allowing reduced forces to meet the demands of high-, medium-, and low-intensity conflict in a world in which the military requirements established in the early postwar years have not vanished entirely.

Force reductions and restructuring already have begun. Secretary of Defense Richard Cheney has requested the services to formulate budgets reflecting significant cuts in fiscal year (FY) 1991 and additional cuts of as much as $180 billion over the next three years that, if implemented, would amount to an annual reduction of 5 percent after inflation, as opposed to the original Bush administration proposals to increase the defense budget by 1–2 percent per year during this period.

Although Secretary Cheney has indicated that these cuts would result in reductions in force levels, base closings, and the elimination of or reductions in some weapons procurement programs, force structure cuts will dominate. The air force reportedly plans to close 15 bases worldwide, eliminate 5 fighter wings, reduce purchases of F–16 fighters, retire Minuteman II ICBMs and some conventionally-armed B–52 bombers, and slow the procurement of B–2 bombers and advanced-medium-range-air-to-air missiles (AMRAAM). The navy proposes to mothball two aircraft carriers. The army could eliminate three active divisions and drop plans to modernize the M–1 tank. None of the services proposed cuts in major new weapons procurement. However, the Pentagon's research budget, including funding for high technology consortia like Sematech and Defense Advanced Research Projects Agency (DARPA) programs, reportedly is threatened by the anticipated deep cuts in the U.S. defense budget.

The Secretary has suggested that the modernization of the strategic nuclear force, along with naval and air capabilities, remains critical to the United States, and that disproportionate cuts will fall on active ground forces. Cuts cannot and should not be apportioned equally among the services. A reduced army, for example, will require greater mobility and, therefore, an enhanced naval and air lift capability.

The impact of such force structure cuts is uncertain but does not appear inconsistent with the requirements of the current and future security environments. However, some critics in Congress and elsewhere see the projected cuts as being more reactive to the budget deficit than responsive to dramatic events in Eastern Europe and the Soviet Union. They question whether the cuts have any relation to changes in the military environment and whether they are guided by a realistic threat assessment and a long-term strategy. As Senator Sam Nunn has said,

My own impression is that Secretary Cheney's orders to the services reflect fiscal change not a real threat assessment. . . . I think these cuts he's talking about now, when you get down to it, are not in relation to events in Eastern Europe. That's the background music, and that's what makes the politics of it more acceptable to an awful lot of people, both on Capitol Hill and in the country. . . . I believe that if you are going to make cuts related to the reduced threat you have to ascertain what the threat is.[3]

Future Defense Technologies

Whatever the military threat, technology has been and will continue to be an important element in any U.S. response. Today's research horizons reveal a multitude of technologies that could revolutionize defense. However, the ability of the United States to capitalize on such advances to provide future military options may well be limited by political, bureaucratic, economic, and technological factors.

Throughout the twentieth century, the militaries of the West and especially the United States have driven the development of new technologies through procurement and R&D programs, from aviation to nuclear energy, computers, integrated circuits, and composite materials. These technologies have influenced strongly the shape of military forces and of the civil economies of the West and the world. Such militarily driven technologies have furthered Western competitiveness and enhanced Western security. Recently, however, the civil sector has assumed the leading role in critical technologies. Furthermore, many technological advances are emanating from Japan and Western Europe, both of which devote a greater share of R&D to funding programs designed for the civil sector than does the United States.

Contrary to the popular perception, defense technology has been evolving only slowly in recent decades, in contrast to the revolutionary changes of four decades ago. The rate of technological innovation is outstripping the integration of technologies into currently deployed systems. At present, many currently deployed systems employ technologies dating to the 1970s or earlier; 40 years ago, the employment of 20-year-old technologies would have relegated systems to obsolescence. There is a great disparity between the technologies that are commercially or otherwise available and those that have been exploited fully in military missions. This state of affairs is no doubt attributable, in part, to the revolutionary advances of the 1940s and 1950s and the stable international climate that has persisted since. The premium has been on evolution rather than revolution in deployed forces as it was in strategy and diplomacy.

On the basis of current and projected technologies, some observers have forecast the dissolution of the large conventional land armies and the impossibility of strategic surprise—which have dominated warfare for centuries. Several decades of evolution of competing technologies, measures, and countermeasures will result in revolutionary advances in lethality and real-time reconnaissance and surveillance. This will place a premium on autonomous, long-range standoff weapons as well as continuous, all-weather surveillance and reconnaissance, at the same time that large platforms and manned platforms will become less important.

If these forecasts are correct, what might be projected about future capabilities and their strategic significance? Increased warning times, and the associated reduced likelihood of surprise, will result from the implementation of improved reconnaissance and surveillance technologies. New systems will exploit multimode sensors to integrate information gleaned from target emanations across broad spectral ranges and different energy types, such as acoustic, thermal, optical, and other electromagnetic bands.

Prompt, automated target identification will be accomplished by high-speed, real-time processing of this data, using expert systems and new mathematical analysis techniques operating on microelectronic neural networks, or perhaps on integrated optical circuits. Combinations of ground-based, space-based, and remote-controlled or autonomous airborne sensor platforms offer the promise of continuous, all-weather coverage of selected regions, and will be redeployable rapidly in times of crisis. Because camouflage techniques, such as stealth, tend to mask only part of a target's signature, it may be expected that integrated, broad-coverage sensors ultimately will prevail in the technical competition between surveillance and deception.

These sensor technologies also could be employed in the development of smart or even brilliant weapons, capable of real-time target acquisition and very high kill probability per round. Improved signal processing and multichannel communication networks will enable better, more mobile, and more rapidly responsive command and control, in turn enabling a more flexible and survivable operational capability. Forces thus can be engaged simultaneously, rather than sequentially, and in depth across a broad front. Accordingly, the advantages once associated with large standing forces eventually will fade along with those of surprise.

Unprecedented weapon lethality will put a premium on unmanned, rather than manned, weapon platforms. Autonomous, long-range stand-off weapons will become increasingly important. Options will exist to defend, or to attack, high value targets using tactical directed energy weapons (DEW) or kinetic energy weapons (KEW). Counter-sensor or counter-communications weapons will employ explosive optical munitions or high-power microwaves. These and other new technologies will make the battlefield of the twenty-first century very different from that of today.

At present, however, this sort of forecast only indicates what might be possible. Today, the West has a decisive lead in most of these technologies, but this suite of technical capabilities is being pursued by the Soviet Union as well, and it can be anticipated that many of these capabilities will be disseminated to or developed in the Third World by the twenty-first century. Although the Soviets have begun the process of reducing weapons and converting certain military resources to civilian use, they appear committed to modernizing their formidable ground forces, navy, and strategic nuclear forces. The prospects for technological innovation are great, and the Soviets anticipate a technological revolution in military affairs comparable to the introduction of nuclear weapons. According to the Commission on Integrated Long-Term Strategy,

Dramatic developments in military technology appear feasible over the next twenty years. . . . These developments could require major revisions in military doctrines and force structures. The U.S. leads in developing many of the relevant technologies, which may be a source of concern to the Soviets. But the Soviet military establishment is already engaged in a major effort to understand the military implications of new technologies, and appears to have concluded that revolutionary changes in the nature of war will result. . . . But high tech is not an American monopoly. . . . the Soviet military establishment is striving to match or even surpass our weapons technology, and will increasingly do so unless we increase our research efforts.[4]

In the Third World, some of the most advanced conventional military capabilities already are spreading. These include the M–1 Abrams main battle tank, F–16 fighters, Exocet antiship missiles, SS–21 surface-to-surface missiles, advanced conventional submarines, and nuclear submarine programs. Programs to develop space-launch, satellite, and ballistic missile capabilities are growing as are those to develop chemical, biological, and nuclear weapons. Such capabilities, and perhaps even more advanced ones, will be developed and deployed in the twenty-first century, changing fundamentally Third World contingencies facing the United States.

Until now, the United States has met such contingencies with a mix of high tech and low tech responses, but these are no longer adequate. Low-tech solutions can be found for dealing with some problems of so-called low-intensity conflict (LIC), but will prove less relevant as more adversaries are armed with advanced weaponry. Past dependence on systems designed for other missions and theaters of operation to meet such threats should give way to a strategy designed to maximize U.S. technological advantages. Many of the technologies being developed in the strategic defense, advanced conventional weapon, and arms control verification areas might be adapted for LIC applications.

The premise that the United States should use, where appropriate, advanced technologies in low-intensity conflict situations requires a fundamental change in thinking. When this premise has been applied, the results have not always been those antici-pated. In the Persian Gulf, for example, the use of the Aegis missile system led to the Iranian airbus disaster. Moreover, there has been a reluctance to deploy in the Third World technologies developed to counter the Soviet threat out of a fear that the Soviets might monitor the results of their use or obtain access to them and either adapt them for their own use or seek countermeasures. Finally, there has been virtually no systematic thought about the application of these technologies in LIC, meaning that requirements and promising technologies have not been identified or funded. Circumstances may compel this rethinking. The proliferation of surface-to-air missiles and of antiship missiles in areas of interest to the United States and its allies requires high technology choices. By one analysis,

> In the Third World, no less than in developed countries, U.S. strategy should seek to maximize our technological advantages. In some cases, technologies developed for fighting the Soviets will be enormously useful. Here too we will want to use smart missiles that can apply force in a discriminate fashion and avoid collateral damage to civilians. Advanced technologies for training will also offer us more effective ways to help friends cope with terrorism and insurgency.[5]

To some extent, the revolutionary possibilities inherent in the defense technologies that now exist or are anticipated by the beginning of the next century enhance the uncertainty and instability of the current security milieu. On the other hand, and more important, they offer the means to address the unprecedented security challenges of the decades ahead. If one believes that the world is poised on the threshold of a military technological revolution, and that the prospect of East–West conflict in the next 10 years is low, then a greater emphasis should be placed on R&D and modernization than on maintaining current active force levels. Traditional Western reliance on technology will grow, not diminish in the years ahead. Indeed, Western reliance on advanced technologies in the emerging threat environment will remain necessary precisely because of anticipated Soviet moves toward a high technology military and the continued proliferation of high technology capabilities in the Third World.

Impediments to Defense Technology Development

Will the United States be able to retain its technological edge and apply emerging technologies to these military missions? There are serious political, bureaucratic, economic, and technological obstacles to achieving this level of responsiveness, and it is by no means certain that available and emerging technologies will be exploited by the West in the future.

Politically, improving East–West relations have diminished perceptions of the need for increased or even level defense spending. As argued above, deep cuts are likely. Arms control frequently is held to be preferable to unilateral cuts as a way to implement such reductions. Arms control threatens, however, to limit or eliminate technological options, either by providing for limits on modernization and the introduction of futuristic technologies, by foreclosing them inadvertently through agreed limits on platforms or other controls, or by making such advances politically unpalatable. The United States must avoid compromising technology options in the arms control process. Prudence would dic-

tate insistence on increased R&D budgets as the price for an arms control agreement. Realistically, the United States may choose unilaterally to foreclose specific technology options in the future, but formally and categorically to close them would erode seriously the ability of the United States to respond rapidly to emerging threats.

Bureaucratically, military R&D is caught up in the larger issue of the proper management and protection of high technology processes and products in the West. Investment is directed in accordance with critical technology lists developed by the Pentagon and others, which to date have been flawed because they focus on the problems of yesterday and today, but not tomorrow. There may be a set of critical strategic technologies that cut across many of the critical technologies in the Department of Defense's (DOD's) Critical Technology Plan, including electronics, computers, information processing, materials, and so on. According to Siegfried S. Hecker, the director of Los Alamos National Laboratory,

Certain technologies are or will remain critical for many decades because they either underpin or drive other, more specific, technologies. These critical technologies require a special investment strategy to ensure stability, perseverance, and the attention of first-rate institutions that can provide a continuity of effort.[6]

Hecker identifies three such critical technologies for which a broader technology base is required—supercomputing, superconductivity, and materials synthesis and processing. The development of high performance computing and high temperature ceramic superconductors, and the prospect of atomically engineered materials with tailor-made properties for specific applications have potentially revolutionary applications in both the civil and military spheres. Exploring the civil and military implications of each of these technologies will be vital if the United States is to protect and promote its economic and military interests in the decades ahead.

Strengthening the scientific base for R&D in these technologies is essential if the United States is to be able to realize their revolutionary promise. To do so, Hecker suggests such steps as higher investments in research; the creation of consortia comprising research universities, government laboratories, and private industry; and the establishment of centers of excellence that can bring together capabilities in theory, computer modeling, specialized experiments, and diagnostics.

The ability of the United States to pursue a strategy of greater emphasis on R&D for these and other strategic technologies is constrained severely by the emerging adversarial relationship among DOD, the Congress, and the defense industry. The defense establishment and service rivalries have slowed technological innovation. Service bureaucracies, along with Congress, frequently have attempted to preserve current deployments and production programs at the expense of long-term military R&D as budgets decline. The Defense Appropriations Bill for FY 1990, for example, retained funding for the purchase of F–14 fighters and the V–2 Osprey tilt-rotor aircraft, both of which Secretary Cheney sought to terminate.

Government and industry funding for defense-related R&D has been uneven and is projected to decline significantly in the decade ahead. Government actions have reduced industry willingness to devote re-

sources to R&D. Stringent cost control, more intense competition, heightened risk-aversion, and a focus on the evolution of existing product lines have eroded the defense industry's commitment to technology-base research and development. According to one analysis,

> U.S. budgeting for research and development has been constrained and uneven, and from the mid-1960s to the late 1970s, the technology base was substantially eroded. During the period 1965–1980, U.S. spending on military research and development declined about 20 percent. . . . In the 1980s, a turnaround for the United States began, but more recently our spending on the technology base was cut back again. At the same time, the substantial R&D undertaken by U.S. defense industry (reimbursed in part by the Department of Defense) has changed significantly in its character. While this effort was highly innovative in the 1950s and 1960s, it has become increasingly conservative in the 1970s and 1980s. Today, it has become far more an effort to reduce technical risk than to innovate. In some measure the Pentagon is responsible for the new emphasis. The main criterion for reimbursement used to be the innovativeness of the work; today the controlling question is apt to be whether industry's R&D is sufficiently related to an ongoing weapons program.[7]

Confronted by uncertainty, bureaucratic complexity, and the decline of traditional military markets, the defense industry already is looking at diversification into commercial and select high-growth military spheres, joint ventures with foreign firms, and other options, even though the full impact of the market changes has not yet been felt. For example, the Rockwell International Corporation no longer has major production programs for military aircraft and is expanding in military areas with better prospects for future growth, and the latest restructuring plans of Honeywell Inc. involve the sale of its marine and defense businesses.

The budget cycle also is damaging to rational planning for military R&D. DOD has been supportive of a two-year budget as an initial step in redressing this problem. The increased focus on cost rather than performance further distorts the planning process for R&D, as both the perception and reality of the high costs of advanced military systems make them vulnerable in military, administration, and congressional circles. An acquisition process requiring as much as 20 years to move a major weapon system from R&D to deployment both increases costs and limits technological innovation. The drawn out development process and resulting delays in the implementation of new technologies actually reduce the return on investments in defense R&D and thus reduce the incentives for such investment. Comparing the U.S. to the Soviet procurement process, the Commission on Integrated Long-Term Strategy concluded,

In translating scientific knowledge into deployed military systems, the Soviet Union has recently been far more successful than we have. Our current approach is piecemeal and haphazard. The procurement process is rigid, slow, confrontational, and micro-managed in ways that endlessly work against the efficient use of our resources. Defense Department officials try to minimize program risk by writing excessively detailed specifications, which unfortunately guarantee that compliance will be expensive, technically conservative, and uncreative. Throughout the acquisition process, such risk is avoided by focusing on today's technologies and on familiar old operational concepts—even though the system being procured will typically be needed for many years into the future. To be sure, conservatism in procurement has also been fostered by the past absence of an integrated long-term strategy. In its absence, the system keeps responding to only a few standard contingencies and overlooking many likely demands on U.S. forces in the future. For the coming years, we will need an acquisition process that fosters cohesion, speed, and incentives for innovation. The Defense Department has made a fair amount of progress toward revitalizing the acquisition process by implementing the recommendations of the Packard Commission. But the reforms need to be moved further.[8]

The need for a technology base capable of sustaining rapid responses to a changing and uncertain international environment is critical, especially at a time of reduced threat perceptions, budgetary difficulties, and the prospects of delayed or deferred force modernization decisions. There is a real risk that the United States will commit itself to military systems that may not be optimal or even useful for future military requirements. There is an equally grave danger of being wholly unprepared for future contingencies. Prudence dictates a shift in emphasis from deployed to deployable forces, entailing an R&D program designed to provide a range of rapidly producible and deployable weapon systems.

A host of concerns will compel a growing reliance on computer simulation for system testing and evaluation: increased budgetary constraints on developing complex military systems, environmental and arms control concerns, and the problems encountered by the United States with inadequate testing. "Virtual prototyping" is especially promising. It involves a computer-generated (virtual) environment in which material and system prototypes can be tested, compared, and evaluated, providing a cost-effective approach to evaluating multiple options, the possibility of early training and doctrine development, and a real-time crisis management option. Increased emphasis will need to be placed on the development of subsystems that can be combined as needed to form integrated systems for different applications. Additionally, hardware development must be coordinated with the simultaneous development of the requisite manufacturing capability. Investment in such approaches, which trades off current military capabilities for future ones, may be necessary. The capability for defense industrial mobilization has atrophied but must be restored for this approach to succeed, permitting the future mass production of new weapon systems as concrete threats emerge.

Economic factors, like the political and bureaucratic ones discussed above, also will constrain the U.S. ability to pursue a prudent technology development strategy. The budget deficit and the certainty of decreased defense spending come at a time of rising weapon costs. The expense of modern technologies has made it more difficult to maintain a wide range of options, because a decision to fund one set of technologies can be made only at the expense of others. Yet, this trend should not be inevitable; advanced technology does not necessarily cost more. For example, in the field of computing and data processing, increased speed and reliability have been achieved without an accompanying increase in cost. Similar possibilities certainly exist for the development of future defense capabilities based on high technologies.

Economic factors also complicate the large and growing challenge faced by the United States in maintaining its defense industrial base. The Pentagon and Congress historically have sought to preserve critical areas of the defense industrial base, including defense laboratories and production facilities, for both political and security reasons. However, there has been a reduction in the number of defense contractors, a trend likely to continue. The problem confronting the United States is how to restructure the defense industrial base during this process, and to preserve vital capabilities and expertise. According to one observer,

> There's no question that budget cuts will force a more rapid consolidation in almost all the subsectors of the weapons industry. The question is to what extent the Department of Defense will participate in the consolidation and make sure that valuable defense assets don't just go floating away in the wind.[9]

There are also technological obstacles to a robust military R&D effort. Dual-use technologies generated by the civilian economy raise issues of technical dependence and technology transfer, leading often to the erection of legal, administrative, and other barriers to the rapid exploitation by the military of such technologies. With the globalization of high technology capabilities, the penetration of the U.S.

industrial defense technology base by imports, the increasingly significant issue of foreign ownership, and the loss of U.S. technological leadership in many areas, the prospect of technological dependence has emerged, posing a serious challenge to the U.S. control of high-leverage technology breakthroughs.

The impact of declining defense budgets on U.S. technological leadership is being debated widely. A series of congressional legislative initiatives have been put forward to establish a civilian equivalent to DOD's DARPA. As Senator Al Gore (D-Tenn.) has said, "The military has been a very important patron for science and technology. To the extent that it vacates the field there are no apparent substitutes."[10] In promoting greater governmental support for civilian science and technology as a substitute, he argued that "Military R&D has been too powerful in this country relative to civilian R&D."[11] At issue today is whether, or to what extent, governmental science and technology policy should continue its focus on military R&D or shift to greater emphasis on civilian and dual-use technology. To the extent that economic competitiveness comes to define a critical aspect of U.S. national security in the 1990s and beyond, the efficiency of support for military R&D in terms of its civil benefits will have to be reassessed.

In light of increasing technological innovation in the civilian sector of the economy and the growing importance of dual-use technologies in the military sphere, the relative emphasis of U.S. policy must be addressed if a viable governmental R&D strategy designed to maintain U.S. leadership in critical technologies is to be developed and implemented. Government labs are now engaged in the process of making the capabilities of certain technologies they have developed available to the civil sector through technology transfer and collaboration with industry. This process could contribute significantly to promoting both security and economic competitiveness. However, because no nation will dominate the full range of militarily relevant technologies in the future, the United States must be able also to exploit technologies developed outside its borders. Rationally planned, selective cooperation with allies across the Atlantic and Pacific involving R&D in dual-use technologies may also be promising, although it is not without problems.

Conclusions

The current changes in the international security environment are more profound than any since the late 1940s. History has not ended; in Europe it is being revived, and throughout the world it is accelerating. While the emerging world is perplexing, offering both great opportunities and grave dangers, the emerging strategic landscape is not *terra incognita*. The East–West confrontation of the postwar era is waning, and the prospect of conflict in Europe between NATO and the Warsaw Pact is perhaps lower than at any time in the last 45 years. However, the United States and the West will be required to meet the challenge posed by Soviet military capabilities for the foreseeable future. Furthermore, emerging political, economic, diplomatic, and military challenges, which derive from developments such as the global diffusion of power, the proliferation of advanced weaponry, and the rise of terrorism and the drug trade, will become more demanding and cannot be ignored in the future. From the global information revolution that is fueling democratic movements around the world, to the dissemination of advanced weapons that is changing the face of regional and international security, technology has been a driving and defining force in the process of change. Indeed, technology, long one of the foundations of Western economic dominance and Western security, offers the hope of addressing the uncertainties and dangers of the emerging world within current budgetary and other constraints.

Technology is only an instrument, however—it is a means, not an end. Technology can serve national security only if it can be integrated into strategies and a force structure that are themselves grounded in reasonable threat assessments. In the current threat environment, characterized by uncertainty and flux, it is essential that a range of technological options be developed. This requires a viable strategy for military R&D and the requisite resources for maintaining and strengthening a robust and responsive defense technology base and improving defense industrial mobilization capabilities. To implement such a strategy successfully, it will be necessary to break through a series of domestic political, bureaucratic, economic, and technological constraints that have slowed the U.S. ability to integrate new technologies into deployed weapon systems and driven spiralling weapon costs, while undermining R&D.

Moreover, given the globalization of technology, the increasing importance of the commercial sector in technological innovation, and the growing significance of dual-use technologies for the military, the preservation of U.S. interests will compel a significant measure of interdependence. In the face of isolationist pressures, how can interdependence be strengthened and rationalized? Rather than rapid force withdrawals and a race toward burden shedding (as opposed to burden sharing), the debate within NATO and between the United States and its East Asian allies should revolve around rationalizing the contributions of all allies to Western defense on the basis of what each can best contribute. The U.S. contribution to Western security will not always consist of forward deployed forces. The United States, for the foreseeable future, can best contribute to Western security through the fruits of a renewed commitment to technological leadership.

For the past four decades, U.S. technological dominance has served it well. While no single nation is likely to enjoy such dominance in the next four decades, the United States has the capability and the interest to retain leadership in critical, strategic technologies. There is no reason to believe that this technological leadership will be any less important to our security and competitiveness in the future than it was in the past.

———

The views in this article are those of the authors and should not be taken as official positions of the Los Alamos National Laboratories or it sponsors. This essay, like the accompanying essays of Chuck Vollmer and Thomas Welch, had its origin in the conference on "Conventional Forces and Arms Control: Technology and Strategy in a Changing World," sponsored by Los Alamos National Laboratory's Center for National Security Studies and its associate director for defense research applications, and held at the laboratory September 25–27, 1989. The authors of this essay gratefully acknowledge their indebtedness to the insights and judgments of the conference participants; especially important for our thinking were the remarks of John Browne, John Immele, Edward Luttwak, Fred Iklè, Jean-François Delpech, Robert Selden, Robert Cooper, and Chuck Vollmer. We also would like to acknowledge the thoughtful comments provided by Brad Roberts and Steven Maaranen.

Notes

1. Theodore Von Karman, *Toward New Horizons*, a report to General of the Army, Henry H. Arnold, on behalf of the Army Air Force Scientific Advisory Group, 13 volumes, volume 1 published by the Central Air Documents Office, November 1945.

2. "Excerpts From Bush's News Conference After NATO Meeting," *New York Times*, December 5, 1989, p. A–8.

3. Susan F. Rasky, "Lawmakers Criticize Cheney on Cuts," *New York Times*, November 27, 1989, p. A–9.

4. *Discriminate Deterrence*, Report of the Commission on Integrated Long-Term Strategy (Washington, D.C.: Department of Defense, 1988), pp. 8–9.

5. *Ibid.*, p. 21.

6. "Comments on critical defense technologies," statement of Siegfried S. Hecker, Director, Los Alamos National Laboratory, to the Senate Armed Services Committee, Subcommittee on Defense Industry and Technology, May 16, 1989.

7. *Discriminate Deterrence*, pp. 45–46.

8. *Ibid.*, p. 47.

9. Richard W. Stevenson, "Hard Choices for Arms Makers," *New York Times*, November 29, 1989, p. C–2.

10. John Burgess, "Effects of Military Cuts on Technology Under Debate," *Washington Post*, December 1, 1989, p. F–1.

11. *Ibid.*, p. F–2.

III. Security in Europe

Vienna, Versailles, and Now Paris: Third Time Lucky?

W. R. Smyser

IN SEPTEMBER 1814, a glittering assembly of European monarchs and statesmen met in Vienna to establish a new and peaceful European order in place of the one that the French Revolution and the Napoleonic Wars had torn apart. Among the distinguished delegates were the emperor of Austria, the czar of Russia, the king of Prussia, the duke of Wellington, and Charles-Maurice de Talleyrand. When their delegations left Vienna in June 1815, they felt confident that they had succeeded.

In March 1919, a less glittering but equally distinguished assembly met in Versailles to establish a new and peaceful European order in place of the one that World War I had torn apart. The delegates included President Woodrow Wilson and the leaders of every major European power except Germany. When the delegates left Versailles in June, they also felt confident that they had succeeded.

In November 1990, a much larger assembly of European and North American statesmen met briefly in Paris to sign a treaty of their own and to approve other agreements negotiated and signed in many cities. They also wanted to establish a new and peaceful European order that would write an end to the long European civil war that had begun in 1914 and not

W. R. Smyser is a Washington consultant in political economy and strategy.

been settled in 1919. When they left, they felt as confident of success as those who had been at Vienna and Versailles.

Given the mixed and even sad results of the first two attempts at a European peace, we can rightfully ask whether we can really expect that the latest try will be any more successful than its predecessors. For the Paris agreements do not stand alone. Instead, they are part of a continuum of almost 200 years of attempted peacemaking, a continuum marked more by failure than success.

As the United States and others begin to implement the Paris agreements, it is not only appropriate but even necessary to begin evaluating the results of the Paris meeting within the historical continuum, trying to see what has succeeded and what has not, what may succeed and what will not. We will attempt such an evaluation here.

Scholars have had a long time to evaluate the first meetings in this continuum, at Vienna and Versailles, and they have generally agreed that the Vienna conference created a more stable system than that of Versailles. But the record also shows that both the Vienna and Versailles systems broke down.

To begin a systematic evaluation, one can make some broad generalizations about the three peace conferences:

The first conferees, at Vienna, pursued certain guiding principles by certain methods. For the international order, their guiding principle was balance and their method was the inclusion of all major powers, victors and vanquished, in the European system. For the domestic order, their principle was monarchic legitimacy and their method was restoration.

The conferees at the second assembly, at Versailles, pursued diametrically opposite principles and methods. For the international order, their principle was vengeance and their method was reparations; for the domestic order, their guiding principle was democracy and their method was self-determination.

The principles and methods of the Paris signatories were closer to Vienna on international matters and closer to Versailles on domestic matters. Internationally, the governing principle was again balance and the method was an almost universal inclusion of victors, vanquished, and neutrals, either as signatories of the peace treaty for Germany, as members of the Conference on Security and Cooperation in Europe (CSCE), or as signatories of the Charter of Paris. For the domestic order, the governing principle was again democracy and the method was again self-determination.

The difference between Vienna and Paris on domestic principles may, however, be more apparent than real. Although the nations at Vienna favored restoration and opposed the pressures for democracy that were then beginning to be broadly felt throughout Europe, they sought restoration not only to block popular government but also to prevent another dictatorship of the Napoleonic type. The negotiators at Vienna and those at Paris both actually feared the same phenomenon: the illegitimate tyrant

who needs crisis and war to consolidate and justify his rule. At Paris, as at Vienna (and at Versailles), the negotiators favored regimes that to them, at least, appeared legitimate.

It goes without saying that the governing principles and methods followed at Vienna must have had some merit. They helped to keep the peace of Europe for almost a hundred years, although they did not prevent intermittent wars on a subcontinental scale. The Vienna system did ultimately break down, but only after almost a century of general peace in Europe.

It also goes without saying that the principles and instrumentalities of Versailles had no such success. They established not a peace but an armistice. They not only failed to prevent another conflict but they can even be charged with having created the political and economic conditions that made one inevitable.

As one examines the components of a European peace, one cannot help but note how little those elements have changed over 200 years. The players may be different, and the techniques of diplomacy or war may be different, but the realities of geography and of international relations are the same as those that faced the statesmen at Vienna and Versailles.

Determinants of Success or Failure

One cannot evaluate all the many elements that go into treaties as universal and complex as those included in this continuum, so we will only look at nine criteria that appear to have most clearly determined success or failure after Vienna and Versailles, beginning with the arrangements for Germany and ending with the role of diplomacy.

The Position and Role of Germany. The role of Germany remains the central problem of any European order and also the most difficult. Although it can only be finally determined by the Germans themselves, the surrounding framework must be established by others. Most important, the Germans and the others must agree on that framework.

The statesmen at Vienna did not know the "German question" as their successors came to know it. Although Napoleon had restructured Germany and had broken its earlier moorings to the Holy Roman Empire, neither he nor his immediate successors could anticipate the powerful role that the Germans could and would play in the center of Europe once they were united. Nonetheless, they understood that even Prussia had to be given status as a major player and had to have reasons to support the Vienna system.

The Vienna settlement also contained a lesson that was forgotten at Versailles: One must give even the loser in a war some interest in preserving the settlement. That was reflected in the way the statesmen at Vienna dealt with France—then perceived as the scourge of Europe. They gave France a voice in its own future and in the future of Europe.

With respect to Germany, the Paris arrangements appear to have laid a solid foundation. Germany has been reunited and is granted a central role in Europe. It has even helped to negotiate that role. It has also accepted limitations with respect to its borders, its troop levels, and its weaponry. It cannot be threatened, but it also need not threaten or appear to threaten—in part because it is defended by others as well as by its own forces.

The Paris agreements even improve on Vienna because they place a united Germany at the center of Europe. In retrospect, this may have been the main failing of the Vienna arrange-

ments, for German unification helped undo the European peace. This time, a united Germany is part of Europe. It is firmly linked to the West but, in the Bismarckian manner, it has reestablished the Reinsurance Treaty with Russia's successor through the Soviet–German pact of September 1990.

The German portion of the Paris settlements, therefore, appears to be most auspicious. All those who signed the Paris agreements can note this with pride. They must also pledge themselves to make certain that it remains as intended. A strong but peaceable Germany that is open in all directions can stabilize Europe, but an errant Germany can unhinge the continent more quickly and more devastatingly than any other single phenomenon.

The Position and Role of Other Europeans. No matter what a treaty might provide for Germany, it must also make arrangements for future cooperation among the other major European powers. Versailles failed not only because of its treatment of Germany but also because the victors did not sustain in peacetime the partnership that had brought them victory in war. They were not only hostile toward Germany but also suspicious of each other. The United States withdrew from Europe. France and Britain fell out, resuming their colonial rivalries (especially in the Middle East) while maneuvering for advantage in Europe. The Western allies compounded the problem by failing to agree on a policy toward the revolutionary government in the Soviet Union.

By 1922, there was no common understanding among the World War I victors on any of the major problems facing Europe. Germany and the Soviet Union turned toward each other, and the Versailles system began to collapse almost immediately after its inception.

In this respect, of course, even the Vienna system had its failings. The Holy Alliance suffered from irreconcilable ideological differences. Other instruments of cooperation also broke down. But, even as the victors differed, argued, and sometimes fought outside Europe or on its periphery, they had no reason to disturb the central arrangements that had been made in Europe itself. They could keep and respect the general peace. Only the unification and the impatience of Germany, as well as the crises attending the decomposition of the Ottoman Empire in the Balkans and the corrosion within Austria–Hungary, finally demolished the old order and brought on the continental war.

In this respect, the Paris agreements are well launched. They have brought the states of Eastern as well as Western Europe and even of North America into a common diplomatic framework. Germany, France, and Britain have signed the agreement and appear fully ready to support it. So does the Soviet Union, whose role and future may be uncertain but will remain important. By achieving this, the agreements have established a framework in which the states of Europe can find their own roles and can mutually adjust those roles. Each has a stake in the system, and all can work to preserve it.

The Balancer Beyond the Sea. Continental Europe has often required the power of a state outside the continent itself to maintain its balance. All too often, one or another European state, whether France, Germany, or Russia, has tried to assert hegemonic control over the entire continent. The best defense against this has been to keep a state from across the water in the

European balance. This has always represented one of the most difficult tasks for any European settlement. Great Britain largely withdrew from continental European affairs after Vienna except on issues affecting its national interests very directly, and its role after Versailles was at best unclear. In both cases, the European balance was weakened as a result.

The United States should have assumed the role of the transmaritime balancer after World War I to counteract the power of a united Germany. But when, after Versailles, it withdrew from Europe and failed to play that role, renouncing the agreements it had helped (albeit sometimes reluctantly) to negotiate, the Versailles arrangements became to all intents and purposes unenforceable and the United States also lost whatever chance there might have been to improve them. By the time it returned to Europe, the seeds for the next war had long since been planted. With the upsurge of Soviet power after World War II, the United States was again called upon to play the role of transmaritime balancer, and only its decision to remain in Europe made stability possible. It will almost certainly have to continue to play a similar role even if the Soviet Union breaks apart.

A continued U.S. presence in Europe is one of the most important if usually unspoken conditions for the success of the Paris agreements, although it is neither possible nor even necessary now to finalize the level of that presence. But the risks of a possible U.S.–European break are already visible in economics, in trade, and over such non-European crises as the Gulf War. Although such a break may not now appear as significant as a crisis over European security policy, its importance should not be underestimated on either side of the ocean.

The United States still has a role to play in European security. Despite glasnost and perestroika, the risk of a more militant Soviet policy toward Western Europe cannot be dismissed. In that event, the United States can play a helpful and perhaps even necessary role. It can even play a role during times of détente, to make certain that there is no misunderstanding as to where its interests might lie with respect to the European balance.

If the tenor of recent anti-U.S. demonstrations in Europe can be seen as a sign of deep-seated political attitudes, it is clear that many Europeans—especially the young—do not see the world as Washington sees it. But those are demonstrations against U.S. policy in the Gulf and not against a U.S. presence in Europe. A link with the United States may not always be enthusiastically welcomed in Europe, especially in some parts of the political spectrum, but it remains appreciated by most Europeans. Even the Soviets, after first suggesting that the common European house did not need a room for the United States, changed their minds.

But the United States and the Europeans can and should begin a quiet consultation about the long-term U.S. role. That role cannot be, and need not be, the same as during the Cold War, but it should not be dismissed, and it should not fall prey to transient issues and conflicts of interest. The United States should have a voice and an influence, not only for the peace of Europe but also for its own. On the other hand, it cannot expect that role or that influence to be as great as it was during the Cold War.

If that role and influence are maintained, the role of the balancer across the sea will be more significant after Paris than it was after either Vienna or Versailles. In that respect, the Paris agreements may be taking a step forward.

The Economic Consequences. Treaties often have unintended economic effects. The Vienna settlement, by confirming Prussia's right to the portion of the German Rhineland that contained the Ruhr valley, helped to make Prussia a great industrial power and to unite Germany under Berlin's aegis. The Versailles settlement, as John Maynard Keynes forewarned, destroyed the prospects for a true European peace by creating the conditions for the German economic collapse that helped bring on the Great Inflation, the Great Depression, and Adolf Hitler.

Although conditions in Europe are now far less desperate than they were after the Napoleonic Wars or the two world wars, they are far from ideal. One of the principal effects of 45 years of communism in Eastern Europe is that the gap in economic and political development between the Western and Eastern halves of the continent is greater than at any time since the fall of Rome. That gap contains the potential for poverty, even hunger, for mass migration, and for long-lasting capital shortages. It also contains the seeds of political instability, both in Eastern Europe and the Soviet Union.

Perhaps the best that can be said of the Paris agreements is that they do not inhibit a cooperative East–West approach to solving those problems. Neither, however, do they mandate it. One of the most important requirements for the success of the European settlement will be to extend generous help from West to East, to those states and peoples that were beaten down by World War II and then by the Cold War.

Although the Paris arrangements did not include a specific economic component, they did make certain assumptions about economics. They assumed open trading borders, a certain level of prosperity, and continuing economic and trade cooperation between Europe and North America. Actions that undercut those assumptions will jeopardize the viability of the accords themselves.

The European Institutional Framework. In this respect, the arrangements after Paris are unprecedented. Europe is under a network of organizations that cover the continent from East to West and from North to South. On a continentwide basis, the main organization is the Conference on Security and Cooperation in Europe (CSCE), a loose but potentially promising structure that its participants pledged at Paris to reinforce. For Western security purposes, there are the North Atlantic Treaty Organization (NATO) and the Western European Union (WEU), as well as a legion of other security arrangements and arms limitations. For trade and economic cooperation, there are West European organizations centered around the European Community, the European Monetary System, and countless others with general or specific purposes. Some of those West European organizations can perhaps be stretched across the entire continent in time.

If there is, however, a single lesson to be learned from both the Vienna and Versailles settlements, it is the fragility of institutions. The League of Nations quickly joined the Holy Alliance and many other institutions on the dustheap of history.

Those experiences should serve as warnings. Organizations do not outlive the conditions and the needs that created them. They must constantly adapt, or be adapted, to play useful roles under new circumstances. There is good reason to believe that more organizations will maintain themselves after the Paris agreements than after Vienna and Versailles because many are performing functions that can be as useful in a united Europe as in a divided Europe, especially if some of the Western organizations obtain East European members. But one of the tasks of international leadership, East and West, will be to discern the new roles that organizations can play and then either to change the structures that now exist or create others that can usefully replace them.

Mechanisms for Preventing War. War prevention remains at best an imperfect science, if it can even be termed a science at all. Diplomatic arrangements generally do not succeed in establishing a just and lasting peace, in part because they have to deal with past problems as much as anticipate new ones. Even now, despite the opportunities that scholars have had to analyze historical experience, different theories contend about how wars begin and about how they can best be prevented. Whatever those contending theories may be, it can be argued that World Wars I and II had different causes.

World War I may have had several causes: The failure of the European system to deal with Germany's rise; the excessive readiness of major powers to commit themselves in support of smaller and more reckless allies; the large forces in being; the mutually exacerbating tensions created by mobilization schedules intended to activate those forces quickly and even preemptively; the absence of a forum for conciliation or for mutual exchange of information on security preparations; finally, and perhaps most important, the readiness of statesmen to accept war even if they did not seek it.

World War II, in contrast, could be said to have had only one cause, Adolf Hitler, who was convinced that nobody would or could block his ambitions. But others must bear some of the responsibility for the war because they did not make clear to him and to other Germans soon enough that there would be a price to pay for aggression.

Different theories about the causes of war have led to different theories of war prevention, some of which have alternated in fashion. Immediately after World War II and after Hitler, the widely accepted model for war prevention was deterrence by overwhelming force, preferably by alliance arrangements and if necessary with nuclear-tipped weapons instantly available for retaliation. It was in such arrangements that the United States found its postwar European vocation. NATO became the structure that brought together German and other conventional forces, U.S. nuclear forces, and the determination of all Western powers to resist a Soviet attack. Whatever the costs and the rigidities of those arrangements may have been, it cannot be denied that they worked, because the post-Potsdam order brought Europe a longer period of peace than it had enjoyed in recorded time.

Once a deliberate Soviet attack appeared less likely, the old questions about the causes of war arose again. Some analysts expressed the fear that the mutual defense commitments intended to deter another Hitler could perhaps unintentionally duplicate the process that led to World War I. If this analysis proved correct, deterrence could be a mistake because the deterrent forces themselves would precipitate the conflict they were intended to prevent. Arguments of this kind flourished during the 1970s and 1980s, and Western policy in Europe became confused and uncertain as well as controversial.

The Paris arrangements have resolved this dilemma by trying to prevent war by either cause. Under those agreements, NATO, with united Germany as a member, keeps its function of trying to prevent war by providing defense and threatening retaliation. On the other hand, CSCE and the arms-control agreements, with their complex of confidence-building, inspection, and verification measures, are designed to forestall or interrupt any repetition of the sequence of events that led to World War I. The object of the Paris agreements as a whole is to create a system that protects the West but does not create an automatic system of mutual escalation. In this sense, Paris goes far beyond Vienna or Versailles.

There is no precedent against which the effectiveness of this combination of measures can be tested. But the fact that the combination exists, and that it has been accepted on both sides of the old Iron Curtain, suggests that the combination can secure the peace as well as any other that statesmen, diplomats, and scholars might now conceive and construct.

Domestic Political Structures. All the signatories to the Vienna, Versailles, and Paris agreements have had certain expectations about the types of government that would rule the countries of Europe, from the restorationist preferences of the Congress of Vienna to the almost universal acceptance of democracy contained in the Paris declaration.

But the results reached at Vienna and Versailles should lead us to question whether the wishes of the negotiators will prevail for very long. The agreements at Vienna did not prevent the revolutions of 1830 and 1848, nor even earlier local changes. The agreements at Versailles did not prevent the seizure of power by Benito Mussolini within a few years and by Hitler later. And the agreements reached in Paris can do no better in guaranteeing the kinds of governments that Europe will have.

Such historical pessimism may raise questions about the future peace and stability of Europe. It is widely assumed by now that democracies are less likely to go to war, and one of the best reasons to hope for a peaceful and stable European future may be the unprecedented number of democracies that are either established or establishing themselves across the continent. What we do not know, and what the past cannot assure us, is whether they will last.

In this respect, therefore, Paris may be no better than its predecessors. Even if one is prepared to accept at face value the many hopes for freedom so eloquently expressed across the continent, one cannot help but remember all the fledgling democracies that have perished in Europe as elsewhere. One can only hope that the lessons of the wars and the dictators have sunk deeply enough into universal consciousness to prevent a return to absolutism anywhere.

Flexibility in the Face of New Problems. Humility must be the watchword of all who attempt to predict European and Atlantic prospects. Nobody could have foreseen the events of 1989 and 1990, and indeed nobody did foresee them. By the same token, it can safely be said that much of what will happen in Europe between now and the turn of the century will surprise not only the Europeans but even their most knowledgeable and sensitive friends. One can perhaps only hope that future surprises, like those of 1989 and 1990, will be pleasant.

Vienna and Versailles should serve as warnings. The events that followed those gatherings soon invalidated many of the attitudes that shaped the thinking and the policies of the participants. Yet those meetings took place at moments when the prospects for change were no greater than now and probably smaller. It is easy and tempting to make a list of all the political, economic, and sociological shifts and upheavals that might occur during the next decade, but the list would probably represent an embarrassment if it were to be reviewed in the year 2000.

Because governments cannot predict events, they must remain flexible. They must decide in advance that they will contain and channel threats to the peace, not letting them disturb the arrangements for security and stability that have been painstakingly built. The Europeans should perhaps be more prepared to be flexible than others, but Americans need to be as well.

A Real Role for Diplomacy. One of the most important differences between Vienna and Versailles was the role that the participants gave to diplomacy as a means for keeping the peace. At Vienna, diplomacy was assumed to have a real function in peacemaking and peacekeeping. Following an eighteenth-century tradition that was carried on throughout much of the nineteenth, states saw diplomacy as one of the best means to preserve national security. They established ties and regarded such ties as strategic and political assets that could help to prevent wars or help to win them. Diplomats could resolve conflicts of interest, reconcile hostile forces, and enhance a nation's safety and well-being. Strategy combined diplomacy and force in complex combinations that only the most competent practitioners, like Talleyrand or Otto von Bismarck, could manage effectively, but that could enhance a nation's safety at the lowest possible cost.

Diplomacy did not function after Versailles, in part because of U.S. suspicion of "secret treaties secretly arrived at" and in part because of the moralistic tone that dominated the conference and its aftermath. That tone, as adopted by the Allies, prevented any real dialogue of reconciliation until the mid-1920s. When later perverted by Hitler, it prevented reconciliation during the 1930s.

No true diplomacy could be practiced for at least two decades following World War II. Force was given the primary and often the only role in national security. As nations broke their word and could seemingly be deterred only by threats to their existence, strategy became the domain of the military instead of the diplomatists. And diplomacy was used not to accommodate but to express maximum goals or to seek to consolidate maximum advantages. Only the détente arrangements of the late 1960s and early 1970s broke the spell and again legitimized the concept of negotiation.

The Paris agreements offer some hope for a return to genuine diplomacy through trans-European contacts designed to realize the full potential of the agreements and to move beyond them. The United States can and should play a role in those processes. Although the style of diplomacy can no more return to that of the nineteenth century than the arts of war can return to the age of the musket, one of the challenges left by the Paris agreements will be for those who signed them to find the combination

of diplomatic and military policy that will create a true strategy of peace and stability.

Advancing Boldly into the Past

The new Europe is in many ways like the old Europe. It is almost as if the twentieth century, the two world wars, and the Cold War, may have been an aberration or a bad dream. Now that those wars are over, one sees the return of patterns that had been long submerged or ignored. Some of those patterns are potentially troublesome.

Even after the Paris accords, there are still North–South and East–West divides across the European continent. Some of the divides are economic and can perhaps be remedied or eased. But deep religious and cultural differences remain, especially between Western Europe and Eastern or Southeastern Europe, and they cannot be so easily solved. Ethnic tensions persist, between and within states. Western Europe fears migration from all directions, and the fear of open borders may do more to block the plan for a European Community Single Market by 1993 than any economic problem. One can truly argue with equal conviction that in Europe everything has changed and that nothing has changed.

The Paris agreements, therefore, are left with the same troubling and troubled legacy that plagued both Vienna and Versailles. They must maintain peace and stability on a continent that has long been and will remain in ferment. They provide a legal framework that attempts to solve or at least contain certain potentially explosive issues, but the issues themselves have not been solved for centuries and may well be beyond solution.

The Paris agreements offer more avenues than their predecessors for finding solutions if people and nations are willing to find them. They also offer certain incentives. Most important, perhaps, they try to create structures and interests that will prevent every local quarrel from spreading across the continent and from involving others. But Europe today, as in the past, is not a place where either statesmen or diplomats can ever safely say their work is done.

No Rest or Respite

On the basis of this evaluation, and within the context of the long historical continuum, one can welcome the results of the Paris talks and of the many negotiations that preceded them. By almost any standard, they offer a much better foundation than Versailles for a stable peace in Europe and beyond. They also offer better prospects than Vienna. For the first time in two centuries, the statesmen may have laid the foundations for a lasting European peace.

The Cold War, paradoxically, served as a substitute for a peace conference after World War II. The states of Europe and the world were even well served by having that conference postponed. No result envisaged by the victors' Council of Foreign Ministers after 1944 offered the prospect for a settlement as balanced as that signed in Paris, and none would probably have survived as long as the Paris agreements may.

Even the Paris agreements, however, whatever their merits may be, are no better than their application in the future. They will need constant attention and adjustment if they are not to fail as their predecessors did. For the Cold War served not only as a peace process of sorts. It also served as the deep freeze that kept many of the old ills of the continent in a state of suspended animation while the giant powers and their great alliance systems faced off across the continent and fought over its ideological future.

With the end of the Cold War, with the return of European unity, and with the Paris peace, the old Europe returns even as a new Europe emerges. The Paris agreements, like those reached at Vienna and Versailles, will finally be successful only if they are regarded and treated as part of a long process that began during the Napoleonic Wars and that must continue past 1991. The object of that process remains the general peace as well as the solution of specific problems.

The third try can be lucky, as legend would have it, but only if all those who signed the Paris agreements, including the United States, will work as firmly and consistently to guarantee the future success of the agreements as they worked to achieve the agreements themselves.

The views expressed in this essay are the author's own and do not necessarily reflect those of his affiliations, past or present.

The Future of the Atlantic Alliance: Whither NATO, Whether NATO?

François Heisbourg

SECURITY AND DEFENSE relationships between North America and Western Europe have been witnessing somewhat contradictory developments. On the one hand, the removal of the canonical Soviet threat is throwing rising doubts, in Western Europe as in the United States, on the future viability of the transatlantic compact. On the other, the attractions of membership in the North Atlantic Treaty Organization (NATO) appear well-nigh irresistible to the new democracies of Central and Southeastern Europe. The post-Communist states, however, are probably less eager to participate substantially in military burden sharing than to use membership of NATO as a way of locking themselves into the West, on their way toward the ultimate prize—membership in the European Community (EC).

Beyond the particular attraction NATO exercises on post-Communist Europe, it is important to recognize that the Atlantic Alliances's future is far from assured and that the content of the European–American security relationship is bound to be deeply trans-

formed as the traditional adversary disappears. At best it will become a transatlantic covenant based on the recognition of a uniting Western Europe: at worst the cold war partners will drift apart.

To assess the prospects for the European–American security relationship, this paper will first analyze the changing nature of the interests of the United States (and Canada) in Europe. It will then evaluate the dynamic of West European integration in the face of new security challenges. Policy recommendations will follow.

U.S. Security Interests in Post–Cold War Europe

In the emerging, non-Metternichian, post–cold war security system, a country's interests are not exclusively, or even primarily, dictated by such external factors as geographical location, access to resources and markets, or the ambitions of outside powers. Domestic considerations—economic, societal, or political—are important, and on occasion predominate. Post-coup leaders in Moscow clearly do not define their country's interests according to the same considerations as their Brezhnevite predecessors. Somewhat similarly, as the United States no longer needs to focus its energies against a permanent, over-armed So-

François Heisbourg is senior vice president for strategic development at Matra Défense/Espace. He is former director of the International Institute for Strategic Studies in London.

viet threat, the nature of U.S. interests is changing. Whatever will contribute to the revitalization of the U.S. productive base broadly defined—for example, improvements in education, infrastructure, and research and development (R&D)—will be more readily deemed to be in the national interest than was the case during the "second Cold War" under the security-conscious but financially irresponsible Reagan administration. Or, if one is less charitable about the way domestic considerations define the U.S. national interest, the accent will be put on whatever allows the United States to continue to enjoy low levels of saving and artificially low taxes. Whichever interpretation is closest to the mark, one result will apply in all cases to the partners of the United States: they will be dealing with a more inward-looking American interlocutor, with a set of priorities driven largely internally. The perpetuation of even the most basic principles of U.S. policy since 1945, such as support for a global and liberal trading system, will depend on this domestically set agenda rather than on the external parameters of international security.

This trend is the result of the collapse of Soviet power, although the continued erosion of the U.S. productive base would have affected relations in the Alliance even under cold war conditions. This Soviet collapse has a corollary. Because U.S. vital interests are no longer permanently threatened by an imposing foe capable of challenging them directly as well as in peripheral theaters such as Vietnam and Angola, the United States will generally have a more "laid-back"[1] attitude toward security affairs, notably in Europe. Threats to U.S. vital interests will arise only in a sporadic fashion, as in the Persian Gulf, and will not in-

volve a superpower adversary. Furthermore, conflicts that would in the past have carried with them the prospect of exploitation by the Soviet Union, thus calling for countervailing action, no longer demand such U.S. involvement. The war between the Serbs and Croats, which has witnessed a justified and logical lack of U.S. intervention, is an example of this new trend, standing in stark contrast to those scenarios prepared by NATO in the 1970s in case Yugoslavia should become the cockpit of superpower confrontation after Tito's death. This pattern is naturally not without qualification. For a great power such as the United States, even if it is inward-looking, the definition of a vital interest will continue to include issues that have a basic bearing on the functioning of an international system in which it cannot fail to have a major economic or political stake. Events in Western Europe, Northeast Asia, and the Persian Gulf will therefore continue to be particularly important to it. The same may be said of loss of central control of nuclear weapons in the former Soviet Union or of nuclear weapons proliferation more generally. Even so, post–cold war Europe is no longer the seat of a confrontation during which the United States, along with its West European allies, had to consider any crisis in the region as a potential threat to its vital interests, and in which the East–West face-off was justification enough for a large and permanent U.S. presence in Europe.

This does not mean that a U.S. presence in Europe and Northeast Asia has become superfluous, simply that the traditional military conditions that called for it have ceased to prevail.

In this new landscape, several areas will continue to be of special importance to the United States with regard to Europe, some of which may lose, and others gain, salience over time.

- The residual, traditional, Soviet or Russian military presence is probably reason enough to justify keeping U.S. forces in Europe at least until 1994, when the last soldiers under Moscow's control will, according to current plans, have been removed from Central Europe.
- The contribution of U.S. forces in Europe and of NATO infrastructure to the victory in the Persian Gulf has underscored the importance of so-called out-of-area contingencies as a rationale for a U.S. presence in Europe and therefore for a U.S.–European compact.
- The United States naturally has an enormous stake in Western Europe's economic prosperity. Although U.S. trade with the EC is smaller than with Asia, it has the domestic political advantage of generating a slight surplus for the United States, in contrast to the yawning deficits of U.S.–Asian trade. Tight security relations do not necessarily result: the fact that EC–Asian trade is now worth two-thirds of EC–U.S. trade is not leading to an EC–Asian security compact.[2]
- Broader, but also less easy to measure, is the influence of the twentieth-century experience of the United States as a large industrialized power with economic and political links to Europe. Events have repeatedly confirmed the proposition that a massive challenge to liberal democracy in Europe sooner or later puts U.S. vital interests in peril: U.S. commitments in 1917, 1941, and the late 1940s were not happenstance occurrences. Further-

more, even if Japan's economic rise continues in the coming decades, it is unlikely that the U.S. share of global economic activity will diminish in relative terms to below what it was at the time of World War I.

- If the general proposition is accepted that the United States has a vital interest in the maintenance of political and economic liberalism in Western Europe, then the question in the post–cold war era will be: What type of security relationship will best ensure that a major challenge to these characteristics will not arise, or if it arises, will not succeed?

Europe's New Security Challenges

Several risks, some external, others internal, challenge Western Europe's security with the removal of the erstwhile Soviet threat. In examining these, a word must be said about the definition of Western Europe.

Western Europe is defined here as comprising the 13 European members of NATO who are also members of the EC (11) and the European Free Trade Area (EFTA)(2). In practice, as countries such as Sweden, Finland, and Austria move toward the EC, and as the "hopeful three" (Poland, Hungary, and the Czech and Slovak Federal Republic [CSFR]) join the Council of Europe and gain associate status in the EC, that definition will progressively have to be broadened and will in effect coincide with democratic Europe (which does *not* include all of post-Communist Europe, as authoritarian examples of "national communism" in parts of the Balkans and the former USSR attest).

It is important to distinguish from the outset between threats to security, which entail the existence of an armed capability at the service of a less than friendly or congenial power, and security risks. Whereas coping with threats will entail "hard security," notably defense options, risk management will rely heavily on nonmilitary initiatives and institutions. Risks, if mismanaged, or out of sheer bad luck, may transform themselves into threats calling for the countervailing deployment of military forces. A wide grey area connects risks and threats, but this simple distinction lies very much at the heart of the elaboration of a satisfactory security regime for Western Europe. The use of legal, diplomatic, economic, institutional, and other similar tools to prevent risks becoming threats will be key to the new European security agenda.

The four security risks listed below will be, or already are, heavily influenced by the consequences of a widespread "return to the past" (or at least a return to its uglier features). This is a past to which post-Communist societies in the East but also the industrialized societies of the West feel tempted to look as the painful but intellectually simple framework of the cold war certainties crumbles. There is no greater single reason for anxiety about the future of European security, and this tendency to look back significantly complicates the immediate and tangible challenges already facing democratic Europe.

The first security risk is the residual Soviet or Russian threat. This is sufficiently real to prompt the Central and Southeast Europeans to negotiate bilateral treaties with their Eastern and Western neighbors, such as the treaties signed by Hungary and the CSFR with the USSR shortly after the failed coup of August 1991.

The second risk flows from the loss of central control of nuclear weapons

in the former USSR and the acquisition of weapons of mass destruction by unstable regimes to the East and the South, along with delivery vehicles able to reach Western Europe. The combination of nuclear weapons with the ambitions of rabid nationalist groups could be all too potent.

The third risk arises from the process of accommodating new countries into the European concert. The three Baltic states can be accommodated with comparative ease, but the emergence of Ukraine will represent a major challenge. In effect, this state of 52 million inhabitants is the largest European nation after Russia and the first large new power to appear on the European scene since Italian and German unity in the mid-nineteenth century. Ukraine will probably harbor feelings of insecurity, internal and external, because it contains a large Russian minority and has borders that were, for the most part, drawn in Kiev's favor in the wake of the Stalin-Hitler Pact (to the West) and under Nikita Khrushchev's rule (the annexation of the Crimea). Hungary, Poland, Romania, Russia, and Slovakia all have potential claims on Ukraine. The many cultural similarities between Russians and Ukrainians could well become a factor of polarization (as between Serbs and Croats or between Catholics and Protestants in Northern Ireland) rather than of easy cohabitation. Other challenges of lesser magnitude but of greater complexity will flow from the emergence of other new states (Croatia, in particular).

The fourth risk stems from cultural and social pressures, notably from the Islamic countries, in the form of immigration to a Western Europe whose electorates are increasingly intolerant of such population flows. This has become the foremost domestic political issue in several European countries (notably France, Austria, Belgium, and Germany) and is often presented as an internal and external security threat by hard-right political parties.

The "return to the past" in the East has come about largely because nationalist sentiment, often repressed under Communist rule, now represents one of the few forms of social identification acceptable in many societies where the Communist period has become taboo.[3] Nationalism has predictably characterized those ex-Communist countries where civil society was the most effectively suppressed.[4] Whereas people in Poland (with first the church and later Solidarity), Hungary (with its relatively tolerant version of "goulash communism"), and the Czech part of the CSFR (with its small but vocal and brave group of intellectuals and dissidents) have benefited from the existence of "alternative societies" under Communist rule and were able to develop various forms of social identification, the Balkans, Slovakia, and much of the former Soviet Union have been the theater of single-minded ethnic self-affirmation.

This phenomenon has been exacerbated by the adoption of nationalist sentiment by former Communist officials, for whom it has become a convenient raison d'être, and is no less corrosive when it is sincerely embraced: Franjo Tudjman of Croatia; Slobodan Milosevic of Serbia; Boris Yeltsin of Russia; Leonid Kravchuk of Ukraine, all bear an ethnic message notwithstanding wide variation in their democratic inclinations (or lack thereof).

Ethnic conflict, under such circumstances, is not surprising. It may be contained within geographical limits in certain instances for some time (as is currently the case in Croatia). Challenges to existing international borders

or situations comparable to that arising as a result of Iraqi repression in Kurdistan will inevitably occur, however, if current trends continue, leading to more or less military forms of internationalization. In Yugoslavia, 550,000 people had lost their homes by December 1991, of whom 45,000 had fled to Hungary and Austria, raising the specter of major cross-border population movements. At least three states (Albania, Bulgaria, and Hungary) could feel impelled to act, or to prod the international community into action, if minority groups in Kosovo, Macedonia, and Vojvodina for which they feel responsible were the object of atrocities. Furthermore, the possible collapse of working democracies in Budapest, Prague, and Warsaw as a result of potential economic failure and social tension could aggravate these trends, for example by eroding restraints that have held the Hungarians back from any attempt to revise the borders inherited from the post–World War I Treaty of Trianon, which left sizable Magyar minorities in Romania, Serbia, Slovakia, and subcarpathian Ukraine.

The return to the past and fear of the future also has its West European manifestations. Although the currents are less violent than those prevailing in the Balkans or the Caucasus, an unusual combination of circumstances is contributing to a worrying growth of inward-looking xenophobia and authoritarianism in sizable segments of West European public opinion. Although Jean-Marie Le Pen's movement is the most spectacular, longest-lasting, and most broadly based example of this phenomenon, significant electoral or street-level manifestations, or both, exist in practically every West European country from Italy to Norway. The feeling that society is losing old values without gaining new ones; disorientation as the familiar landscape of the Cold War disappears; fears concerning national identity in the face of perceived mass migration;[5] incomplete acknowledgment of the darker side of the past (as in Austria, the former German Democratic Republic [GDR], or France); or chronically high levels of unemployment—all may be playing a role in this respect.

The good news is that these movements have generally not generated a strong and overt animus against the EC, and, most important, they have not won a plurality in any European country. The bad news is that some of the good news may not last. Hard-right movements could find it profitable to add a plank to their platform that would be ultra-Thatcherite and opposed to EC integration. Extreme-right movements have powerfully contributed to setting the domestic agenda, notably on immigration, often bringing out the worst in politicians and their electors. They have also contributed, most notably in France, to the growing discredit of parliamentary democracy, lowering the morale of the citizenry in the process.

It is not excessive to speak, in the French case, of the collective equivalent of a nervous breakdown, which hardly creates the conditions for constructive policy, even excluding the prospect of a hard-right electoral victory. It is all the more remarkable that West European integration is proceeding under the circumstances. Some comfort may be drawn from comparing the conditions today with those under which the European Economic Community was created in 1957: France was then in constant political crisis and bogged down in the war in Algeria. Nevertheless, if a widespread anti-integrationist movement were to develop in the EC, the direct security

implications would be severe, because it could preclude the emergence of Western Europe as a more coherent actor in its own collective foreign affairs and raise the prospect of a return to the power politics of before 1914.

The Dynamics of European Integration

Although the treaties agreed upon at the summit in Maastricht (December 9–11, 1991) will not lead to as "perfect" a union as the United States, the EC is emphatically not simply a more or less glorified free trade area. The preamble of the 1957 Treaty of Rome already referred to the establishment of "an enduring and closer union"; and even if the Maastricht Summit has forgone the "F" (as in federation) word, an "ever closer union" has been set as the goal.

The EC is incomprehensible without a grasp of its origins in history, notably the consequences of the two world wars that destroyed the continent. Paradoxically European integration has much the same roots as some of the more unpleasant movements mentioned earlier. In happy contrast to these same movements, the European unification movement confronts history squarely, in effect attempting to face it down. This helps to explain why the end of the Cold War and the unification of Germany have accelerated rather than slowed down European integration, a development that purely economic and diplomatic logic would not have dictated. Germany fears a return to the power politics of its brutal past, a fear shared, naturally enough, by its neighbors. The conclusion is that if you want to avoid more old-style Germany, you need more (federal) Europe. Of course, this can only happen if Germany actively supports such a policy, and that is indeed the case. At the same time a strong feeling persists, not least in Germany, that a window of opportunity element is involved.[6] In several years' time, a united Germany will begin to reap the economic benefits of its massive investment in the former GDR:[7] in the absence of a Europe moving toward federation, such a Germany would, willy-nilly, be compelled to act as the overwhelming central power it would then have become, to the great chagrin of those Germans, and their neighbors, who have no stomach for neo-Wilhelminian excursions.

The European unification process is a drawn-out but also a relentless process, more akin to the advance of a glacier than to the rush of an avalanche[8]—34 years have passed since the Treaty of Rome was signed, and nearly 40 years since its "father," the European Coal and Steel Authority, was established—with occasional surges setting the stage for future progress.

The last surge was the decision in 1985 to create the Single European Market, effective by the end of 1992. The next step should result from the Maastricht Summit: the success of that meeting's implementation is of particular importance in light of the window of opportunity factor. The newly approved treaties on Economic and Monetary Union (EMU) and European Political Union (EPU) will greatly change the Europe of the year 2000, with significant implications for European security. Of course, the follow-on to Maastricht may not turn out that way, indeed the whole process could melt away (possibly under the effect of a sudden anti-EC backlash from disoriented public opinion). The empirical evidence, however, is that the Community can on occasion stall, as in those low moments in the early 1980s when the cruel taunt of Euro-

sclerosis was launched, but the EC has never gone backward. The picture that follows is therefore more than merely plausible.

First, the European Union will be moving toward a single currency before the decade is over. Before that happens, the establishment of the European federal bank will create an ECU bloc,[9] in effect leading to a tripolar international monetary system, where dollar, yen, and ECU will be the three reserve currencies.

Second, although West European nation-states will continue to have nationally based diplomacies and foreign policies, a European foreign policy will gradually dominate the scene. In this respect, practice is preceding rather than following theory. The important news is not that the EC has failed to resolve the Yugoslav crisis: that task is about as simple as providing an answer to the Israeli–Palestinian conundrum. Rather, on a major foreign policy issue, with strongly divergent views between Community members, there has actually been a single EC policy toward the crisis whereas there is, as yet, no formal obligation for the EC's member states to tie themselves to a united policy. Germany, for instance, might have recognized Croatia and Slovenia on its own in the summer of 1991, thus ushering in competing diplomatic stances by the West European powers in the unhappy Balkans. When those countries were recognized, on January 15, 1992, it was the result of a difficult but unanimous EC decision. Awful things may lurk around the street corners of Sarajevo, but the next world war is not at present one of them.

Third, because the line between foreign and security policy is a fuzzy one, and because a laid-back United States is not providing the lead on Europe's new security problems, security and even defense policy will become part of the Community's ambit, albeit at one remove in the latter case. (That remove is the Western European Union, whose 9 members all belong to both the EC and NATO.) Anglo–French disagreement was not a notable issue on this score during the run-up to Maastricht. By October 1991 the British had accepted the prospect of a European *defense* entity in the Anglo–Italian proposal, and the French, in the Franco–German proposal, had accepted that a significant part of their forces could be subordinated to a non-French authority: those were the important developments.

Three points have to be made here. First, broader security, such as assistance to Central Europe, is already well within the Community's purview, and notably that of the supranational European Commission as far as the economic aspects are concerned. Second, the EC's action in the broader security arena complements that of bodies such as the Conference on Security and Cooperation in Europe (CSCE) or the Council of Europe:[10] when the CSCE mandated the sending of cease-fire observers to Slovenia, the EC was the operative body. If the Council of Europe agrees on a mandatory status for ethnic minority rights, only the EC can provide the indispensable tangible backup (e.g., in the form of political isolation or economic sanctions). Third, and this is of particular importance in terms of the interface between the EC, the WEU, and NATO, an effective European military force will probably not be fielded until a crisis situation arises, prompted for example, by the internationalization of the Serbo–Croat conflict. In this respect, pre-tailored forces, such as the recently proposed Franco–German corps (which the Spanish may join) can have their uses,

notably as a prop for stationing or cross-stationing forces. In practical terms, however, the military and national composition of an EC plus WEU mandate will, or at least should be, determined by the particular requirements of a contingency not predictable in its specifics.

This European integration will not, in itself, weaken NATO. Despite the traditional differences of emphasis between Paris and London, there is now general agreement that the Western European Union will be institutionally linked to both the EC and NATO when it moves to its new home in Brussels. In practice, this should be made easier by the fact that all WEU members are members of NATO as well as of the EC. If the WEU, in the fullness of time, merges with the EC, a direct interface would then exist between NATO and the EC. Such a merger, however, promoted by Germany and France, will probably not happen soon for a simple reason: many of the new members of the EC, and at least one old one (Ireland), will probably not want to subscribe to the automatic security commitment of the WEU treaty.[11]

Finally, the EC of the year 2000 may well have taken on board 3 to 6 new members (Austria, Sweden, Finland, maybe Switzerland, Norway, and Malta) and by then negotiations for Hungarian, Polish, and Czech membership will be in full swing (or even completed). Further down the road, an EC of 20 to 30 members is entirely conceivable. This enlargement will, in some instances, lead to the expedient of two-speed arrangements: this has been the case for the strictest version of the exchange rate mechanism of the European monetary system created in 1979, to which several countries have yet to adhere totally (United Kingdom, Italy) or even partially (Greece). Such is also the case for the so-called Schengen agreements, whereby 9 of the EC 12 will abolish their intra-EC border posts. Such variable geometry could also be the formula adopted in "hard" security affairs, with the WEU 9 moving faster than the EC as a whole. Even the prospect of such ad hocery does not detract, however, from the basic point that enlargement creates a need for further deepening. This is what happened when Greece, Spain, and Portugal joined: the Single European Act followed in fairly short order.[12]

The prospect of a doubling of EC membership between 1995 and 2010 could well prompt a tightening of the EC decision-making process to prevent the latter's collapse. If a given level of common policy-making is to be preserved and, inevitably heightened, large numbers call for more federation rather than for confederation.

U.S. Policy Options

It would be surprising if, in such a vastly changed landscape, the substance of U.S.–West European security relations escaped unchanged. One could imagine a bit less U.S. involvement, a bit more European participation, in a security system revolving around a more political NATO, but this sort of incrementalist (or decrementalist) evolution will probably not provide an adequate basis for a healthy transatlantic relationship in the future. Radical changes in the strategic environment will call for radical rather than marginal policy decisions.

The European–American security compact could be built on the following premises:

- a reduced but focused role for NATO;

- the maintenance of a U.S. military presence in Europe; and
- U.S. support for the establishment of a specifically West European security and defense organization.

The United States should not be afraid to encourage NATO to maintain a clear and relatively narrow focus for its activities rather than broaden its political and geographical scope to the point where it would become functionally indistinguishable from the CSCE. During the Cold War, when NATO essentially relied on its military function to fulfill its mission of deterrence and defense, it was necessary to emphasize that NATO was also a political, value-based, organization. Now it is becoming necessary to remind the world that NATO is also a military organization. If it loses its defense characteristics its democratic values alone may not be enough to sustain it because those values are now so broadly shared, from Buenos Aires to Seoul as well as from Vancouver to Vladivostok. NATO will survive as a distinct organization if it fulfills missions that no other body is equipped to deal with: military cooperation close enough to sustain operations such as Desert Shield and Desert Storm; North American–West European consultation in the security and defense arena on issues such as nuclear weapons in Ukraine; collective defense of NATO territory; and providing a framework for a U.S. force presence in Europe. Accomplishing those missions also entails a lower profile for NATO because most of the real-life risks do not fall under its purview. Recognizing the role that specifically European organizations can play (or rather, attempt to play) in such contingencies is the best course that NATO can follow: in this respect, NATO's "strategic concept" adopted at the

Rome Summit in November 1991 breaks new ground. Conversely, it will do NATO's standing no good if it is seen as thrashing about in quest of a role at risk of institutional conflict with already existing organizations: NATO's new Cooperation Council may well discover that there are few wheels left for it to invent, notwithstanding its useful function as liaison between former adversaries.

U.S. interests will be well served by maintaining a permanent, albeit much reduced, military presence in Europe. There is convergence between the logic of history (better to be in Europe than to have to get there the hard way) and of geography (risks to U.S. interest in the Middle East as well as Europe can be readily countered from Europe). If the United States is to remain in Europe, several decisions of particular importance must be addressed.

First, should the United States seek to secure funding of U.S. forces in Europe, in line with the 50 percent share of the bill footed by Japan for stationed U.S. forces? However tempting such burden sharing may be from a narrow accounting viewpoint, such payments carry the risk that U.S. forces will over time be seen as mercenaries, with the potentially negative consequences of such an image in both Europe and the United States. A "rent-a-grunt" policy would not encourage a number of European countries to maintain a robust force posture capable of sharing the more basic burden of joint action against a common foe on the battlefield. The question poses itself rather differently in Japan, which is politically inhibited from participating in overseas military action. The United Kingdom, France, and the WEU acting collectively have no such constraints:[13] politically smart burden sharing (in the form of a seri-

ous European defense capability) is called for, even if financial contributions to specific operations—for example by Germany during the Persian Gulf War—are still welcome when physical participation is not possible.

Second, is a U.S. nuclear presence in Europe desirable? Robust nuclear deterrence—and none is more robust than the U.S. variety—may prove to be useful as proliferation of nuclear weapons raises new challenges in various parts of the former USSR and Middle East. In-place deterrence, close to the more troubled areas, is best. For this purpose, airborne nuclear weapons alone should suffice: ground-launched atomic shells and missiles will no longer be required as the Soviet threat disappears. Furthermore, modernization is not urgent, although the issue will have to be addressed a few years from now.

Finally, should the United States favor the designation of a European Supreme Allied Commander, Europe (SACEUR), as a sign of the Europeanization of security in NATO? However flattering to some European egos, or tempting for some neo-isolationists in the United States, there is little to commend such an idea. A SACEUR of U.S. origin is one of the clearest, most effective ways of signaling the indivisibility of the U.S.–European security compact, particularly at a time when there are doubts as to the future of the U.S. commitment, and directly contributes to strategic coupling. If Europeanization is to occur, and be recognized, it will happen in the European organizations.

Indeed, the most important contribution the United States can make to ensuring a healthy, long-term, security compact with Western Europe is by deliberately supporting moves by the Europeans to establish their own defense entity. This is already being done in general terms, most recently in NATO's Rome declaration. It is in line with the constant U.S. policy since the 1950s of favoring the establishment of a uniting Europe; indeed, the expression "European pillar" was coined by President John F. Kennedy in 1962. Generalities are no longer enough, however, now that European political integration is becoming a practical proposition. Washington will have to decide what its attitude will be on the specific proposition that Western Europe will increasingly elaborate joint positions before discussions occur in NATO and that European defense arrangements will be made alongside, not within NATO. Of these propositions, the former—traditionally considered anathema by the State Department—will be more difficult to handle than the latter. Creating a European force structure may appear to be a major break with the principles of Atlantic solidarity; in practice, that need not be the case for the simple reason that the bulk of so-called NATO forces, some of which are earmarked for assignment to SACEUR (or Supreme Allied Commander, Atlantic [SACLANT]), are nearly all national armies under national command.[14] In practice therefore, national forces can be earmarked simultaneously to several authorities, with the choice of effective control being decided as a function of circumstances; this is what occurred in an ad hoc fashion during the war in the Persian Gulf. There should be no basic difficulty in engaging more systematically in such "multiple hatting" (NATO, WEU, and national) of forces. Some requirements will be associated with such a move, notably in terms of compatibility of communications systems. The Europeans will also have to build up their air transport, in-flight refueling, and strategic reconnaissance capabili-

ties. The recent decision to establish a European ground station for the French-led *Helios* observation satellite in Spain is a first step in this direction.[15] These are areas in which NATO capabilities are quasi-nonexistent and national assets insufficient.

The political and psychological difficulties evoked by hammering out European positions on security issues before the North Atlantic Council enters into the game will be rather more difficult to handle. The Europeans will readily react to U.S. criticism on this score by saying that they have to face a similar situation, with U.S. policies often being the product of laborious interagency (and/or congressional) compromise, and hence preferred on a take-it or leave-it basis. A taste of the same medicine, however, can hardly be considered welcome in Washington. In practice, however, things may not be quite as painful: the disappearance of the cold war agenda that called for a clear and constant U.S. leadership role in NATO on practically every issue creates a different environment for European consultation. If NATO were to seize on the Yugoslav issue (for example, if combat spilled over into Italy or Greece), the United States would not find it particularly inconvenient that the EC had taken the lead on the Yugoslav crisis since June 1991. New realities will make preestablished joint European approaches less perilous and less irksome from a U.S. viewpoint than would have been the case in the past.

Naturally there are limits to what the United States can accept in its future security relationship with Western Europe. The establishment of a "Fortress Europe" associated with the breakdown of a set of rules for global trade sanctioned by the General Agreement on Tariffs and Trade would surely challenge the perpetuation of a transatlantic security compact, both because trade and economic issues take on greater salience as the overriding cold war threat dissipates, and because a global trading regime is one of the bases for Western prosperity—and, indeed, as the Great Depression taught us, for Western security. A vital interest is involved here that could under extreme circumstances take precedence over the transatlantic relationship. The same logic applies the other way around: a closed "Fortress America" in trading terms would be equally damaging to that relationship from the perspective of a Europe no longer in fear of Soviet expansionism. Fortunately, such dire developments are far from being a foregone conclusion.

Ultimately, if integration of the European Community stays on track, and if North America plays along, including in the security arena, a transatlantic security compact will survive on the basis of the existing Washington Treaty of 1949 but with an organization that from its current North Atlantic (NATO) incarnation will become increasingly bilateral, in effect Euro-American.

Failure of European integration would, over time, lead to a return to the traditional, pre-1914 type of power relationships in Europe, with divergent policies toward post-Communist partners in Eastern Europe and the former Soviet Union. Such a Europe would be fragmented, probably inward-looking, and, in the absence of a shared and permanent threat, would not provide a solid basis for the Atlantic Alliance. The Europeans would represent a risk to themselves and to their extra-European partners. The United States has every reason to exert itself in favor of European union, even if this implies a shift away from

the defense-driven, U.S.-dominated, Western coalition of the cold war era toward a lower-profile, more equally balanced, European–American compact.

Notes

1. I owe this expression to the discussions of the Aspen Strategy Group meeting on "New World Order? Lessons from the Gulf War," Aspen, Colo., August 11–16, 1991.

2. In 1991, EC trade with the United States was worth $202 billion, whereas EC trade with Asia was worth $137.3 billion.

3. This analysis rests to a large extent on Laszlo Lang, "Economic Developments and Population Movements in Eastern and Central Europe" (Paper presented at the IISS Conference on "New Security Considerations in Central and South Eastern Europe," Wilton Park, Sussex, U.K., October 9–11, 1991).

4. See, for example, François Heisbourg, "Avoiding Another World War," *Independent*, op.ed., September 1, 1989.

5. In France, for example, the legally resident foreign population stood at 3.7 million people in 1982 and 3.6 million in 1990, according to census figures. This overall stability was accompanied by a rapid increase of foreign residents from non-EC countries, principally from the Maghreb.

6. Apparent in the author's discussions with German politicians.

7. That investment was approximately 5 percent of GNP, proportionally exceeding Marshall Plan aid levels.

8. On this comparison, see Giles Merritt, "A Dull Summit Could Keep Europe Moving," *International Herald Tribune*, December 4, 1991.

9. Capitals are used here because ECU is the English acronym for European Currency Unit, as well, in the lower case, as the name for a prerevolutionary French coin, the ecu.

10. Based in Strasbourg, the Council of Europe was created in 1949 to bring together the European democracies. It is most notable for its Court of Human Rights, whose mandatory jurisdiction on individual human rights issues is recognized by nearly

all of Europe's democracies. At the end of 1991, 26 countries (including all the EC and EFTA members, plus Poland, Hungary, and the CSFR) were members of the Council.

11. Article 4 of the Brussels Treaty includes automatic military assistance by all members in case of attack on one.

12. British, Irish, and Danish entry in the early 1970s had been more readily manageable in institutional terms in the framework of the initial six-country EC.

13. The WEU gave its political blessing to, and provided the locus for, coordination of convoy protection in the Persian Gulf in 1987–1988 and implementation of the United Nations embargo against Iraq in 1990–1991.

14. The major exception is NATO's fleet of E–3A Sentry AWACS aircraft.

15. The *Helios* military observation satellite will become operational in 1994, with a resolution approaching that of its U.S. and Soviet counterparts.

The Graying of NATO

Hugh De Santis

A LITTLE MORE than two decades ago, inspired by the climate of détente, the members of the Atlantic Alliance set out upon the task of making the North Atlantic Treaty Organization (NATO) more relevant to the times. The product of their deliberations, the Harmel Report of 1967, shifted NATO's traditional emphasis on defense to one that combined military security and progress toward East–West political reconciliation. In the wake of the revolutionary upheavals that have taken place in Europe since the summer of 1989, members of the Alliance are once again reexamining the relevance of NATO. In contrast to the 1960s, however, the changes that they are currently experiencing are likely to transform the European political system. Rather than bend, spindle, mutilate, and fold NATO into a political–security institution that barely resembles itself and is scarcely relevant to the conditions of a reunified Europe, this paper contends that allied policymakers ought to be planning for its eventual dissolution.

This is not to say that NATO should be disbanded tomorrow. The precipitous dismantling of an institution that has successfully underwritten European security for four decades would be in neither allied nor U.S. interests. But NATO will not endure indefi-

nitely. The bipolar world order that spawned the Atlantic Alliance and the defunct Warsaw Pact is gradually being replaced by a looser, more dynamic multilateralism reminiscent of the pre–World War II period. NATO belongs to the period that now may be more appropriately called the "aftermath of war," the period of global reconstruction and realignment that extended from 1945 to the removal of wartime controls on Germany in May 1990. The real postwar era of national rediscovery and self-assertiveness is just beginning.

It is, therefore, curious that the United States and its allies, at the very moment that the division of Europe has ended, are seeking ways to sustain the utility of NATO. In fact, efforts to shore up NATO may actually serve to retard European unity. What is needed to promote integration and reduce instability in the postwar era is a new security framework built on the Western European Union (WEU) and a network of mutual assistance agreements linked to that organization and, indirectly, to NATO that would ultimately form the basis of a Europeanized collective defense organization.

NATO's Near-Term Utility

Thus far, allied officials have clung to the view that NATO's declining utility, let alone eventual demise, has been greatly exaggerated. One gets the impression that even entertaining public doubts about the durability of

---

Hugh De Santis is professor of international security affairs at the National War College in Washington, D.C.

the Alliance is heresy. Part of the explanation for the reluctance to contemplate the disestablishment of NATO, however, can be laid to psychological inertia. It is decidedly easier and far less anxiety-provoking to make a decision for yesterday. The past produces few surprises, and it cannot be changed. But to alter one's accustomed patterns of behavior in favor of untested procedures is to risk the unknown and possibly invite failure.

Sentiment reinforces NATOphilia. Over the years, policymakers, pundits, and political analysts have grown attached to an institution they have been quick to defend against detractors during periods when its cohesion has been challenged from within and without the Alliance. Those who have grown old with NATO are hard-pressed to oversee its disintegration. Alas, such romantics ignore the fact that it is European stability, not NATO, that needs to be preserved.

But there is a more pragmatic reason for the ringing endorsement the Alliance has received from the White House, NATO Secretary-General Manfred Wörner, and various public policy institutes on both sides of the Atlantic. At the present time, there is no other institution that can adequately perform its basic security function. Considering the potential for political turbulence in postwar Europe, no serious student of transatlantic affairs would advocate NATO's demise until it became clearer what a successor security organization would look like. Until then, NATO will continue to be essential for the maintainance of peace and order on the continent.[1]

A powerful array of political, military, and psychological factors can be adduced to underscore the importance of NATO in the transition from bipolarism and bloc-to-bloc relations to the more state-centered multilateralism

that is being foreshadowed by the end of the Soviet empire in Eastern Europe.

As a military alliance, NATO has contributed to the longest period of peace in Europe's history. Governments on both sides of the Atlantic are understandably loath to part with an institution that has kept Europe from renewed warfare for more than 40 years. In addition, NATO is still necessary to counter the military potential of the Soviet Union. Perestroika aside, the Soviets have continued to modernize their strategic forces. Moreover, the recent crackdown in Lithuania, the Soviet military's retrograde influence on the conventional and strategic arms reduction talks, and its barely veiled criticism of Mikhail Gorbachev's support for U.S. military action against Iraq suggest that a more confrontational posture toward the West cannot be ruled out.

In the same way, NATO provides a continuing buffer against the nightmare of German neutralism or nuclearization. In a politically fluid, NATO-less Europe, it is not unimaginable that Germany would opt to develop its own nuclear deterrent rather than rely on a militarily retrenched United States or a weaker and thus even less reliable Anglo-French strategic force.

Politically, NATO provides an institutionalized security structure within which security issues can be discussed in an open manner. Despite frequent disagreements among the diverse sovereign states that compose its membership, it has achieved a greater and more sustained level of cohesion on its essential purpose than any other European institution since World War II, perhaps including the European Community (EC).

No less important, NATO serves an essential psychological function in this period of European upheaval. It gives assurance to the allies that the United States will remain committed to European peace and security; in so doing, it inhibits the prospect of new and possibly destabilizing alignments. By the same token, the democratic principles on which the Atlantic Alliance rests have justified the U.S. presence in Europe to an American public that remains suspicious of Old World intrigues and congenitally opposed to amoral power politics.

NATO's Long-Term Disutility

Arguably, the same conditions that gave rise to NATO more than 40 years ago could extend its life even in the emerging postwar Europe. The Soviet Union, as demonstrated by the recent crackdown in the Baltic states, could attempt to reassert its influence, if not strategic dominance, over parts of Eastern Europe. Despite the demise of the Warsaw Pact and the de-ideologization of Soviet foreign policy, the proximity of Soviet power could still pose a continuing security threat to Europeans. Under such circumstances, the European allies might well feel more comfortable relying on NATO and the U.S. deterrent to safeguard both their security and U.S. interests.

Realistically, however, a prolonged reversion to the status quo ante, with or without ideological dogmatism, is improbable. Soviet military power would only temporarily curtail the secessionist proclivities of the Baltic and trans-Caucasian republics. More important, such actions would deny Moscow access to Western credit markets, thereby mortgaging the future of Soviet economic and, in turn, military competitiveness with the advanced industrialized world. In all likelihood, the pendulum would eventually swing back to reformism and cooperation with the West.

Even if perestroika were eclipsed by a return to rigid authoritarianism, the perception of threat in the West is not likely to trigger the same anxiety that it did before Gorbachev's ascendancy. In the cold war period of more or less constant East–West confrontation, it was Soviet strategic and political dominance in Eastern Europe, not ideological rhetoric, that created the fear of invasion in the West. In the wake of the democratic uprisings in Eastern Europe, however, there is little prospect that the Soviets would be able to reassert control over their erstwhile postwar fiefdom. Indeed, Soviet military retrenchment has unleashed the suppressed nationalistic passions of the East European peoples. Furthermore, Germany would surely exert political and economic pressure to inhibit the expansion of Soviet influence.

Whether or not the reformist trend set into motion by Gorbachev continues to define change in the USSR, NATO is likely to become an anachronism in the 1990s. At best, it will be a psychological crutch for Western political leaders who are unwilling to face the future; at worst, it could be an impediment to European stability and to amicable transatlantic relations if its presence were to foster an illusion of well-being that precluded the creation of alternative security structures to deal with the qualitatively different challenges of postwar Europe.

In the first place, NATO is principally a military alliance. Soviet reform and new thinking in foreign policy have denied the West an enemy and accordingly undermined NATO's raison d'être. The communiqué issued after the July 1990 NATO ministerial meeting in London said as much. Agreements on conventional armed forces in Europe (CFE) and strategic arms reduction (START) and the resumption of perestroika will further erode the image of the Soviet threat. If the Soviet Union is no longer the enemy, against whom is NATO directed?

Not only is the Soviet threat receding, the Warsaw Pact no longer exists. The disappearance of an antagonistic alliance cannot help but reduce the military legitimacy of NATO. Without the Warsaw Pact, NATO will be seen increasingly as a relic from the cold war era.

In fact, the normalization of Soviet relations with the West and the reunification of Germany will aggravate conflicting threat perceptions among the European partners of the Alliance. The Spanish, Italians, and, less visibly, the French advocate redirecting NATO's forces from the central front to the southern flank to counter potential security risks from North Africa and the Middle East. Turkey is no less concerned about the threat posed by its southern neighbors—Iran, Syria, and Iraq—as well as by Soviet Russia, its historical nemesis. The Scandinavian states similarly have worried that the progressive relaxation of military tensions in central Europe may cause NATO to discount the threat to their northern flank posed by Soviet forces on the Kola peninsula. In short, the achievement of security along the borders of the old East–West division may lead to the polarization of political–military interests within the Alliance.

Redefining the threat is also likely to create tensions between the United States and the European allies. On the one hand, Washington wants to keep the focus on the Soviet Union to ensure both solidarity in the Alliance and continued U.S. influence in Europe. But excessive concern with the ebbing Soviet threat will make it difficult for

U.S. policymakers to mobilize the Alliance's support for non-Soviet contingencies outside the NATO treaty area. As the Soviet threat recedes, the out-of-area issue is likely to become more salient in the future. But European governments will be exceedingly reluctant to undertake NATO-sanctioned military actions outside Europe lest they arouse security concerns in Moscow that could undermine the Soviet Union's willingness to tolerate independent states on its western borders.

From a political viewpoint, it is hard to imagine any West European state, except possibly the United Kingdom, justifying the perpetuation of NATO on the basis of an extra-European threat. In this case, past is prologue; neither European publics nor governments can be expected to extend NATO's mandate outside the treaty area, including Eastern Europe. The glaring lack of allied unity during Operation Desert Shield/Storm underscores the point.

Indeed, the politics of postwar Europe are likely to trend toward particularism rather than globalism. As reflected in the growing self-absorption of Germany—a condition that is bound to create strains with France—the European allies are investing their energy in the politics of Europeanization. To be sure, they would still like the United States to underwrite their security until some other European entity can supplant it. The United States, too, would like to preserve its dominant security role on the continent to maintain its status as a world power and to inhibit the European Community from formulating policies that will restrict its export of goods and capital. But the U.S. desire to sustain its influence in Europe and the allied preference to limit its role to that of security caretaker do not augur well for the longevity of the Alliance.

Alternatives to NATO

If NATO's days are numbered, which institution is likely to replace it? Until recently, many European officials believed that the new security order should be built on the foundations of the Conference on Security and Cooperation in Europe (CSCE), a Soviet-inspired forum that ironically became the catalyst for détente during the Cold War.[2] Buoyed by the collapse of the Soviet empire and the sweeping public repudiation of communism from Berlin to Bucharest, Germany's foreign minister, Hans-Dietrich Genscher, and Václav Havel, president of the Czech and Slovak Federal Republic, trumpeted the CSCE as the harbinger of the millennium of peace in Europe.

In contrast to NATO, the CSCE contains all the European countries except Albania. It also includes the Soviet Union, thereby enhancing the prospect of European integration. Unlike NATO and, to a lesser degree, the WEU or the Council of Europe, the CSCE is not freighted with the cultural baggage of the Cold War. As the child of détente, the CSCE shares with the Harmel Report a vision of a reunited Europe committed to progress on political, security, economic, and human rights activities. Finally, the membership of the United States and Canada in the CSCE gives it a Euratlantic character. More important, it enables it to address European aspirations without sacrificing the stabilizing presence of the United States.

Convinced that the democratic paroxysms of 1989 prefigured the emergence of a peaceful and prosperous Europe, the leaders of the CSCE states convened in Paris in November 1990 to celebrate their new world order. Officials and pundits alike compared the gathering to the Congress of Vienna in 1815.[3]

As a result of Gorbachev's retreat from reform and growing nationalistic tensions in Eastern Europe, however, the ebullient faith in the CSCE has waned. Even the philosopher-prince of Czechoslovakia seems to have questioned his earlier faith in the power of the CSCE.[4] In light of the polyethnic confusion that reigns in Yugoslavia, Havel may have concluded that a 34-nation body was too cumbersome to transact business efficiently. It has been difficult enough to sustain cohesion in NATO, the ultimate purpose of which its signatories unequivocally endorse. To expect the now 35 nations to agree on a common security program when many of them have mutual grudges to settle is pure fantasy.

The recent establishment by the CSCE of an executive secretariat, a conflict prevention center, and a mechanism to monitor national elections eases the problem of managing a large and diverse membership. But even if such bodies facilitated common security policies, there would be no way to enforce their implementation without the threat of military sanctions. The peaceful revolutions of 1989 and 1990 seem to have mesmerized too many people into believing that collective security would be the rationally ordained outcome of democratic reform.[5] Unfortunately, the end of the Cold War has not transformed human nature. The CSCE might succeed in damping down regional quarrels between its member states, but it would be no more capable of preventing armed conflicts among revisionist states than was the League of Nations unless it were prepared to use military force to enforce its collective decision-making authority.

To compound the security problem, a CSCE-centered Europe, whether it nurtures peace or not, is not likely to sustain an active U.S. commitment. The U.S. public has never been interested in the CSCE. Given that public's chronic complaint about having to defend rich and ungrateful allies and its new worries about an emerging European economic fortress, the emphasis on a CSCE "architecture" for postwar Europe may accelerate the process of U.S. military retrenchment at the expense of continental stability.[6]

Disillusioned with the CSCE, Euro-optimists seem to be gravitating toward the European Community. Although West Europeans continue to believe that NATO and the U.S. military presence are necessary for their near-term security, a majority of them would prefer to see the Community form a common defense organization to protect their interests in the future, according to a recent EC poll. Similarly, a U.S. Information Agency (USIA) opinion survey conducted in June 1990 found that over 70 percent of French society and more than 40 percent of Britons and Germans sampled favored a security structure that revolved around the EC.[7]

It is only natural that Europeans would hope that the considerable progress the EC has made toward economic integration might eventually extend to political and security matters. For the French and others who suspect that the U.S. presence in Europe may soon be coming to an end, the EC represents the only institutionally viable way of providing for European security and ensuring that Germany remains institutionally tethered to the West.

At its present state of development,

however, the EC is just as ill-suited as the CSCE to assume the security trusteeship of a reunited Europe. Efforts to establish an adjunct defense role in a body that includes neutral or security-phobic members such as Ireland, Denmark, and (Turkey aside) Greece are bound to founder. The key to the development of a peaceful Europe is economic integration. To divert the EC from its single-minded pursuit of this crucial objective by burdening it with a security function that it is unprepared to accommodate is to retard and possibly undermine European unity.

Besides, economic unity in the West is not a foregone conclusion. Neither the vaunted monetary union nor the social charter that is intended to give economic progress a human face is yet a reality. Still chafing over Bonn's precipitate decision to establish a currency union with East Germany, the former president of the West German Central Bank, Karl Otto Pohl, recently cautioned against a premature move toward EC monetary union. Meanwhile, Bonn's preoccupation with German unification and Mitteleuropa apart, Italy, France, Spain, and Portugal are advocating closer regional ties with the North African members of the Arab Maghreb Union. Adding a complicating security issue to the EC's agenda at this critical moment in postwar Europe would only widen these divisions.[8]

If neither the EC nor the CSCE is capable of replacing NATO, one could always opt for a new security organization. But one might wait forever for a new security structure to emerge. Membership, the role of nuclear weapons, and burden-sharing arrangements would provoke disagreements far more intense than anything the allies have encountered in the past. While the allies tiresomely debated the future, Europe might enter a dangerous period of drift. In the process, Germany might eventually opt for neutrality or a policy of military unilateralism. And the United States would sooner or later be pressed by Congress and public opinion to remove its forces from the continent.

Besides, there is no need to create a new edifice when there may already exist a better alternative to NATO than either the CSCE or the EC or some hybrid of these and other organizations: the Western European Union.[9] The WEU is the only European institution whose members have pledged to defend one another. Moreover, given its explicit commitment to European integration, it is the security analogue of the EC and the CSCE in their respective economic and political domains.

True, the WEU has not had a distinguished history as a collective defense organization. Established in 1955 as a successor to the Brussels Treaty Organization to monitor German rearmament, its security functions were preempted by NATO after the Federal Republic's entry into the Alliance. Except in Paris, where it still excited *troisième voie* fantasies of a French-led European defense organization, the WEU served thereafter mainly as a souvenir of security cooperation immediately after the war, a sort of monument to good intentions. In the United States, it was all but forgotten until its resuscitation during the intermediate-range nuclear forces (INF) crisis, when the overly sensitive administration of President Ronald Reagan publicly renounced its deliberations and gave it more attention and status than it deserved.

Since then, however, the WEU has taken on new life. At the end of 1987, as the outlines of change in the Soviet Union became more sharply etched, it adopted a "Platform on European Security Interests," which called for more active cooperation among its signatories in support of rather than in opposition to NATO in the areas of arms procurement and arms-control verification. Free of legal constraints on its activity outside Europe, the WEU authorized European participation in the 1987 reflagging of Kuwaiti tankers and in the U.S.-led coalition against Iraq in the Gulf War.

Quietly, interest in the WEU is intensifying in allied capitals. On December 6, 1990, the German chancellor, Helmut Kohl, and President François Mitterrand of France sent a letter to the heads of the European Council expressing the hope that the WEU would become the centerpiece of European security. Rumors are also circulating that the WEU may move its headquarters from Paris to Brussels, which would allow the member states to accredit their ambassadors simultaneously to NATO.[10]

Still, the European allies are treading softly on the issue. The Kohl–Mitterrand letter reportedly triggered a stern demarche from the United States to allied capitals. In response, Genscher and the French foreign minister, Roland Dumas, issued a bland statement on European unity that subordinated the WEU to NATO.[11] Fearful of alienating Washington and thus precipitating a U.S. withdrawal from the continent, the allies, led by the British and the Dutch, have resumed referring to the WEU as a "European pillar" within NATO.

But this transatlantic dance cannot continue indefinitely. The tune is already changing, and the partners risk getting uncomfortably out of step. Whether the United States likes it or not, Europe is Europeanizing. Consequently, U.S. influence will inevitably decline. But a reunited Europe

119

must also accept the responsibility for its own defense. It cannot, therefore, expect the United States to maintain an indefinite military presence on the continent.

To be sure, U.S. leadership will be needed in the short term to provide stability and reassurance to an unsettled continent. But the role of the United States as well as NATO in the unfolding postwar Europe can only be transitional. In the long term, the Western European Union, or whatever it may then be called, is the most likely steward of a united Europe's security.

Europeanizing European Defense

The most vexing security problem facing the Euratlantic policy community is the issue of integrating the former members of the Warsaw Pact in a collective defense framework without alienating either the United States or the Soviet Union. There are two dimensions to the problem: political–military and military–strategic.

At the political–military level, too rapid an attempt to incorporate the East European states into a Western security structure such as NATO could worry Moscow and invite renewed Soviet political interference, possibly even intervention, in the region. Too dilatory a response to the former Pact states would produce a power vacuum that would sooner or later result in military clashes and possibly a regional war.

At the military–strategic level, a precipitate embrace of the former Pact allies would probably inhibit the Soviet Union from further reducing its nuclear arsenal, including its stock of short-range, battlefield weapons. Moscow's unwillingness to make further strategic arms reductions, assuming that a strategic arms reduction

(START) treaty is signed, could also lower the nuclear threshold in Europe.

A cautious, deliberate response to the changing security environment, on the other hand, would help to achieve a third zero, that is, the withdrawal of all nuclear artillery and short-range ballistic missiles from Europe. Germany will surely demand their removal to ensure the departure of all Red Army troops from its eastern states by 1994. But the elimination of all ground-based nuclear weapons is likely to erode the military utility of the Atlantic Alliance. It would accelerate U.S. military retrenchment, thereby leaving the British and French nuclear forces as the sole theater deterrent to the Soviet Union. Both the U.S. departure and the continued presence of British and French nuclear forces, in turn, are likely to provoke anxiety in Bonn, and they could lead Germany to develop its own nuclear deterrent or, at least, to insist on participation in joint nuclear planning, targeting, and use.

Neither London, Paris, nor Moscow would find such a situation tolerable. Nor would they feel much more comfortable if a third zero led to European denuclearization. The removal of nuclear weapons may simply transfer anxieties to the conventional sphere, where the Germans, their agreement with Moscow to reduce the size of the Bundeswehr notwithstanding, could again become a dominant military force in Europe.

The risk in the ad hockery of the decision making in which the United States, the Soviet Union, and the European states have engaged since the summer of 1989 is that no one will have the foresight to think beyond the exigencies of the present and devise a new concept from which a set of security relationships for postwar Europe can evolve. What is urgently needed is an integrated approach that includes, at the multinational level, a U.S.-led NATO as a support structure for a new security system and, at the national level, a panoply of mutual assistance agreements in the East that would be incorporated first into the WEU and eventually into a European collective defense organization.

Paradoxically, the Gulf War and the abrogation of the Warsaw Pact appear to have reinvigorated public support for NATO in Western Europe. Mindful of the dangers of a security vacuum following the collapse of the Warsaw Pact and the revived influence of conservative forces in the USSR, East European leaders have also advocated closer ties to NATO. Even Romania and Bulgaria have expressed interest in an associate membership in the Western Alliance. Although the surge in NATO's stock can be expected to taper off relatively soon, the need for security attachments, especially in the emerging European democracies, will probably intensify in the months ahead. Until such time as a collective defense umbrella can be extended over the entire continent, the newly democratizing states will have to rely on localized associations and mutual assistance agreements to safeguard their security and to build mutual confidence that they intend to resolve differences peacefully.[12]

The recent declaration of Hungary, the Czech and Slovak Federal Republic, and Poland to work toward political, economic, and security integration may be the first of such localized regional arrangements. The tripartite agreement to consult on security questions, promote economic and cultural cooperation, and ensure the rights of ethnic and religious minorities actually dates from early 1990. Caught up in the euphoria of democratic revolt, however, Havel and his foreign minister, Jiri Dienstbier, subsequently dropped the idea in favor of the idealized CSCE process until the vicissitudes of political change exposed the fragility of East European security.[13]

The tripartite declaration is not a military alliance directed at some other state or group of states. Nor is it a mutual assistance pact. But its consultative approach to security lays the basis for a more extensive agreement in the future that could affirm the inviolability of Czech–Hungarian–Polish borders, institutionalize military cooperation, and establish conditions for mutual security. Such a localized security arrangement would facilitate the release of resources that might otherwise be invested in military competition to economic, educational, and ecological endeavors that would make the region more attractive to foreign investment and to eventual membership in an enlarged European Community.

The signatories to this *east central European association* would not be precluded from affiliation with other regional groupings. At the end of 1989, considerable attention was given to the so-called Hapsburg reunion of Austria, Hungary, Yugoslavia, and Italy. By 1990 the Czechs had voiced interest in making it a pentagonal structure. To be sure, the evolution of such a *south central European association* will depend in part on the resolution of the internecine turmoil in Yugoslavia. The emergence of a confederal Yugoslavia would surely contribute to the development of a mutual security pact. But even the division of Yugoslavia would not preclude a confederation of Slovenia, Croatia, and perhaps Bosnia–Herzegovina from achieving such an association. In both cases, the signatories' accord on border and mutual security issues would free financial and human capital for multinational social and economic undertakings.

It is not farfetched to imagine similar localized security pacts taking shape in the Baltic region and in the Balkans. Whether or not the Soviet Union continues to retreat from reform in the future, the Baltic states will probably eventually regain their independence. Individually, they would fare no better economically than would Slovenia or Croatia. Collectively, however, they would strengthen their competitive position, particularly if they were joined by Poland in a *northeastern European association*. True, there are still outstanding Polish–Lithuanian territorial issues to be resolved. But the willingness to transcend their historical resentments in favor of mutualism and collective security would greatly contribute to economic development in the region.

In contrast, a *southeastern European association* would undoubtedly be an extraordinarily complex and problematic undertaking. The Greeks and Bulgarians have apparently resumed bilateral discussions that date from the 1930s. Today, as before, their interest in a treaty derives from their common dislike of Turkey. Nevertheless, even here the situation is not hopelessly bleak. To avoid alienating its partners in NATO and the EC, Greece might consider it tactically prudent to moderate its enmity toward Turkey. So might the Bulgarians, whose attachment to a regional association that included the Turks would draw them closer to both NATO and the European Development Bank.

The same security and economic considerations could induce Romania, its historic dispute with Bulgaria over northern Bukovina notwithstanding, to become party to a Balkan pact. Assuming such critical mass could be achieved, it would be hard for Albania

and Yugoslavia—whether in its present configuration or as a rump confederation of Serbia, Montenegro, and Macedonia—to remain aloof for long, since they would be isolated in their efforts to contest disputed borders in northern Epirus and Macedonia. In such an eventuality, Turkey might also choose to align itself with a Balkan security structure in the continued hope of gaining membership in the EC.

There is certainly no guarantee that such associations will lead to amicable political and economic cooperation. Quite the contrary, political disputes and periodic armed clashes are bound to occur as newly independent states resume the process of de-Ottomanization that was interrupted more than a half century ago. In fact, the associations bring to mind the hapless mini-alliances of the 1920s and 1930s, which fostered mistrust rather than cooperation. Unlike the interwar period, however, the envisioned regional associations would not be purely balance-of-power arrangements. As stated in the tripartite declaration between the Hungarians, Czechs, and Poles, their ultimate purpose would be to create conditions of social, cultural, and economic cooperation that would facilitate their integration in a reunited Europe.

Unlike the pre–World War II alliances in Eastern Europe, which the French and English encouraged to help contain Germany, the regional associations would be directly linked to the process of European integration in two ways. Insofar as it is feasible, each association, and its overlapping memberships, would be joined by at least one representative of the WEU or EC. Germany, for example, would be a natural partner in the east central European group, as would Italy in the transalpine association to the south.

The Scandinavian states, which are also likely to become more politically and economically integrated as Europe reunites, could establish cooperative relations with Poland and the Baltic states. The enlargement of the Balkan association would be harder to achieve. Neither Greece nor Turkey is wealthy enough to be an economic catalyst of integration, and each remains mistrustful of the other. Possibly a combination of Germany, Italy, and France could help link the southeastern European states to the West.

The inclusion of economically powerful West European states in the envisioned regional associations would lend a considerable measure of direction, energy, and support to economic integration. No less important, it would give the democratizing states hope that their economic sacrifice and political restraint would eventually lead to their integration in an expanded Common Market.

East–West linkage can be institutionally reinforced by establishing consultative relationships between the regional associations and the WEU and EC. Until unity among the Twelve is achieved and the East European states become economically more mature, it is premature to consider enlarging the EC. But it would advance the process of cooperation in the East if representatives of the regional associations could develop informal working relationships with the EC, including the European Parliament. Furthermore, it should be possible to establish conditions for eventual associate membership in the EC.

To avoid creating a power vacuum that would exacerbate tensions within the regional associations and revive Russo–German competition, the fledgling democracies in the East must also be quickly brought under the umbrella of Western security. The soothing rhetoric of cooperation by allied bureaucrats to the contrary, NATO membership will never be more than a pipe dream for the emerging democracies. The WEU, in contrast, offers a real and accessible road toward security cooperation in a Europeanized Europe.

In anticipation of its enhanced security role in the emerging postwar Europe, the WEU should plan to move its headquarters from Paris to Brussels, where it can more efficiently coordinate with the NATO bureaucracy. In addition, states that are members of the WEU and NATO could assign the same ambassador to both institutions. While this move is in train, exchanges could begin between the WEU and representatives of the recently announced east central European association. Military and political leaders from Hungary, Czechoslovakia, and Poland could be invited to attend plenary sessions. In addition, certain officials could be selected annually to work with the WEU's security institute.

Adjunct participation in WEU deliberations could likewise be extended to other regional associations. In turn, as the localized mutual assistance agreements facilitate security and economic cooperation, and as lingering Soviet suspicions of Western intentions fade, the WEU—or, by then, the European Security Union (ESU)—could, on a case-by-case basis, extend formal membership to the former Pact states, including eventually Russia, at which point the regional associations could be dissolved.

In the same way that the regional associations will necessarily be the scaffolding for political and economic cooperation in the former Soviet satellite states, NATO must also buttress the WEU until the evolving process of security integration makes it possible for the latter to assume responsibility for the common defense of Europe. Depending on the pace of conventional and strategic arms reductions, this means that NATO, at minimum, will continue to safeguard the security of Western Europe against the distant likelihood of attack from a still militarily formidable Soviet Union. But it also means that NATO will indirectly extend its guarantee to the new democracies of Eastern Europe, as the WEU, or ESU, enlarges its domain to incorporate the states in the regional associations. To provide the emerging European defense organization with the capability to defend the territorial integrity of Europe, NATO will also have to transfer units from its integrated command—or whatever is left of it after the substantial withdrawal of U.S. troops—or, at least, assign units dual tasks in the WEU.

Clearly, there would be limits to NATO's extended security obligations. A future conflict between Romania and Hungary over Transylvania, a civil war between Czechs and Slovaks, or the breakup of Yugoslavia would not justify NATO involvement. But a Soviet attack against Poland, say, or some other East European state that had joined the WEU, would be a casus belli for the Atlantic Alliance, in accordance with Article 5 of the North Atlantic Treaty, if Poland's WEU allies, by virtue of their dual membership in NATO, were dragged into the conflict under Article 5 of the Brussels Treaty.

There is little question that the United States and some European allies—Spain and Portugal, as examples—would be keen on avoiding such invocation of NATO. But the Soviet Union could not be certain that NATO would not respond to an attack against a WEU ally, just as it could not exclude France's independent nuclear force from its strategic planning during the cold war period.

But such dire prognostications need not materialize. The formation of regional associations in Eastern Europe and their gradual assimilation into the WEU could, over time, build confidence and mutual trust among the participating states and, assuming continued progress in the CFE, in the Soviet Union as well. As it becomes clearer to Moscow that it is the WEU, not NATO, that will provide security for the common European home to which Gorbachev made frequent reference in the early visionary period of perestroika, Moscow may also choose to participate in the process of Europeanization by affiliating with either the southeastern or northeastern associations, or both. The natural apprehension that Soviet reinvolvement in Eastern Europe would arouse in the neighboring states would be offset by the security provided by membership in a large collective defense structure stretching from the Atlantic to the Urals, the Bay of Biscay to the Baltic Sea, and the North Sea to the Black Sea.

Throughout this process of integration Europe would be simultaneously denuclearizing. The removal of all ground-based, short-range weapons, including nuclear artillery, from the continent is predictable. Furthermore, motivated by the desire to speed the withdrawal of Soviet troops from its territory and to establish closer ties to the new democracies in the East, Germany is likely to reject the deployment of air-delivered nuclear weapons (so-called TASM).

To be sure, the British and French will maintain their nuclear deterrents to bolster the development of the WEU and to hedge against Soviet or, more likely, Russian expansionism. Nonetheless, to alleviate anxieties in

Bonn that British and French nuclear forces were aimed at Germany, and to preclude German nuclearization, London and Paris would probably be forced to scale back the size of their nuclear arsenals in proportion to the reduction of conventional and strategic arms in Europe.

The Soviet Union would still possess strategic weapons. But so would the United States. Given the enormous uncertainty that will attend the process of European unification, and the nagging worry about the dispersal of nuclear weapons to the restive Soviet republics, it seems unlikely that either Moscow or Washington will agree quickly to a START II treaty. Although the condition of strategic standoff will be far from ideal, it will give assurance to all participants in the process of Europeanization, the United States and the Soviet Union included, that the transition from bipolarism to multilateralism will not undermine the state of mutual deterrence that sustained European stability during the Cold War. Although the European states would maintain defense forces tethered to the WEU, or ESU, they would have no incentive to build nuclear forces.

Like the regional associations and the Warsaw Pact, NATO will gradually wither away. The skeletized force of two U.S. divisions and three air wings in the mid-1990s, say, will be phased out by the end of the decade. To allay allied anxieties about the return to neo-isolationism in the United States, however, U.S. officials would be well advised to underscore their continuing commitment to European security. At a minimum, this would require the United States to leave prepositioned equipment in Europe for the foreseeable future, maintain adequate airlift and sealift capability to respond to crises, if necessary, and foster a con-

sultative relationship with the WEU Council on a broad range of defense topics, especially nuclear weapons policy.

Planning for the Future

The envisioned evolution of European security in the emerging postwar period does not anticipate some millennium of peace. The resumption of the interrupted process of nationalism in Eastern Europe may overcome efforts to establish cooperative structures. Societies that mortgaged their futures to the illusion of a socialist utopia may not be able to defer economic and social gratification. Further, it may be a fantasy to believe that Turkey, which is likely to experience rising Islamic fundamentalism and a growing security threat on its southern borders, can be fitted into the mosaic of a Europeanized Europe. But to repose one's hopes for the future in the strength of institutions like NATO that belong to another time in the history of both Europe and the United States is to induce a dangerous complacency that invites instability.

Conflict cannot be prevented in the emerging postwar Europe. It can be contained, however. In order to do so, the United States and the European allies must first part with their illusions. Efforts to superimpose prefabricated architectures on the new Europe without examining and shoring up, if necessary, its existing foundations are bound to fail. Viewing the future through the lens of 1949 gives an equally distorted picture of reality. Neither approach is rooted in the present.

At the same time, political leaders in the United States and Europe must have some vision of the future that they would like to see emerge from the present. The EC should figure prominently in their thinking—it has the quintessential role to play in the new Europe as the engine of economic unity. So should the CSCE. Just as the CSCE provided a process of interaction that sustained détente in Europe during the superpower chill of the 1980s, it can perform an equally valuable service as a conciliator and mediator in the ethnic, religious, and territorial disputes that lie ahead. But Western leaders also need to develop a new concept of security to replace the alliance structure that has served peace so well for the past four decades. The WEU appears to be the only viable institutional base on which a new structure can be built.

The WEU is no panacea for the problems that await the new Europe; it may struggle to manage the process of integration. Unlike NATO, however, it points the Euratlantic community in the direction of tomorrow rather than yesterday. That alone is a hopeful sign. For its part, the United States should assist rather than resist the development of the WEU. After all, no country has made a greater contribution on behalf of European unity. Besides, the security and stability that a collective defense organization will provide to a continent that is about to resume responsibility for its own affairs can only enhance the long-term geostrategic interests of the United States.

An earlier version of this paper was presented with Robert C. Hughes in April 1991 at the Fourteenth Annual NATO Symposium held at the National Defense University, Fort Lesley J. McNair, Washington D.C. I am grateful to Bob Hughes for his helpful comments.

Notes

1. See "The United States and NATO in an Undivided Europe" (The Johns Hopkins Foreign Policy Institute, Washington,

D.C., 1991), which emphasizes the enduring importance of NATO.

2. See the speech by the British foreign secretary, Douglas Hurd, "The CSCE: Need for a New Magna Carta" (British Information Services, British Consulate General, New York, October 2, 1990). Also see "A New Security Structure for Europe" (British American Security Information Council, Washington, D.C., 1990).

3. William Touhy, "Drinking a Toast to Europe's Future," *Los Angeles Times*, November 13, 1990, pp. H–1, H–6.

4. William Drozdiak, "Havel Urges NATO to Seek Ties with East's New Democracies," *Washington Post*, March 22, 1991, p. A–18.

5. See, for example, Stephen Van Evera, "Primed for Peace: Europe After the Cold War," *International Security* 15 (Winter 1990–91), pp. 7–57.

6. Patrick Buchanan, among others, has recently raised the burden-sharing issue in "Would the Red Army Fold So Quickly?" *Washington Times*, March 4, 1991, p. E–3.

7. Teresa Hitchens, "Most Europeans Favor Common EC Defense," *Defense News*, March 4, 1991, p. 8; "European Publics Still View NATO as Essential, but Divide on Alliance Nuclear Strategy" (USIA, Washington, D.C., July 2, 1990), p. 12.

8. Ferdinand Protzman, "Germany's Top Banker Gives Europe a Warning," and Alan Riding, "Spain Seeks to Mend Europe's Ties to North Africa," *New York Times*, March 20, 1991, pp. D–2 and A–13, respectively.

9. Early reference to the centrality of the WEU in a Europeanized Europe can be found in Hugh De Santis, "The Reshaping of NATO," N-3043-DAG/USDP (Santa Monica, Calif.: The RAND Corporation, January 1990), pp. 30–32.

10. See Elisabeth Guigou, French minister for European affairs, interview with *Les Echos* in Foreign Broadcast Information Service–Western Europe (hereafter FBIS–WEU), March 25, 1991, pp. 2–3.

11. FBIS–WEU, March 25, 1991, p. 1.

12. "West European Publics Support U.S. Actions and Leadership in Gulf Crisis. . . ." (USIA, Washington, D.C., September 13, 1990), p. 30; Frederick Kempe, "East Eu-

ropean Nations Edging Closer to NATO," *Wall Street Journal*, February 15, 1991, p. 9; *NATO News Items* (Norfolk, Va.: SACLANT Public Information Office, February 6, 1991), p. 1.

13. Press release, Hungarian Ministry of In-

formation, Budapest, February 15, 1991, pp. 1–3. See Havel's speech to the Polish Sejm and Senate on January 21, 1990, "The Future of Central Europe," *New York Review of Books*, March 29, 1990, pp. 18–19.

Central and Eastern Europe: Imperative for Active U.S. Engagement

Adrian A. Basora

FROM THE SPRING of 1989, when Poland and Hungary emerged as beacons of hope in the declining Soviet empire, to the final breaching of the Berlin Wall, the eyes of the world were fixed on Central and Eastern Europe. Western steadfastness against Soviet encroachment had triumphed; the Cold War was finally being won. The entire region seemed destined for democracy and economic reform, with the United States playing a leading role.

Now, only three years later, the euphoria has faded, difficulties predominate, and the focus has shifted eastward as the Soviet Union itself has fallen apart. In Europe, the United States and its West European partners are increasingly caught up in the anarchy consuming what was once Yugoslavia, increasingly absorbed with debate over the merits and demerits of military intervention as day-to-day relief and truce operations falter. The here and now of civil war—with calls for "Europe to take the lead" in stop-

ping it—have blotted out any U.S. consensus on a longer-term policy framework for the larger region. Many Americans now view the overall transformation of Central and Eastern Europe as yesterday's priority, and they are abetted by concomitant calls for a drastically reduced U.S. role in Europe as a whole in order to shift resources to domestic needs.

This swing of the pendulum, all too common in American public life, is dangerous. Such a loss of focus, with the consequent danger of eroded commitment, poses a threat to essential U.S. national interests. Rather than withdrawing as problems multiply, the United States should reconfirm its active engagement in Central and Eastern Europe—an engagement based not on altruism but on basic U.S. security. Beyond the vicissitudes of determining immediate steps toward the former Yugoslavia—greatly exacerbated by the politics of an election year—Americans must maintain a clear view of the larger canvas for working out basic U.S. security and economic interests in Europe. Consolidation of the new democracies is an essential building block if the United States is to help construct a new European and a new transatlantic order that will protect these U.S. interests. Alone of all the participants, the

Adrian A. Basora is U.S. ambassador to the Czech and Slovak Federal Republic. He is a career foreign service officer with prior service at the National Security Council and in Paris, Madrid, and Bucharest.

United States—both by history, its present unique power position, and the very nature of its society—has a chance to promote this consolidation through an active role in sustaining it.

The thesis argued below is straightforward: Without active U.S. leadership, a real risk of prolonged instability exists in Central and Eastern Europe that would have corrosive effects throughout the whole continent. Western Europe would be deeply affected, as would the former Soviet Union. In these circumstances, U.S. political and economic influence and access would be undercut not only in the struggling nations of Central and Eastern Europe, but also in a Western Europe increasingly delinked from the United States. The result would be a weakening of the transatlantic axis upon which U.S. security depends and the distancing of Washington from its essential partners in world affairs.

The central conclusion is clear: The need to secure the peace in Central and Eastern Europe goes beyond maintaining consistency with past policy toward that region. It is an essential element in overall U.S. policy toward the Eurasian continent. The world has changed drastically, but Americans are in danger of snatching defeat from the jaws of victory if— with the disappearance of superpower confrontation in Europe—they now desert the basic principles and policies that achieved that change. A stable, friendly Central and Eastern Europe is important as the United States pursues its fundamental, *global* interests such as the spread of democracy, increased international prosperity and openness to U.S. exports and investment, and a more peaceful, livable world. And it is critical to the health of *Europe and of the transatlantic com-*

munity—the principal pillars of U.S. security and prosperity.

The Rationale for Active U.S. Engagement

Elimination of the former Soviet threat and of communism in Central and Eastern Europe does not guarantee the shape of the region's future institutions. Building viable new economic and political systems, incorporating the free market and democracy, is now the challenge. Some argue that the United States no longer has the will or the need to help these now-independent nations meet that challenge and thus to keep its side of the bargain implicitly made with Europe after World War II. Success will require both will and endurance, not often the stuff of daily headlines.

In fact, that bargain remains as essential today as it was four decades ago to basic U.S. interests in a stable Europe; the United States now cannot afford *not* to incorporate the newly freed states of Soviet-dominated Europe into that bargain any more than it could afford to ignore the danger to Western Europe posed by that Soviet domination back in the late 1940s. The cost of support, in cooperation now with the resurgent West European partners of the United States, should be relatively modest—especially if compared to the massive outlays that went into World War II, the Marshall Plan, and the building of the North Atlantic Treaty Organization (NATO). Neither massive bilateral assistance, nor new troop deployments to the region, nor any other new, major commitments of resources need be made. The United States can conduct the necessary role in Central and Eastern Europe at current resource levels in partnership with Western Europe.

We shall look in a later section at the specifics of this approach. It is sufficient to note here that, paradoxically, the relative decline of U.S. preeminence in Europe strengthens the argument for this essential residual role. Precisely because U.S. resources and leverage in the world are no longer so predominant as they once were, the European bloc of countries has become increasingly critical to the advancement of U.S. interests worldwide. Real urgency certainly exists for addressing U.S. domestic problems—many left unattended by the burden of the Cold War; in this context it is important to pare back those international commitments that are less essential to U.S. security and well-being and that others can help meet. In Europe, however, where these basic interests are at stake and the costs relatively bearable, these residual U.S. commitments are essential. It is a false dichotomy to argue that the United States can address *either* its domestic problems *or* help these newly free European states build a new order. In fact, it must do both. U.S. strength and security at home and abroad require that it pursue both efforts in tandem.

What is the threat to U.S. interests that potentially emanates from Central and Eastern Europe? The answer lies in the threat to Europe as a whole, to its growing integration, and to its transatlantic ties to the United States. Barring a resurgence of nuclear or other major military threats to the east from states once part of the Soviet Union, this newly freed Central and East European region can generate—either directly or indirectly—some of the most serious menaces to Europe foreseeable in the coming decade.

A devastating example already exists in the lands of the former Yugoslavia. As is so terribly evident there, long-suppressed ethnic passions and latent boundary disputes have emerged in Central and Eastern Europe with far greater force than most observers had anticipated in 1989–1990. If not strongly discouraged, such confrontations could well continue to spread throughout the region—also having a negative impact both in republics of the former Soviet Union and in Western Europe.

Although the danger of spreading ethnic bloodshed is most obvious throughout the rest of Yugoslavia and elsewhere in the Balkans, replication of this atavistic phenomenon is by no means unthinkable in the northern tier of Central and Eastern Europe. It is also all too clear that such ethnic conflicts can be emulated farther to the east, a point tragically underlined by the Azeri–Armenian conflict.

In Central and Eastern Europe itself, rising tensions among ethnic groups—whether or not they generate the horrors of Yugoslavia—will eventually lead to a competitive search for allies. To the east, the magnet of this deadly rivalry could possibly draw in Russia, Ukraine, or other successor states to the Soviet Union. The shifting sands of ethnic competition would be all the more ominous if at that point authoritarian regimes had taken power in Moscow, Kiev, or both. With governments driven by the emotional issues inherent to nationalism, the risk in the region of nuclear proliferation, or at least of nuclear intimidation, would substantially increase.

Nor would Western Europe be immune. The fact is, European integration does *not* have unstoppable momentum. Much of the past impetus came from the Soviet superpower threat as well as a strong and supportive U.S. presence. Even when these influences were at their peak, Western Europe's centrifugal forces were strong enough to impede integration over significant periods. Were events in Central and Eastern Europe now to descend into ethnic rivalry, traditional centrifugal forces throughout the whole of Europe could once again be strengthened. Violent separatist movements—such as those in Spain, Northern Ireland, and Corsica—could well be reinvigorated. Add to that the probable influx of large numbers of refugees fleeing ethnic strife in the East, and one can imagine a real threat to the stable social and political fabric of Europe—West and East.

Furthermore, with ethnic nationalism out of control, the governments of Central and Eastern Europe would be cast upon the sea of power rivalries with no security framework any longer in place. They would remain weak and insecure; they would inevitably seek external patrons, as happened in Yugoslavia. Some would seek alliances with Germany, as the Slovenes and the Croats did and as Budapest, Prague, or Bratislava could be tempted to do if they began to perceive serious external threats. Warsaw's traditional fears of Germany would undoubtedly lead the Poles to court the French and others in an attempt to strengthen their own relative position. Germany, whose enhanced power is already strongly felt, would thus loom even larger over Europe. This dominance in turn could lead to countermoves by Paris and London, and possibly by Kiev, Moscow, and others—gradually recreating a new balance of power diplomacy reminiscent of the pattern that led Europe and the world into two devastating wars in the first half of the twentieth century.

Although such negative power dynamics would initially be muted by the current momentum toward integration in the European Community (EC), that momentum could soon be eroded and finally reversed. In Central and Eastern Europe, these dynamics could also reverse the recent healthy trend toward dialogue and cooperation between Warsaw, Prague, and Budapest; each would seek to compete with and balance its neighbors' ties in the West. In such a new "Old Europe," NATO would gradually be rendered irrelevant by the new system of separate alliances. Disunited and riven by tensions, it would be unable to prevent perennial crises or stop small "wars" among competing European groupings.

Within Central and Eastern Europe itself, endemic ethnic strife would turn the clock back to yesteryear. It would perpetuate political instability, divert the attention of leaders, and result in misuse of scarce resources. The already difficult task of economic reform would be further complicated. Focus would be on ethnic grievances or on "foreign enemies," rather than on building a new civic culture and undertaking the many daunting efforts and sacrifices needed to consolidate reform in the region.

These dire scenarios may not come to pass, but they are plausible enough to require serious steps to avoid them. Moreover, less stark scenarios that fall short of outright bloodshed still evoke dangers worth avoiding. For example, even if the civil warfare in Yugoslavia does not spread beyond that country, *nonviolent* ethnic dissension can also prove very costly to achieving post-Communist stability. One case in point is the demise of the Czech and Slovak Federal Republic. Although, as approached at present, the ethnic issue there seems unlikely to lead to violence, the difficult negotiations on the future of the federation have already taken a heavy toll in political divisiveness and in delayed reform. They have also slowed the economic transition by diverting the attention and energies of the country's leaders and by creating uncertainties that dampen the interest of potential investors.

The scenarios for potential setbacks to reform in Central and Eastern Europe, whether on the Yugoslav or on the Czech and Slovak models, all point to the need for strong external help and encouragement—not just in containing ethnic issues but also in sustaining political and economic reform. The goal must be a "virtuous cycle" of transition to democracy, the free market, and peaceful settlement of ethnic and other disputes. Bringing these three elements together will achieve full and rapid consolidation of reform in Central and Eastern Europe. Such an outcome would have the important additional benefit of providing encouragement—and pertinent success models—for the long and difficult task of reform that lies ahead in the Soviet successor states.

To repeat, however, this virtuous cycle requires strong outside support—and, without such support, either erosion or dramatic reversal of the reform trend is increasingly likely.

Europeans Cannot Do It Alone

Even allowing for the gravity of danger that can result from ethnic strife, why should the United States take the lead among outsiders in consolidating the peace in the former Soviet satellites? After all, were not the Marshall Plan

and four decades of U.S. military protection enough of an investment in European stability? Should not the West Europeans now solve the emerging problems in their own backyard?

Unfortunately, a wholly European solution, however desirable, is unlikely to occur in the coming decade. The consolidation of reform and avoidance of entrenched ethnic divisiveness in Central and Eastern Europe can move along only one of two paths: rapid incorporation into the European Community, or the maintenance of a broad-based, long-term international effort (including a strong U.S. role) to assure stability and assist the regional reform effort.

Those who argue for the first path, minimizing the need for U.S. involvement, assume incorporation of many or all of the Central and East European countries into the European Community within the next few years. To dramatize the likely impact, they point to the experience of the not too distant past: Spain, Portugal, and Greece were helped to accelerate their economic growth and to consolidate their democracies by the prospect and ultimately the reality of EC membership. The same can happen in the East, it is maintained.

In the real world, however, looking at the current EC integration and expansion agenda, a decade appears an overly optimistic time frame for bringing in even the front-runners—Hungary, Czechoslovakia, and Poland, let alone others in the region less far advanced. The time taken could be much longer, particularly if the current political or economic reform efforts of these leading candidates were to slacken. Overall, three questionable assumptions are made by the proponents of the "EC incorporation" solution:

- that the current momentum of the EC will permit *two* significant expansions of membership within the next decade (countries like Austria, Sweden, and Finland are already well ahead in the queue);
- that events in Central and Eastern Europe itself will not alter the EC integration momentum; and,
- that the current 12 members of the EC will be willing to provide generous, long-term transitional assistance to a large number of Central and East European candidate countries both before and after they join the EC.

None of these assumptions appears valid. The Maastricht Summit of December 1991, the negative Danish ratification vote, and the lukewarm French endorsement in September 1992, demonstrated the uncertainties of the current unification momentum; they underlined the absence of any guarantee that EC integration will progress smoothly, rapidly, or on a predictable schedule. Furthermore, events in Central and Eastern Europe could conceivably create dissension among West Europeans, slow the EC's progress, and call into deeper question the willingness of current EC members to foot a large bill for rapid entry.

Historically, EC integration has seen periods of substantial forward movement followed by periods of little or no progress. Differences and divisions over what happens next are already apparent. The current German conviction is that the EC can and should enlarge rapidly to the east at the same time that it continues to move ahead on integration within itself. France, the EC Commission, and others, however, are strongly committed to the thesis that further "deepening" is required before the EC is ready for a major expansion. Although Austria, Sweden, Finland, and one or two other small, affluent members of the European Free Trade Association (EFTA) are likely to gain admission in the mid-1990s, the French preference for delaying still larger expansion is very likely to win out. And not only for EC institutional reasons; as time goes by, the probable lengthiness and difficulty of political and economic transitions in Central and Eastern Europe will become clearer, as will the high costs for preparing the region's rapid full membership.

Strong reinforcement of this point comes from the extraordinarily high costs of financing the integration into West Germany of 16 million former East Germans—estimated at $100 billion per year for the first few years. It would be imprudent to assume that West European taxpayers—especially farmers and unemployed workers—would look kindly on a similar effort for 64 million Poles, Hungarians, Czechs, and Slovaks, or for double that number if all of Central and Eastern Europe were included.

The most likely scenario, therefore, is for long delays in accession to the European Community—and then accession only by those countries successful enough with deep and prolonged economic restructurings to make them roughly comparable to Spain when it joined the EC in 1986. On this basis, no more than two or three of the more advanced countries of Central and Eastern Europe—presumably from the northern tier—are likely to gain admission even in a 10- to 12-year time frame. In the meantime, other structures will be required for the security, economic, and political needs of the Central and East European region—at least during a long transitional period.

Recommended U.S. Policy

Against this backdrop, the overarching goal of U.S. policy should be to ensure that political, economic, and institutional reform in Central and Eastern Europe becomes irreversible, and that at least the most apt candidates are anchored into the Western security and economic system. Ultimately, much of Central and Eastern Europe should become an integral part of a broadened and modern transatlantic community. The essential first steps, and thus the short-term U.S. objectives for countries of the region, should be:

- to foster the success of their economic transitions;
- to help consolidate effective democratic government there as quickly as possible; and,
- to create a stable security environment for these reforming countries.

As already argued, this calls for active U.S. engagement. Yet, obtaining long-term public and congressional support is bedeviled by the tendency to frame the debate in polar opposites. At one extreme of the economic debate, for example, is the contention that only an effort on the scale of the Marshall Plan is adequate to the task. At the opposite extreme is the view that any significant national outlays are misguided or unrealistic in view of the problems that the United States currently faces at home.

On the military/security side, a similar polarization occurs about whether or not the United States should send large forces to intervene in conflicts like the Yugoslav civil war. Unless the nation is willing to do so, it is asserted, it is useless to be actively engaged at all.

In fact, however, there is fertile middle ground for effective action, ground that lies between the extremes of massive engagement and virtual nonengagement. The cost of occupying this middle ground need not be excessive. By discriminating, the United States can make an important difference in Central and Eastern Europe—at the same time preserving broader U.S. equities on the European continent. The outlines of such an approach are sketched below:

1. On the economic restructuring front, the United States needs to reassert promptly the active leadership role that it played in reform in 1989 and well into 1990. Washington's "leading partner" role began at the 1989 Paris Summit of the Group of Seven (G–7), when President George Bush urged united support for the reforms then beginning in Poland and Hungary. The result was the creation of the Group of 24 (G–24) assistance effort; the EC was given a coordinating role, with the clear understanding that the United States would be a full partner. The G–24 effort worked according to this plan during its early months, with the United States taking much of the initiative, most notably on the Polish stabilization fund and on emergency food aid.

Since then, however, the European Commission has gradually become more dominant both organizationally and in policy terms, and the relative U.S. contribution has declined—starting with the Persian Gulf crisis. Because this lowered U.S. profile has now become established, some Europeans have begun to conclude that Washington has decided to abdicate its role as leader. In fact, however, U.S. aid has remained a very respectable proportion of grant assistance—which is the most critical form of assistance.

135

Through greater publicizing of this record, along with patient diplomacy, these misperceptions can be dissipated.[1]

That is only part of the problem, however. The time has come for overhauling the whole aid structure. The need is to de-emphasize both bilateral financial assistance and the G–24 mechanism that was created to solicit and coordinate it. The number of receiving countries now covered by the mechanism has become unmanageable, and their needs have changed as well. The G–24 initially proved highly useful as a forum to encourage political support and the pledging of aid; yet, from the start it was less successful as an aid coordination mechanism. Now that the political goals have been achieved, with the freeing of all of Central and Eastern Europe from Soviet domination and the subsequent dissolution of the USSR itself, the need is to examine that coordinating mechanism.

With most of Central and Eastern Europe now committed to market reforms and with more than two years' experience as to what does and does not work, the emphasis should now be on the pursuit of effective economic reform policies and efficient aid delivery, looked at on a country by country basis. There is no longer a need for the type of contingency support funds initially required to give credibility to untried stabilization and reform programs in these newly independent states. We are beyond that.

In this regard, the recent trend in Poland toward rejection of foreign investment, rapid privatization, and macroeconomic stabilization is a disturbing one. To prevent further retrogression in the decade ahead, greater focus on individual countries will be needed, perhaps through mechanisms such as consultative

groups under the World Bank and the International Monetary Fund (IMF). Technical assistance and economic policy advice, along with private investment and increased trade access, must be the key ingredients of the Western contribution. Where larger amounts of financial support are warranted, such as for balance of payments or sectoral transition financing, the IMF, World Bank, and European Bank for Reconstruction and Development (EBRD) can provide most or all of the capital. It follows that the across-the-board mechanism of the G–24 should play a gradually decreasing role.

The United States should therefore encourage a move as quickly as possible toward country-specific aid coordination through setting up consultative groups for individual countries. Under the World Bank and the IMF, these would have the active participation also of the EBRD and the Organization for Economic Coordination and Development (OECD). Alternatively, for those recipients that have become OECD "Partners in Transition," the groups could be organized under an OECD umbrella, as was done in the past for Turkey and Yugoslavia.

These consultative groups would need to cease the current emphasis on pledging new funds (additional to those already available from the World Bank, the IMF, and the EBRD). Rather, they should stress the prompt disbursement and effective use of aid already contracted bilaterally, as well as that massive multilateral aid either already in the pipeline or potentially available. Particular stress should be put on the following: donors must speak with one voice in their economic policy advice to each recipient; technical assistance must be adequate and well targeted; and conditions must be created to attract private investment flows. The United States can take the lead in promoting this multilateral approach with little or no extra cost to either the American or the European taxpayer.

This multilateral approach would also permit the United States to translate its strong influence at the IMF and the World Bank into quiet leadership of support for economic reform throughout Central and Eastern Europe. At the same time, of course, the United States should also, as the largest shareholder, play an active role within the EBRD. That is, it should assure an effective EBRD emphasis on private-sector development—with that effort complementary to, rather than competitive with, the World Bank and the IMF.

Through any and all channels, the United States will need to work hard to protect its own direct long-term economic interests in the region. Americans must assume that the economic restructuring of Central and East European countries will ultimately succeed, and that success will bring with it their eventual entry into the EC, or at least close linkage to it. Therefore, unless the United States is actively engaged throughout in shaping these economic changes, U.S. investors and exporters will face serious competitive disadvantages, beginning in the coming decade. This danger is a further argument for emphasizing the role of the World Bank. Its projects carry guarantees of fair access for U.S. suppliers. The same is true of the OECD, which emphasizes open and equitable trade and investment regimes.

It is also urgent to push for the implementation of bilateral investment treaties in those Central and East European countries where they are not yet in force, because, in the last analysis, private investment will be the most critical element of economic success, ultimately providing the prosperous, pluralistic society needed for stable democracy. Such success can only come from effective domestic policies within those countries that attract U.S. and other investors on an equal footing and at little cost to the U.S. government or other aid donors.

2. On the political reform front, the United States has played a significant role from the start—most notably with President Bush's April 1989 speech at Hamtramck in support of the Polish "Roundtable Agreements," followed by his historic visits that July to Warsaw, Gdansk, and Budapest. Yet, much remains to be done. The spectacular nature of the anti-Communist revolutions of 1989–1990 initially made the mundane task of democratic consolidation seem deceptively easy by comparison. Even a brief glance at the history of Central and Eastern Europe, however, or a comparative look at the problems of democratic transition in other regions, makes it clear that the task ahead is complex and difficult. Success has to be measured in years, not in months.[2]

The U.S. goal should be obvious: support for accelerating the consolidation and deepening of democracy in Central and Eastern Europe through both direct and indirect means. Critical *indirect* contributions must include the creation of stable, reliable security arrangements for the region as well as assistance for the successful economic transitions discussed above. Without a secure environment and a modicum of prosperity, the new leaders will face daunting odds in their efforts to consolidate effective democratic government. They already confront a severe dilemma—the very democracy they seek to nurture subjects them to extraordinary public pressures to choose short-term expediency over what will be economically beneficial in the longer term.

Beyond helping mold a more favorable economic and security environment, the United States can reinforce its leading support role by continuing *direct* help to individual countries for the consolidation of political reform. It should continue bilateral technical and material assistance for the building of democratic institutions. Washington should also seek to reshape the political "basket" of the Conference on Security and Cooperation in Europe (CSCE), giving maximum external support to the most critical aspects of the democratic process.

During the years after the 1975 Helsinki Final Act the CSCE process— together with the example of the increasingly accessible democracies of Western Europe and North America— had a powerful impact in Central and Eastern Europe and even in the Soviet Union. The post-Communist transition poses markedly different problems. Still, a similar pattern of regular CSCE reviews to measure progress against formally agreed standards can still help point out the direction of reform—and keep up the pressure on laggards such as Romania. These same standards should also be applied as criteria for eventual membership in the EC, in NATO, and in other regional organizations with a political character.

U.S. programs in these countries are already well launched. The nation needs to continue to emphasize those that build up the cadres and capabilities of political parties, the free press and media, universities, and other institutions that form the underpinnings of democracy. Exchange programs, ranging from high school students to mid-level political, academic, and media leaders should be continued and in some cases deepened.

3. *On the security front,* the United States should work carefully but quickly to build up a de facto secure zone that encompasses at least Poland, Hungary, and the former Czechoslovakia, and possibly other reformers of Central and Eastern Europe in the future. At the same time, the United States should build up the CSCE and, if necessary, other institutions capable of deterring or defusing the types of intraregional ethnic and boundary conflicts besetting Yugoslavia and Moldova.

The first step in implementing this strategy would be to further develop bilateral military and politico-military relationships with countries of Central and Eastern Europe as quickly as possible. This should be done under the general umbrella of the North Atlantic Cooperation Council, but with special emphasis on the northern tier countries. What the United States should be working toward is a clear (though not publicly emphasized) objective: to extend the full coverage of the NATO security sphere to key reforming countries as soon as feasible, perhaps through eventual full or associate membership.

The so-called Visegrad countries— Poland, Hungary, and Czechoslovakia—are already cooperating well among themselves on security and other issues. They merit differentiated attention because of their strategic location, the more advanced stage of their reforms, and because they have made clear repeatedly that they desire NATO membership. If and when other countries of the region reach advanced stages of political and economic reform, the way should have also been prepared for their incorporation through deepening cooperation—assuming that they border on NATO members and want membership.

It is still too early to predict whether *full* NATO membership will be feasible for the Visegrad three, or later for any other Central and East European countries. Nevertheless, security ties are effectively already emerging under the aegis of the North Atlantic Cooperation Council and a variety of other liaison programs, as well as the special declaration by the NATO ministerial meeting at the time of the August 1990 coup attempt in Moscow. These ties should be further developed as quickly as possible. For example, the training of individual military and civilian defense personnel in the United States and in other member countries can be accelerated; there should also be a gradual transition to military staff consultants, adoption of NATO equipment standards, and eventual inauguration of periodic joint exercises.

The process for reaching the ultimate goal of full NATO membership will need to be carefully managed. It is important to avoid arousing hostility or paranoia in Moscow, Kiev, or elsewhere in the former Soviet Union. Just as was done in Moscow during the German unification process, it should be made clear to the leaders of the former Soviet republics that they face no hostile intent from the Atlantic Alliance, and that they themselves can benefit from active cooperation with an enhanced NATO—even though their membership is not in the cards.

In this regard, it is clear that extension of the Alliance to the east has limits. The absorption of a number of small and medium-sized *European* nations, with deep and long-established ties to Western Europe, is one thing. Membership for Ukraine, Russia, and the Central Asian republics, all with potentially hostile neighbors and a history of enmity toward one another, is quite a different proposition. It is difficult to imagine how NATO as a co-hesive instrument of security could survive such a wholesale expansion.

Nevertheless, although NATO cannot come to encompass *all* democracies to the east, a powerful geostrategic rationale does exist for including *some* of them. To repeat, just as the accession of the eastern *Länder* of Germany to the Alliance was a key step toward consolidating reform in Central and Eastern Europe, and one that could successfully be sold to Moscow as a nonthreatening and stabilizing step for all of Europe, so the same rationale should dictate careful though steady movement toward the same end for the northern tier of Central and Eastern Europe.

NATO is, of course, not the only instrument by which to graft Central and Eastern Europe onto the Western sphere of security and stability. The CSCE can and must play an important role, particularly in setting and constantly reemphasizing the moral and legal parameters for interstate and intergroup relations throughout Europe.

The CSCE can only be reinvigorated and kept relevant, however, with strong U.S. engagement and initiative. This is the lesson of the CSCE's history to date—and the obvious implications of membership by large nuclear powers such as Russia and Ukraine. Furthermore, as we are seeing in Yugoslavia, the United Nations (UN) will at times have a role to play. Here again, leadership by the one remaining global power—in close partnership with other UN Security Council members—is essential to success.

In sum, finishing the job that the United States began in Europe over 50 years ago remains as essential to U.S. interests today as it was then. Fortunately, the resources needed to complete the job are far more modest than when the United States entered

Adrian A. Basora

World War II, or launched the Marshall Plan, or geared up to win the Cold War. Those enormous investments can and should now yield rich dividends for the United States—economically, politically, and in terms of fundamental American national values. This harvest is within reach *if* the United States continues to keep sight of its original goals and *if* it recognizes that it still has an essential role to play in Europe and in the transatlantic partnership that has served it so well.

This article was prepared during a semester of research and discussion at the Center for the Study of Foreign Affairs of the State Department's Foreign Service Institute. The views and opinions expressed here are solely the author's and do not represent those of the U.S. government. The author wishes to thank George Sherman, a colleague at the Center, for his invaluable assistance.

Notes

1. The United States provided 20 percent of the Polish Stabilization Fund, 10 percent of the capitalization of the European Bank for Reconstruction and Development (EBRD), and overall has an excellent record on grant assistance and on actual disbursements to Central and Eastern Europe. It is in the area of export credits and guarantees that other donors have been more "generous"—but in many cases, these credits are on "hard" terms, which greatly limits their value to Central and East European countries.

2. See Samuel P. Huntington, *The Third Wave* (Norman, Okla.: University of Oklahoma Press, 1991).

Peacekeeping in the New Europe

James E. Goodby

YUGOSLAVIA HAS IMPLODED. Peace seems irretrievable as blood feuds threaten to make that area—it can no longer be called a nation—a semipermanent battleground. Military force has been deployed and sometimes used in several cities of the former Soviet Union, including Moscow. Ethnic claims and quarrels have erupted in the Czech and Slovak Federal Republic. Romania and Bulgaria are wrestling with minorities problems that threaten a breakdown in public order. The use of military force is obviously no less unthinkable in the new Europe than during the depths of the Cold War. Is the contradiction between order and justice in Central and Eastern Europe so profound that violence will become more commonplace and more intense than during the Cold War?

In this essay, I will first point out some of the difficult issues posed by intrastate conflict. To illustrate the problems in concrete terms I will then describe the experiences of European and United Nations (UN) mediators in Yugoslavia during the latter half of

James Goodby is Distinguished Service Professor at Carnegie Mellon University. During a 35-year career as a foreign service officer, he was head of the U.S. delegation to the Stockholm Conference on Disarmament in Europe, vice chairman of the U.S. delegation to the strategic arms reduction talks (START), and ambassador to Finland.

1991. These experiences add up to a valuable—and tragic—case study in peacekeeping in the new Europe. Yugoslavia may be a sad example of the kinds of security problems Europe will be facing in the post–cold war era. If so, it will be of crucial importance to absorb and act on its lessons. I will discuss some of the lessons that I think emerge from six months of trying to stop the fighting between Serbia and Croatia. One of these lessons is that Europe and the United States should be better prepared the next time. That includes being better prepared to exercise diplomacy's military instrument. In the last part of this essay I will outline some steps that might be taken to begin contingency planning for the use of peacekeeping forces in Europe.

New Threats to Peace and Stability

The Cold War was peaceful in the important sense that war did not break out between the Soviet Union and the United States or between the nations of Eastern and Western Europe. It was not a peaceful time in other respects. Aside from repressions imposed by the former regimes in Central and Eastern Europe in which blood was shed—sometimes secretly, sometimes openly—military force was used by the USSR in East Germany in 1953, in Hungary in 1956, and in Czechoslovakia in 1968. Poland was threatened with military force in 1981, and the former regime itself imposed martial law. Shoot-to-kill orders were carried out by East European border guards against people trying to flee to the West. Obviously, Central and Eastern Europe were hardly models of tranquillity during the Cold War.

One difference stands out between conflict in the cold war era and in the present period. During the Cold War some sovereign states were invaded and, in effect, occupied by others. In the post–cold war period, that kind of conflict seems very unlikely. Violence on a large scale will certainly occur, however, because internal instabilities are likely to persist for at least the next generation in Central and Eastern Europe, and almost certainly for longer. The breakup of Yugoslavia has created conditions that the *Economist* very early on quite rightly labeled "war in Europe." The coup in Moscow came perilously close to precipitating a civil war; such conflict seems almost inevitable in parts of the former Soviet Union.

Internal struggles, it is important to note, may become threats to international peace and security. This was the principle adopted by the UN Security Council in deciding to authorize intervention in Iraq to aid the Kurds. The principle is equally valid in Europe, especially since the Helsinki Final Act and subsequent documents negotiated by all participants in the Conference on Security and Cooperation in Europe (CSCE) have made a government's treatment of its citizens a matter of proper international concern. But acting on the principle is extremely risky when it involves the use of armed force. During the period when the Bush administration was considering its options for dealing with

the growing war in Yugoslavia, many advisers thought that civil war in that country would pose a threat to international security only if the major powers became involved. For them the right solution was simply to isolate or quarantine the war zone. This is realpolitik logic. In the face of intractable differences between Serbs and Croats, this may have been prudent advice but it seems likely that dangerous precedents are being set in Yugoslavia that will endanger future peace and stability. At the end of 1991, after 10,000 people have been slaughtered, it is evident that it is a miscalculation to think that a war in the center of Europe can rage on indefinitely without harmful effects beyond the war zones. The poisons released by the Serbo–Croatian war have already seeped into the Western alliance.

It is prudent to recognize that intervention in an internal conflict could lead the nations of Europe to take sides against each other, with disastrous results. Although the major powers have shown little interest in having their own military forces become involved in any way in the ethnic or intrastate conflicts of Eastern Europe, statements by the pre-coup Soviet government came close to threatening war if other countries, for any reason, decided to intervene in Yugoslavia. A Soviet statement in early August 1991 referred to European considerations of peacekeeping forces in Croatia and warned that "to enter . . . on one side of the conflict would mean to come into conflict automatically with others inside and outside Yugoslavia. And the conflict would grow into an all-European one."[1] That statement may have been the last gasp of military hardliners, but it was intended to—and did—signal that intervention in internal quarrels carries the risk of a general

European war. Even without any act of military intervention by the major powers, however, internal conflicts on the scale of the Yugoslav war may become threats to international peace and security. According to one report, the Hungarians have warned the Bush administration that they must consider intervening to help ethnic Hungarian communities in Yugoslavia if the lives of those people are endangered.[2] Bulgaria and Greece have direct interests in the fate of Macedonia and so does Albania in Kosovo. As it became clearer toward the end of 1991 that Serbia intended to annex large pieces of Croatia, and the intensity of the fighting correspondingly escalated, the implications for other parts of Europe of a violent but successful Serbian seizure of territory began to come into focus. The KGB even described the scene in Yugoslavia as a harbinger of things to come in the former Soviet Union.[3]

Neither the North Atlantic Treaty Organization (NATO) nor the European Community (EC) can be counted on to provide a stable haven for the Central and East European countries, not to mention the Soviet republics, for a long time to come. The region will continue to exist in a kind of security limbo while the construction of a post-Communist order in the former Soviet Union proceeds on its spectacularly disorderly way. This is the kind of environment that balance of power theorists and practical politicians alike would have no difficulty in identifying as a temptation to fate. So long as Central and Eastern Europe remain relatively unstable, incidents may occur there that will become threats to international peace and security. Quarantine, or nonintervention, might successfully isolate the fighting, but what kind of a new world order does this

imply? Yugoslavia already has shown us the answer to this question.

European and UN Mediation in Yugoslavia

In the main, it was the European Community that bore the burden through most of 1991 of working for cease-fires, monitoring these cease-fires, and searching for formulas to get negotiations started between Croatia and Serbia. A review of the Community's efforts is instructive. It shows a Community divided over the fundamental question of whether it was worth saving a Yugoslav federation and at odds over whether armed force should be used under any conditions. The record reveals that the Community negotiated with few instruments of coercion, and chose to deny itself those it had throughout most of the period from July through October 1991. The voice of the United States, the world's only superpower and self-proclaimed advocate of a new world order, was muted, no doubt because of the realpolitik logic cited above. Even the task of orchestrating the sounds of public opprobrium was neglected. The picture that emerges is one of selfless, even heroic maneuvering by brilliant West European and UN diplomats harnessed to national commitments that can only be described as half-hearted.

The mission was truly heroic—it nearly led to fatalities among the mediators. It was certainly creatively and energetically carried out. From early July 1991 onward, it was one of the chief preoccupations of the Dutch foreign minister, Hans van den Broek, in his capacity as president of the EC Council of Ministers for the latter part of 1991. EC mediation was successful almost immediately in the case of

Slovenia. The Community negotiated an agreement that called for the federal Yugoslav army to return to barracks in both Slovenia and Croatia and for the two republics to suspend for three months the declarations of independence they had made on June 25, 1991.[4] The agreement was carried out in Slovenia, where EC observers were quickly introduced, but not in Croatia, where over 11 percent of the population is Serbian. Clearly a major reason for the success in Slovenia was the decision of the Serbian military leaders to concentrate their limited resources on Croatia.

The Community resorted to a whole arsenal of mediation techniques. As its efforts to resolve the Yugoslav dispute expanded, it organized a peace conference, invented an arbitration mechanism for the settlement of disputes, offered ideas for the reconstitution of Yugoslavia, and sent observer teams to monitor cease-fires that had been brokered by EC mediators between Serbia and Croatia. Repeatedly, Community spokesmen talked about economic sanctions, but over four critical months the EC failed to impose sanctions on Yugoslav republics that refused to end the fighting and seek a diplomatic solution to the war.

The peace conference was chaired by Lord Carrington, former British foreign minister, former NATO secretary general, and one of the most successful mediators of the past 40 years. The conference met for the first time on September 7, 1991, in The Hague and held several meetings over the next months. Its full complement of participants included the leaders of Yugoslavia's six republics, the eight-member collective Yugoslav presidency, and EC ministers. Those issues that could not be resolved by negotiation were to be handed to a five-member arbitration board whose decisions would be binding. The five members would be the heads of constitutional courts in France, Italy, and Germany, plus one judge each from Croatia and Serbia. The board would be required to reach a decision within two months after Carrington submitted a case to it.[5]

The EC put forward formal proposals designed to nudge the Yugoslav republics not just toward a cease-fire but also toward a long-term settlement. The proposals would have replaced the Yugoslav federal structure with a "free association of republics with an international personality." Guarantees for the rights of minorities would be provided, ethnic enclaves would be disarmed, and a customs union and programs for economic cooperation would be established. There would be no unilateral changes in borders. Early in October 1991 an agreement along these lines had seemed possible, partly because it required Croatia to continue in some form of association with Serbia and required Serbia to renounce the use of force to change its borders. All the republics except for Serbia, Montenegro, and Slovenia (which considered itself fully independent) had accepted the EC plan for restructuring Yugoslavia. On October 7, however, the three-month delay in implementing their declarations of independence expired for both Slovenia and Croatia. They then proceeded to nullify their legal connections with the Yugoslav federal government. By the end of October, the president of Serbia, Slobodan Milosevic, was dismissing the EC plan as a violation of Yugoslavia's federal constitution.

President Mikhail Gorbachev's efforts at friendly persuasion were equally fruitless. On October 15, the presidents of Croatia and Serbia met with Gorbachev in Moscow and issued a communiqué calling for an immediate cease-fire and the beginning of negotiations within a month under the sponsorship of the United States, the Soviet Union, and the European Community.[6] This promising opening failed to materialize.

At a meeting in Belgrade on October 23, the leaders of Serbia began to unveil their plans for a Greater Serbia as the successor state to Yugoslavia.[7] On November 8, the European Community announced that it was imposing economic sanctions. These included suspension of a 1980 trade and cooperation agreement, limits on imports of Yugoslav textiles, elimination of benefits under the General System of Preferences, and exclusion of Yugoslavia from an EC-backed economic recovery program. A more direct blow to the federal army's war-making capability was the Community's intention to seek a UN-ordered oil embargo against Yugoslavia. Most of Yugoslavia's oil imports come from the Soviet Union and Libya.[8] On November 9, President George Bush personally declared that the United States would support these sanctions.[9]

Most of the Community's mediation effort had been directed toward the limited objective of a cease-fire. Getting agreement to cease-fires proved to be an easy thing to do, but none of the combatants took them seriously and none of them took hold. One problem was that irregular forces were not fully under the control of the Serbian or Croatian governments. Twelve cease-fires were brokered and broken before the EC decided to impose sanctions. A thirteenth was negotiated and ignored shortly afterwards. Observers were sent to Yugoslavia, however, and some precedents were set that may be relevant for future peacekeeping operations. For example, at a meeting in Prague on August 8 and 9, 1991, the CSCE's Committee of Senior Offi-

cials—Yugoslavia concurring—agreed "to include other CSCE participating states invited by Yugoslavia" in the observation teams. Yugoslavia agreed to accept observers from the Czech and Slovak Federal Republic, Poland, Sweden, and Canada.[10] The observers are therefore CSCE sponsored, not just EC mandated. The costs are borne by the governments that furnish monitors. This is a model that is apt to be used again. It allows groups within the CSCE to engage in peacekeeping operations at their own expense while the full membership legitimizes the effort.

The EC did not want to send peacekeeping units to areas where a cease-fire had not yet taken hold. This has been one of the main obstacles to inserting peacekeeping forces into the war zone, and various ideas were floated to deal with it. For example, the EC mission to Yugoslavia in early August suggested that monitors of a cease-fire should consist of "units of the federal armed forces, representatives of the authorities in Croatia and representatives of the Serb population in Croatia in coordination and cooperation with European Community monitors." That EC suggestion failed when Serbia boycotted a scheduled meeting with the EC ministers and Yugoslavia's collective presidency.[11]

Yugoslavia also had its own cease-fire monitors, charged by the federal government with enforcing an "absolute and unconditional cease-fire" approved by the six Yugoslav republics. The observers consisted in part of plainclothes federal police from Macedonia and Bosnia-Hercegovina.[12] One of the members of the cease-fire commission reported on August 23 that the commission was unable to enforce a cease-fire because the federal army seemed unwilling to defend both Serbs and Croats. Instead, he said, he saw Serbian guerrillas wearing army uniforms and driving vehicles with army licence plates.[13]

Recognizing that the Community was placing self-imposed limits on the effectiveness of its mediation efforts, some EC members understood almost at once that escalation of the EC commitment might be necessary. As early as August 1991, Hans van den Broek said that he had "no great objections in principle" to deployment of an armed European peacekeeping force in Croatia.[14] The *New York Times* reported on August 1, 1991, that officials from France, Britain, and Luxembourg had privately acknowledged that military personnel might have to augment the EC observer teams.[15] Croatia would probably appeal to the Helsinki Conference and the United Nations for peacekeeping forces to be sent to the country, said President Franjo Tudjman of Croatia in early August, also according to the *New York Times*.[16] Nothing happened.

The president of the European Commission, Jacques Delors, remarked that "the Community is like an adolescent facing the crisis of an adult. It now only has the weapons of recognition and economic aid. If it were 10 years older, it might be able to impose a military peacekeeping force."[17] France had suggested in July that EC observers should carry sidearms for their own protection.[18] On September 11, 1991, French President François Mitterrand, referring to peacekeeping forces for Yugoslavia, stated that "if, for legal reasons, the United Nations excuses itself, France expects the European Community to take the initiative."[19] On September 17, the *New York Times* reported that Dutch officials had proposed a "lightly armed" force for Yugoslavia, not to impose a cease-fire but rather to use a European show of arms to discourage a resumption of warfare after a new cease-fire had gone into effect.[20]

John Tagliabue, the Balkans correspondent of the *New York Times*, perceptively summed up the situation as of September 15, 1991:

[E]fforts to establish a cease-fire, despite the presence of dozens of cease-fire monitors operating under the flag of the community, were failing miserably . . . the little war was increasingly becoming a test of the effectiveness of forging a common European foreign policy in a post–cold war world. With ethnic rivalries and nationalist conflicts like those in Yugoslavia abounding throughout newly democratic central Europe, the test was not going well at all.[21]

As if to underscore this judgment, the European Community foreign ministers, meeting on September 19, failed to reach agreement on organizing an armed peacekeeping force. Germany, France, and Italy had backed the Dutch proposal but Britain had blocked agreement. The British foreign secretary, Douglas Hurd, drew on British experience in Northern Ireland to make two points that certainly need emphasis in considering peacekeeping operations:

- It is easier to put troops in than take them out;
- The scale of effort at the start bears no resemblance to the scale of effort later on.[22]

It might be noted in passing that if the level of violence in Yugoslavia could be reduced to that prevalent in Northern Ireland the investment of peacekeeping forces for a few years would save thousands of lives.

The Western European Union (WEU), despite British hesitations, was asked by EC ministers to draw up contingency plans for the use of armed forces. Options developed by the military staffs of the WEU included a 30,000-man force, a lightly armed corps, and a force of 10,000 or fewer.[23] None of these plans was ever activated. The possibility of intervening with naval forces was endorsed on November 18, when the WEU foreign and defense ministers offered warships to protect Red Cross ships evacuating the wounded from Yugoslavia. Britain, France, and Italy were prepared to make warships available. Foreign Secretary Hurd said, however, that the offer would have to be negotiated with Serbia and Croatia.[24] The idea of small-scale intervention was discouraged by public statements by U.S. officials suggesting that the scale of any military effort to halt the fighting in Yugoslavia would be prohibitively large.[25]

The Serbs and Croats have themselves at various times favored the interposition of external forces and have said so publicly. For example, in its response to the EC peace settlement proposals in early November, Serbia stated that the federal army would withdraw from Serbian-populated enclaves in Croatia following the deployment in those places of an international force adequate to protect the Serbs in Croatia.[26] On November 6, President Tudjman reportedly said that "ideally some ships from the [U.S.] Sixth Fleet should be sent into the Adriatic and air traffic should be blockaded just as it was in the Persian Gulf war."[27] The most serious proposal was a letter to the UN Security Council reported in the media on November 9, in which the remaining members of the Yugoslav federal presidency asked for UN peacekeeping forces to provide a buffer between Serbian and Croatian forces.[28]

Chancellor Helmut Kohl of Germany and President Mitterrand, as early as September 19, had proposed that the Community seek a UN mandate for a peacekeeping force to establish a "buffer zone" between the warring forces in Yugoslavia.[29] The federal army had flatly opposed the introduction of peacekeeping forces, but this position was overruled in the letter to the UN from Yugoslavia's federal presidency. The Croatian foreign minister immediately welcomed the idea of peacekeeping forces and on November 13, Lord Carrington pursued the idea in conversations with the Serbian and Croatian presidents.[30] Not surprisingly, the Serbs wanted the peacekeeping forces to be inserted along the line established by the Serbian incursion into Croatia, while Croats wanted the forces to be placed along the republic's old borders.[31] Nonetheless, when the three EC members of the UN Security Council—Britain, France, and Belgium—drafted a resolution to implement the EC decision to seek an oil embargo, included in it was a request to the UN secretary general to seek a cease-fire that would last long enough to permit the deployment of UN peacekeeping forces between the Serbian and Croatian forces. Included also was a proposal for a mechanism to tighten compliance with a UN-imposed embargo on arms shipments to Yugoslavia.[32]

Activating the United Nations machinery created one immediate result. It shifted the burden of seeking a cease-fire from the European Community mediators to a UN team headed by former U.S. Secretary of State Cyrus Vance and Marrack Goulding, head of the UN Secretariat's peacekeeping operations. Lord Carrington had stressed the requirements for a cease-fire before EC peacekeeping forces could be introduced and Vance was just as emphatic about this prerequisite. No UN peacekeeping forces would be considered unless the warring factions had accepted a lasting and effective cease-fire.

On November 17, the day that Vance arrived in Yugoslavia to assess the prospects for introducing UN peacekeeping forces, the defenses of Vukovar, a city of key importance to Croatia, were overcome after three months of a siege conducted by the federal army and Serbian irregulars. The federal army at once began to move its tanks and artillery to the nearby Croatian cities of Osijek and Vinkovci, inhabited largely by ethnic Croatians. This movement was accompanied by new cease-fire negotiations among the Croats, Serbs, and the UN mission, which led to the signing of a fourteenth cease-fire by Tudjman, Milosevic, and Yugoslav defense minister General Veljko Kadijevic in Geneva on November 23. The cease-fire conditions were similar to those of earlier cease-fires. They included a requirement that Croatia should allow federal forces trapped at bases inside Croatia to go to Serbia. Another condition was that all paramilitary or irregular forces on either side would also observe the cease-fire, a very difficult objective to achieve.

Vance expressed the view that when they were deployed, UN troops should be inserted in an "inkblot" fashion to deal with "flashpoints," that is, areas where the situation was particularly tense.[33] This would sidestep the issue of whether UN forces would form a buffer at the border between Serbia and Croatia, as Croatia wanted, or between Serbian and Croatian forces where they were as of the time of the cease-fire, as Serbia wanted.

The fourteenth cease-fire lasted long enough for Vance to report to the UN Security Council that it seemed to be working. Thus encouraged, the Security Council on November 27 unanimously adopted a resolution that enabled Vance to return to Yugoslavia to work out arrangements for the deployment of up to 10,000 UN peacekeeping troops. Two aspects of the Security Council's action require special note. The European Community decided not to press for an oil embargo, thus once again dropping any real element of coercion. Second, the support of the Yugoslav delegation to the United Nations was indispensable to win the votes of India and other like-minded countries. Significantly, the role of the UN in resolving internal—as opposed to external—disputes was seen by these countries as unwanted meddling in domestic matters.[34]

Shortly after this hopeful action by the UN, Croatian President Tudjman announced that Croatia would accept UN troops in battle zones in the republic, not just on the border. Adding to the euphoria, federal army forces began a peaceful withdrawal from barracks near Zagreb. By December 1, however, coincident with Vance's return to Yugoslavia, the intensity of fighting had begun to increase. The UN mediator was obliged as soon as he arrived on the scene to express disappointment at the lack of progress.

Thoroughly frustrated by their experiences in Yugoslavia, the European Community's monitoring team in that country had drafted a highly critical report for the EC presidency. The report leaked as the fourteenth cease-fire began to collapse. The federal army's strategy, the report said, was to "pour heavy artillery fire onto a target . . . send in undisciplined irregulars, then move into the villages to reassume overall control." Military intervention by outside forces could deal with the situation, the report suggested: "There is good reason to believe that selective show and use of force—to intimidate and hit the J.N.A. [Yugoslav Peoples' Army] in places where it hurts can cow its bluster and bluff." The monitors accused the federal army of fighting only "for its own status and survival."[35] At the same time, the German government renewed its threats to recognize Slovenia and Croatia by the end of the year, whether or not other members of the EC agreed to do so. Bonn also imposed a ban on air, sea, and land links with Serbia. Partly to encourage recognition, the Croatian parliament decided to grant ethnic Serbian enclaves in Croatia a degree of self-rule.

Meanwhile, as Vance worked to create conditions that would win the Security Council's agreement to deploy UN peacekeeping forces in Yugoslavia, the Serbs increased the pressure on Osijek. Touring the city on December 3, Vance was reportedly shocked by the damage and subsequently protested to the Yugoslav defense minister over the shelling of the city.[36] Dubrovnik, too, came under renewed attack. In Bonn, Chancellor Kohl told the presidents of Croatia and Slovenia that Germany would grant them recognition before Christmas, a move opposed by the United States, Britain, and France. Some of Yugoslavia's neighbors, however, warned that they might follow Germany's lead. The concern of those opposing recognition was that this should await an overall peace settlement and that Serbia's response would be to escalate the conflict, rather than to negotiate.[37] Stepping up its own pressure on all the republics, the United States announced on December 6 a series of economic sanctions, to take effect on December 21.

On December 12, UN Secretary General Pérez de Cuéllar announced plans for a UN peacekeeping force of more than 10,000 troops. The force would consist of 10 infantry battalions and police units. It would be deployed in regions where Serbs and Croats lived in proximity to one another and would assist in humanitarian work, including resettlement of displaced people. The federal army would be withdrawn from Croatia. But the secretary general stipulated that "an effective cease fire" would have to be in place before the plan could be implemented. Clearly, from the secretary general's report, Serbian irregular forces continued to block an effective cease-fire.[38]

Efforts in the Security Council to organize a peacekeeping force coincided with efforts by Washington to block German diplomatic recognition of Croatia and Slovenia. On December 12–13, Deputy Secretary of State Lawrence S. Eagleburger gave "stern warnings" to the 12 members of the European Community that premature and selective recognition of Yugoslav republics would damage prospects for peace and lead to greater bloodshed. These warnings followed letters to the EC from Lord Carrington and Pérez de Cuéllar also cautioning against early recognition. In the Security Council, the British and French sought to head off the German action by sponsoring a resolution calling for military observers to be sent to Yugoslavia to begin arrangements for deployment of the UN peacekeeping force once a cease-fire had taken hold. The two delegations also proposed a clause that would warn against "political actions," that is, recognition that would harm the reconciliation process.[39] All this was to no avail. The German foreign minister, Hans-Dietrich Genscher, responded to the UN secretary general by asserting that denying recognition would only encourage the Yugoslav Peoples' Army in its "policy of conquest."[40]

The UN Security Council on December 15 adopted a resolution that watered down the nonrecognition appeal and authorized the dispatch of 18 to 20 military, police, and political observers to Yugoslavia. Reportedly, the United States had objected to a more ambitious French–British proposal to send as many as 100 military observers there.

President Bush added his voice to the debate on December 15 by saying "we want to see a peaceful evolution." Adding that the United States had been "strongly supportive" of the UN and of the EC, President Bush said "their advice has been to go slow on recognition, and I think they're right."[41]

Germany's advice carried the day, however, in the EC foreign ministers' meeting in Brussels on December 16. The ministers agreed unanimously that they would extend recognition by January 15, 1992, to any Yugoslav republics that asked for it by December 23, provided certain criteria were met. These included protection of minority and human rights, adherence to democratic principles, and respect for existing borders. The decision, however, would permit EC members to extend recognition even if the standards had not been met.[42] Thus, as the new year dawned, the conflict in Yugoslavia would cease being a civil war and become an international European war. The media speculated that fighting soon would spread to Bosnia-Hercegovina.

Lessons for the Future

Were there errors of commission or omission in the EC's mediation effort in Yugoslavia? The Serbs and Croats had irreconcilable agendas and seemed to prefer slaughtering each other to compromise. The general assessment of the leaders of the Yugoslav republics is that they are not men of great political stature and vision. The prospects for success—meaning a reasonably effective cease-fire accompanied by serious efforts to reconstitute the basis for relations among the Yugoslav republics—were never very bright.

Still, any critique of the EC effort must begin with an acknowledgment that the Community's hand was weakened by its apparent public repudiation of the use of armed force under almost any circumstances. In discussing the use of peacekeeping forces, it is essential to make a distinction between *peacekeeping* and *peace enforcing.* The former relates to a situation where a cease-fire has taken hold and where the principal parties to a conflict want help in preserving a shaky peace. Such forces are lightly armed and their mission may be compared to that of police forces. Peace-enforcing missions, in contrast, may operate in environments were a conflict is still raging. Their purpose is to impose a peace, rather than to preserve it. For such a purpose, well-equipped regular units are necessary and their mission is similar to that of a military campaign.

Some EC members, most notably France, seemed favorably disposed toward peace-enforcing operations but most of the EC debate was evidently focused on peacekeeping operations. It was the reluctance of some EC nations, particularly Britain, to authorize the use of peacekeeping forces under conditions of a shaky cease-fire that was most indicative of a lack of full commitment to the mediation effort in Yugoslavia. This meant, in practice, that the conduct of irregular forces, rather than republican governments, determined whether peacekeeping forces could be introduced. The tragedy of Yugoslavia was allowed to mount in intensity and to become a disastrous precedent for all the other disputes in Eastern Europe while the Community denied itself anything like the ultimate argument. The possibility that force would be used to deny military objectives to an attacker or to exact punishment for violations of a cease-fire by irregular forces was a consideration that neither Serbs nor Croats ever had to face. It was this void in the diplomatic process that obviously troubled the EC monitors and led to their cri de coeur to the EC presidency.

The risk of escalation to large-scale military involvement is always present once any military action is taken. Foreign Secretary Hurd was right to warn of that. The risks of not acting also may be serious, especially if Yugoslavia is a test case for how nations will behave in the post–cold war world. There were specific, quite limited tasks that could have been accomplished with the use of armed forces. These included protection of observers, reconnaissance overflights of disputed areas, constabulary duties, and protecting food and medical shipments to besieged towns. More open-ended and more hazardous tasks would have included overseeing the disarming of and providing protection for Serbian enclaves in Croatia and relieving federal army troops blockaded in garrisons in Croatia. The Community also discussed the idea of inserting military units as a show of force to deter violations in areas where cease-fires had been negotiated. There were moments when that might have been feasible. Carrying out these tasks would not automatically have resulted in the need to deploy several divisions of West European combat forces. Yet an inordinate fear that this might happen seems to have prevented a rational exploration at the political level of lim-

ited military actions, whether peacekeeping or peace enforcing, even the threat of which might have made a difference.

A second and related factor that contributed to the EC's inability to halt the fighting was the very low profile assumed by the United States regarding Yugoslavia throughout the latter part of 1991. The Bush administration preferred to leave the running to the Community and was immensely pleased with the Community's agreement to this policy. Occasionally, the United States made clear its support for the EC's effort and occasionally it denounced the actions of Yugoslav republics, particularly Serbia. It *chose* this course; it was not obliged to. It is also true that the allies, through misjudging the situation, missed an opportunity to concert their policies when the idea was raised in the North Atlantic Council in the fall of 1990 by the United States.

The U.S. effort in Yugoslavia bore no resemblance, of course, to the successful diplomatic offensives by the president and Secretary of State James A. Baker III in the cases of the Persian Gulf War and the Arab–Israeli peace conference. It is hard to escape the conclusion that the absence of a high-profile U.S. involvement weakened the EC mediation attempts and discouraged some members of the Community from contemplating the use of limited force in Yugoslavia. The lesson could be pushed still further: it is probable that the West European nations, divided as they still are, will not engage in peacekeeping operations in Central and Eastern Europe that require the use of armed force unless the United States is at their side. "Where the United States does not tread, the alliance does not follow."[43] The experience also showed once again that even the United States cannot set the rules of the game while sitting on the sidelines. Opposing recognition of Croatia and Slovenia was a policy that brought the United States into a head-on collision with its major European allies. The United States had little chance of winning that policy argument when it was contributing so little to the peace process.

There were two other factors that hampered the mediation effort, both questions of process, rather than principle. The first was the reluctance of the EC to escalate its pressure more rapidly than it did. It should not have taken 12 broken cease-fire agreements to persuade the Community that it had to raise the ante. By the time the Community decided to impose sanctions the war itself had caused at least as much damage to the country's economy as the sanctions were ever likely to cause. The time to impose sanctions probably would have been in July when the potential economic losses might have loomed larger in the minds of Yugoslav leaders. The indecision on this issue was another reflection of how difficult it is for 12 nations to conduct a common foreign policy.

Another process problem was the fact that other institutions that could have been actively and visibly engaged took a more passive stance than was necessary or desirable. The threat to international peace and security represented by the conflagration in Yugoslavia was not sufficiently dramatized or publicized during the latter half of 1991 in any of the forums that might have been utilized for this purpose.

The UN adopted an arms embargo, and the Security Council discussed Yugoslavia from time to time. "No one can tell us what the U.N. can do that would be useful," a U.S. official was reported to have said in September.[44] Late in the year, however, as we have

seen, the secretary general appointed a special representative, Cyrus Vance, who played a useful, even crucial role in developing the possibilities for application of peacekeeping forces in Yugoslavia. The UN was hampered, of course, by the worries of countries that wanted the UN to stay out of intrastate quarrels.

The CSCE's Committee of Senior Officials held several meetings in Prague without much notice by the media. The foreign ministers of the CSCE assembled only once, in June, for their inaugural meeting as the Council of Ministers in Berlin. The presidency of the CSCE Council of Ministers was held by German Foreign Minister Genscher, a strong supporter of the CSCE, but because of suspicions, especially in Yugoslavia, about German intentions in the Balkans Genscher was not able to be as effective in this role as his energy and skill would have indicated. The mandate that the nations fashioned for the CSCE Council of Ministers virtually precluded them from meeting for emergencies like Yugoslavia anyway. The result has been that the CSCE has been practically invisible throughout the Yugoslav conflict.

NATO, of course, issued communiqués but the Yugoslav issue was never portrayed as the main business of high-level meetings of the alliance. This was especially noticeable at the Rome NATO summit meeting of November 7–8, 1991. Assembling at a critical juncture in the Yugoslav agony and in a country adjoining Yugoslavia, the heads of state were preoccupied with whether U.S. forces should remain in Western Europe and with a new strategic concept for NATO. Of course they addressed the Yugoslav crisis by opposing the use of force to change existing borders. There was little recognition of the fact that Yugoslavia, not strategic concepts, was shaping the new world order.

The European Community had trouble making key decisions because of internal differences. Would things have gone better if one of the other institutions—NATO or the UN—had been handed the Yugoslav assignment at the outset? Considering the limits that the nations potentially involved imposed upon themselves respecting the use of military force, it does not seem likely that the Community's performance could have been much improved. It is, after all, national governments and not international institutions that determine what is possible. What Britain, France, or the United States were not prepared to do in one institution they were not likely to do in another.

Yugoslavia may be unique. But it also may be a paradigm for the kind of security threat that Europe and North America will face in the decades ahead. A central lesson of Yugoslavia is this: borders can be changed by force so long as the struggle is between successor states to a former union, and in such circumstances the international community will not react with force of any kind. This could be as deadly a lesson as Munich was in its time.

Steps Toward Contingency Planning

When anything like Yugoslavia happens again the international community should be better prepared for it. Among other things, a Europe-based peacekeeping force should have been trained and ready for use. The functions of such a force and the conditions under which it might be used should have been thoroughly studied. Realistic means should have been devised to help governments assess the risk of limited use of force as against the risk of major escalation of force on the one hand or the risk of no use of force at all, on the other. Facing unfamiliar problems in 1991, the governments that might have been effective in moderating the fighting in Yugoslavia shrank from taking resolute action. Next time, the kinds of problems that Yugoslavia presented should be seen in a broader perspective. If the pattern of Yugoslavia is repeated even once more, the road to war in Europe will be so well marked and the road away so obscure that war must become the norm. A commentary of Winston Churchill's comes to mind:

> We shall see how the counsels of prudence and restraint may become the prime agents of mortal danger; how the middle course adopted from desires for safety and a quiet life may be found to lead direct to the bull's-eye of disaster. We shall see how absolute is the need of a broad path of international action pursued by many states in common across the years, irrespective of the ebb and flow of national politics.[45]

And yet, a beginning toward international peacekeeping may have been made in the case of Yugoslavia. What positive lessons there are need to be taken to heart. The experience suggests that at least two levels of involvement by international institutions will come into play in this kind of situation. The first is the legitimizing action provided by the international community through a broadly based institution like the United Nations or the Conference on Security and Cooperation in Europe. The second is the operational responsibility assumed by some subset of those institutions. This has been the pattern tentatively established with regard to Yugoslavia and it seems likely to be repeated.

Thus, the UN or the CSCE in this model would give its approval to the principle that some action is necessary. Ideally, the state or states most directly concerned should join in this consensus. At this point, a smaller, action-taking institution or group of states would take over. This could be NATO, or the WEU, or a group of states that band together on an ad hoc basis, perhaps within the CSCE framework, for the purpose of mounting a peacekeeping operation.

This model could be important for the East Central European states and the Soviet republics, which need reassurance that collective security will work for them too. The former Warsaw Pact nations have not exhibited much interest in the CSCE as a security mechanism. They know that it is structurally impaired by its decision-making procedures. The requirement for unanimity almost guarantees that it will not be an action-taking operational organization. They also know that the United States almost never exhibits leadership in the CSCE in security matters and this, to them, is proof enough that there is no security to be found in this organization.

NATO could help correct this situation as an operating arm of the CSCE. But peacekeeping operations, as pioneered by the United Nations in many parts of the world, require skills that are different from those for which armies are normally trained. Because this is the type of operation that is likely to be most needed in East Central Europe, NATO should give priority to training some units in these skills. Indeed, if NATO is to be relevant to the real security problems of Europe, it is essential that the alliance accelerate such preparations.

The WEU also could prepare itself to take on such assignments. So could the CSCE, through its Conflict Pre-vention Center, if the nations authorized the center to undertake contingency planning and gave it a proper military staff.

There are five types of peacekeeping operations that might be needed in the future. The reality of these examples has been demonstrated in Yugoslavia. These are:

- to carry out humanitarian functions, such as organizing shipments of food and medicine under hazardous conditions;
- to observe a situation that contains some risk of conflict;
- to patrol borders or other sensitive areas;
- to establish a buffer zone between adversarial military forces; and
- to protect enclaves of ethnic minorities.

Such situations would probably subsume all of the possible crises that can be envisaged in Eastern Europe: ethnic disputes within one state, political subunits of one state on the verge of conflict with one another, and two states that are on a collision course over some unresolved issue.

The Yugoslav situation has highlighted the need to think through some of the practical organizational problems of peacekeeping that may arise in Europe. Contingency planning in NATO, the WEU, or the CSCE Conflict Prevention Center should be authorized so that governments will understand the issues that will have to be decided if they are ever to authorize military force in crisis situations. These include the authority to send and receive forces, national origins of forces, command arrangements, and readiness status. Three possible models for peacekeeping forces are illustrated in figure 1.

Model I is a system like the CSCE–EC relationship today. It is the most

Figure 1
Three Models of Peacekeeping Forces

Decisions Required	Model I	Model II	Model III
Authority to send forces	UN or CSCE	UN or CSCE	UN or CSCE
Authority to receive forces	Host central government approval or all factions involved	Host central government approval or all factions involved	Host central government or government of local jurisdiction
National origins of forces	NATO, WEU, and/or some CSCE members on ad hoc basis	Any CSCE member	Great powers only
Command arrangements	Commander appointed by NATO/WEU/subset of CSCE	Commander selected by director of Conflict Prevention Center with approval of states contributing	Commander selected for one-year term by contributing states. Each state serves in turn.
Readiness status	Responsibility of operational organization	Standards set by Conflict Prevention Center to permit deployment within 48 hours	Deployment possible within 24 hours. Joint exercises
Funding	Funding by nations contributing forces	Special assessment for all members	Great power funding

likely kind of peacekeeping because it assumes a UN or CSCE sanction for actions carried out by a smaller organization. A NATO peacekeeping operation sanctioned by the CSCE would be one example of how this model might work. Model II is a system based on the assumption that the CSCE itself could become operational through its Conflict Prevention Center. Model II envisages the possibility that the CSCE would develop its own peacekeeping capabilities relying, of course, on forces provided by member states but with a permanent and sturdy CSCE infrastructure that would provide some institutional glue. Model III assumes a case where the major military powers of Europe and North America jointly form peacekeeping units, under the aegis of the UN or the CSCE. Neither Model II nor Model III seems very realistic at present.

Each of these models assumes that the CSCE could supplement or substitute for the United Nations in future peacekeeping decisions, especially with regard to the very important legitimizing function. These expectations may not be realistic. The CSCE's role in the current Yugoslav crisis has been much more limited than might have been expected when the CSCE heads of government issued their "Charter of Paris for a New Europe" in November 1990. There are many reasons for this. Initial Soviet opposition to a peacekeeping role for the CSCE in Yugoslavia has been cited above. The aspirations of France and some other European nations for a common defense and foreign policy within the European Community tilted them toward the WEU. The unanimity rule in the CSCE gives Yugoslavia a veto over any decision in that body, thus suggesting that other institutions might better handle the operational aspects of peacekeeping in Europe. As for the United States, a press report claims that "European officials said the Bush administration has made clear that it wants no part of cease-fire monitoring efforts and only a passive role in mediation."[46] This, of course, made the EC an ideal choice for the United States.

There are sound reasons for developing regional peacekeeping machinery in Europe. The UN debate on the Yugoslav question in November 1991 showed clearly that non-European UN members are prepared to block peacekeeping operations for reasons having nothing to do with Europe. Ideally, the UN should encourage issues to be handled in a regional context so that the UN itself will not become overloaded. Conversely, as Henry Kissinger argued recently, "if global collective security is pursued too literally, regional institutions like NATO will gradually wither, and a threshold will be created below which local pressures and even aggressions may flourish."[47] If the UN were the only legitimate body for peacekeeping operations in Europe, the CSCE would gradually cease to have even a pretense to responsibility for security in Europe.

However it evolves, one of the main questions for countries participating in the CSCE is whether its requirement for consensus should be further modified in order to make this institution more effective in fast-moving crisis situations. If this cannot be done, the CSCE will probably be doomed to being a talk shop. Its crisis management potential, even in passing the

operational baton to NATO or the WEU, will not be fully realized.

It does not have to be this way. It is not too late for the members to turn their attention to strengthening the CSCE as a peacekeeping instrument, even while giving operational responsibility for peacekeeping to other mechanisms. Changes in methods of reaching decisions are needed, probably to include a qualified majority vote under clearly defined conditions. Investing in the contingency planning and operational capabilities of the CSCE's Conflict Prevention Center in Vienna is essential. NATO can help enormously in this respect. There should be an infusion of NATO talent and experience in Vienna. If amour propre is a problem, let it be a joint NATO–WEU contribution. Links to the United Nations should be forged so that the CSCE can develop into a regional peacekeeping organization in the meaning of the United Nations Charter. All of this demands U.S. leadership. Providing this will also provide at least some of the reassurance needed by the nations of East Central Europe and by the republics of the former Soviet Union.

Conclusion

Experience in Yugoslavia points out the need to think about the unthinkable—international intervention in internal struggles. It bears repeating that intervention in civil wars carries great risks and usually should be avoided. International peacekeeping forces may be necessary, however, to help contain the conflict within the borders of the affected state and to avoid dangerous precedents concerning frontiers. Mediation efforts must be accompanied by some element of military coercion if they are to be successful. And if one accepts the dictum that "all wars must

156

end," some wars might end with all the parties asking for peacekeeping forces. In such cases, third-party intervention with military force could be indispensable. Europe is very poorly prepared to deal with such problems. Furthermore, the involvement of the United States in maintaining peace not only in Western but also in Central and Eastern Europe is essential to long-term stability there. The evidence of traditional divergences of view between Germany, France, and Britain on East European issues has been quite clear in the case of Yugoslavia. It is equally clear that the voice of the United States cannot be heard very well if Washington is only offering advice from the sidelines. Most important, the unwillingness of the majority of the states directly concerned with the issue of peaceful change in the Balkans to consider the use of armed peacekeeping forces except under the most ideal conditions, and perhaps not even then, is a major setback to hopes for a new peace order in Europe. The stakes are too high to let this happen again.

Notes

1. Blaine Harden, "Yugoslav Republics Fear Crackdown," *Washington Post*, August 20, 1991, p. A–8.

2. Strobe Talbott, "Fiddling While Dubrovnik Burns," *Time*, November 25, 1991, p. 56.

3. Serge Schmemann, "A Moscow Report Expresses Fear of Following 'Path of Yugoslavia,'" *New York Times*, October 4, 1991, p. A–6.

4. Stephen Engelberg, "Europeans Try Again to Calm Yugoslavs," *New York Times*, July 28, 1991, p. A–3.

5. This is based on the reports by Blaine Harden and William Drozdiak under the headline "Yugoslav Peace Conference Scheduled," *Washington Post*, September 4, 1991, pp. A–21–A–22.

6. For more details, see the following articles. Blaine Harden, "Yugoslav Sides Accept Peace Pact," *Washington Post*, October 5, 1991, p. A–1; Paul Montgomery, "Serbian Chief Rejects Peace Plan at Yugoslav Parley in the Hague," *New York Times*, October 19, 1991, p. A–2; *idem*, "Bid on Yugoslavia Is Again Fruitless," *New York Times*, October 26, 1991, p. A–5; Chuck Sudetic, "European Countries Warn Serbs to Accept Plan or Face Sanctions," *New York Times*, October 29, 1991, p. A–10.

7. Chuck Sudetic, "Top Serb Leaders Back Proposal to Form Separate Yugoslav State," *New York Times*, October 24, 1991, p. A–17.

8. Alan Riding, "European Nations Declare Sanctions Against Belgrade," *New York Times*, November 9, 1991, p. A–1.

9. Stephen Greenhouse, "U.S. Goes Along with Sanctions on Yugoslavia," *New York Times*, November 10, 1991, p. A–1.

10. "Yugoslavia Agrees to More Truce Observers," Special to the *New York Times*, August 9, 1991, p. A–5.

11. Chuck Sudetic, "Serbs Refuse to Negotiate in Croatia," *New York Times*, August 5, 1991, p. A–6.

12. Blaine Harden, "Croatians Seek High-Tech Arms on World's Black Market," *Washington Post*, August 15, 1991, p. A–38.

13. Blaine Harden, "Clashes in Croatia Escalating; Army Pullout Deadline Looms," *Washington Post*, August 24, 1991, p. A–11.

14. Blaine Harden, "80 Croatian Police Reported Slain," *Washington Post*, August 3, 1991, p. A–15.

15. Alan Riding, "Europeans Try to Ease Croatia Crisis," *New York Times*, August 1, 1991, p. A–3.

16. Sudetic, "Serbs Refuse to Negotiate in Croatia."

17. William Drozdiak, "Lack of an Armed Option Limits EC's Yugoslav Peace Initiative," *Washington Post*, September 5, 1991, p. A–23.

18. Riding, "Europeans Try to Ease Croatia Crisis."

19. William Drozdiak, "Mitterrand Seeks Talks on USSR," *Washington Post*, September 12, 1991, p. A–25.

20. Alan Riding, "European Force is Proposed for Croatia," *New York Times*, September 17, 1991, p. A–3.

21. John Tagliabue, "Croatia's Dying Dream," *New York Times*, September 15, 1991, p. E–2.

22. Alan Riding, "Europeans Not Sending Peace Force to Croatia," *New York Times*, September 20, 1991, p. A–4.

23. Alan Riding, "Community Action," *New York Times*, October 1, 1991, p. A–8. According to conversations between the author and a well-informed source, Poland, Austria, and Hungary had also engaged in contingency planning for peacekeeping operations in Yugoslavia.

24. "Warships Offered for Yugoslav Aid Corridor," *New York Times*, November 19, 1991, p. A–7.

25. This was the sense in which the deputy secretary of state and former U.S. ambassador to Yugoslavia, Lawrence Eagleburger, spoke on the MacNeil–Lehrer Newshour in early November. See also Talbott, "Fiddling While Dubrovnik Burns."

26. Laura Silber, "Serbs, Croats Press War of Words, Guns," *Washington Post*, November 5, 1991, p. A–17.

27. Chuck Sudetic, "Yugoslav Fighting Breaks Cease-Fire," *New York Times*, November 7, 1991, p. A–10.

28. "Serbia Asks for UN Troops," Associated Press from Belgrade, *Washington Post*, November 10, 1991, p. A–49.

29. Riding, "Europeans Not Sending Peace Force to Croatia."

30. Chuck Sudetic, "House-to-House Fighting in Croatian City Nears End," *New York Times*, November 14, 1991, p. A–8.

31. Laura Silber, "EC Mediator Sees Hope for Yugoslav Truce," *Washington Post*, November 14, 1991, p. A–37.

32. Paul Lewis, "Three European Nations Propose a UN Peace Force for Yugoslavia," *New York Times*, November 14, 1991, p. A–1.

33. David Binder, "Yugoslav Rivals Sign a Cease-Fire," *New York Times*, November 23, 1991, p. A–21. Reuters, United Nations, "U.N. Sets Stage for Peace Force in Yugoslavia," *Washington Post*, November 28, 1991, p. A–67.

34. Paul Lewis, "U.N. Promises to Send Force to Yugoslavia," *New York Times*, November 28, 1991, p. A–1.

35. Chuck Sudetic, "Observers Blame Serb-Led Army for Escalating War in Croatia," *New York Times*, December 3, 1991, p. A–8. Laura Silber, "EC Lifts Yugoslav Sanctions, Excepts Serbia, Montenegro," *Washington Post*, December 5, 1991, p. A–9.

36. Reuters, Zagreb, "Lag in Cease-Fire in Yugoslavia Hindering U.N. Role, Envoy Says," *New York Times*, December 5, 1991, p. A–5.

37. Stephen Kinzer, "U.S. Is at Odds with German Backing for Slovenia and Croatia," *New York Times*, December 8, 1991, p. A–18.

38. Paul Lewis, "UN Peacekeepers Seen For Croatia," *New York Times*, December 13, 1991, p. A–6.

39. David Binder, "Bonn's Yugoslav Plan Faces More Flak," *New York Times*, December 14, 1991, p. A–3.

40. Evelyn Leopold, "Informal Accord Reached On Yugoslav Peace Force," *Washington Post*, December 15, 1991, p. A–42.

41. Paul Lewis, "UN Yields to Plans by Germany To Recognize Yugoslav Republics," *New York Times*, December 16, 1991, p. A–1.

42. William Drozdiak, "EC Envoys Agree on Recognition of Croatia, Slovenia Next Month," *Washington Post*, December 17, 1991, p. A–15.

43. This is a quotation from Charles Krauthammer's "The Unipolar Moment," *Foreign Affairs* 70, no. 1, *America and the World 1990/91*, p. 24.

44. John Goshko, "Yugoslavia Is Puzzling

Problem for U.S., Allies," *Washington Post*, September 22, 1991, p. A–31.

45. Winston Churchill, *The Gathering Storm* (Boston: Houghton Mifflin Co., 1947), p. 18.

46. Drozdiak, "Lack of an Armed Option Limits EC's Yugoslav Peace Initiative."

47. Henry Kissinger, "What Kind of New World Order?" *Washington Post*, December 3, 1991, p. A–21.

IV.
International
Security

Russia's Post-Revolution Challenge: Reform of the Soviet Superpower Paradigm

Stephen R. Covington and John Lough

BORIS YELTSIN, PRESIDENT of Russia, proclaimed in his June 1991 inauguration address that "Great Russia is rising from her knees. We will without fail transform her into a prosperous, peace-loving, law governed, and sovereign state."[1] The Russian people have roundly rejected Communist central authority, and a new Union of sovereign states has emerged from the economic and political ruins of the former regime. Russia's rebirth as one sovereign nation in this new Union has the potential to end Russia's cruel history of isolationism and totalitarianism, allowing the republic to take its rightful place as part of Europe. The absolute bankruptcy of the old political and economic system places Yeltsin and the Russian nation in a position as well to realign the Union's traditional national security priorities.

Russia now faces enormous challenges in this endeavor as it simultaneously rebuilds a nation and refashions a Union after the collapse of the

Stephen R. Covington is research fellow at the Soviet Studies Research Centre, Royal Military Academy, Sandhurst, England, and a senior analyst in the Central and East European Studies Group, SHAPE, Belgium. John Lough is a senior lecturer at the Soviet Studies Research Centre.

Communist Party of the Soviet Union (CPSU) and the central government. Russia's reconstruction will encounter every obstacle currently plaguing the nascent democracies in Central Europe. After decades of Soviet-style "barracks socialism," Russia will require all of its resources and energy, squandered for so long in the abyss of cold war ambitions, to revive and reinvigorate the Russian nation. This process alone will prove to be excruciatingly perplexing, with extended periods of political paralysis and economic disarray over the coming decade.

Russia and the new "Union of Sovereign States" also inherit the superpower paradigm of the Communist regime—its armed forces, its war economy, its resource priorities, and its military-theoretical framework. The most intractable obstacle for the new democratic leaders of Russia is reforming this superpower system. Political opposition to reform was vanquished with the coup of August 1991, but the inflexibility of "old thinking" was clearly mirrored in the structure of the Soviet Union's military system. This system was specifically designed to endure the calamities of a World War II–type great war. It is the result of over 50 years of military development and national priorities shaped by World War II and the Cold War. It remains resistant to rapid change even in the current period of profound national weakness because it was built upon a paradoxical foundation of profound social, economic, and technological limitations that eventually deformed and stultified the natural capacities of the former USSR. Its rigidness, resistance to change, and low tolerance for even the most modest adjustment complicate and may delay a decisive transformation of Union security policy.

The question now is not simply will Russia pursue reform, but can Russia achieve radical reform without social convulsions or the collapse of its military system? Coping with the legacy of the Soviet superpower system will place enormous pressure on Russia's democratic leaders as they attempt to balance economic reform, political sovereignty, and military security. This essay addresses Russia's struggle for control over the national security agenda, the possible directions of a new Union security and defense regime, and the critical, perplexing challenges facing the Russian state and the Union over the next 10 years as they attempt to remold the Soviet superpower paradigm.

Prelude to the August Coup: Russian Reconstruction or Soviet Reform?

Boris Yeltsin's June 1991 triumph in Russia's presidential election marked the beginning of a new political situation in the Soviet Union. Russia's peaceful democratic revolution had shaken the legitimacy of the Communist system at its very roots. A conspicuously ill-defined degree of Russian sovereignty had been achieved, however, without overthrowing the former system. Russia's rebirth did not remove the cardinal institutions—the last bastions of power—of the CPSU, still entrenched in the central government, nor had it broken the Party's control over the economy or its army. The Russian and Soviet power structure coexisted in a curious state of dual powerlessness, with each political entity seeking political renewal and economic recovery. An open clash of divergent national security policies and priorities between Russia and the central government veiled a decisive struggle for political power and control over the Union. The outcome of this clash between Russia's program of reconstruction and the central government's plan for Soviet reform would determine the future political hierarchy of the Union.

The Russian leadership was preoccupied with the development of institutions, legislation, and policies that would accelerate the process of Russia's renewal and economic recovery. The Russian government questioned the legitimacy of old security policies because it understood the severe economic and social dilemmas of the country. More important, initiatives in the security and defense sphere were the sine qua non to achieve Russian economic recovery and political stabilization. Demilitarizing the nation, removing Communist Party controls from the economy, breaking the monopoly of the military-industrial complex on the nation's resources, and reconfiguring the size and function of the army were important elements of national security reform. They were equally essential steps in removing the influence of the Party in Russia.

Yeltsin's speeches before the election typified the breadth of the Russian challenge to the Communist political system and superpower paradigm.[2] Yeltsin opposed any foreign aid, including aid to Cuba. He was opposed to nuclear tests in Semipalatinsk and Novaya Zemlya. He opposed calling up the reservists to assist in the harvest. In January 1991 he urged Russian officers and soldiers to not participate in the Soviet military's actions in the Baltic republics. Yeltsin sought Russian jurisdiction over production facilities throughout Russia, including military factories. He also ranked ecological security as a high priority, which would inhibit the military's unbridled exploitation of Russian land.

The Russian leadership also sought to pursue defense conversion on a far greater scale than the former central government had so far dared. The strategic need to match the military potential of the world around them had been the permanent security directive imposed by the Communist leadership since World War II and the principal reason for the Russian nation's economic misery. Even if the costs of conversion far exceeded the economic benefit for the consumer market, Russia's leaders sought to proceed with large-scale demilitarization of the economy to strengthen its statehood and to reduce the power of the CPSU in the Russian economy.[3] Russia simultaneously pursued the destruction of Communist control over both local government and economic relations amongst industrial enterprises. Yeltsin's decree of June 20, 1991, banning organized political activity at the work place and in local government aimed to ensure that a Russian government would no longer compete with the Communists for executive power in Russia.

New approaches to military policy that, above all, supported the security of Russia were also important in her transition to genuine sovereignty. Unless Russia obtained greater influence over military activities and the military-industrial complex on her territory, the new leaders of Russia would be forced to accept the notion of limited sovereignty. Notions of military reform circulating in the Russian parliament therefore focused on removing the most critical elements of the central Communist power structure. The Russian Republic draft concept on military reform, therefore, was as much a political manifesto as it was a draft military reform program. Its drafters believed that the Party-military apparat blocked military, economic, and political reform.[4]

The Union treaty portended a fundamental change in political decision making and in economic relations between the republics and the Center. The negotiations on the treaty from April to July 1991, taking place without the direct participation of the central government, were reshaping the political hierarchy of the Union according to the vital interests of the republics and not the select ambitions of the increasingly redundant Center. The end of the Center's monopoly on matters of security and defense would break through the secrecy of the military and the military-industrial complex, removing a major barrier to military and economic reform. A compromise arrangement between the Center and the Russian Republic also ceded to Russia some control over taxation and banking arrangements, weakening the basis of then–Prime Minister Valentin Pavlov's "anti-crisis program." This decentralization would drastically influence the Union defense budget. Moreover, participation in the development of the central government's budget would allow the republics to shape the budget into something more consistent with their own economic realities and vital interests.

As a result, the traditional approach to developing Union security policy and the traditional template for building a military superpower were being undermined by Russia's political offensive and the role accorded to the republics in the Union treaty. Control over national preparedness was shifting out of the grip of the Party-military elite and into the hands of the republics. Every quarter of the traditional Soviet political and superpower paradigm was under siege from the revolution outside the Kremlin walls. It was this revolution from below—the pressure from outside the narrow circles of Party-military decision making—that pushed the Soviet Union along a course of fundamental reform. These initiatives placed a huge strain on the Center's attempts to refashion a Union based on retaining as much power for itself as possible. Cumulatively, they placed enormous pressure on the Party's capacity to preserve its political and military system.

Mikhail Gorbachev's original policy of defense sufficiency sought to reduce strategic confrontation and lower strategic competition to a level adequate to guarantee the USSR's security while the Party leadership restructured the country's economy and army for a new round of intensified strategic competition in the twenty-first century. Perestroika itself had been the justification for diverse political aims in the Soviet Union. In the Party-apparat view, however, perestroika was a strategic national security program designed to overcome strategic disadvantages in military, political, and economic correlations of national power. Over the course of three five-year periods, the Soviet military leadership planned to acquire and infuse advanced technology into its economy and military.

Well before the August coup this long-term national security program had been overwhelmed by a succession of domestic calamities. In 1991, the Party-military elite was coming under even greater pressure. The strategic retreat from Eastern Europe, political turmoil, and economic chaos had left the Soviet army unprepared for a great war. The quality of the soldiery, a long-established concern, was worsening.[5] Soviet weaponry was perceived to be at an increasing technological disadvantage vis-à-vis that of the leading Western armies, and some of the elite officer corps returned from Eastern Europe demoralized and homeless. The armed forces' political cohesion, too, had been undermined. Most critically, the economic base that supported the military machine was already fractured in places. Economic disarray and chaos had already produced a spontaneous conversion in certain areas of the defense industry as traditional supply networks broke down and government orders were reduced. Even so, perestroika's 1990–1991 transformation from a national security program into a national survival program had not broken the central government's desire to sustain the traditional superpower structure.

The Party conservatives clearly believed Gorbachev's perestroika had failed to fulfill its promises. Six years of economic, political, and military restructuring had not resolved any of the strategic dilemmas confronting the Soviet military. In fact, these old strategic dilemmas were more acute in a fundamentally new, more disadvantageous strategic environment. This new strategic environment was perceived to have violated, if not rendered invalid, many of the principles of Soviet defense sufficiency.

The collapse of the Warsaw Pact and negotiations on limits on conventional forces in Europe (CFE) violated the principle of military-strategic parity in the minds of the General Staff. The Gulf conflict reaffirmed Marshal N. V. Ogarkov's forecasts of the character of future high-tech conventional warfare, exposing the vulnerability of a World War II–type defensive strategy when conducted by numerically and technologically inferior forces. Although the end of the Cold War had lessened tensions considerably and reduced the likelihood of war in general, the disastrous consequences of war—if one were to occur under current conditions—had raised concerns for Soviet security. This heightened sense of vulnerability, exacerbated by the military's perception that they had lost both the Cold War and World War II and the disarray associated with the unplanned, accelerated timetable for withdrawal of Soviet forces from Eastern Europe, had strengthened their desire to preserve the remains of their declining military power at the expense of reform.

The military also recognized that six years of perestroika had widened the technology gap between the West and the USSR. The Soviet military's program of reorganization for high-tech conventional warfare was paralyzed. Heightened Soviet concerns about force correlations with the West pushed the Soviet military to block economic reforms that undermined the priority of the defense industry in Soviet economic planning. This priority remained unchanged despite the precipitous decline in both Soviet economic production and social conditions.

The Party-military leadership believed that the internal erosion of Soviet power threatened to destroy the Soviet Union and its military system. The General Staff strongly contended that the preservation and modernization of the Union and the military system were needed—not reform. Distinct political convictions within the upper echelons of the officer corps had also motivated the General Staff to protect the army's role as an instrument of the Communist Party—not as an institution of the state. The March 1991 statement of Marshal D. T. Yazov, then minister of defense, that the "Soviet military's 1.1 million man contingent was the vanguard of the communist party and the [basis] for the party's political and moral authority" was as much a statement about his political convictions as it was a clear expression of the growing disillusionment of the military with the Party leadership's inaction.[6] Opposition to reform, however, was not solely based on political conviction.

CPSU control over national preparedness was placed in jeopardy by the Union treaty. The Party-military elite could create a superpower built to sustain strategic competition with the West only through the maximal extraction and exploitation of national resources. In addition, the deficiencies, inefficiencies, and technological inferiority in the building blocks of national strength and in the armed forces themselves justified the military-political leadership's direct control over national preparedness. This grip on national preparedness allowed the military elite, in conjunction with the Party, to divert the nation's resources to meet challenges to Soviet ambitions. Over time, this approach produced a distorted war or prewar economy, a highly militarized society, and the world's largest armed forces.

This direct control indeed was the foundation—the cardinal prerequisite—for producing and sustaining a military superpower shaped by the parameters of strategic competition with the West. Only this approach could maximize the military potential of the nation. Any fundamental reform of this traditional approach would lead to a substantial and unpredictable decline in military potential. In the view of the General Staff, not only would cardinal changes risk violating the principle of Soviet economic and military parity with the West, but they would also jeopardize the security of the nation. Moreover, attempted renovation of the Party in the perestroika years reminded the General Staff that any attempt to restructure an existing system even slightly risked precipitating its collapse. In essence, after years of debate and discussion on the reform of the Soviet military system and the Soviet army, the Party-military elite concluded that its military system, its approach to providing for the defense of the country, and its army, were simply not reformable.

This conclusion could be seen in the High Command's pronouncements on military "reform." First, they contended that the existing Union was the sole mechanism that could protect traditional national security constructs and facilitate an acceleration of military development. Any realignment of the Union, whether pan-Slavic or any other structure, would weaken its war organization. For example, Yazov remarked in spring 1991 that dividing the Soviet Union once again into princely kingdoms, as in Russia's past, would only hasten the conquest of Russia by foreign armies.[7]

Second, the High Command saw traditional demands and sacrifices imposed on society as being in line with the international situation and economic capacities. In fact, Soviet military planners continued to use the combined defense industrial capacity of the West as the baseline measurement for determining the size and technological character of the Soviet military-industrial base. Despite the clear advantages gained through the end of the Cold War, the retreat from the arms race, and the lowering of military confrontation, this basic formula remained enshrined in Soviet thinking about defense economics. For example, targets for Soviet tank production were apparently based on an estimate that the United States and Western Europe could produce together 75,000 tanks a year within six months of mobilization.[8]

Third, Soviet planners opposed genuine defense conversion, considered it "criminal," and believed conversion, in their definition, was entirely consistent with the strengthening of defense.[9] As a result, the General Staff attempted to spread conversion thinly, keeping a prodigious economic capacity that could be rapidly reconverted to military use.

Fourth, Soviet military requirements were still based on classic threat perceptions. CFE reductions in no way diminished Soviet expectations that a future conventional war would be waged on the scale of previous world wars. Whereas Soviet civilian reformers asserted that the inability of the Soviets to achieve their political aims in the Afghan War signified the increasingly limited utility of military power, the General Staff had apparently concluded that the Afghan experience only signified the inadequacy of the limited application of military power. As a result, General Staff planning sought to have a 3 to 3.2 million man army by the year 2000, supported by an 11 million man reserve.[10]

Finally, the High Command planned to introduce entirely new generations of military equipment during the last half of the 1990s. This plan retained, not reformed, the critical building blocks of the traditional Soviet superpower paradigm. It was also

168

designed to protect the institutions of traditional Communist power through the turn of the century.

In essence, the military faced technological shortcomings, economic constraints, and societal ills on a vastly greater scale than they anticipated. They were attempting to mold a military superpower for the twenty-first century along traditional parameters out of a nation that, in the absence of immeasurable sacrifice, was ill-prepared to match the military potential of the late-twentieth-century world around it. Yet economic weakness, social unrest, and political disarray had not engendered a desire to reform the system, however paradoxical this may seem to Western thinking. Instead, military leaders had conspired to encourage preservation of the system at the expense of reform even in the face of the intensifying limitations and constraints of the nation.

The Party-military apparat could not accept genuine economic or political reform either. An attempt to move to a market economy and market pricing was likely to expose a far more accurate account of the real costs of Soviet superpower status and debilitate the Party-military's ability to marshal the country's war economy. This alone would put the existing Party-military monopoly of national preparedness under great pressure. Similarly, devolution of political power to the republics would have diluted the country's war mobilization capacity. Either reform process would have affected deeply the General Staff's ability to use the economic, social, and technological capacity of the nation to sustain a military superpower along traditional lines.

In sum, Russian interest in removing the influence of the Party from the society, the economy, and the central government and its intent to pursue a foreign policy designed to return Russia to Europe after 70 years of a "failed experiment," directly challenged the CPSU's political power base and its centralized control over national preparedness. As a result, the Party conservatives' highest priority and most perplexing challenge was to preserve the traditional political system and its superpower paradigm, maintain the nation's traditional organization for war, and sustain a traditional preponderance of military power while accepting national weakness in certain areas of the civilian economic sector.

In response to these demands, the Soviet Cabinet of Ministers and the CPSU-dominated institutions in the central government developed an alternative plan in spring of 1991 aimed to renew the Union, reestablish central government authority, preserve Party control over the nation, pursue economic liberalization, and allow wider sovereignty for the republics. The Center's plan assumed that even a new Union would maintain the military paradigm of old, built on traditional approaches and implemented through the traditional institutions of Soviet power. This plan intended to preserve the USSR's superpower status through the Center's direct control over national economic and military-technological resources. This intent was at the heart of the power struggle between Russia and the central government. It threatened to jeopardize both Russia's economic recovery and its embryonic democracy.

The Russian and central governments therefore had widely diverging goals. The Russian leadership sought an acceleration in reform that could only be achieved with the collapse of the former system. The conservatives in the central government saw Russia's initiatives as threats to both their privileged position of power and the structure of the traditional Soviet superpower paradigm. Eduard Shevardnadze's revelations that the hardliners wanted to use military force in 1990 to prevent the unification of Germany were a sobering indication of the Party-apparat's priorities and problem-solving theories and a powerful indicator of the August coup.[11]

The Failed Coup of August 1991

The August coup has been widely interpreted as an action taken by Communist hard-liners to transform the Soviet Union once again into Stalin's orthodox, totalitarian regime. Political conviction indeed did play a part in the attempted coup. The coup, however, was not simply a political action to preserve the "Socialist Fatherland." It was an attempt—the last convulsion of the Party-military elite—to preserve Leonid Brezhnev's Soviet Union. The leadership of the military-industrial complex, the Party apparat, the Ministry of Defense, the KGB, and the MVD attempted to salvage, in effect, the Soviet Union's cold war national security policy, its cold war formulations on defense policy, and its war economy before fundamental political and economic disintegration of the "old" Union was codified in the Union treaty. In short, maintaining absolute control over national preparedness—the economy, the force mobilization base, and the armed forces—was the aim of the attempted coup.

The senior military leadership supported the aims of the coup for a number of reasons. First, the leadership of the High Command had always looked upon military reform as though it were an isolated process, an end in itself, shaped not by the real economic and scientific-technical capacity of the nation it defended but by the traditional parameters of strategic competition

with the West.[12] Meeting the requirements of strategic competition was the highest priority of the military leadership. Second, their insular existence as a secret state organization above society was critical in removing the military elites from the realities surrounding them. The system of special privilege, developed to appease elites that could not have power, removed them further from the nation they were ordered to defend. Consequently, the military's inability to comprehend the fundamental character of Soviet society contributed to their inability to understand social and economic conditions. The military leadership's understanding of their nation was shrouded in ideological blindness or blurred by a political culture where reality was subordinate to the tenets of a Leninist ideal.

The restoration of the "old" Soviet system in the midst of political discord and economic disarray therefore appealed to the military leadership. It promised political and economic stabilization and national and military strategic parity with the world around them. In particular, however, Marshal Yazov and other senior officers believed that the coup leaders' national policies would have sustained a military-industrial complex removed from the consumer economy, continued militarization of society through universal conscription of its citizens, and maintained Party-military control over national preparedness. In their attempt to preserve the "old Soviet Union," however, the Party-military apparat actually accelerated its disintegration.

The August coup, then, was a last-gasp attempt to preserve Brezhnev's Soviet Union. It failed, and a new Union political structure has surfaced. The coup also discredited the cold war security paradigm pursued by the

Party apparat, the conservative military, and the military-industrial complex. Clearly, the political drive imposed by the Communist regime to preserve a traditional superpower fixated on strategic competition with the West is now as illegitimate and artificial as the Communist system that created this goal.

The failed coup has also relieved Europe of a tremendous future burden. If the General Staff had pursued its 10-year plan in the 1990s based on the traditional criteria of strategic competition and profound economic shortsightedness, Europe could have confronted an even more unstable, yet arguably more capable, military superpower built upon an ever more weak, fragile, and distorted economic and political system. In the immediate wake of the coup, however, alternative concepts for a security and defense regime for the Union of sovereign states were raised that have substantial implications for future Union security policy.

An Alternative Security and Defense Regime

The genuine shift of political power from the Center to the republics will change national security policy decision making in the new Union. The experience of the August coup has left a very strong apprehension lest any Union apparatus, including the military, operate above republic governments without their direct political control. As a result, the former National Security Council (NSC), composed of the leaders of the KGB, MVD, and the Ministry of Defense, has been replaced by a new body composed of republic representatives; in the case of the State Council, the presidents of the 10 republics.

This new NSC composition is de-

signed to ensure that future Union security policy will reflect the mutual interests of the republics, not the select ambitions of the Center. With this type of body making national security policy decisions, Union security policy cannot be based on a simple balance of military power with the West without equal weight given to a balance and convergence of interests between Russia and the republics and between the republics and the Center. In addition, the new role of the former republics in economic policy promises that Union military policy would be more firmly founded on a genuine appreciation of the country's economic capacity, not spurred solely by traditional parameters of strategic competition.

This new approach to national security policy formulation will also change the political control over the Union armed forces. The chief of the General Staff appointed by Gorbachev after the coup, General of the Army V. N. Lobov, suggested that a new organization of national defense will come about after the forging of a new Union.[13] In his view, a new Union defense policy and budget would be developed based on coordinating the policies agreed amongst the republic ministers of defense and coordinated by the central Ministry of Defense. Each republic would constitute a single military district in which republic, not Union, governments would be responsible for carrying out the draft and supporting troops on their territory. Each military district also would be composed mostly of soldiers from that specific republic. The central General Staff would retain control over troop management, planning, organization of training, exercises, and strategy, and the allocation of modern weaponry. Control over nuclear forces would remain centralized. General

Lobov's vision may not be the exact model eventually adopted by the new Union. This model, however, is indicative of enormous changes in the character of future political control over the armed forces when contrasted with the Communist centralized model.

In the most optimistic scenario, future Union security policy would return Russia to its natural role as a great European military power with interests in Asia. As a consequence, this reformation of security policy would change initial assumptions of continued strategic competition with the West in even Gorbachev's original thinking. New parameters for the size of the Union army would emerge, leading to further force reductions over the next several years. Such reductions could only be achieved through a transformation in military policy and military doctrine.

The debate over the Soviet army's strategic offensive or defensive preferences may be replaced by a debate over the country's nuclear policy. Russia may pursue, and the Union may adopt, a Western policy of nuclear deterrence and flexible response as a way of providing for the security of the country while minimizing requirements for conventional forces. In this respect, nuclear stability at minimum levels would compensate for the technological and numerical shortcomings in Soviet conventional forces exposed by the Gulf conflict. It would also free the republics from the burden of matching conventional military developments in the West and allow these republics to place the maximum emphasis on economic recovery and the well-being of their citizens. This approach to military doctrine would resolve many of the questions concerning the proliferation of nuclear weapons among the republics. The security of the republics would conceiv-

ably be guaranteed by a Union nuclear arsenal, the size of which would be determined by the republics.

The creation of a new Union army controlled by a State Council with republic representation promises to provide a new, broader-based, and more stable system of political control for the armed forces, changing their political character. This transformation will end the traditional political stranglehold of central government ministries over all elements of the former Union's superpower status. Nevertheless, even if the political leadership elects to turn away from strategic competition, the new Union will still remain the largest conventional European military power and a strategic nuclear power.

Still, the reform of the defense and security regime faces enormous political, economic, and military-philosophical and military-structural challenges. To raise a new regime from the ashes of ideological and strategic-military competition with the West will be a complex undertaking. Severe obstacles remain in place, slowing military reform and complicating Russia's emergence from the former system.

Future Challenges and the Legacy of the Paradox of Soviet Superpower

The collapse of the Soviet Communist system and the former Union has ushered in a new era, a new political situation in the former Soviet Union. The old political mechanisms and structures proved to be inadequate to cope with the strategic dilemmas of economic disintegration, social disorientation, and military reform. This new political structure, however, has not resolved any of the strategic dilemmas that confronted Gorbachev for over six years. It has simply inherited them. This new Union structure now must stand the test of implementing reform. This process of renewal will be extremely difficult and unstable.

First, Russia and the other republics have changed the political structure and hierarchy of the Union. Yet, the relationships among the republics and between the republics and an emasculated Center remain ill-defined. The phenomenon of dual powerlessness that has plagued the former Soviet Union for over two years could continue, slowing Russia's reemergence and stalling its political drive. In addition, the failed coup compressed what was to be a protracted political struggle between the Party and Russia into three days. The rapid collapse of the Party apparat has left a massive power vacuum, which even President Yeltsin and Russia are finding it exceedingly difficult to fill completely. Moreover, the democratic structures of neither Russia nor the Union had matured sufficiently before the coup to allow for a stable post-Party political-economic transition. The Russian people themselves are embittered, distrustful of promises, and weary as well from the rigors of daily survival. This may deprive the Russian leadership of the support and commitment necessary to carry through vast, and inevitably painful, reforms. In this respect, the absence of the mature and deeply rooted democratic institutions essential to cope with enormous social transformations will place economic and political reform in peril for the next several years.

Genuine economic reform will require a sweeping transformation of society and the economy, not just its political superstructure. Gorbachev has been able to override opposition to reform by presidential decree. President Yeltsin has accelerated the collapse of the Party through presidential decree. Presidential decrees, however, do not solve the real dilemma of implementing political, economic, and military reform in society, a dilemma made more intractable by a Union with decentralized political and economic power and centralized armed forces. Moreover, the leaders of the new Union first have to transform the defense thinking of the Ministry of Defense, still a powerful institution in the new Union, before a new security regime can be adopted.

In the month following the coup, the Ministry of Defense salvaged its institutional power base in both the Union and Russian governments. The actions of Marshal Yazov and others discredited the senior Party-military leadership, not the military institution itself. In fact, the passiveness of the soldiers during the coup, the unwillingness of several officers to follow orders from the coup committee leadership, and the shift of allegiance on the part of several military units to defense of the Russian White House transformed the army in the minds of many Russians from the last bastion of Communist reaction to a trustworthy institution of Russian national salvation. This renewed role of the armed forces in Russia's sovereignty will make it exceedingly difficult for other, arguably weaker, institutions of state power to neglect the army or treat it with indifference. This was demonstrated early in Boris Yeltsin's presidential decrees following the coup, which gave servicemen increases in pay, tax benefits, and housing priorities.[14]

Nor will the General Staff abdicate its responsibility for ensuring the national defense of this new Union. Its formulations for the defense of the country will still influence the reconstruction of a Union defense regime. The General Staff, however, does not have a military-theoretical framework in place to accommodate a radical transformation of security and defense policy. For over six years, the General Staff has employed only standard formulas and traditional criteria. General M. A. Moiseyev stated in April 1991 that the General Staff had not even begun to formulate military-scientific criteria for defense sufficiency.[15] Moreover, the High Command's six-year struggle to preserve the military system was undertaken with the assumption that no far-reaching changes in the structure of the armed forces or defense theory would begin before 1996. As a result, the General Staff is unprepared to cope with a time-constrained, radical transformation of its military system and its armed forces. The military theory is not developed, nor has the political situation stabilized sufficiently to provide a strategic context for redeveloping military doctrine.

The Soviet minister of defense, Marshal Y. I. Shaposhnikov, has consequently stated that a considerable number of studies are now required for the future elaboration of defense policy and military requirements.[16] Achieving a radically new approach to security and defense, however, will depend on how well the Soviet High Command copes with abandoning its traditional approach to war and war prevention, which is deeply rooted in Russian experience. Is the General Staff, still approximately 98 percent Russian in composition, prepared to change its approach? The new political leadership's ability to shift national security priorities and adopt a new security policy depends on this reform of the military mind.

It is critical to recognize how deeply much of the General Staff's approach to security and defense is rooted in the Russian tradition. It is because of these antecedents that the collapse of Communist ideology will not automatically free the General Staff of its "old thinking" on military policy. For example, the allocation of vast resources for war was not just based on the ideological principle that the peacetime preparation for war against class enemies of socialism was the highest national security priority. Russia's history of repeated invasions by great European and Asian powers has led Russia's military planners to anticipate only a *great* war.

General Staff thinking was shaped by this history, which has made removing war from Russian soil a national undertaking requiring every resource of the nation mobilized under strong centralized control. Memories of the experience of World War II, still strong in Russian society, sustain popular support for a strong defense regime. If the General Staff concludes that a future European war will again call upon the resources of the nation as a whole, it will be extremely difficult to justify substantial reductions in the manpower or national-economic capacities for defense. In the past the General Staff has considered such changes to be profoundly destructive, jeopardizing both stability and security.

In addition, the military is accustomed to being responsible for establishing nationwide priorities and implementing measures for a multinational Union in peacetime to ensure the general preparation of the nation and the armed forces for war. Russia's sheer size and its unique geography have contributed to the military's requirement for centralized planning and control. It has also produced a military philosophy that stresses large-scale ground, air, and naval operations over vast areas.[17] As a result, strategic mobility will remain a cardinal force prerequisite for even the most modest Union defense regime.

The demands of commanding and controlling forces deployed over an area equal to the distance between San Francisco and Brussels in the presence of a generally poor national infrastructure have long combined to make any Russian military leader deploy large forces in peacetime, knowing full well that the country could not accommodate rapid force mobilization and deployment over these great distances in a crisis. Direct centralized control over the armed forces, then, not only made perfect political sense during the Communist era; it also made military sense because it compensated for the peculiarities and scale of the territory to be defended. The military will find it quite difficult to accept a degradation in this centralized military control, especially because the republics now have an equal political say in the building of the army, establishing reserves, and declaring war.

It is not, however, simply a philosophical inability to change defense constructs in the face of rapid change that delays the development of new constructs for national defense. The General Staff has relied on old approaches and traditional constructs in its thinking about defense for the last six years because its military system—the structure itself—has extraordinarily low tolerances for genuine change.

Imperial ambitions are counterproductive for a nation on the path to renewal and economic recovery. Yet the strategic competition of the Cold War remains institutionalized in the defense industry of the Soviet Union. The Soviet industrial economic base was conceived under the threat of war with Germany in the 1930s, developed in the midst of World War II, and expanded further through the logic of the Cold War. How does a leadership reform a war economy developed over the course of 60 years? Russian Prime Minister I. S. Silayev has revealed that 70 percent of the industrial enterprises on Russian territory belong to the defense complex and that production of civilian consumer goods only accounts for 26 percent of Russia's industry.[18] Any massive closing down of these industrial enterprises in Russia greatly risks multiplying the country's economic misery and disrupting its fragile political stability. Even Gorbachev, a frequent critic of a defense industry regime that has produced an internal technological barrier between civilian and military industry, has argued that one of the very few commodities the USSR can sell on the world market is modern weaponry.[19] It may very well be that the new democratic leaders will still not be in a position to challenge the military-industrial lobby.

General Lobov stated in February 1991 that technological superiority over the West was the essential aim of Soviet military weapons development.[20] As Soviet civilian economists have argued, the General Staff appreciates the effects of radical economic change but still has little understanding of the country's impoverished economic and technological base. This was best demonstrated in the High Command's priority of continuing series production of existing military equipment and the stockpiling of obsolete instruments of war at the expense of high-technology capital investment in the general economy.[21] Marshal Shaposhnikov has repeated the all too familiar call for quality in weaponry at the expense of quantity. The research, development, testing, and evaluation process in the Soviet procurement cycle, however, is deeply affected by lower production numbers. Consequently, the General Staff must struggle with the irony that a substantial increase in the technological levels of its military equipment will only come about with the continuation of the traditional reliance on series production.

These procurement reductions not only lower the number and quality of items of military equipment produced each year but also decrease the size of the economic mobilization base for war. Soviet specialists estimate that any converted defense plant will require over 10 years to reconstruct for the production of military equipment. The military would contend that this type of conversion places the USSR in a vulnerable situation in the face of a rapid economic mobilization capacity in the West. In essence, six years of perestroika document that the policy of war communism is far simpler to reform than a war economy.

A post-Communist military strategy is also constrained by a combination of the nation's inherent limitations and the legacy of the former system's priorities. For example, the Soviet army placed an overwhelming and distorted reliance on offensively oriented warfare. This traditional approach was not simply the result of Communist ideology. Rather it was equally the result of a clear understanding of the country's economic limitations in relation to the West. Because war is a contest of national economic potential as much as a battle between opposing forces, Soviet strategists understood that a protracted war would only accentuate the economic limitations of the Soviet state and erode any advantageous prewar correlation of military power. As a result, traditionalists in the High Command may maintain that future military strategy must retain its offensive emphasis to compensate for an inferior and worsening economic base for war.

Soviet military strategy is constrained as well by its force structure and equipment design. The current Soviet army is the product of several generations of emphasis on a unique style of offensive warfare. Three five-year plans of military development have been shaped by the pursuit of maximizing the offensive strike power of the ground forces, in particular, and of the conventional forces in general. Simply reducing the numerical strength of the armed forces limits their options and capacity for war but in no way changes the Soviet army's offensive orientation. Essentially, force structure experiments over the past few years have convinced the General Staff that removing one-half of the tanks from a Shock Army does not create a defensive army but simply creates a Shock Army without half its tanks.

Moreover, the General Staff is reluctant to adopt a strategic plan of military action that does not jibe with this predetermined mission.[22] In the Staff's view, this would constitute an imprudent misuse of military potential at a time when the General Staff may still feel the need to maximize its fielded military power. The Soviet General Staff is inclined by experience, therefore, to believe that it would be extraordinarily difficult to transform an army designed and equipped for shock into an army designed and equipped for reaction. This was reflected in the General Staff's 1990 emphasis on the strategic counteroffensive operation as the most decisive phase of a strategic defensive battle and in the renewed emphasis on the strategic offensive in Soviet military doctrine.[23] Consequently, the military leadership will have an extremely difficult time adopting a defensive military strategy of flexible response if it feels compelled to seize the operational and strategic initiative at the outset of hostilities.

In sum, the military feels its war capacity shifts precariously between absolute superiority and defenselessness with even the finest readjustment of its force posture and strategy. Successful military reform will require a fundamental reappraisal of traditional stability modeling, a clear understanding of the country's economic and scientific-technical status, and a capacity to come to grips with the new strategic environment without resorting to old solutions firmly ingrained in the Russian military tradition and institutionalized in the former system's political and military priorities.

The critical challenge facing the new democratic leadership of Russia and the Union during this era of profound weakness in every sphere of national endeavor, however, is the task of reforming the paradoxical paradigm of Soviet superpower. The former system's superpower capabilities were not built upon a flexible foundation of economic and social strength. The system was molded by the constraints of inherent and enduring economic and social weakness. Every component of the system was designed to compensate for deficiencies in other areas. For the sake of cold war superpower ambitions, these limitations were allowed cumulatively to stretch and distort the natural capacities of the nation, deforming its economic structure. The Party-military apparat's military paradigm developed a superpower capability despite the character of its economic and scientific-technical base. Grossly distorted civilian economic development was the price paid for a country run on a reliable—and permanent—war footing. It remains an unwieldy and inflexible base for the

pursuit of a rapid and radical transformation of the economic and social system and a constraint to the democratic evolution of the political system.

Conclusions

Russia and the other republics will attempt to initiate fundamental reform of their military, economic, and social-political structures. The foundation for the reform process is fragile aspirations, vague notions of democracy, economic disarray, political misgivings, and a general sense of resignation in society. The scope of this endeavor alone makes for a very uncertain outcome and an unpredictable Europe in the decade ahead. Moreover, many of the difficulties in reforming the Union after 70 years of Communist rule have yet to be encountered. Not only is every component of national reform totally interdependent, but each republic's success or failure along this path will have a significant impact on regional stability and European stability as a whole in the post–cold war era. The collapse of the former Communist political system and the security structure of the new Union of Sovereign States gives promise that this national restructuring will take place through a peaceful political process.

Russia is certain to exert a powerful influence on the national security and defense policy of the new Union. Prior to the August coup Russia's leaders stated unequivocally that Russia must either remain a military superpower at the expense of economic reform or pursue economic reform at the expense of its traditional approach to superpower building. There were no hybrid approaches, no trade-offs, and no ready-made panaceas that would allow Russia both economic recovery and maintenance of its military superpower status along traditional lines. Moreover, the past few years of perestroika testified that any half-measured, hybrid attempts would neither produce economic reform nor sustain a superpower. Clearly, the radical, decisive domestic and security policy initiatives Russia pursued prior to the coup were equally critical components of its political struggle, which was designed to usurp power from the Communists in the central government and take firm control over the national agenda. Russia's decisive initiatives were taken to break down the system for political gain. Now Russia faces the challenge of reforming the very same structure for the purpose of creating a stable base of national sovereignty and independence. Moreover, the defense industry's dominance of Russia's industrial capacity will be a persistent constraint on pursuing reform.

As a consequence, much of Russia's pre-coup deliberate plan to tear down the Soviet superpower paradigm will be modified. It will extract the country from the vicious cycle of strategic competition with the West. It will retain in good measure, however, a healthy, robust, defense capability. Europe will not witness the demilitarization of the Union. The new Union will remain a conventional military superpower by any definition because of its unique geostrategic situation and will integrate a European defense regime with its own security requirements along its southern and far eastern rims. Its nuclear arsenal will ultimately guarantee the country's security and stability as it painfully rebuilds its collapsing and deformed infrastructure.

Over the next 10 years, this reform process will redefine national security policy and reconfigure the criteria for superpower sufficiency. The new Union security policy will eventually pursue a new round of intensified arms reductions—nuclear and conventional—as it attempts to secure a stable and advantageous balance of power and interests with nations around its periphery. Consequently, arms control will remain a very important security instrument for the future with new partners, new criteria, and new geographical parameters. This new security policy and new arms-reduction regime, however, will only come about after the elaboration of new models and reweighing of new determinants of security and stability. These new models for strategic stability are as critical to future European security as is the new Union structure to regional political and economic stability. The High Command must come to accept that European wars are not winnable because of new global and military strategic models, not simply because the Russians are currently unable to win one under present conditions. The acceleration in European transformations makes genuine reform of old strategic models in the High Command urgent. This revolution of the mind is crucial, and its successful accomplishment will have significant implications for European stability and security at the turn of the century. In this context, even the new leaders of the General Staff have questionable credentials as radical security reformers with a firm grasp of the nation's economic condition.

Before it proceeds with changes, however, the West must wait for the new political and military leaders to conceive and develop a new security and defense regime based on a new model of stability and security. A stabilizing Western policy must be based on the conclusions of this reexamination of the criteria of stability and security and the emerging strategic situation. The past six years of change in the former USSR are clear evidence of the very narrow margin between restructuring and reform. Three years ago the General Staff was preoccupied with preserving the Warsaw Pact's capacity for theater strategic operations after unilateral Soviet force reductions. One year ago, with the Warsaw Pact in tatters, the General Staff reaffirmed its traditional military strategy and doctrine and was attempting to maximize its forces under severe constraints imposed by CFE requirements. In August, the Party-military apparat desperately tried to maintain its control over the nation's traditional mechanism for war preparedness and to sustain a cold war–type military superpower through the turn of the century. The Cold War ended with the coup of 1991, not the collapse of Eastern Europe in 1989. It is, then, important to recognize that the decisive collapse of the Party structure has been matched by an equally indecisive appearance of democratic structures. In essence, the process of genuine reform has not been completed, the former system's collapse only signaled its initiation.

The future security policy of the Union of Sovereign States will seek to ensure that Europe will not remain burdened by an unstable military superpower sustained by a deformed, inefficient, and technologically backward economy. It will attempt to build the Union's national security upon "new parameters of sufficiency" that reflect the vital, mutual interests and goals of its members. But the new leaders inherit a military system that perpetuated technological drain and economic instability for decades, to the point that national security was undermined, not strengthened. The shortcomings and limitations inherent in the traditional system produce a military capacity that constrains even broader-based political and economic initiatives in times of peace and could exacerbate decision making in times of crisis. For over 40 years, the Soviet war economy produced an armed force that cast an intimidating shadow over Europe's economic stability and political security. The challenge of European political evolution and economic integration will be made more complex and acute over the next several years by the legacy of the very same Communist superpower paradigm.

The views expressed in this article are those of the authors and do not reflect the official positions of any of the organizations with which they are affiliated.

Notes

1. President Boris Yeltsin's inauguration address at the Kremlin as carried on the Russian Television Network, Moscow, July 10, 1991.

2. For example, Yeltsin's speech at a meeting organized by the group Democratic Russia at the October Theater in Moscow as reported by Radio Rossiya Network on June 1, 1991.

3. V. Rubanov, "National-State and Information-Legal Factors of Military Conversion in the USSR" (Presentation at the third session of the Round Table on Issues of European Security, National Defense University, Washington, D.C., March 14–21, 1991).

4. Vladimir Lopatin, "Draft Concept on Military Reform." Lopatin, deputy chairman of the Russian Liaison Commission to the USSR Ministry of Defense and the KGB, presented this paper at the Swedish National Security Institute, Stockholm, in February 1991. It was published in *Soviet Military and Political Reform*, the proceedings of a symposium sponsored by the Swedish National Defense Research Establishment, in February 1991.

5. In July 1991, the Soviet armed forces reportedly were over half a million short of their complement of conscripts. "Conscription is Over. There is No One to Serve," *Izvestiya*, July 22, 1991, p. 2.

6. Marshal D. T. Yazov, "At a Fundamental Stage," *Krasnaya Zvezda*, April 2, 1991, p. 1.

7. Marshal D. T. Yazov, "Your 'Yes Vote' is For Renewal," *Krasnaya Zvezda*, March 16, 1991, p. 1.

8. "Military Reform and the Ground Forces," *Krasnaya Zvezda*, April 18, 1991, p. 2.

9. Aleksandr A. Prokhanov, "A Visit to General Rodionov's Office," *Den'* (Moscow), no. 9 (1991), p. 1.

10. "The Concept of Military Reform," special edition of *Voyennaya Mysl'*, no. 11 (November 1990), and General M. A. Moiseyev, "Military Reform: Realities and Perspectives," *Krasnaya Zvezda*, June 12, 1991, p. 2.

11. "The Situation is Greater Than Life," interview with Eduard Shevardnadze, *Literaturnaya Gazeta*, no. 14 (April 10, 1991), pp. 1, 3.

12. "The Dynamics of Parity," *Krasnaya Zvezda*, June 25, 1991, p. 2, and "Conversion and Military-Strategic Parity," *Krasnaya Zvezda*, June 5, 1991, p. 2, typify the Soviet military's discussions on requirements for security with little, if any, consideration of the economic capacity of the state.

13. "General V. Lobov: The Army Needs Radical Reform," *Trud*, August 29, 1991, p. 2.

14. Reported by Tass on August 30, 1991.

15. General M. A. Moiseyev, "Problems of Security: A Considered Approach is Needed," *Izvestiya*, April 6, 1991, p. 6.

16. Moscow Radio World Service, interview with Marshal Y. I. Shaposhnikov, 1210 GMT, August 27, 1991.

17. Christopher N. Donnelly's *Red Banner* (London: Jane's Publishing House, 1988), is an excellent study of the influence of Russian traditions and history on Soviet military thinking.

18. "Ivan Silayev: We've Already Won Back the First Half," *Ogonek*, no. 24 (1991), p. 2, and "If There is a Strong Russia There Will Be a Strong Union," *Mezhdunarodnaya Zhizn'*, no. 6 (June 1991), p. 11.

19. Gorbachev's speech in Khabarovsk, as reported in BBC Monitoring of World Broadcasts, SU/1048 B/1, April 17, 1991.

20. General V. N. Lobov, "The Course to the Realization of the Concept of Sufficiency for Defense," *Voyennaya Mysl'*, no. 2 (February 1991), p. 15.

21. A. Ozhegov, Y. Rogovsky, and Y. Yaremenko, "The Conversion of Military Industry and the Transformation of the Economy of the USSR," *Kommunist*, no. 2 (1991), pp. 54–64.

22. The wholesale destruction of Soviet-produced military equipment in the Gulf War has focused analysis on the technological inferiority of the Soviet equipment used by Iraq in comparison with the coalition's modern equipment. But this technological dimension of the Gulf conflict was not as great a factor in the defeat of Iraq as the use by the Iraqi leadership of this Soviet equipment in a defensive operation for which it was never intended. This dysfunctional use of Soviet weaponry actually magnified the technological inferiority of the equipment itself.

23. General Colonel I. N. Rodionov, "About Several Elements of Soviet Military Doctrine," *Voyennaya Mysl'*, no. 3 (March 1991), p. 7.

Old World Disorders

James C. Clad

ALTHOUGH THE RELENTLESS unraveling of established political order within the former Soviet Union, Yugoslavia, and other Central European states has seized Western attention in recent months, much more redrawing of the world's political map lies ahead—especially in regions we still describe, for want of a better word, as the Third World. The magnitude of this change can scarcely be overemphasized; by comparison to the fault lines opening beneath dozens of bogus "nation-states" created after World War II, Europe's ruptures will come to look like simple hairline fractures.

With every passing week the news from Europe makes us realize how much the old, bipolar confrontation propped up many rickety states or suppressed the ethnic discord within them. But we have yet to realize that most of the world's feeble sovereignties lie well outside Europe; after two waves of state-creation following World Wars I and II, a superabundance of cardboard governments now clutters the membership rolls of international organizations. Within them, as in Central Europe, ethnic discord threatens the state; within them, far more than in Europe, a collapse of even minimal civic standards augurs the rapid disappearance of the state.

One notion has sustained the exis-

tence of third world sovereignty—the European model of the nation-state. Self-determination for colonial peoples became global orthodoxy 40 years ago as the decolonization period began, meshing two, incompatible ideas. The first was the notion that separate peoples require a separate state. The second was insistence, by colonizer and colonized alike, that frontiers positioned during the colonial era should remain as markers for this new "national" identity, even if (as was invariably the case) they were drawn with little heed to achieving coincidence of ethnic geography with boundaries.

This contradiction hardly slowed the decolonizing momentum. Sovereignty alone, it was thought, would prove a transportable and expandable concept, adding scores of new building blocks to the international system. Transportable, yes, but not workable: like flying buttresses of stone holding up cathedral walls, superpower rivalry lent these entities a semblance of solidity. So did the dozens of conventions, protocols, and other instruments that characterize the international system of customary state relations.

But political priorities are another matter. And today, without great power rivalry, there is scant reason to care if territories such as Somalia, once described as a strategic patch of sand, have degenerated into warring sandboxes. If the resolution of the Yugoslav, Moldovan, Georgian, Azeri, and other Central European crises now depends (as American and European di-

James C. Clad, a journalist and former diplomat, is a senior associate at the Carnegie Endowment in Washington, D.C.

plomacy implicitly shows it does) on those who inhabit these lands, the Western powers are even more disinclined to intervene in the Third World to determine the outcome. Only one result is clear: the outcomes cannot square with a continuation of the original, decolonized state erected 20 or 30 years ago.

The remainder of this article looks beyond the fading of global confrontation to another, and far more compelling, reason for the lengthening of the roll call of "national" failures. The disappearance of the outside buttressing occurs at a moment when decay *within* these flimsy sovereignties dooms many to dismemberment or chaos.

In the Third World, as noted, few territorial lines correspond to national affinities. Frontiers too often cut across peoples rather than define them. The second wave of state-creation in our fast-ending century occurred just 35 years ago; it went far beyond the European and Middle Eastern focus of the first wave of the post–World War I era, which crested on the Wilsonian ideal of self-determination.

The entities spawned by the second wave, during the 1950s and 1960s, are now slipping into chronic failure. The demographics alone portend growing Malthusian distress in places like the Philippines, Kenya, and Bangladesh. Successive economic strategies—articulated by patronizing outsiders (Marxists or free-marketeers) or by local wise men (Tanzania's or Cambodia's own brand of indigenous socialism)—have failed.

One by one, the aid experts' prescriptions—privatization, smokestack industries, training, "basic needs," appropriate technology, or whatever—have been tried and discarded. Meanwhile, it is getting harder and harder

for indigenous elites to find excuses. Even the currently fashionable, free-market dogma cannot fill the gap. The international free-trading economy may have bestowed wealth on a lucky group of East Asian countries (and on lucky enclaves within those countries), but export-led industrialization cannot become a universal model.

The reason is simple. If the predominant local "civic culture" favors extraction rather than investment, whatever modest comparative advantage accrues from producing better bananas or hosting the cheapest sweatshop industries will do little to permanently deepen and broaden their economies. Some "national" economies, in any event, are permanently disadvantaged by an out-of-the-way position, by local costs, or by diminutive size. Most South Pacific or Caribbean microstates are already resigned to marginality, while other territories, large in size but slender in resource endowment (or the hard commodity of humankind), have experienced stagnation for two decades.

Meanwhile, third world poverty grows worse with the incessant pressure of numbers. The lure of out-migration to the West assumes a burning, immediate appeal, vitiating any remaining attraction of the original—albeit invented—postcolonial nationalism. Negative reactions in the West to third world migrants—bound to arise in the United States as well—augur poorly for these hopes. Nor is democracy the panacea. In a great swath of the non-Western world, little correlation exists between political participation and economic success. Asia's most voluble country, the Philippines, has recurrent elections and a vibrant if sensationalist free press; these survive robustly beside abject administrative failure and economic distress. Contrast this to the authoritarian ways of Singapore (or Taiwan or Korea), which do little to impede their growth.

During the 1980s, many popular disturbances in Asia seemed motivated by pro-democracy yearnings. Yet the 1986 eviction of Ferdinand Marcos has brought scant improvement in the governance of the Philippines. The Korean opposition, in 1987 and afterward, shows plenty of authoritarian yearnings. Cruelly quelled in 1988, many of Yangon's students retain Burmese chauvinist attitudes to adjacent minorities. And the hyperbole over the events in Tiananmen Square in June 1989 ignores the hard truth that absolutely none of the People's Republic of China's (PRC) neighbors, then or now, wanted to see a narrowly based "democratic" turmoil displace firm leadership in Beijing. Sadly, perhaps, the PRC's export growth continues—inconveniently alongside continuing authoritarian Communist rule.

Now we read of a new wave of democracy sloshing over Africa. Elections in former strongman states bring patronage-hungry parliamentarians into tattered capital cities. Although touting the free market, Africa's "democratic" patrimonialism may—for want of serious civic culture—deliver results little different from the extractive excesses of dictatorships supposedly fading from the scene. Indeed, when it comes to governance, seasoned folk wisdom in much of the non-Western world favors *retaining* politicians, not evicting them, especially those with long tenure and sizable girth. In the scramble for spoils, it is the inexperienced politicians who push corruption levels through the roof.

The argument can be expanded by reference to a successful Asian economy. In Bangkok, the local Chinese and foreign business communities

agree that the "efficiency factor" of corruption eroded under former prime minister Chatichai Choonhavan's government—thrown out by the Thai military in January 1991. What do they mean by this? Southeast Asian economists describe "inefficient" corruption as lacking the once-only, pass-on cost to investors that "efficient" corruption contains. Now, under Thailand's military-dominated regime, corruption is more factorable again—even if jolted by displays (as in May 1992) of military ruthlessness against civilian dissent.

To take another example, in Nepal an electoral system reluctantly accepted by the monarch's self-aggrandizing family has *quickened* despoliation of that mountainous country's few remaining timber resources since free elections in 1990. Long-time opposition politicians, notably within Nepal's Congress party, have seen the chance to win and distribute favors—a result that is swiftly adding to the number of despoilers of Nepal's already degraded environment. "Democracy" enables more vociferous support for ethnic Nepalese rebels who butcher policemen in the neighboring Buddhist kingdom of Bhutan (where King Jigme Wangchuk protects the environment and maintains a far more approachable government than the one in "democratic" Nepal).

Against a dismal political culture, what difference can written charters or basic laws make? Take the newest constitution adopted in Colombia. One of the world's longest such laws, it brims with civic goodwill. Dozens of clauses guarantee liberties and grand entitlement but the parchment promises cannot paper over a political culture founded on guerrilla armies, drug cartels, and acute poverty. The Thais have received their seventeenth constitution since 1932, one that entrenches military nominees in the Senate. The Filipinos are working under their ninth constitution. It makes little difference to the standards of governance.

As it happens, a favored few in the Third World *do* enjoy democracy as the West knows it, although not very often in their own countries. Many people of humble means find freedom by moving to the West. And coincident with the annihilation of distance by air travel and by telephone, ever more of the Third World's elite have become thoroughly cosmopolitan. Privileged families park their money and their children in North America or in Western Europe while treating their homelands as medieval fiefs. Many emigres, such as prominent Filipinos or Central Americans, run extensive patronage empires by telephone while overseas Chinese conduct their business the same way from Vancouver or Perth.

The huge disparities in capital flow out of the poor countries of the world certainly favor the rich First World. The U.S. banking system should be thankful for these assets, which have played no small part in preserving positive equilibrium in U.S. capital flow accounts. But as Robert T. Naylor's *Hot Money and the Politics of Debt* describes it, much of this one-way flow results from emigres pocketing aid money commissions, drug profits, or monopoly gains.[1]

As recent writing within the World Bank about governance makes clear, the quality of administration found in too many third world sovereignties is often indistinguishable from simple looting. Of course, many exceptions exist. Industrious, successful enclaves survive within wider lethargy and failure. In spite of the Philippine malaise, the tiny island of Cebu expands its export zone. Against the torpor of rural India, the dynamism of Puna and the high-tech suburbs of Bangalore make for stunning contrast. Strikingly competitive businesses occasionally surmount the immediate importunities of grasping local politicians or warlords.

But the record of success is short. These and other exceptions cannot outweigh the failure that has predominated throughout the Third World during the last 30 years. And the reason for this state of affairs goes well beyond the presence, or absence, of democracy or even good government, reaching instead right down to the core of identity itself.

No "There, There" Out There

From the perspective of loyalty and legitimacy, there is simply not much "there, there" in two-thirds of the entities masquerading as nation-states. To be sure, this lack of political cohesion in ex-colonial and non-Western territories has become more glaring as cold war politics disappears: without the Great Game with the Soviets, the rich Western world now has fewer reasons to care.

What matters today is the order of priorities for the rich, Group of Seven countries. Rescuing "sovereignties" without foundation will not matter much unless, as in Kuwait, strategic reasons counsel otherwise or, as in Yugoslavia, the proximity is too embarrassing. And yet, even in this force-fed collection of mutual hatreds, a sense of fatalism pervades Western Europe. There will be other, nasty ethnic wars, but so what?

Compassion fatigue now accounts for a slowing response from Western public opinion to successive crises, whether to mass refugee movements or to the effect of brutal civil wars. In this lies a growing recognition that runaway population growth is incessantly adding new generations of potential victims. Floods from deforested Himalayan slopes, a direct consequence of demographic pressure, wash ever more devastatingly into Bangladesh—where successive governments neglect preventive measures. In Southeast Asia, a 1991 flash flood on the denuded but crowded Philippine island of Leyte took more lives than 20 years of civil war with Communist insurgents. Famine, unemployment, insanitary urban congestion—all have a similar tie to administrative failure and Malthusian distress.

Some exceptions, I again stress, exist. Indonesia and Nigeria have managed to create a transcendent nationalism of broad appeal to most citizens, even if a corrupted military in both countries intervenes at will. Like these two countries, other third world states with generous portions of products consistently in high demand (oil, timber) have added to their physical and social infrastructure, as have those occasional success stories like Malaysia or Taiwan, which have won a measure of export-oriented industrial success. But we speak, alas, of specific exceptions to a general trend toward failure.

The implications of this failure for international migration are staggering. Already, some early signs point to a sea change in attitudes toward migrants in the United States, a change mirroring European misgivings apparent since the early 1980s. A tough-minded report on refugees from the Federation for American Immigration Reform, released in July 1991, urges a ceiling on migrants and better efforts to counter migrant abuse of lackadaisical enforcement of American immigration laws.[2] In the indifference to Haitian migrants leaving their unhappy country can be found a harbinger of attitudes in flux: even the United States, the quintessential nation of migrants, may experience a new version of the "drawbridges-up" mentality that animated the 1920s.

The migrants' inexorable push toward Europe and North America is caused by much more than poverty-driven hopefuls. There remain those who, as noted, rule their own failing territories by virtue of birth and position. To them the lure of the West is now so powerful that it supplants primary loyalty to the postage-stamp sovereignties created in the hurried administrative abandonment we call decolonization.

For all these disparate reasons I would argue that we are witnessing a *disintegration* of what now seems, in retrospect, an artificial building block fashioned in the salad days of decolonization: nation-states. Already, many "sovereignties" are slipping into indistinct chaos—Somalia, Zaire, Liberia, Suriname, or Haiti. In remote villages from Myanmar to Azerbaijan, revenge-minded and ethnically based "liberation fronts" settle their vendettas by gunfire, not through ballot-box exercises. Even in territories the sovereignty of which seems well settled—as in Indonesia—new insurgencies and ethnically based challenges, from Sumatra to West Irian, are gaining impetus.

Within other territories, vast regions have already become the preserve of bandits or gruesome insurgencies, as in India's northeast, much of equatorial Africa, the grey zones of Croatia and Romania, or the Andean Latin American countries. In a few countries a type of informal overlordship has occurred. In Liberia during the early 1980s, the finance minister had to have his checks countersigned by a Western overseer; if he had not agreed to this procedure the international moneylenders would not have honored his draft. Earlier Polish mismanagement also offers an example of when, for practical purposes, international creditors willingly shave sovereignty right down to the bone.

Demanding Better Governance

Can anything be done? Having watched successive third world "development" disappointments and having witnessed too many separatist struggles, I am not very hopeful that the large trend can be quickly, or easily, reversed. But at least a start can be made if we prod the World Bank and other aid donors to insist upon immensely better governance as an absolute precondition for continuing support. Some say this smacks of recolonization. Some see refusing to lend unless certain conditions are met—a decline in defense spending, a resumption of fiscal reality, or the start of serious efforts at demographic control—as amounting to a new era of imperialism.

Yet the broad picture of power no longer sustains these quibbles: if insisting on this type of enlightened conditionality, well outside the earlier International Monetary Fund (IMF) economic reform criteria, means greater infringements of sovereignty, so be it. In any event, the critical reassessments come at a time when Western priorities are changing. Reconstructing Central Europe and reintegrating Russia into the Western concert of nations will continue to divert scarce resources away from third world aid programs. Reserves of capital, let alone of concessional capital, are short. In addition, both Western Europe and North America must make, and eventually will make, enormous new infrastructural investments to counter Northeast Asian competitiveness.

In any event, too many regimes

have become aid junkies. Pouring new money into the old failures like Zaire or Myanmar seems perverse. Anyway, we do not have the luxury of tolerating as much failure as we did before, either at home or abroad. Some programs may show the way, such as the Multilateral Aid Initiative for the Philippines. Financed by Western donors and Japan, the plan ties increased aid to serious, demonstrable efforts to liberalize the economy. (It remains to be seen whether the Filipinos can deliver what they have promised.)

Quietly, Japan is imposing a much broader range of conditionality in its aid than was the case even two years ago. From Kathmandu to Yangon, and from Colombo to Beijing, Japanese diplomats in recent years have also moved, away from the limelight, to restrain autocratic rulers from dropping their dismal standards still further. I have seen at first hand how Tokyo's aid conditionality has influenced events in Nepal and Sri Lanka. In Nepal the pressure helped convince King Birendra to submit to democratic elections; in Sri Lanka, Japan's stance (coupled to pressure from the British and other Western countries) has helped to improve international monitoring of the terrible civil war in that country. In Beijing, the Chinese leadership knows that the size of future yen credits depends, in part, on restraint in Chinese arms exports. And the Japanese also count just as much in current moves to encourage Beijing to help rein in North Korea's nuclear weapons acquisition ambitions. Japan's hand is also visible in most if not all the gains squeezed from the PRC—accession to the Montreal Protocol on Greenhouse Gas Emissions or visas for visiting human rights monitoring groups.

In visits to India and other South Asian nations during 1990, Toshiki

Kaifu, then prime minister of Japan, also pulled few punches, telling his surprised hosts that the region's mindless defense spending and bureaucratic economies were doing them little good. The same message is heard elsewhere in the Third World. It is, more often than not, a mirror-image of the message we are giving, ourselves, to reluctant listeners.

In addition to the worthy aims of Japan and other aid donors, the new aid conditionality must focus on demanding new restraints on population growth and a strict accounting of aid leakage due to corruption. This should apply especially in countries (as in the Philippines) oblivious to, and religiously intolerant of, arguments based on well-founded alarm over population growth.

In the U.S. inner cities, the expression "Tough Love" comes from experience in taking addicts off drugs without *any* further coddling; the notion can apply just as well to helping the Third World kick the dependency habit. Impoverishment as a benighted condition has received relentless attention since decolonization. Yet the most impoverished feature of all—the lack of civic culture in these "states"—must receive renewed attention. As demonstrated by India's reluctant and terribly overdue move toward dismantling its bureaucratic command economy, the maxim "Duress Works Best" may provide the best guidance. Only an acute balance of payments crisis in 1991 plus some stiff IMF backbone has accomplished a shift in the elite's attitudes. Another maxim, "Challenge and Response," became a favorite of the British historian Arnold Toynbee as he considered why some nations fail and others succeed.

I have few illusions that aid conditionality, no matter how stringent, can do much to improve matters very quickly. The diplomacy behind it would need to be multilateral, quiet, and determined, and would face just as much resistance from old habits in aid agencies in the developed world as from irritated recipients anxious to preserve maximum leeway in their use of foreign exchange. Still, tougher conditionality, not only for economic reform but for improved governance and environmental protection, promises a modest chance to breathe a little life back into nation-states that now have little purpose other than to enrich those who control their crumbling bureaucratic apparatus.

Alongside the more traditional structural adjustment conditions imposed by the IMF, we have every right to insist on serious population control programs plus staged cuts in defense spending. (India's foreign arms procurement from 1984 to 1989 was $17 billion, the world's highest; Iraq's over the same period was $12 billion.) The immigration reform lobby's report mentioned above urged the exercise of "leadership to sanction and isolate, politically and economically, repressive governments that generate refugees."[3] Increasingly we are going to be hard pressed to find fault with this thinking. The list of conditions should grow longer still. The question is, will there be any convincing authority on the other side of the table to listen to the arguments?

Disintegration by Self-Determination

Just as an embryonic global identity seemed within grasp, framed by photographs of Earth from space or by the urgent environmental agenda, no countervailing logic can obstruct the power of self-determination. In this closing decade of a tumultuous century, it seems odd that so much unrav-

187

eling is happening in this world at precisely the moment when the integrative impulses had looked unstoppable, whether in forging a suprastate in Europe, fashioning a continental trade regime for North America, or fixing an increasing number of economies firmly in the interstices of a global free trade regime.

Yet we cannot avoid any longer a recognition of the disintegration of any meaningful civic order in parts of the world still masquerading as sovereign states. Not only do the official boundary lines no longer even approximate divisions among competing ethnicities, but dozens of the "nation-states" that trebled the roll call of the United Nations (UN) after 1948 may not stand the test of time.

Indeed, the UN's membership could easily even *treble again* by the time the century has played itself out. Many national names, such as "Liberia" or "Somalia," have ceased to convey any meaning at all in the traditional sense of an organized polity with some semblance of a central government. Other names, like Czechoslovakia, Yugoslavia, and the Soviet Union, are spawning 20 new replacement names.

Because of this trend, the United States must avoid the impulse to become the guarantor of the globe's existing borders (a principle it seemed to fight for in the Persian Gulf War). Ever tighter selectivity must prevail. Ethio-pia, Yugoslavia, Russia, India, Pakistan, Indonesia, Myanmar, and so many others suffer most of all from a terrible mismatch of "national" boundaries and true national or local identity. So many lack a critical mass of leaders who even try to transcend ethnicities far narrower than the "nation" they purport to rule.

Poor governance, relentless demographics, and antagonistic ethnicity are the main culprits for the emerging world disorder. Of these, ethnicity presents the most immediate threat. The key question, which the years ahead will answer for us, is this: Without the forced discipline of great power competition, will scores of improbable nation-states lose whatever remaining cohesion they now have? And add one more: If their prospects for longevity are poor, are we not burdening ourselves with a Sisyphean labor to keep them propped up and breathing?

The author alone is responsible for the views expressed in this article, which do not reflect any institutional viewpoint of the Carnegie Endowment.

Notes

1. Robert T. Naylor, *Hot Money and the Politics of Debt* (New York, N.Y.: Linden Press/Simon and Schuster, 1988).

2. Federation for American Immigration Reform, "A New Approach to Immigration" (Washington, D.C., July 11, 1991).

3. *Ibid.*, p. 17.

Third World Politics and Security in the 1990s: "The World Forgetting, By the World Forgot"?

John Chipman

FAR FROM THE epicenter of the political earthquake that shook Europe in 1989, the developing states of the Middle East, Africa, Asia, and Latin America have nevertheless been affected by the ensuing shock waves. As if in reinforcement of their perceived position on the periphery of world politics, leaders throughout the developing world have pointed to the East European revolutions of 1989 and the general Western response to a reforming (and imploding) Soviet Union and seen in the new nature of West–East politics challenges to their own standing in international society. The reemergence of traditional disputes in East Central Europe and the increased salience of local problems parallel the problems in the developing world that continue to derive from incomplete processes of state-building and the management of internal strife. The sources of insecurity in East Central Europe having become analogous to those of the political South, the nature of West–East relations, much to the dismay of many in the Third World, has come to imitate the previous con-

John Chipman is director of studies at the International Institute for Strategic Studies in London.

cerns of North–South politics and therefore diminished the specificity (and possibly amount) of development aid to the Third World.

This still unproven thesis of marginalization from the flow of development assistance has been expressed at a time when, given the broad trend of superpower withdrawals from military engagements in the developing world, the management of most regional conflict in the Third World certainly appears less pressing. Superpower participation in often arcane third world disputes and the sometimes fanciful strategic calculations that accompanied justifications for intervention lent international prestige to otherwise parochial quarrels. States in the developing world often lamented the participation of the superpowers in regional conflict. They also appreciated that they could draw advantages from this competition. The capacity to play East against West is gone, and the poorer states in the developing world are thus struggling with how to deal with great power acceptance of their geopolitical insignificance. Some of the richer third world states are with greater enthusiasm seeking to acquire a wider array of the military instruments of power. But, in general, faced with the reality of continued, even intensified, local instability to which regional powers may not be so indifferent, states in the developing world cannot readily borrow power from the outside to buttress their own capacities. With competition for superpower patronage now less relevant, most developing states must rely on the uncertain assurance offered by existing national military power to bolster national identity and prestige, even if these are not always appropriate tools with which to address the problems they face.

An exception to this emerging rule of the post–cold war era that actors in the Third World might be able to count on the indifference of the outside community to their actions was provided by the Middle East crisis beginning in the summer of 1990. The special place still retained by the Persian Gulf in U.S. strategic calculations and the clear breach of international law committed by Iraq's annexation and thus attempted murder of the state of Kuwait in August 1990 produced an unprecedented international condemnation and military deployments by the United States and over 20 other states to the region. It demonstrated that the UN Security Council could act in unison on the basis of unanimous resolutions and that the superpowers could act in virtual loose alliance together and with a host of other countries to put pressure on a state that had made itself a pariah in a world system many thought would become more benign. The outcome of the 1990 Persian Gulf crisis will reshape attitudes toward the management of conflict in the Middle East and to the utility of economic sanctions and military force in reversing the results of aggressive action in the developing world. In his speech to

Congress on September 11, 1990, President George Bush argued that it was necessary to build a new world order where "the rule of law supplants the rule of the jungle" and deemed the crisis the start of "a new partnership of nations" and "the first test of our mettle." But it is doubtful that the Persian Gulf crisis, almost no matter what its outcome, will prove the archetype for international responses to regional conflict in the 1990s. The particular political importance of the balance of power in the Middle East, the question of oil, and the nature of Saddam Hussein's actions were a truly special combination of features that allowed for quick and unambiguous action by the United States and most of the rest of the world.

The sources, implications, relevance, and balances between "good" and "evil" in most other cases (actual or prospective) of regional conflict are much less clear. In fact, much regional conflict simply does not matter. The United States continues to see itself engaged in the problems of Latin America, now primarily because of the drug problem, and the Soviet Union will be affected by developments in Central Asia, especially insofar as these are related to the management of an Islamic revival. By and large, superpower concern for regional conflict—even in the Middle East—is expressed through irregular diplomatic efforts to bring parties to a negotiating table. Although in 1990 the superpowers are still supporting opposite sides in civil wars—in Angola and Afghanistan—their participation is not at a level that either inspires international concern or gives them substantial influence over the course of these wars. Great power attachment to the international diplomacy of conflict resolution should not, however, be confused with the same urgency of purpose that previously accompanied competitive military intervention.

In this international environment, where the role of the superpowers in regional conflict is in general decline, and where the developed countries of Europe and North America will concentrate on encouraging and creating new conditions of security in Europe, the direction of third world politics and security will more than ever before be locally determined. The likelihood of domestic forces multiplying and of local actors diversifying their regional ambitions is high. This pluralism of domestic and regional activity will, in turn, make it difficult for great powers easily to engage themselves again in regions from which they have withdrawn. The increasing autonomy of local actors (whether states or insurgent groups) and their appreciation of their own local influence will create facts and contexts that will complicate the assessments of outsiders and make the effects of political, economic, or military intervention often incalculable.

In the 1990s, therefore, understanding regional security in the Third World will mean appreciating, more than ever before, the international relations of parochialism. Regional security in the Middle East, Africa, Asia, and Latin America is regularly affected by the external effects of policies implemented to attenuate domestic problems and by the domestic consequences of the external reactions to locally inspired change. Policies pursued by governments to deal with ethnic disputes, secessionist movements, national revival groups, economic depression, or drug issues become security problems for others and inspire reactions that are not always pacific or neutral. The domestic policies of one's neighbor quickly become part of one's own.

The differences between national and regional perceptions of security, as well as the challenge of managing domestic demands for change are among the overarching dilemmas of third world politics and security. In the bipolar world of the past—for which many in the Third World appear sadly nostalgic—the complexity of state security was hidden by the simple geometry and simplistic politics of East–West and North–South relations. The issues that now define third world security are far more subtle, and the definition of regional relationships no longer simply corresponds to the rules of geography.

Five elemental sets of pressures impose themselves on many developing societies: the persistence of feudal or traditional structures and the desire for modern systems of state management; the pressure for democracy and the perceived need of political leaders to maintain more autocratic forms of order; the challenge of maintaining national cohesion and the attractiveness of regional systems of political organization; the aspirations to political and economic independence and the reality of reliance on external aid; and the preeminent desire for military self-reliance that sometimes obscures the urgency of nonmilitary threats to security.

The coexistence of many of these in numerous third world states perhaps justifies the tendency of the great powers to disengage themselves from the intricacy of most third world insecurity. Nagging doubts about whether influence abandoned is peace gained will mean that outside powers will not be able entirely to ignore the outcome of these pressures in some regions. The dramatic events of the

Persian Gulf in the summer and autumn of 1990 will result in changes in the balance of political influence, domestic stability, and military balance of power in the Middle East that will change interstate relations and domestic relationships significantly. But after months of musical chairs diplomacy and alliance shifts (likely to occur at an *allegro vivace* pace), the place will still be unstable and although a vital principle of international law will have been defended, some will ask whether it was all worth it. Equally, outside powers and the United States in particular are denied the luxury of simply redefining the nature of threats in and from the Third World to construct new defense policies as coherent and comprehensive as those that could be elaborated in the period of the Cold War. It will be almost impossible to construct overarching themes to guide policy in an age where regional conflict is sui generis, interests are variable, and the distribution of power and influence so diffuse.

Feudalism versus Modernity

Problems of political stability—and therefore security—in many states of the developing world are often conditioned by the competition between central state power and more traditional forms of influence within state boundaries. The tension between aspirations for modern forms of state management at the center and the reality of long-established—sometimes ancient—practices of local control acutely affect domestic order and perceptions of national identity. The current instruments of political organization (bureaucracies and parties) can rarely displace entirely the more archaic systems of social order that persist in developing countries. Their inevitable coexistence means that

leaders in capitals may have to compromise their desire for a unitary system of government with the practical needs of managing complex social orders. Almost by definition, this also means that the capacities of outsiders to influence local events using the traditional mechanisms of international diplomacy are limited.

In the Afghanistan of the 1990s, for example, recognition of the local influence of tribal groups has persuaded the Communist regime to make arrangements that effectively devolve power to provincial leaders. In 1985, Babrak Karmal, then general secretary of the People's Democratic Party of Afghanistan (PDPA), complained that party life was "rife with factionalism, tribalism, corruption, and regionalism."[1] These did not represent ideological currents or opposition opinion within the Communist Party so much as the tribalism inherent in Afghan society. By 1989 the Najibullah regime had decided to recognize this reality more openly by offering local autonomy, weapons, money, and even titles to local leaders in the country (such as Ismailis in Baghlan province) who could help by keeping open communication to the cities.[2] In this way, central state power has been strengthened by devolving power to trusted but still independent allies. The medieval rules of feudalism thus now appear more relevant to ensuring political order than formal arrangements for decentralization. Afghan leaders at the center, to reinsure their own power, have conceded roles on the periphery to traditional actors. No outsider seeking to influence the outcome of the present civil war can afford to ignore the complex algebra of these internal relationships.

Indeed, throughout the developing world the relationship between formal power at the center and traditional sources of power in outlying regions varies between discreet alliance (as in Afghanistan) through uncomfortable indifference to clear opposition. In Nigeria, for example, the central government made a major mistake when it chose a new Sultan of Sokoto in November 1988 without the support of the local kingmakers: the result was heavy rioting in the north and a major challenge to the military federal government. Few African governments can act without taking into account the positions and local influence of traditional chiefs. Sometimes central governments are able to disturb the traditions of country populations in the interests of national security or out of modernizing zeal. Brazil's Calha Norte policy was in the late 1980s directed toward moving entire Indian settlements away from borders with Colombia and Peru in order to prevent illegal trade. The deforestation of the Amazon, which was carried out for economic reasons but which has also displaced some tribes, has been attenuated because of the concern of environmentalists.

If it is true that modernist forces can sometimes overwhelm traditional social and political orders, the opposite problem is also encountered. Superficially modern societies in the developing world are sometimes challenged at the center by traditional groups who seek a deceleration of history, a return to a past they better understand, and a reversal of the achievements of modernity. They aim to relegate the modern techniques of political order and social control to the background, giving preeminence instead to ancient ideologies or beliefs as more effective tools of organization. Disaffected by the fruits of modern society, these groups, if they come to power, often advocate a degree of isolationism from global affairs.

The rise of Iran's theocracy in the revolution of 1979 is perhaps the classic example of this phenomenon. The desire to establish a political order based on the tenets of early Islam became quickly subject, however, to the exigencies of modern life and specifically of the war with Iraq. Gradually the interests of the revolution had to give way to the interests of the state. Managing a war economy sometimes meant compromising the revolutionary spirit, both in terms of social justice and the desire for economic independence.[3] Eventually the need to blend religious piety and secular pragmatism came to be reflected in Iran's political institutions: most of the clergy both in and outside parliament are concerned to keep the elements of the Imam's legacy but also to allow the administration to work toward that degree of integration in the world economy consistent with the needs of the state. As yet there is no challenge to the primacy of theocratic rule, but the concessions made to pragmatists are illustrative of the way different types of political and social order can coexist even in revolutionary developing states.[4] Again, the record of outside actors in attempting to pick the radicals from the moderates in Iran's political order is an indicator of the difficulties foreign states have in dealing with developing societies pulled between modern and feudal conceptions of civil society.

If, as for Charles Péguy, "Tout commence par la mystique et finit par la politique," the intermingling of the two in so many parts of the world poses challenges to the practice of foreign policy by the developed states. Where opposition groups with retrogressive political agendas operate against the central power they also severely limit the modernizing programs of governments and their capacities to

193

deal with the outside world. Peru's Maoist Sendero Luminoso movement plays on native Indian distrust of Lima's white elite and, having controlled large parts of the countryside during the past decade, has frustrated any conceivable plans for rural economic development. Its interaction with narcotraffickers has not only raised the intensity of conflict but has also made combating the drug problem awkward. Certainly the United States must be cautious in Peru (as in other areas, such as Myanmar) that its efforts to arrest international drug traffickers do not involve it in civil wars or ethnic rivalries. India's involvement in the conflict between Sinhalese and Tamils in Sri Lanka between 1987 and 1990 helped to revivify the Janata Vimuthi Peramuna (JVP) movement, which espouses an ultra-Sinhalese nationalism. While the leadership of the JVP has since been crushed, its appeal in the south cannot be discounted, particularly if programs for greater social justice are stymied by the imperatives of the continued conflict with the Tamils.

These illustrations are meant merely to indicate that managing modern aspirations and economic challenges just when traditional, historically rooted demands are made on the state remains one of the most recurrent dilemmas in the vastly different areas of the developing world. When the problems of the modern world are grafted on to the legacies of more primordial disputes, solutions offered for one category of issues may have dangerous repercussions on the other. State management is thus made awkward by the elemental tension between the imperatives of the modern world and the attractiveness, for many, of traditional society. The management of domestic stability in these circumstances depends on ensuring that

the advances of modernization do not destroy the social fabric and that the demands of tradition are not so retrogressive that the state is disenfranchised from an ever more interdependent modern world.

This problem is compounded by the fact that the pluralism of privately held political opinion, religious belief, and social practice in the developing world is rarely equaled by the opportunity to have these represented publicly at the political center. Regimes in the developing world that have intentionally confused their own security with that of the state are now faced with growing demands for liberalization.

The Challenges of Democracy and the Management of State Power

One of the effects of the East European revolution of 1989 that has been most commented on throughout the Third World—but most spectacularly in Africa—has been the rise in local pressure for democratization. This has produced a need for leaders in the developing world to pay heed to the international trend in favor of full participation in domestic politics, and it has often had unpredictable effects on domestic order. The early months of 1990 saw uprisings in Gabon, Côte d'Ivoire, Benin, and numerous other francophone states where personal rule implicitly and sometimes explicitly supported by the various presidents of the French Fifth Republic was no longer considered a satisfactory means of government. The traditional and often entirely sound argument of many African leaders that the proliferation of political parties would be coextensive with the existence of ethnic groups and that therefore democracy could lead to disintegration will no longer be able to deter democratic movements in Africa, particularly if the participants believe they have the tide of history with them. With international attention focused on this trend, regimes such as those of Daniel arap Moi in Kenya and Sese Seko Mobuto in Zaire, long favored by Western governments, will not necessarily be able to rely on moral support from the outside to buttress their authority. The World Bank Report on sub-Saharan Africa of November 1989 openly called for greater pluralism and more honest government, arguing that "because countervailing power has been lacking, state officials in many countries have served their own interests without fear of being called into account."[5]

Further to the north, the states of the Maghreb are grappling differently with the democratic impulse. In Algeria, Chadli Bendjedid has encouraged a process of economic and political reform from above, but the victories in municipal elections in 1990 of the Front Islamique du Salut (FIS) over the ruling Front de Liberation Nationale (FLN) will have worried those concerned by an Islamic revival. Tunisia has taken a more secular view of the democratic process, prohibiting the main Islamic group, Nahda, from forming a legal political party.

Though there have been some demands in the Arab Middle East for greater democracy, the desire for pluralism usually has been met by the argument that traditional structures offer adequate avenues for debate. In Kuwait, for example, demonstrators throughout the first half of 1990 called for the reopening of the National Assembly, closed in 1986 at the height of the Iran–Iraq war. Officials defending the refusal to restore parliamentary democracy in the country argued that parliament only reproduced political and religious divisions and that Kuwait's *diwaniya* system, whereby officials held open house on certain days of the week at which petitioners could air complaints, was a sufficient substitute for Western-style democracy.[6] Iraq's invasion of Kuwait made this debate moot, but reaction to it raised two further questions. What will be the long-term effect of the large and primarily U.S. military deployment to the feudal states of the Gulf on the capacity of their leaders to hang on to autocratic and hereditary principles of leadership? Will the broad tension between "rich and poor Arab," which Saddam Hussein tried to exploit in the early weeks of the crisis, eventually result in more "people power" in the Middle East? Even in that region, while the problem may be defined differently than elsewhere, the demand for more pluralism of political participation will become more vociferous.

Yet it must be underscored that however awe-inspiring the events of 1989 in Europe might have been, to apply a domino theory to the kinetics of democracy has limited justification in observable fact. The wish that this be otherwise may be the father of much analysis in the case of Cuba. Many in the United States and elsewhere began to predict Fidel Castro's demise after the fall of Nikolae Ceausescu in Romania. But despite the economic pressures Fidel Castro confronts owing to the fall of socialism in Europe, his own grip on power remains impressive. A "palace coup d'état" may be in the offing, but it must be recalled that the Cuban revolution was national, not imposed from outside, and however irrational his logic or fabricated his conspiracy theories, it appears that Castro can still turn foreign hostility to the revolution to his advantage by appealing to a sense of national independence. Although there has been some debate on economic reforms in preparation for the fourth party congress in 1991, there is little chance that the more important proposals for decentralization of the economy can be met when economic circumstances dictate central control. Liberalism and pluralism seem as far away as does a strong and organized internal opposition.

The existence of parties and the fact of elections elsewhere in Central America have been more encouraging but the task of consolidation is enormous. Violeta Chamorro's National Opposition Union (UNO) government coalition has been, since her electoral victory in February 1990, a victim of the Sandinista promise to "rule from below." Two weeks of strikes in July 1990 brought the country to the edge of another civil war. The capacity of the elected government of President Alfredo Cristiani in El Salvador to rule remains conditioned by the interests of the military and their capacity to govern "from alongside," as well as by the power of the Farabundo Martí National Liberation Front (FMLN) to disturb both village and urban life. Peace negotiations in El Salvador must therefore result in the establishment of a new social contract if they are to be successful.

An implied social contract is, indeed, often a precondition for democracy. The tragedy in so many parts of the developing world is that the practices of leaders with narrow bases of support is rarely such as to create an atmosphere of ordered and peaceful dissent. Even where formal democratic practices exist, the capacity of those outside power sometimes entirely to frustrate the normal activity of elected governments makes of democracy a more than usually ineffective means of government. The power of provincial leaders in Pakistan, especially in the Punjab where the opposition Islami Jamhoori Ittehad (IJI)

is especially strong, to obstruct policies developed by Prime Minister Benazir Bhutto was extremely high. The military was able to exert its effective veto over Pakistani politics when, on August 6, 1990, President Ghulam Ishaq Khan dismissed the Bhutto government, charging that it was corrupt and inefficient in its rule. The army's desire to have more policing powers in Sind and its general disapproval of the regime were, however, perhaps more important reasons for this action. The holding of elections following this constitutional coup d'état would not change the fact that the ritual of democracy may be more respected in Pakistan than its practice in the day-to-day life of the country.[7] Sometimes elections are held and the results are not even notionally respected by those who hold both official and coercive power. Following the election held in Myanmar in May 1990, the ruling military junta refused to hand over power. The leader of the victorious National League for Democracy, Aung San Suu Kyi, two months after the election was able to celebrate only completion of a full year under house arrest.

The need felt by many third world leaders to defend institutional, sectarian, or ethnic interests makes difficult the creation of an atmosphere conducive to peaceful competitive politics. The frequent identification of ruling political parties with clans or sects, as in the cases of the Baathist regimes in Syria and Iraq, inhibits a development of loyalty to the state that is separable from loyalty to an ethnic group. There remain many presidential palaces in the developing world where the remark of former President Habib Bourguiba of Tunisia—"What state? I am the state"—would be held in cynical high regard. The "weakness" of new states will for some time still be used as an excuse not to allow internal discussions that might "damage" national cohesion. The disorganizing effect of democratic practices will be the ultimate line of defense of the autocratic scoundrel. If the 1990s will see a greater spread of the democratic ideal, it remains the case that in most developing societies the establishment of political institutions and struggles for power will often take place simultaneously—and therefore awkwardly. Unfortunately, rare will be the opportunities, even for the best motivated of outside powers, to help build a national consensus for a peaceful yet competitive political process in the Third World without becoming embroiled in domestic rivalries.

National Cohesion and the Pressures of Regionalism

The high degree of autocratic control in developing states has often been justified—especially in the cases of those that emerged out of the post–World War II process of decolonization—by the need to "build nations." Nation-building, which has concentrated on forging a single identity and sense of purpose to present to the outside world, has not always been compatible with the aims of regional alliances or organizations. The fissiparous tendencies within many developing states and the new greater capacity of regional powers (given the likely unwillingness of the superpowers to involve themselves in third world conflict that remains at low intensity) are impediments to regional cooperation. While, therefore, North America and the European Community (EC) are both engaged in and promoting the idea and the practice of a new form of bloc politics—regional economic and political integration—many regions in the world are still ill-prepared to engage in a new process of pactomania. Although many leaders in the developing world pay lip service to the idea of regional cooperation, largely in opposition to the perceived or actual interventionist policies of the great powers, the record of such cooperation is mediocre.

The high incidence of ethnic conflict, especially in Africa and Asia, means that the forces of secessionism still appear greater than those for integration. The ideology of national self-determination remains attractive and can find easy support among citizens of provinces or remote areas who are victims of uneven state development or of the success of a particular ethnic group with a firm grip on the central organs of power. The international relations of parochialism are also such that the strength of ethnic groups, either holding or dissenting from central power, can often rely on aid and succor from neighboring states.

Sometimes such groups are virtually created and almost entirely sustained by external powers, as in the cases of Iranian support for Hezbollah activists in Lebanon, or South Africa's links with Renamo in Mozambique. In other cases the links are less direct, and the objects of support more evidently autonomous, as in the examples provided by Ethiopian support for the Sudan People's Liberation Army (SPLA) in Sudan and for the Somali National Movement (SNM) in Somalia, or the putative assistance provided by Pakistan to Sikh extremists in India, or Indian help (often denied) to Sind separatists in Pakistan or to Chakmas in the Chittagong Hill Tracts in Bangladesh. These links, which tend to be more subtle than overt and heavy military assistance (such as China's aid to the Khmer Rouge in Cambodia), are no less complicating for regional security because they touch at the core of central state control over the population. Leaders in the Third World whose nation-building tasks are incomplete are bound to feel particularly threatened by such activity.

The potential nature of regional conflict in the future suggests that it may be easy for countries with narrow agendas to involve themselves in the internal disputes of neighboring states. Organized rebellion against state authorities by ethnic groups, secessionist movements, or drug lords acting in collaboration or through terrorists shows no signs of subsiding. Numerous states are bound openly to exploit the existence of rebel entities to advance their own external ambitions. Because direct military involvement by the superpowers is now less regularly anticipated, many leaders fear the "Lebanonization" of regional conflict. In early 1990 this fear came to be expressed most notably by leaders in the Horn of Africa because of the rise in Israeli support for Haile-Mariam Mengistu's Ethiopia (in order to help preserve the territorial integrity of the state and in return for greater emigration of Falashas) and the apparently greater interest of Arab states in supporting Eritrean secessionist groups. Whether such assistance, military and other, actually could materially affect the battles on the ground was less important than the political fear that the region was falling prey to regional influences at a time of superpower indifference to local events.

Against this continued trend of intraregional tension and prospective Lebanonization of conflict in some areas, it is important to gauge the countervailing desire for regional cooperation. The now long and basically successful history of the Association of Southeast Asian Nations (ASEAN) is often held up as an example, although the glue of a common Indochina policy may soon begin to wear thin. Few other regions display the potential for continuing amicable relations necessary to achieve the same level of consultation. The South Asian Association for Regional Cooperation (SAARC) explicitly excludes bilateral issues from its meetings. Indo-Pakistani tensions over Kashmir or Indian policy in Sri Lanka may be treated in "corridor meetings," but they cannot receive general and official attention. Continental-sized groupings, such as the Organization of African Unity (OAU) or the Organization of American States (OAS) have rarely been able (for very different reasons) to mediate in subregional conflicts. Smaller groups may have a greater chance for limited success. But although, for example, the South African Development Coordination Conference (SADCC) has achieved some levels of economic integration among the member states in Southern Africa, interstate tension (as between Zimbabwe and Mozambique) can still be high, and the relevance of SADCC to the achievement of the Southwest Africa accords of 1988 was nil. The attempt by the Economic Community of West African States (ECOWAS) to provide a five-nation peacekeeping force in Liberia in August 1990 only resulted in greater confusion.

During the 1980s, and especially in 1989, the greatest surge of regional groupings took place in the Arab world, but none has had a preeminent role in managing regional stability. The Gulf Cooperation Council (GCC) did not craft the policy that led to the deployment of Western navies to the Gulf—Kuwait did—and was certainly divided about its consequences. The existence of the organization did not help to facilitate Western deployments: the United States and West European states negotiated access rights on a bilateral basis. In August 1990 it took some time for the GCC states to agree on a policy to deal with Iraq's aggression against a member state, and although all eventually took a common line it remains doubtful whether the GCC could operate efficiently as the principal local security organization. Any outside attempt to collaborate in the creation of a post-crisis stable balance of power (an extremely delicate business) would have to take into account a broader range of countries than those represented in the GCC. The creation in 1989 of the Arab Cooperation Council (ACC: Egypt, Jordan, Iraq, Yemen) comprising states left out of other arrangements raised the hopes of some that a new organization could better help shape inter-Arab politics. This was all changed in August 1990, and although Jordan, Iraq, and Yemen may still be said to have a loose relationship with each other, the organization is all but dead. Most such arrangements in the increasingly disunited Arab world have been meant only to serve narrow and sometimes fleeting political agendas of state leaders rather than to set up permanent security structures. The establishment in 1989 of the Union du Maghreb Arabe (UMA: Algeria, Morocco, Mauritania, Tunisia, and Libya) was made possible by Algerian–Moroccan rapprochement and may have a greater chance of survival. Through its goal of political and economic integration for the region it reduced the importance of the Polisario struggle for the western Sahara in regional relations. Its existence raises the political costs of major disputes between the member states because so much capital has been invested in the ideology of integration. Although this (like other regional alliances) may impose constraints on the activities of radical powers (Libya), it will not be able to prevent radical activity defined as necessary to the state.

Given this general record, one may be justified, therefore, in being cautiously pessimistic about the prospects in the 1990s of greater integration of the Central American economies and of those of Latin America as a whole, as proposed by Secretary of State James A. Baker III and President Bush in June 1990. Were the situation in Nicaragua to improve, and peace talks in El Salvador and Guatemala to bear fruit, greater integration of the Central American economies might be politically feasible. Yet most Central American states remain very concerned to protect limited exports markets, and the transition to creating more complementary economies in the region will be difficult. Before June 1990, almost no official thought had gone into the prospects for integration in the capital cities of the region.

Equally, the history of economic integration in South America is pretty sorry. While Argentina and Brazil continue to sign further trade agreements between themselves to which Uruguay has partially attached itself, each of these countries puts up barriers to trade whenever it feels the need. The experiences of the failed Andean Pact have left psychological traces. A former Uruguayan minister of industry and minister of foreign affairs opened a recent article on Latin American integration with the stark sentence: "I judge Latin American integration impossible."[8] Regional organizations still have a measure of attractiveness throughout the developing world, but the imperatives of national development, both political and economic, remain such as to override most projects for integration.

199

The Politics of Independence and External Assistance

The most ambitious third world attempt at bloc politics, global nonalignment, is now being rendered almost irrelevant. This is so because of the reduced polarization of East–West affairs, which makes policies of political equidistance between the two superpowers more meaningless than ever, and because of the dramatic diversity of the so-called nonaligned states. Yet most third world states remain jealous of their independence, and their leaders are sensitive to the need to balance good relations with the states or institutions that may give them financial and other assistance with the requirements of national independence and sovereignty. No state can remain permanently isolated (though some like Iran, Cuba, South Africa, and others try or may be forced to adopt near-autarkic policies) from the normal current of international economic activity. Few are likely to accept the degree of dependence chosen by the states of francophone Africa that belong to the franc zone and are reliant on France for economic, financial, and military assistance. Yet attempts by some of the poor states to protect themselves from an international economic order that moves too fast for them by instituting exchange controls, passing protectionist legislation, and placing restrictions on the free movement of persons may often harm prospects for needed investment or technical know-how. Such reactions to perceived vulnerability and penetrability often lead to further isolation and deprivation.

This psychology of economic and financial protection in the name of national independence is now being further tested because of the widespread fear that Western economic aid will be shifted from the South to the East.

Throughout the latter part of 1989 and the first half of 1990, leaders from every region of the developing world showed themselves concerned by this as yet not established trend. Clearly, some U.S. assistance to Caribbean states has been reduced and some bilateral European aid to countries in the South has stagnated. But U.S. aid to countries such as Panama and Nicaragua will probably go up, while EC aid to the Lomé group of countries showed a real increase in November 1989, and the Community in early 1990 promised increases to the Maghreb states.

The aid environment is, however, much more competitive for those developing countries above the poverty threshold whose economies bear some similarity to those in Eastern Europe. These countries are now having to pass much more attractive investment legislation if they are to retain some prospect of foreign private investment. The poorer countries, more dependent on public aid, will in the current climate have to pass higher tests of good government and public accountability in order to receive economic aid. Even without the events of 1989, a buildup both of aid fatigue and aid cynicism within Western donor states would have made this necessary. Because of the East European revolutions, the specificity of aid to the developing world has been lost. There are just too many *demandeurs*, and the interests of realpolitik, which in part govern assistance to the East, are greater than perceptions of North–South interdependence. All this will require domestic political and economic changes in the developing world in response to external pressure from donor states and institutions that a few years ago would have been dismissed as unwelcome interference.

This familiar tension between sovereignty and aid reliance is now compounded by the challenges to national economic decision making arising from international concern over environmental exploitation and resource use. This exists at two levels: North–South and regional. On the North–South level, concern for environmental protection has produced tensions because moves by developing states to increase income (often to pay external debts) by rapid industrialization or resource exploitation has inspired the ire of Northern states now more ostensibly concerned about global environmental issues. The most obvious case of this is Brazil's deforestation of the Amazon, which, aside from disturbing Indian populations, is also said to contribute to the greenhouse effect. Specific proposals of "debt for nature swaps" notwithstanding, there is still considerable progress to be made in delineating adequate codes of conduct on the environment that do not so impinge on the national sovereignty of developing states that they make economic advances impossible to achieve or inspire emotional rejection of all environmental safeguards.

More significant for regional security is the tension over use of resources within specific regions. Access to the Kuwaiti oil fields and to the money this would bring him inspired Saddam Hussein's actions against the al-Sabah ruling family, but in the long term other resources are equally important. Water use in the Middle East raises one of the more acute examples of the relationship between national economic strategy and international stability. Certainly the pressure to exploit agricultural lands, particularly in the face of accelerating population growth, means that water is bound to become a more obvious element in regional relations. Because sources of water cross boundaries, there can be few

water exploitation policies whose effects are neutral on neighbors. For example, construction of the Ataturk dam in the Turkish section of the Euphrates River affects the downstream exploitation of water by the Iraqis and the Syrians. Closure of the dam for 30 days in January 1990 created a crisis between Turkey and the other two states. Tripartite negotiations over this problem have rarely been satisfactory. Israel has diverted water from the Litani River that crosses southern Lebanon, thus reducing the amount of water available to Lebanese farmers. Israeli dependence on water from the Golan Heights and the West Bank remains high. Because the water tables in the West Bank are declining and the Palestinian population increasing, Israeli authorities have allowed Palestinians in the territories to consume only at 1967 levels. Egypt depends on the Nile for some 95 percent of its water resources, but water flow to Egypt is dependent on consumption in Uganda, Sudan, and Ethiopia. In the last 18 months, Egyptian interest in regional cooperation in the Nile Valley has increased as Egypt has come to realize its potential vulnerability. If Egypt were to insist on a strategy of food self-sufficiency, its water problem would be aggravated and its relations with Ethiopia, whose cooperation on water management issues has been inconsistent, would decline.[9]

Analogous international rivalries have been exacerbated by issues concerning resources (primarily forest use) in South and Southeast Asia. The fact that in many parts of the developing world economic futures are determined by the successful management of natural resources points to the significance of sound environmental policies for strategic stability. The natural or induced decay or destruction of the resources on which economic stability rests, or around which international attention focuses, can therefore intensify existing conflict and create the conditions for new rivalries.

The Military Imperative and Nonmilitary Threats to Security

The fact that in July 1990 Iraq chose to deploy troops on its frontier with Kuwait to protest the latter's breach of OPEC production quotas, and the fact that Arab states later met to agree on a higher oil price to defuse the crisis, point to the obvious coercive value of military power to ensure fair use and distribution of resources. Iraq's later attack on Kuwait demonstrated yet again that the military choice is still live and that imbalances of power offer temptations to unsavory leaders who believe that might makes right. Although the sources of instability are rooted in the history of state structures, the exacerbating effect of economic and environmental factors, and the complexity of regional relationships, they are naturally aggravated by the persistence of the military solution as the ultimate option of state leaders and their internal or external opponents. Even the poorest states in the developing world have, through their arms acquisition programs, entered the modern world with vigor. Ethiopia, by some measures the poorest country in Africa, has the continent's largest standing army with over 300,000 men under arms. Three of the other poorest African countries, Sudan, Chad, and Mozambique, have nevertheless sought to maintain the ability to conduct armed conflict. In these and other poor countries of the Third World affected by civil conflict, war has become politics by other means; government is the management of conflict; opposition has meant insurgency; and guerrilla activities have become a life-style.

In some of the world's poorest areas of conflict combatants have been insulated, often by the generosity of the international community, from the consequences of their actions. Throughout much of the recent fighting in Ethiopia, for example, the West has provided considerable food aid to alleviate great famines. Such aid has been used by the combatants in their conflicts with each other; convoys have been attacked by rebel groups; and the government for a time resisted allowing the use of the port of Massawa, in rebel hands in 1990, from being used by donors to deliver supplies. Throughout the Horn of Africa, refugee populations have been created by conflict, and the refugee camps established by the United Nations High Commissioner for Refugees (UNHCR) are in many areas the main source of decent rudimentary housing as well as of food and water. Particularly in Somalia, refugee status is actively sought by internally displaced people. Refugee camps there (as in many other places), being areas of minimal infrastructure, have been the object of military attacks by opposition groups. The fact that combatants in many poor regions of the world do not, at least in terms of famine relief or refugee assistance, have to face the consequences of war is not an argument for slowing or cutting humanitarian aid to these areas, but it is a partial explanation for why military action remains an option in poor, embattled areas.

Richer states have sought to make great leaps forward in their ability to produce and export arms for reasons of prestige, regional rivalry, and external markets. Brazil's medium-technology arms industry has made that country a leading actor in the South–South arms trade. More states appear close to crossing the nuclear threshold. They are doing so, in South Asia, the Middle East, and Latin America, in circumstances in which it is not clear that robust mutual deterrence structures that would make nuclear inventories stabilizing factors can be developed simultaneously with the rise in possession. The proliferation of chemical weapons and their actual use during the Iran–Iraq war points to how hard it is to bring new types of weapons within deterrence frameworks. Iraq's threat in 1990 to use chemical weapons if attacked by Israel borrows from the language of deterrence effectively deployed in Europe over the last 40 years, but in the special context of the Middle East it is reasonable to be skeptical about the stabilizing effects of sophisticated weaponry. (In the fall of 1990, people rightly wondered both in the United States and Europe whether the sale of further combat aircraft to Saudi Arabia might not in the long term be regretted. Especially in the Middle East, attempts by outside powers to construct and maintain balances of power, given the shifting bilateral and wider alliances of the region, hold great risks of leading to grief). The general spread of ballistic and cruise missile delivery systems indicates a growing capacity for over-the-horizon combat that may heighten regional perceptions of threat and raise the possibilities of preemption no matter what particular balance of power is eventually achieved in the area.

This general interstate proliferation of armaments and their delivery systems, which complicates both the prospects for arms control and for conflict management, is coupled to an active diffusion of intrastate armaments that heightens the internal opportunities for armed conflict. The sophisticated small-arms trade is such that

guerrilla groups throughout the world are able to garner for themselves quite impressive inventories. The permeability of borders means that states close to conflict zones will find that arms circulate uncomfortably freely: the war in Afghanistan has meant that in Pakistan arms are easily available to various groups. In such situations the state loses one of its usual major attributes: monopoly control over armed force. The capacity of those who oppose state policies to translate this into armed opposition is becoming more pronounced. Where semifeudal political structures are married to the diffuse possession of arms, the chance of conflict is all the higher. This factor only increases the need state leaders perceive for outside assistance and arms suppliers, just as it raises the level of tensions that can produce conflict.

Despite the growing understanding of, and emphasis on, the nonmilitary aspects of international security, states in the developing world in the 1990s are bound still to be concerned by the military component of power and influence. Rare will be the opportunities for states to emulate Panama's action in early 1990: disband their armed forces and concentrate only on the challenge (in the cited case awesome) of economic and social reconstruction. Expenditure on armaments will remain higher than justified by the level of national resources, and the incidence of conflict greater than beleaguered peoples should be asked to tolerate. Regional powers will still seek the establishment or maintenance of a regional security order that is consistent with long-held ambitions and the requirements of domestic security.

But except in the case of a very major conflagration, the great powers are unlikely to be perturbed by most regional conflict that takes place in the

1990s. The disengagement of the superpowers from most regional conflict and the elimination of their rivalry as an ordering principle of international relations means that the global significance of local conflict in the Third World is much diminished. The local salience of traditional disputes may have increased, but their international importance is more difficult to measure. The condemnation of the international community of Iraq's attack on Kuwait may well serve to deter some from taking analogous action. But by and large it will be rare that the outside world, and particularly the United States, is confronted with a case where the defense of international law and the interests of realpolitik coincide so happily. Civil wars throughout the world will not offer easy opportunities to invoke international law as a spur to action from outside, whereas much international conflict will not offer as clear evidence of the breach of law as was the case in the Gulf in 1990. Much regional conflict will remain at a sufficiently low intensity (from the perspective of outsiders, although not of the participants), to ensure, however sadly, the relative indifference of the international community. Few newspapers in the summer and early autumn of 1990 filled their front pages with the many continuing military conflicts in third world areas outside the Persian Gulf.

Conclusion: The Incoherence of Third World Politics and Insecurity

The fact that there is no coherent threat within or from the Third World limits the possibilities for establishing a grand strategy to deal with the instability of the developing states. Economic and technical assistance from North America, developed Europe, Japan, and Australasia is in demand from both the East and the South. Some of the principles that have (or should have) guided development assistance to the South are now relevant to the East. The developed powers will continue for reasons of humanitarian concern, and sometimes for reasons of realpolitik, to support allies and friends in the developing world, just as they encourage their new friends emerging on the European continent. Diplomatic efforts will be made to resolve conflict, and military aid will be proffered to long-standing allies and to others in instances where the transfer of military equipment or the granting of a precise guarantee is seen to have a powerful stabilizing effect. But the reasons to do this will be more ad hoc than in the days when anticommunism provided an overarching rationale for much of Western military and diplomatic activity.

The tremendous reservoir of military power that exists in the United States, which planners will no doubt wish to make more rapidly deployable in the coming years, means that the United States will be capable of intervening abroad. Some countries may seek effectively to rent U.S. power (as Kuwait did when it asked for reflagging of its ships, or as Saudi Arabia did in August 1990) but the complexity of third world insecurity is such that it is hard to imagine many instances where U.S. interests would be sufficiently at stake to sacrifice U.S. lives. One wonders whether an ambitious attempt to enforce international law, known to be honored more in the breach than in the observance, could have the sustained support of the U.S. people. Becoming the UN's policeman is unlikely to be an attractive option for U.S. presidents. Acceptance of the natural anarchy of international affairs may be unsatisfying, but it is easier, and therefore in the long term more tempting, than to give a blanket commitment to uphold the rule of law in all areas.

Given the ambiguities of third world security, we must be cautious about falling prey to a "rent a threat" psychosis. Whatever the challenges to Western interests sometimes made by leaders of Muslim states, there is no Islamic threat against which one can easily deploy military resources. Fighting the drug problem, illegal migration, or nuclear, ballistic, and chemical proliferation are all appropriate ends of foreign policy, but they cannot form the foundations of that policy. In the absence of a general threat against which a coherent defense policy can be constructed, it may also be ill-advised to fashion too grand a mission or design that would govern foreign policy. The defense of international law is one such case, but so, too, is the promotion of democracy. The consolidation of democracy is a goal that, for example, the United States rightly gives itself in Europe and in Central America, but as the principal theme of its foreign policy throughout the world it would be unsustainable, not only for lack of resources, but because there will always be compelling reasons of realpolitik to put to one side considerations of the political structure of foreign states. This is precisely what happened when the United States and many other Western democratic states rightly decided to deploy force in defense of Saudi Arabia and to seek the eventual restoration of the Kuwaiti royal family to its throne.

That said, North Americans, as well as the people of Western Europe, now have a great opportunity to return to first principles (or to develop them) in their policies toward the Middle East, Africa, Asia, and Latin America. Development assistance, which will come to be seen more and more as an integral part of security policy, can be more directly aimed to ensure that democratic processes are respected where they exist and nurtured where they are nascent. The end of the Cold War, however, does not mean that a new Wilsonian order is upon us. Internal and international relations in the developing world are entering a period of greater anarchy. While they muddle through in their bilateral relations with these states, the instinctive reaction of the world's large and developed powers should be more to stand by and watch rather than to become overly engaged in promoting specific regional security regimes. The United States or European states will not be able, especially in areas like the Middle East, to reshape and hold balances of power without getting dangerously enmeshed in ever changing domestic and international politics. In these circumstances the onus to create the local conditions for development and security will be, rightly and more than ever before, on the regions' leaders themselves. That will be a good thing.

An earlier version of this essay was presented to the Aspen Strategy Group meeting on "American Strategy for the 1990s," Aspen, Colorado, August 12–18, 1990.

Notes

1. Speech recorded in official daily newspaper *Haqiqat-i Engelab-i Sawr*, December 21, 1985, cited by Olivier Roy in "The Lessons of the Afghan War," *Adelphi Paper* (London: Brassey's for IISS, forthcoming 1991).

2. Hamish Macdonald, "Back to Feudalism," *Far Eastern Economic Review* 145 (July 13, 1989).

3. See David Menashri, "Iran: Doctrine and Reality," in *The Iran-Iraq War: Impact and Implications*, Efraim Karsh, ed. (London:

Macmillan; Tel-Aviv: Jaffee Center for Strategic Studies, 1989), pp. 42–57.

4. Salamat Ali, "Hand of God," *Far Eastern Economic Review* 149 (July 5, 1990), pp. 24–25.

5. See *Strategic Survey 1989–1990* (London: Brassey's for IISS, 1990), p. 63.

6. Victor Mallet, "Kuwaitis Step up Demand for Democracy," *Financial Times* (London), January 16, 1990.

7. See Mahnaz Ispahani, "Pakistan: Dimensions of Insecurity," *Adelphi Paper* 246 (London: Brassey's for IISS, 1989) for a still-relevant discussion of Pakistan's security dilemmas.

8. Santiago Rompani, "La Integración Imposible: America Latina," *Revista Occidental* (Instituto de Investigaciónes Culturales Latinoamericanas, Mexico) 7, no. 1 (1990), p. 11.

9. Tony Allen, "Water in the Arab Middle East: The Nile, Changing Expectations and Priorities," *Arab Affairs*, no. 8 (Winter 1988–1989), pp. 50–51.

Regional Security, Arms Control, and the End of the Cold War

Geoffrey Kemp

THE END OF the Cold War has raised expectations in the United States, Europe, and the Soviet Union that military budgets will be cut, arms-control agreements will be signed, and a peace dividend will allow for retrenchment and greater investment in domestic programs. There also is great hope that the appeal of arms control and force reductions, as well as democracy and the free market, will spread to other regions of the world.

A case can be made for optimism. The pressures on national defense budgets are intense, and the only question remaining is which components of the force structures of the North Atlantic Treaty Organization (NATO) and Warsaw Pact will take the greatest cuts. No politicians are going to argue against such cuts unless there is an international crisis directly impinging on Western security. The unconstitutional removal of Soviet President Mikhail Gorbachev would be the event most likely to prompt a more conservative attitude to defense retrenchment. Likewise, in Eastern Europe and the Soviet Union, it will take a disaster of great magnitude to increase defense investment.

Furthermore, in recent years there has been an encouraging easing of many problems of international security in the developing world. The Soviet Union has pulled its forces out of Afghanistan and has agreed to major cutbacks of forces in East Asia, especially along the Sino–Soviet border. Vietnam is withdrawing from Cambodia. The superpowers have helped broker an end to the Angolan war and Namibian independence is now a reality. In Latin America the appeal of Marxist guerrilla movements armed and supported by the Soviet Union is on the wane. On the more functional issues of arms control, the Soviet Union has agreed to abide by the terms of the Western-sponsored Missile Technology Control Regime (MTCR) to limit missile transfers to conflict regions and, with the United States, has agreed to significant cuts in its arsenal of chemical weapons.

There are, however, three good reasons to be more skeptical about the prospects for reducing regional conflict and implementing regional arms-control agreements. First, superpower retrenchment itself will create a vacuum, and regional powers will move quickly to fill the void. Second, sources of conflict in key regions of

Geoffrey Kemp is senior associate at the Carnegie Endowment for International Peace. He served as special assistant to the president during the first Reagan administration.

the world have not gone away and in some areas, such as the Near East and South Asia, the prospects for war are growing. Third, and perhaps, most telling, there is no sign that countries in regions of conflict have the political incentives at this time to work together to reduce tensions; in fact, the evidence points in the other direction—many of them are rearming with top-of-the-line military equipment.

Superpower Retrenchment and the Regionalization of Conflict

The end of the Cold War will accelerate a process that has been underway for some time, namely the regionalization of regional conflicts.[1] Each region is likely to adapt to retrenchment in its own way. In some cases, for example Latin America, the United States will retain considerable influence. In other areas, such as Africa, neither the United States nor the Soviet Union is likely to have much impact on events in the coming decade. In important regions such as the Middle East and East Asia, however, the United States and the Soviet Union will retain vital interests even as their capacity to influence events diminishes, compelling increased cooperation with major regional powers. This is likely to lead to new strategic alignments and a continuation of classical geopolitics and balance of power policies.

With the diminution of superpower power has come a gradual removal of the collective security shields that both the Atlantic alliance and the Eastern bloc have provided to regions around the Eurasian landmass and, on occasion, have extended to areas in Africa and Latin America. Collective security not only has carried with it the assurance of superpower support in times of crisis—including the occasional use of superpower military forces—but it also provided subsidized access to arms, supplies, and economic aid. As the collective shield, the arms, and the aid all begin to wither, those regions formally protected by these cold war accoutrements will seek alternative means to assure their security.

U.S. allies in Europe and Asia are worried about a cutback in U.S. forces that is too precipitate. They fear that the drawdown of U.S. forces in Europe, the Mediterranean, the Indian Ocean, and Southeast Asia will compel states in those areas suffering local rivalries and conflicts to increase their own military capabilities or to look for another hegemon for protection. Fears of U.S. withdrawal are most apparent in Europe, where the concern is tied to the issue of a united Germany and its potential for domination of the continent. In the Pacific and East Asia there is concern that if the United States reduces its presence and abandons its military bases in the Philippines and Japan, it will be only a matter of time before Japan or China emerges as the hegemonic regional power.

There also are parallel concerns that the breakup of the Soviet empire will create instability around its huge border. Long-muted regional conflicts in Eastern Europe already have reemerged all around the region, as well as inside the Soviet Union. Poland, in particular, feels vulnerable as it views the prospects of a united Germany, a breakup of the Warsaw Pact, and uncertainty over the future of the Baltic states.

Along the southern periphery of the Soviet border, ethnic violence is prevalent. Fighting between Azerbaijanis and Armenians at one point called into question the Soviet army's ability to protect nuclear weapons installations in the region.[2] There is speculation about the Balkans once more becoming a potential catalyst for conflict. The Soviet Union's decision to cut back on support for radical regimes in the Arab world has caused a geopolitical earthquake in that region.

Who will be the new hegemons, aside from Germany, Japan, and China? If the Koreas ever reunite, a third regional superpower could emerge in East Asia with potentially traumatic implications for regional security. The leading candidates in Southeast Asia must be Indonesia and Vietnam, with India playing an increasingly assertive role in the more westerly precincts. All three of these countries, however, are so burdened with economic problems that their capacity to expand defense capabilities may be limited.

On the subcontinent itself, India already dominates its neighbors. In fact, it is seen by some as a regional bully. Sometimes Pakistan's importance is brushed over too quickly, although by any standards, Pakistan is a potentially important regional military power, especially in the context of Gulf geopolitics. It is, after all, a nuclear weapons state.

In the Gulf, the current focus is on Iraq's emergence as a hegemon, a prospect that sends both thrills and chills throughout the Muslim world. On the one hand, Iraqi leader Saddam Husayn is seen as a strong man capable of standing up to Iran, Israel, and the West; on the other hand, he is viewed as a rapacious bully determined to use his military might to force the smaller Arab oil-rich states to pay his bills and the rest of the Arab world to accept his leadership pretensions.

Eventually, Iran once more will re-emerge as a power to be reckoned with in the Gulf, irrespective of the nature of its regime. In their more somber moments the Iraqis are aware that the best ally they had toward the end of the fighting with Iran was the late Ayatollah Ruhollah Khomeini, whose impact on the conduct of the war led to disastrous military decisions. A more "moderate" Iranian leader would pose serious problems for Iraq and the smaller states of the Gulf Cooperation Council (GCC). How the GCC countries try to juggle their security needs in the face of two such antagonistic and strong powers will be a test of their diplomatic ingenuity in the future.

In the Arab–Israeli context, Arab countries are struggling to adapt to the impact on their security of Soviet retrenchment. In the short run this has been beneficial for Israel. Not only has the Soviet Union cut back on arms supplies to radical states such as Syria, but it also has opened its doors to Jewish emigration to Israel. It is estimated that 400,000 to 900,000 Soviet Jews may go to Israel in the next 10 years.

To counterbalance these two "shocks," the Arabs have attempted to patch up differences and present a common front against Israel. This has proved elusive. Egypt, the key Arab country, cannot afford to alienate the United States, which still provides over $2 billion in aid every year. Iraq, the pretender to the leadership of the Arab world, remains at odds with Syria.

Latin America presents a different case. It never has been plagued with the ethnic and religious rivalry common to the Near East, Asia, and Africa. Furthermore, most of the guerrilla and radical movements in Latin America have been influenced primarily by Marxist ideology rather than nationalism and ethnicity. As a consequence, the collapse of Soviet power and authority has led to a shift on the part of the mainstream Latin radical movements toward politics rather than violence as a way to achieve social change.

In Africa it is possible that Nigeria and a politically stable South Africa could emerge as the dominant powers south of the Sahara, but this is far from clear. Africa is so overwhelmed by economic and social problems that its importance on the geopolitical stage is likely to decline in the coming decade.

Traditional Conflicts with New Ingredients

Despite the surge to democratic rule in Europe and parts of Latin America and the hope that the freedom virus of 1989 will spread, the basic sources of conflict in most regions of the world remain unresolved. Moreover, new sources of antagonism have emerged as well. At the top of the list is the gap in the rate of economic development.

In the Gulf states and East and Southeast Asia, several countries have prospered due to either the export of oil or the development of high technology industries. The small countries of the Arab Gulf are modern, affluent societies. To be sure, they face serious problems in the years ahead, but these are more political than economic in origin. Singapore, Hong Kong, Taiwan, and Korea are now referred to as newly industrialized countries (NICs); Thailand and Malaysia have shown strong economic potential in the past few years. In Latin America, Chile has reemerged with a strong economy. Elsewhere in the Western Hemisphere, however, the absence of economic growth and a parallel rise in the conditions of social chaos, including rapid population growth and an educated but unemployed youth, suggest increasing political instability. The

same is true for the Arab countries not exporting oil, whose youthful populations are becoming more and more discontent with the status quo. This has led to a rise in Islamic fundamentalism.[3]

Without sustained economic growth and the resolution of the debt crisis, political discontent is bound to grow. Yet, there is unlikely to be enough capital to finance the huge debt burden of the poor countries while at the same time finding the funds to bail out the bankrupt Communist regimes in Eastern Europe and the Soviet Union. The financial needs for the reconstruction of the Eastern bloc are huge. While the prospects for an economic bonanza are attracting Western capital, there remain enormous environmental costs to be met. One estimate is that it will take $200 billion to deal with industrial pollution alone.[4]

In addition to problems of debt and population dynamics, most regions, including parts of Europe, are still bedeviled by historic disputes over borders, economic zones, water sources, and immigration. These issues, together with new environmental problems such as deforestation, flooding, and industrial pollution, have emerged as important factors on the national security agendas of many countries. For instance, what initially may appear to be an environmental issue often can manifest itself as a national security issue at the regional level. For example, if as a result of flooding in Bangladesh, caused by the cutting of forests in Nepal and the gradual rise in sea levels in the Bay of Bengal, less and less land is available to cultivate, illegal immigration from Bangladesh to India is likely to increase. This poses burdens for local authorities and further antagonizes relations between immigrants and the indigenous population. It is easy to see how in such circumstances violence can erupt and relations between poverty-stricken states can be stretched to the breaking point.

At a more general level, the efforts by environmental movements in the West to stop such activities as cutting down the rainforests of Latin America and Asia often alienate the countries in those regions, who argue that they cannot afford to pay the price for pristine environmental activity unless they receive economic help from the industrial powers, who, they contend, are responsible for most of the global pollution.

Regional Conflict and Regional Arms Races

The evidence in the key regions around the Asian landmass is that regional conflict is alive and well. The best hard data to confirm this point relate to fears about new wars and the statistics of arms proliferation, which reflect in a very clear and ominous way the investment many countries are making in their military forces at a time when the talk in Washington is of disarmament.

Indeed, while Presidents George Bush and Mikhail Gorbachev met in Washington at the beginning of June 1990 for a summit bantered about as the formal end of the Cold War, there was speculation that the Near East and South Asia were once more on the brink of war, this time made more scary by the presence of weapons of mass destruction. The Arab–Israel conflict remains unresolved and the chances for a breakthrough in the peace process have been reduced thanks to the chaotic state of Israeli politics and the short-sightedness and self-defeating policies of the Palestinians and the majority of the Arab governments. While the Iran–Iraq war

may have ended, there is no peace agreement or even peace process underway. On the subcontinent, after optimism in 1989 that India and Pakistan were at last on the verge of ending their bitter conflicts, the crisis in Kashmir erupted and the two countries moved closer to war than at any time since 1971. In Southeast Asia fighting between Cambodian insurgents and government troops has intensified, while confrontation between China and Vietnam over control of the Spratley Islands in the South China Sea is seen as a possibility. There are at least three elements of the regional arms races that are new and disturbing. First, the quantity and quality of arms found in regional conflict areas have reached unprecedented levels and the ability of local military forces to project power far beyond their borders has increased. Second, the Iran–Iraq war demonstrated the effectiveness, under certain conditions, of chemical weapons and surface-to-surface missiles (SSM) and has raised fears about the further spread of weapons of mass destruction, including nuclear weapons. Third, new suppliers—the so-called second tier—have entered the arms market and can provide some of the weapons that previously were the monopoly of the superpowers and the Europeans.

Force Levels and Power Projection. The regional powers spend most of their defense budgets on modern conventional weapons, not on the more publicized surface-to-surface missiles and weapons of mass destruction that have captured attention in the recent past. The numbers are impressive. Egypt, India, Iraq, Israel, and Syria all have more main battle tanks in their inventories than either Britain or France, the former colonial powers. Israel and Iraq have more armored personnel carriers and India has more combat aircraft than all NATO countries with the exception of the United States. India has the world's third largest army and the seventh largest navy. Syria and Egypt have forces far larger than Spain.[5]

While raw numbers are not as large in other regions of the world, there has been a significant trend toward force modernization and the expansion of defense budgets. Military developments in East Asia are particularly significant. Japan already possesses the fifth largest navy in the world and has plans to acquire a number of guided missile destroyers and two aircraft carriers, which would make it the preeminent naval power in the region.[6]

With 394 combat aircraft, 1,600 main battle tanks, and armed forces 1,249,000 strong, Vietnam remains a formidable military power, although whether it can afford to modernize its forces remains to be seen.[7] Indonesia, Malaysia, and Singapore have begun to cooperate on matters of defense. In February 1989, a memorandum of understanding was signed to give Singapore's armed forces extensive training in Indonesia.[8] Singapore has commissioned its first West German–designed corvette, and has received 8 U.S. F–16 aircraft. Thailand, which already has 18 F–16 fighters, has acquired 400 new armored personnel carriers of Chinese design and is hoping to obtain 300 main battle tanks that the United States is withdrawing from Europe.[9] Finally, Malaysia has concluded a major arms deal with the United Kingdom for a total of £1 billion that is said to include an unspecified number of Tornado fighter jets, Rapier surface-to-air missiles (SAM), and a refurbished submarine.[10]

Numbers alone provide merely a broadbrush view of the arms race. In terms of the quality of the weapons,

the picture is equally striking. The array of conventional equipment includes top-of-the-line American-made items such as the Abrams main battle tank, F–15 and F–16 fighters, and the improved Hawk SAM. The best Soviet equipment also has been transferred, including MiG–29s, which have gone to India, Syria, and Iraq, and SU–24s, which have gone to Libya, as well as a Soviet Charlie–I class nuclear submarine that was received "on loan" by India, bringing up to 17 the number of submarines in the Indian navy.[11]

Britain, France, and China have sold their best fighter aircraft to a number of countries. In addition to the deal with Malaysia, Britain concluded two agreements with Saudi Arabia in 1986 and 1988 covering the sale of 118 Tornados, 48 Hawk light fighters, 90 Black Hawk helicopters, and a number of trainer aircraft.[12] These two agreements, worth $10 billion and $20 billion respectively, represent the largest aircraft sale ever between the United Kingdom and a Middle Eastern country. China also has supplied a large number of fighter aircraft to North Korea, Pakistan, and Egypt.

Several regional countries now have conventional military forces that can operate at increasing distance from their borders, posing potential threats to a wider number of neighbors, as well as to other forces operating in these regions. Of particular interest is Iraq's recent military buildup, which has raised anxieties in Israel as well as a number of Arab states. India's growing power projection capabilities, demonstrated with interventions in Sri Lanka and the Maldives, are indicative of India's determination to become a major regional power.

Chemical, Biological, Nuclear Weapons and Missiles. The spread of weapons of mass destruction and their delivery systems, especially missiles, is at the focus of new concerns about proliferation. Although nuclear weapons remain in a class by themselves, the use of chemical weapons in the Iran–Iraq war and the low-keyed response of the international community have made them an attractive alternative to nuclear weapons for technically deprived countries wishing to develop military capabilities for both deterrence and war-fighting.

Vietnam, North Korea, Taiwan, Libya, Syria, Iran, and Iraq, as well as Egypt and Israel, are believed to have active chemical weapons programs. Iraq, however, is reported to maintain the largest chemical weapons program in the Third World, and is believed to be producing mustard gas as well as nerve agents, including sarin and tabun.[13] Iraq also is believed to have a research and development center that may be used for biological weapons research and development.

Chemical weapons do not equate with nuclear weapons in terms of destructive power. Against a well-protected, forewarned population or military force, the effects of even the most lethal nerve agents can be limited. Thus, for chemical weapons to be most effective, they have to be used without warning against defenseless, unprotected populations. It is this characteristic that makes them so abhorrent.

Even more frightening than the prospect of chemical weapons use is the prospect that there will be greater efforts to develop and use biological weapons. Biological weapons are comprised of living organisms that can cause often infectious, incurable diseases such as anthrax, the plague, or tularemia.[14] Only tiny amounts of these bacterial agents are necessary to create widespread infection; in an aerosol attack, 0.077 ounces of tularemia would produce a cloud 325 feet high, taller than a 20-story building, and 0.62 miles square, with infectious doses multiplying every minute.[15] More than 400,000 people could die within five days of such an attack, with many more deaths following in the surrounding areas.[16] Biological weapons have the potential to be much deadlier than chemical weapons and, according to CIA Director William Webster, yield the widest area coverage per pound per payload of any weapon system in existence.[17]

The CIA has stated that at least 10 countries in the world currently are working to produce biological weapons, and any nation with a pharmaceutical industry conceivably can assemble biological warfare agents.[18] Although biological weapons have not been attributed specifically to any countries in the Near East and South Asia, it has been reported that Iraq possesses a biological warfare facility near the village of Salman Pak, 35 miles southeast of Baghdad.[19] An Israeli official has stated that the Iraqis have developed a military capacity without having manufactured actual weapons, that less-advanced Syrian biological research exists, and that Libya has attempted to buy information on biological warfare.[20] The charges have been denied by Iraq, one of the 111 signers of the 1972 Biological Weapons Convention (BWC) that bans such weapons.[21]

Advances in biotechnology also are making possible the eventual mass production of toxins for weapons use. These are chemical substances found in living organisms that can be reproduced with genetic engineering techniques. A good example is rattlesnake venom, an organic toxin, which when mass produced could act as a chemical weapon for which there is no antidote.[22] Toxin weapons represent a dangerous blurring of the distinction between chemical and biological agents, as they are derived from living organisms, but the toxin itself, whether collected from the living organism or genetically reproduced in a laboratory, is not alive and acts as a poison rather than as a disease.

Biological weapons, although more deadly and potentially much more destabilizing than chemical weapons, possibly rivaling nuclear weapons, have not been given the same attention that chemicals have received. This is perhaps because they do not pose as immediate a threat as do chemicals and, indeed, their potential—and limits—are not yet fully understood. Biological weapons also are perceived as "unusable," in the same sense that nuclear weapons are unusable, meaning that the cost of their use so far exceeds any gains that it seems unthinkable. However, as with nuclear weapons, the cost of failed deterrence with biological weapons could be devastating.

Surface-to-surface ballistic missiles with widely varying ranges, payloads, and accuracies are present in the arsenals of Algeria, Egypt, Iraq, Iran, Israel, Kuwait, Libya, Yemen, Saudi Arabia, Syria, both Koreas, Taiwan, Argentina, and Brazil. Most of these missiles are obsolescent, Soviet-designed unguided rockets and first-generation guided missiles with limited range and poor accuracy that are not deployed in large numbers. Although most of these systems are far from state-of-the-art missile technology, some countries have been successful at modifying and enhancing their capabilities. Faced with the lack of a retaliatory capability when Iran began to launch missile attacks on Baghdad, Iraq embarked upon an ambitious project to extend the range of its Soviet-supplied Scud-B guided missiles. By reducing the size of the warhead compartment and leaving more room for the missile propellant, Iraq developed the 600–700 km range Al-Hussayn missile and the 900 km Al-Abbas.

The most significant event in the development of indigenously modified Scud-B SSM systems came in early December 1989 when Iraq test-fired a 48-ton, 3-stage, 25-meter long satellite launch vehicle named Al-Abid (the Worshiper), and at the same time it claimed it had "come through the most complicated and important stages in the development and production of two different SSM systems, each of which has a 2,000 km range."[23]

Israel also has an impressive missile arsenal, with U.S.-supplied short-range Lance missiles, as well as the indigenously developed Jericho I and II missiles. Israel also is believed to be involved in a research and development effort aimed at extending the range of the Jericho II missile to 1,450 km. There is speculation that this new Jericho IIB system was test-fired on September 14, 1989, when a 1,300 km range missile is reported to have fallen 400 km north of the Libyan city of Bengazi.[24] Israel continues to push full speed ahead with the Shavit, its satellite launch vehicle, which on April 2, 1990, placed into orbit the 160 kilogram (kg) Ofeq-2, Israel's second satellite.[25] Depending on the estimates, an Israeli missile based on the Shavit could have a range of 5,200 to 7,200 km, both of which are sufficient to hit all targets within the Middle East and even Moscow.[26]

Syria possesses a small number of more accurate but short-range Soviet SS–21s. It is reported to be trying to purchase Chinese-made 600 km range M–9 missiles, which are currently under development, after the Soviet

Union refused to sell it the longer-range SS–23 missiles, which are slated for destruction as a result of the Inter-mediate-Range Nuclear Force (INF) treaty with the United States.[27]

Saudi Arabia's missile, the Chinese East-Wind, presently has the longest range in the region (2,700 km). Although Saudi Arabia has taken a number of measures to reassure the United States that it has no aggressive intentions and does not plan to develop chemical or nuclear warheads for its missiles, the low accuracy and high price of this system raise questions about its military effectiveness if used only with conventional warheads.

India and Pakistan both have short-range missile programs under development. On September 27, 1989, India test-fired a 250 km range, single-stage, liquid-fueled missile named Prithvi. The Prithvi, which can carry a payload of 1,000 kilograms, and is, therefore, nuclear-capable, is reported to be almost ready for delivery to the Indian army and air force.[28] Other tactical missiles developed by India are the Trishul and Akash SAM systems, and a modern antitank missile system. Pakistan currently is developing two short-range missiles, the Hatf I and II, with ranges of 80 and 300 km respectively.

More significant, however, is India's intermediate-range missile capability. In May 1989, India test-fired the Agni, a 2-stage, 14-ton, 19-meter long rocket, with an estimated potential range of over 2,500 km.[29] Although the Agni is claimed to be the result of indigenous engineering efforts, technology transfers in the fields of satellite launch vehicles and guidance systems from West Germany, France, and the United States partly are responsible for the success of the Agni program.[30] Although India continues to claim that the Agni is merely a tech-nology demonstrator and has no military uses, the strategic implications of the Agni are quite clear.[31] The Agni's symbolic nature was underscored in the words of one Indian official who stated: "As long as China can reach New Delhi with its ICBMs [intercontinental ballistic missiles], India will remain in a weak position. . . . Can any self-respecting country accept that?"[32]   The Afghanistan conflict has highlighted the growing relevance of missile technology to modern warfare. The use of surface-to-surface missiles during the 11-year conflict, and particularly since the withdrawal of Soviet troops in February 1989, has been very extensive. The Afghan army has been generously supplied with Soviet-made Scud-B missiles; more of them were used in Afghanistan in 1988 than in the entire "War of the Cities" between Iran and Iraq.[33] In November 1988, the Afghan army began firing Scud-Bs on mujaheddin bases around the eastern province of Nangarhar, as a reprisal for the use of multiple rocket launchers against civilian populations.[34] The change from a guerrilla war to a more conventional confrontation during the siege of Jalalabad by mujaheddin forces increased the effectiveness of SSM systems used by the Afghan army. Over 400 Scud-B missiles were fired against mujaheddin troop concentrations around the city of Jalalabad, partly contributing to the defeat of the rebel offensive.[35] In the 10 months following the withdrawal of Soviet troops in February 1989, between 900 and 1,000 Scuds were fired by the Afghan army.[36] There also have been numerous reports of Scud missiles being fired against guerrilla bases in Pakistan, with one missile falling as close as 30 km northeast of Islamabad.[37]

In East Asia, both North and South Korea as well as Taiwan have deployed SSM systems. North Korea possesses a number of unguided Frog–7 rockets it obtained from the Soviet Union, as well as a reverse-engineered version of the Soviet Scud-B which was made possible with Egyptian help.[38] North Korea also is believed to be developing a 450–600 km extended range "Scud PIP," which would enable it to hit any target on the Korean peninsula.[39] South Korea is armed with U.S.-supplied unguided Honest John missiles and with an indigenously developed 2-stage solid propellant SSM with a range of 110–160 miles. This missile is believed to be a converted version of the U.S. Nike Hercules SAM. South Korea also is pursuing an extensive space launch program and has announced that it intends to launch a space vehicle by 1991 (some experts believe that it aims to obtain long-range and even intercontinental ballistic missiles).[40]

Taiwan has the 60-mile range Green Bee, which is derived from the U.S. Lance, and is developing the 620-mile range Sky Horse, which would enable it to hit a wide range of targets in mainland China.[41] Recent intelligence reports suggest that Indonesia may be in the beginning stages of a ballistic missile program. It is developing a missile designated as the RX–250 that could be based on the sounding rocket technology utilized by Indonesia since 1987.[42]

Within Latin America both Brazil and Argentina have developed SSM systems. Argentina's Condor II project recently was abandoned, although Brazil continues to push ahead with a family of missiles whose ranges vary from 90 to 620 miles, and with the 185 mile range SS–300 and the 740-mile range SS–1,000. Neither country, however, is known to have deployed missiles.[43]

Intelligence reports concerning nuclear weapons present overwhelming evidence that Israel is a fully fledged nuclear weapons power and that India and Pakistan have nuclear weapons production capabilities. Iraq's interest in the acquisition of nuclear weapons has been a continuing source of concern. Despite Israel's raid in June 1981 on the Osiraq nuclear reactor, which destroyed it, there is strong circumstantial evidence that Iraq has continued to pursue its nuclear weapons program, possibly in cooperation with other countries, including China.[44] A sting operation arranged by U.S. and British officials led to the arrest in spring 1990 of a number of Iraqi citizens attempting to smuggle nuclear detonators called krytrons out of London's Heathrow airport and into Iraq. Iraq continues to deny that it is attempting to acquire nuclear detonators and has described the issue as an attempt by Western media to discredit Iraq and give Israel an excuse to launch a strike against Iraq's nuclear and military installations.[45]

Iran and Libya also have sought nuclear weapons in the past. Iran launched an extensive nuclear weapons program under the shah, but the revolutionary government showed little interest in pursuing the program further when it came to power in 1979. In November 1987, Iraq dealt the Iranian nuclear establishment a severe setback when it bombed the Bushehr reactor construction site (left uncompleted in 1979).[46] Rumors again have begun circulating that Iran is gearing up its nuclear program, with one report stating that Iran is seeking to have nuclear fuel production capability.[47]

North and South Korea, as well as Taiwan, are possible candidates to join the nuclear club. Although Taiwan and South Korea have been dissuaded from acquiring these weapons through U.S. military assurances, North Korea's nuclear energy program remains a major concern. Recently, intelligence reports have disclosed the existence of a nuclear fuel reprocessing plant in Yongbyon, 100 km north of Pyongyang. This plant can obtain plutonium from spent nuclear fuel, which then can be utilized for the construction of a nuclear weapon. Moreover, despite being a signatory to the 1972 Non-Proliferation Treaty (NPT), North Korea has not allowed the International Atomic Energy Agency (IAEA) to inspect its nuclear facility at Yongbyon. Taiwan has signed the NPT and is currently believed not to be pursuing a nuclear weapons program, although it has an extensive civilian nuclear power program and the capability to produce a nuclear explosive device.

New Suppliers. A third reason for concern about the military buildup in regions of conflict relates to the changing relationships among the supplier countries and the impact this will have on efforts to implement arms-control regimes. In the past, the U.S.–Soviet rivalry has provided a bonus for many Third World countries that were able to obtain large quantities of military grant assistance or low-interest loans by playing off one side against the other. In exchange, both countries had the power—used but rarely—to exert great influence over their clients.

Although the drawdown of competitive aid programs will mean less assistance and leverage in the future, it will not mean that the superpowers will opt out of the arms market. Each superpower retains strategic interests in these regions and each will have a large arms industry seeking profitable ventures with regional countries that can pay the price. Furthermore, the Third World arms market not only keeps Britain and France actively in-

volved as weapons suppliers, but it also has attracted a large number of new suppliers, including China, Argentina, North Korea, South Korea, and Brazil. China has emerged as an important arms supplier, providing a wide selection of basic weapons, including combat aircraft, tanks, missiles, artillery, submarines, and small arms. During the mid-1980s, when the Iran–Iraq war was at its peak, China was the largest arms exporter in the developing world. Although its export capacity is in no way comparable to those of the United States and the Soviet Union, China has carved out a corner of the arms market as a supplier of less sophisticated conventional technology sold at cut-rate prices.[48] It also should be remembered that in Eastern Europe and the Soviet Union there are thousands of skilled weapons specialists who now may take advantage of the freedom to travel to work for profit in those countries able to pay hard currency. Trying to put a cap on the transfer of people will be much more difficult than controlling technology.

Argentina, Brazil, and Singapore also are emerging as weapons suppliers to the Third World. From 1977 to 1987, Latin America and East Asia increased their world arms export market shares from 0.4 to 1.7 and 1.3 to 3.2 respectively.[49] Although Brazil and Argentina appear to be concentrating on the high end of the weapons supply spectrum—including missiles, aviation and avionics, and armored combat vehicles—Singapore's strength is in smaller weapons and ammunition. There are growing indigenous arms capabilities in all of these regions, with Israel and India in possession of the most sophisticated industries. Israel has been active in the arms market for many years, and in 1988 it exported a record $1.47 billion in arms to 61 nations. The first half of 1989 saw a 40 percent increase in sales of Israel Aircraft Industries, 75 percent of which was accounted for by increases in exports.[50] Last year India announced that it, too, would begin to promote foreign arms sales.[51] Egypt, Iraq, Iran, and Pakistan also have strong production capabilities in certain categories of weapons, especially ammunition and small arms.

In sum, the diversification of the arms market and the increasing sophistication of some of the weapons produced by new suppliers suggest that although the United States and the Soviet Union probably will remain the most important suppliers, in part due to their great capacity to provide weapons in large quantities in times of war, their dominance is slowly eroding. If the East Asian economic powers, especially Japan and Korea, decide to enter the market in a big way, they quickly could achieve a very strong competitive position. The idea of Honda or Toyota making jet fighters may be premature, but it is not impossible given the anticipated changes in Japan's strategic status.

Implications for U.S. Policy

What do these trends mean for U.S. diplomacy and national security policy in the 1990s? One thing is clear; a new age of internationalism cannot be assured. In the absence of sustained global economic growth it appears less and less likely. If internationalism is not possible, can the United States distance itself from the traumas of this new world and retreat to a neo-isolationist posture with international involvement primarily focused on economic matters?

Although neo-isolationism may be appealing to some, it is unrealistic. The ideological zero-sum games of the Cold War may be over, but geopolitics, as an important component of international relations is not dead. Geopolitics may now have to share the spotlight with other items on the agenda, but it will remain a driving factor in the way the world works. In a regionalized, competitive world, with numerous sources of unresolved conflict, the United States is destined to remain a key world power with global interests as well as the need to retain the military capacity to intervene directly or indirectly in those regional conflicts where its interests are most clearly at stake. This means that it will have to adapt to the new regional political and military environment by seeking and maintaining security ties with close friends and allies with whom it shares similiar values, as well as others.

For example, although U.S. strategic interests in the Persian Gulf are not preordained or absolute, so long as the United States pursues an energy policy that depends more and more on this region for oil, it cannot "opt out" from the security problems of the region just because it is becoming weaker relative to the regional powers. For the foreseeable future, the United States will remain committed to the security of Israel and some of the moderate Arab countries. Similarly, there is no way any administration can ignore the impact that a dramatic change in the balance of power in East Asia would have on U.S. interests throughout the region, including the all-important economic component. To be able to influence events in this key region the United States must retain a viable, albeit reduced, forward military presence. It also must continue to use arms sales and arms assistance to support key regional players.

How does such a policy coexist with the need to work to limit weapons proliferation and seek regional arms-control arrangements as a way to control the spread and danger of local conflict?

U.S. policy toward regional conflict and arms control will remain torn between the desire to limit weapons proliferation and the need to continue to support friends and allies and to be prepared, as a last resort, to intervene in certain contingencies with U.S. military force. In both the Near East and East Asia, the United States has such enormous interests at stake that arming its friends is necessary, in part at least to assist its own military capabilities should it ever have to intervene to protect Korea, Israel, or Saudi Arabia or to secure Gulf oil supplies. Yet, in doing so, its own assertive policies on arms sales and a forward, if reduced, military presence become part of the problem of implementing regional arms-control arrangements. There is no neat and easy solution to this dilemma. Until there is peace in the Middle East, or an alternative energy source is found, or the Koreas unite, no U.S. administration will or can abandon these two regions.

In the meantime, what can be done about the dangers of regional conflict and arms races? There is a growing consensus among the industrial powers that something should be done to put limits on the transfer to regions of conflict of weapons of mass destruction and of some of the most sophisticated conventional technologies. There is, however, a significant ideological gap between the industrial powers and many of the regional states that see arms-control initiatives as an attempt to interfere with their national security needs at a time when the old collective security umbrellas are being removed.

Most regional states believe that arms-control arrangements must either parallel or follow progress on the resolution of regional conflicts, not precede it. The exception would be informal arrangements to avoid conflict (for example, the so-called "red lines" that have existed between Israel and its neighbors) and the Indo–Pakistani agreement not to attack each other's nuclear facilities.

There also remain analytical problems of relating arms-control measures to regional security needs. It is difficult to separate out the impact of nuclear, chemical, missile, and conventional proliferation and treat each item separately if one takes into account the realities of national security in the region. From a practical perspective, however, disaggregating the components of the arms race so far has proved to be the only manageable—and partially successful—way to focus attention on them.

The United States must continue to work within the framework of several multilateral channels to control nuclear and chemical weapons and surface-to-surface missiles. Efforts to promote a worldwide ban on chemical weapons seem to be making the most progress. In September 1989, at a meeting between Soviet Foreign Minister Eduard Shevardnadze and U.S. Secretary of State James A. Baker III, the United States proposed cutting superpower chemical arsenals by 80 percent in anticipation of the conclusion of a global chemical weapons convention.[52] President Bush followed this announcement with a proposal before the UN General Assembly for the United States and the Soviet Union to reduce their chemical stockpiles by 98 percent within eight years of the conclusion of a chemical weapons convention, followed by the destruction of the remaining 2 percent over two years once all states with a chemical weapons production capability had signed the treaty.[53] The Soviets countered with a proposal not only to reduce stockpiles, but to prohibit U.S. and Soviet production and to renounce the use of chemical weapons under any circumstances.[54]

On May 9, 1990, the Bush administration offered to stop the production of chemical weapons in an effort to attain a compromise by the May 1990 summit date.[55] In exchange, the Soviet Union was asked to agree to reduce its current stockpile of chemical weapons to 5,000 tons, and to retain a 2 percent supply of chemical weapons even after a global ban is negotiated at Geneva.[56] During the May 1990 summit an agreement was signed between the United States and the Soviet Union regarding chemical weapons. Both countries agreed to reduce their current stockpiles to 5,000 agent tons by 2002 and immediately to discontinue production of chemical weapons without waiting for a global ban to come into effect.[57]

Concerning ballistic missile proliferation, a group of seven states—the United States, Canada, France, Italy, Japan, the United Kingdom, and West Germany—formed the MTCR in April 1987, to deal with the growing threat posed by the spread of ballistic missile technology. The MTCR focuses narrowly on those missiles that are considered to be nuclear-capable (which is defined as those having a range of at least 300 km and a payload capability of at least 500 kg). The agreement consists of a set of parallel export controls in each member country, dependent for enforcement on the laws of each state. The agreement prohibits the transfer of conventional SSMs, space launch vehicles, key subsystems for SSMs, and facilities to produce them. Other items to be limited are on-board computers, inertial navigation systems, liquid and solid rocket fuel, testing equipment, flight control equipment, materials for rocket body and engine parts, and technology and know-how for the above items. Any of these items sold must be accompanied by the assurance that they will not be diverted to rockets.[58]

Since its inception, the MTCR has become a focal point, specifically in the United States, in the fight to stop the spread of *all* ballistic missile technology in the Third World. Its current status as an export control agreement between states, rather than as a formal treaty, leaves it open to different interpretations by each of the member states. The MTCR is further stymied by the fact that two principal surface-to-surface missile suppliers to the Third World, the Soviet Union and China, are not members, although the Soviet Union has said that it will abide by the "export guidelines of the existing regime."[59] (The exception will be Scud missile supplies to Afghanistan, which will continue until the United States stops arming the guerrillas.) Any attempt to use the MTCR as the basis for a more comprehensive ballistic missile control agreement would have to take all of these factors into account. The MTCR also is a highly discriminatory mechanism because it makes no demands on its signatories for cutting their own arsenals and offers no incentives for compliance to those it is directed against.

In the realm of nuclear weapons, the NPT divided the world into the nuclear "haves" and "have-nots" with the purpose of halting the spread of nuclear weapons technology in exchange for promoting the spread of peaceful nuclear energy technology. Embodied in the treaty is a commitment by those nuclear weapon states party to the treaty to work toward global nuclear disarmament. With 139 member states, including three nuclear weapon states—the United States, the Soviet Union, and the United Kingdom (France and China are not members)—the NPT is the most sweeping, comprehensive, and probably most successful technology control regime in existence.

At the same time, however, the NPT has not been signed by Israel, India, Pakistan, Brazil, Argentina, or South Africa. Security concerns and the desire for great power status have proved to be more important considerations for these countries than the amorphous goal of halting nuclear proliferation. India has led the fight against the discriminatory nature of the NPT. After the August 1990 NPT review conference, the treaty will run for five more years, until it expires in March 1995, unless it is renewed or a new agreement is signed.

There presently are no international institutions that deal with conventional arms control—in fact, most of the industrial countries that are working together to control nuclear, chemical, and certain missile technologies are competing with each other for sales of high technology conventional arms. This paradox is exemplified by the fact that the U.S. undersecretary of state for security assistance has *both* the arms control *and* arms sales portfolios in his office.

If there is a lesson to be learned from the European experience on conventional arms-control negotiations, it is that until there is movement toward the resolution of basic political and geographic aspects of the problem, detailed blueprints for arms control will not succeed. Europe at last is making progress on arms control because the political environment has changed.

Indeed, the most promising avenues for serious arms-control arrangements are those that involve the regional players themselves, with or without the cooperation of the external powers. These can take many forms, including both informal and formal agreements. Although the external powers may be able to slow and, on occasion, intervene on an ad hoc basis to prevent certain inherently dangerous activities (for example, chemical weapons programs in Libya), there is little hope for comprehensive agreements without regional cooperation, especially at a time of superpower retrenchment.

The dilemma is most apparent in the case of chemical and nuclear weapons in the Middle East. It might be possible to focus on chemical weapons or nuclear weapons if some proximate symmetry existed between the adversaries, but unlike the situation in Europe, this is not the case. Israel will not give up its nuclear monopoly in the absence of an iron-clad peace treaty, a treaty that would have to extend to relations with Iraq and possibly Iran. On the other hand, the Arabs cannot be expected to support a comprehensive chemical and missile ban as long as Israel has nuclear weapons. The rally of Arab support behind Iraqi President Saddam Husayn highlights this trend.

Thus, we have a Catch-22 situation. High-level arms-control initiatives on major weapons systems prior to an ongoing peace process are unlikely to work unless the countries of the region agree to them. However, the political problems of reaching a peace settlement and deciding where one state's security ends and another's insecurity begins are so complex that a decision to postpone major arms-control initiatives encourages a continued arms race that has built-in dangers and can lead to war.

How can these two positions be reconciled? The practical answer must be to pursue *limited* arms-control objectives *prior* to peace negotiations and to accept that substantive progress on resolving the tough issues of nuclear and chemical weapons and SSMs will have to wait until the political environment improves. The best time to negotiate a ban or strict limitations on weapons of mass destruction would be the period following a peace settlement between the primary adversaries. In contrast, the most inappropriate time to raise the issue of, for example, Israel's nuclear weapons, would be during the period when Israel is being asked to make territorial concessions and perhaps to agree to the creation of a Palestinian state. At that moment, Israel will be preoccupied with security issues and its population will be divided on the correct action to take. The case for territorial compromise will rest on the types of security guarantees that can be negotiated. Until the format of a peace settlement finally is settled, no Israeli government will give up nuclear weapons.

In conclusion, it is easy to develop schemes for greater U.S.–Soviet cooperation to end regional conflict, including greater restrictions on the transfer of certain technologies and weapon systems. This has some encouraging possibilities, but if such actions are undertaken in such a way as to convey a superpower condominium, they will backfire. Superpower cooperation that ignores the realities of regional politics could end up leading to more conflict and greater efforts to circumvent restrictions on weapons technology. In contrast, superpower cooperation that directly involves the regional powers holds the most promise for success. In the meantime, the United States will have to plan for continued, although more limited, intervention capabilities in regions crucial to its national interest.

This paper draws upon ongoing work at the Carnegie Endowment on arms proliferation and arms control funded with support from the MacArthur Foundation and the U.S. Institute of Peace. The author would like to thank Alvaro Tafur and Shelley Stahl for their help in preparing this paper.

Notes

1. For a sophisticated treatment of this question see Earl C. Ravenal, "The Regionalization of Power: General Unalignment in the Future International System" (paper presented to the 31st annual meeting of the International Studies Association, Washington, D.C., April 10–14, 1990).

2. The most recent attack on a Soviet nuclear weapons facility took place in mid-February 1990. See "Soviet Rebels Storm an A-Bomb Facility," *Washington Times,* February 19, 1990.

3. For a comprehensive review of the problems facing the Arab world, see "The Arab World Survey," *The Economist,* May 12, 1990.

4. Frederick Painton, "Where the Sky Stays Dark," *Time,* May 28, 1990, pp. 40–42.

5. The numbers are as follows. For main battle tanks: Egypt, 2,425; India, 3,650; Iraq, 5,500; Israel, 3,794; Syria, 4,050; Britain, 1,290; France, 1,815. For armored personnel carriers: Iraq, 7,100; Israel, 10,380; Britain, 3,437; France, 3,275. For combat aircraft: India, 836; Britain, 821; France, 628; United States, 3,205. Source: *The Military Balance 1989–1990* (London: International Institute for Strategic Studies, 1989).

6. For current Japanese force levels see *The Military Balance 1989–1990;* for Japanese naval expansion plans see "If Nanny Retires," *The Economist,* May 12, 1990, p. 38; and "Asia Puts its Wealth in Military," *Washington Times,* February 12, 1990.

7. *The Military Balance 1989–1990,* p. 178.

8. *Ibid.,* p. 151.

9. "If Nanny Retires," p. 38; and *The Military Balance 1989–1990.*

10. *The Military Balance 1989–1990,* p. 151.

11. *Ibid.*, p. 159.

12. Ian Curtis, "Saudi Arabia's European Connection," *Defense and Foreign Affairs*, January 1989, pp. 15–16.

13. W. Seth Carus, *The Genie Unleashed: Iraq's Chemical and Biological Weapons Program* (Washington, D.C.: The Washington Institute for Near East Policy, 1989), pp. 12–19.

14. Robert D. Shuey, *et al.*, "Missile Proliferation: Survey of Emerging Missile Forces," p. 31.

15. Gary Thatcher, "Poison on the Wind: The New Threat of Chemical and Biological Weapons," *Christian Science Monitor*, December 15, 1988.

16. ABC World News Tonight with Peter Jennings, January 17, 1989, reported by Charles Glass, in *Current News Early Bird*, Special Edition on Chemical Weapons, February 28, 1989, no. 1781.

17. Statement of William H. Webster, director of the Central Intelligence Agency, before the U.S. Senate Committee on Governmental Affairs, Hearings on Global Spread of Chemical and Biological Weapons: Assessing the Challenges and Responses, February 9, 1989.

18. *Ibid.*

19. See Stephen Engelberg, "Iraq Said to Study Biological Arms," *New York Times*, January 18, 1989; David B. Ottaway, "Official Denies Iraq Has Germ War Plant," *Washington Post*, January 19, 1989; and "Iraq Has Developed Biological Weapons, Says Israeli Official," *Financial Times*, January 19, 1989.

20. "Iraq Has Developed Biological Weapons."

21. Ottaway, "Official Denies Iraq Has Germ War Plant."

22. See testimony by Barry J. Erlick, senior biological warfare analyst, U.S. Army, before the U.S. Senate Committee on Governmental Affairs, Hearings on Global Spread of Chemical and Biological Weapons: Assessing Challenges and Responses, February 9, 1989.

23. See "Hussayn Confers Names on Rocket, Missile Systems," INA, 1125 GMT, December 9, 1989, translated in Foreign Broadcast Information Service–Near East Service (FBIS–NES), December 12, 1989, p. 20; "Satellite Carrier System Tested," Voice of the Masses, 1230 GMT, December 7, 1989, translated in FBIS–NES, December 8, 1989, p. 23.

24. "Soviets Claim Israel Has Launched BM," *Jane's Defence Weekly*, September 23, 1989, p. 549.

25. "Official Communique Issued," Jerusalem Domestic Service, 1500 GMT, April 3, 1990, translated in FBIS–NES, April 4, 1990, p. 26.

26. Different estimates of the range of the Shavit by the Lawrence Livermore Laboratories and the Department of Defense were cited in Stephens Broening, "Israel Could Build Missiles to Hit Soviets, U.S. Thinks," *Baltimore Sun*, November 23, 1988.

27. David B. Ottaway, "China Warned Against Selling Syria Missiles," *Washington Post*, June 23, 1988; and "Syria is Studying New Missile Deal," *New York Times*, June 22, 1988.

28. On the test of the Prithvi, see Richard M. Weintraub, "India Succeeds in Missile Test Launching," *Washington Post*, February 26, 1988; and Sanjay Hazarika, "India Tests Its Own Surface-to-Surface Missile," *New York Times*, February 26, 1988. On the missile's range and payload, see "Shooting Ahead," *India Today*, March 31, 1988, p. 170; and Aaron Karp, "The Frantic Third World Quest for Ballistic Missiles," *The Bulletin of the Atomic Scientists*, June 1988, p. 14.

29. See Barbara Crossette, "India Reports Successful Test of Mid-Range Missile," *New York Times*, May 23, 1989; Richard M. Weintraub, "India Tests Mid-Range 'Agni' Missile," *Washington Post*, May 23, 1989; and "Advanced Surface-to-Surface Missile Tests Planned," Hong Kong, Agence France Presse, 1550 GMT, May 26, 1989, in FBIS–NES, May 30, 1989, p. 60.

30. Gary Milhollin, "India's Missiles—With a Little Help from Our Friends," *The Bulletin of the Atomic Scientists*, November 1989, pp. 31–35.

31. "India ICBM Could Signal Nuclear Weapons Program," *Defense and Foreign Affairs Weekly*, May 8–14, 1989, pp. 5–6.

32. Statement by an undisclosed official quoted in "India Proposes Building of

ICBM," *Defense and Foreign Affairs Weekly*, June 5–11, 1989, p. 1.

33. Barnett R. Rubin, "End the Cold War in Afghanistan," *Washington Post*, November 29, 1989.

34. "Army Begins Firing Soviet Made Missiles," Hong Kong AFP, 1350 GMT, November 3, 1988, reported in FBIS–NES, November 4, 1988, p. 47.

35. "The Ox Won't Budge," *The Middle East*, August 1989, p. 22.

36. Martin Fletcher, "Soviet Crew 'Firing Missiles at Rebels' in Afghanistan," *The Times*, December 10, 1989; "Diplomats Note 'Major Soviet Arms Shipment,'" Hong Kong AFP, 1119 GMT, January 9, 1990, reported in FBIS–NES, January 9, 1990, p. 53.

37. "Afghans Fire 'Scud,'" *Jane's Defence Weekly*, January 20, 1989, p. 99. See also "Kabul Forces Fire Scud Missile at Peshawar Area," Islamabad Domestic Service, 1500 GMT, April 7, 1989, translated in FBIS–NES, April 10, 1989, p. 56; and "Protest Lodged Over Afghan Scud Missile Firing," Islamabad Domestic Service, 1500 GMT, June 6, 1989, translated in FBIS–NES, June 7, 1989, p. 68.

38. *World Military Expenditures and Arms Transfers 1988* (Washington, D.C.: U.S. Arms Control and Disarmament Agency, 1989), p. 19; and Joseph S. Bermudez, Jr., and W. Seth Carus, "The North Korean 'Scud B' Programme," *Jane's Soviet Intelligence Review*, April 1989, p. 177.

39. "The North Korean 'Scud B' Programme," p. 178.

40. W. Seth Carus, "Missile Proliferation in the Third World," testimony before the U.S. Senate Armed Services Committee, Subcommittee on Defense Industry and Technology, May 2, 1989.

41. Duncan Lennox, "The Global Proliferation of Ballistic Missiles," *Jane's Defence Weekly*, December 23, 1989, pp. 1384–1385.

42. "Indonesia Advances Towards Space Race," *Washington Times*, March 31, 1988.

43. "Missile Proliferation: Survey of Emerging Missile Forces," Congressional Research Service, October 3, 1989, p. 42.

44. "Iraq and the Bomb," *Mid East Markets*, December 11, 1989, p. 13.

45. Carlyle Murphy, "Arabs Rally Around Iraqi Leader, Allege West is Biased," *Washington Post*, April 12, 1990.

46. Leonard Spector, *The Undeclared Bomb* (Cambridge, Mass.: Ballinger Publishing Co., 1989), pp. 221–224.

47. The report out of Cairo refers to a Kuwaiti newspaper quoting diplomatic sources in Japan that Iran purchased large quantities of material for nuclear weapons production in Japan in 1987. See "Nuclear Weapons Program Reportedly Started," Cairo, MENA, 1340 GMT, April 21, 1989, reported in FBIS–NES, April 21, 1989, p. 46.

48. For details of the global trends in arms exports, see Stephanie G. Neuman, "The Arms Market: Who's on Top?" *Orbis* 33:4 (Fall 1989), pp. 509–531. For a more extensive discussion of Chinese arms sales policy, see Jennifer Reingold and Shelley Stahl, "Notes on Chinese Arms Exports to the NESA Region" (paper prepared for Carnegie Endowment Project on Arms Control and the Proliferation of High Technology Weapons in the Near East and South Asia, October 1989).

49. *World Military Expenditures and Arms Transfers 1988*, p. 10.

50. See "Israel Defence Export Figures," *Jane's Defence Weekly*, June 24, 1989, p. 1299; and "Export Boost for IAI," *Jane's Defence Weekly*, October 21, 1989, p. 887.

51. See Sanjay Hazarika, "India Plans to Increase Arms Imports and Exports," *New York Times*, February 5, 1989.

52. Michael R. Gordon, "U.S. Asks Soviets to Agree to Cuts in Chemical Arms," *New York Times*, September 25, 1989.

53. See David Hoffman, "Bush Urges Chemical Arms Cuts," *Washington Post*, September 26, 1989; Maureen Dowd, "End the 'Scourge' of Chemical Arms, Bush Says at U.N.," *New York Times*, September 26, 1989; and Michael R. Gordon, "Neutralizing Poison Gas," *New York Times*, September 26, 1989.

54. See Paul Lewis, "Soviets, Welcoming Bush's Plan on Chemical Arms, Go Further," *New York Times*, September 27, 1989; and Don Oberdorfer, "Soviet Calls

for End of Chemical Arms," *Washington Post*, September 27, 1989.

55. Michael R. Gordon, "In a Switch, Bush Offers to Stop Producing Chemical Weapons," *New York Times*, May 9, 1990.

56. *Ibid.*

57. "Summary of U.S.–Soviet Agreement on Chemical Arms," *New York Times*, June 2, 1990.

58. *Missile Technology Control Regime*, United States Department of Defense Fact Sheet, April 16, 1987, pp. 1–4.

59. Joint Soviet–American Statement released by *Tass*, Moscow, February 10, 1990.

Whose Collective Security?

Edward C. Luck and
Toby Trister Gati

THE FOUNDERS OF the United Nations (UN) had it right, but it took 45 years and the end of the Cold War to prove it: given the proper international environment, the entire global community can mobilize a collective response to aggression through the UN. The international community was determined to oust Iraq from Kuwait by diplomatic, political, economic, and, finally, by military means, but it was, in the end, a Security Council authorization to use force—even if it was not a "UN force" itself—that provided the mandate to the 28 nations allied with the United States to undertake the Persian Gulf War. After the ceasefire agreement was signed, the UN returned to center stage to carry out that agreement's disarmament provisions, especially the dismantling of Iraq's nuclear, chemical, biological, and ballistic missile capabilities, its restrictions on the sale of Iraqi oil and the use of funds for humanitarian purposes, and its procedures for returning properties taken during the occupation of Kuwait.

The UN's founders had hardly intended, however, that one member state should play such a dominant role in marshaling the world's military

The authors are president and senior vice president for policy studies, respectively, of the United Nations Association of the USA (UNA-USA), an independent organization that carries out policy research, international dialogue, and public education about the UN and U.S. policy in the UN.

might and that in doing so it should ignore the collective security mechanisms outlined under chapter VII of the UN Charter. Moreover, they would have been shocked to witness the collapse of the Soviet Union just when the possibility of U.S.–Soviet cooperation in defense of peace—for four decades the dream of every supporter of a more activist UN—seemed within reach.

If the original vision of the United Nations has new life, then, there are also many unanswered questions about the shape of future international security arrangements. Indeed, by turning to the United Nations as a critical component of its Gulf strategy, the United States brought to the surface both the hopes and the fears surrounding any discussion of collective security. If today's transformed international environment raises the hope that the collective might of the international community can protect the weak against the strong, as originally intended in the UN Charter, it also raises concerns that the strong will seek to impose their vision of world order on the weak, without regard for the principles of national sovereignty and noninterference in domestic affairs also enshrined in the UN Charter. The ambivalence of many states toward a stronger UN is now coupled with apprehension about a pax Americana, even a UN-centered one, without a Soviet counterweight.

If collective security has a future, it

is not yet clear what it will look like. Americans are far from eager to assume the role of global policeman, but neither are U.S. political leaders ready to suggest putting even part of U.S. military forces under an international or UN command. Other countries have similar concerns. During the Persian Gulf War, national leaders of the major contributing states hailed the new era in international relations, but none expressed a willingness to cede authority to the UN so that it might implement existing provisions of the charter regulating the use of force. The detailed structures for implementing collective security outlined in the UN Charter need to be reviewed in light of the changing international security environment of the world after the Cold and Persian Gulf wars. For if a "new world order" is to be created, a way must be found to strengthen the institutional capability for responding to global threats to the peace.

Here, the role of the United States is crucial. It is the only country with the combination of political, economic, and military strength necessary to defend the interests of smaller countries against powerful neighbors. At the same time, as seen in the Gulf, preponderant military power cannot always be brought to bear without the active support, both political and increasingly financial, of other states in the international community. Not every crisis will rivet U.S. attention as did the Iraqi invasion of Kuwait or call for a massive U.S.-led response. But if the United States does not take the lead, then who will? In a world characterized by repeated outbreaks of low-level fighting between neighboring states and disregard for the welfare of civilian populations caught in the cross fire, by mistreatment of ethnic or national minorities, and by large-scale human rights violations, the greatest threat to international stability may be a situation in which everyone knows something should be done but no one wants to take the lead.

It is at this point that "the system" should take over—a system of collective responsibility that would engage the international community in tasks ranging from preventive diplomacy, to economic sanctions, and to joint military action as needed to maintain international peace and stability. The UN Charter provides for such a system and it is the purpose of this paper to consider ways in which its collective security provisions can be strengthened and reinvigorated to take advantage of exciting new possibilities in the post–cold war world.

National decision makers in many parts of the world, not least in Washington, D.C., are rediscovering the potential utility of the range of coercive actions permitted the UN Security Council under the charter's chapter VII, with its 13 articles detailing the possibilities for a concerted multilateral response to threats to international peace and security. There is no lack of authority or tools, as amply demonstrated in the diplomatic, economic, and military efforts to expel the Iraqi invaders from Kuwait. But this was a highly unusual situation that provides no clear precedent for the future. If the UN's full potential as an instrument of collective security is to be realized, four clusters of questions need to be addressed with some urgency:

- Who should have the authority to decide when to invoke the charter's collective security provisions, or more precisely, which countries should be represented on the Security Council and how should it take its decisions?

- Who should be authorized to oversee the implementation of sanctions and the use of force once these steps have been mandated by the council?
- When should the UN decide to become involved in a local conflict and when should it leave this burden to regional organizations or to the parties themselves?
- Who pays the bill when the UN is asked to serve as world policeman and how are the funds to be raised?

The UN Charter speaks to all of these concerns to some extent, of course, but fuzzy answers that seemed acceptable in the days when the UN was usually left sitting on the sidelines are inadequate as the organization enters the center ring of international security politics for the first time. In the days ahead, these provisions are likely to be tested as never before.

Who Decides?

It is clearly the Security Council—the subject of all 13 articles of chapter VII—that has full and unrivaled responsibility for determining when and how collective security steps will be undertaken. Only the council has the authority under international law to make decisions that are binding on all member states. So with the new-found cooperative spirit among the five permanent members—none has cast a veto on a substantive issue in almost two years—has come increasing discussion among the whole UN membership about the composition of the council itself. The more active and assertive the council becomes, the more the 150-plus member states not on the council will mutter about decisions it makes in their name but without their input.

The Persian Gulf War was a striking case in point. Although initially there was widespread excitement in the UN about the close collaboration of the five permanent members of the Security Council, over time the disenfranchised expressed growing apprehensions. They included both developing countries, concerned about their exclusion from UN decision making, and leading developed countries like Germany and Japan, which were expected to shoulder much of the cost of the UN-authorized operations but were largely excluded from key decision-making sessions. Simply put, during the Gulf crisis most UN members were left out of the process of consultation and deliberation that led up to the resolution authorizing the use of force. Even the 10 elected, nonpermanent members of the Security Council professed frustration that the permanent five met alone under U.S. leadership to design security policy and then presented them with a fait accompli to be voted up or down. For the rest—more than nine-tenths of the UN's total membership—the system seemingly afforded no say at all. They were not involved in the consultations, and their assent was unnecessary according to the charter even on decisions that could bind their actions.

This is particularly galling to the larger states in the developing world that exert enormous influence over events in their regions and in the General Assembly yet have no comparable input into UN security policy. Because it is in the developing world, after all, that the UN again and again becomes involved, developing countries large and small are uneasy about the way future decisions on critical war and peace issues may be resolved at the UN. The fact that U.S. power is no longer counterbalanced by another superpower only heightens these concerns. Paradoxically, the renewed emphasis on consensus in UN decision making has resulted not only in a less acrimonious process but also in suspicions in some developing countries of a more subtle, behind-the-scenes dominance by the United States. Even the low-key, restrained U.S. stance in the selection of a new secretary general in the fall of 1991 was at first misinterpreted by some of the smaller countries as a U.S. device for getting its way without having to express its preferences publicly.

Even some American allies, who once complained that the United States failed to use the UN, now fret that it may use the world body too much, turning it into a mere instrument of U.S. foreign policy. On the other hand, if the middle and smaller powers seek to make the UN a mechanism for constraining U.S. power, then trouble could lie ahead. The UN cannot succeed without strong, constructive U.S. leadership, while the United States needs the UN to manage and promote a fair international division of labor and burden-sharing arrangements on security as well as development issues. The Security Council could not work under cold war conditions, but sustaining a balance of interests in a post–cold war world in which the United States is the only remaining superpower will also be a challenging proposition for all concerned.

The larger economic powers in the industrialized world do not fear UN encroachment on their domestic order, but, like many developing countries, they too resent their exclusion from decision-making circles. Because they are assessed substantial amounts for UN operations that the Security Council authorizes and they are obliged to suspend economic relations when the council imposes sanctions, UN enforcement actions have real consequences for them. Accustomed to being part of the inner circle that makes decisions in other areas of international policy-making, some of the Group of Seven (G–7) economic powers complain that this is tantamount to "taxation without representation." Japan has been especially vocal in recent years in insisting it should be part of the Security Council circle; Germany has also begun to voice similar concerns. Certainly if key economic powers like Japan and Germany showed a greater willingness to participate directly in peacekeeping and enforcement operations, as the British and French did in Desert Storm, it would enhance their claims for permanent Security Council seats.

The case of Japan demands special attention. The Persian Gulf War shook politics in Japan more than in any other country and raised questions among the Japanese about their country's status in the international community. The question of whether or not Japan should send support troops or even nonmilitary personnel to the region was especially divisive. The Japanese government did agree to send minesweepers to the Persian Gulf after hostilities ceased. The promised legislation to permit not only greater logistical, communications, and medical support of UN peacekeeping operations, but also participation of the Japanese Self Defense forces in peacekeeping has failed to pass in the Diet for the second time. For many, this is just one more sign of Japan's unwillingness to accept its global responsibilities. At the UN, whose charter still refers to the Axis "enemy states," the Japanese are particularly sensitive about being excluded from levels of decision making commensurate with their economic influence. A permanent voice in the Security Council might prod Japan to consider more seriously how and toward what ends its influence will be used in the world, although China is likely to resist a permanent seat for Japan, and France and the United Kingdom have opposed any changes that would bring their special status into question. All three, of course, can veto any amendments to the charter, including changes in the composition of the Security Council.

The issue of the council's composition is clearly coming to a head. The corridor talk on this question at the UN is far more serious than in the past and, with the organization's rapidly expanding security role, it is framed with a good deal more urgency. Amending the charter may be tantamount to opening a Pandora's box, but it was accomplished on several occasions in the 1960s and 1970s without significant harm. In each case, moreover, the primary purpose was to increase the size of UN bodies to more fully reflect the organization's growing membership. The Security Council, for example, was enlarged from 11 to 15 members in 1965.

A number of formulas are being floated that would keep the council to a manageable size, retain the same veto-carrying permanent members, and give both major donors and major developing countries a more permanent voice in the council's deliberations. We would recommend that, first, Japan and Germany be given permanent but not veto-bearing seats and the "enemies clause" (article 107) be deleted and, second, that Africa, Asia, and Latin America each be given an additional rotating seat, also without a veto, so that big countries like India, Nigeria, and Brazil can sit on the council with greater regularity. These steps would raise the total membership of the council from 15 to 20. The future

of the Soviet seat, with its veto, depends on developments within the Commonwealth of Independent States, as well as on the ultimate legal and political judgment of the international community. It seems to us, however, clearly preferable on both international legal and political grounds to have Russia as the legal successor state to the Soviet Union and the other republics as independent, separate UN members. Giving the council seat to Russia would be the best way to ensure the continued excellent cooperation of Security Council members. In any case, the breakup of the Soviet Union has spurred a more urgent look at the makeup of the council and has whetted the appetite of other large countries for a permanent seat.

Over the longer term, a more radical restructuring of the Security Council might be contemplated. Although the whole structure of the UN is based on the member state system, the growth of regionalism is likely to persist in both the economic and security realms. With the end of the global competition between the United States and the USSR, international politics are increasingly defined in regional terms, especially on security issues, and here the biggest problems are local, not global. This suggests two steps, one simple and short term, the other complex, controversial, and long term. The easy part is for the five permanent members to expand consultations within their respective regions on the major issues that are before the council or likely to arise in the foreseeable future. To a certain extent this has already taken place within the European Community (EC) and among the G–7, but the process should be regularized. Over time, if the sense of regional identity grows and regional organizations begin to assume a larger security role, the UN Charter might be amended to give a voice and possibly a veto to each major region (North America, Latin America, Western Europe, East Central Europe, Africa, East Asia, and South Asia) on UN intervention in that area. The current permanent members would retain permanent seats, at least in the near term.

Who Enforces the Peace?

The war with Iraq displayed both the strengths and the weaknesses of the UN system of collective security for all the world to see. The UN itself proved to be a remarkably good forum for rallying an international political response to naked aggression, yet when it came to using force, the carefully laid out provisions in chapter VII of the UN Charter were never invoked. The UN's authority was proclaimed everywhere—including most vividly in the U.S. Senate—up to the point of authorizing the use of force, and again the UN came front and center in the effort to clean up the mess left by Desert Storm. But the world body seemed to fade once again into irrelevance when the fighting was in progress.

There were, of course, good reasons for this pattern: after all, the evolution of international relations has not yet reached the point at which most nations are ready to accept international command of their forces in combat. And there is reason to question whether a UN command could have prosecuted the war as efficiently as the coalition and with as little loss of life among allied troops. But there were political costs to excluding the world body completely, including a loss of credibility both for the United Nations and for the concept of a "new world order."

Clearly, the international community is still improvising rather than institutionalizing mechanisms for dealing with regional crises. The mobilization of a global consensus was possible in the Persian Gulf not only because the Iraqi actions were so egregious but also because the United States was willing to take the lead politically, diplomatically, and militarily (although not financially). Future crises may follow a similar pattern, but many states feel that eventually the role of world policeman should rightly belong to the world community as a whole rather than to any one country—no matter how strong—and that authority and responsibility should be shared more equitably among all nations. A number of recent opinion polls, moreover, have shown that the U.S. public is not eager to have the United States play the role of global policeman and would far prefer to send the UN's blue helmets to handle regional crises rather than the U.S. Marines. Whether this represents a growing confidence in the UN, a desire to have other countries carry more of the burden, or a new isolationist spirit remains to be seen.

For all its shortcomings, no one has been able to advance a more credible plan than the UN Charter for carrying out collective security. Moving beyond "pacific settlement of disputes" under chapter VI of the charter to enforcement actions under chapter VII, however, has put the UN into largely uncharted territory. The Kuwaiti crisis of 1990 led to a highly improvised application of the collective security *principles* in the UN Charter, while the charter's *provisions* for UN enforcement of security (Military Staff Committee, UN troops, UN command) were circumvented.

Whether the UN collective security structures envisioned almost half a century ago, with the various peacekeeping mechanisms that have evolved since, can be reshaped to make the UN a potent agent for international security—and whether the major powers have sufficient commitment to making them work—is an open question. The resistance of major military powers to consideration of a unified or UN command and the general reluctance of member states to negotiate "special agreements" for standby forces under article 43 of the charter bespeak the difficulties involved.

Article 43 goes to the heart of the matter because the UN at present has no forces automatically at its disposal and must appeal to the members to volunteer forces even for noncombatant peacekeeping missions. This sometimes results in significant delays in responding to urgent crises, reducing the world body's credibility as a potential deterrent to would-be aggressors. In a long-forgotten passage of the 1945 UN Participation Act, which defined U.S. relations with the new United Nations organization, Congress acknowledges that article 43 agreements, should they be concluded between the United States and the UN, could well turn the command of those U.S. forces over to the Security Council and thus possibly to non-American officers. This might be seen today by many Americans as ceding too much of the president's authority as commander-in-chief to a multilateral body. Certainly, in an operation as large and risky as Desert Storm, to do so would seem unrealistic, although it would be less so in more limited operations of less strategic importance to the United States.

It should not be forgotten, however, that the United States would retain a veto in the Security Council over the commitment of any UN forces. There are no precedents, moreover, so it would be quite possible to consider negotiating article 43 agreements with the UN that would stipulate that the standby forces would be put at the UN's disposal only under conditions and circumstances specifically agreed to by the president and/or Congress, and only with their consent. In other words, the United States could designate certain units, and perhaps give them special training for participation in prospective UN collective security operations, without committing them to the UN in advance.

This topic remains controversial, but we believe it is time for the United States to open quiet consultations with the other permanent members of the Security Council about the possibility of all five nations negotiating simultaneous article 43 agreements with the UN. As the countries protected by the veto, as well as by their nuclear deterrents, the five are best positioned to open this new chapter in collective security. The size of the designated forces need not be enormous, but they should fit the needs of rapid deployment and force projection missions. Logistical support, communications, and intelligence capabilities should be shared with the UN whenever possible. Although it might take some time to negotiate such agreements, as well as to get all five permanent members on board, the very suggestion that these major military powers were consulting on how to bring force to bear under the UN umbrella should in itself serve as a powerful deterrent to potential aggressors, especially after the experience of the Persian Gulf War.

Other UN member states should also be encouraged to negotiate standby agreements. Because these countries would not be able to veto the deployment of their article 43 forces by the UN, it was suggested at a UNA–USA meeting in Moscow in spring 1991 that these countries be given the right to determine whether or not their forces would take part in a particular enforcement operation. This would provide them with essentially the same assurances that possession of the veto gives the five permanent members, while making it possible for them to prepare for future enforcement operations.

A second key building block of the UN collective security system was meant to be the Military Staff Committee, consisting of the chiefs of staff of the five permanent members or their representatives. Again, the elaborate article 47 provisions regarding its operation were largely set aside during the cold war era. In the buildup to the Persian Gulf War, the committee met once at a relatively high level, chiefly to scare the Iraqis by showing the determination of the major powers, but no real efforts have ever been made to create a unified command structure under UN auspices. Should article 43 forces ever come into existence, command and control questions—and the role of the Military Staff Committee—would take on greater urgency.

In the meantime, the committee could undertake more modest, but important, roles to test the prospects for cooperation and to prove its utility. Its first task under the charter, "to advise and assist" the Security Council on military matters, makes considerable sense, especially if the UN's security role is to expand in the future It has been said that war is too important to be left to the generals, but surely questions of how to maintain the peace should not solely be the preserve of diplomats unaided by the best professional military advice the military has to offer. Among the questions on which the Military Staff Committee is to proffer advice is "the regulation of armaments, and possible disarma-

ment." In the case of Iraqi disarmament, the UN is taking unprecedented steps to disarm a major military machine. As the whole body more and more approaches arms control and disarmament as an integral component of peacemaking and peacekeeping efforts specific to regional conflicts, the technical expertise of military specialists will be increasingly important to its work, as has been the case in Iraq. Activating the Military Staff Committee to aid in these tasks, in other words, need not represent a commitment to, nor even a step toward, multilateral command and control of national forces—something the charter says would "be worked out subsequently" in any case. If the committee had been functioning fully prior to Iraq's invasion of Kuwait, it might have been helpful in several ways. First, its very activity might have been a useful deterrent, suggesting the possibility of a broad-based international response to Iraq's aggression. Second, the charter states that the committee shall be responsible under the Security Council for the "strategic direction of UN forces." This could have included, first, sorting out the general division of labor among the various national contingents deployed in the Gulf theater and, second, laying out overall military and strategic objectives in the Gulf operation, possibly including limits on the use of force against largely civilian targets. Even modest results from general consultations on these subjects could have proven beneficial politically, particularly in the uncertain months leading up to the commencement of hostilities. Third, a little-noticed clause in article 47 speaks of the establishment of "regional sub-committees," to which local UN member states would presumably send military representatives. This might have proven a politically acceptable way to expand the commitment of the moderate Arab states and others in the coalition with less political arm-twisting by the United States and less need for these Arab leaders to defend their cooperation with the United States to skeptical domestic advisers.

When Should the UN Intervene?

With increasing opportunities for UN intervention has come a growing need to choose when UN involvement is most appropriate and a renewed debate about where national sovereignty ends and international responsibilities begin. The UN Charter gives the Security Council considerable freedom to "determine the existence of any threat to the peace, breach of the peace, or act of aggression . . . and to decide what measures shall be taken" (chapter VII, article 39). And, under article 99, the secretary general is authorized to bring to the attention of the Security Council those items that "in his opinion" may threaten international peace and security.

Although the preamble lays out a series of principles and purposes that sound universal, the remainder of the charter describes a decision-making structure that is highly political and selective. In practical terms, then, most of the responsibility for deciding when, where, and how these sweeping principles will be applied rests with the members of the Security Council. Theirs necessarily must be a subjective rather than an objective judgment. Thus, council members chose to respond vigorously to the Iraqi invasion of Kuwait, but they showed no inclination to get involved in the strife in Liberia, Ethiopia, or the Sudan that raged at the same time. To some observers, this selectivity undermines the credibility and integrity of the in-

stitution as a global peacekeeper, but to others it is a sensible bow to reality in view of the UN's limited capabilities and capacity for influencing events. A keen sense of when to get involved and when to stay out, moreover, helped to sustain the organization through such politically difficult times as the Cold War.

In the past, Soviet–U.S. tensions—reflected in the penchant of the two states to use their vetoes—ensured that the UN would get involved in relatively few crises. Today, the unprecedented cooperation among the permanent members, as well as their more narrowly defined interests in the developing world, could provide—in fact already has provided—a much wider menu of problem areas calling for UN attention. With the UN's continuing physical and financial limitations, however, this growth of tempting opportunities calls for a corresponding sense of restraint and for selectivity.

Will it simply be, as many smaller nations complain, that the UN will get involved only when the interests of the five permanent members are demonstrably involved (Kuwait being a case in point) but when none of them can or wants to handle the situation unilaterally? In that case, how will the security interests of developing countries that are not deemed strategically important get addressed? There is a growing danger, for instance, that conflicts in Africa will be essentially excluded from the map of Security Council interests. Over time, it may be useful to try to develop generally applicable rules of intervention regarding when the collective security provisions of chapter VII should be invoked. For example, specific kinds of events, threats, or situations might automatically trigger Security Council action, such as the possibility that weapons of mass destruction might be used in a regional dispute, clear evidence of genocide, a huge flow of refugees that threatens to destabilize neighboring countries, massive human rights violations, the overthrow of democratically elected governments, or flagrant violation of earlier Security Council decisions. Not one of these questions has a simple answer, but each is worth grappling with if the concept of a new world order is to be based on sustainable and broadly credible political and legal norms.

The increasing demand for UN security services, especially in internal or transnational conflicts, has also raised pointed questions about the capacity of the organization to deal with so many security problems simultaneously. Some of these questions deal with the personal time, talents, and priorities of the secretary general, who cannot be everywhere at once, while others deal with the organization, staffing, and communications capabilities of the UN Secretariat for overseeing so many far-flung operations. These issues are especially timely at a point when restructuring the secretariat is being given serious attention by the member states, and a new secretary general, well-versed in international diplomacy, seeks to put his stamp on the organization. The old question of the relationship between the UN and regional organizations takes on a renewed urgency under these conditions.

The UN Charter does not assume that the Security Council will address all security problems or that it will necessarily be the first recourse in case of threats to international peace and security. Article 52, in fact, calls on member states to "make every effort to achieve pacific settlement of local disputes through . . . regional arrangements or by . . . regional agencies before referring them to the Security Council." Chapter VIII, probably the least explored territory in the charter, addresses the possibilities for coordinating the efforts of regional bodies and the Security Council aimed at both peaceful resolution and enforcement of council decisions.

Such coordination of global and regional action might have been a politically, and perhaps militarily, attractive option in the Gulf crisis, especially given the symbolic importance of bringing Arab states into the coalition. Unfortunately, in the Middle East as in other areas of strategic importance, adequate regional partners for the UN do not yet exist. In the past, when regional organizations were weak and divided or where a superpower had a clear interest, the venue for action more often than not was the Security Council. Where regional organizations exist, as in Africa, Latin America, or Europe, the track record of regional-global cooperation has been mixed at best. The recent crises in Haiti and Yugoslavia, on the other hand, engendered a greater degree of cooperation between the UN and regional organizations in dealing with stubborn local conflicts. Developing a fuller global-regional partnership would also help address the endemic problem of alienation among developing countries within the UN security structure.

One of the most fundamental questions facing the UN today is whether principles of collective security—and other global norms—apply to individuals and groups within states or only to relations between member states themselves. If the latter, then nations could be allowed to do to their own people what international norms do not permit them to do to other nations. On the other hand, if the international community can tell states how they should treat their own populations, how are these verdicts to be enforced? Many still feel reluctant to condemn the violation of human rights or disregard for basic human needs when these result from internal political breakdown or civil war. It is only in recent years that the international community has come to accept the idea that certain domestic policies (e.g., apartheid, genocide, and other massive human rights violations) should not be tolerated by the community of civilized nations. Yet the Security Council remains cautious about labeling even gross rights violations within established borders as "threats to international peace and security" requiring chapter VII action, at least beyond economic or arms transfer sanctions in especially egregious and persistent cases.

The aftermath of the Kuwait crisis dramatically raised these issues in a way that was distinctly unwelcome to many governments. The intervention by the Western powers to create "safe havens" to protect Iraq's Kurds and other minority groups from their government, for example, may have set a precedent with far-reaching consequences for traditional notions of state sovereignty. Recent suggestions by the French that international law recognize a "duty to intervene" in cases where a government's actions are creating a humanitarian catastrophe has set off alarm bells in a number of capitals, especially in the developing world.

With refugee crises around the globe and famine present or looming in parts of Africa, this controversy will not go away. Many governments assert that the "duty" concept is a dagger directed at them, threatening to formally reduce their sovereignty and affording the great powers, through the Security Council or worse yet unilaterally, an excuse to intervene in domestic conflicts. The dilemma posed by the conflict between government claims to sovereignty and human claims to survival will almost certainly become one of the major issues of international law and security in the 1990s.

Who Will Pay the Bill?

There has clearly been no "peace dividend" for the UN peacekeeping, arms monitoring, and collective security budgets. The more these services are demanded by the international community, the higher the costs to the world body. Once a small fraction of UN spending, with the launching of the Cambodia operation the costs of peacekeeping operations alone may soon exceed the whole regular budget of the United Nations. Although puny compared to the costs of national defense or of local conflicts prevented or contained, these expenditures loom very large in UN eyes. If the UN begins to undertake collective security operations directly, then its expenses will multiply many times. Operation Desert Storm, for example, cost 10 times as much as the annual outlays of the entire UN system, including all of the specialized agencies. Even a more modest collective security operation would be very expensive by UN standards.

These new demands come at an awkward time for the UN, which is still struggling to overcome the painful effects of massive U.S. financial withholdings during the mid-1980s and of smaller delinquencies by other member states. The United States has begun to pay off its arrearages, but they still exceed $500 million (or one-half of the UN's regular annual budget), of which more than $100 million (as of October 1991) is owed to peacekeeping alone. The United States is clearly a lot more ready to enunciate a new world order than to help pay for it. And although the Russians are clearly supportive of the principles of the UN Charter and supportive of recognizing the right of the international community to intervene, they may not be able to contribute even their assessed dues on time, much less extra for new peacekeeping operations in the next few years.

Although separate assessments are made for most new peacekeeping operations, the prospects for successfully completing new assignments are inevitably affected by the overall financial health of the institution. The most obvious problem has been the virtual elimination of the UN's modest reserve funds, leaving no discretionary funds that could cover the start-up costs for a new operation until the hat can be passed around the member states for longer-term support. Subsequent delays in payments from major donors, like the United States, tend to compound the problem. There is a built-in nine-month mechanical delay in the payment of U.S. regular dues, which are due each January but paid at the earliest when the next U.S. fiscal year begins in October. And U.S. funding for peacekeeping operations is particularly problematic when new operations, unanticipated by the federal budget cycle or the agreement to reduce the budget deficit are begun. Although the United States cannot solve the UN's financial problems alone, it could at least set a good example for others.

When the United States and other major contributors are unable to come up with the funds in a timely fashion, the ability of the UN to maintain peacekeepers in operation is dependent largely on the willingness of countries contributing troops to wait for compensation or on emergency supplemental support by a few states. When it was time to dispatch UN observers to the Iraq–Iran front following the UN-brokered armistice, for example, there were no funds to get them there until a member state agreed to make an extraordinary payment. More recently, the efforts of the UN Special Commission to ferret out Iraqi weapons of mass destruction were hampered by the lack of adequate transportation and logistical support from member states, which otherwise professed keen interest in the operation. Many months after the operation had begun and had proved its extraordinary value, still no funds had been appropriated by the UN member states to fund it.

The issue of financing looms even larger when one moves from peacekeeping to enforcement actions. Although Operation Desert Storm demonstrated a clear U.S. willingness to provide military leadership and troops for collective action, a central aim of U.S. foreign policy was to share the financial burdens more broadly. The Bush administration appears to have persuaded its coalition partners to pay more than $48 billion in cash and other contributions toward an estimated $60 billion in war costs, with additional Saudi Arabian payments likely. In future crises, however, the countries that foot the bill may be unwilling to allow the United States the degree of military and political control it had in the Persian Gulf and may link issues of financing to greater participation in strategic decision making. The UN, of course, can offer a forum both for sorting out the division of labor in carrying out such operations and for developing a formula for sharing the financial burden.

Another endemic problem has been the separation of substantive and budgetary decision making within the

UN. Under the charter, the Security Council has authority over the former and the General Assembly over the latter. This anomaly in the UN's structure—a bit reminiscent of Washington's system of checks and balances but more clumsy in practice—could cause serious difficulties down the road, especially if the resentment of the council's prerogatives grows among those countries excluded from its deliberations. Haggling between the council and assembly over the size and cost of the Namibian operation delayed the deployment of the peacekeeping forces and almost jeopardized the success of their mission. Japanese officials have complained that their minor role in the decision-making process for the UN-brokered peace agreement in Cambodia, which looms as the largest, riskiest, and most complex security mission ever undertaken by the UN, has not been commensurate with the financial burden Japan will be expected to carry in the implementation of the agreement.

There have been many creative suggestions for producing a larger and steadier flow of income for UN peace and security operations, which often cannot be anticipated in the regular budget cycle. These proposals have ranged from a tax or assessment on international commerce or on arms sales, to a renewal of the UN's reserve fund, to shifting U.S. contributions from the State Department to the Defense Department budget. Rebuilding the reserves should be the first priority, especially as the United States begins to pay its arrearages. Although it might be unwieldy in practice, the concept of an international levy on arms transfers is very appealing because the greater the volume of weapons proliferation, the greater the funds available to the UN to contain the consequences of their use. The possible establishment of a UN arms trade registry might provide a data base for such an undertaking. Developing countries, which depend on arms supplies from the major arms producing countries, are likely to have strong objections to such a system, however, because it would let countries with indigenous arms manufacturing capabilities off scot-free. Whether or not this is the best approach, clearly some kind of regular financing mechanism is needed, given the increasing number and importance of UN efforts at both enforcement and peacekeeping. Anything approaching a "new world order" cannot be obtained on a shoestring, especially an ad hoc one.

Conclusion

Global threats to the United States have receded, perhaps creating a false sense of security. Regional instabilities, many based on ethnic hatreds and thwarted national aspirations, are multiplying at an alarming rate. Certainly the United States cannot resolve all of them with the use of force, nor should it aspire to do so. Multilateral crisis management, peacekeeping, and collective security should be as fundamental to the defense of U.S. national security interests in the 1990s as participation in the North Atlantic Treaty Organization (NATO) has been during the past 45 years. The threats we face are different today and so should be the mix of responses.

If the White House and Congress are serious about a new world order, they should begin by putting their own house in order. A first step would be to put some real money and political capital behind their lofty rhetoric. Just as the U.S. government mobilized an international coalition against Iraq, so, too, it can energize international diplomacy to develop at least a rudimentary collective security system based on broader consultations, modest commitments of forces to the UN, and financial burden sharing.

Certainly there is the risk of failure. But the unprecedented opportunities to build new security structures that are present today will not last forever. Untapped potential is wasted potential. Without U.S. leadership in forging a new collective security system based on the UN Charter, the only alternatives when the next bully comes along will be another large-scale commitment of U.S. troops or letting an aggression go unpunished. Surely the political and security risks of either of these outcomes are greater than those inherent in a determined effort to bring the UN Charter back to life.

This article presents the authors' personal views, which do not necessarily reflect the official position of the United Nations Association of the USA.

Religion and Peace: An Argument Complexified

George Weigel

BEIRUT, AND INDEED all of Lebanon, the Golden Temple of Amritsar, Kashmir, Belfast, Tehran, the Temple Mount in Jerusalem. These being the typical reference points for most discussions of "religion and peace," it is little wonder that Western elites—our academic institutions, the prestige press, our governments—tend to think of religion, in its impact on international public life, as a source of, rather than a remedy for, violent conflict.

But the fact that these are taken to be the primary reference points, however, is not itself an accident, because it reflects the broader inclination of elite Western opinion to view religion as an irrational, premodern phenomenon, a throwback to the dark centuries before the Enlightenment taught the virtues of rationality and decency and bent human energies to constructive, rather than destructive, purposes. Nor should it be considered a secret that this elite Western suspicion of religion frequently involves a caricature of religious conviction.

It would be foolish for people of faith to deny that religion can be a source of violent conflict. It has been; it is today; it will be in the future. But it would be imprudent, unwise, and just plain wrongheaded for both religious skeptics and statesmen to ignore

George Weigel is president of the Ethics and Public Policy Center and the author of several books on ethics and international affairs.

the fact that religious conviction has also functioned as a powerful warrant for social tolerance, for democratic pluralism, and for nonviolent conflict resolution. This essay will explore the latter, often uncharted, territory in the conviction that, as religion is not going to fade from the human landscape, it is important to understand how religious faith, and the personal and social values that derive from it, can serve the cause of peace.

The Unsecularization of the World

Although rarely recognized, the "unsecularization" of the world is one of the dominant social facts of life in the late twentieth century.

This is true of the United States which, despite the predictions of two generations of secularization theorists, remains an incorrigibly religious society.[1]

It is true of central and eastern Europe; indeed, the revolution of 1989 would not have taken the form it did, and might possibly never have happened at all, without the efforts of the Roman Catholic church in Poland and Czechoslovakia and the Evangelischekirche in the late German Democratic Republic.[2] One could also mention in this regard the roles played by various Orthodox churches in Romania, Bulgaria, and throughout the republics of the Soviet Union.[3]

"Unsecularization" aptly describes

the situation in Latin America, where the traditional Roman Catholic religiosity of the population is being forcefully challenged not merely, or even primarily, by secularization but by forms of evangelical and fundamentalist Protestantism whose social impact could be supportive of economic liberalization and political democratization.[4]

"Unsecularization" also characterizes the Asian subcontinent, where Hinduism, Buddhism, and Islam, and variants on each, remain powerful social (and indeed political) forces.

Finally, "unsecularization" characterizes much of the Arab world, in which a particularly militant form of Islam is a powerful (some would argue, the most powerful) social and political dynamic.

The social, political, and geopolitical impacts of man's persistent yearning for communion with the divine are, of course, diverse in the extreme, as these examples of "unsecularization" indicate. That modernization puts great stress on traditional communities—familial, ethnic and tribal, religious—is, further, an empirically established fact.[5] But that modernization inevitably leads to radical secularization of the Scandinavian sort is a much more dubious proposition with little empirical warrant. The world is not going to become Sweden (or Cambridge, Massachusetts, or the CBS executive dining room) in the foreseeable future. Religion is, so to speak, here to stay. The task, then, is to discern the theological and political conditions under which religion serves the cause of nonviolent conflict resolution.

Religion and Cultures of Tolerance

The political *structure* of societies is a function of the political *culture* of so-

cieties. The forms and functions of governance are not the result of a kind of social virgin birth. Rather, they express the fundamental, constitutive self-understandings and values of a people—understandings and values that are frequently religious in origin and nature.

How, then, does religion contribute to the evolution of societies that prize social tolerance, that cherish pluralism, that prefer nonviolent to violent means of resolving conflicts over public life: societies that, by the values and dynamics of their own political cultures, will be likely to prefer nonviolent means for resolving conflicts among, as well as within, political communities?

The case with which we are most familiar is, of course, that of the West. Western democratic societies are the result of a complex process of cultural, economic, social, and political evolution, and it would be a prime example of the fallacy of *pars pro toto* (confusing a part with the whole) to ascribe to religion the sole place as a causal force in the development of Western democracy. Greek philosophy, Roman law, feudalism, and the Enlightenment each played a key role in shaping Western democracy—and its preference for legal and political, that is, nonviolent, conflict resolution—as we know it today. But Judaism and Christianity made essential contributions to the political *culture* of the West, the culture from which the democratic structures of our societies have grown.

How did this happen? Three dynamics in the history of this culture-forming process should be noted.

First, the ethical monotheism of Judaism, spread throughout the Western world by the Jewish diaspora and by Judaism's child, Christianity, taught that "there are universal ethical principles which stand over the action of individual human beings and societies as a whole."[6] The debate over the content of those principles and their applicability to public life has, of course, been continuous for over two millennia. But "immediate agreement" on the content and implications of these universal principles "was taken to be less important than the common conviction that all parties are under the same truth," and the parallel conviction that, in this debate, "revelation and reason, faith and experience, all count as evidence."[7]

Jews and Christians believed, and taught, that these universal ethical principles were based on God's nature and God's will for His creation, but several of the key forms of Judaism and Christianity also taught that knowledge of these principles was discernible through a disciplined moral reflection on the structure of creation itself, a reflection sometimes described as the "natural law" method of moral reasoning.

This teaching had a tremendous, if usually unappreciated, social or public impact on the political culture of the West. For if ethical monotheism teaches that "all persons in principle have access to [the universal moral norms],"[8] then it follows that "all have certain responsibilities, and all in principle may, indeed ought to participate in the edification and evaluation of others and of the society at large."[9] Jewish and Christian understandings about the universal "availability" of moral insight were an important cultural factor in opening up the possibility of a politics of persuasion in which all men would have a moral claim to participate.

Second, Judaism and Christianity also occasioned a profound shift in the social structures of Western societies.

Because these great religious traditions insisted that the key communities of identity were the synagogue or the church, they radically altered the force of claims made by other contending communities: the family or tribe and the polis. Societies in which the family or tribe or the polis is the dominant locus of personal and social identity are centripetal in nature: they tend toward cultural, social, and political monism. The claims of the synagogue and the church, on the other hand, desacralize politics and clear the social space for pluralism, thus further enhancing the prospects of a politics based on persuasion and consent rather than on divinely sanctioned coercion.[10]

To be sure, the monistic impulse has never been expunged from some forms of Christianity (particularly, although not exclusively, in the worlds of Eastern Christianity), and it is also evident today in various types of what is usually termed "ultra-Orthodox" Judaism. Nevertheless, the logic of Judaeo-Christian ethical monotheism drives toward pluralism rather than monism in the construction of societies and polities, and thus the political logic of the "Judaeo-Christian ethic" was an important building block of democratic *culture*.

Third, the process described in the two points above also had a kind of feedback mechanism within it. The evolution of pluralistic democracy over the past two centuries and the 70-year struggle between the West and the monism of Marxism–Leninism have not only been influenced by Judaism and Christianity, they have themselves influenced Jewish and Christian theological understandings. Catholicism's experience of a liberal democratic society in the United States, for example, was an important element in the 190-year evolution of Catholic theological understanding that eventually yielded the Second Vatican Council's 1965 "Declaration on Religious Freedom."

Religious conviction and democratic culture have, therefore, experienced a dialectical or reciprocal relationship in the West. Yet the key point to grasp is that tolerance in Western societies is frequently grounded, even today, in religious conviction. Or, as Richard John Neuhaus has nicely put it, Jews and Christians in the West have come to understand that "it is the will of God that we be tolerant of those who disagree with us about the will of God."[11] This religious warrant for domestic social tolerance and civil amity has, in turn, been one of the cultural factors mitigating the more bellicose instincts in Western societies and predisposing Western democracies to prefer nonviolent to violent means of conflict resolution in international public life. Societies whose political cultures prize tolerance and teach the importance of civilized conversation as a means of resolving differences even in matters of (to borrow from Paul Tillich) "ultimate importance" would seem, ipso facto, more likely to look toward other than violent means of redressing grievances and settling disputes among nations. In any event, that seems to have been the way things have worked out empirically.[12]

To sum up, Judaism and Christianity have made three seminal contributions to the evolution of relatively pacific democracies in the West, societies in which (and for which, in their encounter with the world) nonviolent means of conflict resolution are understood to be morally, as well as pragmatically, preferable: the concept of a universal moral law that is in principle knowable by all men; the concept of the independent integrity and moral

priority of the religious community as the key community of identity, a claim that desacralized politics and cleared the ground for pluralism and the politics of consent; and, more recently, the *religious* affirmation of religious freedom and social tolerance, which is an important building block of a political culture capable of sustaining an experiment in democratic pluralism, itself the world's most successful example of nonviolent conflict resolution.[13]

The Just War Tradition and the Pursuit of Peace

On the narrower question of religion and the problem of war, I would also argue—in what will perhaps strike some as a paradoxical fashion—that Christianity in particular has made an important contribution to nonviolent conflict resolution through the evolution of the just war tradition and Christianity's gradual acceptance of that tradition as its mainstream normative framework for reflecting on problems of war and peace.

The classic just war criteria of the *ius ad bellum* (by which it is determined that the resort to armed force is morally justifiable) and the *ius in bello* (by which morally justifiable conduct within war is assessed) have, of course, been abused throughout history. But they have also served as a restraint on political officials and military personnel, and they continue to shape both the U.S. policy debate (as in the 1984–1986 exchange between George Shultz and Caspar Weinberger on the use of U.S. military forces abroad) and the U.S. Uniform Code of Military Justice.[14]

More broadly, the *ius ad bellum* principles (just cause, right intention, proper authority, likelihood of success, last resort) have been an important cultural current in shaping international law and international organizations, even though the central "nonintervention" principle of modern international law is, in some respects, in tension with the understanding of the international system found in classic just war theorists.[15]

Moreover, the religiously informed just war tradition has had an important moral and cultural impact on Western democratic societies and their approach to problems of international conflict. The just war tradition assumes that we live in a morally coherent universe in which all human actions, even in extremis, are susceptible of moral judgment. In other words, and according to the just war tradition, we do not live in hermetically sealed, separated compartments labeled, respectively, "morality" and "politics" (or "war"). Rather, just war theorists, rejecting the moral simplifications of both pacifism and what we might call bellicism (the holy war or crusade tradition), argue for the possibility of rational moral judgment even under duress. John Courtney Murray described the public impact of the evolution of the just war tradition in these elegant terms:

> The [political] community is neither a choir of angels nor a pack of wolves. It is simply the human community which, in proportion as it is civilized, strives to maintain itself in some small margin of safe distance from the chaos of barbarism. For this effort the only resources directly available to the community are those which first rescued it from barbarism, namely, the resources of reason, made operative chiefly through the processes of reasonable law, prudent public policies, and a discriminatingly apt use of force. . . .
> The necessary defense against

barbarism is, therefore, an apparatus of state that embodies both reason and [armed] force in a measure that is at least decently conformable with what man has learned, by rational reflection and historical experience, to be necessary and useful to sustain his striving toward the life of civility. The historical success of the civilized community in this continuing effort of the forces of reason to hold at bay the counterforces of barbarism is no more than marginal. The traditional [just war] ethic, which asserts the doctrine of the rule of reason in public affairs, does not expect that man's historical success in installing reason in its rightful rule will be much more than marginal. But the margin makes the difference.[16]

Father Murray's reflections may help us to understand, moreover, that the just war tradition is more than a set of moral guidelines for determining when the resort to armed force is justified, and more than a catechism of rules setting boundaries on the use of military force once war has been entered upon. Rather, the just war tradition contains within itself what I have called a *ius ad pacem:* a theory of statecraft that is religiously and morally supportive of nonviolent legal and political approaches to conflict resolution. Just war theory points, in other words, toward a concept of peace while determining the ways and means in which discriminate and proportionate armed force can contribute to the pursuit of that peace.

The "peace" in question is thoroughly worldly; it is not the peace of the Kingdom of God, where the lions lie down with the lambs, nor is it the secular utopia of a world without conflict. Rather, the peace envisioned by just war theory—the peace that functions as a kind of moral and intellectual horizon against which the use of force may be measured and toward which the use of force ought to be ordered—is the peace that St. Augustine called *tranquillitas ordinis*, "the tranquillity of order," or, as I have interpreted it, the peace of "dynamic and rightly-ordered political community."[17] The peace of just war theory, in other words, is the peace of politics and law as nonviolent means of conflict resolution. Far from being an obstacle to the nonviolent resolution of conflict, then, the just war tradition, in its formal criteria (especially the *ad bellum* criterion of "last resort") and in its logic, gives a highly developed moral warrant to conflict resolution through other than military means, even as it holds open the moral possibility that the defense of innocents and the pursuit of a lasting peace may, at times, require the proportionate and discriminate use of armed force.

This concept of a *ius ad pacem* will continue to play an important role in the moral culture of the West as we face the necessity of refining the traditional *ius ad bellum* ("war-decision law") and *ius in bello* ("war-conduct law") criteria under the impact of new forms of international conflict by both state and nonstate actors and new military technologies. The current situation in the Persian Gulf, which would have been even more potentially disastrous without Israel's energetic exercise in nuclear nonproliferation vis-à-vis Iraq's Osirak reactor in 1981, has brought to the fore crucial questions involving the ethics of preemption, the proscription of violence against noncombatants (e.g., in the case of "human shields" surrounding legitimate military targets), and the nature of "proportionality." Questions of the morality of deterrence, this time around in terms of chemical weapons,

are also being pressed upon us. In a sense, the issues engaged in the Gulf are a dramatic magnification of the stress put on traditional understandings of the just war criteria by the phenomenon of contemporary terrorism—stresses felt, for example, during the U.S. confrontation with Libya during the early 1980s, stresses that are daily part and parcel of political life in Israel.

The just war tradition is, then, in need of what theologians would call a "development of doctrine." Such a development might usefully take place, at least in part, in conversation with those international legal scholars who have come to understand the inadequacy of the nonintervention principle as the sine qua non of contemporary international law. But in its capacity to restrain violence, in its broader understanding of how the use of military force has to be ordered to the pursuit of peace, and in its concept of statecraft, the just war tradition remains an invaluable resource for developing both the moral culture and the political actors capable of sustaining efforts to broaden the sphere of nonviolent conflict resolution.[18]

Religion and Peace: A Brief Global Survey

The following survey of current arenas of conflict may help illustrate some of the dynamics of the complex relationship between religious conviction and the nonviolent resolution of conflict within and among nations.

Central and Eastern Europe. The impact of religious conviction and religious organizations on the revolution of 1989 in central and eastern Europe remains the least-reported facet of that astonishing and heartening complex of events. And yet, as Timothy Garton

Ash has demonstrated in his reportage from the region, the political revolution of 1989 was preceded by a moral and cultural revolution, one of whose ignition points was the "most fantastic pilgrimage in the history of contemporary Europe"—the visit of the newly elected pope, the Pole John Paul II, to his homeland in March 1979:

> In a beautiful, sonorous Polish, so unlike the calcified official language of communist Poland, [John Paul II] spoke of the "fruitful synthesis" between love of country and love of Christ. At Auschwitz he gave his compatriots a further lesson in the meaning of patriotism, recalling, with reverence, the wartime sacrifices of the Jews and Russians, two peoples whom few Poles had learned to love. He spoke of the "inalienable rights of man, the inalienable rights of dignity.". . .Invoking the romantic messianism of Adam Mickiewicz, he spoke of the special lesson which Christian Poland had to teach the world, and the special responsibility which this laid on the present generation of Poles. "The future of Poland," he declared from the pulpit of his old cathedral, "will depend on how many people are mature enough to be non-conformists."[19]

According to Garton Ash, the pope's pilgrimage was more than a "triumphant articulation of shared values"; it also engendered a mass "popular experience of—there is no better word for it—solidarity. . . . That intense unity of thought and feeling which previously had been confined to small circles of friends—the intimate solidarity of private life in eastern Europe—was now multiplied by millions." The result would loom large in political history:

For nine days the state virtually ceased to exist, except as a censor doctoring the television coverage. Everyone saw that Poland is not a communist country—just a communist state. John Paul II left thousands of human beings with a new self-respect and renewed faith, a nation with rekindled pride, and a society with a new consciousness of its essential unity.[20]

Perhaps the most remarkable dimension of the Polish revolution lay in the linkages forged between that mass, religiously derived sense of national unity and purpose, so evident in the worker-based trade unionism of the Gdansk Solidarity leadership, and the political activism of secular (and often Jewish) intellectuals in the Committee for Social Self-Defense (usually known by its Polish initials, KOR). In any event, the result was a revolutionary impulse with staying power (it is difficult to imagine the Polish revolution surviving the martial law period from 1981 to 1983 without the motivation and discipline provided by the Church)[21] and with a commitment to nonviolence. For the intellectuals in the KOR group, nonviolence was a commitment derived primarily from a sense of the possible (the other side had all the weapons), but also from intense historical study and moral reflection, particularly during the martial law period.[22] Garton Ash in fact stresses the moral component of the Poles' commitment to nonviolence against those who would reduce it to a merely pragmatic calculation: "It was a statement of how things should be. They wanted to start as they intended to go on. History, said Adam Michnik, had taught them that those who start by storming bastilles will end up building their own."[23] For the masses, though, it seems likely that the commitment to nonviolence was most powerfully warranted by the continual preaching of this theme by a pope who had, in the Latin American context, vigorously rejected those currents in the theologies of liberation that seemed to favor revolutionary violence against the "first violence" of oppressive social systems.

The same dynamics and actors—intellectuals, workers, Church—shaped the "velvet revolution" of Czechoslovakia, where Václav Havel's motto, "living in the truth," provided a splendid parallel to the pope's exhortation to "call good and evil by name."[24] Indeed, President Havel's magnificent New Year's Day address to his countrymen on January 1, 1990, was a compact, highly charged statement of the priority of the moral revolution over the political revolution and a clarion call to cleanse the "devastated moral environment" of Czechoslovakia so that the seeds of a democratic political culture might take root in fertile ground.[25] That religious conviction might have a key role in that process of democratic consolidation was presaged by the importance among the Prague intellectuals of the Catholic priest Václav Maly and by the mass impact of the petition for religious freedom initiated in 1988 by a Moravian peasant, Augustin Navrátil, vigorously endorsed by the octogenarian Catholic primate, Cardinal František Tomášek, and eventually signed by over a half-million Czechoslovaks.[26] At the time, the Navrátil petition looked like a brave act of defiance without a discernible public impact; in retrospect, it was an important step in teaching the people of Czechoslovakia that they could, in fact, live "in the truth."

Similarly, in the late, unlamented German Democratic Republic, the Lutheran Evangelischekirche pro-

vided, throughout the 1980s, an organizing ground for the civic opposition to the regime, an opposition that first formed around the issue of religious conscientious objection to conscription and that took its inspiration from the life and death of the theologian Dietrich Bonhoeffer, a martyr to Nazi tyranny.

We may also note that the countercase to nonviolence, during the revolution of 1989, was Romania, where religious leaders (such as Laszlo Tokeş) were key figures in the agitations that led to the downfall of Nicolae Ceauşescu, but where the hierarchy of the Romanian Orthodox Church had been thoroughly coopted by the regime and was thus in no position to aid in the creation of a parallel or alternative "civil society" from which a nonviolent revolution might have sprung.

No doubt the relationship between religious and political conviction and between religious and political institutions in the new democracies of central and eastern Europe will shift during the process of democratic consolidation. Friction along these lines is already evident in Poland, especially in terms of the church's role in education.[27] But if one is looking for striking examples of how certain forms of religious conviction can provide powerful warrants for nonviolent approaches to conflict resolution, even under the most strained circumstances, one need not look much further than to the revolution of 1989 and its antecedent movements throughout the 1980s in Poland, Czechoslovakia, and the former German Democratic Republic.

The Soviet Union. The highly disciplined and nonviolent nature of the Lithuanian revolution of 1990 was due in no small part to the role of the Catholic resistance in Lithuania over the past 15 years and to the ideas that have informed that activism on behalf of religious freedom. Indeed, one can argue that the ground on which the current independence movement and its nonviolent character were formed was initially tilled in the mid-1970s by the Lithuanian Catholic Committee for the Defense of Believers' Rights and its remarkable samizdat publication, the *Chronicle of the Catholic Church in Lithuania*. Before Vytautas Landsbergis and Kazimiera Prunskiene, so to speak, there were Father Alfonsas Svarinskas, Father Sigitas Tamkevicius, and Sister Nijole Sadunaite. Moreover, the continuing importance of Catholicism in the life of the Lithuanian people makes it likely that the Lithuanian revolution will remain (as it did despite massive Soviet provocations in the spring of 1990) nonviolent because of the commitment to nonviolence repeatedly urged by John Paul II.

The role of religion in several of the other restive republics of the Soviet Union has been, of course, far more complex. The emergence in the Russian Republic of a Christian Democratic movement, led by former Russian Orthodox dissidents and with some affinities to the Christian Democratic movement in Western Europe, suggests the possibility that a revolutionary political force committed on religious grounds to nonviolent change could emerge and make common cause with those secular radical democrats whose choice for the nonviolence of politics and legal change has different warrants. Conversely, in Ukraine, the nationalism and corruption of the russifying Russian Orthodox patriarchate of Moscow, on the one hand, and the intense linkage between Eastern-rite Catholicism and nationalism in western Ukraine on the other, have combined to produce scuffles, some attacks on people, and a general atmosphere of confrontation rather than reconciliation. Were this situation to get even more precarious, one might expect that the current Soviet leadership would be prepared to make virtually any concessions in order to have John Paul II make a pastoral visit to Ukraine.

The relationship between religion and nonviolent conflict resolution during the dismantling of Lenin's Soviet Union is thus likely to be as complex as the Union itself. Leaning toward a religiously grounded preference for nonviolence are those parts of Catholicism most directly linked to John Paul II and to the Polish experience, together with those reformist elements in Russian Orthodoxy that have distanced themselves from the machinations of the patriarchate of Moscow for some years now.

Latin America. The picture in Latin America is as complex as the region. The romance with revolutionary violence (heavily influenced by Franz Fanon) in which some Latin American theologians of liberation indulged themselves from the late 1960s through the early 1980s has been blunted by Vatican interventions at the level of both ideas and personnel,[28] and by the evident preference of "the people," in whose name liberation theology claimed to speak, for the rule of law and for democracy: in short, for nonviolent means of resolving conflict and pressing urgent claims for social change. Moreover, the hierarchy of the Catholic church has shown itself to be an adept midwife to democracy in certain countries (most prominently, in Chile), and a strong, if sometimes lonely, voice for nonviolence in other nations (Nicaragua, El Salvador).

249

Nevertheless, as suggested above, the most dynamic force in Latin American religion and politics over the next decade may well be the new evangelical and fundamentalist (more accurately, pentecostal) Protestants. Viewed historically and theoretically, this "Protestantization" of Latin America may, as one observer has suggested, follow the pattern of social impact of its immediate antecedents— the Wesleyan revolutions in eighteenth-century England and the nineteenth-century United States: "Protestantization" will involve the *embourgeoisment* of the affected populations and will provide religious and moral warrants for both entrepreneurship and democracy, thus leading to a kind of pacification of social life.[29] Viewed through the lens of present-day politics, however, the situation may be rather more complicated than that. Guatemala, which will become the first country in Latin America with a Protestant majority during the 1990s, has also witnessed a disturbing linkage between evangelical Protestantism and the far from nonviolent activities of former president Efraín Ríos Montt. "Protestantization," in other words, is no guarantee of a future in which nonviolent forms of conflict resolution prevail, although on balance, and speaking in broad generalities, the pentecostal phenomenon in Latin America could prove good news for those interested in the nonviolent resolution of conflict.

South Africa. The picture is extremely complex in South Africa as well. Some South African blacks have flirted with local variants of liberation theology and have endorsed revolutionary "second violence" against the "first violence" of the apartheid system. Other black South African religious leaders have been steadfast in their condemnation of violence; Archbishop Desmond Tutu is a primary example.

Of perhaps greater significance for the long haul, however, are two religious groupings in South Africa that have received relatively little attention from the Western press and from Western policy analysts. The first is the Dutch Reformed Church which, under the leadership of Dr. Johan Heyns, has disentangled itself from the ideology of apartheid associated with Hendrik Verwoerd, and has in fact condemned the system as biblically unwarranted. This "development of doctrine" has already had a great impact in the Afrikaner community and was certainly one stream of influence shaping the post-apartheid policies of the government of F. W. de Klerk. Moreover, should the Afrikaner community begin to unravel, with racial radicals turning to violence as a means to curb the de Klerk initiatives, the Dutch Reformed Church could play a key role in depriving the rejectionists and their resort to violence of moral legitimacy.

The second religious grouping that may have an impact on nonviolent forms of conflict resolution in South Africa is comprised of the various African Indigenous Churches, often called the "independent black churches" or the "Zionist" churches. Although census figures are not very reliable here, the best estimate is that some one-third of South African blacks (i.e., 6.3 million people) belong to these churches, whose theological conservatism has led to a largely apolitical stance toward the social order.[30] The independent or Zionist churches would not, therefore, provide the kind of positive, religiously grounded, moral warrants for nonviolent approaches to social change that, say, the Catholic church provided in Poland. But these churches may, by the very fact of their existence and by their theological disinclination to engage in political strife, provide an important black counterweight to those forces, aligned with either the African National Congress (ANC) or the Inkatha Movement, which are increasingly turning to violence in the run-up to a post-apartheid South Africa.

The Islamic World of the Middle East. Islam is poorly understood in the West, with various stereotypes competing for media and political attention. It is, therefore, important to remember, with Bernard Lewis, the significance of Islam for millions of lives over a period of many centuries:

> Islam is one of the world's great religions. . . . Islam has brought comfort and peace of mind to countless millions of men and women. It has given dignity and meaning to drab and impoverished lives. It has taught people of different races to live in brotherhood and people of different creeds to live side by side in reasonable tolerance. It inspired a great civilization in which others besides Muslims lived creative and useful lives and which, by its achievement, enriched the whole world.[31]

This is not the Islam with which most Americans, indeed most Westerners, are familiar. Nor are Western commentators and policy analysts sufficiently aware of the complexity of the jihad tradition within Islam and the important work that has been done in developing the Islamic just war tradition in ways that parallel the Western equivalent's effort to restrain political violence.[32] And it would doubtless come as a surprise to many Westerners to be told that there are, today, Islamic scholars who are working to develop a Qur'anic theory of

religious tolerance, and even a Qur'anic theory of what we in the West would call "civil society." On the basis of these realities, one should not prematurely dismiss Islam as a potential religious ally in the pursuit of peace and the development of nonviolent means of conflict resolution within and among nations.

Even so, where is the modern Islamic society in which pluralism is legitimated, where nonviolent means of political succession are institutionalized, where religious liberty is protected for all? One can concede, as indeed one should on the basis of the empirical evidence, that what is often (and loosely) termed "Islamic fundamentalism" is not the predominant form of Muslim belief in the modern world. But one must still confront the countervailing empirical evidence that militant forms of Islam play an extraordinarily important role in regional and world politics, even as other, less bellicose, Islamic currents of thought struggle for a hearing in those regions.

Might one look, without minimizing present difficulties or romanticizing the past, toward what in Western terms would be called a "development of doctrine" in Islam on this matter of religion and peace? Perhaps the crucial determinant of the future of the intra-Islamic debate on the relationship between religious conviction and the proper ordering of society will be the fate of recent attempts to ground the right of religious freedom within Islamic-dominated societies on the Qur'an. For religious freedom is, arguably, the first of human rights and an essential foundation for a polity committed to giving priority to the nonviolent resolution of conflict.[33]

The Sudanese scholar and activist Mahmoud Mohamed Taha (executed by President Ja'far Mohamed Numeiri in January 1985) worked for some 30 years to develop what he termed the "second message of Islam," which included an Islamic jurisprudence "that allows for the development of complete liberty and equality for all human beings, regardless of sex, religion, or faith."[34] One might also cite, as an important contribution to this discussion, the work of Abdulaziz Sachedina, who has tried to develop a Qur'anic argument for religious freedom from within a self-consciously Shiite perspective.[35] Mahmoud Mohamed Taha was not, to be sure, an advocate of the Western, secular polity, and his call was for tolerance within an Islamic state; in that sense, one can say that the discussion as he formulated it paralleled Roger Williams, but not James Madison. And Taha's translator, Abdullahi Ahmed An-Na'im, concedes that the development of an Islamic theory of religious freedom would necessarily involve a kind of "reformation" in Islamic approaches to the interpretation of sacred texts. But the very fact of that admission presumes the possibility of such a pathbreaking new hermeneutic of Islamic law.[36]

The conversation with Islam that is just beginning on these issues will be short-circuited at the outset if it ignores either of two realities that, it should be freely admitted, are in tension with each other. On the one hand, modern Islamic societies exhibit a pronounced tendency toward monism: they link family or tribe, polis, and religious community into a unity that is, by definition, antipluralistic. And insofar as the cultural affirmation of pluralism as a positive social good seems an important element in the evolution of societies committed to a preference for nonviolent conflict resolution within and among political communities, there are problems that simply have to be faced on this front.

On the other hand, there is the historic experience of Islam in the Middle Ages, which testifies to the capacity of Islam to accord religious legitimation to societies that display considerable tolerance. There is, further, the contemporary fact of what we may call, on the central and east European model of the 1980s, "dissidents" within the Islamic world, whose potential influence on the future of Islamic self-understanding ought not be prematurely gainsaid. These include not simply religious leaders like Mahmoud Mohamed Taha and scholars like Abdulaziz Sachedina and Abdullahi Ahmed An-Na'im, but cultural leaders like the Egyptian Nobel laureate Naguib Mahfouz and major political figures like Anwar Sadat. These men, and others like them, are, clearly, a minority in the Islamic world. For precisely that reason, though, locating, supporting, and engaging such "dissidents" in active conversation ought to be a priority for Western scholars and policy analysts concerned about Islam's relationship to the pursuit of a post–cold war world order in which nonviolent conflict resolution plays an increasingly important role.

Indeed, Sadat's personal odyssey may be taken as a kind of paradigm of possible development in the Islamic world. The Sadat who began his public career in sympathy with the Muslim Brotherhood, and who argued on a Qur'anic basis for a policy of refusal to negotiate with Israel, eventually came to justify his peacemaking efforts in explicitly Qur'anic terms. That this led, finally, to Sadat's assassination is an important warning against excessive optimism about the short-term possibilities of development here. But the facts of Sadat's evolution cannot be denied. The model is there, for those who wish to emulate, and indeed amplify, it. I am not optimistic that such an amplification will soon reshape the politics of the Islamic Middle East. All the more reason, then, to get the needed conversation started—and precisely on the level of theology and moral theory.

Postlude

Politics is a function of culture, and at the heart of culture is religion: so thought Paul Tillich, and so have I argued in this paper. Whatever else may or not happen in the last decade of this millennium, it is as certain as anything can be in this contingent world that religious conviction will continue to play a crucial role in the politics of nations. If that is a surprise to some, then so be it.

Religious conviction is today, as it has ever been, a source of conflict within and among political communities. But it should also be remembered that it has not been religion that has made an abattoir of life in the twentieth century. Lenin, Stalin, Hitler, Mao Tse-tung, and Pol Pot maimed and murdered on an unprecedented scale, in the name of a politics which explicitly rejected religious or other transcendent reference points for judging its purposes and practices. Radical secularization, therefore, is no guarantee of peace, just as vibrant religious conviction is no guarantee of war. These are simple points. Unhappily, U.S. academics and policymakers seem to have no end of trouble grasping them. That intellectual failure is itself an obstacle to effective religious support for the nonviolent resolution of international conflict.

From Conflict Resolution in the Post–Cold War Third World *(Washington, D.C.: United States Institute of Peace, forthcoming). Used by permission*

of the publisher. The views expressed in this article are those of the author alone and should not be taken as representing the opinion of the Ethics and Public Policy Center, the United States Institute of Peace, or any other agency.

Notes

1. See Richard John Neuhaus, ed., *Unsecular America* (Grand Rapids, Mich.: Eerdmans, 1986), pp. 115–158, for useful summaries of the research data.

2. See Timothy Garton Ash, *The Uses of Adversity: Essays on the Fate of Central Europe* (New York: Vintage Books, 1990), and *We the People: The Revolution of 1989 Witnessed in Warsaw, Budapest, Berlin, and Prague* (Cambridge: Granta Books, 1990).

3. The complexity of the interaction between religion and the pursuit of peace with freedom and justice is, of course and as noted below, illustrated by the current tensions between Ukrainian Catholics and the two forms of Orthodoxy in Ukraine.

4. See David Martin, *Tongues of Fire: The Explosion of Protestantism in Latin America* (London: Basil Blackwell, 1990).

5. See Peter L. Berger, *The Capitalist Revolution: Fifty Propositions About Prosperity, Equality, and Liberty* (New York: Basic Books, 1986).

6. Max L. Stackhouse, "Democracy and the World's Religions," *This World* 1 (Winter/Spring 1982), p. 108.

7. *Ibid.*, pp. 108–109.

8. *Ibid.*

9. *Ibid.*

10. One key episode in this historical development was the exchange in 494 between Pope Gelasius I and the Byzantine emperor Anastasius I, in which the pope wrote, "Two there are, august emperor, by which this world is ruled on title of original and sovereign right—the consecrated authority of the priesthood and the royal power." By asserting the independence of the Church from the sovereign authority of the emperor, the pope also asserted (deftly, to be sure) a radical limit on the emperor's authority: the emperor was incompetent in certain areas (in fact, the most important areas), which belonged by God's will to another sphere of power.

And thus a small step toward the religious legitimation of pluralism was taken.

11. Richard John Neuhaus, "What the Fundamentalists Want," *Commentary*, May 1985, p. 43. That this understanding arose, perhaps paradoxically or perhaps providentially, in a line of development that followed the European wars of religion does not diminish the force of the point. In one sense, it could be argued that the Peace of Westphalia and the political arrangements that historically followed that attempt at the desacralization of politics were a matter of Western Christianity catching up with St. Augustine.

12. This phenomenon is not without its dangers, of course. Societies which prize tolerance, dialogue, and civility in domestic life may come to think of conflict as somehow epiphenomenal, a matter of bad communication or misunderstanding—particularly when personalist psychology has begun to function as a weltanschauung or all-purpose explanatory framework for discerning the truth of things. This seems to have been the case in certain elite and activist circles in the West during the 1980s. Other possible outcomes notwithstanding, recent events in the Persian Gulf have provided an important check to this temptation.

13. This is not to argue, of course, that religious warrants are the only culturally available norms for legitimizing religious freedom and social tolerance, a claim that would be historically and empirically absurd. Other moral legitimations of democratic pluralism are clearly in play in the United States and indeed throughout the Western world. On the other hand, it is the religious warrants for religious tolerance that are least accounted for in much of the contemporary scholarly and media debate.

14. For a discussion of the Shultz/Weinberger exchange and other issues of the reception of the just war tradition in modern U.S. life, see James Turner Johnson, "The Just War Idea and the American Search for Peace," in *The American Search for Peace: Moral Reasoning, Religious Hope, and National Security*, George Weigel and John Langan, SJ, eds. (Washington, D.C.: Georgetown University Press, 1991).

15. See J. Bryan Hehir, "Intervention and International Affairs," in Weigel and Langan, *American Search for Peace.*

16. John Courtney Murray, *We Hold These Truths: Catholic Reflections on the American Proposition* (Garden City, N. Y.: Doubleday Image Books, 1964), p. 275.

17. See George Weigel, *Tranquillitas Ordinis: The Present Failure and Future Promise of American Catholic Thought on War and Peace* (New York: Oxford University Press, 1987).

18. Pacifism has, of course, made important contributions to the idea that nonviolent means of conflict resolution are to be preferred to armed force. On the other hand, it must be noted that contemporary pacifists have found themselves, on more than one occasion in recent years, sanctioning violent responses to what is often termed the "first violence" of "unjust social structures." For a discussion of this phenomenon, see Guenter Lewy, *Peace and Revolution: The Moral Crisis of American Pacifism* (Grand Rapids, Mich.: Eerdmans, 1988). Lewy's thesis is debated in Michael Cromartie, ed., *Peace Betrayed? Essays on Pacifism and Politics* (Washington, D.C.: Ethics and Public Policy Center, 1990). My own "theses for a pacifist reformation" are included in the latter volume.

19. Timothy Garton Ash, *The Polish Revolution: Solidarity* (Sevenoaks, U.K.: Hodder and Stoughton, 1985), pp. 28–29.

20. *Ibid.*, pp. 29–30.

21. See Garton Ash's analysis in his *Uses of Adversity*, pp. 47–60.

22. On this point, see Bronislaw Geremek, "Postcommunism and Democracy in Poland," *The Washington Quarterly* 13 (Summer 1990), pp. 125–131.

23. Garton Ash, *We the People*, pp. 139–140.

24. Václav Havel, "The Power of the Powerless," in *Living in Truth,* Jan Vladislav, ed. (London: Faber and Faber, 1987), pp. 36–122, and Garton Ash, *Uses of Adversity*, p. 48.

25. It is interesting (to say the least) that the *Washington Post* saw fit to edit out of the lengthy excerpt of Havel's address that it reprinted on its op-ed page the Czechoslovak president's explicitly religious warrant for the kind of society he wanted to see emerge from under the rubble of the to-

talitarian state. Said Havel, "Our first president wrote 'Jesus and not Caesar.'. . . . This idea has once again been re-awakened in us. I dare say that perhaps we even have the possibility of spreading it further, thus introducing a new factor in both European and world politics. Love, desire for understanding, the strength of the spirit and of ideas can radiate forever from our country, if we want this to happen. This radiation can be precisely what we can offer as our very own contribution to world politics" (Foreign Broadcast Information Service document FBIS-EEU-90-001, January 2, 1990).

26. On the Navrátil petition, see Garton Ash, "The Yeoman and the Cardinal," in *Uses of Adversity*, pp. 214–221.

27. See Adam Michnik, "The Two Faces of Eastern Europe," *New Republic*, November 12, 1990, pp. 23–25.

28. See the two seminal statements from the Congregation for the Doctrine of the Faith, "Instruction on Certain Aspects of the 'Theology of Liberation'" (August 6, 1984) and "Instruction on Christian Freedom and Liberation" (March 22, 1986). The first instruction offers a powerful critique of politicized religion; the second describes the multiple ways in which Christianity contributes to the moral—and political—liberation of man.

29. See Martin, *Tongues of Fire*, pp. 205–232.

30. The figures are from *South Africa 1989/90*, the official yearbook of the Republic of South Africa.

31. Bernard Lewis, "The Roots of Muslim Rage," *Atlantic*, September 1990, p. 48.

32. On the jihad tradition and its complexity, see Rudolph Peters, *Jihad in Medieval and Modern Islam* (Leiden, Netherlands: E. J. Brill, 1977) and Mehdi Abedi and Gary Legenhausen, eds., *Jihad and Shahadat:*

Struggle and Martyrdom in Islam (Houston: Institute for Research and Islamic Studies, 1986). Nonviolence as a means of political action is also being discussed in an Islamic context, albeit with many of the difficulties that have plagued Western nonviolent and pacifist thought over the past 20 years; see Ralph Crow, Philip Grant, and Saad E. Ibrahim, eds., *Arab Nonviolent Political Struggle in the Middle East* (Boulder: Lynne Rienner, 1990). For an argument developing what the author believes is the "striking similarity" between the formal structures of Islamic just war theory and its Western counterpart, see John Kelsay, "Islam and the Distinction Between Combatants and Non-Combatants," in *Cross, Crescent, and Sword*, James Turner Johnson and John Kelsay, eds. (Westport, Conn.: Greenwood Press, 1990).

33. See George Weigel, "Religious Freedom: The First Human Right," *This World* 21 (Spring 1988), pp. 31–45, and "Catholicism and Democracy: The Other Twentieth-Century Revolution," *The Washington Quarterly* 12 (Autumn 1989), pp. 5–25.

34. Abdullahi Ahmed An-Na'im, "Introduction," in Mahmoud Mohamed Taha, *The Second Message of Islam*, translated by Abdullahi Ahmed An-Na'im (Syracuse, N.Y.: Syracuse University Press, 1987), pp. 21–22.

35. Abdulaziz Sachedina, "Freedom of Conscience and Religion in the Qur'an," in David Little, John Kelsay, and Abdulaziz Sachedina, *Human Rights and the Conflicts of Culture: Western and Islamic Perspectives on Religious Liberty* (Columbia, S.C.: University of South Carolina Press, 1988), pp. 53–90.

36. See Abdullahi Ahmed An-Na'im, "Human Rights in the Muslim World: Socio-Political Conditions and Scriptural Imperatives," *Harvard Human Rights Journal* 3 (Spring 1990), pp. 13–52.

V. Proliferation and Arms Control

Arms Control and the End of the Cold War

Brad Roberts

ARMS CONTROL WAS a stepchild of the Cold War. As the threat of nuclear confrontation between the United States and Soviet Union seemed to increase in the 1950s and 1960s, along with fears that such a war would lead to mutual annihilation, policymakers sought means to stabilize the competition between the two sides without resort to war. The result was both an arms-control process and an arms-control product. The process of arms control, that is, the negotiation of limits on military capabilities, became a significant—and at times the only—way to conduct a political dialogue between the two superpowers. It also served to reassure allies and the interested public that nuclear armageddon was not imminent. The product of arms control, in the shape of formal agreements, made the armaments competition between the two sides more manageable and contributed to some easing of the economic costs associated with maintaining defenses. Between 1959 and 1992, more than 30 arms-control agreements were signed by the United States, culminating in the deep cuts in nuclear and conventional forces of the early 1990s.[1] During the Cold War arms control was at the center of U.S. concerns and made all earlier experiences

Brad Roberts is editor of *The Washington Quarterly* and a research fellow at CSIS.

with negotiated restraints on the use of force appear tangential, as in the case of the Geneva Protocol of 1925, or inconsequential, as in the naval agreements of the interwar period.

With the June 1992 summit of Presidents George Bush and Boris Yeltsin, the golden era of arms control has come to full fruition. The conclusion over the last five years of a very ambitious arms-control agenda between the two cold war adversaries raises a legitimate question about the future role and promise of arms control and its relative prominence in U.S. policy. The United States no longer lives at the brink of strategic conflict with an opponent threatening it with annihilation. The restructuring of the East–West relationship in ways well suited to the interests of the erstwhile Western pole has devalued arms-control talks as a way to manage conflictual relations. This has led to a review of the place of arms control in U.S. strategy, one manifestation of which is an incipient debate about the future of the U.S. Arms Control and Disarmament Agency (ACDA).[2]

The sense that arms control's day is over is reinforced by the widespread conviction that after the Cold War the security of the United States must be seen in new terms that emphasize economic, social, and environmental factors, among others. By this argument, arms control has been devalued as irrelevant to a new international agenda for which military instruments themselves are not especially useful.

But the world has not changed this radically. Instead, it has grown even more complex. To be sure, there are problems of prosperity and well-being for which common international responses appear increasingly valuable. But the classic question of security in the interstate system has not disappeared with the passing of the Soviet empire. In a way, the pursuit of national and international security has grown more rather than less complex in the post-Soviet era as the study of security issues has been unleashed from cold war constraints that have for decades defined if not skewed the global debate about security.[3] Old problems of security and stability in Europe, Asia, and the Middle East have come into sharper focus after the Cold War. New problems have emerged, especially those related to the spread of unconventional weapons and advanced conventional capabilities in areas of military competition outside the East–West context. But new opportunities have appeared as well, both for the practice of statecraft free of the bipolar standoff and for the exploitation of common economic and political challenges to strengthen multilateralism as a principle of international affairs.

Does arms control have an important role to play in this new era? This article offers a speculative analysis. It reviews the three focal points of U.S. arms-control policy in the decade ahead: the continuing East–West agenda, the multilateral or global agenda, and regional measures. It then goes on to discuss the two principal determinants of the impact arms control will have on the management of international conflict: the ability to de-

sign and implement effective compliance mechanisms and the propensity to seek negotiated measures, what is termed here the sociology of arms control. It concludes that arms control will continue to be a prominent U.S. policy instrument, but not as before. Looking ahead, it is reasonable to expect that the number of arms-control products will grow as existing agreements are joined by new instruments, many of which will not involve direct U.S. participation. In particular, the regional agenda will require new U.S. attention and leadership. But arms control as process will also remain important. This is clearest in the relationship of the United States with the successor states of the Soviet Union, where the implementation of existing measures will require a degree of U.S. stewardship well beyond that of past practice in the arms-control field. But the arms-control process will also be valuable as a way to arrive at more cooperative international approaches to common problems of security.

The Continuing East–West Agenda

The East–West arms-control agenda has not disappeared with the end of the Cold War. Arms control will have a continuing impact in three areas.

The first is in the implementation of existing agreements. Confidence about the ability of the successor states of the Soviet Union to implement the major agreements of recent years—those on Intermediate-Range Nuclear Forces in Europe (INF), Conventional Forces in Europe (CFE), and Strategic Arms Reductions (START I and II)[4]—rises and falls with each new piece of news from that troubled region. The West, particularly the United States, has labored to ensure that these states assume the responsibilities accepted by the old Union government. It has also sought to use the arms-control process as a way to create incentives for the new states to centralize the command and control of the nuclear weapons of the erstwhile Soviet military. It may well be that the structures of zones and the allocation of weapon systems among them is simply too rigid for the new geostrategic realities in Europe. On the other hand, it is clear that many of the leaders and publics of the successor states see participation in binding arms-control agreements as an important sign of their acceptance and legitimacy as new states in the international system.

The demands of implementation will exceed previous experience. In the past, implementation of arms-control agreements entailed essentially monitoring and verification of compliance and attempts to resolve issues of noncompliance through committees established for that purpose or in the larger political environment. In the future, effective implementation will require not just a sharp eye on the actions of U.S. treaty partners but a willingness and ability to take certain stewardship responsibilities for the agreements themselves. Thus the verification tasks will be supplemented by those associated with brokering differences of view among states in a fluid international environment, amending measures as circumstances change and facilitating enactment of treaty commitments on the ground. One symptom of this broadening agenda is the growing role of the U.S. On-Site Inspection Agency in the implementation programs of the countries of the former USSR. Another symptom is the effort by Western states to stem the "brain drain" of Soviet weapons scientists to the devel-

oping world; although not precisely arms control, these efforts are important and useful adjuncts to U.S. arms-control policies.

Problems associated with the destruction of weapons have emerged as key unanticipated challenges to the implementation of existing agreements. Especially in the area of nuclear and chemical weapons, it appears that Russia does not have the fiscal means, the political will, or the technical ability to undertake the timely destruction of weapons in ways that will not damage the environment. If rapid progress cannot be made in destroying these weapons, it will sow doubts not just about the ability but also about the will of remnants of the old system to implement agreed measures.

The second arms-control topic remaining for the East–West agenda is the pursuit of follow-on agreements. In June 1992, there is a widespread sense in Washington and the media that the most ambitious possible East–West arms-control agenda has now been concluded, and that the future does not hold significant new agreements. With the rapid drift of international events and ever-changing thinking about the place of nuclear weapons in the post–cold war environment, this sentiment should not go unchallenged. Some interest remains in deeper cuts in the nuclear arsenal and, at some future time, in an arms-control agreement that also addresses the arsenals of the other advanced nuclear weapon states: Britain, France, and the People's Republic of China (PRC). Further unilateral arms-control measures by either Russia or the United States appear unlikely at this writing, given the apparent preference of both states for codifying restraints in formal measures so that they will have the benefits of verification and compliance mechanisms. Some arms-control steps, however, such as those related to the redeployment or elimination of short-range nuclear forces, are likely to remain informal in character.

The third 1990s remnant of the old East–West arms-control agenda is European security. The Conference on Security and Cooperation in Europe (CSCE) remains firmly in place and in spring 1992 gained a new forum for negotiating arms-control measures. Interest also remains strong among some Europeans in a follow-on CFE treaty (called CFE–1A), which would add manpower limitations to the armaments limits of the original agreement.

There is a sharp debate within the transatlantic community about whether these various negotiations should be used to deal with problems of possible future force reconstitution and peacekeeping or whether there should be some pause in the effort for negotiated measures and a shift of emphasis toward working with existing transparency and confidence-building measures. The United States has been undecided on this point, although it has rejected any effort to use the CSCE arms-control process as a way to negotiate constraints on forces in the continental United States.

The Global Agenda

The East–West arms-control agenda is only one element of the agenda of the 1990s. A second focus of arms-control energy will be the multilateral, global agenda. Such arms-control mechanisms are likely to grow in importance with the breakdown of the bipolar world order and with the industrialization of parts of the developing world and the proliferation of military technology and capability, especially of unconventional weapons.

Efforts to strengthen the existing regime controlling the use of unconventional weapons will be the top priority. The Nuclear Non-Proliferation Treaty (NPT) is facing new trials in the early 1990s with the pull of events in the Middle East, South Asia, and the former Soviet Union. Following discovery of Iraq's sizable but secret nuclear weapons program going forward under the very nose of inspectors from the International Atomic Energy Agency (IAEA), measures associated with verification and compliance with the NPT are likely to enjoy growing support.[5] In 1995 states parties to the NPT will convene to consider the extension of the treaty either for another 25 years or for a shorter period. States opposed to the special rights of the pre-1967 nuclear weapon states may garner enough political support among the disaffected of the developing world to throw its extension in doubt. The status quo–oriented West tends to view this possibility as remote, arguing that most states of the world will see their security better served by an imperfect treaty than by the unrestrained acquisition of nuclear arms. Some other states believe strongly that unless a comprehensive nuclear test ban is implemented the established nuclear powers will have failed to make sufficient progress toward implementation of their commitments under the NPT. New issues are certain to crop up in the global debate about nuclear weapons in the years ahead, suggesting that it is too early to be confident about the outcome of the 1995 extension debate, especially given the many new demands upon the NPT regime to improve its performance as well as the uncertainties in regions where nuclear issues are of continuing or growing relevance.

The Biological and Toxin Weapons Convention (BTWC) of 1972 will also face growing scrutiny in the 1990s. Two decades after it was written, doubts are increasing about the seriousness with which some states take their commitment to the convention, with reports of between 10 and 15 countries possessing offensive biological warfare capabilities. These countries might see these capabilities as "the poor man's atom bomb."[6] The treaty lacks both verification and compliance provisions. The importance of a more effective regime has caught the attention of many policymakers impressed by the argument that the BTWC must keep pace with a changing technological environment: the biotechnology revolution may have created significant new risks of biological warfare, or may do so in the future, which has raised the stakes in the success or failure of the regime.[7] The means to strengthen the convention and to boost confidence in its effectiveness have been the subject of periodic review conferences, most recently in September 1991. Verification mechanisms developed for other global treaties will not easily be grafted onto the BTWC, given important features of the relevant technologies and production facilities, although work is ongoing to identify options to improve the monitoring of treaty commitments and to weigh those options in terms of the security benefits relative to their costs, either fiscal or in terms of lost proprietary information in the commercial sector. In the meantime, serious attention must be given to implementation of confidence-building measures and the equally important objective of getting all states parties to implement existing commitments.[8]

In the chemical area, negotiations appear in summer 1992 to be leading to the conclusion of a comprehensive disarmament treaty, the Chemical Weapons Convention (CWC). States parties to the convention would undertake to destroy existing arsenals and not to build or transfer chemical weapons to others. This agreement would represent a significant advance on the Geneva Protocol of 1925, which was an undertaking not to use these weapons and remains in force. Unlike the BTWC, the CWC would provide for some verification and compliance mechanisms. Unlike the NPT, it would require disarmament by states of both the developing and the developed worlds. The willingness of the United States to forgo chemical weapons appears consistent not with the disarmament ideology of the 1920s but with a prudent reading of national security interests in the 1990s. Under the CWC, the United States will trade away a military instrument last used in battle by the United States when Woodrow Wilson sat in the White House in exchange for a dampening of the pressures toward chemical weapons proliferation.

These global regimes are important not only for their effect in limiting the global spread of unconventional weapons; they also have the important benefit of generating norms of state conduct. Those who see the world in realpolitik terms decry the role of norms in politics, arguing correctly that norms are irrelevant to those determined to act with contempt for the standards of others. But policy realists too often miss the importance of norms in generating the political consensus necessary to punish behavior not consistent with those norms. Something of this mechanism was at work in the sharp international response to Iraq's annexation of Kuwait. Norms based on the selective rejection of categories of weapons deemed unacceptable create the foundation for sanctions, embargoes, and arguably more direct enforcement actions. Without the norms embodied in the global nuclear, biological, and chemical regimes, the international community would be far less ready to cope with the consequences of widespread access to the relevant technologies. The Outer Space Treaty of 1967, the Seabed Arms Control Treaty of 1971, and the Environmental Modification Convention of 1977 also embody norms likely to assume growing salience in the decades ahead as global industrial development puts the means to cause significant harm in each domain in the hands of an ever larger number of states.

A strengthening of these regimes will require concerted effort on the part of the United States and its allies. They must make astute use of periodic review conferences to gain consensus about problems and responses. As argued below, particular attention will be given to the inspection issue and to whether or how existing verification regimes can be improved to deal with new threats.

But effective multilateral arms control will require more than just some tightening of the existing legal framework. Complementary policies must be pursued as well. Policymakers should increase the diplomatic attention given proliferation issues. They must also cultivate those military capabilities that will shape the expectations of potential cheaters; this points to the continuing need for investment in technological superiority and defenses against specific types of weapons as well as the preservation of alliances and the political bases for collective security.

The 1990s will also witness the emergence of a new set of multilateral arms-control issues. The 1991 decision of the United Nations (UN) to set up an annual registry of conventional weapons traded internationally suggests a growing global interest in arms-control transparency measures and in the use of negotiated measures to cope in new ways with the problems of competitive relations.[9] In a way, the registry idea represents a bit of old thinking about arms control—that it is weapons themselves that create security problems. But it also represents a new appreciation of the fact that the uneven flow of arms can and has produced not just competition but war, either by nourishing the ambitions of aggressors or deepening fear among the vulnerable. The UN initiative to police Iraq's compliance with the April 1991 cease-fire agreement points also to the possibility of a growing UN role in monitoring and verifying treaty compliance. The UN Special Commission's unique experience in the use of information provided by various national intelligence agencies has stirred interest in supporting new UN roles in this area.[10]

But because the global proliferation of military capability involves so many elements other than nuclear, biological, and chemical weapons, there is a widespread hope in Washington that arms control will take on a larger nonproliferation function in the years ahead. This hope is misplaced, because U.S. policymakers will find it impossible to employ traditional nonproliferation approaches as arms-control tools.

The weapons proliferation problem cannot be dealt with by placing a permanent barrier between the haves and have-nots, although this is exactly the focus of nonproliferation policy as it was pursued in the cold war era. The fact that the biological and chemical disarmament agreements impose equal burdens on the militaries of the developed and the developing world is one factor accounting for their future promise; the unequal burdens assumed under the NPT are a factor pointing to a very sharp future debate in the new century about the lingering rights of the pre-1967 nuclear states. The inherently discriminatory character of nonproliferation mechanisms is incompatible with an era in which technology, industrial capability, and expertise are slowly spreading throughout the world. Permanent firebreaks between the haves and have-nots will only fuel the ambitions of the have-nots to acquire what they have been denied. Such discriminatory mechanisms are necessarily stopgap measures, intended to buy policymakers time to arrive at more fruitful ways to address the will rather than the means to acquire weapons. This is not to deny their important interim value in constraining access to technologies that enable aggressive states to cross significant capability thresholds, that is, those related to the reach and essential military effectiveness of missiles or their warheads.

Thus, conspicuous by their absence so far from this review are the supplier regimes such as the Missile Technology Control Regime (MTCR), the Australia Group in the chemical area, and other collaborative export-control efforts designed to deny military-related technology to targeted countries. Export-control approaches will remain important in U.S. policy for many years to come, but they are a poor substitute for complementary and ultimately more durable approaches. Efforts to negotiate international limits on conventional arms transfers to regions in conflict are likely to be implemented in the years ahead, but their potential utility must be understood as limited in the same way as other supplier regimes. A complete embargo of weapon sales by Western suppliers to regions in conflict may precipitate rather than ameliorate instability. This will compel suppliers finally to come to some agreement among themselves on what constitutes stabilizing and destabilizing transfers. Especially in the Middle East, limits on conventional arms transfers are likely to be supported by the supplier states only as an interim measure so long as they effectively contribute to achievement of a longer-term peace settlement in the region. This points to the essential linkage of such supplier regimes to future regional arms-control measures.

In sum, U.S. policy aimed at stimulating regional measures, strengthening global regimes, and integrating ad hoc supplier restraints could have a very powerful effect in stemming weapons proliferation or at least in coping with its most serious consequences, but only if pursued in this integrated way.

Regional Measures

Beyond the East–West and global arms-control measures, a new set is emerging in the early 1990s as a serious possibility—regional measures. Interest in regional arms control has been stimulated by the end of bipolarity and superpower preeminence, combined with the proliferation of advanced conventional and unconventional weapons in regions of chronic conflict. Latin America has advanced furthest in this new direction. For example, Argentina, Chile, and Brazil, building on the Treaty of Tlatelolco, agreed in September 1991 to create and police among themselves a zone free of nuclear, chemical, and biological weapons under the so-called Mendoza agreement.[11] In East Asia, elements of an informal arms-control regime between the two Koreas overlap with North Korea's entry into the multilateral NPT. In South Asia, the nuclearization of both India and Pakistan has prompted fears of an arms race and war, nudging them to begin a dialogue about informal and formal measures to limit the risks. And in the Middle East, where some limited arms-control measures have long been implemented such as the demilitarization and international policing of the Sinai, appeals in recent years by Presidents George Bush, Mikhail Gorbachev, and Hosni Mubarak have helped to stimulate renewed interest in regional arms-control measures.

In each of these regions, there is an active exploration of the models of arms control, including not just those from the East–West experience but also earlier efforts such as the various measures of the years between World Wars I and II. Such a historical review shows arms control in three different guises: disarmament (whether comprehensive or of selective systems), arms control (meaning measures embodying choices by states to limit weapons acquisitions or direct them in ways not threatening to neighbors), and confidence-building measures (embodying undertakings related to state behavior in the military domain that reduce the risk of war through misperception and miscalculation, that increase transparency of military actions, and that may work over time to change the political terms of reference of conflict). Arms control qua disarmament and major force-structuring agreements of the START and CFE types appear today to be remote possibilities in the Middle East, South Asia, and East Asia.[12] More fruitful endeavors may well be found in the areas of confidence-building measures and the codification of arms deployments at existing thresholds of force levels or capabilities.

A key issue with regard to regional arms control is its fit with the global agenda. If regional efforts succeed in producing over time a series of diluted agreements without the verification or compliance mechanisms of the global measures, their future efficacy will be in some doubt. They may, in fact, contribute to insecurity in time of crisis and near conflict because of their failure to create real confidence about the behavior and intentions of possible adversaries. Such weak measures would erode the global regimes. On the other hand, regional measures that match or exceed the standards of the global regimes could prove valuable complements to the latter.

New forms of arms control might also burgeon from the creative talent of newcomers to the arms-control process. The problem of dual-use technologies (i.e., technologies such as those in the aerospace, chemical, biological, electronic, and systems integration fields that have both civil and military applications) may stimulate novel responses by states not members of supplier cartels. It would not be surprising, for example, to find likeminded states in South America and Africa agreeing to self-imposed restraints on military applications backed by effective self-policing mechanisms in exchange for access to critical dual-use technologies.

The achievement of formal regional negotiated measures will be difficult for a number of reasons. Many of the factors critical to arms control in the East–West context are not characteristic of those conflicts, although there is no reason to believe that sharp bipolarity and the presence of mutual assured destruction are necessary conditions to arms control. There are important questions about the timing and scale of such undertakings and whether confidence-building measures really have anything to contribute to relations between historical enemies.[13] But if the East–West experience is any indication, arms control may contribute as much in the 1990s as a process of dialogue and signaling about political intent as it will in formal measures.

Compliance

How much or how little arms control occurs in the years ahead will be a direct function of how effective current and future regimes prove to be. Tending arms-control agreements has rarely attracted the same energy or public enthusiasm as creating them, but the success of their implementation will be critical in determining whether arms-control instruments will acquire such broad support as elements of national security strategy as they did in the West during the Cold War.[14]

The ability of arms-control measures to secure compliance by states parties is a function of two factors. One is the political context within which compliance is sought. Expectations of compliance will be shaped by the degree to which the general relations among states parties are peaceful rather than conflictual and by the level of interest shown by those with political, economic, or military leverage to secure compliance. Obviously, these dynamics differ markedly from region to region. The other factor is the compliance mechanisms designed into the treaty itself. Will parties to the treaty be able to detect cheating of a militarily significant character in a timely way through inspections specified in arms-control agreements backed by whatever separate intelligence resources are available to them? Will the inspection regime be perceived to be sufficiently rigorous to increase the costs of cheating or otherwise influence the calculations of risks and benefits by leaders contemplating noncompliant behavior?

The focal point for this debate in the early 1990s is how intrusive inspections must be to achieve the required results. The near brush with unconventional weapons in the Iraqi arsenal has led to widespread criticism of the limited mandate for inspections conducted by the IAEA and the absence of verification provisions under the BTWC. Iraq's ability to pursue research and development programs for nuclear (and biological) weapons despite periodic inspections in recent years has fueled international demands for a right under future or modified arms-control measures to highly intrusive inspections virtually anywhere and any time, without right of refusal.[15]

The intrusiveness issue has emerged as a sort of litmus test of one's commitment to effective compliance measures. The United States, for example, was widely criticized as abandoning the struggle for an effective CWC when in 1991 it backed away from its former rhetorical position of "anywhere, any time" inspections. But the Iraqi experience holds other lessons as well. It shows that finding the proverbial smoking gun will prove very difficult when inspectors are confronting a well-prepared adversary who has had time to bury, either literally or figuratively, proof of malfeasance, and that inspectors need not just a right to intrude in sensitive areas but also to conduct regular and indeed systematic inspections so that patterns of activity become known over time, leading to what are essentially political decisions about the level of confidence gained or not through the inspection process. This political context is often overlooked in the debate about inspections. It means that suspicions about individual sites will be weighed in the context of the larger relationship of that state to others. What is politically possible under a cease-fire order vis-à-vis the Iraqis is arguably not acceptable for states not at war.

Advocates of highly intrusive measures have also generally failed to account for the costs of such measures. Potential costs include not just the fiscal—including the substantial investment that would be necessary for the United States to maintain in readiness all facilities potentially subject to short-notice intrusive inspection—but also the loss of legitimately sensitive or proprietary information. Especially in Europe and the developing world, little attention has been paid to the costs and risks to industrial facilities of falling under the purview of intrusive treaties. In the United States, these issues have received some consideration. The U.S. chemical industry has shown interest in the stipulations of the CWC, much more so than the biotechnology industry in the BTWC or indeed industry in general that might be subject to "anywhere, any time" on-site inspections. Advocates of intrusiveness also generally have not weighed those costs against benefits. One of the emerging criticisms of START, for example, is that it will benefit the United States rather less than originally envisaged while costing a great deal for the quite elaborate verification provisions.

This is not to argue that intrusive measures are undesirable; rather, it points to the need to balance competing priorities. It points also to the fact that the debate about intrusiveness has become a substitute for a debate about compliance more broadly. Intrusive inspections are not a panacea for the problem of compliance; effective and comprehensive inspections are the foundation of a larger strategy relating to verifying whether or not a state is living up to its commitments and to enforcing compliance where that becomes necessary.

This compliance debate grew highly politicized during the Cold War. The dispute about whether or not the Soviet Union was complying with its arms-control treaty commitments became superheated in the United States in the 1970s and 1980s and led other states to shy away from the subject for fear of being co-opted by one side or the other. This was most evident in the debate about U.S. allegations concerning the use by Soviet or Soviet proxy forces of biological and toxin weapons in Afghanistan and Southeast Asia—the so-called Yellow Rain debate. No states, not even allies of the United States, wanted to take sides in the dispute for fear of the domestic and international political consequences. In retrospect, it has become clear that the Soviets were in fact cheating in the biological area by their continued programs in the offensive domain.[16] This episode also showed that in the absence of an obvious smoking gun, suspicions fall upon the accuser as well as the accused. Indeed, even given blatant proof of violations, as in the case of the Soviet radar facility at Krasnoyarsk, the political interest of some in sustaining an existing treaty seems to overwhelm the capacity to deal with noncompliance. The annual reports of the U.S. president to the Congress on Soviet arms-control compliance never produced the consensus necessary to deal with patterns of noncompliance as accepted political and military facts. This appears to have been less the case in the area of strategic arms, where the United States and Soviet Union were able to use the General Advisory Council to resolve problems of compliance with the Strategic Arms Limitation Treaty (SALT I) privately.

The end of the Cold War has created a widespread hope that the end of bipolarity will lead to a depoliticization of arms-control compliance issues and that existing compliance mechanisms will be able to operate to their full potential to deter and detect cheating and provide the foundations for enforcement. Will this hope be realized? Will it matter?

On the East–West agenda, issues of compliance seem to have receded. The widespread skepticism about Soviet compliance and the perceived high risks for the West of Soviet noncompliance have passed from the scene. The more pressing question today is not so much the will of the successor states to comply with existing arms-control commitments as their ability to do so given the other demands upon their resources and energy. The exposure of their weapons programs to international public opinion through existing verification mechanisms will weigh in their perceptions of their priorities, however, and effective compliance mechanisms are likely to prove quite central to any debate about future arms-control agreements between or among the successor states of the Union.

On the global agenda, there is a real possibility that arms-control negotiations long paralyzed by East–West division may now suffer the consequences of North–South division.[17] For some in the nonaligned movement, the debate about global agreements has become a vehicle for contesting the distribution of power and

influence in the post–cold war era. They abhor any agreement that preserves the long-term military or economic dominance of the developed world and may prefer to scuttle negotiated measures—or to sign them with the expectation of cheating—than to be seen to be acquiescing in the political agenda of the North. If they are to join regimes constraining their military choices, they are likely to do so only if the regimes give evidence of fairness and equity. This accounts for resistance to further have versus have-not regimes or to regimes that otherwise preserve special rights of enforcement or representation for specific categories of states. Hence the importance leading members of the developing world attach to global treaties that fully reflect their views and concerns.[18]

On the regional agenda, changing global politics may have some salutary effect on the ability of the UN to act as a guarantor of compliance. The UN's relative effectiveness to date in policing the cease-fire terms with Iraq and the evident coalescence of U.S. and Russian views on important regional security issues bodes well for the UN's functions in this area, although there is the risk that the PRC and perhaps future new members of the Security Council will exercise a veto in ways that frustrate UN engagement. In regions where the involvement of outside powers has a firm historical foundation and a certain level of legitimacy, such as the Middle East where the United States is concerned, the UN is unlikely to prove a substitute for that great power involvement. But the UN might become a facilitator of policing actions by regional organizations as yet not created or empowered to take on this task. Its effectiveness will also be determined by the specific rights accorded it by arms-control treaties. Its capacity to act to enforce arms-control commitments will be stronger in those instances where the UN itself has formal responsibility, as in postwar Iraq, and weaker where compliance findings are the responsibility of individual states.

Thus, there is no guarantee that the improved promise of the UN in strengthening the politics of compliance will translate into perfect compliance by all states to all new and future arms-control treaties. It is, therefore, also necessary to speculate about compliance by enforcement through military action in those instances where a state's broken commitments have led to war or appear to be doing so. Without some expectation that a renegade state will confront armed resistance, the leaders of such a state might care little even if inspections confirm noncompliant behavior. Much hope has been invested in the strengthened collective security operations of the UN, but there is also reason to doubt that it will always find the will and means to respond to aggression as it did in Kuwait. Efforts to strengthen the capacity of the UN to act in such circumstances may pay off by deterring potential cheaters from breaking with existing arms-control agreements. They would come to see that aggression employing those assets would prove futile.

Unilateral enforcement actions by any one party are likely always to be subject to at least some international criticism, just as people today reiterate their criticism of Israel for its 1981 bombing of the Osiraq nuclear plant in Iraq even after the existence of Iraq's nuclear programs became more widely known. Preemptive strikes in circumstances short of war will always have detractors and supporters arguing the implications of actions not taken. The UN as such will have limited po-

litical capacity to conduct such measures, except in circumstances such as those prevailing in Iraq today. Regional organizations may assume some growing role in this area, because regional consensus may be easier to achieve than global consensus in isolating and punishing renegade states because of the propinquity of the threat.

The United States appears to be attaching a growing priority to enforcement actions tied to and endorsed and legitimized by international entities, whether global or regional (such as the CSCE and the Organization of American States). Its ability to act in concert with others, or alone where deemed necessary, will be tied to military programs giving it the flexibility to do so. This suggests the relevance of a U.S. military instrument of sufficient strength, peacekeeping competence, and familiarity with other militaries to make its power projection credible.

In speculating about the future of arms-control compliance, it is important to bear in mind that a great deal of experience will be reaped in the 1990s. This experience will be as important in shaping the predispositions and abilities of states to deal with problems of noncompliance as was the cold war era.

The Sociology of Arms Control

As an institution of human and state behavior, arms control must be understood in relation to the broader political and intellectual environment of which it is a part. To exploit fully the opportunities listed above requires the setting aside of some old ways of thinking about arms control and problems of international security.

Among arms controllers in the United States (and also elsewhere in the West and perhaps in the erstwhile

East), thinking about arms control has been shaped by a number of factors that may not, in retrospect, be relevant to creative thinking about the arms-control tasks of today and tomorrow.

One factor is the era of strategic bombing that preceded the creation of the atom bomb and the resultant tendency to equate weapons of mass destruction with strategic weapons. This is not a good guide to understanding the important differences between nuclear, biological, and chemical (NBC) weapons, the different risks associated with each, and the motives driving their acquisition. The U.S. tendency to impute to NBC weapons programs in the developing world the same strategic purpose they have for the United States—deterrence—obscures other potential motives, whether military or symbolic, and the possible interaction of those motives with other national priorities. This makes it difficult to calculate the incentives states might have for agreeing to arms-control measures.

Another factor is the U.S. propensity to quantify military relationships and to view stability as inherent in specifically crafted and minutely measured force ratios—"bean counting" as it was decried in the 1970s. But regions where the number of competitors is relatively large or does not divide clearly into two sides and where the differences of geography, development, and military capability are sharp, stability may inhere not so much in exact parity but in equitable balances among military competencies, decreased reliance on specific use-or-lose weapons, and perceptions of the unwillingness of interested outsiders to acquiesce to aggression.

A third factor is the technological preeminence of the United States and the U.S. tendency to view compliance problems as amenable to technological fixes. The United States was able to begin the arms-control process with the Soviet Union because of its strengths in the national technical means of verification, strengths that states in the developing world do not enjoy.

A fourth factor is the East–West military buildup, which gave birth to a tendency to accept only the highest possible standards for arms-control measures because of their direct relationship to the immediate survival of the United States. It is not clear that all possible arms-control measures can or should live up to the exacting legal standards of the United States or that there are not also security benefits to be extracted from measures that are less than perfect. The United States will not join the CWC or agree to additional verification provisions for the BTWC unless it rethinks along these lines.[19]

U.S. attitudes toward regional arms control will also be shaped by cold war thinking about regional conflicts. For the last 40 years, senior U.S. policymakers have looked at the Third World through the filter of the containment strategy and too often have understood conflicts there only in their geostrategic context. Although it is weakening as the Cold War recedes, the legacy is a tendency to understand only the concerns of friends of the West in the Cold War rather than engaging in a broader rethinking of the dynamics at work in each region. In the future, there will be a much larger role than was possible during the Cold War for preventive diplomacy and peacebuilding in regions in conflict. Arms control is likely to feature as a significant element in such a recrafted strategy.

One measure of the continued primacy of these notions in U.S. arms-control thinking is the apparent failure of the United States to articulate the lessons of its arms-control experience in ways useful for interested observers in the Middle East and South Asia.[20] In June 1992 the United States, together with Russia, hosted a seminar on arms control for interested states in those regions as an adjunct to the Middle East peace process. Informal commentary from a number of regional participants reflected their frustration with Washington's need to tell the arms-control story as a kind of search for the holy grail and the inability of U.S. policymakers to transmit the benefits of their experience in weighing risks, calculating uncertainties, and coping with the politics of compliance.

Without active participation and leadership by the United States, progress on the three-part arms-control agenda under discussion here is doubtful.[21] The United States cannot do much to compel the adoption of regional arms-control measures. But given its political influence, sophisticated verification capabilities, and military strength, which enable it to cushion some of the risks for some of the states involved in the negotiations, the United States has the potential to serve as facilitator, monitor, and guarantor of some global and regional measures.

But it will do so only if it has a clear perception of the stakes. The success or failure of efforts to achieve meaningful arms control in regions in conflict will have tangible consequences for the security of the United States. In both Asia and the Middle East, it has a direct role as the guarantor of the security of one or more states, and the drift toward war in either region is likely to involve U.S. forces. Moreover, a general deterioration of the international security environment

would make it much more difficult for the United States to reap the peace dividend at the end of the Cold War and would force upon it politically divisive choices about the kind of role it should play in maintaining peace in an anarchic world.

The critical U.S. policy choice is between a strategy emphasizing reliance on military means, for which funding and political support may not be forthcoming absent international legitimization, and one emphasizing pursuit of a more cooperative "order" that narrows military risks, isolates renegade states, and preserves options for diplomacy and force. Because no armed opponent now appears capable of or intent upon threatening U.S. survival, the United States may feel it not worth the effort to pursue the second strategy. Policymakers should recognize, however, that unless more effective responses are found to the problems of weapons proliferation and control, the risks to the United States may again escalate as more states acquire the ability to significantly increase the costs of U.S. power projection or directly to threaten the territory of the United States. A good beginning has been made in this direction in 1991 and 1992 with U.S. efforts to facilitate a peace process in the Middle East, promote a regional dialogue in South Asia, and broker the bilateral agreement between the Koreas. But good beginnings are valuable ultimately for what follows.

In the developing world as well as the developed, important aspects of old thinking continue to shape the way arms control is understood and evaluated. Salient factors include the following. The first factor is the long-term dominance of the North–South security agenda by a few states whose views are unrepresentative of the rest. The near-nuclear states such as India and others with major investments in weapons and military capability have co-opted many states of the developing world into a crusade for global equality and justice. But this crusade appears more oriented to the legitimization of their own national choices than to the fact that most states of the developing world have no interest in unconventional weapons or in military solutions to problems of national development and security. One indication of the gap between a few leading countries and the rest of the international community was India's decision after Iraq's invasion of Kuwait to sell to Iraq chemicals useful for making chemical weapons, surely one of the finest examples of pursuing principle (the right of any sovereign state to the weapons of its choice) to the point of folly.

Second, most diplomats of the developing world who are working today on regional and global arms-control issues received their training during postings at the Conference on Disarmament (CD) in Geneva, a UN-affiliated organization. The mantras of nonalignment have been particularly powerful there, and they include especially a pervasive anti-Americanism, the portrayal of disarmament in near-messianic terms, and the propensity to view interstate conflict in value-neutral terms unless it has clear Western involvement, when imperialism is decried. The easy resort to dogma at the CD has faded in recent years as the prospect of the successful conclusion of a CWC compelled states from the developing world to begin to grapple in a non-ideological way with their interests vis-à-vis the convention, but for decades the CD has served as a training ground for diplomats who seemed to see in arms control a political rather than a security instrument. The result has been a primarily ideo-logical view of global and regional security issues.

A third factor is the rigid equation of military strength with national security and the symbolism of military power as national sovereignty. This is a manifestation of the weak relationship between civil and military officials in many developing countries. It leads some states to acquire weapons that create unintended fear among their neighbors, arousing unpredictable responses and rising insecurity.

A fourth factor is the fragile role of the non-governmental sector in developing countries. In the United States and the West generally, institutions and individuals outside government have usefully served to generate and test arms-control ideas and to weigh the arms-control record without the bureaucratic stake of governmental agencies or the vow of silence imposed upon those with access to classified information. In the Middle East and East Asia, a few such institutions and individuals are beginning to appear, but their continued ability to contribute to the arms-control debate is uncertain, as is the willingness of their governments to open that debate.

Finally, the publics in most developing countries have been fed for decades the state dogma on questions of international conflict and security through a compliant media and academe. A frequent private lament of diplomats from both the Middle East and South Asia is that decades of controlled debate and the resulting ideological blinkers widespread among elites have robbed policymakers of the room for maneuver they need in the new environment to take new risks and establish new international relations.

These factors will be important in shaping the ability of policymakers in developing countries to look to the

273

consequences of their choices, to weigh the risks associated with alternatives, and to debate trade-offs in terms of national and international interests. This bodes ill for arms control, which necessarily entails the acceptance of risk, debates about competing priorities, and decisions to limit or relinquish military instruments otherwise available. These factors will not quickly pass from the scene. Nor should they all. The developing countries make a legitimate case—generally misunderstood or ignored by the United States—about the vulnerability of their own societies and the unequal distribution of power in the world.

There are reasons to believe that perceptions on questions of international security and arms control are changing and will continue to do so. Democratization in the developing world will have a profound effect on arms-control choices made by governments there. It facilitates a modernization of civil-military relations, a process that in Argentina, Chile, and Brazil helped to bring about a redefinition of national security and national priorities. Democratization also brings non-governmental organizations into the policy process, strengthens the role of the independent media, and stimulates public education on international issues—all of which permit a broader definition of national priorities and increase the susceptibility of leaders to international moral norms.

Economic factors are also important. Many states in regions in conflict are also struggling with problems of development, modernization, and debt. They will face increasing choices between weapons programs and other national priorities. Especially where budgetary claims are made for weapons development programs that would isolate the state from valued foreign relations, the international economy, and foreign investment—as when nuclear or other banned weapons are built—national decision makers will face even sharper choices about the allocation of resources. Unless those programs offer undisputed military advantages (and the military utility of chemical and biological weapons is hotly disputed) or the country faces the threat of imminent war, it is reasonable to expect some attenuation of funding commitments to such programs in all but the wealthiest of countries. In the developing world, only a few oil-rich countries like Iraq will be able to funnel millions of dollars into surreptitious weapons programs.

Military factors as well will contribute to some rethinking of arms-control options. As decision makers in regions in conflict increasingly anticipate the possibility of wars in which weapons of mass destruction and advanced conventional weapons are not just in their own hands but in those of others as well, their perception of the stakes in conflict must begin to change. This pattern of perceptual evolution is evident in East–West relations, and there are many reasons to expect that states in other regions will experience the same shift.[22] Leaders may come to believe that there is a threshold beyond which military instruments alone cannot provide security, and that they must look beyond national strategies emphasizing military preparation and symbolic military power to complementary measures that balance military options with more cooperative solutions.

The passage or refashioning of conventional wisdoms among elites in the developing world will not occur quickly. But the process can be accelerated by leaders committed to serious pursuit of negotiated restraints. As Anwar Sadat reminded the world in his trip to Jerusalem, leaders can redefine political reality. The rethinking of national strategies within governments and a willingness to look at arms control in new ways can be stimulated as well. A useful model for this purpose is ACDA. Established in 1961 as a separate agency within the U.S. government and charged with advocacy in the interagency process for policy approaches emphasizing negotiated restraints, ACDA proved instrumental in rethinking the U.S. approach to the Cold War and became a primary vehicle for the pursuit of U.S. strategy. Although its voice in the policy process has waxed and waned with the interest of senior policymakers, its record as a catalyst for more cooperative approaches to questions of international security suggests that it might be a useful model for other governments interested in improving their competence on arms-control matters.

Conclusion

The end of the Cold War has altered the place of arms control in U.S. policy but has not eliminated it. Arms control will remain a major focus of U.S. interest and energy in the decades ahead. But not as before.

In the narrowest sense, arms control as a body of legal treaties relating to the disposition of the military forces most threatening to the United States is likely to be of less salience in the 1990s with the demise of the Soviet Union. But plenty of work remains in the implementation of existing treaties and the strengthening of global regimes. Moreover, the United States has key roles to play as facilitator, monitor, and guarantor of future regional arms-control measures. In a broader sense, arms control as a set of formal and informal undertakings concerning the disposition of military capabilities—either local or global—will continue to have value as a way to shape the threats to regional and international security and to reduce the likelihood that U.S. forces will be called upon as a last resort. In regional conflicts, arms control is likely to become a principal element of preventive diplomacy and a way to diminish reliance on U.S. power projection.

Thus, from the perspective of U.S. policymakers in the 1990s, both an expansion and dilution of the arms-control agenda is in evidence. That agenda includes many more elements than in the cold war era, although they are of less direct short-term importance for the United States. They may nevertheless be critical tools in building a new order of international affairs that is more cooperative than anarchic and that channels the energies of the developing world away from military means of solving conflict and toward the building of stable, prosperous nations and regions.

Notes

1. *Arms Control and Disarmament Agreements, Texts and Histories of the Negotiations* (Washington, D.C.: U.S. ACDA, 1990).

2. In 1991 Congress requested a study of ACDA's performance of its mandated tasks together with recommendations for any reorganization of the executive branch that would strengthen the ability of the U.S. government to carry out arms-control functions. A report from the ACDA inspector general is due by December 1992.

3. John Chipman, "The Future of Strategic Studies," *Survival* (Spring 1992), pp. 109–131.

4. START II is being used unofficially at the time of this writing to describe the package of strategic nuclear measures agreed at the June 1992 Bush–Yeltsin summit.

5. Hans Blix, "Verification of Nuclear Nonproliferation: The Lesson of Iraq," *The Washington Quarterly* 15 (Autumn 1992), pp. 57–65.

6. For a review of these biological warfare allegations, see Elisa D. Harris, statement to the Defense, Foreign Policy, and Space Task Force of the Budget Committee of the U.S. House of Representatives, Hearings, May 22, 1991.

7. Erhard Geissler and Robert H. Haynes, eds., *Prevention of a Biological and Toxin Arms Race and the Responsibility of Scientists* (Berlin: Akademie Verlag, 1991).

8. Barend ter Haar, *The Future of Biological Weapons* (Washington, D.C.: Praeger for CSIS, 1991). See also Oliver Thraenert, ed., *The Verification of the Biological Weapons Convention: Problems and Perspectives* (Bonn: Friedrich Ebert Stiftung, 1992).

9. Michael Moodie, "Transparency in Armaments: A New Item for the New Security Agenda," *The Washington Quarterly* 15 (Summer 1992), pp. 75–82.

10. Rolf Ekéus, "The Iraqi Experience and the Future of Nuclear Nonproliferation," *The Washington Quarterly* 15 (Autumn 1992), pp. 67–73.

11. For full text see *Chemical Weapons Convention Bulletin* (Harvard-Sussex Program on CBW Armament and Arms Limitation), no. 14 (December 1991), p. 19.

12. Ivo Daalder, "The Future of Arms Control," *Survival* (Spring 1992), pp. 51–73. Daalder differentiates between approaches to arms control for states with essentially cooperative relations, such as those prevailing today in Europe, and those with basically competitive relations, and argues that measures beyond modest ones intended to build confidence and security are unlikely to be adopted in the latter case.

13. Geoffrey Kemp, *The Control of the Middle East Arms Race* (Washington, D.C.: Carnegie Endowment, 1992). See also Alan Platt, ed., *Arms Control in the Middle East* (Washington, D.C.: United States Institute of Peace, 1992).

14. Charles Flowerree, "On Tending Arms Control Agreements," *The Washington Quarterly* 13 (Winter 1990), pp. 199–218.

15. See Committee for National Security, *The Lessons of Iraq: Unconventional Weapons, Inspection and Verification, and the United Nations and Disarmament*. Briefing and discussion with Johan Molander, special adviser to the chairman, United Nations Special Commission on Iraq, November 13, 1991 (Washington, D.C.: Committee for National Security, 1991).

16. R. Jeffrey Smith, "Yeltsin Blames '79 Anthrax on Germ Warfare Efforts," *Washington Post*, June 16, 1992, p. A–1.

17. Joseph F. Pilat, "Yet Another Farewell to Arms Control?" in *The Future of Arms Control: New Opportunities*, report prepared by the Congressional Research Service for the Subcommittee on Arms Control, International Security, and Science of the House Committee on Foreign Affairs, April 1992 (Washington, D.C.: GPO, 1992).

18. Nabil Fahmy, "The Security of Developing Countries and Chemical Disarmament," in Brad Roberts, ed., *Chemical Disarmament and U.S. Security* (Boulder, Colo.: Westview Press, 1992), pp. 63–70.

19. Brad Roberts, "Framing The Ratification Debate," in Roberts, *Chemical Disarmament and U.S. Security*, pp. 119–149.

20. For a rethinking of the lessons of the interwar naval arms-control experience for future regional arms-control measures, see Caroline F. Ziemke, "Peace Without Strings? Interwar Naval Arms Control Revisited," *The Washington Quarterly* 15 (Autumn 1992), pp. 87–106.

21. Michael Moodie, "Multilateral Arms Control: Challenges and Opportunities" (Paper prepared for a conference on verification at the Southern Methodist University, April 25, 1992).

22. Kenneth Waltz, *The Spread of Nuclear Weapons: More May Be Better* (London: IISS, 1981).

Four Decades of Nuclear Nonproliferation: Some Lessons from Wins, Losses, and Draws

Lewis A. Dunn

FOR MORE THAN four decades, the United States has opposed the spread of nuclear weapons to other countries. This basic policy has rested on the belief that nuclear proliferation would result in new threats to U.S. security, heighten global and regional instabilities, and quite possibly lead to the use of nuclear weapons. That assumption continues to guide U.S. policy today.

Over the years, U.S. nuclear nonproliferation efforts have relied on three broad sets of specific actions that constitute the basic building blocks of U.S. policy in this area. Initiatives have been lauched and measures have been taken in order to reduce the political incentives that could lead countries to acquire nuclear weapons; technical obstacles have been created in order to make acquisition more difficult; and international nonproliferation institutions have been established.

It is especially timely to reconsider the record of nuclear nonproliferation

Lewis A. Dunn is assistant vice president and manager of the negotiations and planning division, Science Applications International Corporation. He served as assistant director of the U.S. Arms Control and Disarmament Agency.

efforts over the course of the past decade. With open or unacknowledged nuclear proliferation throughout the world, such an analysis could provide useful insights for renewed attempts to head off a world of many nuclear weapon states. Equally, with policy attention focusing on the problems of chemical weapons and missile proliferation, examination of the nuclear nonproliferation experience could provide lessons for those two areas.

This article offers some reflections on nuclear nonproliferation wins, losses, and draws. It focuses on both the policies pursued and the results achieved. In some cases, whether to categorize given policies and their results as wins, losses, or draws is open to differing interpretations; readers undoubtedly will strike their own balance. By way of conclusion, some lessons for chemical weapons and missile nonproliferation are drawn from the nuclear nonproliferation record.

Nuclear Nonproliferation Wins

There are five acknowledged nuclear weapon states: the United States (1945), the Soviet Union (1949), the United Kingdom (1952), France (1960), and China (1964). In addition,

India detonated a nuclear explosive device in 1974, but claimed it was only for peaceful purposes; and Israel is believed publicly to have manufactured nuclear weapons.[1] Top officials in both South Africa and Pakistan have stated publicly that their countries have "the capability" to make nuclear weapons should they desire to do so.[2]

Today, proliferation is quite different from what many officials and observers in the late 1950s and early 1960s thought would be the case. Back then, it was feared widely that 15–20 states, if not more, would possess nuclear weapons by the mid-1970s. Behind the difference between past predictions and the current situation are a series of nuclear nonproliferation wins.

Decisions by West European Countries Not to Acquire the Bomb. In thinking about steps to slow overt or unacknowledged nuclear proliferation, we rightly focus on today's so-called problem countries, such as Pakistan, India, North and South Korea, Taiwan, Israel, Iran, Iraq, Libya, Syria, and South Africa. Two decades ago, however, the list of problem countries was quite different. Rather than Third World countries, that list included the West European countries of France, West Germany, Italy, Switzerland, and Sweden. Japan also should be put in the category of early potential problem countries, even though there was considerably less serious discussion of nuclear weapons acquisition there. With the exception of France, all of these countries eventually chose not to acquire nuclear weapons.[3]

The decision by West European countries and Japan to renounce nuclear weapons is a clear, and often forgotten, nuclear nonproliferation success. Renunciation, however, was not a foregone conclusion: at differing times in the 1950s or 1960s, acquisition of nuclear weapons was an open question in virtually all of the above mentioned countries. Several countries, including Sweden and Switzerland, had nuclear weapon programs. For West Germany and Japan, their subsequent adherence to and ratification of the 1968 Nuclear Non-Proliferation Treaty (NPT), rather than reserving the nuclear option, was not an open and shut issue.

Of the many explanations for this nuclear nonproliferation win, some are tied to U.S. policies, but others are not. Perhaps most important, for countries such as West Germany, Japan, and Italy, the U.S. alliance provided a necessary and credible foundation for their security. In contrast, the security costs of seeking nuclear weapons in terms of contributing to the disruption of the alliance and possible Soviet threats would have been high. For Japan, domestic politics and its so-called nuclear allergy also provided strong disincentives. Sweden and Switzerland both had their own reasons for not acquiring nuclear weapons. Swedish and Swiss military leaders came to question whether nuclear weapons would undermine their posture of armed neutrality. In the Swedish case, shifting domestic politics and a new emphasis on Sweden's role in the forefront of disarmament efforts in the late 1950s also ran counter to acquisition of nuclear weapons.

Third World Incentives and the Nuclear Nonproliferation Norm. The establishment and strengthening of the nuclear nonproliferation norm is another closely related success. The norm has helped contain the spread of nuclear weapons to the Third World, while reinforcing the decisions of most Western countries to renounce nuclear weapons.

This norm encompasses several changes in thinking about nuclear weapons and nuclear proliferation. As demonstrated over a decade ago by India's claim to have carried out only a peaceful nuclear test—as well as by the denials of current problem countries of any nuclear weapon-related activities—global opinion increasingly has rejected the legitimacy of acquiring nuclear weapons. Equally important, a widespread belief has emerged that the spread of nuclear weapons could add to regional and global insecurity. Unlike the early 1960s, moreover, the current perception is that a world of dozens of nuclear weapon states is not the inevitable wave of the future. Similarly, the acquisition of nuclear weapons no longer is seen as a main route to international prestige and recognition.

The U.S. policy of nuclear nonproliferation contributed in several ways to the emergence of this norm. Most important, the United States took the lead, first in the successful negotiation of the NPT, and then in encouraging decisions by nearly 140 nonnuclear weapons states to adhere to the NPT, including virtually all West European countries. This treaty now embodies and demonstrates the norm of nuclear nonproliferation. Presidential antinuclear rhetoric also has strengthened perceptions of the illegitimacy of nuclear weapons.

This norm probably has been most important in containing proliferation incentives in those Third World countries that are not today's problem countries, but that could have been driven to seek nuclear weapons by fear of their neighbors' long-term intentions, by prestige, or by the simple belief that sooner or later all important countries would have nuclear weapons. This group includes, for example, Indonesia, the Philippines, Singapore, Venezuela, Mexico, Chile, Egypt, Algeria, Nigeria, and Yugoslavia. At the same time, the norm of nuclear nonproliferation, as discussed more fully below, also appears to have constrained the efforts of Third World problem countries such as Pakistan to acquire a nuclear weapon capability. Concern about hostile foreign reaction undoubtedly partly explains, for instance, the decision not to move to open pursuit of a nuclear weapons capability in several problem countries, such as India and Pakistan. Finally, this norm has helped to prevent the reconsideration of earlier decisions by most Western countries to opt for nonnuclear status.

The Nuclear Supply Regime. Beginning in the mid-1950s, U.S. policymakers also took the lead in establishing a set of international institutions, procedures, and agreements to regulate peaceful nuclear cooperation and the supply of nuclear materials, facilities, and technology to other countries, which became a nuclear supply and export control regime. This regime now consists of U.S. conditions for agreements on bilateral cooperation; International Atomic Energy Agency (IAEA) safeguards that monitor the peaceful uses of nuclear energy; the so-called Zangger trigger lists that specify the items that NPT nuclear suppliers can export under safeguards, which have become the basis for rejecting export requests from problem countries; and the London Nuclear Suppliers' Guidelines that extend controls to technology and include commitments to restraint in the transfer of sensitive reprocessing and enrichment equipment or technology. At present, efforts are underway to extend the nuclear export control and supply regime to meet the challenges posed by the so-called dual-use exports, items with both nuclear and nonnuclear uses, and by new enrichment technologies.

At one level, successful U.S. efforts to foster multilateral agreement on this set of institutions and procedures that govern peaceful nuclear supply and cooperation are a definite nuclear nonproliferation win. Consider their respective impact in regulating and permitting legitimate peaceful nuclear cooperation and in impeding the nuclear weapons activities of problem countries.

IAEA safeguards have been the principal means whereby recipients of peaceful nuclear equipment and materials could reassure both suppliers and their neighbors that such support was not misused for the manufacture of nuclear weapons. Although problems have arisen and challenges remain, IAEA safeguards on balance have done a credible job in providing that assurance. In their absence, the suspicions of neighboring countries' could well have fueled pressures for steps toward the acquisition of nuclear weapons, as has occurred in regions such as Latin America, where countries have not accepted safeguards on all of their peaceful nuclear activities. Similarly, the London Nuclear Suppliers' Guidelines restrictions on the transfer of sensitive reprocessing and enrichment technology have helped head off the global spread of many small-scale sensitive facilities, avoiding comparable pressures for proliferation.

Nuclear export controls and supplier restraint also have complicated significantly, slowed, or increased the costs of the efforts by problem countries to acquire nuclear weapons. For example, there are public estimates that Pakistan began to seek a nuclear weapons capability in the early 1970s. Export controls bought time for diplomatic initiatives. They also allowed

for unexpected domestic political changes to occur in that region, including in India, Indira Gandhi's assassination and Rajiv Gandhi's election and subsequent defeat, and in Pakistan, President Zia ul-Haq's death and Benazir Bhutto's election. Moreover, in some important cases—quite possibly the Libyan one—such export controls probably have blocked and will continue to impede the acquisition of nuclear weapons for many years.

However, at another level, the limits of export controls and nuclear supplier restraint must be acknowledged frankly. Problem countries increasingly have developed sophisticated methods to circumvent controls. The implementation of regulations by some key U.S. allies may be halfhearted, while high-level U.S. officials sometimes have been reluctant to expend political capital on export control diplomacy. As discussed more fully below, it has been clear since the Soviet detonation of an atomic bomb in 1949 that export controls, secrecy, and denial of technology alone cannot prevent the further spread of nuclear weapons.

Winning Widespread Adherence to the NPT. Widespread adherence to the NPT also stands out as a nonproliferation success by helping to establish a norm of nuclear nonproliferation. In adhering to the NPT, moreover, nearly 140 countries have renounced the right to manufacture or acquire nuclear weapons. Although in a few cases this undertaking might be open to question, for virtually all others, adherence both significantly binds a country's future policy and provides reassurance to its neighbors. In addition, the legal obligations assumed by state-parties under Article III of the NPT have been a major foundation for nuclear supplier restraint and export controls. Similarly, for many countries, the acceptance of IAEA safeguards on all of their peaceful nuclear activities rests on their NPT obligation, also under Article III.

Nonetheless, the commitment of several countries to the Treaty increasingly has become open to question. The most notable cases include Iraq, Iran, and Libya in the Middle East, and North Korea in Asia. If these countries eventually were to acquire nuclear weapons, the NPT's credibility would be damaged. In addition, in 1995 the parties to the NPT are to decide by majority vote whether " . . . the Treaty shall continue in force indefinitely, or shall be extended for an additional fixed period or periods." The adherence of many small Third World countries with potentially little direct security interest in and, therefore, reason to support the NPT could prove a problem in mustering the required majority vote.

Regularizing U.S.–Soviet Nonproliferation Discussions. Another example of successful institution-building is the pattern of regular bilateral discussions between the United States and the Soviet Union on nuclear nonproliferation that has been established. Begun sporadically in the late 1970s, these exchanges have taken place approximately every six months since 1983. The discussions have ranged across the nuclear nonproliferation agenda, and also have proved relatively insulated from the ups and downs of the broader political relationship. For example, even as the Soviet delegation was walking out of the Geneva nuclear negotiations in 1983, the Soviet Union was proposing a new round of nonproliferation talks. Nonproliferation discussions fall into the win category for several reasons.

These U.S.–Soviet exchanges have proved most useful for policy discussions regarding multilateral nuclear nonproliferation institutions, from how to handle challenges to Israel's right to participate in IAEA meetings to cooperative efforts to ensure success at the five-year review of the NPT in 1985. They also have helped to coordinate U.S.–Soviet efforts to buttress nuclear export controls, by upgrading the Zangger trigger lists to include additional items. Sufficient habits of cooperation were built up over time in order to make it possible to use these bilateral discussions for nonpolemical consideration of what steps either side might take to head off problem country nuclear weapon programs. In some instances, actions resulted. Nonetheless, the reluctance of both sides to use available influence with such countries—because of other political interests—as well as the limits of influence frequently stood out.

Nuclear Nonproliferation Losses

The record also contains a number of nuclear nonproliferation losses, suggesting the limits of what U.S. nuclear nonproliferation policy can accomplish and of U.S. readiness to pay a political or domestic price for that goal.

Additional Nuclear Weapon States: Could More Have Been Done? The failure to prevent additional countries from acquiring nuclear weapons or a nuclear weapons capability is the most obvious nuclear nonproliferation loss. In addition to the five acknowledged nuclear weapon states, four other countries widely are assumed either to possess nuclear weapons capability or to be able to acquire it within the short-term. At the same time, the pattern of this additional proliferation activity has changed. Since China detonated a nuclear weapon in 1964, no other country openly has opted for nuclear weapons status. Instead, a new group of neither acknowledged nuclear weapon states nor questioned nonnuclear weapon states is emerging.

A brief consideration of the record with regard to both sets of countries would be instructive. That record makes clear that if a country has strong incentives to acquire a nuclear weapons capability and a sufficiently broad industrial base, it will not be possible to prevent the country from eventually achieving that goal. This became evident at the start.

The early postwar U.S. policy of secrecy and denial, written into law in the 1946 Atomic Energy Act, clearly was aimed at preventing early Soviet acquisition of the atomic bomb. As already noted, the policy was unsuccessful. The Soviet 1949 atomic bomb test demonstrated for the first time, but not the last, the limits of technology controls in the face of a country determined to acquire nuclear weapons.

Although the rigid strictures of the Atomic Energy Act were not necessarily aimed at Great Britain, the postwar breakdown of U.S.–British cooperation on the Manhattan Project and application of the Act served only to delay the first British atomic bomb test. However, U.S. legislation later was revised in 1954 and 1957 to permit increased assistance to Britain's nuclear weapons program. From the 1960s onward, the U.S. sale of submarine-launched ballistic missiles also was essential to maintaining Britain's nuclear deterrent. Both developments reflected a primacy of alliance concerns over more diffuse nuclear nonproliferation interests.

By contrast, the administration of John F. Kennedy made quite extensive efforts in the early 1960s in order to convince the French that an independent nuclear force was illusory and dangerous. This, in part, reflected the broader pressures from the administration to raise the nuclear threshold in Europe and shift toward a greater reliance on conventional forces. These efforts followed previous U.S. refusal to amend restrictive legislation in order to permit aid to France's nuclear weapons program. Not surprisingly, U.S. arguments against French acquisition of nuclear weapons fell on deaf ears. Along with the legislative restrictions, they served mainly to antagonize the French who were committed firmly to becoming a nuclear weapons power.

In the early 1960s, Israel's first steps toward a nuclear weapons capability became a matter of concern. The United States learned that Israel had purchased the Dimona research reactor from France, which eventually provided that country with access to unsafeguarded plutonium that could be used for weapons. The Kennedy administration obtained Israeli agreement for regular visits to the site, in exchange for the sale of Hawk surface-to-air missiles. These visits, however, gradually became pro forma and ended in the administration of Lyndon B. Johnson.[4] In the years that followed, attempts were not made to bring U.S. influence to bear decisively in an attempt to contain Israeli nuclear activities. Other considerations, speculated on below, clearly took precedence.

A decade later, both Canada and the United States sought unsuccessfully to use their diplomatic influence to head off India's 1974 detonation of a nuclear explosive device. In carrying out that test, India took advantage of a loophole in the terms of its agreement covering nuclear cooperation with Canada and the United States. (The agreement did not ban explicitly peaceful nuclear explosions.) The strong adverse foreign reaction that followed India's test—especially from the Canadians—probably contributed to the Indian government's decision not to test again. Nonetheless, by the mid- to late-1980s, heightened concerns about Pakistani nuclear weapons activities led the Indian government to warn publicly that India might be forced to build nuclear weapons.

The case of South Africa is somewhat similar. In 1977, combined pressure from the United States and the Soviet Union was brought to bear in response to indications of possible South African preparations for a nuclear test; and no test occurred. It remains uncertain whether South Africa or some other country secretly tested two years later a nuclear device in the South Atlantic. In any case, as official South African statements make clear, neither renewed external political pressure nor export controls have stopped that country's advance to the point of possessing a capability to make nuclear weapons.

Pakistani officials, including former President Zia, have stated that Pakistan now has the capability to make nuclear weapons, although Prime Minister Bhutto has stated that Pakistan does not possess a nuclear weapon. The development of Pakistan's nuclear weapons capability over the 15 years since India's test have entailed concerted and successful efforts to circumvent nuclear export controls. Nonetheless, these controls did slow Pakistan's advance and buy time for diplomacy to be brought to bear. U.S. willingness to use military assistance as a lever to pressure Pakistan to stop its pursuit of a nuclear weapons capability, however, was tempered by both the continued need to work with Pakistan in order to funnel arms to the Afghan resistance and the real risk that

to terminate assistance would remove the last Pakistani disincentive for an open nuclear weapons program. Besides, even had the United States cut off assistance, past experience with a comparable cutoff in the late 1970s suggests that Pakistan's nuclear weapons activities would not have stopped.

Taken together, these brief sketches suggest that it may be useful to distinguish nuclear nonproliferation losses from policy failures. Some losses are unavoidable, regardless of what the United States and other like-minded countries attempt to do. Export controls can only slow a determined country; U.S. influence may be too little or unavailing. At the same time, several of the cases highlight the limits of U.S. readiness to pay a domestic or foreign policy price for nuclear nonproliferation. In those cases, the debate over whether the United States could have done more and whether policy failed will continue.

The NPT Holdouts. That a group of countries have refused to sign the NPT, despite U.S. efforts to convince them to do so, is another nuclear nonproliferation loss. Four of these NPT holdouts are high on all lists of problem countries: Pakistan, India, Israel, and South Africa. The other countries that appear to be further away from possession of a nuclear weapons capability include Argentina, Brazil, and Chile in Latin America, and Algeria in Africa. France and China, also holdouts, are nuclear weapon states.

In recent years, U.S. diplomacy has continued to seek adherence of these countries to the NPT, and has worked closely with like-minded countries. Sometimes, key holdouts, such as Spain, Saudi Arabia, and North Korea, have changed their position. Still, the odds seem low that any of the other significant holdouts, with the possible exception of South Africa, will change policy.

The reasons for nonadherence vary. For virtually all holdout countries, refusal to adhere is, in part, a means to keep open the option to make nuclear weapons. Rejection of adherence also is buttressed in some cases, such as India, Argentina, and Brazil, by arguments about the NPT's discriminatory character. These arguments emphasize that nuclear weapons states are not required to renounce their nuclear arsenals, nor do they have to accept IAEA safeguards on their peaceful nuclear activities. For China, nonadherence is a residue of earlier attitudes that stressed the benefits for communism of the proliferation of nuclear weapons. French nonadherence is tied up as much with Gallic pride and the logic of independence as with French criticism of the NPT's discriminatory elements. Some French NPT critics also claim to be concerned that adherence to the NPT would make it more difficult to continue the testing of nuclear weapons.

Widespread Civilian Use of Plutonium.
The growing prospect of the widespread commercial use of plutonium is a somewhat different nuclear nonproliferation loss. Although estimates vary, several tens of thousands of kilograms of separated plutonium could be circulating in international commerce by the year 2000. Most of this plutonium will be used as nuclear fuel in light-water reactors in Japan, France, West Germany, Switzerland, and some other West European countries. With time, South Korea again could seek access to plutonium for use in its substantial civilian nuclear power program.

A series of developments over the past decade explain the growing commercial use of plutonium. In the late 1970s, efforts by the administration of Jimmy Carter to convince the Europeans and Japanese not to use plutonium failed. These countries argued that the use of plutonium was necessary for their energy security, particularly in the then-planned programs for breeder reactors. They also moved to reprocess nuclear spent fuel in order to ease the problems of managing nuclear waste.

The administration of Ronald Reagan shifted away from Carter's opposition to reprocessing and plutonium use, partly reflecting the belief that better nuclear supply relations with key West European nuclear trading partners would pay off with nonproliferation cooperation elsewhere. The shift also rested on a less skeptical attitude toward nuclear power generally, and toward the use of plutonium in breeders specifically. A possible compromise position between those of Carter and Reagan in terms of an acquiescence in the use of plutonium in breeders joined with active efforts to discourage plutonium recycling, was never tried.

By the mid-1980s, the growing storage costs for separated plutonium led to a decision by some countries to recycle that plutonium in light-water reactors; it was cheaper to use up the plutonium than to store it.

The increased commercial use of plutonium and its frequent international shipment will place new strains on the ability of countries to ensure its adequate physical security. The risk of plutonium theft, whether by terrorists, extortionists, radical governments, or thieves could well be high. Problems with tracking and accounting for large shipments and stocks of plutonium—especially because some amount in use always will be unaccounted for—will open up the possibility of insider collusion in any such thefts.

Failures of Nuclear Supplier Cooperation. Overall, most nuclear suppliers often have taken quite seriously their responsibilities for nuclear export controls. Nonetheless, periodic failures of nuclear supplier cooperation constitute another nuclear nonproliferation loss, one with implications for other areas of nonproliferation export controls. Two types of supply failure have occurred: specific export control breakdowns and broader inability among the major nuclear suppliers to agree to hold regular multilateral discussions of nonproliferation.

At one time or another, the export control system of virtually all nuclear suppliers has failed to block exports of concern to a problem country, despite good faith efforts by the supplier. Also, there have been instances in which the nuclear export control bureaucracy of a given country has not paid sufficient attention to potentially troublesome exports or to entreaties to stop particular exports of nonproliferation concern.

In addition, since 1977 it has not proved possible to convene a meeting of the entire London Nuclear Suppliers' Group, which brought together both East bloc and the major Western nuclear suppliers. France and West Germany, in particular, have opposed that meeting on the grounds that it likely would antagonize Third World countries, and despite U.S. and Soviet counterarguments, neither country has been prepared to shift its position. The lack of regular meetings of all nuclear suppliers has made it harder to reach consensus on new supply initiatives, such as dealing with the problems posed by so-called dual-use exports with both nuclear and nonnuclear uses. With no regular meetings, a more general discussion of nuclear supply problems, the exchange of information on problem country efforts to circumvent controls, and the consideration of possible common responses to violations of nuclear supply conditions have been impeded.

Nuclear Nonproliferation Draws

Still other developments of the past decades fall into the category of nuclear nonproliferation draws. For this category, the jury is still out. There have been both positive and negative consequences, or there has been a mixture of both success and failure.

Containing the Openness and Scope of Nuclear Weapons Programs. Although U.S. policies have not been successful in preventing completely the proliferation of nuclear weapons or nuclear weapons programs, they have contributed to constraining the openness and scope of nuclear weapons activities in current problem countries. This comprises a nuclear nonproliferation draw. These countries still may proceed to open nuclear weapons programs and eventual deployments; but their current unacknowledged moves toward or apparent acquisition of a nuclear weapons capability are less damaging than open proliferation.

There are several reasons to believe that this outcome is less dangerous. On balance, the unacknowledged possession of nuclear weapons likely will have a less corrosive impact on the perception that widespread proliferation still is avoidable. Such possession probably will have less impact on the incentives of countries other than regional rivals to acquire nuclear weapons. In turn, constraining the size of a country's nuclear weapons program—in terms of the amount of nuclear weapons materials and weapons—can help reduce the threat of nuclear theft or nuclear gifts. Scarce nuclear assets are easier to keep track of and too dear to give away for political, ideological, and economic reasons. Moreover, to the extent that future new nuclear weapon states move beyond small unacknowledged capabilities, crisis instability, and the risk of accidental, unintended, or intentional use of nuclear weapons likely would increase.

Decisions to stop short of acknowledged nuclear weapons pursuit or deployments partly reflect the impact of the more general norm of nonproliferation. Nuclear jawboning by the United States and other countries also has helped. Other regional concerns, including the fear of the reaction of neighbors and outsiders, have had an impact as well.

In addition, export controls probably have affected the size, sophistication, and character of the nuclear weapons capabilities of problem countries. The U.S. ability to block Pakistan's purchase of high-quality steel for use in uranium-enrichment centrifuges, for example, could not but have impeded future production of that material. Global constraints on nuclear weapons testing, both the Limited Test Ban Treaty and the broader anti-testing norm, also would affect the ability of problem countries to produce more sophisticated nuclear weapons—rather than a first fission device.

Some Nuclear Weapons Program Shutdowns? It is well known that in the mid-1970s both South Korea and Taiwan had active nuclear weapons programs, but under political pressure from the United States, both countries shut down such activities. Nonetheless, this termination must be considered only a nuclear nonproliferation draw, because under certain circumstances both programs could spring back to life.

Within South Korea, pressures again may be growing to reconsider a nuclear weapons option, given reports of nuclear weapons related activities in North Korea and rumblings in the United States about withdrawal of some U.S. troops from South Korea. One recalls that the withdrawal of one U.S. division from South Korea in the early 1970s was a major precipitant of the earlier South Korean nuclear weapons activities. Despite the shutdown of its activities, Taiwan publicly is reported to have sought to resume in the mid-1980s steps that would have provided it access to plutonium that could be used for nuclear weapons. Apparently, U.S. influence again convinced it not to do so.

Comparison of the U.S. approaches to South Korea and Taiwan with those to Pakistan and Israel is instructive. In the two East Asian cases, U.S. nuclear diplomacy is reported to have stressed to both countries in the mid-1970s and to Taiwan in the mid-1980s that further steps toward nuclear weapons would call into question the basic U.S. security tie with South Korea and residual political, economic, and security links with Taiwan. Both South Korea and Taiwan took the U.S. warning seriously. By contrast, U.S. nuclear diplomacy has been less effective against Pakistani nuclear activities.

Speculating briefly, the relatively greater dependence of Seoul and Taipei, compared to Islamabad, on the U.S. connection may partly explain the different outcomes of U.S. intervention in these cases. In addition, Washington's greater stake in avoiding the spread of nuclear weapons to the Korean Peninsula—because of the U.S. military presence and possible impact of proliferation on Japan—may have been a consideration affecting both the credibility of U.S. nuclear diplomacy and the readiness to exert it. On the other hand, the main thrust of U.S. policy in South Asia in the 1980s was to convince the Soviet Union to withdraw from Afghanistan.

Turning to the Israeli case, other than attempts in the early 1960s to gain access to Israel's Dimona reactor and periodic appeals for Israel to join the NPT, the public record is blank, in terms of high-level intervention to constrain that country's nuclear activities. Despite Israel's high dependence on the United States and the danger that a nuclear Middle East is the most likely source of a future superpower nuclear confrontation, U.S. nuclear diplomacy toward that country has not been strenuous or effective. Initially, in the mid- to late-1960s, the overall lack of a high U.S. priority to nuclear nonproliferation partly may explain the limits of U.S. nuclear diplomacy. Over time, a reluctant acceptance of a possible, but unacknowledged, Israeli nuclear weapons capability as a sunk cost for U.S. nuclear nonproliferation policy, or as a given that could not be changed, may have been increasingly important in the minds of some officials. An assumption of overall stability—that the Arab countries always would be far behind and that Israel's capability would remain uncertain and unacknowledged—likely played a role. It also is difficult not to presume that domestic political considerations were at work as well, and that the Israeli government would have rejected U.S. attempts to rein in its nuclear activities.

The Treaty of Tlatelolco: An Almost Nuclear-Free Zone. Although the Treaty of Tlatelolco provides the legal framework to make Latin America a

nuclear weapons-free zone, it only can be considered a nuclear nonproliferation draw. Chile and Cuba have not signed, Argentina has not ratified, and despite having signed and ratified, Brazil has yet to wave it into force. As such, the Treaty of Tlatelolco remains as much a nuclear nonproliferation promise as reality.

The United States and Latin American countries repeatedly have urged Argentina, Brazil, and Chile to take the needed steps to bring Tlatelolco fully into force. In response, the latter countries have made various arguments, from calling into question whether the United States was abiding by its obligations under the Treaty to calling for special provisions to safeguard their peaceful nuclear activities. Still, the underlying explanation of their reluctance to bring the Treaty fully into force has been a desire to preserve a nuclear weapons option.

Nonetheless, the Treaty does serve to constrain their activities, to a degree. Brazil, for example, has stressed that in accordance with international law it will take no action inconsistent with Tlatelolco. By its very existence, the Treaty also adds to the norm of nuclear nonproliferation. Moreover, both Argentina and Brazil at some point could decide to adhere. For instance, if fears of a nuclear arms race fueled by mutual suspicions were to grow in Buenos Aires and Brasilia, full adherence to Tlatelolco would offer a ready-made vehicle to provide needed reassurance. Here, too, the jury is still out and some measure of success has occurred.

Nonuse of Nuclear Weapons. Although not the direct result of U.S. nuclear nonproliferation policy, the nonuse of nuclear weapons over the past four decades also has had important nuclear nonproliferation benefits, and, therefore, deserves brief mention.

In particular, nonuse has contributed significantly to the emergence and widespread acceptance of the belief that nuclear weapons were not simply advanced conventional weapons. This oft-remarked nuclear taboo, in turn, has affected the calculations of some of the first generation problem countries regarding the benefits and need for nuclear weapons. Nonuse also supported the growth in the 1960s and 1970s of the norm of nuclear nonproliferation.

More widespread nuclear weapons proliferation, however, could lead to a future use of nuclear weapons. Depending on the specifics, such use could either greatly strengthen the nuclear taboo and associated nonproliferation norm, or undermine it. For that reason and because it had little to do with nonproliferation per se, nonuse is considered a draw.

Some Implications for Chemical Weapons and Missile Nonproliferation

Over the past several years, the United States and other countries have begun to place greater emphasis on measures to control the spread of ballistic and cruise missiles and chemical weapons (CW). A Missile Technology Control Regime, with a list of sensitive items and guidelines for their control, has been concluded among the United States, the United Kingdom, France, West Germany, Japan, Italy, and Canada. China and the Soviet Union remain outside, although the Soviets have indicated interest in creation of such a multilateral control regime. In turn, a group of Western countries, the so-called Australia Group, has compiled a list of key chemicals needed to make chemical

weapons and steps have been taken by individual countries in order to control their export. Negotiations also are underway at the Geneva Conference on Disarmament, which are paralleled by U.S.–Soviet talks, regarding an international convention to ban the development, stockpiling, production, transfer, and use of chemical weapons. President Bush also has proposed a bilateral U.S.–Soviet agreement to reduce each country's CW stocks.

There is a series of lessons for missile and CW nonproliferation from the nuclear nonproliferation record. By way of conclusion, these lessons are sketched briefly, with some thoughts on the similarities and differences of nuclear weapons, chemical weapons, and missile nonproliferation.

First, a key to longer-term success likely will be the establishment of an international consensus or norm in favor of control. The norm of nuclear nonproliferation significantly influenced the calculations and decisions both of potential nuclear weapons states and of suppliers of nuclear technology, and provided the legitimacy for all other nonproliferation measures. No comparable norm now exists in the area of missiles. The Geneva Protocol norm against use of chemical weapons was undermined badly by repeated successful and unpunished Iraqi use of chemical weapons in the Gulf War.

A second lesson is that export controls and technology denial can make it harder, more time consuming, and more complex for countries to develop advanced military capabilities. They can buy time for other measures to be implemented, but, with some exceptions, they alone cannot prevent proliferation and should not be called on to do so. The impact of export controls, moreover, is likely to be even weaker in the chemical weapons area.

Legitimate civilian chemical activities are more widespread, the number of firms and countries involved greater, and the unique constraints of radioactivity to assist control are lacking. For missiles, export controls again seem most useful to slow the process and to buy time. Although access to guidance technologies could be a key bottleneck, this would apply only to countries seeking more sophisticated capabilities.

Third, technical characteristics aside, the nuclear nonproliferation experience suggests that ensuring effective export controls will be a continuing political and not only technical struggle. Problem countries will continue to find new ways to circumvent their impact. More important, other supplier countries often will lack the will, mechanisms, or personnel to implement effective export regulations. A growing number of suppliers will compound the problem. Recent experience with both chemical weapons and missile export controls serves only to reinforce this point.

Fourth, the existence of a legally binding international obligation to enforce export controls can be especially helpful in obtaining the support of other countries to alleviate some of the above weaknesses. In the nuclear nonproliferation area, the NPT made it easier for governments to convince legislatures to place restrictions on trade. A legally binding obligation under the NPT also provided a valuable handle for U.S. arguments with other countries about the need to put in place export control systems and to implement them effectively. NPT membership also could be cited as part of nuclear diplomacy aimed at heading off specific exports. In neither the CW nor missile technology control fields is there now a comparable legally binding obligation. One of the main benefits of a complete and total chemical weapons ban would be its creation of that obligation, via a ban on transfer.

Fifth, the nuclear nonproliferation record also drives home the importance of influencing incentives to acquire advanced military technologies. Steadily growing skepticism about the utility of nuclear weapons, backed by strong U.S. alliances, have been most critical in the nuclear field. By contrast, Iraq's recent successful uses of chemical weapons have sent the opposite signal. The problems of assistance to countries threatened with chemical weapons and sanctions against users have yet to be addressed. With regard to missile proliferation, it may be feasible to take measures via tactical missile defenses to negate directly the benefits for Third World countries of acquiring missiles. Absent that, perceptions of the utility of missiles also are likely to rise over time, again partly boosted by Iraq's use of missiles in the war of the cities as well as by recent Afghan government use of Soviet SCUD missiles.

Sixth, four decades of nuclear nonproliferation clearly demonstrate that nonproliferation efforts in any area must be placed into a broader national, regional, and international political perspective. Consider each briefly.

Nationally, nuclear nonproliferation traditionally has been but one piece— and often in practice a subordinate one—of overall national security and foreign policy. This already has been evident from the start in the chemical and missile nonproliferation areas. It is unlikely to change, barring a dramatic proliferation threat to the United States itself.

In turn, the key to long-term regional nuclear nonproliferation success increasingly seems likely to be political initiatives to defuse the underlying conflicts. In South Asia, the Middle

East, the Gulf, and the Korean peninsula, nuclear nonproliferation cannot be pursued only on its own terms. The need for such political initiatives may increase the difficulties and complexities, but also may open up new opportunities. Similarly, both missile and chemical weapons nonproliferation need to be put into such a broader regional political context. Equally important, the relationships between all three types of proliferation need to be factored into policy development.

Finally, the nuclear nonproliferation record reflects both the benefits and the limits of U.S.–Soviet cooperation. Cooperation between the two countries was essential to put in place a strong nuclear supply regime, buttress the NPT, support the IAEA, and defuse at least some problem country hot spots. Still, U.S.–Soviet regional interests also have differed on occasion, restricting the possibility of common nonproliferation action. Similarly, limits even on their joint influence have been evident. These same strains can be expected in trying to put together a parallel approach to CW and missile nonproliferation.

Conclusion

Looking back at the record of four decades of nuclear nonproliferation wins, losses, and draws makes clear both the potential influence and the continuing limits of U.S. efforts to prevent the further spread of nuclear weapons around the globe. Both what the United States realistically can hope to do and what it cannot do need to be taken into account in revamping U.S. nuclear nonproliferation policies in the decades ahead. Equally, the lessons of the record of the past decades need to be reflected in the new measures now rising to prominence in order to prevent the spread of chemical weapons and missiles. To do so could increase measurably the prospects for their success.

The views contained herein are the author's, and not necessarily those of Science Applications International Corporation or any of its sponsors. The author would like to thank the Aspen Strategy Group for its support of an earlier version of this paper, which will appear as an appendix in a forthcoming Aspen Strategy Group Report on Proliferation.

Notes

1. For a detailed discussion of recent revelations about Israeli capabilities, see Frank Barnaby, *The Invisible Bomb* (London: I.B. Tauris & Co., 1989).

2. See *Time*, March 30, 1987, p. 42; *New York Times*, August 14, 1986; for an overview of the current nonproliferation situation, see Leonard S. Spector, *The Undeclared Bomb* (Cambridge, Mass.: Ballinger, 1988).

3. A clear nuclear proliferation loss, the French case is discussed below.

4. See McGeorge Bundy, *Danger and Survival* (New York: Random House, 1988), p. 510.

U.S. Arms Reductions and Nuclear Nonproliferation: The Counterproductive Possibilities

George H. Quester and
Victor A. Utgoff

THE END OF the Cold War has renewed the hope, in the United States and around the world, that nuclear weapons can be very much deemphasized; and it has also caused Americans to expect substantial conventional arms reductions. In the aftermath of the events since 1989, many Americans have similarly assumed that the superpower example of détente and disarmament will help to discourage nuclear proliferation and the spread of weapons of mass destruction to additional countries around the world.

But there is reason to be concerned that the real impact of U.S. nuclear and conventional arms reductions is counterproductive, in that, if carried too far, they may encourage rather than discourage nuclear proliferation.

Some Positive Reinforcements

There are indeed many ways in which such developments will help to reduce

George H. Quester is a professor in the Department of Government and Politics at the University of Maryland. His latest book is *The Future of Nuclear Deterrence* (Lexington, Mass.: D. C. Heath, 1986). Victor A. Utgoff is deputy director of the Strategy, Forces and Resources Division of the Institute for Defense Analyses. In 1990 he published *The Challenge of Chemical Weapons: An American Perspective* (New York: Macmillan, 1990).

nuclear proliferation. Before moving into the unfortunate counterproductive linkages that are the primary subject of this paper, it is important to enumerate some of these positive reinforcements and to understand how various arms-control goals of recent decades have reinforced one another.

First, the dramatic reduction in Moscow's and Washington's nuclear arsenals may somewhat satisfy world public opinion on issues of fairness and morality because it has been widely asserted that other states cannot be asked to forgo nuclear weapons unless the superpowers are doing so. In the countries where public opinion makes a difference, and where that public opinion is plugged into world opinion (for example, Japan), the apparent termination of the East–West nuclear confrontation makes it all the more difficult for an aspiring politician to suggest acquiring national nuclear forces.

More broadly, the reduction in superpower arsenals will be viewed in many places as at least setting a good example. The pace of these reductions since 1989 can thus be interpreted as evidence that Moscow and Washington are complying with article VI of the Nuclear Non-Proliferation Treaty (NPT), which required the existing nuclear weapon states to engage in negotiations "toward general and complete disarmament." With the crucial NPT Review Conference coming in 1995, at which a vote will be taken on whether the treaty is to be continued, this evidence will provide important ammunition for supporters of the NPT.

Other things being equal, then the trends in superpower policy will also reduce the glamor and newsworthiness of nuclear weapons generally as less attention will be given to nuclear war scenarios and to the potential military applications of nuclear warheads. The possible addition of Germany and Japan to the United Nations Security Council as permanent members would be symptomatic of this new direction because it would break up the accidental pattern in which the five permanent members of the Council became the only five states to openly possess nuclear weapons when the NPT was signed in 1967 (and as signatories were allowed to retain such weapons under the treaty). It is a further symptom that economic prowess is now seen as at least on a par with nuclear prowess where international political influence is concerned.

Toward General and Complete Disarmament (GCD)?

As noted, the superpower nuclear arms reductions can be seen as a move toward GCD; indeed, these cuts amount to a much greater reduction than anyone would have dared to predict five years ago. It is now necessary for the world to face the question, however, of whether it really wants, or could live comfortably with, general and complete disarmament.

Looking to the end of the trail, one must sadly consider the possibility that there might never be a world without nuclear weapons, if only because eliminating the current nuclear arsenals would quickly tempt some other state to race into the role vacated by the superpowers. There may indeed be no way to get there from here, and trying to go too far in the direction of GCD may produce a very unwanted result— the emergence of a series of new nuclear weapon states. A world of no nuclear weapon states at all would thus be dangerously tempting (unless world government is first achieved and all separate sovereignties have been eliminated) to any renegade state wishing to capture a nuclear monopoly like that of the United States in 1946 (and, unlike the United States, perhaps prepared to use such a monopoly to establish an empire). The existence of a pair of finite-deterrence nuclear weapon states might eliminate this most dangerous of temptations, but then too many additional states might still be lured into nuclear weapons production, simply by the seeming ease of matching the status of the existing two.

Two pessimistic possibilities thus have to be considered here as the premises for much of the analysis that follows: first, there may always have to be at least one (perhaps two) nuclear weapon states (or an international organization that possesses nuclear weapons), and, second, to prevent another 15 nuclear weapons possessors from attempting to join such a state or states or international organization, the residual nuclear arsenal held by the one or two "nuclear guardians" may have to be considerably more robust than the one now advocated by proponents of minimum deterrence.

The Enduring Importance of Nuclear Weapons

Regrettably, the realities of international power politics thus hardly support the view that nuclear weapons are no longer important, or that they do not have a weight in international affairs comparable to economic strength. One can illustrate this by considering the standing of particular countries if nuclear weapons were not a factor.

For example, would outsiders be nearly as worried about the future of the former Soviet Union if its successor states did not possess nuclear weapons? The command and control arrangements for these weapons have now introduced serious new nuclear proliferation concerns for many Americans.

The world might also be less solicitous for the stability of the regime in Beijing after Tiananmen if it did not control a nuclear arsenal. And what would be the relative importance attached by the outside world to Britain and France, as compared to Germany and Japan, if the first two states did not possess nuclear weapons? Would they not be regarded as relatively minor powers because they lag behind in economic strength and conventional military strength?

It is similarly not clear whether the United States would be quite as committed to the defense of Israel (although other important factors are at work here) if there were not persistent rumors that Israel had "bombs in the basement." And would everyone pay as much attention to South Asia, a region of depressing poverty, if there were not the continual prospect of nuclear proliferation in Pakistan and India? Similarly the long-term U.S. withdrawal from South Korea might be proceeding more rapidly if not for the nuclear potential now displayed in both the Koreas.

And, conversely, one has to contemplate how different the world assessment of countries like Argentina, Australia, Saudi Arabia, or Sweden would be today if they had acquired nuclear weapons before the nonproliferation regime, such as it is, had settled into place.

The world's sigh of relief that such weapons might at last be eliminated illustrates its enormous fear and dread of the destruction they can inflict. This fear, of course, makes the acquisition of such weapons by any country on the threshold of developing them a very important problem and thus can make such a country feel and be more *important*. Being important has never been low on the scale of national motives in international relations.

Negative Interactions: The Stress on Basic Deterrence

To repeat, the world's enthusiasm about major reductions in the nuclear arsenals of the United States and the former Soviet Union stems primarily from a dread of the destruction such weapons can inflict. The global public is more impressed by what nuclear weapons can do to cities than by what such weapons might accomplish to reverse the military outcome on potential battlefields. But this conveys and reinforces an impression that even a few nuclear warheads, in the possession of a Libya, Iraq, or North Korea, would be very important, and it can thus work to enhance the desire of some of these national regimes for such weapons. Many of the states that have been suspected of an interest in nuclear weapons might well have been influenced by this kind of motivation, for example, the Shah's Iran and present-day Algeria, or Argentina and Brazil before they became democracies, and other states could easily feel the same way in the future.

The strategic analysis that now accompanies the changes in the Soviet and U.S. arsenals repeatedly reinforces these impressions. It will too often be asserted that the primary or only use of nuclear weapons will now be "basic deterrence," so that "extended nuclear deterrence" will be terminated or retained only under the most exceptional circumstances. The argument of Robert McNamara, former secretary of defense, that "the only role for nuclear weapons is to deter their own use" will be quoted approvingly, with an implicit message that the countervalue impact of nuclear weapons is so much to be feared that any military applications are to be dispensed with. But this again suggests that great importance is to be attached to *any* nuclear arsenal, even if a country on the threshold of nuclear capability has only acquired a few nuclear warheads.

No one will argue that national decisions on nuclear proliferation around the globe will simply be the result of whatever importance Americans and others seem to attach to the most rudimentary of nuclear forces. Some national leaderships will indeed not reach for such weapons until they are sure they can achieve more robust nuclear forces.

The important point is rather that any effective nonproliferation strategy must still seek to reinforce, rather than erode, this barrier to entry, that is, must avoid endowing small numbers of nuclear weapons with great significance; the decisions now made on U.S. nuclear and conventional force structure do play an important role here.

Finite Deterrence Reasoning

The primary question for discussion amid debates about whether the totals of nuclear warheads should fall to 3,000, or 1,000, or even lower is now: "How low can we go?" Advocates of the lower levels will often argue that "numbers don't matter," that is, that *any* nuclear retaliatory threat sufficient to destroy most of an adversary's cities is sufficient to satisfy national needs. But this kind of argument about American and Russian levels again transmits an impression abroad that 10 or 20 nuclear warheads, by the same standards, would still be very significant.

The statement of proponents of finite deterrence that "numbers don't matter" can basically mean that the first 100 bombs any nation acquires are much more significant than an incremental move from 3,900 to 4,000 (almost everyone might agree with this), and/or that these first 100 bombs might almost be enough to deter and cancel out the relevance of larger arsenals (here we have a much more contentious point, but certainly a big boost for potential proliferators). The military and political leaders of potential nuclear weapon states will be considering strategic realities, but they will also be taking account of the impressions of their own less expert public opinions and of the impressions of such publics in other countries.

For example, as the nuclear forces of the United States and Russia are reduced, the existing nuclear arsenals of Britain, France, and the People's Republic of China (PRC) will probably also be reduced, although probably by smaller percentages. It is thus almost inevitable that the nuclear forces of these latter countries will look "more important" as the difference between their own and the superpower nuclear forces is diminished, and will attract more analytical attention, perhaps thereby producing more inclination toward emulation in near-nuclear states.

Thus, a country that acquires nuclear weapons may feel it is moving up to a stature comparable to Beijing's at a moment when that stature has become greater in any comparison to Washington's or Moscow's. The nuclear league will look like an easier league to break into, an easier level to approach or match. As the superpowers drop from five digits to four in the totals of their nuclear warheads, it will *seem* more impressive if India (or some state emulating India) reaches triple digits.

We have postulated that world public opinion may conclude that Moscow and Washington are setting a good example, an example that should be matched. But there are countries in the world, Pakistan and India being two prominent examples, where public opinion is much more inclined to favor nuclear proliferation and is not so impressed by such "good examples," that is, where even a democratically elected government may conclude that what has happened between the cold war protagonists is less the setting of a relevant example and more the creation of a vacuum or an opportunity.

Diminished Support for Nonstrategic Nuclear Weapons Development

A probable consequence of the euphoria that has attended the end of the Cold War is that the United States, in addition to reducing its numbers of nuclear weapons, will be reducing its investment in advanced delivery systems that enable it to use such weapons against forces invading the territory of allies. That investment will be portrayed as excessively expensive and/or inconsistent in tone with the end of Soviet–U.S. hostility. It will also be portrayed as inconsistent with nonproliferation because the United States allegedly cannot ask other nations to forgo the acquisition of nuclear

weapons while it enhances weapons in its own arsenal.

Yet the crucial paradox here is that nuclear proliferation might be encouraged rather than discouraged by such a U.S. failure to maintain theater nuclear delivery systems. Such systems work to maintain the ability of the United States to control escalation. First, the United States would be in a better position to discourage and deter any nuclear escalation by another nuclear power, making it to that power's military disadvantage to use its nuclear weapons. Second, the United States could plausibly itself threaten to escalate whenever some other country perceived a military or political advantage in its initial use of nuclear weapons, with the U.S. escalation finely calibrated to reverse these initial advantages with minimum damage to innocent civilians so as to leave the adversary with no good choices except to back off.

Any comparison between a country's rudimentary nuclear forces and continuously developing U.S. nuclear forces would, of course, discourage the country from acquiring nuclear weapons in the first place. Given the economic costs of acquiring rudimentary nuclear capabilities, and the current general world antagonism to proliferation, such forces are less likely to be acquired if they will be so badly outclassed.

Yet the risk is precisely that such U.S. theater nuclear weapon systems will be labeled as "relics of the Cold War," and that their development will not be continued. In particular, more than the *quantity* of nuclear weapons retained by the United States, a failure to maintain the *quality* of such weapons might make an unfortunate difference for some decisions about the bomb taken around the world. Beyond keeping the United States and one or another of the nuclear weapon states in place as nuclear powers, it may thus be necessary for the United States (or a responsible international organization) to be *substantially in the lead* in the sophistication and tactical applications of its nuclear weapons if it is to maximize deterrence of nuclear proliferation.

Conventional Arms Reductions

The end of the Cold War inevitably dictates reductions in U.S. conventional military capabilities; but such reductions, if they go too far, can again have the impact of reducing rather than enhancing the global barriers to nuclear proliferation. For reassuring allies that they do not need their own nuclear weapons, and for warning adversaries that they will not be able to exploit a nuclear arsenal, it will be of great value for the United States to seem capable of intervening effectively at the conventional level.

Desert Storm thus amounted to a valuable display of the kinds of conventional capabilities that might be deployed against any renegade state reaching for nuclear weapons, or against a state that had already acquired such weapons. Yet it is important to note that much of the military capability brought to bear in Desert Storm had been developed and procured for the Cold War, and that some of it might well not have existed if the Cold War had ended earlier. In the conventional case, just as in the nuclear, East–West competition has generated military capacities that would be difficult for any new power to overcome, and that thus constitute an important disincentive to proliferation.

The United States should therefore continue a significant portion of the conventional weapons development that was associated with the Cold War, especially enhancing the capacity for more finely tuned attacks, thus reminding prospective adversaries that U.S. escalation dominance will apply at each level. A state like Iran or Iraq might reach for a rudimentary nuclear force in hopes of deterring U.S. nuclear escalation, and then exploit a local conventional warfare advantage. The optimum strategy for discouraging such proliferation will be to negate both of these hopes, maintaining credible options for U.S. nuclear escalation, as noted above, and maintaining a plausible capacity for conventional defense as well.

The United States will now have to deal with a world in which both India and Pakistan may have *some* nuclear warheads; both the Koreas are not far from such weapons; Israel may have such weapons; and various Arab states are moving closer to having them. The most ambitious of U.S. goals will be to keep such weapons from being used, discourage any more extensive procurement of such weapons, and minimize how much they are openly proclaimed—and *perhaps* even to talk the regional powers into disassembling and eliminating whatever has already been acquired. For any and all these purposes, which may require maintaining a plausible prospect of U.S. military intervention, it will be desirable for the United States to have the graduated array of nuclear and conventional options just outlined.

The Bush administration has indeed indicated that it does not intend to let U.S. conventional military forces degrade substantially in the wake of the Cold War. Although procurement is to be reduced, the administration proposes that the development of conventional weapons capabilities be continued, and, more generally, that strong conventional forces will be maintained, at the least to prepare for the contingency that relations with the successors to the Soviet Union might worsen. Yet this can still leave important gaps.

Eroding Extended Deterrence

Extended deterrence has been a phrase used to describe a variety of U.S. goals. These normally would include protecting an ally of the United States, rather than U.S. territory itself, protecting such an ally against an adversary's conventional or nuclear attack, and doing so by the threat of using U.S. nuclear weapons. But it would be helpful to sort out a little more fully here the array of developments that U.S. policy has been designed to prevent, especially because events since 1989 are fostering a widespread impression that the United States will no longer threaten nuclear retaliation except after the use of nuclear weapons by another power, and perhaps only when such weapons are used against the United States itself.

Extended nuclear deterrence, in the past, included the goals of preventing the use of conventional weapons (in particular tanks) against an ally by an adversary stronger in conventional forces, *and* of preventing the mere threat of such an attack,[1] *and* of preventing the excessive acquisition of conventional weapons (by either side) in the first place (this being what is typically styled an "arms race"). The first two goals clearly contribute to the third, because states are less likely to invest in tanks and other conventional weapons when U.S. nuclear umbrellas make it more difficult to use them or to threaten their use.

Extended nuclear deterrence also had the objective of preventing the use of *nuclear* weapons by any adversary against an ally that did not have them, *and* of preventing the mere threat of such use (what is often labeled "nuclear blackmail"), *and* of preventing additional acquisitions of nuclear weapons in the first place (i.e., preventing nuclear proliferation). Again it follows that the accomplishment of the first two goals contributes to the third, as threshold countries are less likely to reach for nuclear weapons when they cannot easily see themselves using them or threatening their use.

It has to be stressed, moreover, that such extended nuclear deterrence has, at all times, been seen as a straightforward antiproliferation device where *allies* were concerned. Because the United States gave the impression of being ready to use its own nuclear forces in response to an adversary's tank attack or nuclear attack, the likelihood of such attacks was reduced (and the political impact of the mere threat of such attacks was reduced), so that allies such as South Korea, West Germany, or Turkey did not feel a need to acquire their own nuclear forces. The United States has been eager to head off nuclear proliferation for both allies and adversaries (and has also wanted to damp down conventional arms races between such allies and adversaries), and its apparent willingness to use nuclear weapons, even in situations where no nuclear attack has as yet been launched on the United States itself, has played an important role in pursuing this goal.

The demise of the Warsaw Pact and the breakup of the Soviet Union is stimulating a widespread belief that extended nuclear deterrence is now less required for the protection of the North Atlantic Treaty Organization (NATO). Even if the Cold War is over, however, it may nonetheless be premature to conclude that all conventional or nuclear threats against the NATO countries or against the former members of the Warsaw Pact can safely be ruled out and that consequently Germany and the other Central European states would under no circumstances see national nuclear forces as the antidote to such threats.

One has to remember that the new political leaders of virtually every former Warsaw Pact member, and the leaders of the newly independent states that used to be part of the Soviet Union, are novices on nuclear strategy and nuclear policy. If such leaders now perceive even the most rudimentary conventional military threats from Russia or from any other neighboring state, it cannot be taken for granted that they will see nuclear options as irrelevant. It may yet be necessary for the United States to maintain some kind of meaningful reassurance or guarantee here if nuclear proliferation is to be avoided.

NATO facing the Warsaw Pact has been the classic scenario for extended nuclear deterrence. Another has always been protecting South Korea against attack from the North. It may be difficult for anyone to determine whether the Cold War is now definitely "over" on the Korean peninsula, and a termination of U.S. extended deterrence on behalf of the Republic of Korea (even if this is now rationalized as an antiproliferation step to reassure North Korea somehow) might lead Seoul once again to contemplate the national nuclear option.

As part of the same optimistic response to the end of the Cold War, the United States is pulling out some of those deployments of U.S. military personnel and/or theater nuclear weapons overseas that had made it more plausible that the United States would set for itself the same threshold for nuclear escalation as its threatened allies. As with the more theoretical discussions of shifting from extended nuclear deterrence back to basic deterrence, this policy might seem to deemphasize nuclear options more generally around the globe, but it might also drive the particularly threatened countries, among them South Korea, to feel the need for acquiring their own such options.

There have been many different arguments for keeping theater nuclear weapons deployed outside the United States itself over the decades of the Cold War, arguments not always logically consistent with each other, but all made with the goal of making U.S. nuclear escalation more credible and plausible, thus deterring adversaries and reassuring allies. One argument pertains to maintaining a capability for the timely targeting of advancing enemy forces; although nuclear systems based at remote locations might also be capable of attacking such forces, only systems based closer in might be brought to bear in time. Another argument is directed to showing threatened allies that U.S. forces would share their situation, so that there would be less gap between the relevant national interests when the time came for a nuclear escalation. A third argument concludes that nuclear escalation was made more likely simply because U.S. nuclear forces and troops were deployed in the path of the adversary's advance. Even if this last "trip-wire" role is not particularly rational in its mechanisms, it might still connote to all concerned that U.S. extended nuclear deterrence was in place, and thus that local production of separate nuclear weapons was unnecessary.

Given the variety of new military conflicts that may emerge among all the new regimes in the world, a U.S. military presence could be withdrawn too quickly from where it had been deployed for the past four decades, removing old solutions before old problems are definitively eliminated. Given all these conflicts, it may more generally be too early to terminate extended nuclear deterrence.

No-First-Use or Negative Security Assurances

As noted above, we may now be seeing a trend toward an American acceptance of the no-first-use policy long advocated by Secretary of Defense Robert S. McNamara and many others, because the United States would never use nuclear weapons unless another power used them first.

As an alternative to such a total termination of nuclear escalation, it is sometimes suggested that the United States should now reassert the negative security assurances announced at the end of the Carter administration, whereby it renounced (in the context of the 1978 NPT review) the use of nuclear weapons only against states that did not acquire nuclear weapons of their own (thus supplying a greater disincentive to nuclear proliferation than total no-first-use)—*and* that were not fighting against us in alliance with a nuclear power.

The latter condition was most important, because, as of 1979, it denied the extension of this U.S. assurance to the Warsaw Pact and North Korea. By 1989, however, the Warsaw Pact no longer tied its members to the Soviet Union as allies. And by 1991 there was no longer even a Soviet Union for North Korea to be allied with, and any military alliance to the PRC was also in doubt.

For some, such a "negative security assurance" might thus seem to be very suited to nonproliferation goals, rewarding the restraint on acquisition by North Korea or other countries that the United States is trying to foster.

But at the same time it can aggravate a number of the problems noted above, for such a renunciation of U.S. nuclear escalation options may leave unprotected those U.S. allies that feel threatened by the conventional military forces of their neighbors. The past situation of South Korea facing North Korea perhaps remains the prime example, but other such cases are still plausible for the future.

Some Alternative Policy Tracks

How can the United States best dovetail the goal of global nonproliferation and U.S. national nuclear policy? Such policy cannot stop proliferation all by itself, and other factors will have to be in play if the spread of nuclear weapons is to be avoided; but how can the maximum desirable impact be extracted from the coming evolution of U.S. nuclear weapons and nuclear strategy? It will be necessary to reduce the U.S. nuclear arsenal but also to moderate and manage these reductions. U.S. nuclear weapons policy cannot by itself stop nuclear proliferation, yet it can help or hinder attempts to do so, and the task is to minimize the hindrance.

The thrust of the argument here has been that a straightforward and enthusiastic response to the end of the Cold War may be missing opportunities for discouraging nuclear proliferation. It is not enough to state that U.S. concerns should be shifted from the containment of Soviet power to the prevention of the spread of nuclear weapons. Rather, attention must be paid to some of the ways the containment efforts of the Cold War also indirectly discouraged proliferation, so that these disincentives should not get lost in reaping the peace dividend. We address below some policy options that should be given a hearing in light of the importance of the nonproliferation effort. Many of these have already been implicitly outlined in the discussion above.

Clarifying Weak Prospects for an Enduring Regional Nuclear Monopoly. Where countries are paired off, for example, Argentina and Brazil, a part of the solution to problems of proliferation may be to encourage each country to realize that either's acquisition of nuclear weapons would probably be matched by the other, while either may abstain as long as the other abstains. Argentina might very much relish having the only nuclear arsenal in Latin America (however small), and so might Brazil; but neither will want to be part of a pair of new nuclear weapon states in the region. Ironically, it is the very closeness of various states to achieving the bomb that might make each of them stand back from actually producing such weapons, knowing that their own example could all too easily be copied.

The deterrent effect of such pairing is indeed a powerful encouragement to those who oppose nuclear proliferation. The United States and the old Soviet Union have not been alone in their opposition to the spread of nuclear weapons in their own national interest. Nonproliferation serves the interests of many countries and is not a lost cause.

Staying Ahead of Potential Proliferators in the Quantity and Quality of Nuclear Weapons. If we wish to make a maximum contribution to discouraging proliferation, it may be very important to steer the strategic discussion in a direction where the numbers and quality of nuclear weapons matter, despite all the current trends of the discussion in just the opposite direction. Whatever

the appeal of finite deterrence and its resignation to simple countervalue targeting, it has to be recognized that this implies a great importance for a rudimentary nuclear stockpile in any other country—exactly the wrong message to deliver. Rather than going about suggesting that "even a few bombs are enough," the United States must maintain the total *quality* of its nuclear arsenal so that it continues to look difficult to match.

The general argument here is that success in deterring the proliferation of nuclear weapons will depend heavily on taking the prospective value out of their use after they have been acquired. The morally appealing argument is that this would somehow be "naturally" accomplished by terminating any prospects of U.S. use of nuclear weapons; but the sad reality is that the linkages may be just the reverse.

People, of course, may then worry about what the United States might do in imperialistic fashion with its dominance of the escalation scenario. But, as demonstrated in the close U.S. consultation with the United Nations in Desert Storm, such concerns can be assuaged if the United States continues to develop confidence in its willingness to exercise power only on behalf of, and with, the world community. The prospect of having a nuclear arsenal largely directed by the United Nations may still seem unrealistic as of 1992; but, for all the reasons cited, it is a far more realistic long-term avenue to explore than a world without nuclear weapons.

Avoiding Categorical No First Use. Even if the United States were to guarantee the non-use of nuclear weapons against states not possessing such weapons themselves, it follows that it will be very important to *maintain* the option for such first use whenever an adversary has acquired nuclear weapons.

The structure of incentives here always has to be twofold to be meaningful, offering U.S. restraint on use where a potential threshold power offers restraint on acquisition, but *denying* such restraint when that power does not. The more general drift of current thinking toward a blanket policy of no first use must thus be resisted because it would remove one crucial contingency of negative security guarantees. It would certainly not make sense to assure proliferators the advantage of always getting the best opening nuclear shot.

Maintaining and Enhancing the U.S. Lead in Conventional Warfare Systems. As stressed above, some important discouragement of proliferation emerges in the U.S. ability relatively to ignore, rather than be cowed by, nuclear weapons in the hands of another country. A wider array of graduated *nuclear* options works to this end; so will a wider array of *conventional* options.

If the United States deploys a menu of conventional options comparable to that shown in Desert Storm, it enhances the impression that it can hold its own nuclear forces in reserve to retaliate for any use of nuclear forces by its adversaries, and that it can in the meantime punish and/or defeat such countries on the nonnuclear battlefield. Sharing such enhanced conventional military capabilities with allies and other threatened states would, moreover, reassure them that they did not need to reach for nuclear weapons of their own.

This consideration may require that the United States develop, and be ready to acquire and share on rela-tively short notice, conventional weapons that are still more effective than those we have seen to date and more finely tuned to precisely targeted strikes with low collateral damage. The nuclear arsenal of the United States and the major powers would remain in the background, a rung of escalation reserved for any further escalations by a threshold power.

To repeat, too unilateral a U.S. use of the most effective conventional weapons might be counterproductive for the prevention of the spread of nuclear weapons because some regimes would feel themselves so threatened that they would become desperate to acquire nuclear weapons as their most feasible retaliatory instrument. Yet if an enhancement of U.S. conventional capabilities is coupled to more frequent referral to international authority on when they were to be used, the ideal policy mix for the maximum discouragement of nuclear proliferation could well be the result.

The Need to Choose

There is no doubt that the end of the Cold War has given Americans and others a great deal to celebrate. Yet this good news must still not be allowed to obscure the fundamental choices noted throughout this article.

However great the desire to reduce conventional armaments, and to cut back existing nuclear arsenals, *and* to avoid nuclear proliferation, the risks are all too great that these worthy goals will conflict with each other, at least over some important ranges of policy choices. To assume that all good things go together here, when they do not, portends major disappointment; and a disappointment about halting the horizontal spread of nuclear weapons might be the worst kind of disappointment of all. Rather than accelerating and extending reductions in the U.S. nuclear and conventional arsenals, these may need to be slowed and limited if a maximum contribution to halting nuclear proliferation is to be achieved.

This paper reflects the views of the authors alone and is not necessarily endorsed by the Institute for Defense Analyses or the U.S. Department of Defense.

Notes

1. This threat has often been referred to generically as "Finlandization" (regardless of whether it actually ever applied to Finland).

Prospects for Chemical and Biological Arms Control: The Web of Deterrence

Graham S. Pearson

MAJOR CHANGES TO the world scene have taken place over the last three years with the dissolution of the former Soviet Union and the Warsaw Pact, the conflict between the Iraqi and coalition forces of 1990–1991, and the move away from bipolar tension toward regional conflicts and less stability. The same time frame has seen no sign of any reduction in the proliferation of chemical and biological (CB) weapons. Indeed some 10 nations are assessed as having biological weapons programs and almost twice that number have, or are aiming to acquire, chemical weapons.[1]

Following the Persian Gulf War, which saw a real threat of the use of CB weapons, the United Nations (UN) under Security Council Resolutions 687 and 715 established a Special Commission to oversee the elimination of Iraq's weapons of mass destruction and to carry out a monitoring regime to ensure that such a capability is not regained. The lessons being learned from the activities of the Special Commission are of immense importance for both CB arms control and

for would-be proliferators; it is particularly important for the status of the UN, the deterrent effect of its resolutions, and the credibility of the CB arms-control regimes that the UN Special Commission should succeed in its activities and that Iraq should be deprived of its capability for weapons of mass destruction. In addition, negotiation has been completed for the Chemical Weapons Convention (CWC), which is due to be opened for signature in January 1993. Also, the Ad Hoc Group of Governmental Experts considering verification measures for the Biological and Toxin Weapons Convention (BTWC) from a scientific and technical viewpoint has met twice—in Geneva from March 30 to April 10, 1992, and from November 23 to December 4, 1992. The tasks for CB arms control have become more important. Success in these efforts appears increasingly possible. But the challenges have also come into sharper focus.

This essay starts by considering the nature of CB weapons. It sets this discussion in the context of the relative scale of effect of such weapons against a background of the current world scene and of the existing arms-control framework. Recent changes in the international arena influence perceptions about the promise for and limits

Graham S. Pearson is director general of the U.K.'s Chemical and Biological Defence Establishment at Porton Down. Since his appointment in June 1984 he has contributed actively to both CB defense and the CB arms-control debate.

of the arms-control agenda[2] and create new incentives and opportunities for states to work together to limit the proliferation of CB weapons. The aim is to achieve a web of deterrence to complement the imperfections of arms control with other measures so that a potential cheater finds obstacles to every possible avenue to cheating and is led to a judgment that the acquisition of chemical or biological weapons is expensive, of uncertain military value, and politically unacceptable.

The Nature of CB Warfare

The use of CB weapons involves the dissemination of materials that cause harm or death to the attacked population. In both the chemical and biological cases, the primary route of attack requires the material to be disseminated into the atmosphere so that it can reach and be inhaled by the target population. In the case of chemicals, the materials poison the person attacked; biological agents cause infection, with harm and death as the result of the ensuing disease. The potential chemical and biological warfare (CBW) threat spectrum ranges from the classical chemical warfare (CW) agents, such as mustard, nerve agents, and hydrogen cyanide, through toxic industrial, pharmaceutical, and agricultural chemicals, to bioregulators and toxins, and thus to both genetically manipulated biological warfare (BW) agents and the traditional BW agents such as bacteria, viruses, and rickettsia. The CBW spectrum is shown in figure 1: the materials in the four boxes to the left poison while those in the two on the right infect. The relative toxicity of CW and BW agents is shown in figure 2. As might be expected, the quantities required to infect are very much less than those needed to poison. Typically there is a

factor of about 1 million between the quantities of typical BW agents needed to kill a person and those of typical CW agents.

The greatly enhanced potency of BW agents means that the distances downwind over which such agents can have effect are significantly greater than those for CW agents. This is shown schematically in figure 3, which demonstrates that typically for CW agents a kilometer is a representative downwind hazard distance, while for bioregulators and toxins the distance is about 10 kilometers, and for BW agents it is a few hundred kilometers. All of these calculations assume comparable and favorable meteorological conditions. The other difference between CW and BW agents is that the former tend to be rapid acting, with nerve agents resulting in harm or death within minutes, whereas the latter are slower to act because of the need for the microorganisms to replicate themselves inside the host. Consequently, chemical weapons have potentially greater utility in a near-contact battle, while biological weapons are more appropriate for rear areas or for static situations. Biological warfare is essentially a strategic concept.

Comparisons of chemical, biological, and nuclear weapons have been published by both the secretary general of the United Nations, in 1969,[3] and by Steve Fetter of the University of Maryland, in 1991.[4] Both these comparisons (see tables 1 and 2 respectively) demonstrate clearly that chemical weapons have a significantly greater effect than conventional weapons, while biological weapons have comparable effects to nuclear weapons. Both chemical and biological weapons are unique in two respects:

- they produce no collateral damage; and

Figure 1
CBW Threat Spectrum

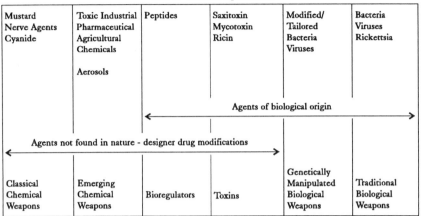

Mustard Nerve Agents Cyanide	Toxic Industrial Pharmaceutical Agricultural Chemicals Aerosols	Peptides	Saxitoxin Mycotoxin Ricin	Modified/ Tailored Bacteria Viruses	Bacteria Viruses Rickettsia
			Agents of biological origin ←——————————————→		
	Agents not found in nature - designer drug modifications ←——————————→				
Classical Chemical Weapons	Emerging Chemical Weapons	Bioregulators	Toxins	Genetically Manipulated Biological Weapons	Traditional Biological Weapons

- they require materials that can be acquired from legitimate peaceful facilities; there is no necessity for expensive nuclear facilities or for conventional military explosives.

Against that must be balanced several disadvantages, including, first, that of a delayed reaction over an area, second, dependence on the prevailing meteorology, and, third, the political reaction to a use or threat of use, which will be stronger than for any conventional method of warfare.

There can be little doubt about the utility of chemical or biological weapons. Chemical weapons were used in World War I, in Italian attacks on Abyssinia in the 1930s, and in the Iraq–Iran conflict of the 1980s. In all these cases, they were used against essentially unprotected personnel. Although the use of biological weapons in conflict has not been so unequivocally demonstrated, it is known that in conflicts involving conventional weapons more casualties result from disease than from the use of conventional weapons.[5] In addition, past offensive

biological programs have demonstrated the utility of such weapons by all means short of their actual use in war.

Divergent views are frequently expressed on the potential utility of chemical or biological weapons. It is frequently suggested that the meteorology is too uncertain, and that the user's troops may be at greater risk than those attacked. All such suggestions about the alleged disutility of chemical or biological weapons need to be carefully evaluated and investigated. Many are of doubtful validity. For example, despite meteorological conditions, an upwind chemical or biological weapons attack will be less sensitive to the accuracy of the delivery means than will a conventional weapons attack. As to the vulnerability of an aggressor's troops, it is important to remember that an aggressor knows what agents are available to it and can select the meteorology or other conditions to minimize the potential downwind hazard to its own forces.

Indeed, because of the uncertainty of the location of the precise hazard

Figure 2
Toxicity of CBW Agents

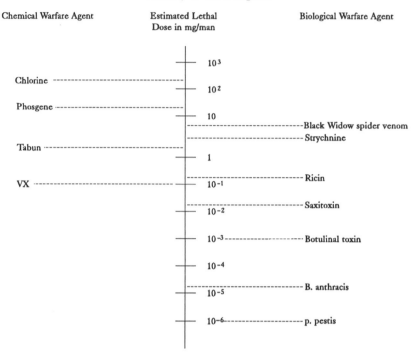

| Chemical Warfare Agent | Estimated Lethal Dose in mg/man | Biological Warfare Agent |

Chlorine ....

Phosgene ....

Tabun ....

VX ....

10^3
10^2
10

Black Widow spider venom
Strychnine

1

Ricin

10^{-1}

Saxitoxin

10^{-2}

10^{-3} Botulinal toxin

10^{-4}

B. anthracis

10^{-5}

10^{-6} p. pestis

Source: SIPRI, *Problems of Chemical and Biological Warfare*, vol. II (Stockholm and New York, 1971).

area arising from a particular attack, it is necessary to adopt a greater hazard area—and consequently a useful force multiplier occurs in that protective measures have to be donned in a much larger area than the actual hazard area because the latter depends on local meteorological variations.

Finally, selection of chemical or biological weapons that result in incapacitation rather than in death can again act as a force multiplier because incapacitated personnel need to be looked after in a way that the dead do not. Although chemical and biological weapons require time to take effect, this is much less of a disadvantage for an aggressor because it can choose

when to utilize the material and can thus select to do so at the optimum time—and this can indeed be an advantage, because it may be far from clear whether an attack has actually occurred and who carried it out.

CB Arms Control in a Changing World Scene

The first step in CB arms control was the Geneva Protocol of 1925, which essentially banned first use because several states retained the right to retaliate in kind should they be attacked with CB weapons. The next milestone was the Biological and Toxin Weapons Convention of 1972, which sought to

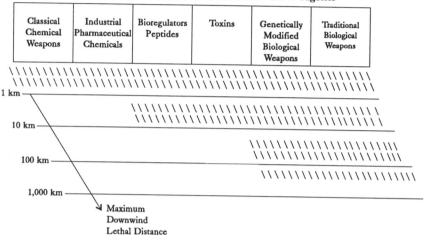

Figure 3
Downwind Hazard Distance for CBW Agents

ban a complete class of weapons. This had, as was usual at the time, no provisions for compliance and verification; nor did it address use. A further 20 years has brought agreement of a text for the Chemical Weapons Convention, which has provisions for verification and inspection as well as for investigations of use. These developments, coupled with the threat in the Gulf conflict of 1990–1991 that Iraq might use CB weapons and information about the former Soviet program, have reminded the international com-

Table 1
Comparative Estimates of Attacks on Unprotected Population
Using a Nuclear, Chemical, or Biological Weapon

Criteria for estimate	Type of weapon		
	Nuclear (one megaton)	Chemical (15 tons)	Biological (10 tons)
Area affected	Up to 300 km²	Up to 60 km²	Up to 100,000 km²
Time delay before effect	Seconds	Minutes	Days
Damage to structures	Destruction over an area of 100 km²	None	None
Normal use after attack	3–6 months after attack	Limited during period of contamination	After end of incubation period or subsidence of epidemic

Source: UN, *Chemical and Bacteriological (Biological) Warfare and the Effects of Their Possible Use*, Report of the Secretary-General, A/7575/Rev.1, S/9292/Rev.1 (1969).

Table 2
Conventional/Chemical/Biological/Nuclear
Warhead Comparisons

Warhead Type	Dead	Injured
Conventional (1 ton of HE)	5	13
Chemical (300 kg of GB)	200–3,000	200–3,000
Biological (30 kg of anthrax)	20,000–80,000	
Nuclear (20 kiloton yield)	40,000	40,000

Source: Steve Fetter, "Ballistic Missiles and Weapons of Mass Destruction: What Is the Threat? What Should Be Done?" *International Security* 16 (Summer 1991), pp. 5–42.

Note: Missile with 1 tonne warhead against large city with average population density of 30 unprotected civilians per hectare

munity of the utility of such weapons and have focused greater attention on the need for effective and comprehensive regimes to ban them.

Against this background, the last three years have seen immense changes in the world scene that few would have predicted. The Soviet Union and the Warsaw Pact have been dissolved, and Iraq invaded Kuwait in August 1990 with Operation Desert Storm as the result. More recently, Yugoslavia has dissolved with bitter racial conflict and "ethnic cleansing." Few can predict with any confidence what developments may occur over the next three years, let alone the next decade, but the prospect of continuing regional conflicts must be high among them.

As noted, following the Gulf conflict the UN established a Special Commission to oversee the elimination of the Iraqi weapons of mass destruction. The UN's willingness to take on a more dominant role in the maintenance of international peace and security is welcome. It is, however, far from clear how far the UN is prepared to take such action against other states or in the event of lesser breaches of international security than the invasion of a neighbor. It is, however, clear that the world is no longer one of bipolar tensions but one in which re-

gional conflicts will dominate and unexpected alliances may be established to meet short-term goals.

In addition, it has been apparent throughout the past decade that the number of states possessing or seeking to acquire chemical or biological weapons has continued to increase. The United Kingdom Defence White Paper of July 1992 stated that a number of states are seeking chemical, biological, or nuclear weapons and the means to deliver them. About 10 countries are assessed as having biological weapons programs and almost twice that number have, or are aiming to acquire, chemical weapons. More than 20 countries outside the North Atlantic Treaty Organization (NATO) possess ballistic missiles.[6]

Although there have been significant developments and improvements in arms-control regimes, it has also become evident that no arms-control regime is guaranteed to be wholly effective. The recent changes in the world scene and increased awareness of the potential impact of CB weapons give a new urgency and incentive to devising a strategy that complements arms control with a range of other measures to form a web of deterrence such that an evader or potential evader will judge that acquisition of chemical or biological weapons would be prohibitively expensive, of doubtful military value, and carry substantial risk of detection that would make it politically unacceptable. The key elements of such a web are:

- comprehensive, verifiable, and global CB arms control to create a risk of detection and a climate of political unacceptability for CB weapons;
- broad CB export monitoring and controls to make it difficult and expensive for a proliferator to obtain necessary materials;
- effective CB defensive and protective measures to reduce the military utility of CB weapons; and
- a range of determined and effective national and international responses to CB acquisition and/or use.

The web of deterrence should lead a state to judge that acquisition of a CBW capability is not worthwhile. This aim of deterring many states can be achieved by a regime in which there is at least a finite possibility of detection of noncompliance; the risk of detection can be sufficient to deter without the discovery of a program being inevitable. The aim is to strike the right balance so that the resources required to achieve the degrees of deterrence and detection are commensurate with the security gains achieved.

CB Arms-Control Agreements

Although no arms-control agreement can be 100 percent effective—and this applies equally to CB arms control—it must be as effective and intrusive as possible because this greatly enhances both the chance of detection of noncompliance and the deterrent effect. The status of first chemical and then biological arms control is reviewed in the following sections.

Chemical Arms Control. The emergence of a final agreed text[7] of the Chemical Weapons Convention from Geneva in August 1992 is to be warmly welcomed because once the convention comes into force it will ensure that the possession of chemical weapons will be illegal and declared stocks of such weapons will be monitored and destroyed and their production facilities destroyed or converted. The scope of the CWC is such that it will include all chemicals misused for chemical warfare; it therefore covers past CW agents, known current CW agents, and possible future agents. The whole of the chemical weapons spectrum, including toxins, is included within the CWC's scope. In addition, provision is made for both routine and challenge inspection regimes so that activities that present a risk to the convention can be inspected and, should noncompliance be demonstrated, appropriate steps taken. Finally a section of the treaty addresses investigations of the allegations of use.

Although the Geneva Protocol signed on June 17, 1925, prohibits the use in war of asphyxiating, poisonous, and other gases and of all analogous liquids, materials, and devices and the use of bacteriological methods of warfare, there have been numerous allegations of the use of CW and BW over the years. Although the UN secretary general has carried out investigations of allegations of use, such investigations are wholly dependent on the accessibility of the site of the alleged attack to UN teams. Many CBW agents are non-persistent; in other words, the hazard is transient, borne on the wind and, as quickly as it comes, dispersed and diluted. The task of acquiring unequivocal evidence of the use of CW or BW agents is therefore a major challenge. The inclusion in the CWC of steps to address such allegations is a useful step forward.

For success, timely access to the location of the alleged attack is vital so that samples can be taken while traces of agent still persist and memories are still accurate as to the precise location in which the attack occurred. Samples need to be acquired at known locations that can be correlated with the collateral evidence that a CW or BW attack took place at that point. Samples have to be taken in such a way as to demonstrate that they have not been contaminated, and the sample trail from point of sampling to analysis needs to be rigorously validated. The analogy is to the acquisition and analysis of forensic evidence for the courts. The aim must be to obtain unequivocal evidence that can be presented to the UN without technical or political challenge.

Environmental samples are greatly preferable to biomedical samples although the latter are frequently more readily available. Biomedical samples are much more difficult to analyze effectively because CBW agents are by their toxic nature reactive with the body and in so reacting are metabolized. In addition, victims from such attacks will be given medication to treat the symptoms, and that medication will also be metabolized in the body. Subsequent analysis of a sample taken a few days after an attack presents a demanding technical challenge, especially if there is uncertainty about the nature of the agent used in the attack. It is hard enough to provide unequivocal evidence of an attack even when the nature of the agent is known.

The CWC offers the prospect of improved arrangements for investigations of allegations of use. This will require the training of teams of experts. They must be mentally and physically prepared to visit the site of alleged attacks to collect evidence by interviewing casualties and obtaining environmental samples for analysis. Such sample analysis will be futile if the teams of experts do not succeed in locating and visiting the actual scene of an attack. If they do succeed, then maps, the global positioning satellite location system, and video and still cameras are needed to provide incontrovertible evidence that the location is indeed correctly designated. Samples need to be collected, witnessed, and sealed. At each stage of the sample trail leading back to the analytical laboratory, any change of custody needs to be documented and witnessed. On arrival at the analytical laboratory, authenticated procedures need to be used to analyze the samples under conditions that can prove that the samples have not been adulterated or otherwise contaminated.

Investigations of allegations of use to date have concentrated on incidents relating to the use of chemicals, and such procedures tend to be focused on a search for the use of an unusual chemical if not for an actual CW agent. This emphasis needs to be broadened under the Geneva Protocol and as part of the secretary general's investigations to include analytical procedures that would detect if a BW agent or material had been used to cause disease. The analytical procedures for the investigation of allegations of use need to be reviewed to ensure that they are equally effective for chemical and biological attack and pose no hazard to the scientists at the analytical laboratory. This is particularly true where biomedical samples are concerned because these may be contaminated with naturally occurring endemic diseases such as AIDS. Laboratory procedures also need to ensure that there are no risks to the scientists carrying out the analysis to determine whether there is unequivocal evidence of a chemical or biological attack. For an investigation to be effective, timely access to the location of the alleged attack is vital. States need to agree to allow an investigating team access to an alleged attack on their territories within a matter of days after such an allegation. It is important to investigate allegations of the misuse of chemical or biological materials wherever these occur so as to confirm misuse, if any, and take appropriate action.

The CWC is due to open for signature in Paris in January 1993 and will enter into force not less than two years after that opening (i.e., January 1995 at the earliest) and 180 days after the 65th state has ratified the convention. Following signature, the Preparatory Commission (PrepCom) will meet at The Hague in the Netherlands to elect a chairman, appoint an executive secretary, and establish a provisional Technical Secretariat. The PrepCom will carry out a range of activities in preparation for the establishment, once the convention enters into force, of the Organization for the Prohibition of Chemical Weapons (OPCW), which will also be located at The Hague.

The PrepCom will be responsible for the recruitment and training of technical and support staff and for the purchase and standardization of equipment required by the OPCW. In respect of training, it will be important to determine an appropriate standard and to devise training courses that demonstrate that the required standard has been achieved. Modular courses leading to an academic qualification appear attractive. The PrepCom will also draw up a program of work and budget for the first year

of operation of the OPCW. In addition, the PrepCom will have a vital role in elaborating the provisions of the CWC through draft agreements, provisions, and guidelines. Examples of these are the following:

- detailed procedures for verification;
- detailed procedures for conduct of inspections;
- models for facility agreements;
- lists of approved equipment for use by inspectors; and
- guidelines for scheduled chemicals in low concentrations.

The elaboration of the detailed procedures for verification and for the conduct of inspections for the CWC will be greatly aided by the lessons learned by the UN Special Commission set up after the Gulf war to oversee the elimination of Iraq's weapons of mass destruction. The Special Commission itself was able to benefit from the considerable amount of work carried out by many states on trial inspections in preparing for and negotiating the CWC.

A crucial element of the Gulf cease-fire arrangements set out in Resolution 687 is the elimination under the supervision of the UN Special Commission and the International Atomic Energy Agency (IAEA) of Iraq's nuclear, biological, and chemical weapons, all ballistic missiles with a range over 150 kilometers, and the so-called Superguns and the means for their production, support, and maintenance. The United Kingdom rightly affords a very high priority to and plays a full part in the work of the Special Commission.

The inspection program has progressively disclosed a capability far greater than Iraq had originally declared, including an advanced program to produce nuclear weapons and a BW research program with offensive military applications. Arrangements for

311

monitoring Iraq's long-term compliance with Resolution 687 have also been agreed in Resolution 715, which provides for a stringent and intrusive regime designed to ensure that Iraq never again possesses or uses these weapons.[8]

Among the valuable lessons learned from the inspections carried out by the UN Special Commission on Iraq are the following:

- intrusive on-site inspections are essential for the disclosure of the suspected capabilities;
- broad-based and sustained political commitment and pressure are essential to make the inspection program effective;
- all available information needs to be collated and continuity provided between inspections;
- the structure, timetable, and duration of inspections have to be flexible so that chief inspectors can achieve their objectives without being unduly constrained; and
- when inspectors are provided by a range of nations on an intermittent basis and with varying expertise, their training and organization require considerable attention.

Valuable studies are being carried out in various countries on the lessons learned from these Iraqi inspections; these lessons must be applied to the improvement of CB arms control.

In addition, it is vital that the regimes under UN Security Council Resolutions 687 and 715 succeed in removing from Iraq its capabilities for waging war with weapons of mass destruction. Should the Special Commission not be effective in eliminating Iraq's capability to produce and use such weapons, states contemplating regional aggression may learn a series of lessons about international resolve that would be extremely unpalatable to other states.

Another activity that will be addressed by the PrepCom is the training of inspectors to carry out the activities of the OPCW; such training will take place in a number of countries and the question of appropriate standards and appropriate expertise will need to be addressed. Inspectors will need to be trained to have appropriate skills—technical, personal, and perhaps linguistic—so that effective teams can be created.

The procedures for the analysis of samples taken by OPCW inspectors in the course of their inspections need to be developed. It seems probable that a system involving accredited national laboratories that will analyze samples distributed blind by the OPCW will be the way forward, with each sample being analyzed by one or more accredited laboratory. Attention needs to be given to an appropriate international standard of accreditation of any laboratory carrying out such analyses. Not only will the laboratories need to be accredited but certified reference materials will be required to ensure that analyses are unequivocal and can be relied upon to draw firm conclusions at the OPCW.

Equipment to be used by inspectors on-site will range from protective equipment to ensure that they are not at risk from any toxic or harmful chemicals that may be present during an inspection through equipment to aid them in carrying out their inspection. The latter equipment may well include some analytical capabilities, but it should be recognized that confirmatory analysis in an accredited laboratory will be required if there is to be confidence that the CWC is effective and is being firmly enforced.

Thus, with regard to chemical arms control, a significant step forward has been made with the agreement of the CWC, and it is now vital that the PrepCom draw on the experience gained by the UN Special Commission so as to elaborate as effective a regime as possible. There is a real opportunity to ban a further class of weapons and to seek to reverse the trend toward increased proliferation of chemical weapons.

Biological Weapons Convention. The Biological and Toxin Weapons Convention was opened for signature in April 1972 and prohibits the production, stockpiling, acquisition, and retention of microbial or other biological agents or toxins, "whatever their origin or method of production, of types and in quantities that have no justification for prophylactic, protective, or other peaceful purposes." Some 120 states have now signed and ratified the BTWC but there are others that have yet to sign or ratify it and initiatives to increase the numbers of signatories are to be encouraged. The BTWC was the first convention to prohibit an entire class of weapons but at the time that it was agreed it made no provision for monitoring compliance or verification. The past two decades have seen significant advances in the willingness of the international community to accept provisions for such monitoring. Intrusive inspections to confirm compliance and to verify that only permitted activities take place are now allowed by treaties such as the Conventional Forces in Europe (CFE) and Open Skies.

The BTWC has a review conference at five-yearly intervals. In the developing climate of arms control and confidence-building measures (CBMs), it is not surprising that at the Second Review Conference in 1986 four politically binding CBMs were agreed by states parties to improve transparency and confidence in the convention. These four CBMs require:

- declaration of all BL4 (maximum containment) laboratories and of all defense BL3 or BL4 laboratories;
- declaration of unusual outbreaks of disease;
- encouragement of publication of results; and
- encouragement of international contacts and conferences.

The Third Review Conference in 1991 resulted in a robust final declaration reaffirming the importance of the BTWC.[9] The CBM regime was improved and three new CBMs were added that are well focused on activities relevant to the convention. In addition, the conference mandated an Ad Hoc Group of Governmental Experts to examine potential verification measures from a scientific and technical viewpoint. In addition, the declaration encouraged measures to prevent BW technology transfer.

The politically binding CBMs agreed in 1991 require:

- declaration of all BL4 research centers and laboratories;
- declaration of national biological defense programs;
- declaration of unusual outbreaks of disease;
- encouragement of publication of results;
- encouragement of international contacts and conferences;
- declaration of legislation related to the BTWC;
- declaration of past activities in offensive and defensive biological research and development programs; and
- declaration of vaccine production facilities.

313

The responses to the 1986 CBMs were disappointingly slow because the number of states having made a declaration only climbed slowly; 13 at the end of 1987, 24 at the end of 1988, 28 at the end of 1989, 36 at the end of 1990, and 41 at the time of the Third Review Conference in September 1991. In contrast, by the end of September 1992 some 35 states had made responses to the CBMs agreed in September 1991. Although small in comparison to the total number of states parties (about 120), this figure is far more encouraging than that of 1987.

The mandate for the Ad Hoc Group of Governmental Experts to identify and examine potential verification measures from a scientific and technical standpoint requires the identification of measures to determine compliance with Article I, which reads:

Each State Party . . . undertakes never in any circumstances to develop, produce, stockpile or otherwise acquire or retain:

(1) Microbial or other biological agents, or toxins whatever their origin or method of production, of types and in quantities that have no justification for prophylactic, protective or other peaceful purposes.
(2) Weapons, equipment or means of delivery designed to use such agents or toxins for hostile purposes or in armed conflict.

The verification measures are to be considered singly or in combination and need to address the broad range of types and quantities of microbial and other biological agents and toxins, whether naturally occurring or altered, capable of use as means of warfare.
The measures once identified then have to be examined in terms of six criteria:

- strengths and weaknesses based on amount and quality of information provided;
- ability to differentiate between prohibited and permitted activities;
- ability to resolve compliance ambiguities;
- technology, material, manpower, and safety requirements;
- financial, legal, safety, and organizational implications; and
- impact on scientific research, cooperation, industrial development, and other permitted activities, and implications for confidentiality of commercial information.

The first meeting of the Ad Hoc Group of Experts (VEREX I) took place in Geneva on March 30 to April 10, 1992, when 53 states parties participated. Thirty-one working papers and 21 background papers were circulated. Background information was provided on the objectives for BTWC verification, the elements of the biological defense program, the lessons learned from other verification regimes, and information relevant to verification. The conference identified some 21 potential verification measures, which were grouped according to whether these were off-site or on-site measures.[10]

The off-site verification measures fall into four groups:

- information monitoring, including publication surveillance, legislation surveillance, data on transfers, and transfer requests and multilateral information sharing;
- data exchange, including declarations and notifications;
- remote sensing, whether from satellites, aircraft, or ground-based off-site; and

- inspection activities to be carried out off-site including sampling and identification, observation and auditing.

On-site verification measures include:

- exchange visits, which may be made under bilateral or multilateral arrangements;
- inspections, including interviewing, visual inspection, identification of key equipment, auditing, sampling and identification, and medical examination; and
- continuous monitoring on-site by instruments and/or personnel.

The second meeting of the Ad Hoc Group of Governmental Experts (VEREX II) was held in Geneva on November 23 to December 4, 1992, when 46 states parties participated. Over 100 papers were circulated. This meeting concentrated on examining each measure, defining the measure, and setting out its characteristics, capabilities, and limitations.[11] Evaluation of the measures against the criteria in the mandate will be carried out at further VEREX meetings in 1993, with the aim of completing the report of the Ad Hoc Group of Experts by the end of 1993 in accordance with the mandate from the Third Review Conference.

Following the first two meetings of the Ad Hoc Group of Experts, it became clear to many experts that an effective verification regime requires two key elements. The first is declarations of relevant activities within a state to provide a baseline of information. It is clear that any judgments of compliance must be made against an appreciation of what is the norm for the country concerned. That norm will be based on various sources of information but will depend primarily on declarations made by a state party. The second element is on-site inspections of the sites and facilities that present the greatest risk to the BTWC. The on-site inspection regime needs a considerable degree of flexibility so that an appropriate degree of intrusion can be made as necessary to confirm compliance.

Although some consider the BTWC to be unverifiable and that the VEREX process should not lead to a verification regime, such a wholly negative view is no longer tenable. The past decade has seen an increase in the number of states assessed to have or to be seeking to acquire biological weapons. The threat of biological weapons being used by Iraq against the coalition forces was real, and the UN Special Commission through its on-site inspections has revealed at least the existence of a biological weapons research program with offensive applications. It is evident that there are verification measures that have at least a finite possibility of detecting noncompliance, and such measures in combination have a very significant deterrent effect.

A spectrum of potential measures to detect and deter violation of the BTWC has been devised, ranging from political declarations through the CBMs agreed at the review conferences to declarations of patterns of national activity and inspections of high-risk sites to intrusive inspections. As we move across the spectrum we find increased confidence, increased deterrence, and an increased number of compliant countries. It will be necessary to strike the right balance so as to maximize the benefits to global and national security deriving from confidence that would-be possessors are effectively deterred.[12] It is important to recognize that the inspection regime will have a significant deterrent effect, and the chance that a state will be deterred from acquisition of a BW capability will be very much greater than the chance that noncompliance will be detected. Nevertheless, there has to be a finite probability of detection of noncompliance to achieve a deterrent effect. For this reason, there must be planned uncertainty in the precise activities of a verification regime so that a potential proliferator remains uncertain as to whether his activities will be detected. Over a period of time, as more and more declarations are made by states and a better pattern of activity or norm for the state is built up, so the deterrent effect of the regime will increase.

CB Export Monitoring and Controls

With arms control as the anchor of the web of deterrence, other elements can be brought into play. A second essential element is export controls.

A state considering the acquisition of chemical or biological weapons capabilities will consider also whether the agents or the weapon systems are available from within the state using national resources or whether it must seek the agents or weapon systems from abroad. As both chemical and biological materials and related equipment have dual uses—that is, for permitted activities as well as for prohibited ones—the adoption of export monitoring and control measures is far from simple. Nevertheless it is important to ensure that materials and equipment are not freely available in order to prevent CBW capabilities from being easily acquired or rapidly exploited for a quick breakout from treaty commitments.

CB export controls need to be designed to avoid inhibiting permitted peaceful trade, yet they should be targeted so that a state seeking to acquire chemical or biological weapons does not find it easy to acquire the necessary skills, materials, and equipment. It should be appreciated that in the long run export controls will not prevent indigenous capabilities from being developed. Focused CB export controls on both materials and equipment add to the burden on the evader and aid deterrence, although alone they are insufficient.

The Chemical Weapons Convention in Article XI on Economic and Technological Development includes two specific requirements:

- That States Parties shall not maintain among themselves any restrictions, including those in any international agreements, incompatible with the obligations undertaken under this Convention, which would restrict or impede trade and the development and promotion of scientific and technological knowledge in the field of chemistry for industrial, agricultural, research, medical, pharmaceutical or other peaceful purposes;
- That States Parties shall undertake to review their existing national regulations in the field of trade in chemicals in order to render them consistent with the object and purpose of this Convention.

The aim of export controls is to impede the misuse of CB materials and equipment for prohibited purposes and is thus entirely compatible with and complementary to the objectives and aims of CB arms control. The Australia Group of countries has sought since 1985 to harmonize and agree export controls on dual-use equipment and materials and its work has been a useful deterrent to proliferation in the period when a CWC was still under negotiation. With agreement on the convention, it is entirely appropriate that the Australia Group's members should review their controls in the light of its implementation. The Group, however, is still likely to have a significant role in the period while the convention's provisions come into effect and in connection with biological materials and equipment that it does not cover.

CB Protective Measures

The third element of the web of deterrence is CB protective measures. These reduce the range of materials that are effective in use by an aggressor. They also reduce the range of materials that need to be the subject of an arms-control regime. In addition, they weaken the military utility of CBW because effective protective measures limit casualties and ultimately reduce the effectiveness of CBW. Furthermore, the provision of broadband protective measures effective against most of the CBW spectrum may force a user to acquire a larger capability, which is more likely to be detected.

A major concern in Operation Desert Storm was that Iraq might use chemical or biological weapons against the coalition forces. This had the effect of ensuring that the coalition forces improved the effectiveness of their protective measures against the threat of such weapons. Fortunately, neither chemical nor biological weapons were used in the conflict, and a contributing factor to their non-use must have been the perception that their use against well-protected and well-trained forces would not result in a significant military advantage.

Perceptions of the value of possession of chemical and biological weapons before and after Operation Desert Storm vary considerably. A number of important lessons were learned by both coalition forces and by CBW possessors. The coalition forces learned the importance of maintaining effective protective measures against both chemical and biological weapons so that the threat of their use will have only a limited impact on military capability. Future conflicts may well not have the long period of preparation that was possible in the Gulf conflict prior to the ground war.

The reactions to the Gulf conflict of governments in two states parties are instructive. The U.K. Defence White Paper of July 1992 stated that the expertise established at the Chemical and Biological Defence Establishment at Porton Down enabled the United Kingdom to make a timely response to a number of threats that emerged during the Gulf crisis.[13] Work will continue on evaluating the threat and hazard, particularly from biological agents, and on the research and development of detection equipment, physical protection, and medical countermeasures. In the United States, the Department of Defense's report to the Congress, entitled *The Conduct of the Persian Gulf War*, highlighted as a major deficiency the unpreparedness of the United States to face biological warfare.

Prior to the Gulf conflict, it was appreciated that chemical weapons had only been used against unprotected target personnel whether in World War I, Abyssinia, or against Iran and the Kurds. The availability of effective protective measures results in a marked decrease in the utility of chemical or biological weapons. The advantages from use of such weapons is reduced to the increased effectiveness of conventional weapons against an enemy handicapped by wearing full protection comprising masks and suits. Effective protective measures not only reduce the utility of a potential CB warfare attack, they also force the aggressor to acquire a sufficient quantity of agent to achieve benefits from the enhanced impact of conventional weapons and reduces the range of chemical or biological agents that can be used effectively. This reduction in the range of available agents is useful to both arms and export controls, which can consequently be better focused.

It is therefore evident that CB arms control must preserve the rights of states to maintain protective measures and indeed should encourage their maintenance in order to enhance both national and international security.[14] Proposals to prohibit defensive measures are unsound and destabilizing because they would decrease national and international security by allowing a wide range of chemical or biological materials to be used effectively against unprotected personnel. Equally, suggestions for pooled protective measures under international control are ill-founded because a defense that is available for a potential aggressor to examine, evaluate, and circumvent is no defense and would again decrease stability. Effective protective measures need to be maintained as a key element of the web of deterrence. CB defense programs are not a threat to arms-control conventions but complementary to them, provided that there is an adequate degree of openness— as indeed is provided for in both the BTWC's confidence-building measures agreed in 1991 and the provisions of Article X of the CWC.

A state seeking to acquire CB weapons has a wide range of available materials if the target nation has no CB defense. Continued improvements of CB protective measures will further reduce the available materials that an aggressor can use. It is important,

however, to recognize that arms and export controls may lead to the selection by a potential aggressor of novel materials that are not the subject of current control regimes. Such regimes need to have flexible amendment procedures that can add additional materials rapidly without encountering political arguments. Further, CB protective capabilities need to be improved so that the physiological burden is reduced, thereby reducing the force multiplier effect of that burden in respect of conventional weapons.

Determined and Effective Responses

Should a state be shown to have acquired CB weapons or used such weapons, there needs to be a range of determined and effective national and international responses—possibly including an armed response—that will result in clear political penalties. The exact nature of these responses needs to be uncertain so that a state considering acquisition of a CBW capability will find it difficult to judge whether the risks are politically acceptable. The prime requirement is that such a state should be in no doubt that there will be swift, painful, and determined international penalties.

Chemical weapons were used in the mid-1980s during the Iraq–Iran War. At that time, no concerted international penalties were imposed on Iraq. This inactivity sent the wrong signals to CBW proliferators and would-be possessors. The recent international changes and the willingness of the UN to become involved following the Iraqi invasion of Kuwait are much more encouraging signs. The serious view taken by the UN in investigating allegations of chemical weapons use in 1992 has also been a positive development. The CWC has a section on sanctions making it clear that noncompliance will be regarded very seriously and result in punitive sanctions. It should be equally clear that noncompliance with the BTWC will be regarded in the same light.

Key Arms-Control Issues

A new opportunity exists today to improve global security by further narrowing if not eliminating the instabilities, threats, and risks posed by chemical and biological weapons. But this is also a great challenge because it will require a sustained effort by states to integrate various policy approaches with the goal of a strong and seamless web of deterrence against the production, possession, and use of these weapons. To review, this requires the following actions:

- CB arms-control regimes need to be made as effective as possible so that a potential evader is far from certain as to whether his activities will not be detected—the agreement of the CWC and the work being carried out on the verification measures for the BTWC offer the prospect of arriving at a situation in which potential possessors of CB weapons will judge that the effort that would be required to conceal such capabilities and the penalties that result should such capabilities be detected are politically unacceptable;
- export of materials and equipment that may be used to acquire a CBW capability need to be monitored and controlled so that a potential proliferator finds the acquisition of such materials and equipment is hard and difficult to conceal;
- effective CB protective measures need to be acquired and maintained because such measures reduce markedly the range of CB materials

that may be used with effect and also reduce the utility of acquiring a CBW capability; and
- the penalties imposed by the world community should a state party be found to be in breach of its obligations should be such that a potential proliferator will be in no doubt that there will be a response by the international community and will judge that that response will be politically unacceptable.

To maximize the benefits for national and international security of this web, a number of activities must succeed. First, the UN Special Commission must be successful in its mission of overseeing the destruction of Iraq's weapons of mass destruction under Security Council Resolutions 687 and 715. The implications for the future of CB arms control if it is judged that Iraq has retained a capability for weapons of mass destruction will be greatly destabilizing. Second, the effectiveness of the Organization for the Prohibition of Chemical Weapons should be ensured. A considerable amount of work needs to be put into the PrepCom to ensure that the elaboration of the CWC enables the maximum benefits to be gained from the convention. Third, the effectiveness of the BTWC must be improved through the development of a cost-effective verification regime that will deter states parties from acquisition of BW capabilities.

Finally, a common political commitment is required. As we move toward the 21st century with the advances that are available to us from science and technology, we must concentrate on developing a cost-effective web based on experience and avoid the temptation to claim that commercial confidentiality or other sensitivities make elements of the web impracticable. The benefits to national and global security need to be weighed against the possible disadvantages, and in reaching such judgments we owe it to future generations to ensure that we make the best use possible of the scientific and technical means available to us. We have a unique window of opportunity to improve the web of deterrence by minimizing the perceived advantages of chemical and biological weapons and thus improving both national security and that of the world community. We must seize this opportunity.

© *British Crown Copyright 1992/MOD. Published with the permission of the Controller of Her Britannic Majesty's Stationery Office.*

I would particularly like to thank both David O. Arnold-Foster of the Ministry of Defence and Brad Roberts, editor of this journal, for their immensely helpful comments, which have helped to improve this essay greatly.

Notes

1. *Statement on the Defence Estimates 1992*, Cm. 1981 (July 1992), p. 7, para. 104.

2. Brad Roberts, "Arms Control and the End of the Cold War," *The Washington Quarterly* 15 (Autumn 1992), pp. 39–56.

3. United Nations, *Chemical and Bacteriological (Biological) Weapons and the Effects of Their Possible Use*, Report of the Secretary-General, A/7575/Rev.1, S/9292/Rev.1 (1969).

4. Steve Fetter, "Ballistic Missiles and Weapons of Mass Destruction: What Is the Threat? What Should Be Done?" *International Security* 16 (Summer 1991), pp. 5–42.

5. Various publications issued by the Medical Department, U.S. Army Office of the Surgeon General, Falls Church, Va., and the Center for Military History, Washington, D.C.

6. *Statement on the Defence Estimates 1992*, p. 74, para. 3.

7. Conference on Disarmament, *Report of the Ad Hoc Committee on CW to the Conference on Disarmament*, CD/1170, August 26, 1992.

8. United Nations, *Plan for future ongoing monitoring and verification of Iraq's compliance with relevant parts of Section C of Security Council Resolution 687 (1991)*, Report of the Secretary-General, Security Council S/22871/Rev.1, October 20, 1991.

9. The Third Review Conference of the Parties to the Convention on the Prohibition of the Development, Production and Stockpiling of Bacteriological (Biological) and Toxin Weapons and on Their Destruction, Geneva, September 9–27, 1991, *Final Document*, BWC/CONF.III/23, 1992 (Geneva: United Nations, GE.91–62715–Jan 1992–500).

10. *Summary of the Work of the Ad Hoc Group for the Period 30 March to 10 April 1992*, BWC/CONF.III/VEREX/2, April 13, 1992.

11. *Draft Summary of the Work of the Ad Hoc Group for the Period 23 November to 4 December 1992*, BWC/CONF.III/VEREX/CRP.25/Rev.2, December 4, 1992.

12. For a further discussion of the deterrent effect of verification regimes, see Graham S. Pearson, "Biological Weapons: The British View," in Brad Roberts, ed., *Biological Weapons: Weapons of the Future?* CSIS Significant Issues Series, vol. 15, no. 1 (Washington, D.C.: CSIS, 1993).

13. *Statement on the Defence Estimates 1992*, p. 74, para. 3.

14. For a further discussion of the continued need for CB defense even when the Chemical Weapons Convention enters into force, see Graham S. Pearson, "The Continuing Need for Chemical and Biological Defence Following a Chemical Weapons Convention," Proceedings of the 4th International Symposium on Protection against Chemical Warfare Agents, Stockholm, Sweden, June 8–12, 1992, pp. 353–358.

The Arrow and the Shield: U.S. Responses to Ballistic Missile Proliferation

Thomas G. Mahnken

IN RECENT YEARS it has become increasingly apparent that the technology to build long-range missile systems, once confined to a select group of states, is spreading throughout the developing world. The Director of Central Intelligence, William Webster, has testified that by the end of the decade 15 states in the developing world will possess ballistic missiles, and 6 of them will have intermediate-range ballistic missiles (IRBMs).[1] The "War of the Cities" between Iran and Iraq and the tests by India, Israel, South Africa, and Iraq of IRBMs represent some of the more tangible signs of the diffusion of such technology. The former commander in chief of the U.S. Space Command, General John L. Piotrowski, testified that in 1989 there were five times more third world ballistic missile launches than in 1988.[2] The continued spread of ballistic missiles throughout unstable regions in the Third World is becoming more than just a problem that can be addressed by export controls and diplomacy. Although ballistic missiles have been used principally for their tactical military effectiveness in recent conflicts, the acquisition of missile sys-

tems of increasing capability, and their assimilation into regional arsenals, will in the future have a greater impact on conflicts in the developing world, including those in which the United States will be involved. Ballistic missiles already threaten U.S. allies in the Middle East and Asia; they could eventually threaten U.S. bases and power projection forces, and even the continental United States itself. The fact that ever greater numbers of states are acquiring ballistic missile technology, that these states see ballistic missiles as a weapon of choice, and that possession and use of such systems could have potentially serious consequences, suggests the need for a more comprehensive framework for U.S. policies concerning proliferation. Sole reliance on policies to hinder the spread of technology should give way to policies to limit its utility after it has spread.

The diffusion of ballistic missile technology is but one of the more visible and disturbing symptoms of a larger geopolitical phenomenon: the rise of a series of regional powers with growing military capabilities to back up their strategic aspirations. The global strategic landscape, once dominated almost exclusively by the bipolar competition between the United States and the Soviet Union, is wit-

Thomas G. Mahnken is an analyst with SRS Technologies, where he works on national security and long-range planning issues.

nessing the emergence of a series of regional powers, including China, India, Iraq, Israel, and Brazil, that not only possess substantial military and economic resources, but are also involved in regional rivalries largely divorced from, although often fueled by, the superpower competition. In order to support their interests against both rival states and their outside supporters, these states are acquiring increasingly capable and sophisticated weapons, both through transfers of state-of-the-art hardware from the major arms exporters and through the indigenous production of major weapon systems. As a result, these states are acquiring qualitatively new military capabilities, including ballistic missiles and space launch and satellite capabilities. For emerging regional powers, such high-technology weapons are seen as necessary instruments of national policy, as a means to help shape the local environment in ways amenable to their interests. To quote two Indian strategic analysts:

> [T]he motivations for acquisition of high-technology weapons are the same for developing nations and developed nations: making use of high technology to gain a military advantage over an adversary. . . . The developing nations feel the need for high-technology weapons for defense against use of such weapons by developed interventionist nations as well as developing nations who may be armed with such weapons by major industrialized powers.[3]

The rise of regional power centers comes in contrast to growing limitations on U.S. global power projection capabilities. For decades, the Soviet threat has justified an expansive global U.S. presence, including extensive alliances and security guarantees, large numbers of forward-based troops, and high levels of foreign economic and military aid. Now, in the face of warming U.S.–Soviet relations (however tenuous or temporary they may prove to be), an impulse favoring U.S. retrenchment is developing. It is likely that this will lead to substantial cuts in the U.S. force posture that will include those units earmarked for power projection contingencies. It is also likely that in coming years the United States will face a significant loss of overseas bases due to local opposition to a U.S. presence or inability to pay escalating demands for rent. U.S. forces may even be forced to operate from the continental United States. The reduction in the number of bases available to U.S. forces abroad will multiply U.S. reliance upon those that remain and hence also intensify the effect of the loss of bases if they are attacked. If the United States wishes to remain a stabilizing influence worldwide, means must be found to moderate the potential effects of the diffusion of advanced weaponry such as ballistic missiles.

Although proliferation has been viewed primarily as a problem best dealt with by restrictions on technology transfer and by diplomacy, the continued spread of ballistic missile systems could become a military threat as rising regional powers are tempted to use such weapons to back up their political ambitions. The possession of ballistic missiles by regional powers may allow them to challenge U.S. legitimacy in peace, reduce U.S. leverage in time of crisis, and hold at risk U.S. and/or allied forces and bases in war.

Understanding the Impact of Ballistic Missile Proliferation

Emerging regional military capabilities can be viewed on three levels: military, politico-military, and geostrategic. In recent wars, including those between Iran and Iraq and between the Soviet-supported Afghan regime and the mujaheddin, ballistic missiles have been used because of their ability to deliver firepower rapidly over long distances with little or no warning. As states acquire larger numbers of higher-performance systems over coming years, they will develop a capability to integrate their ballistic missile forces better into their conventional military operations. An integrated military force, in turn, would provide rising regional powers with a strategic military capability, whether conventional, chemical, or nuclear, to back up their political ambitions and challenge the legitimacy of U.S. involvement in regional affairs.

Military. On a purely military level, ballistic missiles allow states to strike distant targets quickly and with little or no warning. As such, they have been the weapon of choice of both the United States and the Soviet Union throughout much of the postwar era. Ballistic missiles also provide an assured penetration capability, a factor of increasing importance as a growing number of developing states acquire sophisticated air defenses.[4] Ballistic missiles and aircraft could provide a synergistic capability: missiles can be used to suppress air defenses to allow the subsequent penetration of aircraft.[5] To quote the director of India's Institute for Defence Studies and Analyses, Air Commodore Jasjit Singh,

[Ballistic missiles] become additionally attractive against highly defended targets where manned aircraft may face attrition. However, their greatest utility is likely to be against a vast range of targets beyond the effective range

of combat aircraft. . . . The problems of defense for a target country . . . increase tremendously.[6]

Armed with a unitary conventional warhead, ballistic missiles have limited utility except as terror weapons, but the value of terror weapons should not be discounted. More than 1,000 surface-to-surface missiles of all ranges were fired during the War of the Cities in the Iran–Iraq War with significant (although not decisive) effect. While many of these were short-range systems confined to the battlefield, among those fired by Iraq were some 190 650-km Al-Hussein missiles, 160 of which were aimed at Tehran; the missiles caused approximately 2,000 Iranian casualties, evacuation of half the population of Tehran, and a severe disruption in the Iranian war economy.[7] To many observers in the developing world, the war showed the decisive quality of the modern ballistic missile and so increased its attractiveness as a weapon system of choice. As an Iraqi military analyst put it, "[T]he Iran–Iraq War, for the first time in modern history, has conclusively proved and operationally demonstrated that land-to-land missiles could be effective weapons in armed combat or total war specifically, even if they are armed with conventional warheads."[8] More likely, it was the effect such weapons had on an Iranian population already tired of the war and suffering from waning morale, rather than the limited destructiveness of the missiles themselves, that caused their success in the conflict.

According to Director of Central Intelligence Webster, more than 1,000 Scud-Bs provided by Moscow have also been used by the Afghan government to punish and demoralize the mujaheddin.[9] They were used extensively during the siege of Jalalabad, although their military value here too is suspect. The missiles were both easier for the poorly trained Afghan army to operate than aircraft, and, unlike aircraft, were invulnerable to antiaircraft missiles such as the Stinger, which caused heavy losses among Soviet and Afghan aircraft after their introduction into the war.

In addition to standard high-explosive warheads, missiles can be fitted with advanced conventional warheads containing such payloads as submunitions or fuel-air explosives (FAE) that could significantly enhance their destructive effect, especially against targets such as airfields, supply depots, roads, or railyards. According to Kerry Hines, "if delivered by a highly-accurate SRBM [short-range ballistic missile], a FAE warhead probably would produce sufficient overpressure to damage some above-ground concrete structures, such as aircraft shelters and munitions bunkers, and possibly some underground command-and-control facilities."[10] Highly accurate Soviet theater missiles armed with advanced conventional warheads were seen as a major threat to the North Atlantic Treaty Organization (NATO) and provided an original impetus for the development of theater missile defenses in the mid-1980s.[11] Israel, for its part, has been concerned about Syrian use of highly accurate Soviet-supplied SS–21s against Israeli airfields and mobilization centers. To quote Dore Gold of Tel Aviv University's Jaffee Center for Strategic Studies:

> Capable of striking targets within 100 meters of its aim point, the SS–21 clearly gives the Syrian army a missile system with "counterforce" capabilities. . . . Shutting down Israel's northern airfields even for several hours would considerably aid the Syrian Air Force by temporarily altering

the balance of air power. In this way, even a limited ground-to-ground missile force can become an important strategic factor when used in conjunction with a country's air power.[12]

India is reportedly investigating a range of such warheads, including prefragmented munitions, bomblets, minelets, and incendiary warheads for its Prithvi and Agni missiles, although there are still significant technological hurdles to be overcome.[13] Dr. V. S. Arunachalam, scientific adviser to the Indian minister of defense, has gone so far as to state, "India is convinced that missiles provide an optimum option as weapons and their improved accuracy over long ranges make even nuclear warheads unnecessary."[14]

Chemical warheads may provide another attractive option to nations that develop a ballistic delivery capability. Aimed against soft targets such as cities, airfields, or unprotected troop concentrations, chemical warheads delivered without warning by missile could have a devastating effect, although they are highly sensitive to temperature, humidity, and the speed and direction of the wind. The technology to construct chemical weapons is widespread. Of the states that are developing a ballistic missile capability, Iran, Iraq, China, North Korea, India, Pakistan, Syria, Egypt, Israel, and Libya possess or are developing chemical warfare capabilities.[15] Indeed, Syria and North Korea are believed to possess chemical warheads for their ballistic missiles, and there is evidence that Iran, Iraq, and Libya have programs to develop them.[16]

Nuclear-armed ballistic missiles could devastate both civilian and military targets. High accuracy would not be required to destroy most targets, needless to say. Not surprisingly, those states that are most eagerly attempting to develop a missile capability are also those with the most active nuclear programs. Webster has testified that four of the countries now developing missile capabilities already have nuclear weapons or advanced nuclear weapons programs. By the end of the decade, an additional four could develop similar capabilities.[17]

Ballistic missiles already threaten U.S. allies such as Israel, Egypt, Pakistan, and South Korea. In a future conflict, ballistic missiles could threaten not only U.S. allies, but also U.S. power projection forces or bases abroad. The U.S. Central Command (USCENTCOM), for instance, is highly dependent on a small number of geographically dispersed and vulnerable bases in South and Southwest Asia for the projection of U.S. power in the Middle East and South Asia.[18] Much of the matériel needed for operations in the theater is pre-positioned and could become a lucrative target in a future conflict. The loss of facilities on Diego Garcia, for instance, would deny the United States key facilities (e.g., port, airfield, storage facilities) and could severely hamper subsequent operations.

The United States has already been the target of third world ballistic missiles. In April 1986, following the U.S. strike on Qadhafi's headquarters, Libya launched two Scud-Bs at the U.S. Coast Guard facility on Lampedusa, an island off the coast of Italy. Although the missiles missed the island entirely, such may not be the case should the United States face a more sophisticated enemy armed with more sophisticated weaponry.

The most extreme contingency, of course, would involve the use of nuclear- or chemical-tipped ballistic missiles against the continental United States. Indeed, Qadhafi has stated that if Libya had possessed long-range nu-

clear ballistic missiles at the time of the 1986 U.S. air strike on Tripoli, he would have retaliated by attacking New York City.[19] Although the chances of such an event occurring in the near future are low (as the states that are more radical politically are also fortunately relatively underdeveloped technologically), Iraq's launch of the Al-'Abid space launch vehicle in December 1989 and of the Tammuz-1 IRBM shows that extremist states are gaining long-range strike capabilities. The prospect of retaliation against the continental United States could form a substantial deterrent to U.S. global activism in the future.

The emergence of ballistic missile capabilities in the Third World is in many ways analogous to the experience of the Soviet Union with the nuclear-armed ballistic missile in the mid- to late 1950s—the so-called revolution in military affairs. When the first ballistic missiles were deployed in the late 1940s and early 1950s, they were viewed as essentially long-range artillery support for divisional operations—a new means to deliver firepower. As the quantity and quality of forces increased, however, it became apparent that the technical characteristics of the ballistic missile would permanently alter the way one thought about, and in the event conducted, warfare. In particular, it was realized that the advent of long-range nuclear ballistic missiles gave surprise and preemption a new urgency.[20]

Although the numbers of ballistic missiles in third world countries are limited and the technology of many of their systems primitive by superpower standards, this will change as regional powers acquire more sophisticated industrial infrastructures. Third party ballistic missiles will be produced with longer ranges, more accurate guidance systems, and more destructive warheads.[21] In addition, all the political imperatives that drive arms competition—and could motivate the use of such systems—are present in the Third World: intense religious/ethnic/ideological conflicts with a recent and sustained history of violence; authoritarian regimes that have used force to legitimize their rule; and a lack of an agreed framework for the conduct of relations. With both the technical and political preconditions in place, it is increasingly likely that advanced ballistic missiles will be used in the developing world in coming years, with potentially devastating consequences. Although what we have witnessed so far has been confined to the tactical military level, military analysts in the developing world already have begun to assimilate the impact of the ballistic missile, drawing on both the superpower experience and recent wars in the Third World to formulate its implications for their force postures and national security policies.

Politico-Military. A number of rising regional powers are acquiring an integrated military capability in which ballistic missiles are but one component. On a politico-military level, the possession of ballistic missiles by powers hostile to the United States or its allies, especially if coupled with chemical or nuclear warheads, will threaten to allow them both to constrain U.S. influence within the theater and to jeopardize the ability of the United States to carry out operations in aid of threatened allies.

The establishment of a ballistic missile force involves much more than the development and testing of a prototype missile. An operational capability requires the ability to deploy those missiles in an operational basing mode, whether in silos, bunkers, or mobile transporter-erector-launchers

(TELs). Their military utility, further, requires their integration into a command and control network. In addition, as Jasjit Singh has written, "Effective employment of ballistic missiles can be achieved only with integrated and effective reconnaissance, surveillance, and target acquisition systems. There is, thus, a strong case for not only the development and deployment of . . . missiles, but their integration with strike aircraft and surveillance systems."[22] The establishment of a ballistic missile force by developing states is thus likely to be a rather expensive enterprise. Nevertheless, a growing number of states seem willing to incur such costs. Regional ballistic missile forces need not approximate the sophistication of current superpower arsenals: the first Soviet IRBMs were mobile or pad-launched and maintained in a low state of readiness, and current Chinese ballistic missile forces are likewise spartan by current superpower standards.

A number of states are also beginning to acquire space capabilities for reconnaissance and communications, and could be capable of constructing antisatellite (ASAT) weapons.[23] Regional powers have acquired indigenous space capabilities, and several states have bought satellites manufactured by industrialized states or satellite data from the United States, Europe, and increasingly the Soviet Union and China. One arena in which commercial access to satellite information is manifesting itself is in the sale of data from observation satellites.[24]

In a future conflict, a regional state may be able to counterbalance the military power of the United States within the theater through its large general purpose forces, substantial ballistic missile and space capability, and the inapplicability of nuclear deterrence (it is difficult to imagine a U.S. nuclear response without a direct attack on the United States with nuclear weapons). This is not to say that regional powers will be able to outgun the United States in absolute terms. Rather, they will be able to raise significantly the cost of U.S. involvement in regional conflicts. To quote Mohan and Subrahmanyam, "Sophisticated weapons can come in handy for inflicting punishing damage by a technologically superior nation on a less capable one. They also may be useful for developing nations to raise the cost of intervention and to help in defense."[25]

A ballistic missile force, with or without an explicit deployed nuclear warhead, may be capable of acting as a deterrent to outside (including U.S.) intervention. Indeed, Singh has stated, "Time has come for the Indian Air Force to think of integrating its deep strike aircraft with a possible ballistic missile force to constitute a strategic deterrent capability for national defense."[26] Such weapons need not be used in order to affect perceptions of the regional power balance—the mere possession of such capabilities will influence the calculus of local actors in peace, crisis, and war.

Geostrategic. On a geostrategic level, regional powers that combine the possession of long-range ballistic missiles with their own growing economic, military, and political influence, may provide a source of leadership on regional issues that offers an alternative to the United States. A number of rising regional powers, such as China, Brazil, India, Israel, and Iraq, are busy acquiring capabilities that can only be described as symbols of great power status, including nuclear weapons, ballistic missiles, and space assets. Nuclear power for civilian use, and potentially nuclear weapons for military use, are widely perceived as high-prestige programs, although the former may not be cost effective and the latter bear an international stigma. Nonetheless, they are the object of significant nationalistic and patriotic sentiment in the Third World. Ballistic missiles are symbolic of more than pure military power: technologically, the ability to produce them represents a considerably advanced stage of industrial development; politically, the possession of nuclear-tipped missiles is viewed as the acme of national power. The ability of regional powers to deploy weapons such as ballistic missiles represents both symbolic parity with the industrialized states in one prestigious area of national power and superiority over local rivals.

Space assets such as satellites and launch vehicles are another area of increasing activity in the developing world. Space is seen to possess significant civilian and potential military benefit, even if at high cost. Even such states as Afghanistan and Saudi Arabia, with little indigenous space capability, value the prestige of being allowed to participate in Soviet or U.S. manned space missions. In addition, space programs are the object of significant patriotic and nationalistic sentiment in the Third World. In this respect, space technology, like the technology needed to construct ballistic missiles, represents a physical demonstration of a nation's arrival at a position of global importance, however tenuous.

The United States and the Soviet Union established their credentials through the manipulation of three symbols: Sputnik, the hydrogen bomb, and the missile gap. Now rising regional powers are adopting these symbols to signify their fitness to lead in the regional context. To quote Subrahmanyam, "[Agni's] role as a weapon is the least of its roles. It is a confidence builder and a symbol of India's assertion of self-reliance not merely in defense but in the broader international political arena as well."[27] It is indeed ironic that rising regional powers are seizing upon these very symbols of national power just when the United States and the Soviet Union are reducing their own arsenals of nuclear ballistic missiles.

The ability to field advanced military technologies may be seen as a way to acquire respect and influence within the regional context. It fosters the view among its neighbors that the regional power is able to match the United States (and other advanced industrial powers) in its capacity to lead. Whereas in the past regional powers accepted the involvement of the United States in regional affairs because of its prestige, rising powers may in the future possess sufficient prestige of their own to allow greater distance between themselves and the United States.

In essence, the diffusion of advanced military technology is symbolic of the evolution of the international system away from the bipolarity that has characterized the period since the end of World War II. While the emerging strategic environment is not likely to be "multipolar" in the classic nineteenth-century sense, it is likely to witness the rise of a series of second- and third-tier regional powers with substantial military and economic power to support their increasingly ambitious political agendas.

The ultimate concern for the United States would be that, in such an environment, the country would be less willing to remain active worldwide in support of its interests. New means and methods of warfare in the hands of regional powers, coupled with an absence of a U.S.-provided symmetrical response, may create a vacuum that an ambitious regional power could fill. Unable to support its allies directly, the United States might find its influence eclipsed locally by that of a rising hegemonic power. This could lead to a form of de facto strategic impotence. If the United States wishes to remain a stabilizing influence worldwide, it must find the means to moderate the potential effects of the diffusion of advanced weaponry such as ballistic missiles.

U.S. Policy Options

U.S. antiproliferation policy historically has concentrated upon agreements such as the London Nuclear Suppliers Group and the Missile Technology Control Regime (MTCR) to limit or control the transfer of key technologies as a means of slowing or halting the spread of destabilizing military technologies. The underlying assumption has been that while the denial of all technology that could be used to construct ballistic missiles, for instance, might not be possible, the denial of a handful of key components would be enough to halt a program. Put another way, it has been hoped that export restrictions would raise the cost of acquisition—political and economic—high enough to make it unattractive. Experience, however, shows that supplier cartels suffer from two major flaws. First, the existence of a cartel limiting supply raises the economic incentive for cheating among members. Second, this incentive also fosters the establishment of new sources of supply outside the cartel. In the case of ballistic missiles, this is accentuated by the fact that the MTCR is an informal, voluntary association without an institutionalized arrangement to govern interpretation of restrictions.

U.S. policy on missile proliferation has had a mixed record. On the one hand, there is considerable evidence that the MTCR has slowed a number of ballistic missile programs,[28] and U.S. pressure may have led Egypt to withdraw from the Condor-II missile program, which may itself be in trouble.[29] On the other hand, there is evidence that U.S. allies have been less than scrupulous in enforcing the regime's provisions. France, for example, has negotiated to supply Brazil with liquid-fuel propulsion technology that could be used for ballistic missiles,[30] while a number of European companies have been involved in Iraq's missile programs.[31] In addition, while the Soviet Union has announced its adherence to the MTCR export guidelines, there is little hope that China will follow suit. The prospects for an even broader multinational agreement covering advanced technologies seem remote because of the growing number of states involved in high-technology weapon exports, the value of those exports, and the difficulty in controlling many "dual-use" technologies.

In the end, however, arms control fails as a single solution to missile proliferation because it fails to address the root cause of the acquisition of such capabilities: rising regional powers view the possession of such weapons as advantageous for the advancement of their individual national security interests. A number of developing states have shown considerable determination and tenacity in their quest to acquire ballistic missiles and have devoted a significant proportion of their scarce economic resources to the endeavor. Even if the MTCR were perfectly enforced, the fact that regional powers view ballistic missiles as important, both as symbols of national will and instruments of national policy,

and the fact that they are acquiring increasing capabilities to manufacture advanced technology domestically, indicate that it will be difficult to halt the spread over the long term. Thus U.S. antiproliferation policy should expand to encompass measures to mitigate the effects of proliferation when it does occur.

Options After Proliferation

Measures to limit the spread of advanced military technologies such as the MCTR have received broad-based support. There is less unanimity, however, regarding what is to be done when such technologies have already spread. Such a discussion will become all the more important as regional powers acquire and are tempted to use such weapons. The failure to discuss and formulate U.S. options for what to do after proliferation has occurred could put the United States at a critical disadvantage in a future contingency in which it is called upon to project power. Three broad policy prescriptions exist, which could be implemented singly or in combination: deterrence, preemption, and active defense.

Deterrence. Some analysts have argued that the spread of missile technology should be treated as a fait accompli: instead of concentrating its energy on halting the flow of advanced military technology to the developing world, the United States and its allies should focus more attention on measures to contain the adverse consequences of the spread.[32] Indeed, Janne Nolan has urged the identification of policy instruments "which could be used to manage the transition to a world of genuine military pluralism in which states believe it to be their sovereign right to deploy advanced weapons."[33]

329

Some states that already possess a nuclear capability have taken initiatives to reduce tension with their neighbors. India and Pakistan have negotiated an agreement not to attack one another's nuclear facilities, and Argentina and Brazil have initiated on-site visits to each other's nuclear installations. Further confidence- and security-building measures (CSBMs) could include information and intelligence exchanges, on-site inspection of defense production and space launch facilities, and prior notification of missile tests.[34] Such an approach, however, will be effective only to the extent that the underlying political sources of regional tensions have themselves mellowed. Lacking such developments, CSBMs could themselves become the source of recrimination and conflict.

A policy of deterrence after proliferation also entails a number of other problems. Many regional powers possess value structures radically different from those of the United States, Europe, or for that matter the Soviet Union. Such conflicts as those between the Arab states and Israel, between North and South Korea, and between India and Pakistan are more intense, have a recent history of violence, and in many cases have lacked the comparative restraint and moderation that characterized the U.S.–Soviet competition, even in the early postwar years. It is naive to expect cultures that place supreme value upon martyrdom, or regimes that slaughter their own citizens, to embrace Western precepts of deterrence and stability. In addition, such an approach would legitimize the possession of ballistic missiles, and could lead to the legitimation of the possession of nuclear and/or chemical weapons by these states. Although Westerners have accepted mutual de-

terrence between the superpowers (not without considerable tension, however), it is less likely that the U.S. public would be comfortable under threat from a Qadhafi, a Saddam Hussein, or a Kim Il-Sung. Finally, such an approach would foster the view that the superpowers were unable or unwilling to influence regional events.

Preemption. The use of military force is another possible way of dealing with the emerging third world missile threat. One could argue that the airstrike launched by Israel against Iraq's Osirak nuclear reactor represents the shape of things to come. As a policy, however, preemption has two major flaws. First, it is unlikely to be acceptable politically. During the Cuban missile crisis, for example, President John F. Kennedy's ad hoc executive committee considered but rejected preemptive strikes on the Soviet missiles, even though there was no evidence that nuclear warheads had been delivered.[35] The fear of retaliation with even one or two missiles outweighed the tremendous superiority the United States enjoyed at the global nuclear and local conventional levels. More recently, the United States failed to act militarily against the Libyan chemical weapons plant at Rabta, despite the example of a rather successful strike against Qadhafi three years before.[36]

Second, even if acceptable politically, preemption is likely to be difficult militarily. During the Yom Kippur War, for instance, the Israeli air force attempted to suppress Syrian Frog-7 missiles that were being launched at Israeli settlements but was unable to locate them; retaliation was ordered against Damascus instead. Preemption against mobile missiles is likely to be an exceedingly difficult task. As President Saddam Hussein of Iraq put it:

Our missiles are mobile. Today you see them in Baghdad, tomorrow in Mosul, and the next day you launch them from Basrah. . . . We can launch missiles every hour and from different places. For each base [the Israelis] hit or destroy on the ground, we will . . . build another one.[37]

Even the one supposedly successful use of preemption—the Israeli strike on the Osirak reactor—in retrospect appears qualified. It has been reported that Iraq managed to recover fissionable material from the ruins of the reactor and has constructed a dispersed network of chemical, nuclear, and ballistic missile production facilities.[38] Again, to quote Saddam Hussein:

We have been engaged in a war [with Iran] for eight years, and we know the facts of war. . . . Is it logical to build missiles in obvious places? In every civilian and military factory, a piece of the missile is made. Will [the Israelis] strike at every factory in Iraq, visible and invisible? They should hold their breath and think again.[39]

Defense. The United States must act not only to limit the availability of key technologies, but also to limit the utility of those weapon systems that are produced. Key to this effort is the ability to defend U.S. and allied forces and facilities from third party ballistic missiles.

Defense against third world ballistic missiles has received increasing attention recently. Indeed, the 1990 *National Security Strategy of the United States* notes that, "as ballistic-missile capabilities proliferate, defense against third-country threats also becomes an increasingly important benefit."[40] Deployment of theater defenses would counter the third party

ballistic missile threat on the military, politico-military, and geostrategic levels. On a military level, a theater defense would provide the ability to negate those characteristics of the ballistic missile that make it the ideal weapon of surprise attack (speed, accuracy, power of penetration) and protect U.S. and allied forces and facilities. On a politico-military level, it would allow subsequent U.S. and allied military operations to continue without interference. On a geostrategic level, it would allow the United States to retain its ability to influence regional events.

In many ways defense against short- to intermediate-range ballistic missiles is much easier than against ICBMs. First, target warheads travel at a much slower velocity than do those of long-range missiles. Second, since short-range missiles remain within the atmosphere throughout much of their flight, the opportunity to employ countermeasures and penetration aids to overcome the defense is sharply limited. Each of these factors greatly simplifies the task of the defense. Indeed, a number of high-performance surface-to-air missiles (SAMs), such as the U.S. Patriot and Soviet SA-X-12B, have limited capabilities to act as antitactical ballistic missiles (ATBMs). The fact that the stockpile of missiles available to developing countries, and of mass-destruction warheads for those missiles, is likely to be limited would also enhance the effectiveness of an ATBM system.

The United States has a number of programs for active defense against theater ballistic missiles. The PAC-2 is an upgrade of the Patriot SAM designed to provide the missile with a limited self-defense capability against short-range missiles as well as airbreathing threats such as aircraft. The Arrow program began in July 1988 as a joint U.S.–Israeli program under the Strategic Defense Initiative (SDI) to demonstrate and validate the technology to build a new but relatively simple ATBM with a high-explosive warhead. The program is on or ahead of schedule. Three tests of the interceptor are scheduled in 1990 or 1991, and should a decision be made for early deployment of the system, Arrow could be deployed by 1994.

The U.S. Army's Strategic Defense Command is applying technology developed under the SDI to the defense of U.S. forces worldwide. The Extended-Range Interceptor Technology Program (ERINT) is a program to design and test a prototype interceptor capable of disabling ballistic and maneuvering tactical missiles, aircraft, and cruise missiles. ERINT will destroy a missile by impact rather than by high-explosive warhead. The Theater High-Altitude Area Air Defense (THAAD) system will demonstrate the application of technologies developed in the SDI to theater missile defense. The goal of the program is to build an interceptor system that will be capable both of defending a large area and of high-altitude engagement against nuclear- or chemically armed missiles. The THAAD system would overlay the PAC–2 or future point defense system to provide area coverage of U.S. forces, bases, or allies.

Space-based strategic defenses could also have an important role to play in defending U.S. forces, bases, and allies against third party ballistic missile attacks. The Boost Surveillance and Tracking System (BSTS), deployed as part of a Phase I Strategic Defense System (SDS), would detect ballistic missile launches, identify boosters, and predict the trajectory of ballistic missiles during powered flight. Deployed in high earth orbit for optimal viewing, the BSTS would use advanced sensors and processing techniques to track missiles by observing their hot exhaust plumes. These data would then be transmitted both to space-based weapons and ground-based theater defenses. BSTS would also play a crucial role in providing theater commanders with tactical warning and attack assessment. Alternatively, development has been suggested for an independent theater missile launch detection system that would use relatively small space-based sensors on lightweight satellites. It has been argued that such a scheme would provide a more timely means of transmitting data concerning threats to the theater.[41]

In the future, the transfer of defensive technology could become an important factor in providing both direct defense and political reassurance to allies threatened by neighboring states in possession of ballistic missiles. The United States took a key step in this direction when it announced, in March 1990, its willingness to supply Israel with two batteries of Patriot PAC–2 SAMs with ATBM capability. Of equal, if not greater, significance was the fact that the missiles were able to incorporate data from U.S. early warning satellites. Because the missiles facing Israel need only fly for a short time, early warning provided by space-based platforms could be key to an effective theater missile defense.

ATBMs may in the future have to be deployed as an integral part of U.S. power projection forces. For instance, a mobile version of the Arrow, ERINT, or THAAD ATBM and associated ground-based radar could be developed for U.S. amphibious forces. Alternatively, a sea-based theater missile defense using the AEGIS radar system and interceptors fired from the vertical launch system could be developed. A future theater defense architecture might also benefit from a number of technologies under development for the SDI, such as the airborne optical adjunct and hypervelocity gun.

Conclusion

Despite our best efforts, ballistic missile technology will spread. This suggests that U.S. policy should move beyond measures to limit the flow of ballistic missile technology to formulate policies and acquire capabilities to counter the spread of such systems when and where it does occur. In other words, the United States must act not only to limit the availability of key technologies, but also to limit the utility of those weapon systems that are produced. U.S. antiproliferation policy, based on the Missile Technology Control Regime and bilateral and multilateral diplomacy, should be reinforced by acquiring capabilities that will allow the United States to defend its forces and allies and maintain its flexibility in the face of a new, more complex strategic environment.

This paper is based on a presentation given to the American Association for the Advancement of Science Annual Meeting, February 16–19, 1990, New Orleans, La. The views it contains are those of the author and do not reflect those of SRS Technologies or any of its sponsoring agencies.

Notes

1. Senate Armed Services Committee, *Statement of the Director of Central Intelligence*, 101st Cong., 2nd sess., January 23, 1990, p. 15.

2. Senate Armed Services Committee, *Testimony by General John L. Piotrowski, USAF, Commander in Chief, United States Space Command*, 101st Cong., 2nd sess., March 7, 1990, p. 3.

3. C. Raja Mohan and K. Subrahmanyam, "High-Technology Weapons in the Developing World," in *New Technologies for Se-*

curity and Arms Control: Threats and Promise, Eric H. Arnett, ed. (Washington, D.C.: American Association for the Advancement of Science, 1989), p. 229.

4. Syria acquired advanced air defenses (including the SA–5 surface-to-air missile and advanced air defense radars) from the Soviet Union following the 1982 Israeli invasion of Lebanon and subsequent poor showing of the Syrian air force. Libya is another state with highly sophisticated air defenses, also employing the SA–5 and the Senezh command-and-control system: the defenses around Tripoli and Benghazi are reportedly second only to those around Moscow and other Soviet cities in depth and sophistication. See John F. Lehman, Jr., *Command of the Seas* (New York: Charles Scribner's Sons, 1989), p. 373.

5. This synergy was the basis of the Soviet air offensive operation developed in the late 1970s. See Tommy E. Whitten, "The Changing Role of Air Power in Soviet Combined-Arms Doctrine," *Air University Review* 34 (March–April 1983); and Phillip Petersen and John R. Clark, "Soviet Air and Anti-Air Operations," *Air University Review* 36 (March–April 1985).

6. Jasjit Singh, "The Strategic Deterrent Option," *Strategic Analysis* 12 (September 1989), pp. 599–600.

7. Senate Armed Services Committee, Subcommittee on Defense Industry and Technology, *Hearing on Ballistic and Cruise Missile Proliferation in the Third World*, Testimony of W. Seth Carus, 101st Cong., 2nd sess., May 2, 1989, p. 44.

8. Hazim T. Mushtak, "Arms Control and the Proliferation of High Technology Weapons in the Near East and South Asia: An Iraqi View" (Paper prepared for the Carnegie Conference on Arms Control and the Proliferation of High Technology in the Near East and South Asia, Bellagio, Italy, October 23–27, 1989, p. 5, cited in Janne E. Nolan, *Trappings of Sovereignty: Ballistic Missiles in the Third World* [Washington, D.C.: Brookings Institution, forthcoming]).

9. "Administration Alters Assassination Ban," *Washington Post*, November 4, 1989.

10. Kerry L. Hines, "Soviet Short-Range Ballistic Missiles: Now a Conventional Deep-Strike Role," *International Defense Review* 18 (December 1985), pp. 1911–1912.

11. See, for example, *Soviet Military Power*, 6th ed. (Washington, D.C.: GPO, 1987), pp. 41–43; Dennis M. Gormley, "Emerging Attack Options in Soviet Theater Strategy," in *Swords and Shields: NATO, the USSR, and New Choices for Long-Range Offense and Defense*, Fred S. Hoffman, Albert Wohlstetter, and David S. Yost, eds. (Lexington, Mass.: Lexington Books, 1987); and Keith B. Payne and Marc J. Berkowitz, "Anti-Tactical Missile Defense, Allied Security, and the INF Treaty," *Strategic Review* 12 (Winter 1988).

12. Dore Gold, "Ground-to-Ground Missiles: The Threat Facing Israel," *IDF Journal* (Fall 1987), quoted in Payne and Berkowitz, "Anti-Tactical Missile Defense," p. 26.

13. "India Enters the Missile Age," *Sunday*, March 13–19, 1988, pp. 35–37.

14. V. S. Arunachalam, "Defense, Technology, and Development and Indian Experience" (Paper delivered at a conference on "Implications of New Technology for Australia and Regional Security," Strategic and Defence Studies Centre, Australian National University, Canberra, November 29–30, 1989), p. 15.

15. House Armed Services Committee, Subcommittee on Seapower, Strategic, and Critical Materials, *Statement of Rear Admiral Thomas A. Brooks, USN, Director of Naval Intelligence*, 101st Cong., 1st sess., February 22, 1989, pp. 38–39.

16. "Soviet Chemical War Chief Alerts West with Syria Visit," *Washington Times*, April 8, 1988; *Hearing on Ballistic and Cruise Missile Proliferation in the Third World*, Testimony of W. Seth Carus, p. 51.

17. *Statement of the Director of Central Intelligence*, p. 15.

18. James P. Wootten, "Regional Support Facilities for the Rapid Deployment Force," Report no. 82-53F, Congressional Research Service (Washington, D.C., March 25, 1982); James R. Blaker, S. John Tsagronis, and Katherine T. Walter, "U.S. Global Basing (Task 4 Report): U.S. Basing Options," Report HI-3916-RR (The Hudson Institute, Indianapolis, Ind., October 1987).

19. "Al-Quadhdhafi Wants Long-Range Arab 'Missile'" (in Arabic), Tripoli Television Service, 2106 GMT, April 19, 1990.

20. Marshal V. D. Sokolovskii, *Voennaya Strategiya* (Military strategy) (Moscow: Voenizdat, 1962). See also Mark E. Miller, *Soviet Strategic Power and Doctrine: The Quest for Superiority* (Miami, Fla.: Advanced International Studies Institute, 1982), pp. 33–39.

21. Thomas G. Mahnken and Timothy D. Hoyt, "Missile Proliferation and American Interests," *SAIS Review* 10 (Winter–Spring 1990), pp. 110–112.

22. Singh, "Strategic Deterrent Option," p. 601.

23. Thomas G. Mahnken, *Third-Party Space Capabilities: Programs and Implications*, SRS WO 90-2142/1 (Washington, D.C.: SRS Technologies, 1990).

24. See Hugh De Santis, "Commercial Observation Satellites and Their Military Implications: A Speculative Analysis," *The Washington Quarterly* 12 (Summer 1989); Ann M. Florini, "The Opening Skies: Third-Party Imaging Satellites and U.S. Security," *International Security* 13 (Fall 1988); Michael Krepon, "Spying From Space," *Foreign Policy*, no. 75 (Summer 1989); see also the section devoted to the issue in *Bulletin of the Atomic Scientists* (September 1989).

25. Mohan and Subrahmanyam, "High-Technology Weapons," p. 236.

26. Jasjit Singh, "Let Us Not Be Shy of Agni" (in English), *Hindustan Times* (New Delhi), April 19, 1989.

27. K. Subrahmanyam, "The Meaning of Agni" (in English), *Hindustan Times* (New Delhi), June 2, 1989.

28. For instance, the director of the Brazilian Space Activities Institute (IAE) has complained that U.S. export restrictions to the VLS satellite launch vehicle program increased the system's cost by $8.4 million and delayed the first launch of the rocket by two years. See "U.S. Policy Hinders Satellite Program" (in Portuguese), *Jornal do Brasil* (Rio de Janeiro), November 6, 1988, p. 12.

29. "Egypt Drops Out of Missile Project," *Washington Post*, September 20, 1989; "Is Condor Kaput?" *U.S. News and World Report*, March 5, 1990, p. 20.

30. "Arianespace Assures Liquid Fuel Technology" (in Portuguese), *Gazeta Mercantil*

(São Paulo), September 23–25, 1989, p. 16.

31. "A Civilian Project of Mosul University" (in German), *Stern* (Hamburg), January 16, 1989.

32. Karl Kaiser, "Non-Proliferation and Nuclear Deterrence," *Survival* 31 (March–April 1989).

33. Janne E. Nolan, "Third World Missiles— The Limits of Nonproliferation," *Arms Control Today* 19 (November 1989), p. 13.

34. *Ibid.*

35. Ray S. Cline, "The Cuban Missile Crisis," *Foreign Affairs* 68 (Fall 1989), pp. 191–192.

36. Whether military plans to strike Rabta were drawn up is not publicly known. Nonetheless, the option was widely discussed by Congress and the media. In the end nothing was done, and there is substantial evidence that the plant is operational.

37. "Saddam Comments on Binary Chemicals, Missiles" (in Arabic), Baghdad INA, 0620 GMT, April 19, 1990.

38. "Strike on Iraq No Longer an Easy Option for Israel, Analysts Say," *Washington Post*, March 31, 1989.

39. "Saddam Comments on Binary Chemicals, Missiles."

40. *National Security Strategy of the United States* (Washington, D.C.: GPO, 1990), p. 24. See also Howard Banks, "Missile Rattling," *Forbes*, January 8, 1990, p. 44; "U.S. Allies Concur on 'Southern' Threat," *Military Space* 7 (March 12, 1990), p. 1.

41. "Lightsat Might Cue Theater Defenses," *Military Space* 7 (March 26, 1990), p. 1.

The Global Arms Market After the Gulf War: Prospects for Control

Janne E. Nolan

THE GULF WAR has sparked renewed interest in controls on the international arms trade. Years of unregulated arms sales to Iraq, many argue, contributed to that country's hegemonial ambitions and the inexorability of war. Unless curtailed, arms suppliers will now find new clients who may prove even more dangerous than Saddam Hussein.

Will the current outrage about the West's prewar laissez faire policies toward Iraq lead to a reappraisal of arms export policies to other countries? Are the dangers of arms proliferation now so clear that countries will finally cooperate to establish an international system of restraint?

The only possible answer is: It depends. Just as wars in the Middle East tend to unleash contradictory impulses that maximize the opportunities for both peace and renewed conflict, the policy environment after the Gulf War is rife with peril and promise. Each indication of support for tighter regulations on arms sales is matched by an indication that such an objective will

Janne E. Nolan is a senior fellow at The Brookings Institution. Her most recent publication is *Trappings of Power: Ballistic Missiles in the Third World* (Washington, D.C.: The Brookings Institution, 1991).

prove ever more elusive in coming years.

Current rhetoric notwithstanding, there is little consensus domestically or internationally about the relative desirability of controls on conventional weapons. Restraint on the transfer of conventional arms has never proven a fruitful endeavor for international diplomacy, certainly as compared to the regulation of nuclear or even chemical weapons. The nuclear nonproliferation regime owes its genesis to the monopoly on nuclear capabilities maintained by the superpowers for many years. It is held together by a widespread consensus about the unique dangers of nuclear weapons, and it has operated with the clear objective of retaining a permanent hierarchy between nuclear and non-nuclear states. In the case of chemical (and biological) weapons, eliciting multinational support for a restraint regime is possible in large measure because of the less than compelling military utility of these weapons and the moral opprobrium raised by the grave risks they pose for noncombatants.

The proliferation of conventional technologies shares few of these attributes: the monopoly for all but the most advanced armaments is already shattered, the dangers of proliferation are disputed by many, the possibility of a hierarchy is manifestly rejected, and the perceptions of utility overwhelm any moral opprobrium. The only formal conventional arms restraint regime, the cartel of industrial countries known as the Missile Technology Control Regime (MTCR), restricts the sale of ballistic missiles, and that is largely because of their association with the delivery of nuclear or chemical weapons. Even more problematically, conventional weapons have always been seen as the benign alternative to nuclear proliferation, and they remain the most common instrument of dissuasion in efforts to stop new states from going the nuclear route.

Before the MTCR was initiated in 1987, no formal international apparatus existed to guide transfers of conventional technologies to developing countries. There is still very little interest in a regime that would curtail exports of weapons or dual-use technologies. Governments, including those that adhere to the MTCR and the Nuclear Non-Proliferation Treaty, have vigorously resisted controls on transfers of advanced aircraft and nonballistic missiles, despite their pertinence for the delivery of nuclear weapons and potentially for ballistic missile development.

Will the Gulf War change this calculus and heighten international interest in regional and global arms-control initiatives? As discussed below, a selective system of restraints on the supply of certain key technologies may be feasible, but a more comprehensive arms-control regime is likely to prove far more difficult to achieve. Any new initiative to regulate the international arms trade will, to be realistic, increasingly require the cooperation of both developed and developing states.

This essay first discusses the major supply and demand factors that will have to be considered in such an undertaking, and then assesses the relative feasibility and effectiveness of alternative approaches.

Controls on Suppliers

There are several reasons to be optimistic about the prospects for more ambitious efforts at arms restraint by suppliers in the wake of the Iraqi crisis. Iraq has just provided the world with a forceful demonstration of the potential consequences of the current international system of arms supplies. Largely unregulated by formal agreement, sales of weapons to the Third World amount to an arms bazaar worth $30 billion annually. With over three dozen suppliers vying for sales, almost any country with cash and determination can buy advanced weapons, from tanks to fighter aircraft to cruise missiles. Despite the existence of formal regimes to restrict access to nuclear, chemical, biological, and missile technologies, moreover, even renegade states like Libya and Iraq have been able to get access to these technologies through a growing network of covert suppliers.

The costs of undiscriminating arms sales were demonstrated in the recent conflict with Iraq. Coalition forces faced threats posed by weapons of their own design, from modified Soviet Scud–B missiles to French Mirage jets to the latent but mercifully unrealized threat of chemical weapons made with the connivance of German firms. Western technology also gave Iraq a weapon industry of its own that many believed could have made an international embargo irrelevant.

Most of Iraq's arms purchases were perfectly legal and had the support of the supplying government. Some sales were clearly illegal, such as provision by German companies of materials and technical assistance to build up Iraq's chemical weapons industry, but most governments nevertheless refused to interfere. Some, including France and Germany, secretly sanctioned illegal commerce with Iraq. Whatever its limitations, the Iraqi military was a tribute to the industrial world's technical largess and reluctance to restrict free enterprise.

How and why the industrial world indulged Iraq's military ambitions is now a subject of great controversy and recrimination. Whether this sudden attack of self-examination will be sufficient to prompt durable policy changes toward countries other than Iraq remains to be seen.

One factor that is in favor of new restraint initiatives is the unprecedented level of cooperation forged among the industrial countries since Iraq's invasion of Kuwait. The rapprochement between the superpowers, in particular, is a new element in the geopolitical equation that could go a long way toward restraining the pressures for competitive arms sales. Assuming that the Soviet government does not revert back to old forms of rivalry with the West in the Third World, the United States and the Soviet Union will have a common interest in containing regional instabilities. The joint statement signed in January 1991 by U.S. Secretary of State James A. Baker III and Soviet Foreign Minister Aleksandr Bessmertnykh, for instance, pledged that the two sides would seek a common approach to the quest for peace in the Middle East. The Soviet Union has already indicated it will join the MTCR and is turning to the West for advice about ways to regulate the export activities of its own defense industries.

The industrial nations have increasingly adapted to the need for multinational cooperation to combat transnational problems, such as terrorism, drug-trafficking, and certain categories of illegal arms exports. Within the European Community, the move toward economic integration of the West European nations by 1992 has already led to coordination of various facets of their trade policies, including some in the military sphere, and to commensurate improvements in intelligence-sharing and other mechanisms for collective enforcement of trade restrictions. Similarly, the effort by East European countries to acquire Western economic assistance and technology has created a natural incentive for these nations to support Western policies, including restraining certain types of exports.

The MTCR has already had some success in impeding the proliferation of the technology for missile programs. It is credited with helping stop the Argentinian–Egyptian–Iraqi Condor II program in 1990, discouraging Chinese sales of the M–9 missile, and forcing the West German government to crack down on private firms engaged in missile development in Libya and Iraq. It is probably correct that Iraq's missile capabilities would have been further advanced without the regime. Partly as a result of pressure from the U.S. Congress and the threat of legislated sanctions, moreover, governments are paying more attention to these kinds of export violations. Germany, for instance, has put in place entirely new procedures to ensure closer government scrutiny of missile and chemical technology exports.

Another factor favoring a new climate of restraint is the renewal of interest in and support for multinational institutions. After many years of cynical disregard on the part of most leading nations, the United Nations (UN) is increasingly being seen as a mechanism for international mediation and conflict resolution. If this trend continues, the UN could provide much-needed international leadership for encouraging global arms restraint and regional security initiatives.

Judging from recent administration and congressional rhetoric, interest is growing in the United States in tightening up national export policies. Announced in February 1991, the so-called Enhanced Proliferation Control Initiative (EPCI) crafted by the Bush administration is intended to strengthen existing restraint regimes for chemical, biological, nuclear, and missile technologies. Skeptics see this measure as little more than a cosmetic and belated effort to respond to congressional pressures for sanctions against chemical or missile exporters. But if nothing else, the EPCI is an indicator of the higher profile being given by the executive branch to nonproliferation objectives.

Certain kinds of arms export controls may find a new source of support within the U.S. military, especially if an expanded U.S. military presence is maintained in the Persian Gulf region in the future. Heavily armed countries that are politically unstable could pose a direct risk to the security of U.S. personnel and military technology deployed overseas. The services have never been great fans of advanced technology exports in any case, fearing that weapons they use themselves could be acquired by hostile forces should a well-defended client be transformed into an aggressively armed adversary. This is not an uncommon development in volatile regions of the Third World.

Conventional arms restraint is receiving renewed attention in the Congress and among private commentators, as well. Edward Luttwak, for example, has endorsed a proposal for a wholesale arms embargo, "from Marrakesh to Bangladesh," arguing that only "a total arms ban to all countries in the 'violent zone' can succeed."[1] Congressional supporters of such sweeping initiatives include Lee Hamilton (D–Ind.), chairman of the subcommittee on Europe and the Middle East of the House Committee on Foreign Affairs. In January 1991, Hamilton called for a global moratorium on third world arms sales.[2] The rhetoric is reminiscent of the mood in Congress in the late 1970s, when liberals denounced the U.S. domination of the global arms market as the action of a "merchant of death."

A renewed interest in international arms restraint, however, will have to compete with a number of other factors that will make any initiative difficult to pursue. As has happened repeatedly in the past, political interest in restraint may be outstripped by structural imperatives that favor permissive export policies.

The most critical factor militating against more stringent controls on suppliers is the changing and increasingly diffuse character of the international technology market. Protectionist instruments, like the missile cartel, work only in proportion to the clout of the members and their relative monopoly on the products they are trying to control. But over 30 countries produce weapons, and over a dozen of these can produce missiles. Several, such as China and Brazil, are unapologetic about their permissive missile export policies and have indicated they will not become members of the MTCR or any other restraint regime until they have a more equal share of the arms market. In other areas of weaponry, including fighter aircraft or naval vessels, the number of potential exporters is much larger and the consensus in favor of controls even weaker.

Trends in the technology market presage declining control by governments over the disposition of defense-related innovations. Critical technologies vital to defense, from supercomputers to biotechnologies to fiber optics, are increasingly commercial in origin. As developing countries establish their own weapon industries, they too are increasingly capable of tapping into new sources of commercial and dual-use goods without reference to superpower constraints. In the future, only an ever-shrinking percentage of technology will be subject to direct government controls, testing the viability of cartels for all but a few of the most advanced technologies.

The trends toward multinational defense cooperation and liberalized trade between East and West could also give developing countries greater access to military technology. Most industrial countries are dependent on exports; the easing of trade barriers among them may, therefore, raise the level and volume of defense technology available for purchase globally. Absent disincentives, former Soviet bloc states may try to benefit from both Western technology and loosened Soviet control by seeking military clients of their own. The migration of expertise is also defying national boundaries. Since the beginning of the policy of perestroika, for example, dozens of Soviet nuclear engineers have apparently found their way to India and Pakistan looking for employment.

Tighter constraints on domestic investment in defense and increased foreign penetration of the U.S. market mean that U.S. industry may also seek a larger share of the global arms market. Many in industry believe that marketing weapons more aggressively is the only way expensive national research and development programs for futuristic technologies, such as stealth, can be made affordable.

Without higher export revenues, rising weapon costs could make necessary much higher government subsidies to companies involved in advanced research and development. Finding the money may be increasingly difficult as U.S. government budgets become tighter. How the United States decides to support its own high-technology sector could thus have consequences for technology diffusion. Reduced federal financing for high-definition television, semiconductor manufacturing technologies, and other military research and development programs with commercial applications could force companies with an interest in such ventures to turn to the export market to stay economically viable. Although developing states are still far from gaining access to these technologies, the structural linkage between domestic defense industrial policy and other forms of technology diffusion should not be overlooked.

A deepening dependency on exports of dual-use technologies could thus force the United States to liberalize arms and technology export policies in a manner that might not reflect its long-term foreign policy and military objectives. Controls on exports may seem an expendable luxury in a severely constricted economic environment, particularly if the restrictions seem to be cutting into U.S. military preparedness and economic competitiveness. Indeed, some Bush administration officials have begun informally to promote government incentives to encourage U.S. arms exports.

A policy that sought to subsidize the costs of national security and sustain the nation's economic competitiveness by enhancing the capabilities of smaller states to wage war with advanced weapons would seem a paradox, but it is not out of the question. Even today, standard U.S. weapon systems such as the F–16, an aircraft touted by U.S. industry as a product that should be marketed worldwide, are still very advanced by the standards of most developing countries. Because contracts with many developing countries are increasingly accompanied by a demand for access to manufacturing processes, end-use assurances and other such levers of control may become increasingly difficult for suppliers to enforce, further attenuating their influence over the distribution and use of weapon technology. And third world consumers may augment their access to advanced military technology by using U.S. defense firms and even the U.S. military services to advocate more permissive technology-sharing agreements. This in fact occurred in the recent controversies over aircraft development programs with Japan and South Korea.

Another structural impediment to arms restraint is the central role that arms agreements have come to play in the relations between the developed and developing world. Arms sales are used to herald the opening of new relationships, to indicate friendship or alliances, to encourage positive changes in clients' policies, and to sustain goodwill. They are the leading currency of international diplomacy for many countries, including the United States and the Soviet Union. A refusal to provide armaments, by contrast, imposes high costs. It is taken as a sign of disapproval of a country's government or policies to refuse to sell it conventional weapons to which other countries have access. Except for the most advanced technologies, the United States refuses arms requests only from countries with which it has overtly hostile relations.

Political dependency on arms exports was illustrated by the Bush administration's $18 billion post–Gulf War arms package for Egypt, Saudi Arabia, the United Arab Emirates, Bahrain, and Turkey. The apparent conflict between the quest for an arms-control regime and these proposed weapon transfers, the administration hastened to explain, was not real. The weaknesses in these countries' arsenals had to be redressed before they could be expected to negotiate in earnest. For all of its apparent irony, selling arms to countries in order to encourage their participation in a peace process has been the mainstay of U.S.–Middle East policy for decades.

Finally, there is a basic question whether greater priority will be given to national and international regulatory mechanisms for stemming weapons proliferation or to countermilitary responses, such as promoting antitactical ballistic missile programs for key allies or even deploying strategic defenses in the United States. These instruments are not necessarily mutually exclusive, but they represent wholly different approaches to the problem and may not ultimately be politically or bureaucratically compatible. The transfer of antitactical ballistic missiles to certain third world countries, for instance, could exacerbate proliferation problems either by providing technologies useful for missile design or by spurring regional military adversaries to augment their offensive capabilities to defeat the defenses.

However challenging the picture may seem, it is not yet the case that a free market is the only realistic arbiter of technology transactions. Supplier cartels may seem outmoded and transitory in light of the rapid transformations under way in the international system but, however imperfectly, they still constitute one of the few mechanisms by which advanced countries can influence the pace of international developments.

The Demand Side

Regional powers may have a growing interest in arms restraint for several reasons. First, the demand for armaments will be affected by resource constraints. The economic effects of the war against Iraq are taking their toll not only on the coalition partners but also on states throughout the Third World, which faced higher oil prices for many months. Lower budgets for defense expenditures in these countries will especially affect the demand for the most expensive, high-technology systems recently displayed in the conflict. Now that the Soviet Union is dependent on hard currency for its arms sales, moreover, economics will constrain the Soviet market as well.

Second, countries face obvious military threats from missile and other advanced weapons proliferation in the hands of proximate adversaries, as dramatized by the Gulf War. The war underscored the shared vulnerability of states in conflict-prone regions. Even noncombatants are subject to attack when military adversaries are separated only by a common border and when missiles or nonconventional munitions threaten to move the battlefield to other countries or into population centers. In this case, the consequences of aggression were as grim for the perpetrator as for the victims, but many innocents paid for Saddam's mistakes.

The Arab world, in particular, may be learning important lessons from Iraq that could encourage greater re-

ceptivity to arms restraint initiatives. Most states in the region stood by impassively while Iraq was developing its chemical and missile capabilities, and Egypt actually provided military support to Iraq through the Condor missile program. Iraq enjoyed a certain prestige among its neighbors for having amassed an impressive defense infrastructure. Whatever their views about Iraq's regional ambitions, Iraq's neighbors tended to look at the country with a certain indulgence, such as one would afford an enfant terrible of whom one disapproves but is also secretly proud.

The politics in the Arab world have clearly changed. The heightened sense of vulnerability and common purpose during the war has brought about unprecedented cooperation among Arab countries, including rivals such as Saudi Arabia and Syria, and forged much stronger relations with the West. Moderate Arab countries may not argue as forcefully in the future that Arab countries are entitled to any level and type of arms acquisition as long as Israel has nuclear weapons.

Indeed, one of the more encouraging developments to emerge from the region in recent years is the proposal from Egyptian president Hosni Mubarak to ban "weapons of mass destruction" from the region. The Mubarak plan urges joint negotiations on all nonconventional forces but does not insist that there be a formal linkage between Israeli nuclear arms and other types of weapons. The proposal is rife with political and technical problems, but it has not been dismissed by any state, including Israel.[3] What is most important is that states like Egypt are taking the lead in regional security initiatives.

The feasibility of any arms restraint arrangement is so closely tied to regional politics that this issue cannot be discussed adequately in the abstract. States may abide by an arms restraint plan if it is part of a broader political accommodation and if it originated among the partners. For now, the dialogue among adversaries in the Middle East, the Indian subcontinent, the Koreas and elsewhere is far too embryonic to inspire too much confidence about imminent change in arms acquisition policies.

But there are other reasons to be skeptical about the prospects for regional arms restraint. One is the likely effect of the success of U.S. technology in the war against Iraq on the demand for advanced weapons among third world clients. It is clearly a dilemma for U.S. policymakers simultaneously to praise the triumph of U.S. technology in defeating Saddam and to suggest that certain states be denied access to it. The notion of a permanent international technological hierarchy, with the developed world always staying one or two generations ahead of the developing world in its weaponry, may become increasingly difficult to sustain. Countries may not be able to afford or absorb stealth technology for now, but they can certainly seek advanced cluster munitions, fuel air explosives, and sea-launched cruise missiles. In the future, moreover, the pace of technology diffusion may eventually vitiate or severely challenge the ability of the advanced countries to use technological superiority to influence international events. The rapid transformation of technology from state of the art to obsolescence may make the quest for this advantage ever more elusive, especially if increasingly advanced technologies are made available for export.

Another factor that may weaken a restraint regime is the growing number of competitive arms suppliers. With China, Israel, and even North Korea already serving as fairly significant suppliers of technical assistance to other third world weapon producers, this trend appears to have become a matter of intra–third world diplomacy, potentially circumscribing the ability of the industrial powers to impose meaningful trade controls.

In the end, the viability of any arms restraint regime will depend on whether it elicits political support from third world countries. Perhaps the greatest impediment to new security arrangements is the perception of discrimination that arises when developed countries seek restrictions on developing countries that they do not honor themselves. As an Indian analyst has put it, the industrial world's efforts to discourage other countries' acquisition of high technology is "akin to drug pushers shedding tears about the weaknesses of drug addicts."[4]

Toward a Regime of Managed Military Trade

The MTCR, like other forms of supplier controls, has been plagued by its image as an idealistic arms-control initiative designed to save the Third World from itself, rather than as a prudent gesture to stem the deterioration of military environments in which the West may have to protect its own interests. Although it should be obvious, it perhaps needs to be reiterated that countries have abided by export restraints in the past because of an interest in containing military developments in areas in which their own forces might be placed at risk. This may not be an argument that wins supporters in developing countries, but it does have the virtue of reflecting the pragmatic self-interest for industrial states embodied in the MTCR.

The states that retain some control over sensitive technologies can influence demand by raising the financial and political costs of acquiring them. The technology will, nevertheless, eventually be diffused to countries determined to achieve certain military capabilities. Trade restrictions, however, can buy time to devise ways to contain the instabilities posed by global militarization and to address the causes of international conflicts. The added time could also be used to help states develop force postures and doctrines oriented toward deterrence and stability and to devise international norms for managing the potential risks posed by the diffusion of advanced technologies.

The first priority of a regime to control transfers of sensitive technologies must be to develop simpler guidelines capable of winning wide support. The guidelines would have to shorten the list of targeted technologies and provide more flexible rules to decide what should be included in order to accommodate and stay current with rapid changes in the international technology market. As some describe it, a new regime would need "higher fences around fewer goods."

Many experts have suggested that developed countries could increase their influence by focusing on a few so-called enabling technologies, those that make significant contributions to military capability. These could include guidance technology, certain kinds of computer software, and biotechnologies. The diffusion of these kinds of goods is still sufficiently contained that denial of a sale would have a real impact.[5] An export regime would thus rely less on prohibiting technology exports and more on strict requirements for disclosure about the uses of a given technology.

With the exception of a few categories of items that could be restricted a priori, such as biological and chemical agents, decisions about what constitutes a sensitive technology will increasingly have to take into account the specific conditions in recipient states, including their industrial capabilities, local or regional enmities, the sophistication of their military forces, and the overall foreign policy objectives of suppliers and clients. In turn, to understand these conditions will require more emphasis on shared intelligence, verification, and, ultimately, willingness on the part of the receiving country to abide by end-use restrictions.

To reform the export control system, building on existing institutions established for coordinating exports would probably work better than attempting to establish a wholly new apparatus. For all its imperfections, the coordinating committee on multilateral export controls (CoCom) for East–West trade has experience in identifying and tracking technologies, and, although this is where it has proved weakest, in enforcing restraints. With fewer restricted goods, efforts to monitor technology flows by means of shared intelligence, to impose strict penalties for noncompliance, and to participate in joint efforts to pressure non-CoCom members to abide by the organization's guidelines could become more effective. Although there may never be full agreement about the scope and desirability of some safeguards, even general norms could provide a foundation for adjudicating disagreements.

A revised control apparatus could have several regional subgroupings, reflecting changes in power alignments in the international system. Although the basic structure could remain, with power in the hands of advanced industrial countries, additional consultative mechanisms could be established for areas such as East Asia, South Asia, and the Middle East. These regional groups could deepen international understanding about the emerging technology environment, an understanding that has for too long remained oblivious to developments outside the East–West context.

The growing complexities of reforming guidelines for trade suggest that advanced nations should consider elevating a regime to control military trade to the status of an international agency, even if membership remains strictly consensual. Such an apparatus could provide the expertise to anticipate transfers of precision-strike systems, antisatellite systems, and other futuristic technologies that could threaten global stability, and it could help manage their dissemination in a more structured way.

Of course, no single agency could realistically accommodate the diverse interests of dozens of nations and remain effective. Like the nuclear nonproliferation regime, however, an international regime for controlling dual-use conventional technology could complement national policies and bilateral or regional diplomacy. Such a mechanism will have to be established by an evolutionary process based on the development of flexible institutions that can adapt to rapid changes in the international system.

Additional reforms will be needed for even an informal export regime to be workable. One of the most basic problems is the absence of a comprehensive data base for monitoring dual-use technology that can be embodied in both civilian and military products or for identifying its sources. Devising a U.S. export-control policy has long been hampered by this deficiency. In 1989, for instance, the General Accounting Office charged that there was no coordination among U.S. agencies that were supposed to track dual-use technologies available internationally. Without comprehensive information, national and international agencies cannot adjust controls to the realities of the market and cannot consider the effectiveness of alternative policies.

Far greater cooperation between industry and government may also be necessary to identify, let alone monitor, technologies deemed vital to security. As the European countries move to rationalize their high-technology industries by melding commercial and defense activities, for instance, companies will have to do more to ensure the security of their defense-related innovations. The sheer complexity of the international technology market, with its networks of legal and illegal suppliers, is already overwhelming the modest resources available to governments to track technological developments and create effective policy instruments. This kind of cooperation may be especially important in the case of Japan. As the world's leading source of sophisticated information technology, Japanese industry dominates what has become a crucial component for a wide range of advanced military missions, including command and control, intelligence, targeting, and guidance. Without support from Japanese industry and government, any control regime could be readily subverted by Japanese exploitation of market opportunities undertaken without adequate consideration of the collective security interests of other industrialized states.

A more ambitious international apparatus for industry-government cooperation, one that includes high-level official participation, will have to be established. A practical model for such cooperation might be found in efforts to control the spread of chemical weapons. The Chemical Manufacturers Association, whose members account for almost 90 percent of all chemical production in the United States, has actively helped devise the terms and mechanisms of a treaty to ban chemical weapons. According to one analyst, this "unprecedented industry-government relationship has given the diplomatic community access to technical expertise critical to understanding and resolving key outstanding treaty issues."[6] Without industry's assistance, the government could not have identified the thousands of items relevant to making chemical weapons or where they are produced, nor could it have evaluated the risks and benefits of alternative treaty limitations and their verification. And the chemical industry also benefited. The loss of sales that a treaty prohibiting military production imposes is vastly overshadowed by the industry's ability to make sure that any agreement does not impinge on its legitimate commercial activities.

As the developed countries move toward greater integration of their defense industries, they will have to agree about the disposition and security of their shared technologies. Defense companies will have a direct interest in these agreements. As is true of the chemical industry, participation and support for such arrangements may be necessary both to help compile information about sources of technology and to help design and implement workable safeguards that do not interfere unduly with legitimate activities of private enterprise.

The model of the chemical manufacturers may be particularly apt for the space industry. Commercial interests involved in promoting peaceful space cooperation have the most to lose from international opprobrium for the diversion of space technology for ballistic missiles or other offensive military uses. The immediate self-interest of such companies suggests that they help governments restrain missile programs in unstable countries by identifying technologies needed for missile development and devising safeguards that will discourage the adaptation of civilian equipment for military programs. Although some might consider this undue encroachment on national sovereignty, this is one technology for which a few suppliers still have the leverage to influence the pace and content of production programs.

As long as the United States believes it must retain technological superiority to ensure its security, it will try to protect its most advanced military technologies against unplanned dissemination. Export controls may have outlived their usefulness for those technologies that are already widely diffused, but some market restrictions are needed for innovations critical to national defense as well as for less advanced technologies such as nuclear weapons that are believed to be inherently destabilizing.

The problem will always be how to select the technologies that warrant attention, especially as defense innovation becomes increasingly dependent on foreign components and U.S. commercial products and the pace of dissemination and obsolescence accelerates. The MTCR has managed to come to grips with the synergism among particular dual-use technologies that, added together, could augment missile production capabilities. In principle, the lists of controlled items compiled for the MTCR could be the basis for a more comprehensive approach to North–South technology diffusion, were there political support for such an objective. The existing guidelines are sufficiently flexible to accommodate new kinds of high-risk technologies that may become more widely available in coming years, including equipment pertinent to warhead design, improvements in missile accuracy, and range and targeting capabilities.

Assessing the scope and potential effectiveness of export controls, however, requires a better understanding of how the United States and other industrial states will restructure their overall trade and industrial policies. If industrial countries' efforts to foster their competitiveness depend on increased arms and technology exports, even modest controls may be difficult to sustain domestically let alone internationally.

Whether the United States and other industrial countries are prepared to offer client states incentives to limit their weapon acquisition programs, and if so, what kind of incentives, is another unresolved question. The absence of effective coordination among agencies with jurisdiction over trade policy, security assistance, economic assistance, sensitive technology transfers, space policy, and arms control makes it difficult to consider mechanisms from which Washington could gain leverage.

Agencies with responsibilities for international debt management and other concessionary transactions need to be brought into the policy process to see if there may be ways to link financial incentives and military restraints. At a minimum, the policies of the World Bank, the International Development Agency, and other international lending agencies should be reviewed to ensure that assessments of a country's eligibility for credits and loans take into account the influence of its military, including the nature

and relative burden of weapon development and production programs. Consideration should be given to a proposal put forward in 1989 by a task force of the House Committee on Foreign Affairs to establish an International Development Cooperation Council in the White House, with jurisdiction over all international assistance mechanisms.[7] This is one way to encourage coordinated attention by senior officials and to connect development assistance activities with other foreign policy objectives.

The international effort since August 1990 to isolate Iraq, as well as growing international concerns that have been raised about destabilizing developments in countries such as Libya, Iran, and North Korea, could be the basis for a selective multinational arms restraint regime in the near term. These countries could be subject to very stringent trade controls and accompanying sanctions, to be observed by all the industrial countries and their major clients. Such an arrangement might appear to exist largely to penalize states with whom adherents have minimal relations in any case, but perhaps this is not so unreasonable. It emphasizes the need to build on existing consensus. And it affirms the essentially political character of diplomatic instruments: formal, technical controls have to be calibrated against the realities of international politics.

In the longer term, however, export cartels are not a solution for removing the forces that impel countries to acquire advanced weapons. Efforts to restrain weapon acquisitions are more likely to be effective if they are part of broader initiatives to build a genuinely interdependent international system with codified and reliable means of resolving regional disputes peacefully.

In support of such efforts, nations might wish to explore confidence- and security-building measures (CSBMs), including information and intelligence exchanges, on-site inspections of defense production and space launch facilities, and prior notification of missile tests. These and other mechanisms that promote consultation among regional rivals could help to ease unwarranted suspicions about missile production efforts, limit their political and military consequences, and, possibly, reduce some of the incentives now propelling the expansion of these programs.

CSBMs can reduce tensions by mitigating the mystery about rivals' military activities, providing channels for routine interaction, and demonstrating adversaries' interests in reassuring other states about their military goals. Although such instruments are only valuable as indicators of political will and can be violated at any time, they can serve as the beginnings of the diplomatic infrastructure that will be needed for broader accommodation. Examples of existing regional CSBMs include the recent agreement between India and Pakistan not to attack one another's nuclear facilities and to begin negotiations of a nuclear test ban; the process of mutual reassurance taking place between Argentina and Brazil that includes on-site visits to their respective nuclear facilities and declarations of nonhostile intent; and informal U.S. proposals to encourage Middle Eastern countries to abjure the first use of ballistic missiles and to give prior notification of missile launches.

Declarations of intent, like a pledge not to use ballistic missiles preemptively, would obviously not endure in a crisis, but they can be important signs of political conciliation among countries that might not otherwise be speaking to one another. Similarly, on-site visits and prior notification of test launches do nothing to stop entrenched missile programs, but they can help to reduce the climate of suspicion among adversaries.

Other CSBMs that could be considered for a restraint regime include the application of international safeguards and on-site verification at space launch facilities to ensure they are not being used to develop missiles; maintaining missile forces unarmed and unfueled during peacetime, subject to monitoring; prior notification of test launches, as well as agreements to orient systems being tested away from adversaries' territory; regional export controls, such as agreements not to sell missiles or other weapons to terrorist states; and routine bilateral military exchanges between rival states to document the extent and pace of weapon development and acquisition plans and to discuss common security concerns.

Another area of potential U.S. assistance is to provide states with technologies for more effective command and control, survivable basing modes, permissive action links, and other such systems that have long been deemed vital to superpower military stability. This proposal is controversial, however. Some argue that emerging missile (and nuclear) powers should be discouraged from gaining confidence in their forces in order to make it less likely that they would contemplate their use. Others argue that unreliable command and control procedures or unsafe weapons help no one, and that the likelihood of use of new missiles would be reduced if these nations had greater confidence in their ability to use them when they were actually needed.

The decades of effort by the superpowers to manage their nuclear rivalry could provide lessons to new states and help foreshorten the difficult transition from provocative to deterrent postures. Although judgments about the desirability of technological assistance in this area would have to be made on a case-by-case basis, to assume that countries should be discouraged from developing modern force structures may not only be unrealistic but could also unduly prolong the risks posed by force vulnerabilities and unconventional doctrines.

Although achieving more significant curbs on the demand for advanced weapons will depend on progress in the reduction of overall regional tensions, this broader objective can be helped by encouraging states to pursue incremental measures aimed at enhancing confidence. The United States can play an important role in encouraging regional powers to pursue CSBMs, although the choice of initiatives must ultimately come from the states themselves and reflect local realities.

Most proposals for international arms restraint agreements tend to reflect a bias in favor of the great powers, often with little sensitivity to the ambitions of developing states to become more equal partners in the international system. More far-reaching cooperation may be impeded by the smaller states' perception that the great powers are discriminating against them. Defining common norms that can elicit genuine international support will require taking the objectives of developing countries seriously and recognizing that those interests are as enduring as they are diverse.

The views expressed in this article are those of the author and should not be ascribed to The Brookings Institution.

Notes

1. See Edward Luttwak, "Stop Arming the Third World," *New York Times*, November 4, 1990, p. A–29.

2. See "Washington Roundup," *Aviation Week and Space Technology*, January 28, 1991, p. 19.

3. The proposal calls for all states to sign the Non-Proliferation Treaty, for instance, which Israel refuses to do. For further discussion, see United Nations General Assembly, "Establishment of a Nuclear-Weapon-Free Zone in the Region of the Middle East," Report of the Secretary-General, October 10, 1990.

4. C. Raja Mohan and K. Subrahmanyam, "High-Technology Weapons in the Developing World," in *New Technologies for Security and Arms Control: Threats and Promises*, Eric H. Arnett, ed. (Washington, D.C.: American Association for the Advancement of Science, 1989), p. 230.

5. As John D. Steinbruner has argued, "The prohibition of exports should be directed only to direct weapon products and to items so closely related to weapons applications that such an application predominates over all other applications. For militarily sensitive technologies that cannot meet this criterion strictly applied, export licensing should require explicit, accurate, and complete end-use disclosure. For especially sensitive technologies, cooperative verification agreements should be made a condition of export." For further discussion, see Steinbruner, "Forging the New World Order," *Brookings Review* 9 (April 1991).

6. Kyle B. Olson, "The U.S. Chemical Industry Can Live With a Chemical Weapons Convention," *Arms Control Today* 19 (November 1989), p. 21.

7. House Committee on Foreign Affairs, *Report of the Task Force on Foreign Assistance*, 101st Cong., 1st sess., 1989, H. Doc. 101–32.

Transparency in Armaments: A New Item for the New Security Agenda

Michael Moodie

THE UNITED NATIONS General Assembly passed, on December 9, 1991, a resolution on "Transparency in Armaments" (TIA) by a vote of 150 to 0 with Iraq and Cuba abstaining. The People's Republic of China (PRC) and Syria did not participate in the vote (although the former abstained and the latter voted yes in the United Nations [UN] First Committee's adoption of the resolution). Although this resolution was only one of many passed by the General Assembly and received little attention in the media, it nevertheless has potentially important implications for how the global community addresses security issues in the rapidly evolving international environment. It could reflect a willingness to put aside traditional shopworn rhetoric and old security shibboleths in an attempt to come to grips with the security problems of the post–cold war era. Alternatively, it might represent a harbinger of a global security agenda that defines sharp North–South cleavages. Or it could become a sterile exercise, as only too often in the past when rhetoric and posturing by the international community have replaced action and accomplishment

Michael Moodie is assistant director for multilateral affairs in the U.S. Arms Control and Disarmament Agency.

in confronting fundamental security challenges. The purpose of this article is to provide background on this "transparency in armaments" issue and to examine some of those implications.

The UN's transparency in armaments resolution calls upon the UN secretary general to establish a register of conventional arms, including transfers, for which member states are requested to provide data according to categories established in an annex to the resolution. These categories include tanks, armored combat vehicles, large caliber artillery systems, combat aircraft, and attack helicopters—not coincidentally the five categories of equipment limited by the Treaty on Conventional Armed Forces in Europe (CFE). Additional categories include warships and missiles or missile systems, with each of these categories broadly defined in the annex. Each member state is requested to provide data annually by April 30 regarding imports into and exports from their territory in these weapons categories during the previous calendar year. The data are to include specification of the supplying state of any imports and recipients of any exports.

The resolution also requests the secretary general to create a panel of experts to elaborate the technical procedures needed to implement the register and to make any adjustments to the annex necessary for its effective operation. The experts are also to address modalities for possible expansion of the register in such areas as military holdings and national production. A report to the General Assembly on these issues is to be submitted to its next session, which begins in September 1992. This report will be the basis for establishing the standard format or matrix that will be used to report the information, starting in 1993.

Early expansion of the scope of the register is also a possibility. UN member states, therefore, are also invited to send the secretary general, by April 30, 1994, their views on the possible addition of further categories of equipment that the register might include.

The resolution, however, does not limit itself to arms transfers. Member states are also invited to provide the UN with any available background information regarding their military holdings, procurement through national production, and relevant policies. They are also asked to inform the UN of their national arms import and export policies, as well as their legislation and administrative procedures both as regards authorization of arms transfers and prevention of illicit transfers.

Finally, the resolution invites the Geneva-based Conference on Disarmament (CD) to undertake certain activities as soon as possible and report on them to the United Nations in the annual report the CD presents to the UN First Committee. These activities include

- addressing the question of "the interrelated aspects of the excessive and destabilizing accumulation of arms, including military holdings and procurement through national production";
- elaborating universal and nondiscriminatory practical means to increase openness and transparency in this field;
- considering the problems of openness and transparency related to the transfer of high technology with military applications; and
- addressing similar questions related to weapons of mass destruction.

Obviously, the resolution establishes an enormous agenda for both New York and Geneva. Not surprisingly, different UN members attach different priorities to the tasks identified. These differences reflect not only individual national security interests but also a variety of perspectives on the broader questions of the appropriate relationship between industrialized and industrializing countries and the rights and obligations of members of the international community. Given these diverse interests, a major challenge lies ahead in using the register and the other aspects of the resolution to meet the important goal of diminishing excessive and destabilizing arms buildups through greater openness and transparency.

Why This Particular Resolution?

A quick examination of how the resolution evolved and assumed the form approved by the General Assembly highlights some of the issues of greatest concern to the key participants and the questions and implications that must still be addressed.

On March 20, 1991, the Japanese government proposed measures on arms issues related to the Middle East in an effort to increase transparency in international conventional arms transfers. Among those measures was the notion of an international register. In early April, Prime Minister John Major of Great Britain made a similar suggestion to his colleagues in the European Community (EC). In late May, Prime Minister Toshiki Kaifu of Japan proposed to a UN Disarmament Conference in Kyoto the creation of a universal arms transfer register under UN auspices. He also announced his government's intention to submit a draft resolution to this effect to the next plenary of the UN General Assembly. Then Foreign Minister Taro Nakayama repeated this undertaking to the Conference on Disarmament in early June.

Although the idea of a register had had a long history, the proposals offered by the two leaders evoked a strong resonance within the international community in the aftermath of the war with Iraq and the heightened attention of the international community to the problem of destabilizing weapons buildups. The Japanese and British proposals were reinforced by the conclusions of a study by a group of UN governmental experts on the question of transparency in arms transfers that recommended, among other steps, the creation of a universal and nondiscriminatory arms transfers register. The concept of a UN arms transfers register was endorsed by the EC and the Group of Seven (G–7) at meetings later that summer.

To translate their concepts into reality, the British, Japanese, and Dutch (the last acting in their capacity as EC president during the second half of 1991), strongly supported by France and Germany, offered a resolution in the UN First Committee calling for the creation of an arms transfers register. The concept of the register as proposed by the Europeans and Japa-

nese, however, encountered serious criticism from several third world delegations. Pakistan and Egypt, in particular, argued that the EC–Japanese concept was too narrow and would ultimately prove ineffective. If UN member states were genuinely concerned about destabilizing military capabilities, they contended, providing information only on arms imports and exports would do little to build confidence because other aspects of that capability were left unaddressed.

Pakistani delegates, for example, focused on the problem of indigenous defense production and stockpiles as means of securing military capabilities other than through arms transfers. Failure to include information on what weaponry a state could produce domestically would provide a very incomplete picture to other states worried about its capabilities. Confidence would be undermined, not enhanced. Similarly, without a good sense of what weapons and military stores a state had stockpiled, there would be an insufficient basis for making confident military assessments.

Egyptian delegates raised in particular the issue of the relationship between conventional weapons and weapons of mass destruction. That such a relationship existed in the perceptions of many states could not be ignored, and information on only one dimension of conventional capabilities with no data available on weapons of mass destruction would provide an inadequate basis for reasonable national security calculations. For the Egyptians, too, the European–Japanese approach constituted an inadequate foundation on which to build lasting confidence.

Other third world delegations, Brazil and Argentina among them, pointed out that a register limited to arms transfers addressed only finished weapon systems. It was silent on the transfer of technology with military applications either explicitly or in terms of dual use. An increasing number of states, however, were more interested in acquiring the necessary advanced technology and producing the finished systems themselves than in importing complete systems. Was this not part of a state's military capability, too, they asked, and should information not also be provided on technology transfers?

In response to these and other criticisms, supporters of the European–Japanese concept argued that the register should be seen only as a limited step to which states could immediately commit themselves. It would be a political sign of their intention to come to grips with the problem of destabilizing military buildups. As a political action, the register could not become an instrument for analysis of military capability. It represented a limited exchange of information designed to serve political, not military, or even analytical purposes. From the supporters' perspective it was better to do something immediately, even if the shortcomings of the effort were clearly recognized, than to do nothing in the vain hope that an approach addressing all aspects of the problem could be developed.

Weeks of negotiation ensued in the First Committee. Not only was there the tension between those who wanted to take action and those who had serious reservations, but there were also two other problems. One was a difference over whether the resolution should spell out explicitly what data the register would provide or whether that definition should be left to experts once the general approach was approved. The other was the distinction between issues suitably addressed in an information exchange of the kind represented by the register and administered by the UN relatively easily, and the more complicated, multifaceted problems that required additional give and take.

The resolution of these contending pressures produced the document approved by the General Assembly. Creation of the arms transfers register would proceed immediately, but opportunities to pursue the issues raised by some of the third world delegations were also provided both at the UN and the CD. The possibility of expanding the register to deal not just with additional categories of weapons but with other aspects of military capability such as production was also included. The resolution reflected the kinds of compromises often struck at the UN. The question now is how the implementation of the resolution will proceed in light of the differing priorities that shaped it.

Questions and Implications

The evolution of the resolution on transparency in armaments highlights some questions of a longer-term nature that will continue to confront the international community as it deals with this important issue. Those questions relate to the proper perspective on the role and impact of arms transfers, the value of transparency in military matters and the locus of responsibility for effective transparency, North–South differences on this aspect of the arms-control agenda, and the future of international institutions that address security questions such as the Conference on Disarmament.

Are Arms Transfers Good or Bad? Much of the international support for the creation of an arms transfers register was generated by the concern over destabilizing military buildups of the kind the world witnessed in Iraq. Speaking at a press conference in Luxembourg on April 8, 1991, Prime Minister Major, for example, explained his interest in such a register as a result of "one of the most frightening things about Iraq [which] has been the ability of a tin pot dictator to acquire high technology as well as conventional weapons on a truly massive scale." One of the dangers in so strongly supporting the register as a result of the Iraqi experience, however, is that it could lead to skewed perspectives regarding arms transfers. In particular, the fact that there is a link between what happened in Iraq and the register as a response to those developments runs the risk of reinforcing the inaccurate perception that all arms transfers are bad and that the register can solve the problem.

To be sure, the acquisition of enormous amounts of conventional weaponry or the procurement of some kinds of conventional military technology could have a destabilizing impact on a regional military balance. An emphasis on power projection capabilities for most states, for example, would spark serious concerns among their neighbors. The acquisition of enhanced lethality munitions such as fuel air explosives would probably prompt the same reaction. At the same time, not all transfers are destabilizing or illegitimate. Arms transfers to meet defense needs are both consistent with article 51 of the UN Charter acknowledging the rights of states to self-defense and capable of enhancing stability. In that regard they are no less legitimate than domestic defense industrial production.

The problem is that there are no criteria and no easy analytical methods by which to assess the impact of a given transfer, or even a pattern of transfers to a state, on the military balance in its region. The information provided in the register will not provide the answer but only some of the data on which such an analysis would be based.

The value of the register rests in its use as a political measure to build confidence. If a state, exploiting the transparency inherent in the register's information exchange, can demonstrate that it is committed to restraint in its military acquisitions, its neighbors and potential adversaries should feel some modicum of reassurance. It would constitute one step, however small, in breaking down the mutual suspicion that is often the wellspring of competitive arms buildups.

Who Is Responsible? The utility of the UN arms transfers register will depend on the number of states who actually contribute to it. Because participation is voluntary, there is the possibility that only a limited number of UN members will submit the requested data. If that is the case, then the register's value will fall far short of expectations. It would promote the kind of disappointment felt at the fact that of the more than 100 parties to the Biological Weapons Convention (BWC), less than three dozen participated in the information exchange and other confidence-building measures agreed by states parties at their Review Conference in 1986. Just as states parties made a strong effort at the 1991 BWC Review Conference to reverse that poor performance, a strong push will have to be made to garner as much participation in the register as possible.

To a certain extent, past UN consideration of security issues has tended to define arms control as controlling someone else's arms—preferably those of the superpowers and nuclear weapons in particular. As Ronald Lehman, director of the U.S. Arms Control and Disarmament Agency, argued in his speech to the UN First Committee on October 15, 1991,

What is disquieting . . . is the fact that some of the strongest proponents of arms control—so long as it is restricted to the major powers—are often the most reluctant to engage in meaningful arms control in their own regions. These champions of the reduction of others practice a double standard; they consistently fail to see any value in reducing their own.

With the end of the Cold War and the efforts of the United States and the republics of the former Soviet Union to continue the process of significant nuclear arms reductions entailed in the Strategic Arms Reduction Treaty (START), this attitude is increasingly difficult to sustain. As regional conflict and nonproliferation move to the top of the international security agenda, many UN states are uncomfortable that the spotlight has been turned on their security policies and that the pressure is mounting to demonstrate their commitment to dealing effectively with this new agenda.

The transparency in armaments resolution may represent a step away from the old thinking of many UN members. It certainly reflects their recognition of a new set of problems that must be addressed. This is not to argue that old arguments will not resurface. Many states will contend, for example, that the discussion of excessive and destabilizing accumulations of arms cannot be limited only to conventional forces because nuclear arms represent the most excessive and destabilizing military capabilities.

In the final analysis, the performance of UN members in providing

the requested information to the register will provide the genuine benchmark for determining how much attitudes have changed and whether all states will accept some responsibility for encouraging restraint in both supplies and sales of military equipment. In and of itself, such restraint would be valuable. But it could also reflect the broader sense that solving the security problems plaguing the international community is not only someone else's job.

Will East–West Problems Become North–South Problems? One potentially worrisome aspect of the new international security environment highlighted by the UN First Committee's negotiations over the TIA resolution was the fact that many of the strongest supporters of the initial draft were industrialized nations while many of that draft's most severe critics were members of the nonaligned group. Although it is a patent oversimplification to talk about a North–South split over the new global security agenda, it is the case that there are differences in interests and approaches to that agenda between the industrialized and the industrializing worlds. Some of the issues raised by the South during the discussion of the resolution reflected long-standing concerns of the nonaligned group, such as an overriding emphasis on nuclear issues, but new emphases also emerged that suggested that an element of tension between North and South may continue as the new security agenda is addressed.

One example of this potential tension is reflected in the resolution's request to the Conference on Disarmament for discussion of problems associated with the transfer of high technology with military applications. This request will involve the CD in complex and sensitive areas that have both strong nonproliferation implications and serious consequences for the ability of industrializing nations to secure access to technology they consider vital for their further development. Some industrializing nations, for example, chafe badly at the notion that those countries that can develop advanced military technology or sophisticated dual-use technology have organized themselves to coordinate controls on the export of that technology in order to combat proliferation. They see such efforts as the 18-member Missile Technology Control Regime (MTCR) or the Australia Group (which focuses its 22 members on coordinating export controls on potential chemical and biological weapons technology) as supplier cartels that either by design or inadvertently restrict their access to important advanced technology that should be freely available to them.

The continued emphasis on nuclear issues also reflects something of a have versus have-not tension. Some nonaligned states resent strongly, for example, the distinction in the Nuclear Non-Proliferation Treaty (NPT) between the rights and privileges of those nations that could sign as nuclear weapons states (i.e., the United States, the Soviet Union—now the Russian Federation—Britain, France, and the PRC, which had manufactured and exploded a nuclear weapon or nuclear explosive device by January 1, 1967) and the rest of the nations of the world that could only join as nonnuclear weapons states.

This is not to belittle the extreme importance of many of the questions raised by nonaligned states about the future of the world's nuclear arsenals. The collapse of the Soviet Union, for example, has prompted a number of concerns about the status of nuclear weapons in the new republics where tactical and strategic nuclear weapons have been stationed. It has also raised the question of the future of START and the prospect for follow-on agreements. Nor is it meant to underestimate the legitimate concerns of some nonaligned states about the prospect of nuclear proliferation in their regions of the world. In areas such as the Middle East, South Asia, and the Korean peninsula, for example, a number of states are actively pursuing a nuclear weapons capability, some in contravention of their obligations under the NPT. These are not North–South issues; they must be addressed by the entire international community. But they must be considered in a balanced way with other security problems, most of which have important aspects relating to conventional weapons and in the resolution of which the nonaligned nations can play an extremely important role.

The successful conclusion of the TIA resolution negotiations demonstrates that a balance among the security concerns of key states in the industrialized and industrializing worlds can be achieved. It would be unfortunate, however, if that balance were to be so precarious and fragile that it prevented progress being made in any single area because that would be to "get out in front" of some parties' priority concerns. Establishing linkage between progress on one issue to progress in other areas will inhibit the taking of any successful steps. Linking restraint on conventional weapons acquisitions, for example, to progress in dealing with weapons of mass destruction is likely to ensure that progress in neither area is achieved.

All participants in discussions of these issues at the UN and CD and in other bilateral and multilateral exchanges tenaciously defend their na-

357

tional interests. At the same time, none of them has a desire to transform the global arms-control agenda into a North–South confrontation. There is no reason why it should necessarily become one. The arms-control process has historically entailed the reconciliation of contending interests and the relaxation of tensions that may result from divergent security concerns. As long as the commitment to the common objective of finding solutions to global security problems remains paramount, it will continue to do so.

Whither the Conference on Disarmament? The United Nations provides a vital forum in which all members of the international community can highlight global security problems, but the 39-member Conference on Disarmament is the only forum in which representatives of the industrialized and industrializing worlds can actually negotiate security agreements. The request to the CD to examine the issues outlined in the TIA resolution comes at an important time in the CD's history.

At the moment, the primary objective of the CD is conclusion of its negotiations on a chemical weapons convention (CWC). CD members have set a deadline of the end of 1992 to accomplish this objective. If a CWC is completed this year—and everyone can only hope that it is—the CD then faces the question of the subject of its next major effort. The TIA resolution suggests some possible directions the CD might explore. In particular, if carefully managed, the transformation

of its examination of the excessive and destabilizing accumulation of arms into a program of work could yield important results. It could, for example, concentrate attention on destabilizing buildups in various regions of the world and their implications for regional and international security. The CD's work on transparency in armaments would be especially helpful if it prompted states to focus on specific security problems within their own regions, fostering regional arms-control efforts of the kind embodied in President George Bush's Middle East initiative.

Conclusion

The arms-control agenda of the future is already being written. It promises to be significantly different from that of the past in many respects. Although in and of itself the transparency in armaments resolution constitutes but a small step toward dealing with that agenda, it suggests some of the problems and prospects on the horizon. If it, like other future arms-control efforts, is to have real meaning, however, all states—but especially those in regions of the world where violence and instability threaten strife and chaos—must match their deeds to their fine words.

The views expressed in this article are those of the author. They do not necessarily reflect the policies of the U.S. Arms Control and Disarmament Agency or the United States government.

Export Controls and the North–South Controversy

K. Subrahmanyam

THE SEARCH FOR more effective export controls is a growing preoccupation of the industrialized countries, where policymakers prize such controls as essential foreign and security policy tools in the post–cold war era. Countries on the other side of these barriers naturally have a rather different view of such controls, one rarely understood by the advocates of export controls.

Our critique is twofold. First, export controls are by definition discriminatory—they embody a fundamental double standard whereby nuclear weapons and missiles are deemed essential for the security of industrialized countries but dangerous in the hands of developing nations. Such discrimination cannot be the basis for international consensus. Second, export controls fail to deal with underlying problems of international security, which means that at best they are short-term fixes and at worst aggravate basic international problems. Export controls are bureaucratic in nature, arising out of an unwillingness or inability for lack of adequately sophisticated understanding to distinguish between one developing nation and another on the basis of their past rec-

ords, their policies, and the nature of their societies and national ethos. They also promote complacency and may not take into account new technologies that may be adopted. They therefore encourage the nations concerned to circumvent them. Above all, export controls divide the world into North and South, project a racist bias, and have proved to be inefficient instruments for pursuing global nonproliferation objectives.

This article begins with a review of factors determining the limited effectiveness of export controls. It underscores the changing nature of the proliferation problem, one in which proliferation arising from the breakdown of control over the Soviet nuclear arsenal is today a much higher priority than traditional proliferation issues. I then review the politics of nonproliferation in the post–cold war era, highlighting the ways in which outdated thinking among the nuclear states aggravates the nuclear weapons problem. The essay concludes with some recommendations for revising export controls and nonproliferation measures.

The Effectiveness of Export Controls

In applying broadly discriminatory export controls, the industrialized countries have not found the most effective means to deal with proliferation

K. Subrahmanyam is consulting editor (foreign affairs) to the *Economic Times* of Delhi, India. He is a former director of the Institute for Defence Studies and Analyses, Sapru House.

threats. Of the more than 130 developing nations, export controls are not a reasonable concern for some 110. All that is necessary in their cases is to check whether they genuinely need high-technology, dual-use items or whether they are serving as conduits for other nations. The developing nations whose nuclear or missile activities will disturb international peace and stability can easily be identified and watched. Export controls specific to a particular nation are logically more effective in preventing proliferation than across-the-board controls.

The failure to date of the international community to effectively control the flow of weapons and military technology to individual countries has nothing to do with the efficacy of such a country-specific approach. Iraq was not a case of inadequacy of export controls only. It was a case in which, despite everything the world knew about the nature of Saddam Hussein's regime, his aggression against Iran, and his use of chemical weapons, the leading industrial countries continued to arm him, provide him credits, and ignore reports put out by the United Nations (UN) on his use of chemical weapons. It was a failure of policy, a failure of assessment, and an encouragement of a ruthless authoritarian dictator who finally turned on his benefactors.

Proliferation by Pakistan was yet another case of permissiveness—in this case, a military dictator extracted a price from the U.S. government for serving as a conduit of U.S. arms to Afghan mujahidin who were fighting Soviet troops. Pakistan was permitted to go forward to the point of assembly of an explosive device. Pakistan also, according to U.S. sources, as far back as 1984 received technology related to weapon making from yet another authoritarian regime—the People's Re-

public of China (PRC). North Korea, too, has been able to develop its nuclear and missile capabilities, presumably with some help from the PRC, its neighbor. Today, when Syria, Iran, and even Algeria are mentioned as candidates for proliferation, their sources of technology are mostly the PRC and North Korea.

As many Western strategists used to point out when the Western nations were engaged in arms racing and proliferating weapons, it was not the weapons alone that constituted the danger but weapons combined with aggressive and expansionist policies. That is of course true not only in Europe but elsewhere in the world as well. Although such nuanced distinctions between democracies and nondemocracies were made in respect of industrialized countries, Western countries were unwilling to make such distinctions in respect of the developing world.

The attempt to deal with nuclear proliferation as a global generic threat rather than as a problem of aggressor states started in 1968 with the Nuclear Non-Proliferation Treaty (NPT). But it quickly went awry. It was based on the mistaken assumption that by subjecting the reactors of the nonnuclear weapon states to inspection by the International Atomic Energy Agency (IAEA) new countries would be prevented from making the bomb—in this case the plutonium bomb. It was blithely assumed that uranium enrichment through gaseous diffusion would be beyond the capability of developing nations. India's nuclear test in 1974 prompted the London Suppliers' Club to prepare a trigger list as a way to strengthen export controls on plutonium production technologies.[1] Not surprisingly, items not on the list proliferated. Release to Pakistan of equipment it needed for its uranium centrifuge enrichment project was authorized—by the author of the trigger list himself, Claude Sangger—because such equipment did not figure in his list. Similarly no one thought subsequently that the Iraqis would go back to the electromagnetic separation (Calutron) method and therefore they were able to get much of the equipment they wanted. The South Africans had their Jet Nozzle separation (exported from Germany) and it is possible Israelis have laser separation. The French now talk of reducing the cost of enrichment of uranium by laser separation of vaporized uranium compound.

These attempts to prevent the spread of technology are reminiscent of the Greek fable about Prometheus. The Greek gods could not stop the proliferation of what they considered a dangerous technology—fire—and mortals of today are not likely to be any more successful. This is not to decry export controls, which contribute to delaying proliferation efforts, but to warn against complacency about their effectiveness.

The relative ineffectiveness of export controls is also seen in the failure of the major suppliers of armaments on the world market to live up to their commitment to arms sales restraint. In July 1991, the five permanent members of the UN Security Council, which are also responsible for 85 percent of the world's arms exports, undertook to exercise restraint on arms sales. Ringing declarations were made in Paris, London, and Washington. Nevertheless, the United States has booked orders for $40 billion of arms sales to the Gulf area since the end of the Persian Gulf War. It is also to sell 15 F–16 aircraft to Taiwan. The French defense minister Pierre Joxe has talked of the French defense industry competing with that of the

United States.[2] The Russians are selling submarines to Iran. The British have major arms deals with Saudi Arabia. In all these cases, preaching and practice diverge widely. In addition, the Chinese have in the past exported enriched uranium to South Africa and Brazil and C–SS–2 missiles to Saudi Arabia.

Given this background, it is not very likely that the much talked about export controls will actually be adhered to. The past record of export restraint and control does not inspire confidence. How then can one expect states other than the advanced industrial ones to adhere to similar controls?

The PRC well illustrates the challenge posed by new suppliers unwilling to participate in export controls. Although the four Western declared nuclear weapon powers have suspended nuclear tests, given up wholly or mostly their tactical nuclear weapons, started reducing their nuclear arsenals (except for Britain, which continues to proliferate), and are working toward further arms reductions, the PRC conducted a megaton test on May 21, 1992, and an underground low-yield test on September 25, 1992. The Chinese have not indicated their willingness to give up tactical nuclear weapons or to join any arms reduction process. These developments may not worry West Europeans but they are of vital concern to the PRC's neighbors. The PRC is today the last bastion of self-righteous authoritarianism. At Manila, during the conference of the Association of Southeast Asian Nations (ASEAN), the foreign ministers expressed their misgivings about Chinese policy toward the South China Sea.

The new states arising from the erstwhile Soviet Union have aroused concern about proliferation. It is doubtful that they will be able to adopt and enforce effective export controls. In fall 1992, German customs officials intercepted two kilograms of enriched uranium of Ukrainian origin.[3] It is reported that this is only one of scores of such incidents. That would indicate that fissile materials from the republics of the former Soviet Union are coming into the market, first perhaps as samples, which may later be followed by sizable quantities. A deal has been reported in a U.S. journal between a group of scientists from erstwhile Soviet republics and Iran to build three nuclear weapons in Iran.[4] The story has been denied, but it re-emerges from time to time and has significant plausibility. Marshal Yevgenii I. Shaposhnikov, in his address to the Paris colloquium cited earlier, referred to the move to form a southern union of states including the Central Asian republics and pointed out that some of them had their own nuclear programs—a situation with significant implications.

The possible negative consequences of the breakdown of the arsenal of the former Soviet Union was raised by, among others, the Indian prime minister at the UN Security Council summit of January 1992. Unfortunately there has been no effort by the Security Council to contain and attenuate this threat. Instead, the tendency appears to be to brush the inconvenient issue under the rug. A deal has been made between the United States and Russia for the sale of enriched uranium from the latter to the former. Although this is meant to be for use in reactors after dilution of weapon-grade enriched uranium, the transaction has not been brought under the safeguards regime of the IAEA.

Nor has there been international verification of Russia's claim that all tactical nuclear weapons previously deployed in the erstwhile republics of the Soviet Union have been transferred to its territory. Can we exclude the possibility that some weapons may not have been accounted for and have been left behind in the republics? Even if tactical nuclear weapons have been moved into Russia, what about their secure storage, decommissioning, and dismantlement? The Russians have complained about delays in receiving the promised aid for these purposes. Unanswered questions also remain about the Ukrainian attitude. Some U.S. analysts have raised questions about the ways in which the Semipalatinsk nuclear test facility in Kazakhstan and nuclear facilities in other ex-Soviet republics, particularly Ukraine, can be utilized for nuclear proliferation.

There is also the problem of command and control over nuclear weapons, as first evident at the time of the August 1991 coup attempt. President Boris Yeltsin talks about plots to overthrow him unconstitutionally and has consequently outlawed the National Salvation Front. Unconstitutional overthrow implies a coup by sections of the armed forces. Potential coup plotters would presumably like to get at some nuclear weapons and fissile materials in order to use them as bargaining leverage for their own freedom if the coup were to fail. Fears of a coup would also indicate the possibility of a split in the Russian armed forces. If that were to happen, how safe would the Russian tactical nuclear weapons and fissile materials be?

Given this background and extreme economic hardship in the erstwhile Soviet republics, can a transfer of weapons and fissile materials for monetary gain be ruled out? Furthermore, no adequate information is publicly available on the erstwhile Soviet nuclear scientists and technical personnel and their whereabouts. The U.S. Central Intelligence Agency (CIA) is reported to have earmarked efforts to focus on nuclear proliferation. The Russians make a similar claim. What the world requires is reassurance through greater transparency and international verification of the ex-Soviet personnel, weapons, fissile materials, and facilities.

It should be obvious to everyone concerned about nuclear weapons and the risk of nuclear war that in the post–cold war era, the risks of proliferation arising out of the breakdown of the Soviet arsenal are far more immediate and substantial than the traditional proliferation risks. These traditional risks are in fact fairly marginal, given the decision by the vast majority of the states of the developing world not to pursue nuclear weapons.

A major drawback of controls has been the inadequacy of safeguards in nuclear weapon nations that are parties to the NPT. Mention is often made of an international black market in enriched uranium, heavy water, and other special nuclear materials. The Norwegians complain that their heavy water has shown up in India. India denies the charge and asks how Norway, which is a party to the NPT, allowed the heavy water to leave the country without adequate safeguards. Similarly, there are reports that Soviet and Chinese special nuclear materials are available on the international black market.

Current proposals to strengthen the export control regime are defended as necessary responses to the lapses cited above. An honest assessment of their history reveals, however, a set of problems with export controls that will not go away with a bit of tightening here and fine-tuning there. Problems posed by new suppliers, competing interests, and a simple-minded, self-serving

view of the world among the controlling states rob such controls of their credibility and efficacy. The democratic developing nations facing nuclear threats will have to take into account the possibility that Saddam Husseins and Mohammed Zia-ul-Haqs will continue to benefit from this kind of permissiveness on export controls among some of the leading industrial powers.

The Politics of Nonproliferation After the Cold War

The nuclear powers ordained in the NPT—essentially, the victors in a world struggle now five decades past—must recognize how their thinking about their own nuclear capabilities shapes the global nuclear problem after the Cold War. Their current doctrines must be analyzed and their implications considered logically and dispassionately.

The nuclear powers of the West—the United States, the United Kingdom, and France—have no nuclear adversaries to deter because Russia is now accepted as a partner and no longer treated as an enemy. Thus these countries have no need to exercise deterrence against any adversary. Under these circumstances one would expect the nuclear weapon powers and their allies to move toward a world free of nuclear weapons. But they claim that they still need nuclear weapons, not to deter specific adversaries but to maintain deterrence against certain contingencies. These include a Russian reversal from democracy toward hostility, the emergence of a future nuclear-armed Saddam Hussein, and strategic uncertainties, for which nuclear weapons are somehow deemed a form of insurance.

If the claim is accepted, certain logical conclusions follow. If a contingent deterrent against Russia turning hostile and a potential nuclear-armed Saddam Hussein is needed by Western Europe and the United States, it will be needed even more by democratic nations that are located nearer to Russia and areas from which potential Saddam Husseins may emerge, for whom such threats will be more proximate and immediate. It looks as if the doctrines of the United States and its transatlantic allies have not been thought through to their logical conclusion. If the logic of contingent deterrence is restricted to only the white industrial nations, then it raises doubts elsewhere in the world as to whether a racist approach does not underlie the present rationalization. Democracy must be defended against authoritarianism and militarist threats wherever they exist, whether in the North or South, East or West.

Another element of Western logic is revealed in its emphasis on arms-control regimes that falsely segregate one category of weapons from another. For example, a draft chemical weapons ban has been finalized. It provides for a universal nondiscriminatory verification regime and a time interval in which nations are to eliminate their chemical weapons arsenals. Can the logic be sustained of advocating the ban and elimination of one category of weapons of mass destruction but continuing to legitimize the most horrendous of them—the nuclear weapon in the cartelized possession of five nuclear weapon powers?

It is not difficult to accept that, having built enormous nuclear arsenals based on a logic derived from a closed system of nuclear theology, the nuclear-armed nations will need time to reduce their holdings of nuclear weapons and finally eliminate them. The world today better understands the

problems involved in decommissioning weapons and eliminating fissile materials. There is some logic in the plea that the international community has to go through a period of minimum deterrence before reaching a world free of nuclear weapons. That logic should apply in equal measure to states with declared nuclear weapons as well as those states with undeclared weapons or which are otherwise nuclear capable.

Conventional wisdom, which has conditioned people to accept the differentiated legitimacy of nuclear weapons for the five weapon states but not others, also interferes with managing the high risks associated with our present failure to contain the consequences of the breakdown of the former Soviet arsenal. Of course, the danger posed by the retirement and storage of weapons and fissile materials is not a danger found solely in the former Soviet Union. The international community should be in a position to monitor them and track down discrepancies wherever weapons are stored. There have been proposals that the IAEA should be authorized to verify facilities on the basis of intelligence information furnished to it— presumably by the CIA and the Russian agency now undertaking such tasks. One wonders whether such activity, undertaken on a discriminatory basis, with possession of nuclear weapons and weapon-making facilities being legal for nuclear weapon powers and illegal for others, will be in conformity with international legal norms. Even if it is, would it be effective against acquisition of ready-made weapons and fissile materials? Probably not.

It is of course difficult also to predict what will happen in the PRC. When the Chinese people finally repudiate authoritarianism, will there be a great deal of violence? Might the armed forces split apart, with necessary consequences for the nuclear arsenal? Already two decades ago I raised the question of command and control over the large nuclear arsenals of the five nuclear weapon powers and the consequences of political instability in those countries in a conference of the Stockholm International Peace Research Institute. At the time, those objections were not taken seriously. After the Cold War, they have emerged at the top of our list of proliferation concerns.

New Thinking for a New Era

New thinking is needed to tackle the problems of nuclear weapons and the international insecurities of which they are a symptom. That new thinking should take into account the following developments. First, the central problem today is not nonproliferation in the conventional sense. About 150 countries have acceded to the NPT. Barring North Korea and Iran, there are no other suspect candidates for proliferation. Israel, Pakistan, and India form a separate category of nations that already have undeclared arsenals or weapon-making capabilities with the necessary amounts of fissile materials. The real problem is preventing movement of fissile materials and ready-made weapons. There are five declared nuclear weapon powers and three powers with undeclared nuclear arsenals or weapon-making capabilities. The rest of the world has been brought under the NPT regime, with some problems in regard to Ukraine and Kazakhstan. North Korea and Iran have to be watched carefully. Unless the industrialized powers or the PRC are exceedingly careless and permissive, the chances of new nuclear weapon states

emerging by making their own nuclear weapons are not very high. But the risks of fissile materials and nuclear weapons seeping out of ex-Soviet republics to state and non-state actors are much more significant.

Nuclear arsenals are bound to lose their deterrent potential and atrophy over time for sheer lack of use. Saddam Hussein's irrationality and megalomania were nurtured by some interested powers and are not likely to be repetitive events. Although the four Western nuclear weapon nations are not willing to give up their doctrine of deterrence or their reduced arsenals (Britain will still have a larger arsenal), the United States and Russia have stopped production of nuclear weapons and fissile materials and have taken their weapons off alert. A moratorium for nuclear testing is now in force for the four Western countries and chances are bright for their acceptance of a comprehensive test ban from 1997 onward.

Expert opinion today holds that countries that have already produced nuclear weapons or fissile materials in quantity cannot be totally divested of them under acceptable standards of verification. In respect of the three undeclared nuclear weapon or nuclear capable powers, therefore, the practical course is to cap their capabilities. Four out of five nuclear weapon powers have no interest in adding to their arsenals or producing more fissile materials—thus they should have no objection to capping their arsenals and capabilities. The means to adequately verify this level of control may well be found in the just completed chemical weapons ban and its nondiscriminatory verification regime acceptable to all countries. The principle underlying its intrusive verification regime is that chemical weapons are banned and their possession made illegal—for all.

The countries possessing them are permitted a sufficiently long period in which to destroy them.

It is possible to construct a comprehensive nonproliferation regime taking into account these positive developments. One approach would be to amend the NPT, although there are perhaps legitimate fears that it would unravel if any such attempt is made. However, the shortcomings of the present NPT must be rectified. These are:

- it is discriminatory;
- it does not provide for safeguards to prevent seepage of materials and technology from the nuclear weapon powers;
- it does not provide for complete prohibition of testing;
- it does not provide a nondiscriminatory verification regime;
- it does not prohibit the first use of nuclear weapons;
- it does not prohibit research and development to produce new weapons; and
- it does not envisage the ultimate delegitimization and elimination of nuclear weapons.

Because the present NPT cannot be amended but will need to be extended indefinitely, a second treaty should be negotiated that will incorporate all the above objectives and reinforce the nonproliferation regime, thereby restoring to the term *nonproliferation* its appropriate meaning. Further, it will stop the present proliferators from continuing their activities and prevent new proliferators from joining in.

If the present NPT is extended and a new treaty is brought into force, it will be possible to declare the production of new nuclear weapons by any party an offense against international law. All nuclear installations and all nuclear activities would come under nondiscriminatory inspection. In order to ensure that nuclear weapon powers get no privileges, the verification agency should have a majority of decision makers from nonnuclear weapon states and its findings and recommendations should not be subject to veto by the Security Council.

The treaty should permit the nuclear weapon powers to keep their nuclear weapons for a period of 20 years, after which their continued retention would be reviewed. This is to give the nuclear weapon powers time to shake off the conditioning by nuclear theology of the last four decades. It would also create broader consensus within the international community about lingering threats to peace and security, thereby either strengthening the capacity to act in collective self-defense or legitimizing for another fixed period the possession of a minimal nuclear retaliatory capability sufficient to prevent nuclear blackmail by an aggressor. Meanwhile, the no-first-use provision would lay the foundation for the ultimate elimination of nuclear weapons. All nuclear weapon powers and nuclear capable powers would be required to declare their weapon and fissile materials stockpiles, which would enable the verification agency to pursue undeclared weapons and fissile materials anywhere in the world. The verification agency should have its own intelligence agency and might also benefit from intelligence provided by national agencies. Negotiations for a second treaty to reinforce the first should be initiated immediately so that it can be considered along with extension of the existing NPT.

Understanding the North–South Aspect

Nuclear proliferation in itself is not a North–South issue, nor are export controls or missile proliferation. There are Saddam Husseins in the South as there were Hitlers and Mussolinis in the North; Communist authoritarian regimes existed in the North and continue in the South. These problems are converted into North–South issues when countries in the North form cartels, clubs, and groups and do not bring democracies from the South into such arrangements. This parochial attitude converts proposals that should address international security problems in a nondiscriminatory manner into North–South issues, and the proposals put forward by the North appear to be designed to dominate the South—to have a racist bias.

Export controls will no doubt to a limited extent achieve their purpose of delaying proliferation. But the need of Russia and the PRC for hard currency is so great that they may not enforce such controls in spite of their declared commitment. It is not even certain that all European countries will enforce them rigorously and that there will not be more transactions under the table. A country that has the resources—as Iraq did and Iran does and Pakistan was able to raise from the Arab countries—and the determination will always find a way to get around the controls.

The present export control strategy is derived from the philosophy underlying the London Suppliers' Club, the Missile Technology Control Regime (MTCR), the Coordinating Committee for Multilateral Export Controls (CoCom), and the Australia Group. Each was set up during the cold war era by like-minded countries, although the Soviet Union joined some of them and now even the PRC offers to adhere to the MTCR. With the Cold War over, there is a need to reorganize some of these groups on a broader base to include leading democratic nations of the developing world.

On the basis of its 18-year record of exemplary nuclear restraint, its avowed intent not to transfer missile technology, and its recent domestic legislation on chemical precursors, there is no reason why India should not be accepted as a full member of these groups, thereby enabling their parochial and racist image to be rectified. India would be loath to accept any appearance of condescension, namely, any invitation to adhere to these regimes without membership. With regard to the chemical weapons treaty, although India is an enthusiastic supporter of the treaty, it opposes the perpetuation of the white nations' club (the Australia Group) after the treaty comes into operation. As we approach the end of the 20th century this apartheid on international security management appears anomalous and counterproductive.

Political-military establishments tend to be conservative and consequently they will take time to shed the burden of the approach defined by cold war nuclear theology. Greater responsibility therefore falls on the intellectuals, mass media, and groups that draw parliamentarians from many countries to think beyond the conventional framework of East–West and North–South divisions.

This paper was prepared for the Dutch Advisory Council on Peace and Security and presented at a seminar at Clingendael, The Hague, on November 6–7, 1992.

Notes

1. India's test was a peaceful nuclear explosion conducted at the same time as the United States and the USSR were conducting dozens of them. The NPT recognized it in Article V and textbooks have been written about it.

2. Joxe spoke on September 29, 1992, at a colloquium on "Un nouveau débat stratégique," sponsored by the French Ministry of Defense, Paris, September 29–October 1, 1992.

3. *International Herald Tribune,* October 17–18, 1992.

4. See a paper by Vitalii I. Goldanskii of the Russian Academy of Sciences, "Prevention and Management of Proliferation and the Positions and Roles of CIS Scientists," prepared for a symposium on "The Proliferation of Nuclear Weapons: Past, Present, and Future," University of Chicago, Chicago, December 3–5, 1992.

How to Think About—and Implement—Nuclear Arms Control in the Middle East

Avner Cohen and Marvin Miller

THE PROSPECT OF a nuclear-armed Iraq and the reality of a nuclear-armed Israel cast an ominous shadow on the crisis and war in the Persian Gulf in 1990–1991 and focused attention on the danger of nuclear proliferation in the post–cold war era. More recently, suspicious nuclear activities in Iran and North Korea and the potential for the transfer of nuclear weapons materials, technology, and expertise from the former Soviet Union (FSU) have underscored both the global nature of the proliferation threat and the importance of agreements between the regional actors as a complement to the nonproliferation efforts of outside powers such as the United States.

In the Middle East, both the moderate Arab states and Israel now share a common concern about nuclear proliferation and also recognize the need to deal with it on a regional basis. It is one thing to recognize such a need, however, and another to come up with mutually acceptable ideas and modalities for meeting it. Achieving agreement on nuclear arms-control arrange-

ments in the Middle East involves three distinct problems: the linkage between the nuclear issue and the rest of the peace process; the linkage between the nuclear issue and the rest of the arms-control agenda, particularly with regard to chemical weapons and conventional arms limitations; and the difficulties intrinsic to the nuclear issue itself, namely, how to craft a realistic and effective arms-control agreement, given Israel's determination to retain its unacknowledged nuclear capability at least until there is *true* peace in the region and Arab demands for nonnuclear equality and symmetry.

These problems have already surfaced during the first two rounds of the ongoing multilateral talks on regional security and arms control in the Middle East. The Arab states want to put the nuclear issue at the top of the negotiating agenda, pushing "for a full accounting of Israel's nuclear arsenal and demanding the weapons' elimination" as early as possible,[1] but Israel maintains that the nuclear issue should be discussed only after all other arms-control issues are resolved. The problems of linkage are difficult, but hardly insurmountable. For example, the parties could agree to consider the nuclear, chemical/biological, and conventional weapons issues in separate parallel negotiations, with the proviso

Avner Cohen is a visiting scholar at the Center for International Studies at MIT. Marvin Miller is a senior research scientist with the Department of Nuclear Engineering and the Defense and Arms Control Studies Program at MIT.

that the separate agreements would only be implemented as a single package. This essay focuses on the nuclear issue, specifically, on whether making Israel's unacknowledged weapons more transparent would aid or hinder efforts to reach a nuclear arms-control agreement.

The Post–Gulf War Context

Nuclear arms control in the Middle East must start from the implications of the Iraqi nuclear program. Major gaps remain in our knowledge of this program; indeed it is possible that significant activities remain unknown. From what we do know, however, it is credible that Iraq could have assembled its first nuclear weapons by now, or could have done so in the near future, with possibly catastrophic consequences. This realization is very chilling to many Arabs and Israelis alike. Fortunately, Saddam Hussein invaded Kuwait, refused to withdraw, was defeated in the Persian Gulf War, and had no choice but to agree to the draconian provisions of United Nations (UN) Resolution 687.[2] This led to the establishment of the UN Special Commission on Iraq, with its mandate to dismantle that nation's programs to develop weapons of mass destruction and ballistic missiles and to deny Iraq the possibility of resurrecting them. In the nuclear area, however, despite the well-publicized and sometimes heroic efforts by the inspection teams sent to Iraq to carry out this mandate, Iraq still refuses to provide a full accounting of its program or to agree to long-term surveillance of its territory.

The major lesson of Iraq for the nonproliferation community is that states with a limited industrial and technological base can obtain sufficient access to bomb-making technologies and know-how to initiate a large-scale nuclear weapons program and can largely conceal that program both from national technical means of gathering intelligence and the International Atomic Energy Agency (IAEA) safeguards regime. Further, although Iraq's nuclear ambitions were well known, virtually all concerned intelligence organizations had a flawed overview of the state of the Iraqi nuclear project prior to the war. This failure has led to much soul-searching and analysis in the United States and elsewhere to identify both its causes and possible remedial actions. It is plausible that the failure stems from a complex set of technical and political factors, including the tilt by Western governments toward Iraq during the Iran–Iraq War; Iraq's insights into and consequent ability to evade U.S. intelligence capabilities; the difficulty of finding what is not deemed credible, for example, the presence of electromagnetic isotope separation technology; and the lack of human intelligence on the spot until after the war. In response, new resources have been allocated to enhancing U.S. intelligence-gathering and analytical capabilities in the proliferation area. Similar efforts have probably also been made by other concerned governments, among them Israel, albeit on a smaller scale.

At the same time, there is now a much greater appreciation, both inside and outside of the IAEA, of the ability of states parties to the Nuclear Non-Proliferation Treaty (NPT) to conduct clandestine nuclear weapons programs behind the fig leaf of nominal adherence to their nonproliferation obligations. Over the last two years, the IAEA has taken several steps to deal with such clandestine programs. In particular, it has asserted its authority to conduct special inspections both at declared sites and at undeclared locations on the basis of all available information, including intelligence supplied by outside sources.[3]

Finally, the success of Iraq in obtaining the materials, technology, and expertise for a nuclear weapons program—often with the collusion of foreign suppliers and the knowledge of their governments—exposed major deficiencies in existing national and international regulations on nuclear export control. In response, embarrassed governments, for example Germany, have strengthened their laws on exports, and there is now an international agreement for controlling the export of dual-use, as well as specifically nuclear, materials and technology.[4]

In sum, the specter of a nuclear-armed Iraq, as well as similar concerns about the nuclear ambitions of other small countries with large grievances, has led to much rhetoric about the seriousness of the proliferation threat and some concrete actions designed to bolster the denial side of the nonproliferation regime. These words and deeds are laudable, but one can question whether the political will exists to thwart a state determined to acquire nuclear weapons, especially if military action is required. Nor is such action a panacea. As the Gulf war demonstrated, even overwhelming military power is ineffective in destroying clandestine nuclear facilities unless their location is known. Undoubtedly, intelligence capabilities will improve. But so will the ability to hide such facilities where we least expect to find them, whether underground, in urban areas, or in other countries. Determined states may even bypass the major barrier to possessing weapons by purchasing significant quantities of weapons-usable materials, if not actual weapons.

The end of the Cold War has undoubtedly changed the prospects for preventing further proliferation. The picture, however, is a mixed one. The good news is that nonproliferation is less likely to be traded against cold war interests and that nuclear arms reductions in the United States and the FSU support the devaluation of the idea that such weapons can be useful in fighting wars. The bad news is that nonproliferation is more likely to be traded off against economic interests in the FSU, the People's Republic of China (PRC), and other countries, just when the potential for post–cold war fragmentation of the international system exacerbates regional conflicts and heightens incentives for proliferation.

Thus, it is essential to strengthen policies of nuclear denial, but these must be complemented by greater efforts to reduce the incentives to acquire nuclear weapons. In the Middle East, this requires progress toward a political settlement of the Arab–Israeli conflict. Indeed, the prevailing view is that trying to reach agreement between the parties on arms control in general, and nuclear arms control in particular, before the peace process bears fruit would be futile, even counterproductive. But serious discussions about arms control can also *aid* the peace process by increasing each side's understanding of the other's basic security concerns. Moreover, on the long road toward a solution of the Arab–Israeli conflict, concrete arms-control confidence-building measures, both bilateral and unilateral, can help allay suspicions about the other side's true desire for peace.

The good news here is that the formation of a new government in Israel in summer 1992 has given impetus to the negotiations between Israel, the Palestinians, and Syria that began at the Madrid peace conference in October 1991. In addition, the Madrid conference framework provides a specific forum—the multilateral working group on regional security and arms control—for discussion of arms control and proliferation in a regional context. This group, together with four other multilateral forums on other regional problems, was created in January 1992 and has convened twice since. The first meeting, held in Washington in May 1992, was mostly an academic seminar, designed to acquaint the representatives from 12 Arab countries and Israel with the concepts and practices of arms control, with particular reference to the experience of the United States and the Soviet Union in this area. In the second meeting, held in Moscow in September 1992, there was the beginning of a dialogue between Arabs and Israelis about how to proceed with substantive discussions.

Unfortunately, three of the significant regional players are not at the table: Iraq is regarded as a pariah state so long as Saddam Hussein remains in power, while Syria and Iran, although invited, have declined to participate. This alone makes it highly unlikely that any substantive agreements can be negotiated anytime soon. Indeed, the group has not yet even agreed on what topics should be discussed and the priorities of such discussions. The very establishment of such a forum is itself significant, however. For the first time, delegates from Israel and the Arab states sit together, learning about arms control, and can talk to each other about their nations' threat perceptions and concepts of regional security.

Specifically, they can talk about nuclear weapons in the Middle East. In the past, the Arab states have raised the issue of Israel's nuclear capabilities as a threat to peace in such international forums as the UN and the General Conference of the IAEA. Israel has always resisted such pressure, insisting that the nuclear issue can be seriously addressed only in direct negotiations between the parties and in the context of agreement on other aspects of regional security. The Madrid conference has brought Arabs and Israelis together and given them the opportunity, at last, to concentrate on matters of substance, not just procedure.

Further, the events of the Gulf war have led to a rethinking of the nuclear issue by both Arabs and Israelis. On the Arab side, the human suffering, economic costs, and environmental havoc suffered by countries in the region because of the war, and the realization of how much worse the situation could have been if nuclear weapons had been used by Iraq and/or Israel, have caused the old Arab vision of establishing nuclear parity with Israel to lose much of its appeal. Moreover, even discounting the risk of actual nuclear use, possession of nuclear weapons by Iraq or Iran would cause a significant, and dangerous, shift in the balance of power in the Arab world between moderates and extremists, increase the latter's geopolitical ambitions, and lessen the appetite of outside powers such as the United States to intervene militarily to protect allies and oil supplies. In a peculiar way, the Gulf war has led to a shared concern on the part of Israel and most Arab states about the danger of nuclear proliferation in the Middle East, particularly in a resurgent Iraq or a fundamentalist Iran. Thus, below the surface of Arab public demands that Israel sign the NPT and place all its nuclear facilities under IAEA safeguards forthwith, lies a good deal of flexibility and realism about the virtues of reaching an interim nuclear bargain with Israel.

In Israel, too, the Gulf war has forced a quiet rethinking of the nuclear issue. It is now increasingly recognized that even if the twin pillars of Israeli nuclear policy for the past 30 years, that is, ambiguity about its own program and a parallel commitment to prevent Arab nuclearization, are still essential, the means to attain these ends need to be refurbished. In particular, Israel can no longer have confidence in its ability to detect and destroy a nascent Arab nuclear threat unilaterally, as it did in 1981.[5] Cooperation in this regard with other states, particularly the United States, has now become a necessity for Israel.

The concern about Arab and Iranian nuclearization is central to the political thinking of Israel's new prime minister, Yitzhak Rabin.[6] He believes that the Gulf war has given Israel a window of opportunity of perhaps 5 to 10 years to minimize this threat. During this period, Israel should contribute to a vigorous nuclear denial strategy via enhanced political and intelligence coordination with friendly states, and, more fundamentally, it should negotiate peace agreements with its neighbors to reduce incentives and support for nuclearization in the Arab world. In line with past Israeli policy, Rabin thus far has not mentioned Israel's own nuclear program, let alone hinted at a willingness to consider constraints on it. Instead, he is concentrating on achieving some measure of success in the negotiations with the Palestinians and Syria before engaging in serious talks on arms control. Such talks cannot be delayed indefinitely, however, and their chances of success depend crucially on the willingness of both sides to take calculated risks, with due appreciation of the complexities involved, especially with regard to the nuclear issue.

The Complexity of the Nuclear Arms-Control Problem in the Middle East

One long-standing idea for reducing the risk of nuclear weapons in the Middle East is to ban them by establishing a Nuclear Weapons Free Zone (NWFZ) in the region. Both Israel and the Arab states have endorsed this concept for years. This apparent consensus has, however, led to a blind alley because the formal preconditions that each side has stipulated in its proposals for such a zone have been patently unacceptable to the other. The Arab states have insisted on prior adherence to the NPT by all states in the region.[7] Israel, which has refused to sign the NPT, has insisted that the issue of an NWFZ in the Middle East can be addressed only through direct negotiations among all the regional parties and that a nuclear-free Middle East can become a reality only when there is true peace in the region.[8]

Thus in the past each side could claim the moral high ground of support for an NWFZ with the knowledge that it would not have to negotiate seriously about how and when such a zone could come into force. Although some of the formal sources of this impasse have now been removed—the multilateral arms-control talks provide a forum for direct negotiation on the whole array of arms-control issues in the Middle East—it remains highly unlikely that the apparent consensus on an NWFZ could be translated into action anytime soon. The substantive reason is known by all, but stated by none: until Israel feels truly secure, it will continue to regard its unacknowledged nuclear deterrent as an essential ingredient in guaranteeing its very existence and will not relinquish it.

In the interim, Israel might agree to constrain its nuclear capability as a step toward the eventual goal of a Middle East free of nuclear weapons. A basic difficulty remains, however: how to negotiate, or even talk about, eliminating, dismantling, or freezing an arsenal that is more than 25 years old, but does not officially exist.[9] Although Israel was the sixth nation to develop a dedicated nuclear weapons program, its behavior has been radically different from that of the five members of the de jure nuclear weapons club. Israel's policy has been to neither confirm nor deny its nuclear status, only pledging, since the mid-1960s, "not to be the first to introduce nuclear weapons to the Middle East." Although Israel has never explicitly defined what "to introduce" nuclear weapons means, this formulation is implicitly based on an understanding that such an introduction involves some kind of *public* act, for instance, making an official declaration of possession or conducting an acknowledged nuclear test. This Israel has steadfastly refused to do.

Israel's nuclear program was born and shaped many years ago. From the mid-1950s Israel's leaders, particularly its first prime minister, David Ben Gurion, regarded a nuclear deterrent as a necessity, the ultimate guarantee of the country's existence. At the same time, they feared nuclearization of the Arab–Israeli conflict, recognizing that any failure of the resulting "balance of terror" could be catastrophic for Israel. For this reason, Israel has never joined the official nuclear club. The taboo against public discussion of Israel's nuclear weapons in Israel is the natural outcome of this schizophrenic predicament.

In the United States too, since the Johnson administration, there has been a marked reluctance to discuss the nuclear reality in Israel. Even in periods of heightened concern about nuclear proliferation, for instance during the Carter administration, or at low points in U.S.–Israeli relations, the Israeli "bomb in the basement" has been treated by the U.S. government, particularly the Congress, as a special case. As recently as June 1991, Secretary of Defense Richard B. Cheney responded to a question at a news conference in Cairo by saying, "I don't know that Israel has any nuclear capability. They have certainly never announced it."[10]

Since the end of the Gulf war, however, there has been increasing criticism of the U.S. attitude as hypocritical and inimical to the fashioning of an effective global nonproliferation strategy. In particular, some security analysts have suggested that Israel's long-standing policy of ambiguity about its nuclear program is not compatible with arms-control agreements to prevent further nuclearization in the region. A representative view is that of Geoffrey Kemp:

> While Israel has good reasons for developing its nuclear weapons program, and has shown responsibility in not flaunting it, its existence has been a catalyst for other Middle East states to seek their own nuclear capability, particularly Iraq. But until there has been a long period of peace in the Middle East, Israel is unlikely to negotiate away its nuclear force. *In these circumstances, the best way to address the Israeli nuclear weapons program is to engage in a more open discussion of its existence and seek ways to limit its further growth, without, at this time, calling for its elimination.* Pushing Israel too hard on nuclear weapons while demanding that it be more flexi-

ble on giving up land for peace would be counterproductive. But to say nothing about this program, or engage in empty semantics, is equally counterproductive. (emphasis added)[11]

Interestingly, this argument for more nuclear openness or transparency has also been made by some Israeli and Arab analysts, albeit with opposite views about what the final outcome of the nuclear arms-control process should be. For the Israelis, nuclear arms control could provide a means for legitimizing Israel's nuclear monopoly. Even if Israel ultimately agreed to limitations on its nuclear arsenal, the quid pro quo would be Arab acceptance of this monopoly, at least for an agreed period of time.[12] On the other hand, some Arab analysts see more openness as the logical starting point for putting the Israeli nuclear program on the negotiating table explicitly as a weapons issue in order to first cap it and then to negotiate its elimination. If the Arabs are serious about dealing with Israel's nuclear capability, according to this view, they must first acknowledge reality in order to change it.[13]

There are persuasive reasons, however, for believing that open acknowledgment of Israel's nuclear program, at this point, would hinder rather than help the process of nuclear arms control both in the Middle East and globally. In Israel, the absence of any debate about the nuclear issue is more than a matter of imposed censorship; it reflects a genuine political, military, and societal taboo against considering nuclear weapons as real weapons. Official acknowledgment would run the risk of undermining this profound taboo. In particular, it could galvanize open public support for nuclear weapons, hence limiting the flexibility of the government in negotiating agreements involving nuclear limitations.

On the Arab side, open acknowledgment by Israel of its nuclear status would create demands for both more transparency, for example, declarations of how many weapons of what type existed and their means of delivery, as well as for a commitment by Israel to dismantle them verifiably at an early date. Absent such an unlikely commitment, there would be increased domestic pressure on Arab governments finally to end Israel's nuclear monopoly in the Middle East by whatever means necessary, including purchase of weapons. Globally, the sudden emergence of a new, declared, nuclear weapons state would provide support for similar actions by India and Pakistan and complicate efforts to extend the NPT in 1995. Some degree of transparency short of open acknowledgment might be helpful, but how much? As usual the devil is in the details, to which we now turn.

The Balance Between Transparency and Opacity

If open acknowledgment by Israel of its nuclear weapons program is not a good idea, what useful purpose would be served by, in Kemp's phrase, "a more open discussion of its existence"? In particular, would such a discussion enhance the acceptability to both Israel and the Arab states of "ways to limit its further growth, without, at this time, calling for its elimination"?

Since the sensational assertions about the size and scope of the Israeli nuclear program made by Mordecai Vanunu in 1986,[14] and more recently by Seymour Hersh,[15] there has been a growing sense of unease about the rationale for Israel's weapons and the genuineness of its declaratory commitment to get rid of them ultimately through an NWFZ. The principal concern with regard to the former issue for some Arab and non-Arab security analysts is that the assertions by Vanunu and Hersh imply a nuclear use doctrine that goes far beyond the traditional justification of "last resort." For example, according to Norman Moss:

Deterrence for Israel would require a few nuclear bombs, and aircraft and possibly missiles able to deliver them as well as survive enemy air strikes. In October 1986, Vanunu told the London *Sunday Times* that Israel had assembled the material for 100–200 atomic bombs. Vanunu also said that Israel was well on the way to producing thermonuclear bombs. . . . This is far more than required for a last-resort nuclear strategy. It implies that Israel's purpose in possessing nuclear weapons goes beyond this and that it is ready to use or threaten to use nuclear weapons for several national objectives.

Moss also recognizes, however, that:

Developing the Jericho missile and thermonuclear weapons does not necessarily mean that Israel has a strategy that requires them. On the basis of the U.S. experience, it would seem equally probable that once the initial decision was made, more and better weapons were built simply because of technological and bureaucratic momentum. The rationale, if any, followed.

Nevertheless, the existence of an advanced nuclear capability is worrisome:

Future Israeli leaders may have less respect for the nuclear taboo than the superpowers have today and may refuse to see the nuclear bomb as a special kind of weapon to be used only *in extremis*. . . .

Nuclear proliferation means proliferation possibilities.[16]

These concerns have been echoed and expanded upon in a paper by Yezid Sayigh, the coordinator of the Palestinian team to the multilateral Middle East arms-control talks. According to Sayigh:

More recently, Arab anxiety has grown that the Israeli "defensive shield" provided by nonconventional weapons can now be used assertively, as a strategic cover for conventional operations. The fear is that with its extensive first- and second-strike nuclear capability, long-range delivery systems and evolving reconnaissance assets . . . Israel is even in a position to wage an offensive nonconventional war, yet remain relatively immune from counterattack.[17]

These fears, Sayigh asserts, "are not far-fetched." Under opacity, there have been "subtle outward shifts in Israeli doctrine and policy" concerning its nuclear deterrent. In particular, Sayigh maintains that Israel has incorporated nonconventional capabilities in its "force structure and operational thinking"; there were demonstrative deployments of nuclear weapons by Israel during both the October 1973 and Gulf wars in order to convince the U.S. government of the risks of not attending to Israel's pressing security needs; and, finally, Israel has incorporated nuclear battlefield weapons, specifically, artillery shells and land mines, into its "war waging doctrines." Sayigh speculates that this capability, used in conjunction with "some elements in the Israeli space and [anti-tactical ballistic missile] programs, . . . lends itself to an evolving doctrine of controlled nonconventional applications," for instance, to "detonate a single [nuclear] weapon demonstratively, to halt an enemy offensive at an early stage and abort it before it poses a threat to national survival."

The statements by Moss and Sayigh raise two basic questions: to what extent are their assertions about a change in Israel's nuclear capability and doctrine credible and, to the extent that they are credible, is this change incompatible with a policy of last resort, that is, use of nuclear weapons as a means of avoiding the imminent destruction of the state? Israel has thus far not responded to these assertions. They cannot be ignored, however, particularly in the context of negotiations on interim confidence-building measures that would limit the further growth of Israel's nuclear capability. If Israel seeks to legitimize its interim need for *some* nuclear shield, it must convince others that their rationale is still last resort.

With regard to the credibility of these assertions, their primary sources are, as noted, Vanunu and Hersh. In general, the former is persuasive, and the latter a mixed bag. Primarily on the basis of the Vanunu evidence, it appears that Israel has indeed gone beyond the Nagasaki-type bomb to more advanced fission-only and fission-fusion devices. It also appears that *if* advanced low-yield weapons are part of the Israeli arsenal, the primary rationale for their development was, as in the U.S. case,[18] the desire to create options for nuclear use in a way that would minimize harm to both Arab and Israeli noncombatants, thereby obviating recourse to the morally repugnant—hence not credible—targeting of population centers and to permit use, in extremis, over Israeli territory.

Obviously, the perception that low-yield weapons can be militarily useful in war-fighting is dangerous because it weakens the essential taboo against *any* use of nuclear weapons. Unlike the situation in the United States, however, nuclear weapons have not been integrated into the military doctrine of the Israeli Defense Forces (IDF). And, in the event of a threat to the existence of the state that could not be countered by conventional means, for example, a massive enemy ground offensive or extensive use of chemical weapons against Israeli population centers, the selective use of small nuclear weapons, including the demonstrative use conjectured by Sayigh, is surely preferable to the destruction of Baghdad or Damascus.

In 1962, a decision was taken by Israel's political leadership that it would not integrate nuclear weapons into its armed forces.[19] The authors of this essay are convinced that Israeli nuclear weapons are still only a psychological insurance policy for last resort contingencies.[20] The military doctrine of the IDF remains conventional: as long as there are no Arab nuclear weapons, the Israeli army must plan its response to all military threats as if Israel had no nuclear weapons. The experience of the 1967 and 1973 Arab–Israeli wars—during both of which Israeli nuclear weapons were available—only strengthened the lesson that nuclear weapons have no military utility in almost any military situation in which Israel could find itself.

It is also reasonable to assume, with Moss, that technological and bureaucratic momentum has played a role in the development of the Israeli arsenal. Indeed, one would expect that its role in the highly secret, publicly unacknowledged Israeli nuclear program was even greater than in the United States.

In sum, like the declared nuclear weapon states, Israel has very likely developed an arsenal that, in theory at least, gives it more options than the destruction of enemy cities using Nagasaki-type bombs. But there has always been a high barrier against any use of nuclear weapons by Israel. It is important to convince the Arab states of this while avoiding an open discussion of what is in Israel's arsenal and why. Realistically, however, it can be anticipated that the Arab states will raise these matters in any negotiations on confidence-building initiatives in the nuclear area. Israel will surely refuse to participate in such discussions. As a result, initiatives whose purpose is to build confidence could instead raise suspicions of bad faith and would be likely to end in failure. How to proceed?

A Realistic Approach

It is useful to consider this dilemma in the context of specific proposals for nuclear confidence-building in the Middle East. Israel should cap its production of weapons-usable nuclear materials, while the Arab states and Iran should reinforce their declaratory commitment not to produce nuclear weapons by accepting the authority of the IAEA to make special inspections at both declared and suspect nuclear facilities.[21] The U.S. proposal for arms control in the Middle East of May 29, 1991, incorporated this idea but also went beyond it in calling for a verifiable ban on the production of enriched uranium and separated plutonium—not just nuclear weapons—by all states in the region. Indeed, the Arab states and Iran should signal their peaceful intent by not building or seeking to purchase nuclear facilities, including large research reactors, which have no clear relevance to their civil nuclear programs.

The reaction to the U.S. proposal in both Israel and the Arab states was not enthusiastic. For Israel, any change in a nuclear program born of the trauma of the Holocaust and generally perceived to have reaped significant benefits is bound to be difficult. Although, after the Gulf war, there are now more Israelis who are willing to consider arms-control measures in order to prevent further nuclearization in the region, there is still significant opposition to such steps and even to more open discussion of the nuclear issue in Israel. Beyond this, Israelis also insist on the need to link nuclear constraints with other arms-control measures, particularly in the area of conventional arms. And, finally, although the proposal does not refer to existing weapons, but only to future production of weapons-usable materials, the negotiation of protocols to verify nonproduction in both Israel and the Arab states is certain to be a complex undertaking.

For example, even if the Arab states could be persuaded to accept, as an interim measure, a proposal that maintained a de facto Israeli nuclear monopoly, they are not likely to accept any asymmetry in verifying compliance. If Israel insists on stringent verification measures, for example, challenge inspections by teams including Israeli nationals, then it would have to accept similar measures to be carried out by other countries. Challenges to inspect the entire Dimona facility and other sites would be likely, but they would hardly be acceptable to Israel. As in the case of providing assurances to the Arabs about Israel's nuclear doctrine, any attempts to negotiate nuclear confidence-building agreements that create demands for a high degree of transparency are not realistic at this time.

A possible solution is for Israel to shut down the Dimona reactor, and hence cease its production of plutonium, as a unilateral undertaking[22] and to convey assurances about its nuclear doctrine in private discussions and through third parties, especially the United States. By this action, Israel would also join the growing global consensus on the wisdom of a ban on the production of weapons-usable material, contribute to efforts to minimize further proliferation in the Middle East, and lessen the opprobrium of remaining outside the NPT. Further steps toward denuclearization by Israel depend on the success of efforts to bring peace to the Middle East and to minimize the risk of further proliferation. It would be naive, however, to believe that Israel's perception of a threat to its existence and its consequent reliance on a nuclear deterrent would disappear overnight with the signing of a peace treaty. Indeed, Israel may feel less secure when it trades land for peace, and some will argue that nuclear weapons are the ultimate guarantee of a smaller Israel. Realistically, it will take many years of peaceful coexistence and major political changes in the Middle East involving, among the most important, the coming to power of liberal democratic regimes in the Arab states, before Israel will forgo its nuclear insurance.

Nor can this process be significantly accelerated by Israeli acceptance of U.S. security guarantees, possibly in the guise of a formal treaty.[23] Indeed, Ben Gurion himself sought a formal guarantee for Israel's territorial integrity from the United States during the late 1950s and the early 1960s, but he was turned down by Washington primarily because of concern that such a guarantee would increase Soviet influence in the Arab world and thus jeopardize U.S. interests. By mid-1963, however, when President John F. Kennedy was trying to abort the Israeli nuclear program, it appears that Ben Gurion was opposed to trading it for a U.S. security guarantee. Instead, Ben Gurion was interested in U.S. security guarantees *in addition* to Israel's own nuclear program, possibly as a way to keep the program undeclared.

It is highly unlikely that Israel would be ready to exchange its nuclear shield now for U.S. security guarantees. And the United States would also be reluctant to provide such guarantees in a post–cold war environment in which it seeks to reduce its overseas security commitments. However, the United States can—indeed it must—play a pivotal role in brokering a nuclear agreement in the Middle East. In fact, Israel is not likely to consider any constraints on its nuclear program without some prior understandings with the United States in this area. Thus, a willingness on the part of the United States to help Israel maintain a qualitative edge in the military area, including real-time access to satellite data, could reassure Israel about its ability to respond to regional threats. And the United States needs also to reassure the Arab side and thus orchestrate a positive Arab response to Israeli agreement on nuclear constraints.

Israel was not the first state to acquire nuclear weapons and, given its unique geopolitical security concerns, it should not be expected to lead the world into the nuclear-free age. Recognition that Israel's nuclear monopoly cannot, however, be maintained forever may be one of the strongest incentives for political progress and the ultimate meaning of "nuclear learning." In the meantime, emphasis must be on learning how to "lengthen the fuse" between political disputes and the nuclear powder keg.[24]

Notes

1. Ruth Sinai, "Mideast Arms Talks," *Associated Press*, May 11, 1992.

2. UN Security Council Resolution 687 was passed on April 3, 1991; two subsequent resolutions, 707, passed on August 15, 1991, and 715, passed on October 11, 1991, reaffirmed and extended the provisions of 687 by, e.g., demanding that Iraq halt all nuclear activities except for the production of isotopes for medical purposes and approving plans for long-term monitoring of Iraqi territory.

3. For an excellent discussion of the issue of challenge inspections and other measures to improve the ability of the IAEA to deal with clandestine nuclear programs, see Lawrence Scheinman, "Assuring the Nuclear Non-Proliferation System," Occasional Paper Series, Atlantic Council of the United States (Washington, D.C., October 1992).

4. The guidelines and the control list for the dual-use export control regime were published by the IAEA in July 1992 in INF-CIRC 254, part II.

5. Yitzhak Rabin, "Only the U.S. Can Prevent Proliferation," *Davar* (in Hebrew), January 17, 1992; Ze'ev Schiff, "Race Against Time," *Politika*, no. 44 (March 1992), pp. 14–17. This view was also expressed to the authors even more strongly in interviews with Israeli policymakers and politicians in summer 1992.

6. In his inaugural speech to the Israeli Knesset on July 13, 1992, Rabin stated: "Already in its initial stages—the government—possibly with the cooperation of other countries—will give its attention to the foiling of every possibility that any of Israel's enemies should get hold of nuclear weapons." See also his article, "Taking Advantage of the Time Out," *Politika*, no. 44 (March 1992), pp. 28–29.

7. For the history and details of the Arab, particularly Egyptian, position on an NWFZ, see Mahmoud Karem, *A Nuclear-Weapons-Free Zone in the Middle East: Problems and Prospects* (Westport, Conn.: Greenwood Press, 1988).

8. See Joshua Jortner, "A Nuclear-Weapon-Free Middle East," in Sadruddin Aga Khan, ed., *Nuclear War, Nuclear Proliferation, and Their Consequences* (Oxford: Clarendon Press, 1985), pp. 170–177.

9. See Avner Cohen and Benjamin Frankel, "Opaque Nuclear Proliferation," in Benjamin Frankel, ed., *Opaque Nuclear Proliferation: Methodological and Policy Implications* (London: Frank Cass, 1991), pp. 14–44.

10. Transcript of Secretary Cheney's Press Conference, Cairo, Egypt, June 1, 1991, Office of the Secretary of Defense, Washington, D.C.

11. Geoffrey Kemp, *The Control of the Middle East Arms Race* (Washington, D.C.: Carnegie Endowment for International Peace, 1991), p. 180.

12. Shai Feldman, "New Dilemmas," *Politika*, no. 44 (March 1992), pp. 56–59.

13. See Ze'ev Schiff, "Conditional Recognition," *Ha'aretz*, April 17, 1991.

14. "Revealed: The Secrets of Israel's Nuclear Arsenal," *Sunday Times* (London), October 5, 1986; Frank Barnaby, *The Invisible Bomb: The Nuclear Arms Race in the Middle East* (London: I. B. Tauris, 1989).

15. Seymour Hersh, *The Samson Option* (New York: Random House, 1991).

16. Norman Moss, "Vanunu, Israel's Bombs, and US Aid," *Bulletin of the Atomic Scientists* 43 (May 1988), pp. 7–8.

17. Yezid Sayigh, "Reversing the Middle East Nuclear Race," *Middle East Report*, no. 177, vol. 22, no. 4 (July–August 1992), pp. 16, 17.

18. See Matthew Evangelista, *Innovation and the Arms Race* (Ithaca, N.Y.: Cornell University Press, 1988).

19. See Yair Evron, "Opaque Proliferation: The Israeli Case," in Frankel, *Opaque Nuclear Proliferation*, pp. 46–47.

20. Even some of the strongest supporters of Israel's nuclear program subscribe to the view that an Israeli bomb has little military value. See, for example, Yuval Ne'eman, "Five Reasons Against Walking on the Edge," *Politika*, no. 44 (March 1992), pp. 30–32.

21. Avner Cohen and Marvin Miller, "Facing the Unavoidable: Israel's Nuclear Monopoly Revisited" (draft), Defense and Arms Control Study Program, Massachusetts Institute of Technology, Cambridge, Mass., June 1988; and in Frankel, *Opaque Nuclear Proliferation*, pp. 68–71.

22. This suggestion has been made informally by a senior Israeli nuclear analyst.

23. Charles William Maynes, "A Necessary War?" *Foreign Policy*, no. 82 (Spring 1991), pp. 171–172.

24. Joseph S. Nye, Jr., Albert Carnesale, and Graham Allison, eds., *Fateful Vision: Avoiding Nuclear Catastrophe* (Cambridge, Mass.: Ballinger, 1988), p. 7.

Managing New Arms Races in the Asia/Pacific

Gerald Segal

ARMS RACES ARE powered by the twin engines of insecurity and the ability to pay for new weapons. With the ending of the conflict that was driven furthest by these engines—that between East and West—the global total of arms transfers is falling. But in both the Middle East and the Asia/Pacific[1] there is evidence that arms races are expanding. The Persian Gulf War of 1990–1991 has made it obvious how arms transfers affect the Middle East, but relatively little attention has been given to the risks of arms races in the Asia/Pacific. Given the particular importance of East Asia for the international market economy, the high technological standard in parts of the region, and its increasing ability to afford expensive weaponry, the risks of miscalculation are all the more significant. It should also be noted that because of the general unwillingness of leaders, mainly in East Asia, to talk explicitly about external threats to their security, it is often especially hard to identify the full extent of the risks in the region.

Statistics indicate the scope of the problem.[2] In 1991 the Asia/Pacific accounted for 35 percent of all imports of major weapons, more than any other region including Europe. In 1990, developing countries in the Asia/Pacific

accounted for 44 percent of imports of major arms by all developing states, although this figure had fallen from 59 percent in 1989. Despite a decline in the size of the global arms trade, since 1988 the states of the Asia/Pacific could be said to have held up their share of the market. Important questions need to be answered about why the region has managed to buck the trends in the international arms market and what this says about the risks of conflict in the Asia/Pacific. If the region is only beginning to enter into higher-paced arms races, perhaps this is a particularly appropriate time to try to halt the process.

Of course, it is impossible to speak of the Asia/Pacific as a coherent region.[3] Given the vast disparities in levels of development and the variety of local conflicts, it is obvious that the twin engines of the arms race are powered at different rates. In the 1970s, South Asia used to lag well behind East Asia as an importer of major arms, but in the 1980s the developing states of South Asia usually imported roughly a third more than the generally more prosperous states of East Asia. When figures for the developed states of the Asia/Pacific are included, however, East Asia ranks ahead of South Asia as an importer of arms. In the post–cold war world there are good reasons to be worried about the risks of arms races in both East and South Asia. Thus it is necessary to look in more detail at

Gerald Segal is a senior fellow at the International Institute for Strategic Studies and editor of the *Pacific Review*.

the subregional patterns of the arms trade before looking at ways in which this commerce can be controlled.

Who Buys Weapons in the Region?

Of the leading importers of major conventional arms among countries of the developing world in 1987–1991, 7 Asia/Pacific states were to be found in the top 15.[4] Three of the top five importers among all countries included (in rank order) India, Japan, and Afghanistan. The other major importers in the Asia/Pacific in this period were North Korea, South Korea, Thailand, Pakistan, and Taiwan (see table 1).

Two obvious conclusions emerge from these data. First, Asia/Pacific states are among the leading importers of major arms. Second, there appears to be great variation in the reasons for the presence of Asia/Pacific states at the top of these lists. Indeed, taking into consideration the relative wealth of the importer and the extent to which the country is in a state of high tension, one can divide the Asia/Pacific states into four theoretical categories: (1) those with high wealth and low insecurity; (2) those with high wealth and higher insecurity; (3) those with low wealth and low insecurity; and (4) those with low wealth and high insecurity. Categories (2) and (4) are the most worrisome, but it should be borne in mind that some countries with high levels of insecurity, such as Sri Lanka or Myanmar, are primarily concerned with domestic insecurities. Category (3) states are not considered here because they do not figure either as major security risks or as major arms buyers.

High Wealth and Low Insecurity. In the first category there are states such as Japan and Australia which, to some

extent like the states of the North Atlantic Treaty Organization (NATO), import high-technology weapons but with little immediate prospect of using them in combat. These are rich states that can easily afford such purchases, and their percentage of military spending is relatively low. They are not involved in any direct and dangerous conflict, but their countries have more general responsibilities for defense and deterrence of threats that have, in the post–cold war world, become even more diffuse.

To be sure, there is always the risk that these weapons might be used in conflict. Australia and New Zealand, unlike Japan, took part in the allied effort led by the United States in the second Persian Gulf War, although they were hardly in the forefront of the military campaign (the first war in the Persian Gulf was between Iraq and Iran). None of these developed states runs any serious risk of major combat, and the ending of the Cold War has forced them to rethink their security strategy.

It is more than likely that most of these states, as in the case of NATO members, will reduce defense spending and also reduce arms purchases. But major question marks remain over the important case of Japan, which ranks so high in the list. Japan finds itself under increased pressure from some in the United States to spend more on "burden sharing" in defense, and Americans also urge more Japanese purchases of U.S. weapons as a way of helping to balance the U.S. trade deficit with Japan. When the Soviet Union was seen as the major threat in East Asia, it was easier to make the case for increased Japanese spending. But with the disintegration of the Soviet Union and the fact that, unlike in Europe, there is relatively little fragmentation of the former

Table 1
Arms Trade in the Asia/Pacific, 1987–1991

	Arms Imports, 1987–1991 (in million U.S.$)	Arms Imports as % of GNP, 1991	Military Expenditure as % of GNP, 1989	Military Expenditure per capita (in U.S.$)	Arms Imports as % of Total Imports, 1989	Arms Exports, 1989 (in million U.S.$)
India	17,562	6.0	3.1	10	17.1	—
Japan	9,750	0.3	1.0	231	0.7	110
Afghanistan	8,430[a]	210.0	n.a.	n.a.	462.0	—
Korea, North	4,631	10.0	20.0	285	n.a.	400
Korea, South	3,552	1.0	4.3	213	0.6	40
Thailand	3,370	4.0	2.7	33	1.0	—
Australia	2,956	1.0	2.3	368	1.5	80
Pakistan	2,299	6.0	6.8	22	6.4	20
Taiwan	2,174	1.0	5.4	397	0.8	10
Indonesia	1,429	1.0	1.7	8	0.5	10
Singapore	1,276	4.0	5.1	550	0.2	70
People's Republic of China	797	0.2	3.7	20	0.2	2,000
Bangladesh	552	2.7	1.6	3	3.3	—
Cambodia	318	31.0	n.a.	n.a.	n.a.	—
Sri Lanka	274	3.0	3.2	13	0.5	—
Myanmar	268	1.0	3.7	15	9.5	—
Philippines	144	0.3	2.2	15	0.6	—
Laos	133	26.0	n.a.	n.a.	45.7	—
New Zealand	106	0.2	2.2	258	0.6	—
Malaysia	105	0.2	2.9	61	0.3	—
Brunei	34	1.0	n.a.	n.a.	n.a.	—
Vietnam	6	0.0	n.a.	n.a.	n.a.	—

Sources: *SIPRI Yearbook, 1992*; IISS, *Military Balance, 1991–1992*; ACDA, *World Military Expenditures, 1990*.

[a] Arms were transferred rather than purchased; their gross value far exceeded both Afghan GNP and economic imports.

Union in East Asia, the pressure for increased Japanese defense spending should ease. But the Soviet Union's demise has also meant that pressure has grown for a U.S. military withdrawal from the region and no multilateral security networks exist to help fill the vacuum. The result may well be that Japan takes up some of the slack from the Americans, and thus it may well remain a major arms importer.

High Wealth and Higher Insecurities. The second major group of states includes those that face a greater risk of conflict and that have some national wealth, although less than Japan and Australia, and therefore find the burden of arms purchases heavier. Singapore (ranked 10th in the region) and Malaysia (ranked 19th) are obvious cases in point. Thailand's ranking, 6th, was in part caused by its involvement with the Cambodian conflict, and in any case, according to some theories about military regimes, the character of its armed forces was always likely to keep arms spending high.

Of course, in face of a request to control arms transfers these Southeast Asian states can point to reasonable levels of insecurity and their reasonable ability to support defense spending and arms purchases. They can all talk about the uncertainty surrounding the settlement of the Cambodia problem and the insecurity related to the retreat of the superpowers. Some will also talk of worry about the intentions of the People's Republic of China (PRC) in the South China Sea. Other uncertainties include the somewhat more hidden rivalries among the members of the Association of Southeast Asian Nations (ASEAN), and especially that between Malaysia and Singapore.[5] As in the first category, there

is little immediate likelihood that the weapons being purchased will be used, although in the medium term there are real risks of conflict. Although these states are less wealthy than those in the first category, they are certainly all growing economies that find the defense burden much easier to bear than poorer states. Yet these states often have well-educated populations who can handle the higher-technology (and more expensive) weapons and after the Gulf War think it even more essential to acquire the latest. As with the first category, one can feel relatively at ease about these purchases, although there are real risks of arms races in new technology.

Low Wealth and High Insecurity. But such relative complacency is not sensible when we look at the final category of states, which are in much more imminent risk of conflict and where arms purchases are part of an already-active arms race. In many, but not all cases, these are states that are far less developed and cannot really bear such a heavy defense burden without impoverishing their people. This is the category of arms importers that should be of greatest immediate concern. India and Afghanistan rank at the top of this worry list, and Pakistan (ranked 8th in the region and 13th among all developing states) is not far behind.

South Asia has a long and bloody history. This is not the place to explain the course of this history, but it is important to point out that with continuing tension between India and Pakistan, simmering civil war in Afghanistan, and disintegration of the old order in Central Asia, there is plenty of tinder for the fire of arms races and war. Although it is true that Afghanistan itself is likely to move down the list of arms purchasers, its uncertain status will help feed the insecurity and arms races.

Some evidence suggests that both India and Pakistan may also reduce arms imports. The disintegration of the Soviet Union, the ending of the Cold War, and problems in the Indian economy have all led to a sharp reduction in Soviet arms sales to India. Of course, in the short term, the "bargain basement clearance" of arms from the former Soviet Union may lead to an extraordinary increase in arms purchases, and there is also important evidence that many of the cash-strapped parts of the former Soviet defense industry see arms sales as a high priority.[6] As a result, it is especially difficult to get states in regions of high insecurity to think clearly about their priorities in controlling arms transfers. Yet it is already apparent that Pakistan is finding it far harder to obtain large numbers of weapons from its former friends in the United States. Although none of this suggests that India and Pakistan cannot go to war, for example over Kashmir, on balance the incentives for restraint are growing as the ability to fill arsenals, especially with high-technology weapons, is reduced. The odds must be that in the short term, South Asians will also move down the list of arms importers.[7]

Of course, in the medium term concern is warranted. The disintegration of the Soviet Union has led to the emergence of a number of independent states in Central Asia. As none of these units has natural borders and rivalries are more than likely to develop, India and Pakistan may well become drawn in. Kazakhstan may well be a nuclear weapons state, a situation that will further complicate a region that includes apparently nuclear-armed, or nearly so, Russia, the PRC, India, and Pakistan. Already a worrying amount of evidence suggests that some of the new Central Asian states (most notably Kazakhstan) are exploring ways not only to produce weapons, but possibly even to sell them.[8]

Although in the short term relative confidence can be expressed about South Asia, the same cannot be said for some states in East Asia. North Korea (ranked 10th among the world's importers of major conventional arms) and South Korea (ranked 15th) are still locked in the region's most dangerous rivalry. Although South Korea has been making major diplomatic and economic gains in recent years, North Korea has felt itself to be both increasingly insecure and decreasingly able to afford an arms race with the South. The PRC apparently first triggered North Korean concern in the early 1980s when it opened economic relations with South Korea and made the North feel increasingly isolated. The reduction in assistance from the Soviet Union added to pressure on Pyongyang and has been a major reason why the regime has apparently been seeking to develop nuclear weapons. The disintegration of the Soviet Union in 1991 has left North Korea at the mercy of a PRC that is still committed to increased economic reform and opening to the international market economy.

It is likely that North Korea will move down the list of purchasers of conventional arms, if only because there will be few states willing to sell it or, more accurately, give it weapons. South Korea is likely to hold its position as it continues to fear the consequences of uncertainty in North Korea and plan for the crisis that must come with the succession to Kim Il Sung. With the removal of U.S. nuclear weapons from South Korea announced in the autumn of 1991, and continuing uncertainty about North Korea's nuclear intentions, South Korea may well find it easier to purchase conventional arms from the United States as a means of keeping a regional balance of power.

Further down the East Asian coast is Taiwan (ranked 9th among arms buyers in the region and 14th among all developing states), which still confronts the PRC in the unresolved civil war. Although Taiwan is far richer than the PRC, its level of insecurity is far higher, if only because of the vast disparity in size and military power. Although the PRC is able to maintain an indigenous arms industry, Taiwan depends on complex arrangements whereby it can purchase components for arms or arrange coproduction deals. Because of its political isolation, Taiwan must scramble more than most to provide for its own defense and thus the figures for its purchases of defense equipment do not always reflect the larger program of defense deals. For example, the agreement with France to buy six frigates is hard to assess because they are being delivered in pieces and are officially not a sale of complete warships.

It is hard to see the PRC–Taiwan rivalry ending in the near future and therefore Taiwan is likely to remain high on the list. Should the PRC run into increasing problems with the developed world over trade and human rights issues, Taiwan might well find it easier to increase its arms purchases. Taiwan is certainly able to bear such an economic burden with relative ease and indeed a more open system for defense procurement from abroad might actually reduce its overall defense burden.

In sum, although the Asia/Pacific does have some of the world's most important purchasers of major arms, not all the main buyers can be considered as being at major risk of using these weapons in war. The richer states of East Asia are likely to remain the highest up the list of buyers, but only in the case of Korea and Taiwan is there a serious risk of conflict. Tension in Southeast Asia may develop, but more in the medium term. Concern over potential conflict in South Asia may decline in the short term, although worry about political fragmentation in the shatter-zone of Central Asia must make for more worry in the medium term. Indeed, the relatively large number of issues that fall into the category of medium-term worry suggests it is particularly urgent to move now to control potential arms races and conflicts.

Who Transfers Weapons to the Region?

In the 1987–1991 period, the transfer of major conventional arms to the Asia/Pacific was dominated by the then superpowers (see table 2). The Soviet Union accounted for 45 percent of transfers and the United States accounted for 35 percent of the market. West European states accounted for 10 percent, led by Britain with 4.4 percent, France with 2.5 percent, and Germany with 1 percent. The PRC was the only other important seller to the region, accounting for 5.8 percent of the market. The most obvious conclusion from these statistics is that the number of arms suppliers is relatively small. Perhaps, therefore, arms supplies might be controlled with relative ease if there were sufficient political will. But the motives and the circumstances of the arms suppliers differ and may not be so easily controlled.

The Former Soviet Union. Beginning with the nominal market leader—the

Table 2
Arms Imports in the Asia/Pacific by Source, 1987–1991
(In million U.S. dollars)

Importing Country	Total Arms Imports	Exporting Country						
		Soviet Union	USA	France	UK	PRC	Germany	Other Europe
India	17,562	13,871	—	882	1,516	—	254	—
Japan	9,750	—	9,537	49	164	—	—	—
Afghanistan	8,430	8,125	149	1	43	48	—	22
Korea, North	4,631	4,217	—	—	—	414	—	—
Korea, South	3,552	—	3,273	46	150	—	—	69
Thailand	3,370	—	1,635	132	143	1,290	50	90
Australia	2,956	—	2,727	54	61	—	—	10
Pakistan	2,299	—	795	33	158	1,027	—	19
Taiwan	2,174	—	1,373	—	—	—	—	476
Indonesia	1,429	—	486	60	375	—	122	348
Singapore	1,276	—	1,031	101	—	—	144	—
PRC	797	497	113	163	5	—	—	—
Bangladesh	552	—	12	—	—	355	—	—
Cambodia	318	170	—	—	—	20	—	—
Sri Lanka	274	—	12	—	—	158	—	3
Myanmar	268	—	—	—	—	222	—	—
Philippines	144	—	101	—	4	—	5	27
Laos	133	125	—	—	—	2	—	—
New Zealand	106	—	23	—	2	—	—	24
Malaysia	105	—	—	11	52	—	—	33
Brunei	34	—	12	18	—	—	—	4
Vietnam	6	6	—	—	—	—	—	—
Total	60,166	27,011	21,279	1,550	2,673	3,536	575	1,451

Source: *SIPRI Yearbook, 1992.*

former Soviet Union—the picture is relatively simple and yet subject to massive change. The Soviet Union sold to just seven countries in the region, and just three of these (India, Afghanistan, and North Korea) dominated the purchase ledger. Vietnam used to rank far higher up the list, but it declined to acquire Soviet weaponry as it withdrew from Cambodia and concentrated on economic reform. The PRC began purchasing small quantities of Soviet arms in the late 1980s, and although there were signs of a major deal in 1990–1991, the August 1991 revolution in Russia apparently has given the Chinese pause for thought.[9]

Indeed, the revolution in the former Soviet Union will have a major impact on the pattern of arms transfers to the Asia/Pacific region. With new regimes emerging from the entrails of the former superpower, it is hard to envisage a major program of arms transfers, except in the unusual category of the clearing of old weapons stocks in an urgent search for cash. Although it is true that the defense industry in the former Soviet Union is still producing weapons, they are often left uncompleted because the integrated weapons production system has broken down. The decline of interrepublican economic cooperation makes it unlikely that the former Soviet defense industry can be reconstituted. Of course, where finished products can be completed, it may well be that some of the former republics will try to increase sales as a way of earning vital foreign exchange.

But none of the former Soviet Union's partners is in a position to pay cash for such weapons. India in particular, which accounted for 51 percent of all Soviet arms transfers to the region, cannot afford major arms purchases in the near future. North Korea is being denied weapons by the new regime in Russia, which is improving relations with South Korea. Similarly, the Afghan regime is being cut off from most of its military supplies as Russia seeks aid from the West. Thus it is a better than decent bet that in the next few years the successor states to the Soviet Union will cease to be major arms suppliers to the region. The Central Asian states may well be involved in small arms deals with the region but it is unlikely that any former republic apart from Russia will emerge in the longer term with a major arms industry.[10]

The United States. The picture is radically different in the case of the United States. Its market share in the Asia/Pacific is bound to increase to well over two-thirds in the coming years. In the 1987–1991 period it supplied 15 countries, ranging from Brunei to Japan. The more developed countries, and most notably Japan (45 percent of U.S. sales to the Asia/Pacific region), South Korea (15 percent), and Australia (13 percent), accounted for over two-thirds of U.S. sales. The first two of these markets are likely to remain buoyant, and others, including Taiwan (6 percent of U.S. sales to the region) and Singapore (5 percent) are likely to increase in importance. With the defense cuts in the United States the pressure may well grow to export weapons as a way of reducing costs of shorter production runs.

Of course, some U.S. markets are likely to fade. Australia is unlikely to hold its position as, like most NATO states, it cuts back defense spending. Pakistan (4 percent) may well seek to increase its purchases but the United States will probably be reluctant to cooperate. Thailand (8 percent), despite uncertainty about some of its ASEAN colleagues or Myanmar, is likely to hold steady or even decrease its demand as the Cambodian issue is edged toward a less intense conflict.

It seems clear that the major responsibility for arms transfers to the region will fall on the United States and thus the means to control the process will also be primarily in U.S. hands. Of course, the situation is not so simple, if only because there exist significant domestic sources of weapons in the region, most notably in the PRC. Without the cooperation of the PRC, the prospects for arms control are limited.

The PRC. The PRC's attitude is important not merely because it accounts for 5.8 percent of exports to the states of the Asia/Pacific (to nine countries), but more because the PRC itself is a major power in the region and the local power with the most powerful defense industry. The PRC's arms transfers to Afghanistan, Sri Lanka, and Laos are not significant either in terms of these states' total arms purchases or in terms of fueling local conflict. Transfers to Myanmar are not a threat to international security, but they are offensive because of the unsavory nature of the regime.[11]

Only the PRC's sales to Pakistan and North Korea have been a serious cause of concern. If, as seems likely, India purchases far fewer weapons from the successor states of the Soviet Union, then it may be more worrying if the PRC continues to transfer arms to Pakistan, and especially worrying if there is a relative increase because the U.S. and European arms transfers to Pakistan decline. Persistent reports in 1991 cited Chinese M–11 missile sales to Pakistan and a growing concern on

the part of the United States that this sale was destabilizing to the regional balance.[12] Equally, as the former Soviet Union fades as an arms supplier to North Korea, the PRC may fill the gap and thereby keep the pressure on South Korea to keep buying arms from the United States. But at least in this case the PRC has been improving its relations with South Korea and therefore has a more obvious interest in restricting its arms transfers to North Korea. Such Chinese self-interest might well be the basis for international arms control in Northeast Asia, while not necessarily applying to Central and South Asia.

Less optimism is warranted about those conflicts in which the PRC itself is a major player, most notably regarding Taiwan and the South China Sea. Although the PRC's rivalry with Vietnam has declined and therefore the pressure on Hanoi to spend on defense equipment is fading, the pressure on Taiwan and the ASEAN states remains active. If serious efforts are to be made to keep ASEAN states from wasting money on an arms race, then the PRC—the main potential threat for many states in the region—will have to be brought into the arms-control process. As the former Soviet Union pulls out of the region as a major naval power and even the United States scales back its forces, concern grows in Southeast Asia about an unchecked PRC. Southeast Asians also worry that Japan may feel it necessary to fill the gap left by the retreating superpowers, and that this in turn might encourage a further growth in Chinese naval power in the region. This cycle of uncertainty feeds off overlapping territorial claims in the South China Sea and the impetus that is thereby given to states in the region to spend on high-technology weapons, especially in equipment for naval and air warfare.[13]

Western Europe. The final group of arms suppliers—the West Europeans—plays only a marginal role in Asia. Although France and Britain each sold to 12 states, and Germany sold to 5 in the region, in only one case were the Europeans the major arms supplier. By far the largest sales were to India, but even here the Europeans accounted for only 21 percent of the total. As suggested earlier, the Indian market is already beginning to decline, although there must be some prospect for an increase in the European share of the Indian market as the Soviet Union fades as a supplier.

The only exception to the rule of Europeans as marginal suppliers is Indonesia, where 63 percent of arms sales were made by Europeans, led by Britain and Holland. Important markets are also to be found in Singapore, but in most cases the main competitor for market share is the United States, which is unlikely to draw back. Europeans can make a contribution to the process of arms control, and with the disintegration of the Soviet Union they are emerging, along with the PRC, as one of the major parts of any possible deal on limiting arms transfers to the Asia/Pacific.

Who Sells From the Region?

Although in general the states of the Asia/Pacific are clearly major arms importers, they are, as a group, only minor arms exporters. There are some notable exceptions, in particular the PRC, however, that raise real concern about arms exports from the region. South Asian states barely register on the global list as arms exporters, but arms exports in 1989 from East Asia were worth $2.6 billion (0.5 percent of

total East Asian exports), compared to $7 billion by NATO Europe (0.6 percent of total NATO Europe exports). No other region apart from the United States accounted for more arms exports. The rise of East Asian countries as arms exporters has been relatively recent; in 1979 East Asia exported $788 million in constant 1989 dollars (0.2 percent of total exports), compared to $8.1 billion by European NATO states (1 percent of exports).

An obvious conclusion is that East Asia must now be considered as more than just an importer of weapons. East Asians are also important players as arms sellers. Yet further investigation reveals that most of the increase in the East Asian profile can be attributed to a few very straightforward factors. Only 2 countries in East Asia ranked among the top 15 exporters of major conventional arms to the developing world in the 1986–1990 period—the PRC (ranked 4th) and North Korea (ranked 15th). Neither of these states figures among the major exporters to the developed world, and for 1991 only the PRC ranked in the top 15 of total arms exporters (4th place). In the 1979–1988 period, the PRC accounted for 57 percent of total arms sales by states in East Asia and Australasia. North Korea accounted for 17 percent, South Korea for 14 percent (mostly in 1982–1984), Japan for 7 percent, and Australia for 2 percent.[14] By the late 1980s when East Asia began to assume importance as a source of arms exports, only the PRC and North Korea were significant actors. In 1989, fully 73 percent of arms exports from East Asia came from the PRC (North Korea accounted for another 15 percent).

Of the PRC's total export of major conventional weapons in the 1987–1991 period, 45 percent went to Asia/Pacific states. The rest, and by far the largest percentage of the growth in

PRC arms exports in the late 1980s, went to the Middle East. The PRC did particularly good business during the first Persian Gulf War and when that war ended, Chinese arms sales dropped sharply, at least in dollar terms (from $1,930 million in 1988 to $1,127 million in 1991 in constant 1990 dollars). But as a percentage of the overall, and rapidly shrinking, market the PRC's share only fell from 6.3 percent in 1987 to 5.1 percent in 1991.

The second Persian Gulf War clearly reopens the possibilities for the PRC to improve its market share. The PRC has developed a reputation for selling relatively cheap but less sophisticated weapons, although it also supplied medium-range ballistic missiles to Saudi Arabia and in 1991 was reported to have made deals with Iran and Algeria concerning nuclear technology.[15] The PRC has certainly joined the front rank of weapons dealers, although it is true that it has usually not opened markets in the developing world and the largest PRC deals are usually in areas where the other great powers have long been active in the same business. Reports of PRC sales of M–9 missiles to Syria would fall into this category.[16] North Korea has been a much paler shadow of the PRC, with special expertise in exporting missiles.[17]

The relatively restricted number of arms exporters accounting for the impressive East Asian showing in recent years might suggest that limiting exports would be a relatively easy task. But the PRC has long proved difficult to cajole into international agreements of this sort, and North Korea is drifting even further from a position where it might be subject to rational negotiations. The PRC has shown that it can be pressed to take a more constructive approach to international arms control, as seen in its agreement in November 1991 to abide by the terms of the Missile Technology Control Regime (MTCR). The PRC also joined the meeting in Paris in July 1991 to discuss limiting arms sales to the Middle East. But one thing is clear: any agreement to deal with the growth in arms sales in the Asia/Pacific will have to focus on the PRC and North Korea, which constitute the two most difficult problems among the region's major local exporters.

Proliferating Nuclear Weapons

In part because of general concern with the nuclear capability of Iraq, the issue of nuclear weapons proliferation has returned to the top of the arms-control agenda. But it is in the Asia/Pacific region that the greatest risks of proliferation exist. Although the PRC's relations with Algeria, Syria, and Iran regarding nuclear technology and India's rumored deals with Iran are both worrying, the main focus of attention is on Central Asia and Northeast Asia.

With the breakup of the Soviet Union, a set of new states has emerged in Central Asia. One of them, Kazakhstan, has more nuclear weapons on its territory than any other Asian state, as well as a major nuclear weapons test site.[18] Although it is true that the vast majority of the these nuclear weapons are set to be destroyed under the agreement following the Strategic Arms Reduction Talks (START), and the weapons are apparently still under the control of Russian-dominated forces, it is not certain that the agreement will be fully implemented. In any case, even complete compliance would still leave more nuclear weapons in Kazakhstan than in any country in Asia other than the PRC and Russia. Powerful voices in Alma Ata argue for the need to retain nuclear weapons in an environment where security is uncertain. Westerners also fear that some of the new Central Asian states may try to export uranium or even nuclear specialists and their know-how. U.S. officials, including the secretary of state, visited the region in early 1992 and claim to have been given assurances that non-Russian missiles will be disabled or removed by 1995, but other reports from Central Asia suggest far more equivocation. As the question of who controls the weapons in Kazakhstan and Central Asia is sorted out, a great deal of ambiguity will remain about whether Asia has just acquired another nuclear weapons power. Given the uncertainty about so many fundamental issues concerning the former Soviet Union it seems likely that, at least in the medium term, Kazakhstan will become an important player in discussions about nuclear weapons issues in Central and South Asia.[19]

This lack of clarity increases the pressure on the already complex nuclear weapons configuration in Central and South Asia that links Russia, the PRC, India, and Pakistan. Rumors have long circulated about the extent of the Pakistani nuclear program and the part that the PRC may have played in it.[20] Little hard evidence is available in the public domain, but it seems possible that the uncertainties that are developing in Central Asia may well add to the pressure for Pakistan to openly declare its nuclear hand. Under such circumstances it is probably too late to stop the proliferation of nuclear weapons in this region, but the stage may well be set for more formal negotiations on building confidence about the handling of nuclear weapons among what increasingly looks like five nuclear powers.

India appears to be under particular

pressure in the period after the disintegration of the Soviet Union. It was painful for India to note in November 1991 that the then Soviet Union's line had shifted to supporting the notion of a nuclear weapons free zone in South Asia, an idea long opposed by India because of its concerns with PRC nuclear power. But in that month India agreed to consider a proposal for a conference on the issue that would include the United States, Russia, the PRC, India, and Pakistan. India still refused to sign the Nuclear Non-Proliferation Treaty (NPT), although France and the PRC had recently changed their views. India also knew that many Western states would reduce their aid if it persisted with high military spending and an uncooperative approach to controlling the risks of nuclear confrontation. The United States, for one, was, in the absence of an effective Russian leadership, at the forefront of the effort to control the risks of tension in the region. Pakistan, too, felt that it was more insecure in the post–cold war days because it feared Indian conventional military power and no longer had leverage on the West by virtue of its anti-Soviet and anti-Indian policy.[21]

The position in Northeast Asia is less a matter of confirmed nuclear proliferation, but there are far greater risks if the region should become focused on a nuclear confrontation. Of course, the PRC and Russia are acknowledged nuclear weapons powers in the region. The United States had a policy of neither confirming nor denying the presence of nuclear weapons in South Korea, but few doubted the presence of these weapons as a deterrent to another Korean war. In October 1991, as part of a clarification of the U.S. position about reducing nuclear weapons in the post–cold war world, it was announced that the

United States would withdraw all nuclear weapons from South Korea and from ships in Pacific waters. Of course, because the United States could easily fly in weapons from storage across the Pacific, the United States must still be considered a major nuclear weapons power in the Pacific.

These three nuclear powers have long been known to have leaned on their allies in Korea to eschew the development of nuclear weapons. South Korea joined the NPT under strong U.S. pressure, as did North Korea under Soviet pressure. But in the early 1990s, with the military and political balance clearly shifting in South Korea's favor, concern has grown that North Korea is developing nuclear weapons.[22] North Korea initially refused to allow inspections of all its nuclear facilities by the International Atomic Energy Agency (IAEA) because Pyongyang claimed the U.S. weapons in the South should also be examined. When the United States called North Korea's bluff by promising to withdraw all nuclear weapons, the pressure was stepped up on North Korea to agree to a full inspection. Even the PRC exerted pressure, albeit in private, by threatening to establish diplomatic relations with South Korea unless the North undertook a serious détente with the South and agreed to halt its nuclear program. The North has moved on the first condition and yet is still dragging its heels on the second. U.S. officials remain very doubtful about whether the North will allow full inspections and even about the South's ability and interest in carrying out thorough investigations.[23]

Although it seems obvious that both the Soviet Union and the PRC might have been instrumental in helping North Korea start on the road to a nuclear weapons capability, neither Russia nor the PRC wants to see such a program come to fruition. The pressure is on to limit, and quickly, the possibility that Northeast Asia will become a zone with four nuclear powers. But if North Korea should move closer to a nuclear capability, then the pressure may well rapidly escalate for South Korea and Japan to make it six nuclear powers in Northeast Asia. Of course, Japan has lived with the threat of PRC and Soviet nuclear weapons and may well not see a North Korean bomb as requiring a change in its own nonnuclear status. But uncertainty may well grow in Japan about the reliability of the U.S. nuclear umbrella and under such circumstances, a nuclear-armed North Korea may well bring Japan into the nuclear weapons club.

Controlling the Arms Trade

The discussion about how to control the arms trade in the Asia/Pacific is still in its infancy. In a sense this is understandable, if only because the rise of the region as both a market and a supplier of weapons is relatively new. What is more, discussions about arms control in the region have only recently begun to grow more sophisticated. Earlier notions about zones of peace, nuclear weapons free zones, or even a Conference on Security and Cooperation in Asia (CSCA) based on the relatively successful Conference on Security and Cooperation in Europe (CSCE), have now been sidelined. More complex and current efforts to deal with the post–cold war reality are now taking shape.[24] Various strands among them might be woven together in order to smother the risks of major arms races or even conflicts.

Building on Existing Arrangements. One set of initiatives would build on existing agreements and institutions. Current efforts to stop the proliferation of nuclear weapons are being strengthened, especially in light of the obvious loopholes that became apparent as the Iraqi nuclear weapons program was being dismantled. In this respect, the main challenge is the question of North Korean intentions and whether the IAEA mechanisms can be beefed up rapidly enough to monitor them closely. Although serious thought is being given to the kinds of powers that the IAEA might need, it is increasingly clear that it will be difficult to reach agreement fast enough to stop North Korea. The PRC still looks set to block any effort to transfer the matter to the United Nations (UN) Security Council and therefore the main pressure will have to be exerted by the interested great powers. Discussions about a U.S. military option grow more important but it remains true that the risks would be far greater than in the Iraqi case.

The role of the IAEA in the Central Asian case is less urgent, if only because Kazakhstan and perhaps other Central Asian states may have passed quite legitimately through a vast loophole in the system. No one really thought that the collapse of the Soviet Union might give rise to a real risk of nuclear proliferation. Nevertheless, the IAEA could be useful, especially if it were given greater funds, in monitoring the destruction of nuclear weapons in the former Central Asian republics and checking on the disposition of facilities in the fuel cycle of the former Soviet Union's nuclear weapon system.

Other efforts, for example, the development of an effective MTCR, might also be useful in the region. As the number of participants has increased in the wake of the second Gulf War, far more attention needs to be paid to signing up new members in Asia. This arrangement is still far from effective, but it is a good example of multilateral efforts that are making progress.

New Efforts to Control Conventional Weapons. It should be remembered that the existence of weapons per se is not necessarily a problem; rather it is the assessment of the capability and intentions of those who own them that is so crucial. And yet when one ventures into the realm of intentions, subjective judgments complicate efforts to reach international agreement. Nevertheless, international organizations have offered some intriguing notions about ways to limit arms transfers and spending on weapons. Their initiatives are important because it is clear that contrary to the trend in much of the rest of the post–cold war world, defense spending in Asia is rising.[25]

The International Monetary Fund (IMF), led by several Western states, has developed the notion that states that spend more than 4.5 percent of their gross domestic product (GDP) on arms will have their aid cut.[26] On average, Asian nations currently spend 2.1 percent of GDP on arms, with North Korea (20 percent), Pakistan (6.8 percent), Taiwan (5.4 percent), and Singapore (5.1 percent) leading the region. Others probably over the limit but for which detailed information is hard to come by include Vietnam, Afghanistan, Cambodia, Laos, and Mongolia.[27] Of course there are major problems in properly measuring defense spending and in comparing figures between states that are in real danger, those that are in arms races, and those with large enough GDPs to support massive spending that is still below the 4.5 percent global average (such as the PRC). What is one to do with small states, some of which are primarily concerned with domestic threats to stability? And, of course, the United States spends 5.5 percent of GDP on its armed forces. Nevertheless, it may be possible to find a composite list of criteria for those spending excessive amounts on weaponry as set out in table 1. It certainly seems hard to argue with those states that do not wish to provide aid to those that spend vast and unnecessary amounts on weapons.

One of the newest ideas for developing criteria on which to judge states comes from the United Nations and the G–7, which have both explored the concept of an arms register. Although this scheme began as an effort to commit exporters and importers to declaring their part in the arms transfer business and to build confidence through transparency, it has developed into a broader attempt to register the size of arsenals. Such a scheme would certainly have a beneficial effect in the Asia/Pacific, but many states in the region have been among the main stumbling blocks. When the UN General Assembly's First Committee approved a resolution to set up an arms sales register, it was adopted by 106 to 1, but of the eight states that abstained, five were from Asia (the PRC, North Korea, Pakistan, Myanmar, and Singapore). Only one Asian state—Japan—was a sponsoring state. When the General Assembly voted for the arms sales register, the PRC refused to participate.

In some respects, the problem from the Asian point of view was with the very notion of transparency in a political culture that values face and elaborate efforts to protect it. Many Asian states prefer not to confront unsavory issues directly or in public and prefer pragmatic solutions behind closed doors. European and Japanese officials turned initial reluctance into grudging acceptance of the arms register after heavy diplomatic pressure at the end of 1991. The Netherlands led the effort by the European Community (EC), and some concessions were made to the worries of less developed countries that opposed the emphasis on weapons imports instead of exports. In effect, this process was also an invitation to the major importers to come together to restrict arms exports. In 1992 detailed efforts are under way to agree on specific categories of weapons, and it would not be unreasonable for aid donors or even those wishing to transfer high technology to demand full compliance with the arms register before signing a deal. As already noted, a relatively small number of countries export arms to the Asia/Pacific, and an effort that focused on the permanent five of the UN Security Council would cover most of the major arms exporters (93 percent of exports in the 1987–1991 period). But even if the effort were to be concentrated on the aid and technology transfer policies of North American and EC states, in the coming years it might be possible to cajole states into accepting a UN-sponsored "military balance" that could be verified by an international agency and subjected to challenge inspections.

A New Multilateralism? What is so striking about discussions of building better security in the Asia/Pacific region is the virtual absence of any multilateral mechanism. Europeans are blanketed by NATO, the Western European Union (WEU), the CSCE, and now perhaps even a security role for the EC. These structures have helped limit the spread of conflict in Yugoslavia, manage the transition in Central Europe, and prevent panic as the Soviet Union disintegrates. No similar schemes exist to moderate the uncertainties in the Asia/Pacific region.

To some extent there might be a role for a CSCE process that by virtue of its reach from Vancouver to Vladivostok already touched on Asia/Pacific issues. And now that CSCE membership has been extended to the new states of Central Asia (at the Prague Summit in January 1992), an argument could be made that existing mechanisms are already being extended into Asia. But it seems even less sensible to deal with complex security issues on a Eurasian basis when it is already clear that even approaches aimed at the whole Asia/Pacific region are far too vague and vast.

More interestingly, an increasingly sophisticated series of proposals, most notably from the Canadians, have called for the creation of a "habit of dialogue" for "cooperative security" for the North Pacific.[28] But this approach is still in its infancy, as are notions that ASEAN will now take on a major security agenda. It may be that many of the proposals already identified—such as strengthening the IAEA, an arms register, or even nuclear free zones—might be usefully tackled in these subregional forums. It certainly seems necessary to focus arms-control efforts on specific problems and/or specific subregions.

Perhaps a return to basic principles would be most useful. At its core, the arms trade is a result of political insecurity, which is best tackled by a political solution. By themselves, arms transfers are not necessarily a major problem. The dangers begin when it becomes likely that these weapons will be used in conflict and/or states will acquire weapons that they really cannot afford. As already suggested,

weapons acquisitions in the region seem to vary in the degree of danger they present. Some of the old trends are being changed, not by political agreement but by the rapidly changing course of international events. Unilateral arms cuts have taken place along the Sino–Soviet frontier and on the Sino–Vietnamese border. Soviet naval forces have been pulled back to home ports, Vietnamese troops are out of Cambodia, and U.S. forces are withdrawing from the Philippines and being thinned out in many other parts of East Asia. India has pulled its troops back from Sri Lanka and must reduce its defense budget for economic reasons. Much of this can be described as spontaneous arms control—part of the process of informal arms control that was apparent in the 1980s.[29]

But for all the progress toward order in the region, it is apparent that the rapidly changing political events have thrown up aspects of a new disorder as well. Central Asia must be considered among the most dangerous of the new shatter-zones. Arms transfers in neighboring states, which were already changing direction because of the end of the Cold War and altering domestic economic priorities, will change again because of the disintegration of the Soviet Union. New risks will soon be mirrored in new patterns of arms transfers. Attempts to build political confidence in the region must be initiated at once if they are to stand any chance of limiting the subregional arms race.

Further around the Asia/Pacific rim in Southeast Asia, the risks of insecurity are more controllable. These concern the South China Sea and the general question of Chinese irredentism. At least this subregion has more of a tradition of multilateralism, but the ASEAN experience does not suggest that difficult issues will always be handled well, especially in the security sphere. The states of this region, among them states increasingly able to afford an arms race, look set to carry on building up their arsenals, although their use seems less likely than in the states of the far more unstable Central Asian environment.

Northeast Asia presents the greatest risk if tensions develop. The nuclear weapons factor in that region makes it all the more essential that the question of Korean reunification be handled carefully. This subregion seems most ripe for an à la carte approach to security that focuses on specific agreements to control weapons in readily identifiable areas. The primary focus of attention will be on inducing North Korea to be more cooperative and keeping South Korea behind a tough policy of intrusive inspections while this delicate process is managed.

Conclusion

It can be argued that the Asia/Pacific region has only a few major potential flash points and relatively few arms suppliers, and that it offers some evidence that informal and unilateral arms reductions can foster a cooperative atmosphere. But it is also true that this region has a more volatile mix of flash points and funds for war than many other parts of the world. In the absence of any multilateral framework of international cooperation, there are real risks of arms races and even hostilities in the region. If the countries of the developed world are serious about limiting the risk of conflict, they themselves have the ability to control the vast majority of the weapons exported to the Asia/Pacific region. But their efforts will be incomplete without the cooperation of indigenous arms producers, primarily the PRC. This process will no doubt involve pressure

on the PRC to play a more cooperative role, in part through limits on aid if the PRC spends too much on arms or sells weapons in a particularly destabilizing way. But engaging the PRC and the developed world in an arms-control dialogue is also a matter of giving the PRC a greater stake in the new international order. To that extent patience will be required while the PRC comes to recognize that international interdependence is worth embracing. Whether the PRC is pushed or enticed into cooperation, developing a stable, regional interdependence is the single most important task in building security in the Asia/Pacific region.

Notes

1. In this paper, the term *the Asia/Pacific* includes all countries from Afghanistan to New Zealand and up to Japan.

2. Unless otherwise noted, statistics throughout this paper are taken from U.S. Arms Control and Disarmament Agency, *World Military Expenditures and Arms Transfers, 1990* (Washington, D.C., 1991), and *SIPRI Yearbook, 1992* (Oxford: Oxford University Press for SIPRI, 1992).

3. These issues are developed in Gerald Segal, *Rethinking the Pacific* (Oxford: Oxford University Press, 1990).

4. As measured in terms of value of volume of imports. Other, perhaps more "fair," means of measurement of relative position are set out in table 1. The top 15 importers of major conventional arms in the developing world were, in descending order, India, Saudi Arabia, Iraq, Afghanistan, Egypt, North Korea, Israel, Angola, South Korea, Syria, Thailand, Iran, Pakistan, Taiwan, and the United Arab Emirates.

5. See for example, Tim Huxley, "Singapore and Malaysia: The Precarious Balance," *Pacific Review*, no. 3 (1991).

6. For example, *Independent*, February 13, 1992. Postfactum, February 27, 1992, in British Broadcasting Corporation, *Summary of World Broadcasts, Soviet Union* (hereafter BBC,SWB,SU),1319,A1/2–3, on Kazakh plans and SU,1314,i on a report of February 25 on Russian plans. See generally,

Ian Anthony, *The Arms Trade and Medium Powers: Case Studies of India and Pakistan* (London: Harvester/Wheatsheaf, 1992).

7. On some of the short-term efforts see *International Herald Tribune*, January 6, 1992, and *Independent*, January 3, 1992.

8. President Nursultan Nazarbayev of Kazakhstan talking to defense sector managers, reported in TASS, January 14, 1992, reprinted in BBC,SWB,SU,1280,B/9–10. Also Postfactum on January 10, reprinted in BBC,SWB,SU,1277,B/9, and *Izvestia*, February 29, 1992, in BBC,SWB,SU, 1322,A1/1–2.

9. The PRC's agreement to purchase 20 SU–27 aircraft and four trainers has gone ahead. Future deals are under discussion but the PRC remains uncertain about the state of the Russian defense industry.

10. For a discussion of the Kazakh case see a statement by the deputy prime minister reported in Postfactum, January 10, 1992, reprinted in BBC,SWB,SU,1277,B/9.

11. On the $1 billion deal see *Financial Times*, February 11, 1991.

12. *Guardian*, April 6, 1991, and *International Herald Tribune*, May 3, 1991.

13. *International Herald Tribune*, May 11–12, July 9, and September 30, 1991.

14. From Graeme Cheesman, "Asia/Pacific Arms Transfers," *Pacific Research* 4 (August 1991), p. 6.

15. See Yitzhak Shichor, *A Multiple Hit: China's Missile Sales to Saudi Arabia*, SCPS Papers no. 5 (Kaohsiung, Taiwan: Sun Yat-sen Center for Policy Studies, 1991), and more generally Anne Gilks and Gerald Segal, *China and the Arms Trade* (London: Croom Helm, 1985); *Financial Times*, April 26, 1991; *International Herald Tribune*, November 1, 1991.

16. *Times* (London), March 6, 25, 1991, and *Sunday Times* (London), June 2, 1991.

17. Janne Nolan, *Trappings of Power* (Washington, D.C.: The Brookings Institution, 1991), and Andrew Mack, "Missile Proliferation in the Asia/Pacific Region," in Trevor Findlay, ed., *Chemical Weapons and Missile Proliferation* (London: Lynne Rienner, 1991).

18. Kazakhstan has 104 intercontinental ballistic missiles (10 warheads on each) and one bomber base. Nonstrategic nuclear weapons may still be in Kazakhstan, Tajikistan, Uzbekistan, and Turkmenistan. Natural uranium mining is concentrated in Kyrgystan. See details in Kurt Campbell et al., *Soviet Nuclear Fission*, Studies in International Security (Cambridge, Mass.: Center for Science and International Affairs, 1991). Kazakhstan and Tajikistan each have 30 percent of the former Soviet Union's uranium reserves and the former Soviet Union had 45 percent of total world reserves. Details in Radio Moscow World Service, January 19, 1992, reprinted in BBC,SWB,SU,W0214,A/2.

19. For a range of reports on this subject see Channel 1 TV on February 8, 1992, in BBC,SWB,SU,1301,A1/1, *Pravda* on January 21, 1992, in SU,1285,B/3, TASS World Service on January 14, 1992, in SU,1280,B/9, *Trud* on January 9, 1992, about a Tajik deal with Islamic states, in SU,1276,B/7, and *Krasnaya zvezda* on February 21 in SU,1314,B/7 on Kazakhstan waiting for the PRC to get rid of all its weapons. See also, *International Herald Tribune*, February 7, 14, 1992.

20. *International Herald Tribune*, May 13, 1991 and January 2, 1992. The PRC also reportedly sold heavy water to India between 1982 and 1987. For a critical assessment of these reports see Hua Di, "China; One Superpower Worse than Two," *Asia-Pacific Defense Reporter* 2 (August 1991).

21. For some references to these swirling changes see *Far Eastern Economic Review*, November 28, 1991, and *Financial Times*, November 25, 1991.

22. Andrew Mack, "The Nuclear Issue on the Korean Peninsula," *Foreign Policy* no. 83 (Summer 1991), pp. 87–104, and Gerald Segal, "A New Order in Northeast Asia," *Arms Control Today* 21 (September 1991).

23. Gerald Segal, "Concern Over Nuclear Issues in Asia," *International Herald Tribune*, February 7, 1992.

24. Geoffrey Wiseman, "Regional Arms Control," *Pacific Review*, no. 1 (1992); Jayantha Dhanapala, "Prospects of Arms Limitations in the Asia-Pacific Region," *Disarmament* 13, no. 3 (1990), pp. 123–141; Chandra Jeshurun, ed., *Arms and Defense in Southeast Asia* (Singapore: Institute of Southeast Asian Studies, 1989); and Aaron Karp, "Military Procurement and Regional

Security in Southeast Asia," *Contemporary Southeast Asia* 11 (March 1990).

25. See the International Institute of Strategic Studies, *The Military Balance, 1991–1992* (London: Brassey's for IISS, 1991), but see also Desmond Ball, "Asian Defense Spending Set for Dramatic Rise," *Asia-Pacific Defense Reporter*, September 1991, and *Aviation Week and Space Technology*, February 24, 1992, pp. 96–98.

26. *Far Eastern Economic Review*, November 7, 1991, pp. 52–53.

27. Figures from the International Institute for Strategic Studies, *The Military Balance, 1991–1992* and U.S. Arms Control and Disarmament Agency, *World Military Expenditures and Arms Transfers, 1990*.

28. Gerald Segal, "Northeast Asia: A La Carte Security," *International Affairs* 67 (October 1991).

29. See a discussion in Gerald Segal, ed., *Arms Control in Asia* (London: Macmillan, 1987), especially the Introduction.

On Tending Arms Control Agreements

Charles C. Flowerree

AS DRAMA, THE arms control process often resembles a poorly crafted three act play in which the climax is reached at the end of the second act and the interminable third act plays to a drowsy or distracted audience. In the first act, the ebb and flow of negotiations provides the action, while the second is enlivened by the sometimes tense and heated debates leading up to ratification. In the third act, the parties settle down to put into practice that which has been agreed. Only if there are spectacular accusations of noncompliance by one party or another does the third act stimulate wide attention.

Of course, the arms control process is not conducted merely to provide a stage for the participants and diversion for the public. Over the post-World War II decades, agreements on limiting arms or certain forms of military activity have become interwoven tightly with other elements of the effort to maintain national and international security. The means by which these agreements survive and adapt to

changing conditions after they enter into force deserve as much attention as the negotiations that produced them in the first place. They cannot be left simply to fend for themselves. As Princeton professor Richard Falk has pointed out, "parties to arms control agreements have an obligation to tend them."

Unfortunately, in some instances, the after-life of arms control agreements has been as fraught with controversy as their birth. The controversies over Soviet compliance with agreements limiting stegic arms and banning antiballistic missile systems and toxin weapons are cases in point. The discussion that follows will touch on several aspects of the after-life of arms control treaties: the evolution of arrangements for overseeing the proper functioning of agreements, problems and deficiencies in these arrangements, how the parties to certain treaties have attempted to cope with their problems, what lies ahead in the field of arms control, and some suggestions for possible changes and improvements in the way the United States deals with these questions.

Evolution of Mechanisms for the Maintenance of Treaties

In the years following World War I, when the concept of arms control was in its infancy, treaties were based on the notion that a nation's word was its

Charles C. Flowerree is a retired foreign service officer who served in the Arms Control and Disaramament Agency from 1977 to 1982. He was U.S. ambassador to the Conference on Disarmament in Geneva in 1980 and 1981. In 1980 he headed the U.S. delegation to the review conference of the Biological Weapons Convention and was assistant delegation head at the Review Conference of the Non-Proliferation Treaty.

bond. No special provisions for verification of compliance or for periodic reviews were deemed necessary. The Washington naval treaty of 1921 governing the number of capital ships in the fleets of the five major naval powers and the protocol prohibiting the use of chemical and biological weapons adopted at the 1925 Geneva Conference on the Supervision of the International Traffic in Arms were simple statements of undertakings by the parties with no compliance provisions at all. The Geneva Protocol, with minor exceptions, held through World War II and beyond largely because a condition of mutual deterrence inhibited the major powers from using the widely abhorred chemical and biological weapons. The naval treaty, on the other hand, quickly broke down when Japan, chafing at the inferior strength permitted it under the terms of the agreement, decided to ignore these limitations after 1930.

East–West confrontation in the post-war era brought about intense concern about verification of compliance with the obligations assumed under any agreements to limit armaments. Following the failure of the U.S. Baruch plan to place all fissile material under international control, attention turned in the late 1950s to negotiating a complete ban on nuclear testing as a way of limiting the growth of nuclear arsenals.

The test ban negotiations conducted under United Nations (UN) auspices produced the first serious effort to develop a formal mechanism for insuring treaty compliance. Whereas nuclear explosions in the atmosphere could be detected fairly easily and measured by sampling devices under national control, underground explosions, especially in the lower ranges, could be identified positively only by a network of seismic observation stations, many of which would have to be placed within the territory of the two superpowers. Pinpointing an event, identifying it as nuclear in origin, and accurately measuring its yield requires a sophisticated detection system, the details of which would have to be established precisely in any comprehensive agreement banning nuclear explosions. After five years of trying, however, the two Western nuclear powers participating in the negotiations, the United States and Great Britain, found themselves at loggerheads with the Soviet Union over the number and location of the seismic stations required for adequate verification. They also were unable to agree on salient aspects of the organization that would be required for the proper functioning of the system.

In 1963, however, the three principal parties were able to agree on a Limited Test Ban Treaty (LTBT)—applicable to testing in the atmosphere, outer space, and under water—where detection could be accomplished by national technical means. This treaty, to which other countries were invited to adhere, provided no oversight mechanism or consultative arrangement. It did, however, provide for amendment by a majority vote of the parties, which included all three original signatories.[1] Until recently, this provision never was invoked, but several nonnuclear weapon states, which have long favored a test ban in all environments, now have asked for a conference of the parties to the LTBT in order to discuss the possibility of amendment. The three nuclear weapons parties have acquiesced, and a meeting probably will be held in the latter part of 1990 or in early 1991.

In the late 1960s and early 1970s, a spate of negotiations in the Eighteen Nation Disarmament Committee in

Geneva and in its successor bodies produced a succession of multilateral arms control agreements that incorporated some provisions for consultations among the parties and oversight of the functioning of the treaties once they were in force. Initially such provisions were minimal, but they began to be expanded with succeeding agreements:

- The 1967 Outer Space Treaty that, in addition to regulating the use and exploration of outer space, prohibited the orbiting of nuclear weapons and the emplacement of such weapons on celestial bodies, relied solely on consultations among the parties to resolve questions of compliance.
- The Treaty on the Non-Proliferation of Nuclear Weapons (NPT) that entered into force in 1970 added a provision for a conference of the parties in 1975 and, if desired, at five year intervals thereafter to review the operation of the treaty. Thenceforth, review conferences became standard features of multilateral arms control agreements. The NPT was unique in one respect: it relied, in part, on an existing organization, the International Atomic Energy Agency (IAEA), to carry out some of the necessary oversight functions.
- Two succeeding agreements, the Seabed Arms Control Treaty of 1972 and the Biological Weapons Convention (BWC) of 1975, relied on consultations among the parties and review conferences at five year intervals in order to resolve any problems that might arise after the treaties' entry into force.
- A convention on the Prohibition of Military or Any Other Hostile Use of Environmental Modification Techniques (ENMOD) that entered into force

in 1978 added one new feature to the standard follow-up provisions of multilateral agreements. Upon the receipt of a request from a state party, the depositary would convene within one month a Consultative Committee of Experts. Any party would be able to appoint an expert to participate in the committee's deliberations. A summary of the committee's findings of fact would be transmitted to the depositary.

Two regional treaties, the Antarctic Treaty (1961) and the Latin American Nuclear-Free Zone Treaty (1968), took different approaches to the question of treaty oversight. In the Antarctic case, representatives of the contracting parties were to meet two months after the treaty went into force, and thereafter at suitable intervals, for the purposes of consulting on matters pertaining to Antarctica and in order to make suitable recommendations to their governments. Any party whose representatives are entitled to participate in these meetings also has the right to designate observers to carry out inspections in all areas of Antarctica in order to ensure that the provisions of the treaty are being observed. If desired, inspections may be carried out by aerial observation. Any dispute that cannot be resolved among the parties shall, with the consent of all parties to the dispute, be referred for settlement to the International Court of Justice.

The Latin American Treaty established an elaborate, three-tier organization (OPANAL) consisting of a general conference of all the contracting parties, an elected council of limited size, and a permanent secretariat to handle questions arising after the treaty's entry into force. In terms of its structure, the organization for implementing the terms of the prospective chemical weapons convention now under negotiation in Geneva owes much to the Latin American model.

In the realm of bilateral arms control agreements, the Strategic Arms Limitation Talks (SALT I) agreements of 1972 [the Anti-ballistic Missile (ABM) Treaty and the Interim Agreement on the Limitation of Strategic Offensive Arms] set the standard for follow-up arrangements. A permanent Standing Consultative Commission (SCC) was created that, *inter alia*, was to consider compliance questions, establish necessary procedures, and consider proposals for amending and strengthening the agreements. The Intermediate-range Nuclear Forces (INF) Treaty incorporates a somewhat modified version of the SCC called the Special Verification Commission.[2]

To sum up, follow-up mechanisms have become standard features of arms control agreements. The differences among them may be attributed, *inter alia*, to the nature of the agreement—whether multilateral, bilateral, or regional—the compexity of its provisions, the technology of the weapons being constrained, and the political climate in which the treaty exists.

Desired Features of Regimes for Treaty Maintainance

Ideally, any organization established to monitor arms control treaties that have entered into force should be able to facilitate the exchange of information on any subject that could affect the parties' attitude toward the treaty, building confidence in all quarters that the treaty is meeting expectations. An effective treaty implementation mechanism ought to be able to cope, as may be appropriate under the provisions of the treaty, with the following tasks:

- *Treaty Compliance:* As noted, the most commonly recognized responsibility of all treaty oversight arrangements is to deal with compliance questions. This responsibility does not extend to fixing blame or meting out punishment. Rather, consultation and fact finding in order to clear up misunderstandings are the goals. Should the facts indicate a clear-cut violation or should a party be dissatisfied with the responses of another, the issue may have to be taken up elsewhere.

- *Adapting to Changing Conditions:* Changes in circumstances that prevailed at the time of negotiating the original agreement may also require adjustments in treaty operations. The emergence of new nuclear supplier nations, for example, has changed some of the operating assumptions of the Non-Proliferation Treaty.

- *Interpreting Treaty Language:* Ambiguities are the frequent residue of the haggling over language that occurs during negotiations. Sometimes ambiguity is deliberately built into an agreement in order to protect future options for one party or another. For example, the United States preferred not to define precisely the vital term "launcher" used in the SALT II treaty, in part to avoid the possibility that future basing options for the MX missile might be limited.[3] During the operation of a treaty, however, the parties must agree on the meaning of its formulations. Whole new interpretations of the terms of the agreement may arise occasionally, as in the case of the "broad" and "narrow" interpretations of the ABM Treaty provisions regarding the testing or deploying of defensive systems involving "other physical principles."

- *Dealing with New Technological Developments:* The impact of new technologies, such as the continued development of phased array radars or the application of recombinant DNA technology, can create new problems that need to be dealt with in the context of the applicable treaties.

- *Developing Implementing Procedures:* When a treaty calls for weapons or other assets to be dismantled or destroyed, or when it contains provisions requiring other positive actions, the detailed procedures cannot always be defined in the treaty text and may have to be elaborated by the body charged with implementation of the treaty.

To appreciate better the success of existing follow-up arrangements in handling these various functions, it is instructive to examine the workings of two treaty regimes at opposite ends of the spectrum. The bilateral SALT I agreements established a formal arrangement to deal with a comprehensive range of issues that could arise after entry into force, while the multilateral Biological Weapons Convention relied exclusively on periodic review conferences in order to consider questions that could not be handled by *ad hoc* consultations among the parties.

The SALT I Agreements and the SCC

Although the United States and the Soviet Union have engaged in about a dozen negotiations on arms control or related issues such as the "Hot Line" agreement, only twice have negotiations limiting armaments resulted in

treaties that entered into force—the SALT I and INF agreements. The latter is too recent to have developed much of a track record for follow-up, but SALT I provides a classic case for the examination of the after-life of arms control agreements. The Standing Consultative Commission (SCC), a trail blazer in the realm of treaty oversight, was a unique feature of SALT I. Its functions are set forth in Article XIII of the ABM Treaty:

To promote the objectives and implementation of the provisions of this treaty, the Parties shall establish promptly a Standing Consultative Commission, within the framework of which they will:

(a) consider questions concerning compliance with the obligations assumed and related situations which may be considered ambiguous;
(b) provide on a voluntary basis such information as either Party considers necessary to assure confidence in compliance with the obligations assumed;
(c) consider questions involving unintended interference with national technical means of verification;
(d) consider possible changes in the strategic situation which have a bearing on the provisions of this Treaty;
(e) agree upon procedures and dates for destruction or dismantling of ABM systems or their components in cases provided by the provisions of this Treaty;
(f) consider, as appropriate, possible proposals for further increasing the viability of this Treaty; including proposals for ammendments in accordance with the provisions of this Treaty;
(g) consider, as appropriate, proposals for further measures aimed at limiting strategic arms.

The SCC's organization and rules of procedure gave it many advantages as a mechanism to ensure the proper functioning of the treaties for which it was responsible. Each side is led by a commissioner who is directly responsible to his government. The commission is required to meet frequently, at least twice a year, with no limit on the length of meetings nor on the provisions for communicating between sessions. The SCC's mandate is broad enough to allow it to deal with virtually any type of problem that might arise under the treaty regime, and even to improve it.

Equally as important as the scope of its mandate is the SCC's *modus operandi*. Its proceedings are confidential, relieving it of the necessity of issuing communiqués or of holding press briefings after its sessions. These features, no matter how exasperating they may be to the media, allow frank and uninhibited discussions of matters that are sometimes, but by no means always, of the highest sensitivity. The permanence of the organization fosters systematic record keeping that is a great advantage in reinforcing institutional memory. As a matter of practice, the SCC has conducted the first two five-year reviews called for in Article XIV of the ABM Treaty. The third was the subject of a special conference in 1988. These reviews have been made much simpler by the opportunity to raise issues during the intervening years in the SCC regular sessions, in effect providing a continuous process of bilateral review.

Finally, it should be noted that the SCC took on an additional function under the Agreement on Measures to Reduce the Risk of the Outbreak of Nuclear War of September 1971, to consult regarding measures to reduce the danger of inadvertent or accidental nuclear war. Between 1976 and 1985,

several protocols regarding the implementation of that agreement were negotiated in the SCC. Among other things, a message system designed to speed transmission of information during periods of crisis or potential misunderstanding was established.

While compliance questions are the ones that attract the most attention, according to former U.S. Commissioner Robert Buchheim, the majority of the SCC's work has been concerned with clarification of treaty provisions and with performing the treaty's requisite tasks such as devising procedures to be used for the destruction or dismantling of armaments and weapon systems.[4] When necessary, it also develops understandings to govern future conduct under the provisions of the agreements, as well as procedures for implementing these understandings. After the negotiation of SALT II, the SCC was charged with working out agreed procedures for the implementation of certain SALT II provisions to cover weapons systems or activities that were not addressed in the SALT I Interim Agreement, such as the destruction of heavy bombers and submarine-launched ballistic missile (SLBM) submarines, conversion of heavy bombers to tankers, the liquidation of fractional-orbit bombardment systems, and notification of intercontinental ballistic missile (ICBM) launchings for testing or other agreed purposes.

The guiding principle of the SCC has been to raise potential problems for resolution before they get out of hand and become the cause for an undesired reconsideration of an entire agreement. The attainment of this ideal, of course, depends on the desire of both parties to see the agreement flourish. Until the advent of the Reagan administration, the view prevailed that there had been no instances when questions raised by the United States about SALT I compliance had failed to result in a cessation of the Soviet activity in question or, alternatively, had elicited additional information that allayed U.S. concerns.

Although it was a Reagan administration article of faith that the SALT II Treaty was fatally flawed, that administration adopted an interim policy of abiding by the principal limitations imposed by both the SALT I Interim Agreement and SALT II. The "fatally flawed" characterization of SALT II had less to do with its specific provisions than with the underlying concept. Arms control was not perceived as a useful tool for the ordering of U.S. relations with the Soviet Union during the period of the U.S. military build up. Moreover, as the Strategic Defense Initiative (SDI) began to gain momentum, the ABM Treaty was seen as a potential roadblock to its full achievement. This led to the much-publicized effort to interpret its provisions in a way that permits unrestricted testing of SDI components.

It is not the purpose of this discussion to argue the merits of the Reagan administration's case but rather to point to the consequences of its policies. In brief, the traditional role of the SCC of seeking solutions to problems that could threaten the well-being of the SALT I agreements was no longer an important U.S. objective. Denunciation of Soviet violations, rather than quiet diplomacy, became the order of the day. In a letter to President Ronald Reagan sent in November 1985, Defense Secretary Caspar Weinberger called the SCC "a diplomatic carpet under which Soviet violations have been continuously swept, an Orwellian memory hole into which our concerns have been dumped like yesterday's trash."[5] Although the policy of confrontation

changed the character of the SCC, the SCC dialogue, even during this period, produced some understandings on the implementation of the treaties under which it functions.

As the story of the SCC demonstrates, the effectiveness of any oversight mechanism depends in large part on the commitment of all parties to the success of the original treaty.

The BWC: Tribulations of a Multilateral Treaty

When the Biological Weapons Convention was negotiated in 1972, some considered it to be of secondary importance because biological weapons (BW) had little appeal for most military planners, and the United States had already rid itself of its BW stockpile. At the same time, there was a a sense of urgency to reach an agreement in the field of biological and chemical weapons, as the international community had been struggling unsuccessfully for some time to negotiate a ban on both types of weapons. By separating the two, the knotty problem of a chemical weapons ban could be left for subsequent deliberations.

Largely because of the perception that the BW threat was not great, the convention that was negotiated in 1972 had minimal provisions for ensuring proper implementation. Parties were enjoined to consult and cooperate in solving problems that might arise. Complaints about unresolved breaches of obligations under the treaty were to be lodged with the UN Security Council, which was empowered to undertake investigations. The functioning of the convention was to be reviewed by a conference of the parties at five year intervals following 1975, the year the BWC entered into force.

The first review conference turned

out to be more fraught with problems than the framers of the convention could have imagined.[6] There was widespread dissatisfaction with the procedures for handling suspected violations. Sweden came armed with a recommendation to amend the convention, although it did not make clear immediately the precise nature of the amendment. In time, the Swedish delegation revealed that what it had in mind was the formation of a permanent consultative committee of experts representing the parties for the consideration of questions relating to compliance with the provisions of the convention, including possibile on-site inspections. The proposal had the support of a large number of non-aligned delegations, but ran into stiff opposition from the Soviet Union and its supporters. Western countries were sympathetic to its objectives, but had serious reservations about achieving them through this sort of amendment.

Arduous negotiations on the Swedish proposal made little headway until toward the end of the conference the British proposed a compromise that had the support of the NATO delegations. The proposal became the basis for an eventual resolution of the issue worked out in consultations among the British, Swedish, and Soviet delegations. The compromise language of the final communiqué moved only very slightly in the direction of the original Swedish proposal. The communiqué drew attention to the flexibility inherent in the provisions for consultation and cooperation under Article V of the convention and stated that the parties could use "various international procedures which would make it possible to insure effectively and adequately the implementation of the Convention's provisions taking into account the concern expressed by the Conference participants to this effect."

Meanwhile, the United States delegation had been alerted by Washington that there had been an accident in April 1979 near a biological installation of the Soviet military in Sverdlovsk, resulting in the release of spores of anthrax (a proscribed BW agent), resulting in illnesses and deaths.

At the closing session and after the compromise on the handling of compliance questions had been reached, the United States announced that it had received information suggesting a possible violation by the Soviet Union, and that in accordance with the agreed procedures, the United States would be entering into consultations on the matter, keeping all parties to the convention informed of the outcome. The Soviet delegation took umbrage at this statement, denying having engaged in any activity inconsistent with its treaty obligations. The Soviet Union said that the Sverdlovsk incident was caused by the accidental distribution of meat contaminated by anthrax; it was a public health problem and, therefore, was not within the purview of the convention. Although much information that tends to support the Soviet version is now on the public record, the issue still has not been resolved to the official satisfaction of the United States.

The Swedish initiative at the 1980 review conference illustrates the difficulty of trying to change a treaty through amendment. As the Soviets and others pointed out during the conference, an amendment that was not acceptable to all parties would create an undesirable split in the treaty regime with some parties embracing the amendment while others would abide only by the unamended version. During the 1982 session of the UN General Assembly, Sweden and Belgium attempted to overcome the impasse that was blocking efforts to strengthen the compliance provisions of the BWC, but to no avail. During the same session, a French-sponsored resolution, adopted over the strenuous opposition of the Soviet Union, requested the secretary general "to investigate, with the assistance of qualified experts, information that may be brought to his attention by Member States concerning activities that may be construed as violations of the [Geneva] Protocol or of the relevant rules of international law."[7] This resolution, which was aimed mainly at chemical weapons, had only marginal relevance to the problems with which the BWC review conference had been struggling. Tied exclusively to the Geneva Protocol, the resolution was applicable only in cases where chemical or biological weapons had been used. Nevertheless, the resolution established a basis for UN investigations of violations of multilateral arms control agreements. Furthermore, with the effective investigations of the use of chemical weapons conducted by the UN during the Iran–Iraq War, a firm precedent has been established.

Another compliance issue hovering in the background, although it was not recognized as a possible BW problem at the time of the review conference, was the so-called Yellow Rain controversy. Since the late 1970s, the United States had been receiving information about the possible use by Vietnamese forces of toxic substances, purportedly supplied by the Soviet Union, against the hill people of Laos and later against forces in Cambodia opposing the Vietnamese. At first, it was assumed that the substances in question were chemical warfare agents. In April 1981, however, then Secretary of State Alexander Haig stated in a speech in Berlin that the Yellow Rain that had been falling on the hill people of Laos was tricothecene, a form of mycotoxin, a naturally produced toxin.[8] If true, its use would have been a violation of the BWC.

In the absence of another forum, the issue had been hotly debated in the UN General Assembly, which authorized the secretary-general to dispatch a team of investigators to Southeast Asia. The team, denied access to the territory of Laos and Cambodia, failed to turn up any direct evidence of the use there of chemical or biological weapons. On the other hand, the investigators said they could not disregard the circumstantial evidence suggesting the possible use of "some sort of toxic chemical substance in some instances."[9] Since 1981, the United States has continued to hold that Communist forces in Southeast Asia used tricothecene mycotoxins in violation of the BWC. Although the basis for the charge has been challenged strongly outside the government, the annual reports on "Soviet Noncompliance with Arms Control Agreements" that the administration submits to Congress have repeated the charge since 1984.[10]

From this brief recounting of the after-life of the BWC it is apparent that a treaty that was considered of secondary importance when it was negotiated became the source of considerable bilateral and international friction, in part through its failure to provide a permanent body to facilitate consultations on compliance questions. In the matter of the Sverdlovsk incident, U.S. suspicions could have been raised in a less confrontational manner had such a body been in existence. However, given the strong disposition of the U.S. government after 1980 to distrust the actions and intentions of the Soviet Union in matters impinging on national security and the uncooperative nature of the Soviet regime at the time, it is improbable that any structural changes in the treaty would have produced a satisfactory resolution of this issue. Nevertheless, the existence of a more subtle means of raising sensitive compliance questions could have helped the BWC avoid the rough passage it experienced in early recent years.

Despite the rebuff to the Swedish proposal of 1980, there remains a widespread desire to strengthen the BWC. Recent efforts in this direction have followed the route charted in 1980, continuing to work on extending the consultation function under Article V. The 1986 review conference agreed on conditions for convening consultative meetings to consider problems of compliance that might be raised by a state party.[11] It also was agreed that there would be exchanges of data among the parties on research centers dealing with dangerous bacteriological materials. In the spring of 1987, an *ad hoc* meeting in Geneva of scientific and technical experts was convened in order to work on the modalities of the information exchange. How far this kind of approach to the compliance problem can be taken is not clear. One of its obvious limitations is that all actions prescribed under Article V are recommendations rather than obligations. The search for better consultation and compliance arrangements continues. The need is not just theoretical. The problem of BW proliferataion now has reared its ugly head. If U.S. intelligence is correct, there may be as many as ten countries actively pursuing biological weapons development programs.

As the foregoing discussion has indicated, the Biological Weapons Convention is clearly an agreement in need of help. In a later section some possible remedies for its ailments will be examined.

In addition to illustrating the perils of act three of the arms control process, the examples of the BWC and the SALT I agreements show some of the significant differences between multilateral and bilateral agreements in terms of how they can or should be maintained after entering into force. Even within these two categories there are differences in the nature of various agreements that preclude a single prescription for curing their various ailments. The multilateral nuclear Non-Proliferation Treaty, for example, has unique facets that set it apart from arms control agreements applying to weaponry. The NPT relies in large measure on IAEA safeguard procedures in order to insure compliance, but that agency is not organized to undertake the complete range of functions with which a body like the SCC is charged. Also, the NPT faces an expiration date in 1995, at which time important decisions concerning its future will have to be taken. Another special case is the prospective chemical weapons convention which will have the most elaborate implementation provisions of any multilateral arms control agreement.

Lessons from the SCC and BWC Experiences

It is a premise of this discussion that the SCC established by the ABM Treaty meets all the desiderata for arms control oversight mechanisms described earlier in this article. This is not to say that the SCC could not be improved. However, the basic concept for ensuring the proper functioning of bilateral arms control treaties relating to nuclear weapons is sound.

As has been noted earlier, the Reagan administration did not seem to share this assessment when it came into office. However, that admistration's concerns, as has been noted, seemed to stem more from a philosophy that found little place for arms control agreements in its concept of how to deal with the Soviet Union than from concern about the structure of the SCC itself. Support for this assertion can be found in the fact that when the INF Treaty was negotiated, its Special Verification Commission (SVC) was modeled closely on the SCC. Many of the differences between the two organizations are cosmetic. The SVC is charged with "resolving" compliance questions that may arise, while the SCC is to "consider" them. In the real world this semantic difference has little bearing on the possibility of resolving the issues at the commission level. Another difference is in the minimum number of meetings that are required for the two bodies. The SCC meets at least twice a year, while the SVC meets at the request of either party. In the first year of its existence, the SVC has had four long meetings, perhaps an indication that a treaty that incorporates an enormous amount of operational detail requires even more time and attention from its implementing body than one that is less detailed.

In comparing the SCC and the SVC, the real differences lie in the treaties under which they function. The INF Treaty has elaborate provisions for verification by one party of the activities of the other, while the ABM Treaty under which the SCC functions relies on the use of "national technical means" for verifying compliance. In both cases, however, the SCC and the SVC have the same responsibilities with regard to compliance—they deal with questions that may arise from the conduct of verification operations, but the conduct of these operations is the responsibility of others.

The SCC model has several other possible applications. The Joint Consultative Commission (JCC) established by the still unratified treaty on Peaceful Nuclear Explosions (PNE) already is modeled on the SCC. Presumably, the JCC could be adapted to the PNE's companion Threshold Test Ban Treaty, if both ever are ratified. The future Strategic Arms Reduction Talks (START) treaty is, of course, an agreement suited to the SCC-type of implementation mechanism. In the nuclear area, all agreements with the Soviet Union are candidates for this type of arrangement, provided the Soviets agree, and there is no reason to believe that they will not continue to do so.

In regard to multilateral agreements, possible improvements in the Biological Weapons Convention also could be applicable to other treaties. The BWC needs two kinds of continuing bodies—an expert group to keep abreast of developments in the field of microbiology and a consultative committee to deal with compliance questions and other issues concerning the operations of the convention. In his thoughtful and thorough examination of the BWC's first ten years, *The Diplomacy of Biological Disarmament*, Nicholas Sims suggests an "entirely new kind of committee," one that would be charged not with handling compliance issues or undertaking fact-finding missions, but with watching over the general health of the treaty regime.[12] This "Committee of Oversight" would be staffed at the expert level and would maintain links between the convention, the microbiology professions, and the World Health Organization, abetting international cooperation in the peaceful applications of microbiology. In activities more directly relevant to the functioning of the treaty regime, it could tackle such problems as making more precise the definitions of substances covered by the convention, or possibly establishing procedures for the rapid identification of pathogenic micro-organisms and toxins in order to determine whether their presence in an infected population was of natural occurrence, the consequence of an accident, or of something more sinister.

Sims suggests that such a committee could be elected by one review conference and report to the next. The parties would have to absorb the costs of its operations, but, as Sims notes, the treaty thus far has been run on the cheap. Any serious effort to give it muscle is going to cost money.

As for the consultation and treaty implementation functions, a possible solution that would avoid the pitfalls of the amendment process would be for the review conference to elect a bureau composed of a few senior officials to serve as a continuing point of contact for the parties until the following conference. The Preparatory Committee (PREPCOM) for the review conference in the past has followed an analagous practice. For the 1986 review conference, the PREPCOM elected ambassadors from three countries to comprise the bureau with responsibility for chairing the committee in rotation and for handling "technical and other matters" in the months between the conclusion of the PREPCOM's work and the convening of the review conference itself. The proposal suggested here would have the bureau elected by the review conference function in the latter capacity between conferences. For example, when a party wished to request a meeting of the kind envisaged by the agreements at the 1986 review conference, it could do so by communicating with members of the bureau who collectively would be responsible for follow-up ac-

tions. No amendment of the convention would be necessary to put into effect such an arrangement. The fact that the bureau would be an elected body knowledgeable about the convention should make it acceptable to all parties.

This sort of arrangement could be applicable to other multilateral agreements that lack a consultative mechanism to function between review conferences. The ENMOD Treaty has a provision for a Consultative Committee of Experts to act as a fact finding body, a precedent cited by Sweden in its effort to amend the BWC in 1980. However, the procedures for convening the ENMOD Committee are cumbersome and the terms of reference imprecise. It is important to recognize that the purpose of a continuing body such as the bureau would not be to investigate allegations concerning compliance, but rather to facilitate what has been most sorely needed: the consultation process.

One obvious question regarding the implementation of the BWC is why not place biological and chemical weapons under the same international supervisory organization (the Organization for the Prohibition of Chemical Weapons), as is now contemplated for the CW Convention, or devise a similar organization for the BWC? While the two types of weapons have many similarities as far as their banning is concerned, verification of nonproduction of biological weapons is even more difficult than for chemical weapons. Furthermore, the old impediments to amending a treaty in force still stand in the way. After the CW convention has been in effect for some time and the whole process has had time to mature, the possibility of placing both types of weapons under the same, or similar, international oversight authorities may well look more feasible.

As for regional arms control treaties, like the prospective agreement on Conventional Forces in Europe, nothing has been said here thus far about how implementation mechanisms for such agreements might be structured. So far, this issue does not seem to have been addressed in the CFE negotiations. An SVC-type organization might be adapted to the CFE's requirements, but until the provisions of the future treaty are better known, particularly those dealing with verification, any attempt to elaborate further would be premature.

Arms Control Agreements and National Policies

In all instances, whether an arms control treaty is bilateral, multilateral, or regional, it is in the interest of the United States to have a relatively low key channel through which it can express its concerns about matters of compliance. Robert Einhorn had some cogent observations on this score.[13] He wrote that when concerns over compliance are not alleviated, the choices open to a treaty party are: (a) do nothing and let the unresolved issue fester, (b) renounce the agreement, (c) attempt again to get the other party to provide needed information, or to agree that its behavior is prohibited and that it will not be repeated, or (d) propose practical solutions that give assurances about the future behavior of the other party, even if it does not eliminate uncertainties about—or pass judgment on—past actions by that party. Examples of this latter approach include proposing the negotiation of new, common understandings that

clarify ambiguities or terminate questionable activities, or proposing agreements on additional verification measures.

These considerations highlight the importance of incorporating in arms control agreements verification and compliance arrangements that are capable of protecting the security of the United States (or the security of any state party to the treaty), by identifying militarily significant violations early enough to permit the United States to take whatever compensatory actions are necessary. These treaty arrangements also should instill confidence in the U.S. public that its interests are being protected and that the agreements are functioning fairly and effectively. As far as the public and often the Congress are concerned, the perception that the Soviet Union is in violation of an agreement often is more telling than elaborate assessments of whether a violation is militarily significant.

The question of public perception points up another requirement for ensuring the well-being of treaties in force—maintaining public and Congressional support for and confidence in the agreements. The most obvious and effective means of achieving this objective would be for the executive branch to share more information with Congress and the public in order to counteract the confusion that often stems from the cacophony of official and unofficial voices. In the past, the executive has been reluctant to share much of the information that might clarify a confused situation, for fear of compromising intelligence operations needed for verification purposes or out of concern that release of this information would cause the Soviets to become less forthcoming in future discussions of treaty compliance. This latter concern can be mitigated by not releasing sensitive information while the issue to which it applies is under discussion with the Soviets. As for the risk of compromising intelligence operations, a case can be made that this fear often has been exaggerated in the past. After all these years, U.S. and Soviet knowledge of each other's capabilities in verifying arms control agreements is very high. If the U.S. government believes an arms control agreement to be in the best interest of its national security, the risk of exposing intelligence capabilities must be weighed against the great importance of maintaining public support for and confidence in the agreement. In this regard, confidence and understanding will depend not simply on the quantity of information that is shared but also on its balance and objectivity.

Another factor that bears on the importance of maintaining public support for arms control agreements is the increased cost these days of verifying them and assuring their proper functioning. These costs are a small price to pay for an arms control agreement that is in the interest of national security and that promises to reduce substantially future outlays for armaments. Nevertheless, in an era of staggering deficits, all major expenditures presumably will receive careful examinations by budget cutters. The question of overlap and duplication among the various treaty oversight mechanisms easily could attract their attention.

The INF Treaty ushered in a new era in verifying agreements with its adoption of an elaborate regime, including on-site inspection, for the purposes of monitoring compliance. This activity, scheduled to endure over a period of 13 years, will cost the United States hundreds of millions of dollars.

Presuming a successful conclusion of the ongoing START negotiations, verifying the projected reduction of 50 percent in strategic nuclear arsenals will not come cheaply, nor will the limitations projected under a future agreement on conventional forces in Europe. Looming ahead also is the proposed international authority to supervise the operation of a chemical weapons convention whose costs are likely to be on the same order as those for implementing the INF Treaty.

Ideally, consolidation of the oversight mechanisms of treaties that have many common elements should be an objective of future arms control negotiations. Treaties dealing with nuclear weapons, for example, could be placed under an SCC/SVC-type organization. There would be substantial savings in administrative costs under such an arrangement. Personnel requirements also would be reduced, with the possibility of some individuals representing the United States on more than one treaty implementation body. Each treaty regime would have the benefit of ready access to relevant records and the institutional memory of the umbrella body. In short, the arrangement would be both efficient and cost effective, characteristics that are all too rare in the arms control area, not to mention others.

Unfortunately, in the real world, acceptance of such a radical approach is highly unlikely, even if the Soviets were to agree. Bureaucracies are not noted for their enthusiasm for passing up opportunities to create new fiefdoms with high level grade structures, and there are few negotiators who believe they cannot create something better than their predecessors. Already the INF Treaty has gone its separate way.

The principle of consolidation might be applied at home, however, if not in the field. It would be sensible for each involved Washington agency to designate a special organization to look after the implementation of arms control agreements. United States delegates to meetings with other treaty parties should be drawn from an experienced and stable cadre. An often noted feature and not inconsequential advantage of Soviet delegations in these meetings is the long experience of most of the participants. The task of overseeing the implementation of arms control agreements is difficult, time-consuming, and often frustrating work, and to be effective it must be carried out day-by-day, out of the limelight or glare of publicity.

Conclusion

A high tide has been reached in the ebb and flow of activity in the negotiation of agreements on arms limitations or elimination. Adding to worries about the East–West confrontation, which fueled the search for agreements in the past, is a new concern about the proliferation of weapons of mass destruction that is motivating the effort to achieve new agreements, or to strengthen old ones. Nuclear proliferation remains a concern, although a less frightening one than when the NPT was negotiated, and recent disturbing developments have focused attention on chemical and biological weapons as proliferation problems.

As has been noted, modern arms control measures have become increasingly complicated, as nations have grown more reluctant to leave the details of enforcement to the good will of the parties. The February 1989 version of the rolling text of the chemical weapons convention exceeds 150 pages (and is rising), compared with the single sheet on which the Geneva Protocol of 1925 was printed.

In the consideration of possible improvements in treaty maintenance mechanisms, it is important always to bear in mind that without the unstinting support of all parties, no arrangement—no matter how carefully crafted—can rescue an agreement in trouble. To borrow from Robert Einhorn again,

> If they both [the United States and the Soviet Union] believe their national interests can be served by negotiating and adhering to arms control agreements, they will have the incentive to adopt the pragmatic and constructive approaches needed to make the implementation process function reasonably well, even with its inherent shortcomings. But if either or both of them do not feel they have an important stake in the conclusion and continued operation of arms control agreements, the process is destined to fail—no matter what efforts are made to try to improve on recent experience.[14]

Finally, assuming there is a desire to make arms control work, the importance of regular and persistent attention to the implementaion of agreements cannot be stressed too strongly. For governments to realize the benefits they originally sought in arms control agreements, some government officials must live with them full-time, all the time.

Notes

1. U.S. Arms Control and Disarmament Agency, *Arms Control and Disarmament Agreements* (Washington, D.C.: GPO, 1982).

2. Text of the INF treaty is from the Arms Control Association, *Arms Control Today* 18:1 (January/February 1988). All other references to the text of treaties are from *Ibid.*

3. Robert J. Einhorn, "Treaty Compliance,"

Foreign Policy 45 (Winter 1981–1982), p. 29.

4. Robert W. Buchheim and Dan Caldwell, *The US–USSR Standing Consultative Commission: Description and Appraisal* (Providence, R.I.: the Center for Foreign Policy Development, Brown University, 1983).

5. Quoted by Michael Krepon, "How Reagan is Killing a Quiet Forum," *Washington Post*, August 31, 1986.

6. Nicholas A. Sims, *The Diplomacy of Biological Disarmament: Vicissitudes of a Treaty in Force, 1975–85* (London: Macmillan, 1988).

7. UNGA Document A/37/98D, December 13, 1982.

8. U.S. Department of State, *Special Report No. 98 Chemical Warfare in Southeast Asia and Afghanistan* (Washington, D.C.: GPO, March 22, 1982).

9. UNGA Document A/37/259, December 1, 1982.

10. See, for example, Department of State, *Special Report No. 12 Soviet Noncompliance with Arms Control Agreements* (Washington, D.C.: GPO, February 1, 1985).

11. *Final Document, Second Review Conference of the Parties to the Convention on the Prohibition of the Development, Production, and Stockpiling of Bacteriological (Biological) and Toxin Weapons and on Their Destruction,* Geneva: United Nations: BWC/CONF. 11/3; 1986.

12. Nicholas A. Sims, *The Diplomacy of Biological Disarmament*, pp. 298–304.

13. Einhorn, "Treaty Compliance," pp. 41–42.

14. Einhorn, "Treaty Compliance," p. 47.